CHOUJIN X

1

SUI ISHIDA

SUI ISHIDA was born in Fukuoka, Japan.
He is the author of the immensely popular
Tokyo Ghoul and several *Tokyo Ghoul* one-
shots, including one that won him second
place in the *Weekly Young Jump* 113th
Grand Prix award in 2010.

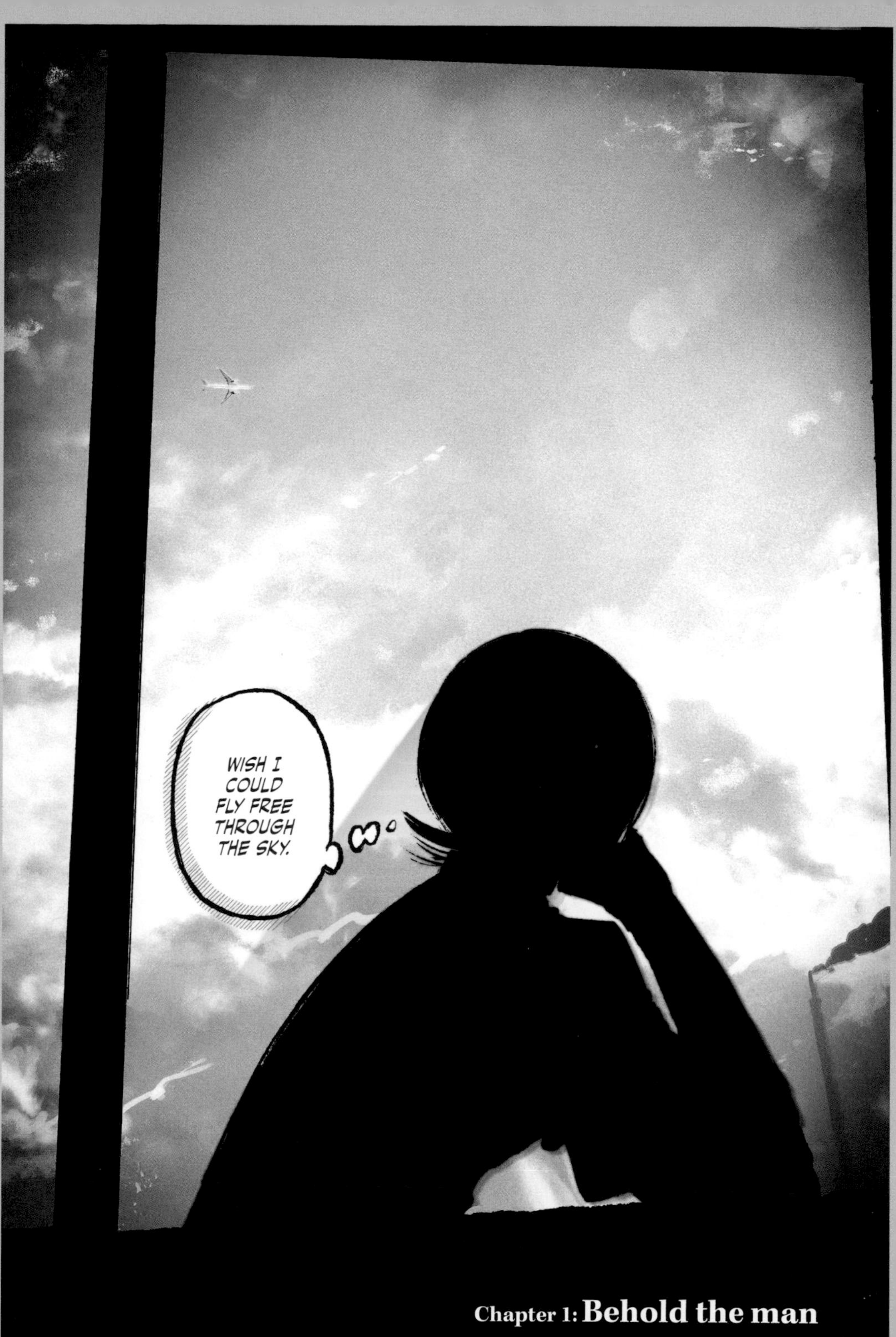
WISH I COULD FLY FREE THROUGH THE SKY.

Chapter 1: Behold the man

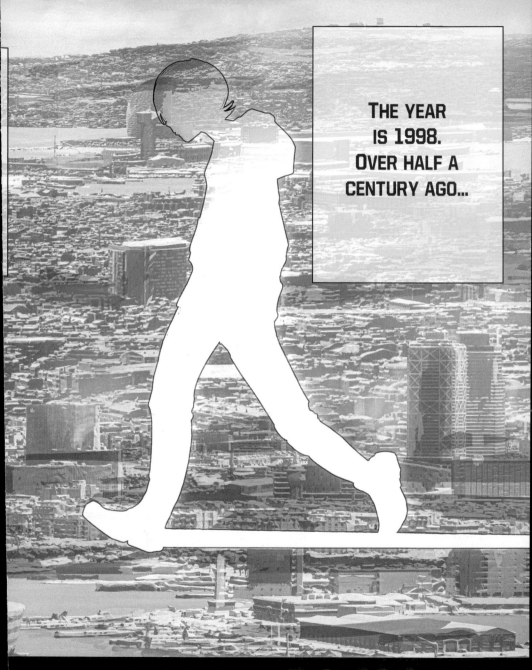

THE YEAR
IS 1998.
OVER HALF A
CENTURY AGO...

Chapter 1: Behold the man

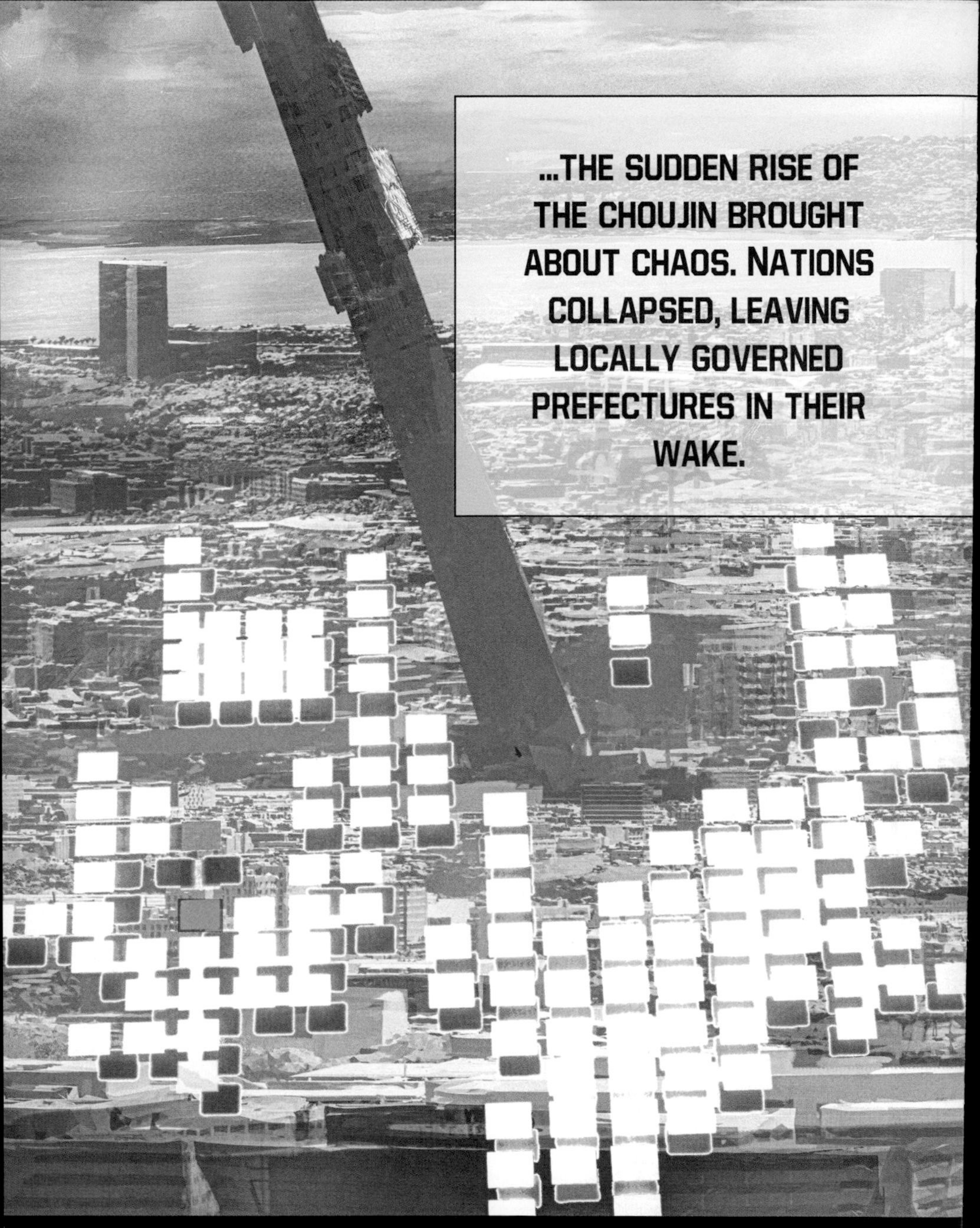
...THE SUDDEN RISE OF THE CHOUJIN BROUGHT ABOUT CHAOS. NATIONS COLLAPSED, LEAVING LOCALLY GOVERNED PREFECTURES IN THEIR WAKE.

CHOUJIN X 1

STORY AND ART BY SUI ISHIDA

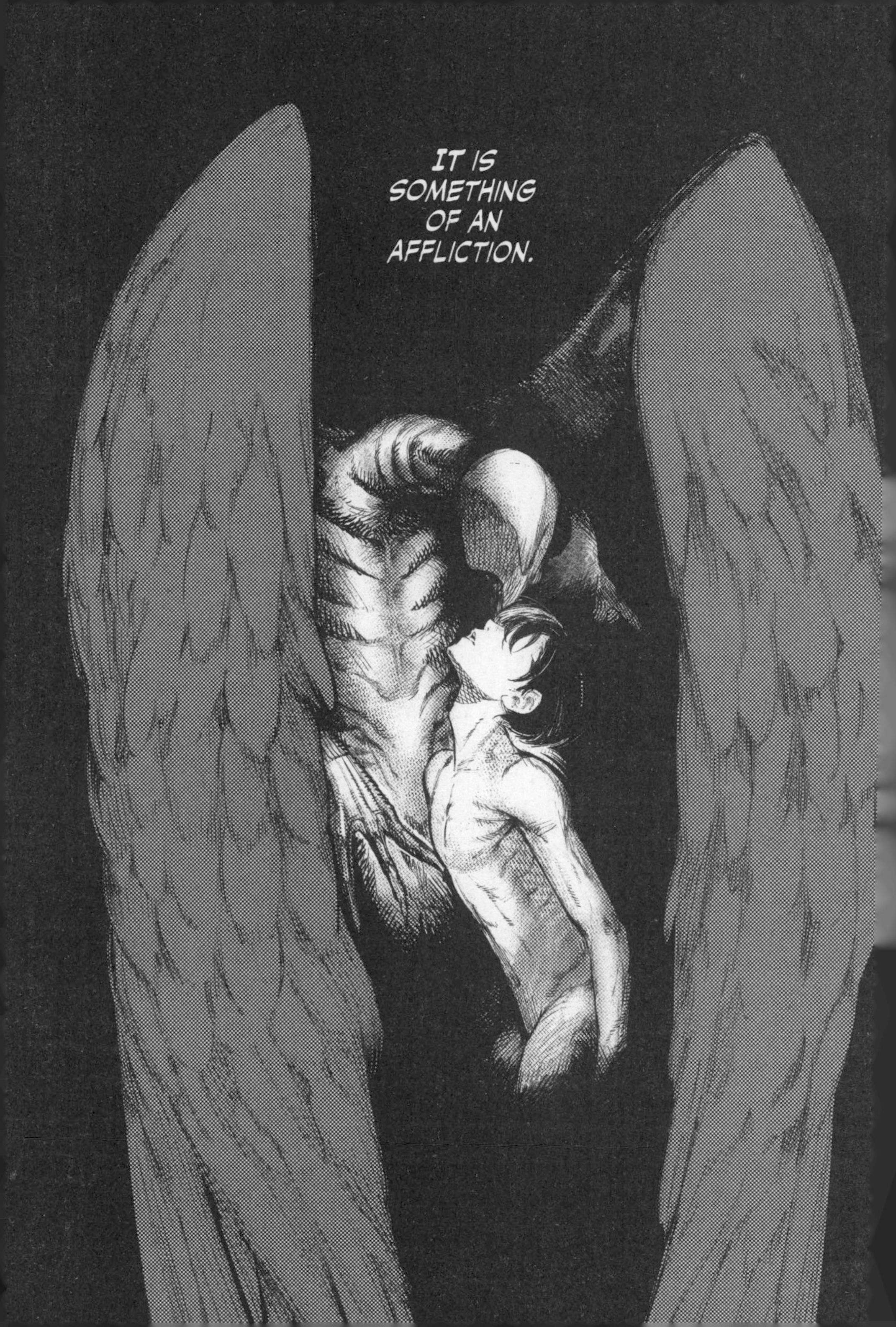
IT IS SOMETHING OF AN AFFLICTION.

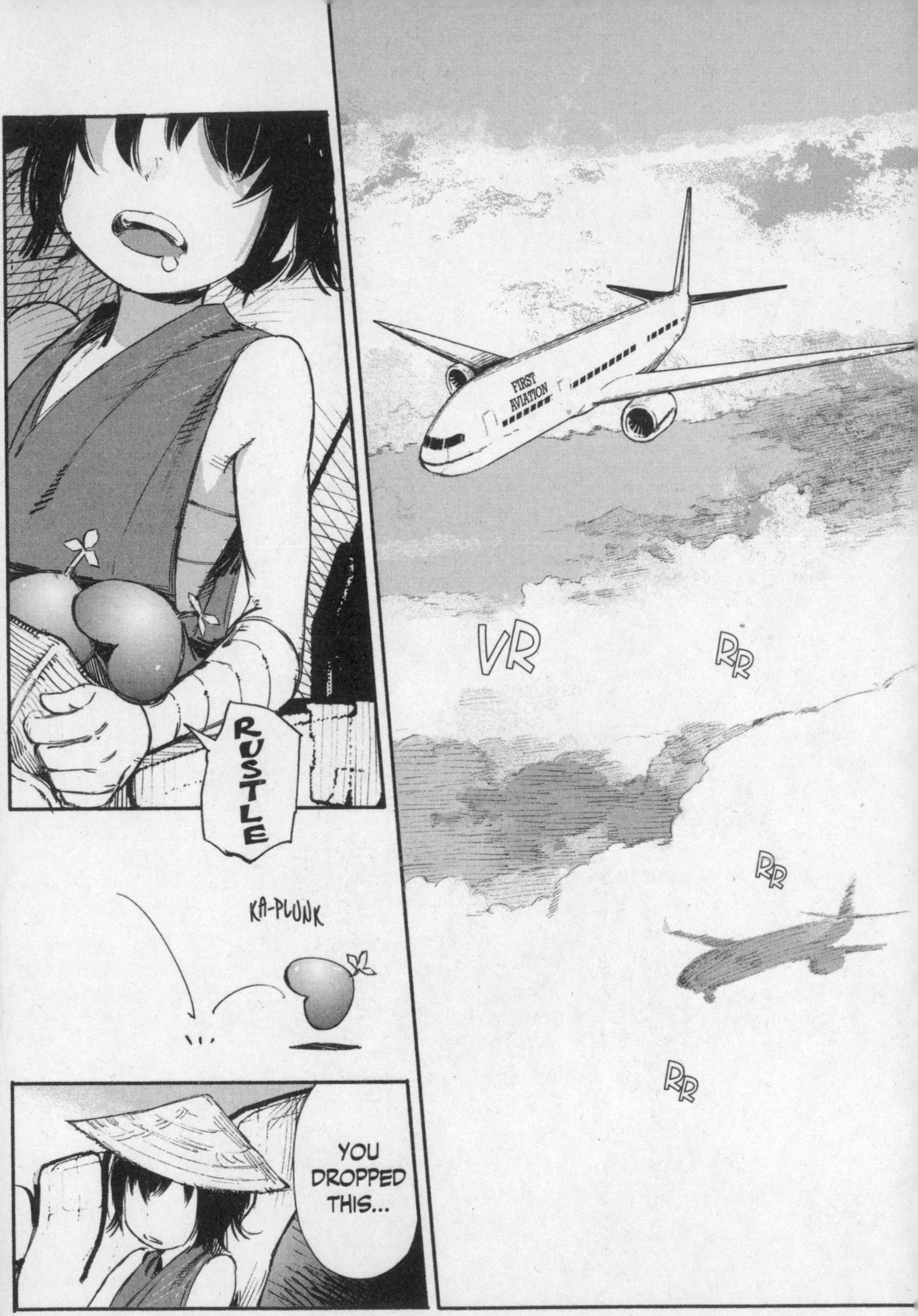
FIRST AVIATION
VR
RR
RR
RR
RUSTLE
KA-PLUNK
YOU DROPPED THIS...

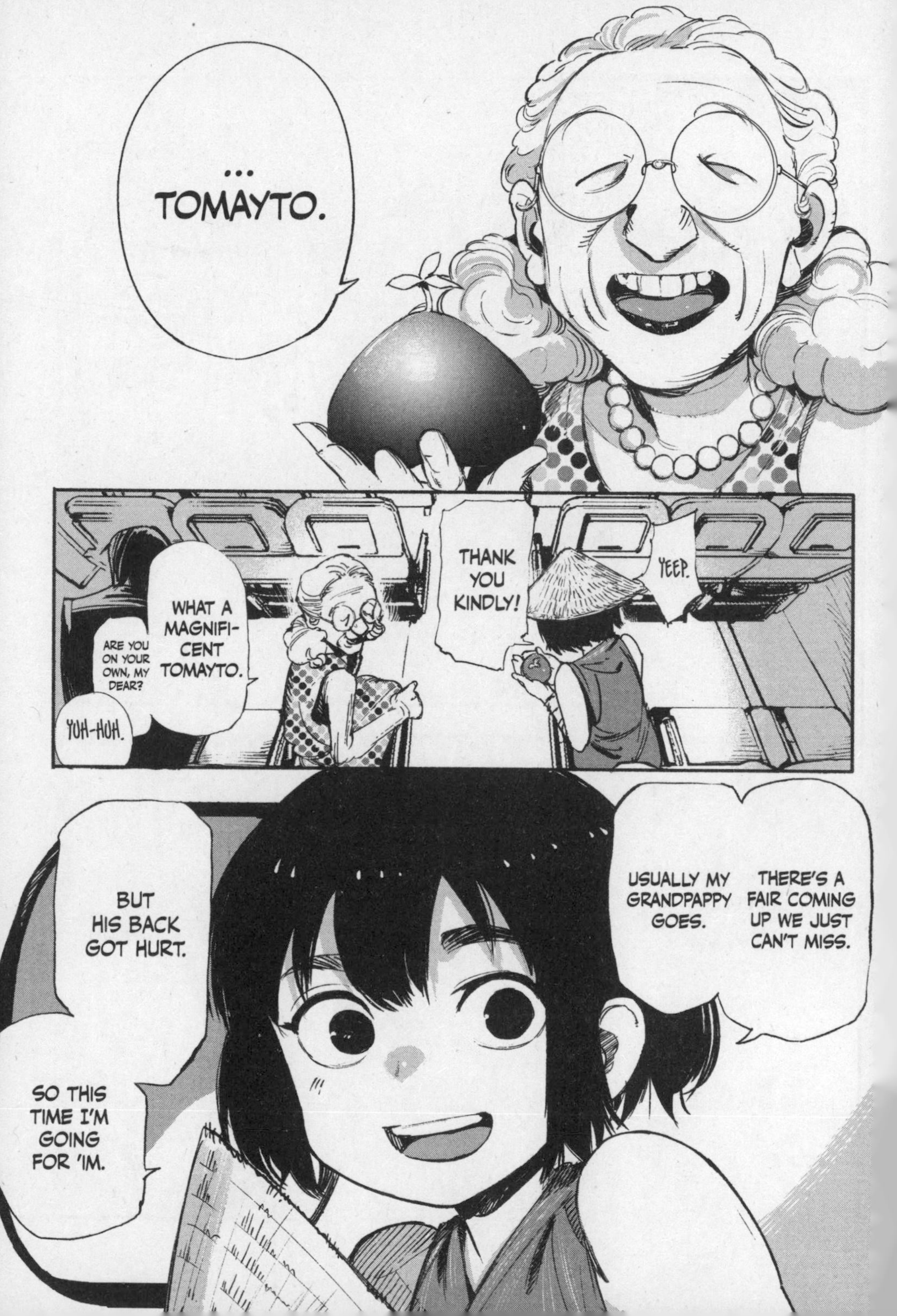
... TOMAYTO.
YEEP.
THANK YOU KINDLY!
WHAT A MAGNIFI-CENT TOMAYTO.
ARE YOU ON YOUR OWN, MY DEAR?
YUH-HUH.
THERE'S A FAIR COMING UP WE JUST CAN'T MISS.
USUALLY MY GRANDPAPPY GOES.
BUT HIS BACK GOT HURT.
SO THIS TIME I'M GOING FOR 'IM.

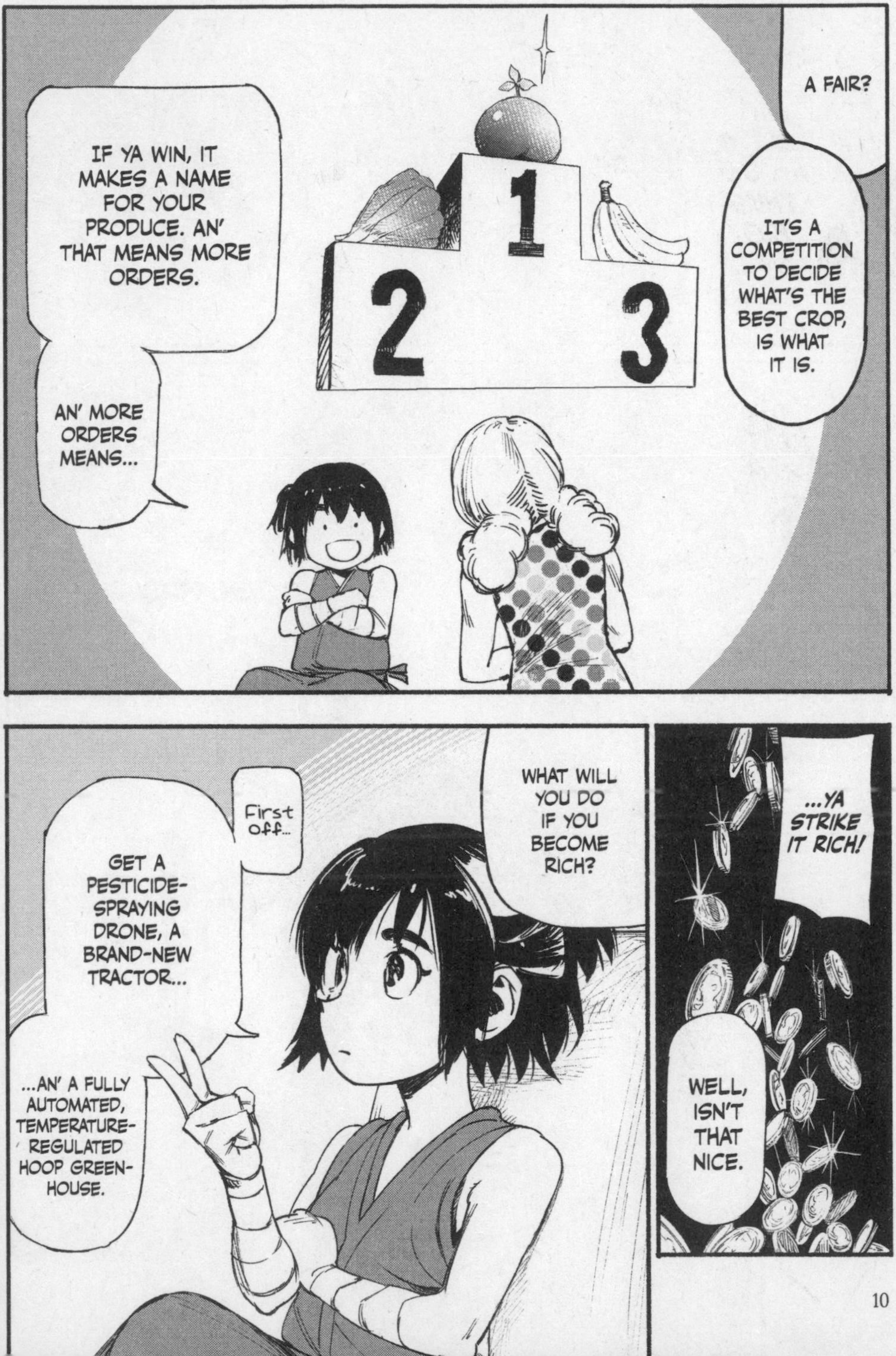
A FAIR?
IT'S A COMPETITION TO DECIDE WHAT'S THE BEST CROP, IS WHAT IT IS.
IF YA WIN, IT MAKES A NAME FOR YOUR PRODUCE. AN' THAT MEANS MORE ORDERS.
AN' MORE ORDERS MEANS...
...YA STRIKE IT RICH!
WELL, ISN'T THAT NICE.
WHAT WILL YOU DO IF YOU BECOME RICH?
First off...
GET A PESTICIDE-SPRAYING DRONE, A BRAND-NEW TRACTOR...
...AN' A FULLY AUTOMATED, TEMPERATURE-REGULATED HOOP GREEN-HOUSE.

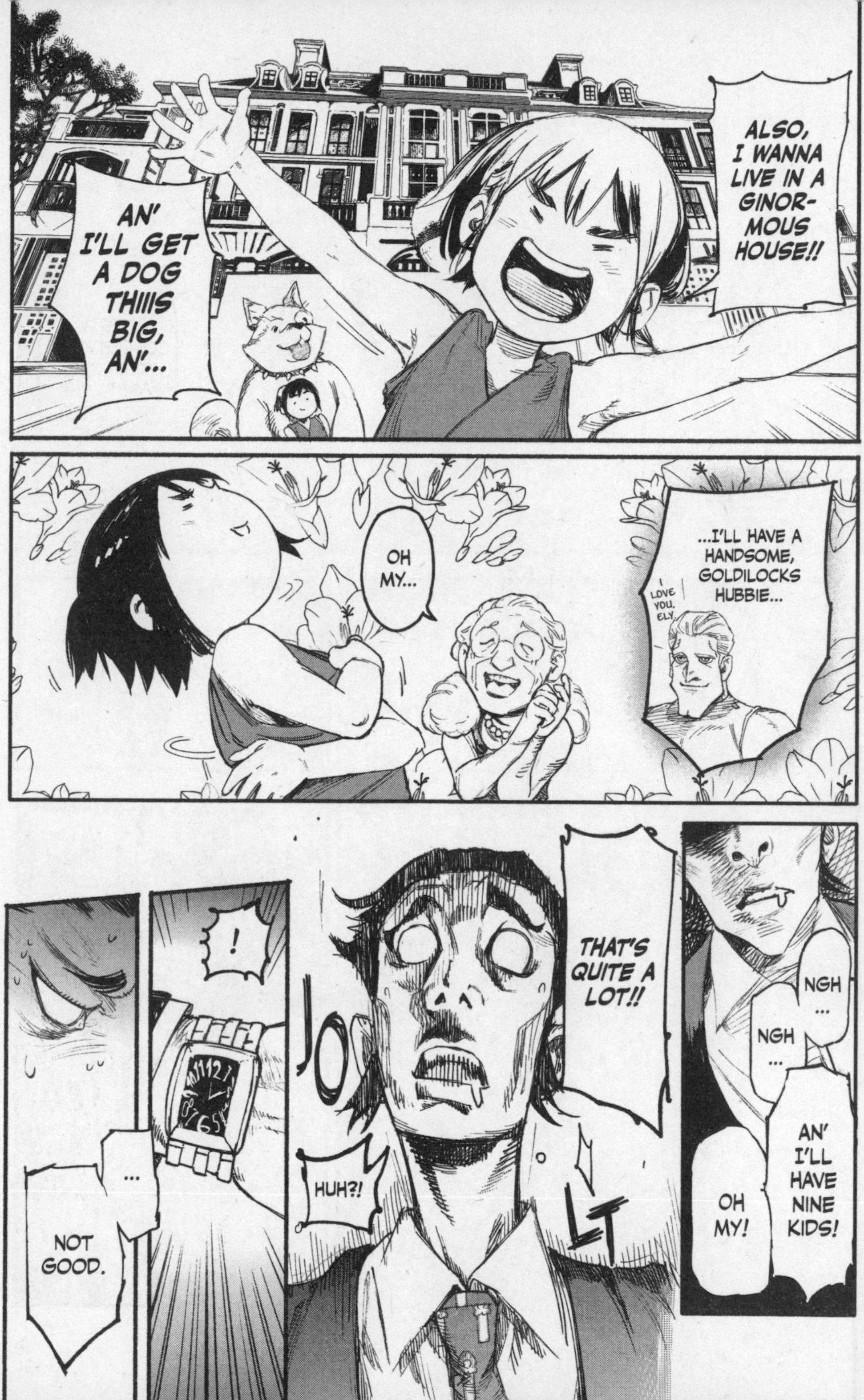
ALSO, I WANNA LIVE IN A GINOR-MOUS HOUSE!!
AN' I'LL GET A DOG THIIIS BIG, AN'...
...I'LL HAVE A HANDSOME, GOLDILOCKS HUBBIE...
I LOVE YOU, ELY.
OH MY...
NGH ...
NGH ...
AN' I'LL HAVE NINE KIDS!
OH MY!
THAT'S QUITE A LOT!!
HUH?!
!
...
NOT GOOD.

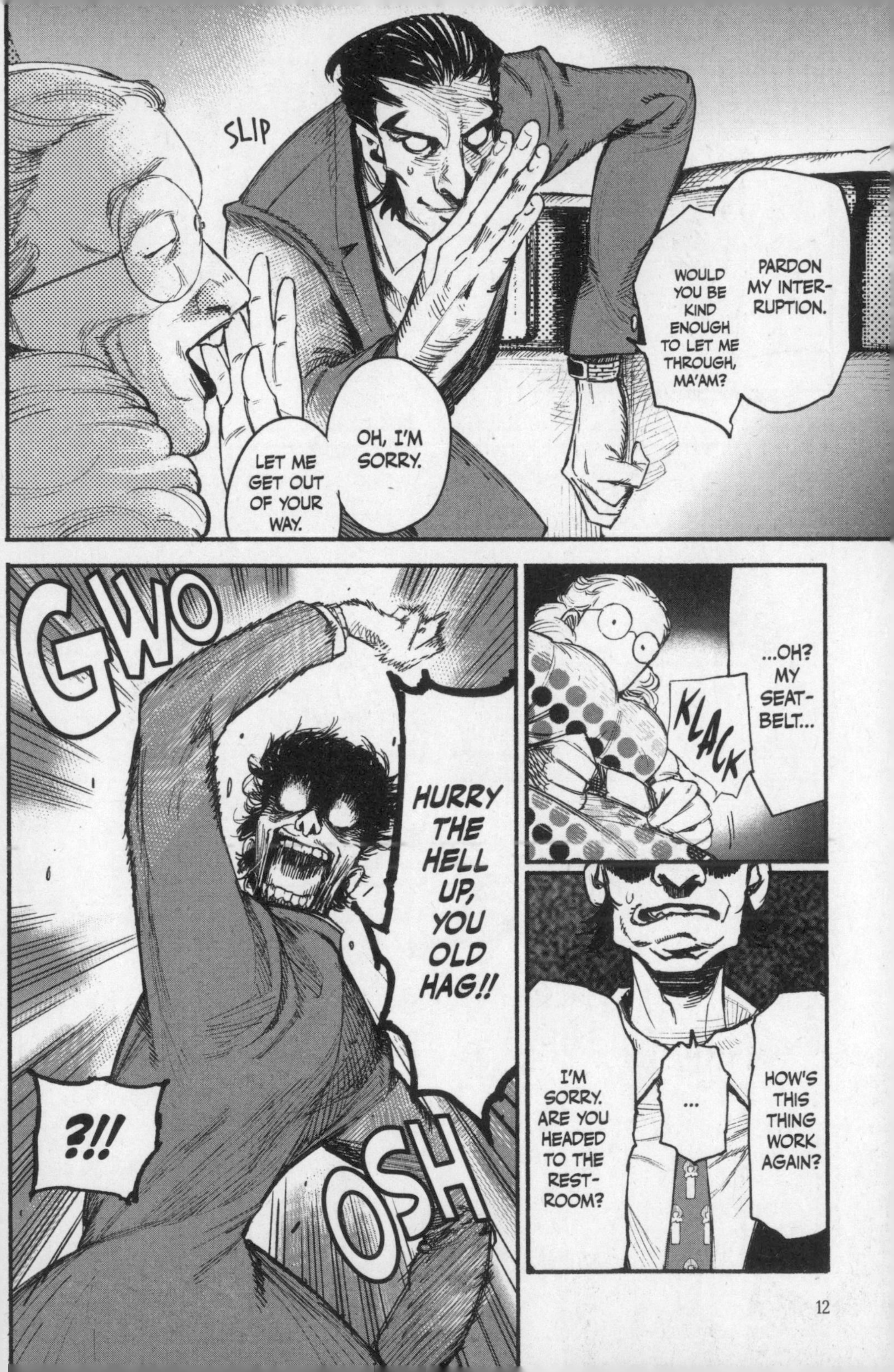
PARDON MY INTER-RUPTION.
WOULD YOU BE KIND ENOUGH TO LET ME THROUGH, MA'AM?
SLIP
OH, I'M SORRY.
LET ME GET OUT OF YOUR WAY.
...OH? MY SEAT-BELT...
KLACK
HOW'S THIS THING WORK AGAIN?
...
I'M SORRY. ARE YOU HEADED TO THE REST-ROOM?
GWO
HURRY THE HELL UP, YOU OLD HAG!!
?!!
OSH

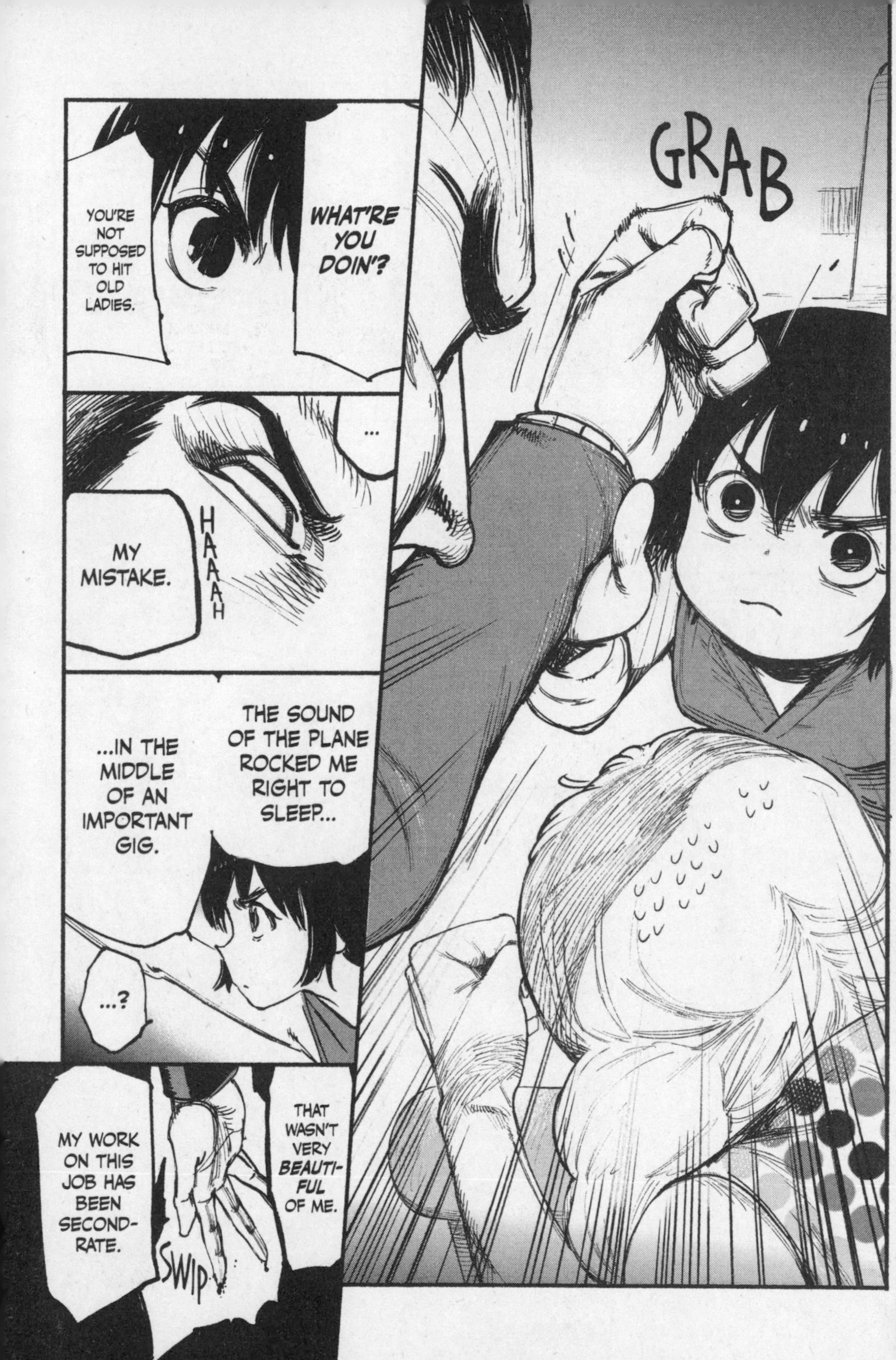
GRAB
WHAT'RE YOU DOIN'?
YOU'RE NOT SUPPOSED TO HIT OLD LADIES.
...
HAAAAH
MY MISTAKE.
THE SOUND OF THE PLANE ROCKED ME RIGHT TO SLEEP...
...IN THE MIDDLE OF AN IMPORTANT GIG.
...?
THAT WASN'T VERY BEAUTIFUL OF ME.
MY WORK ON THIS JOB HAS BEEN SECOND-RATE.
SWIP

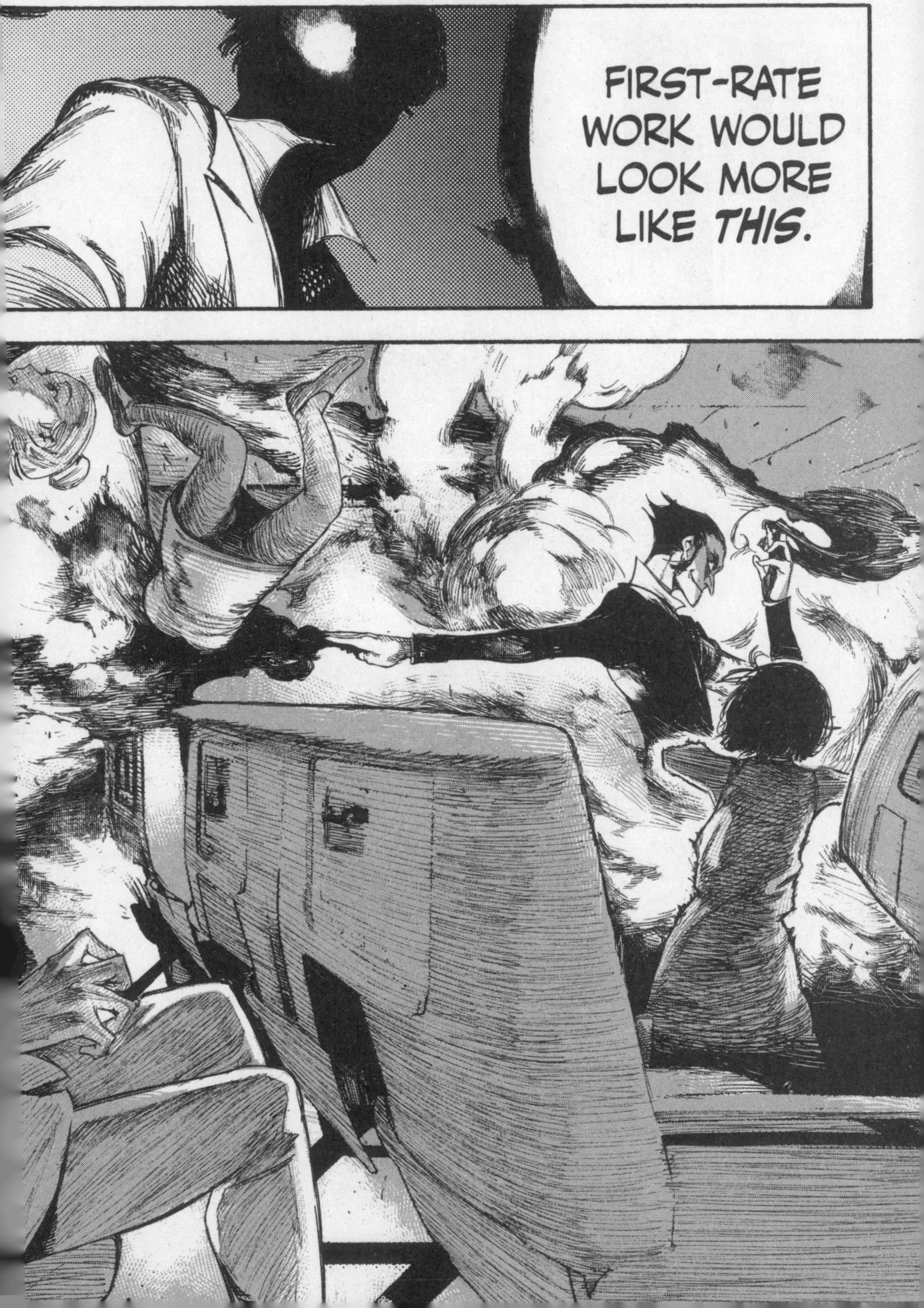
FIRST-RATE WORK WOULD LOOK MORE LIKE *THIS*.

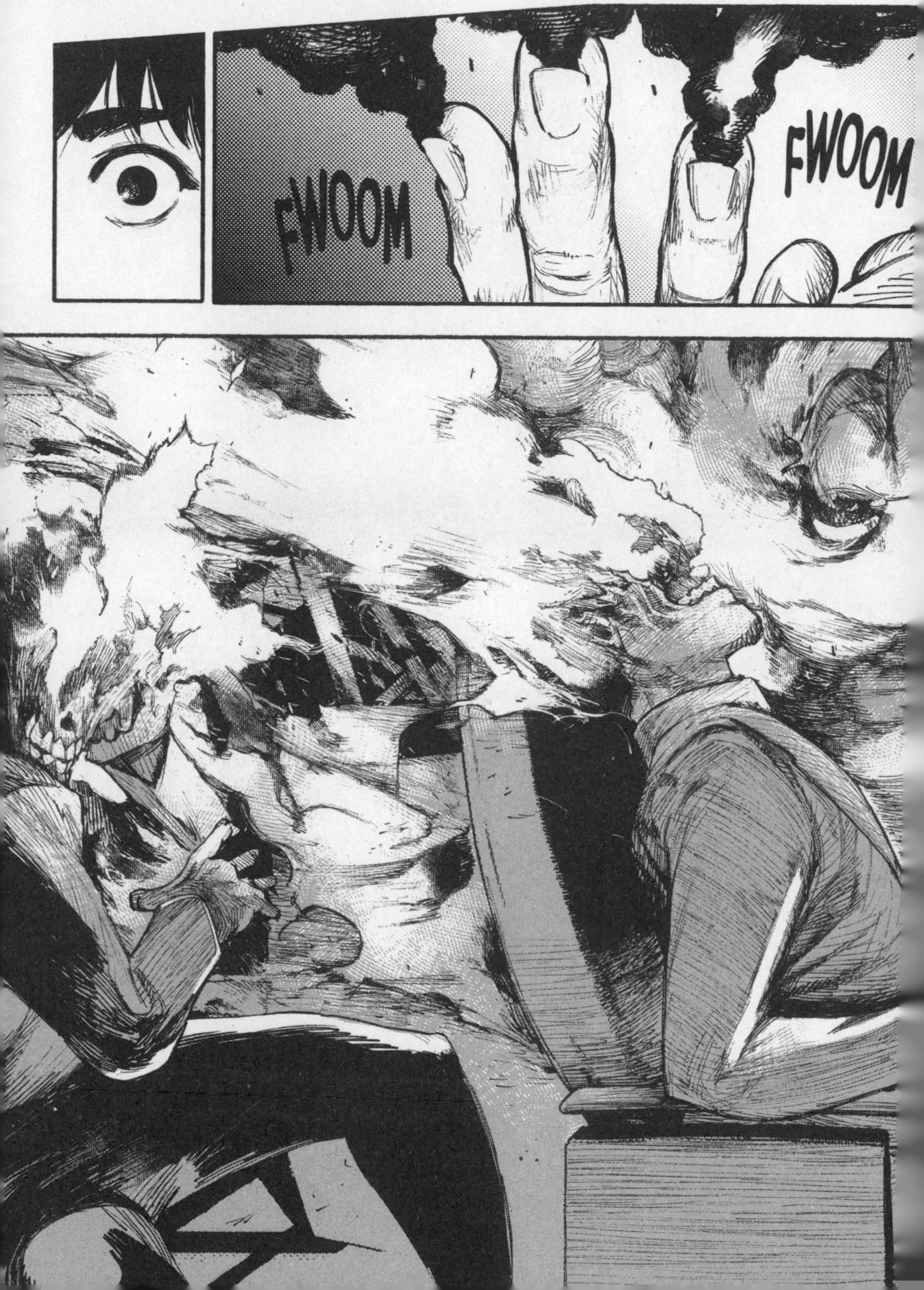
FWOOM
FWOOM

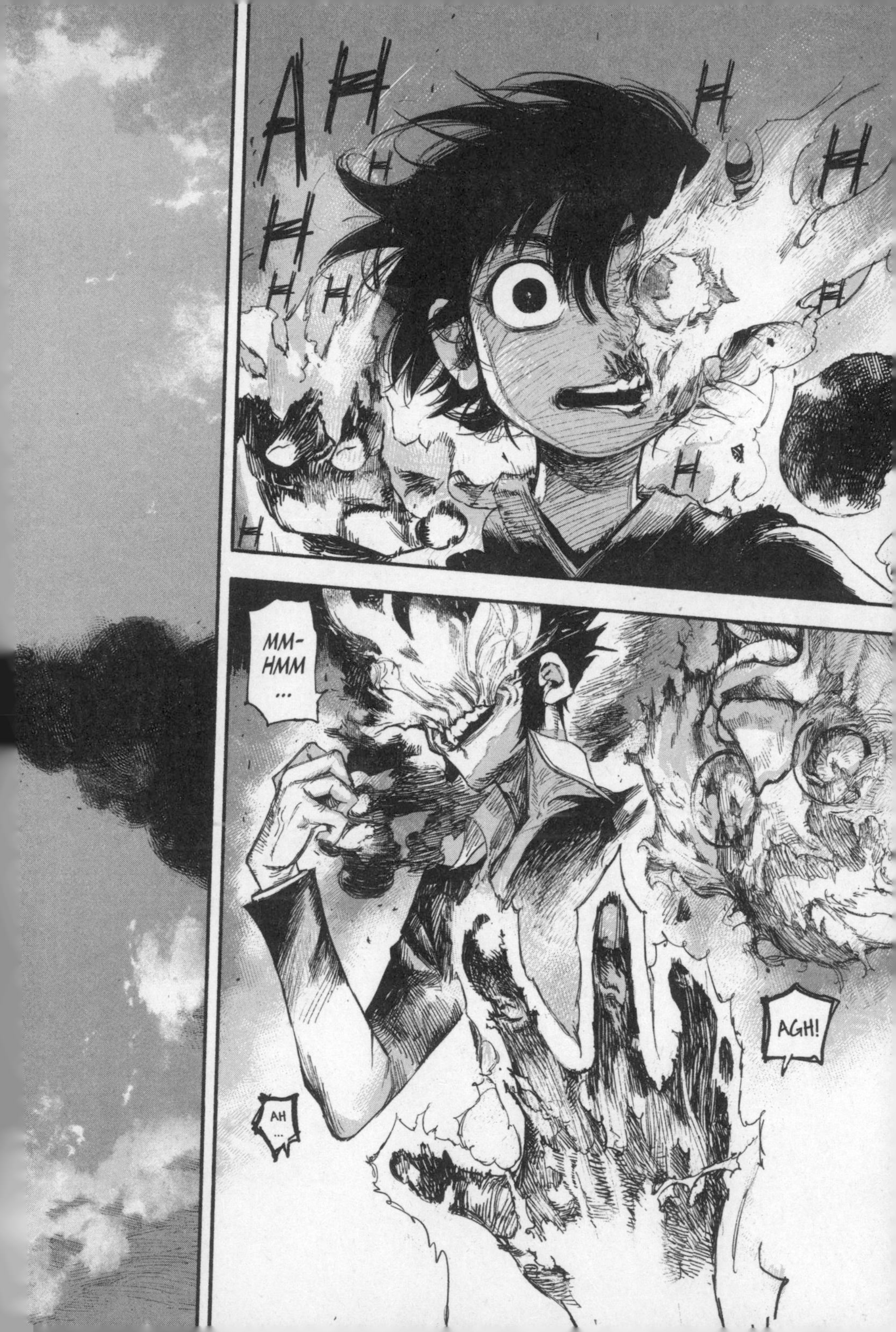
AHHHHH
MM-HMM ...
AGH!
AH ...

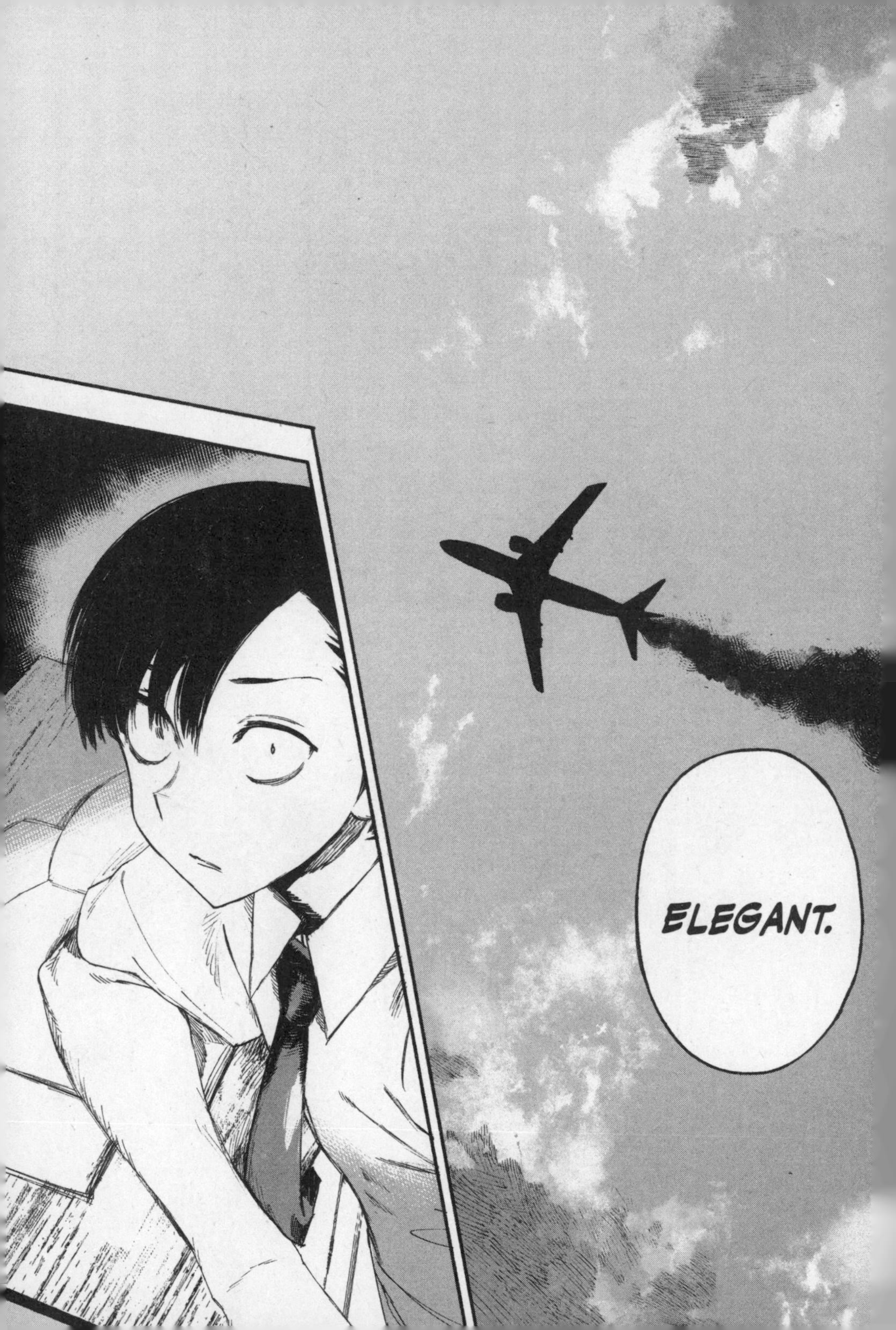
ELEGANT.

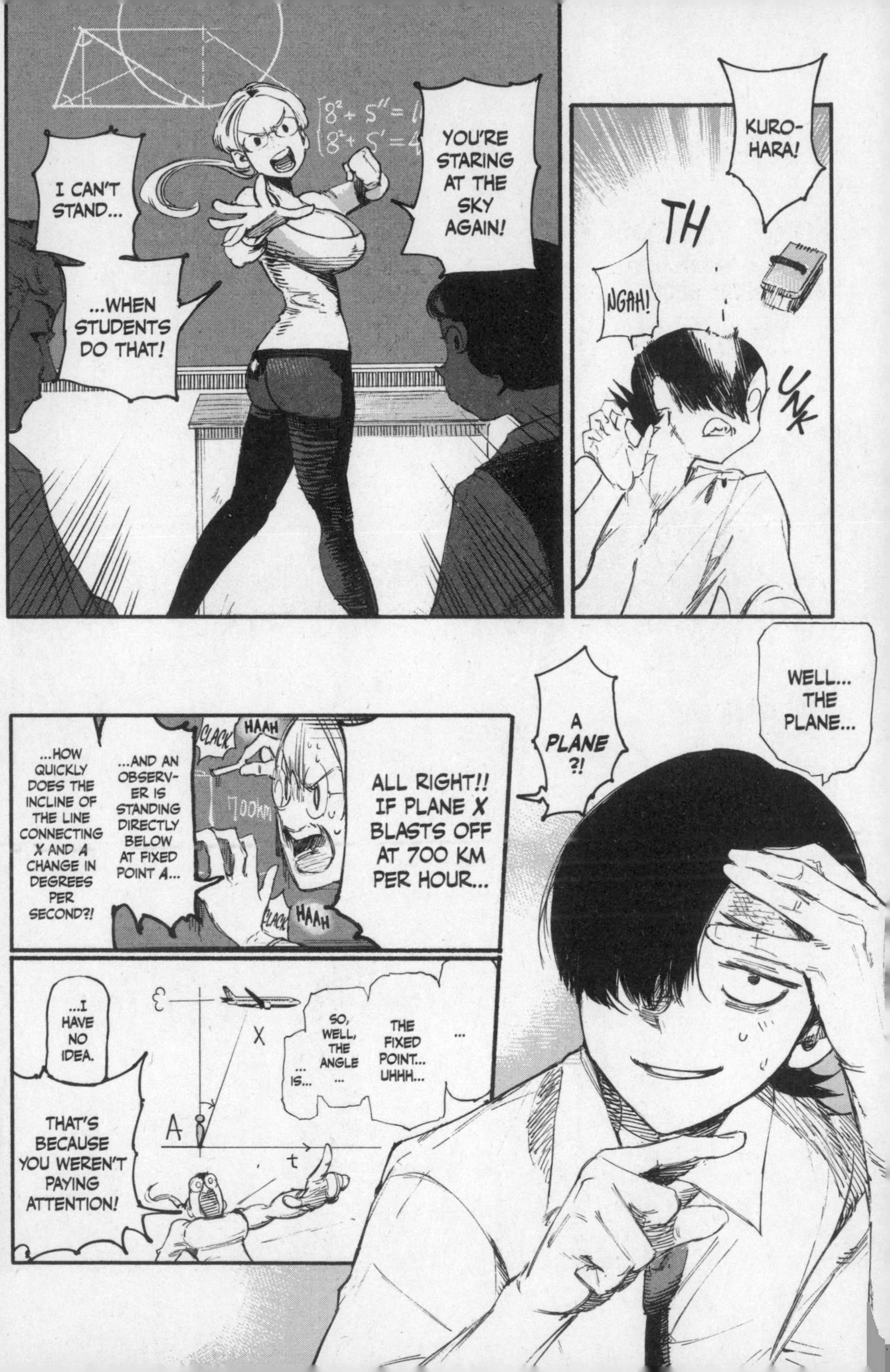
KURO-HARA!
TH
NGAH!
UNK
YOU'RE STARING AT THE SKY AGAIN!
I CAN'T STAND...
...WHEN STUDENTS DO THAT!
WELL... THE PLANE...
A PLANE ?!
ALL RIGHT!! IF PLANE X BLASTS OFF AT 700 KM PER HOUR...
...AND AN OBSERVER IS STANDING DIRECTLY BELOW AT FIXED POINT A...
...HOW QUICKLY DOES THE INCLINE OF THE LINE CONNECTING X AND A CHANGE IN DEGREES PER SECOND?!
CLACK
HAAH
CLACK
HAAH
...
THE FIXED POINT... UHHH...
SO, WELL, THE ANGLE ...
... IS...
...I HAVE NO IDEA.
THAT'S BECAUSE YOU WEREN'T PAYING ATTENTION!
X
A
t

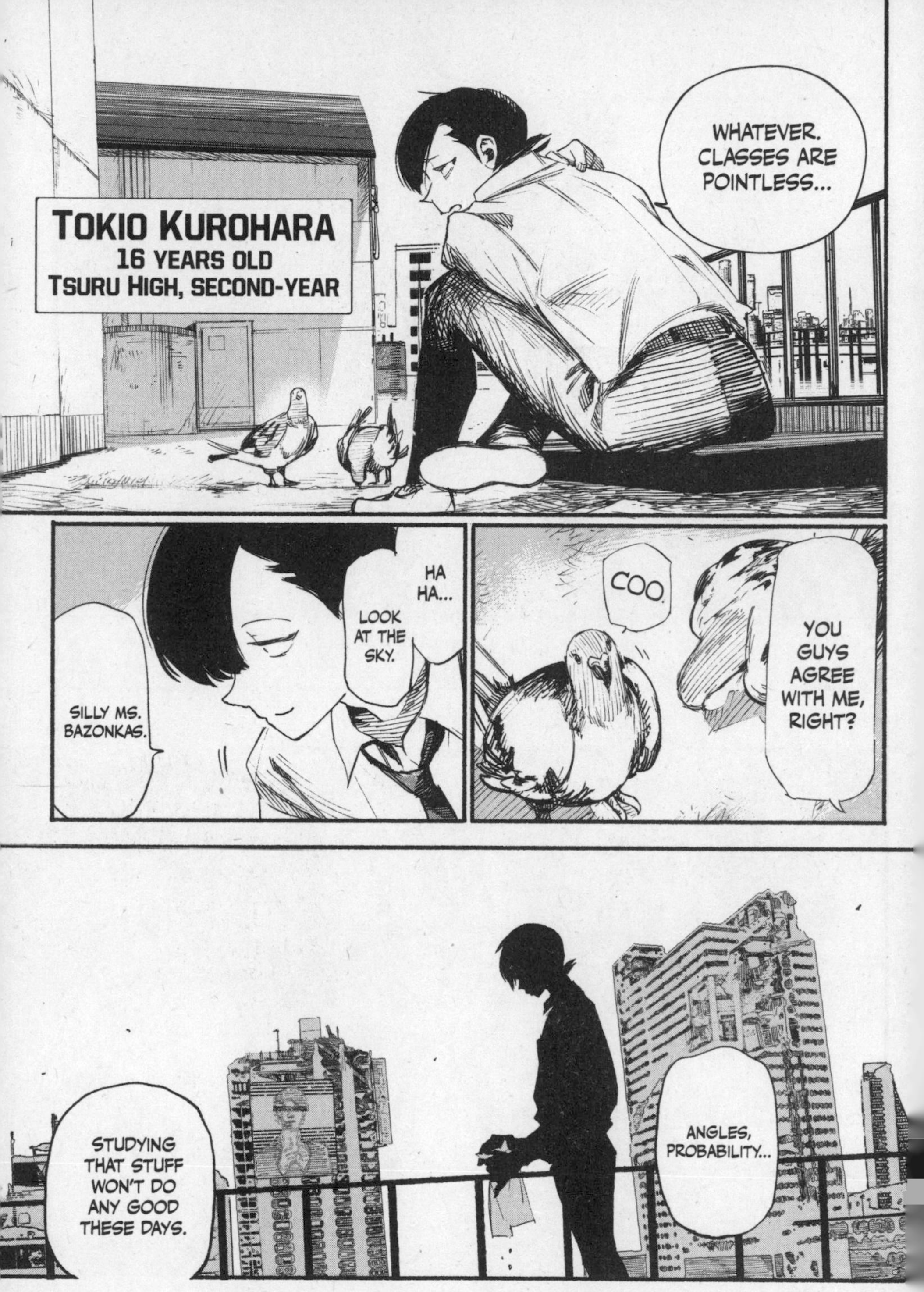
WHATEVER. CLASSES ARE POINTLESS...
TOKIO KUROHARA
16 YEARS OLD
TSURU HIGH, SECOND-YEAR
YOU GUYS AGREE WITH ME, RIGHT?
COO.
HA HA...
LOOK AT THE SKY.
SILLY MS. BAZONKAS.
ANGLES, PROBABILITY...
STUDYING THAT STUFF WON'T DO ANY GOOD THESE DAYS.

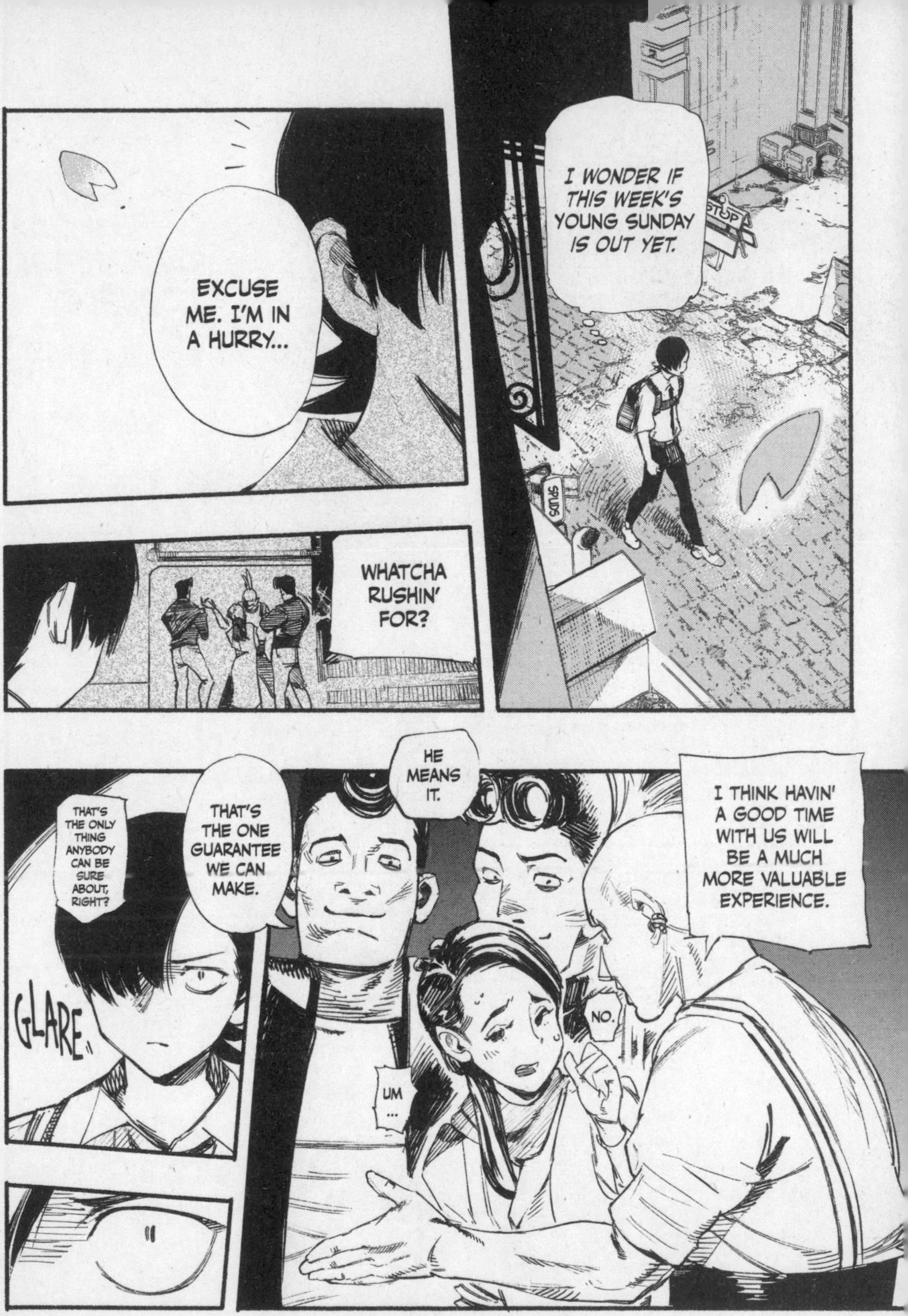

I WONDER IF THIS WEEK'S YOUNG SUNDAY IS OUT YET.
STOP
EXCUSE ME. I'M IN A HURRY...
WHATCHA RUSHIN' FOR?
I THINK HAVIN' A GOOD TIME WITH US WILL BE A MUCH MORE VALUABLE EXPERIENCE.
HE MEANS IT.
NO.
UM ...
THAT'S THE ONE GUARANTEE WE CAN MAKE.
THAT'S THE ONLY THING ANYBODY CAN BE SURE ABOUT, RIGHT?
GLARE.

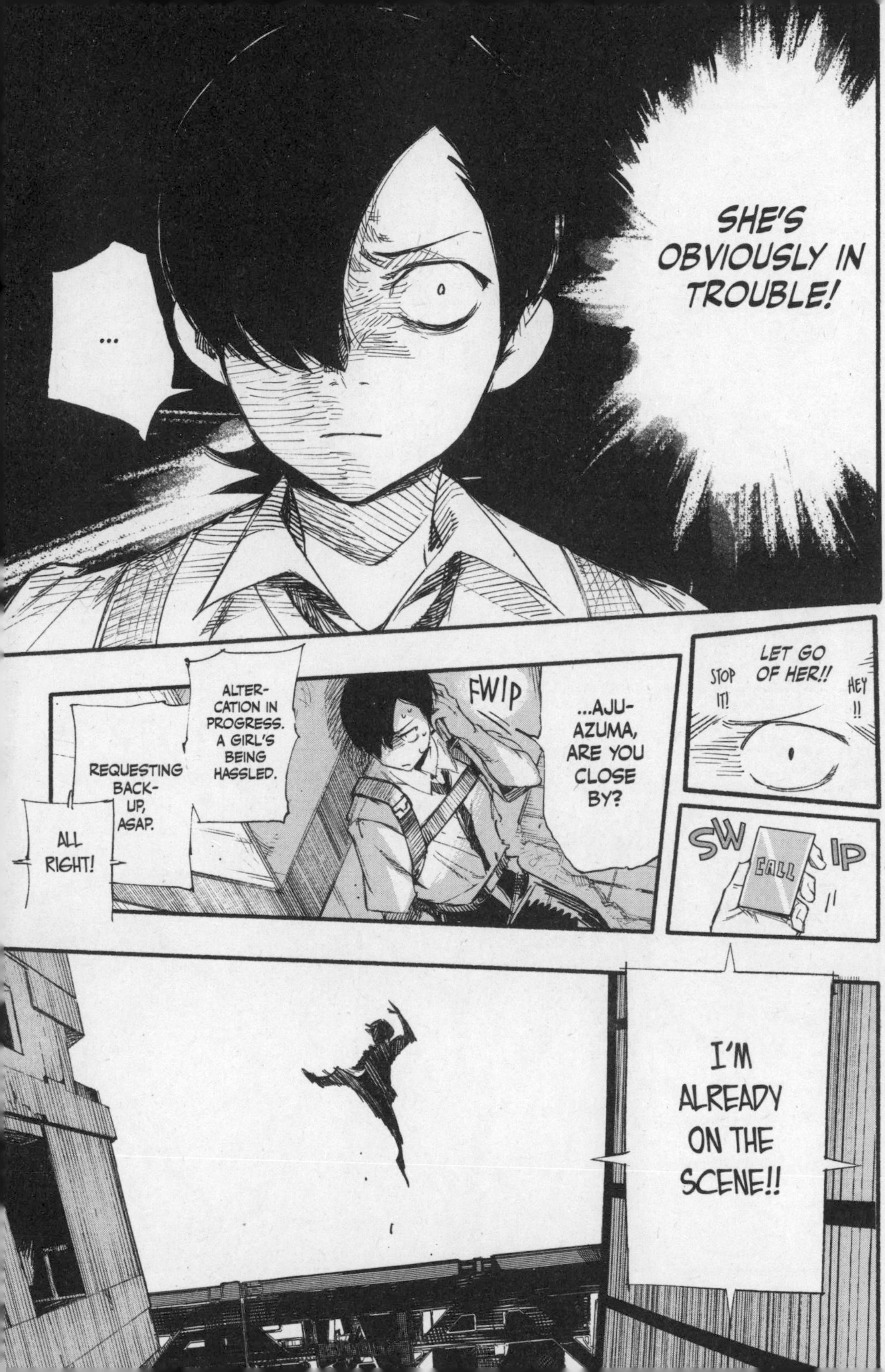
SHE'S OBVIOUSLY IN TROUBLE!
...
HEY !!
LET GO OF HER!!
STOP IT!
SWIP
CALL
...AJU-AZUMA, ARE YOU CLOSE BY?
FWIP
ALTER-CATION IN PROGRESS. A GIRL'S BEING HASSLED.
REQUESTING BACK-UP, ASAP.
ALL RIGHT!
I'M ALREADY ON THE SCENE!!

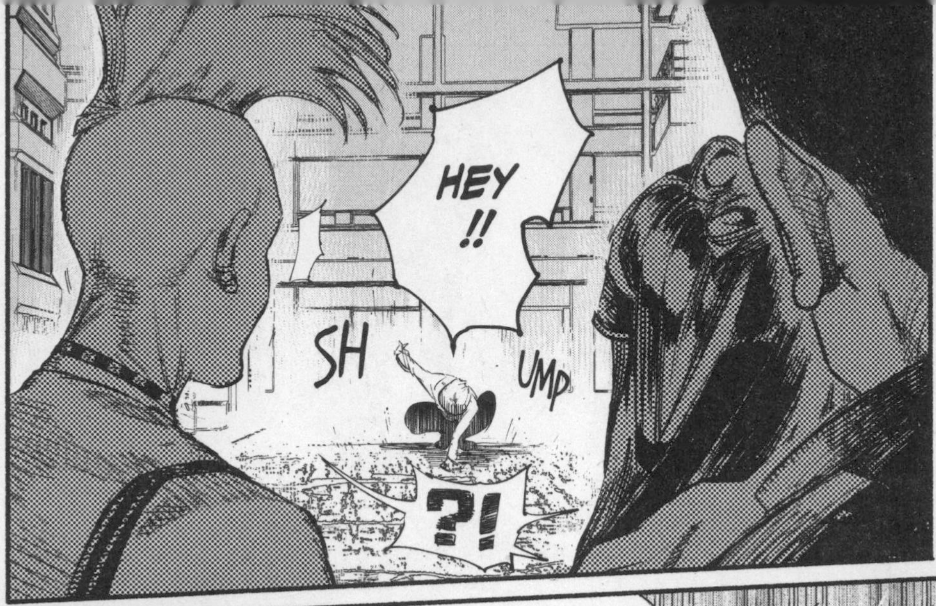
HEY !!
SH
UMP
?!

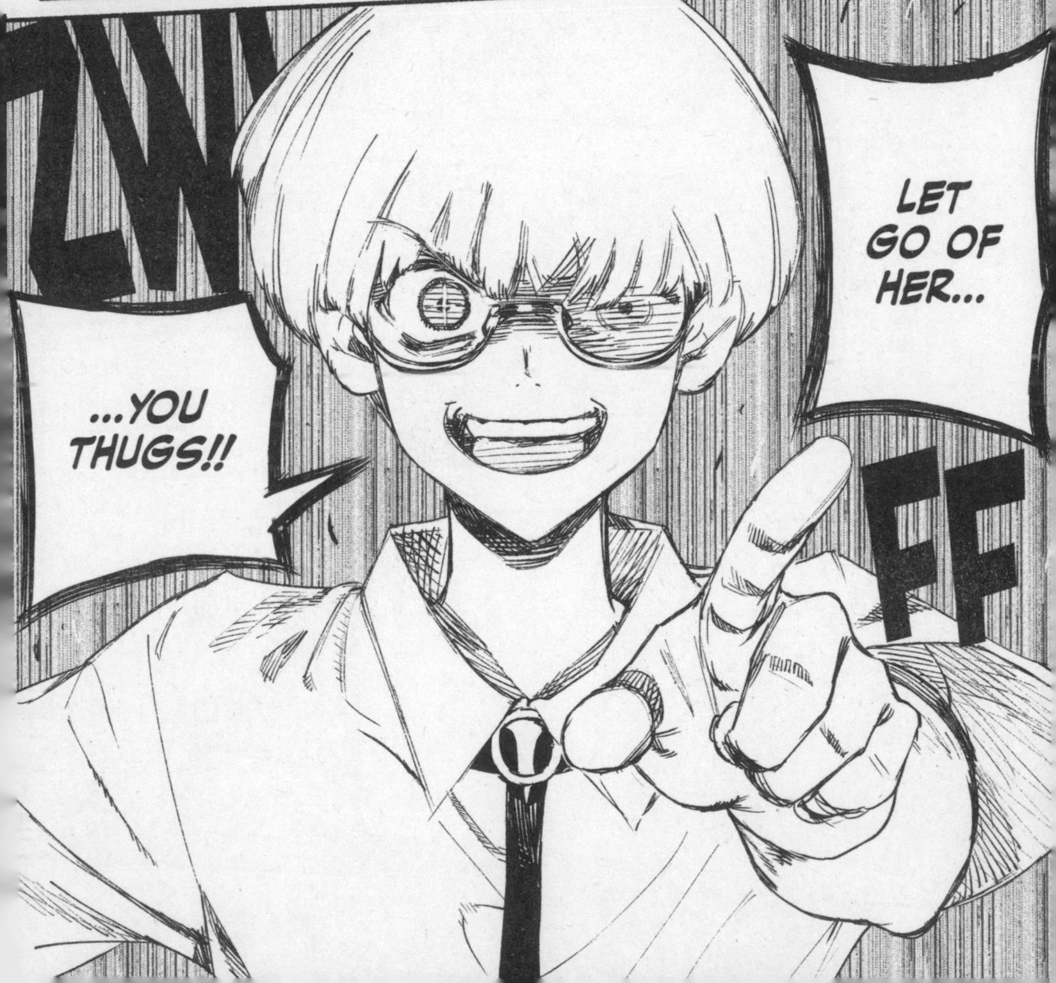
LET GO OF HER...
...YOU THUGS!!
FF

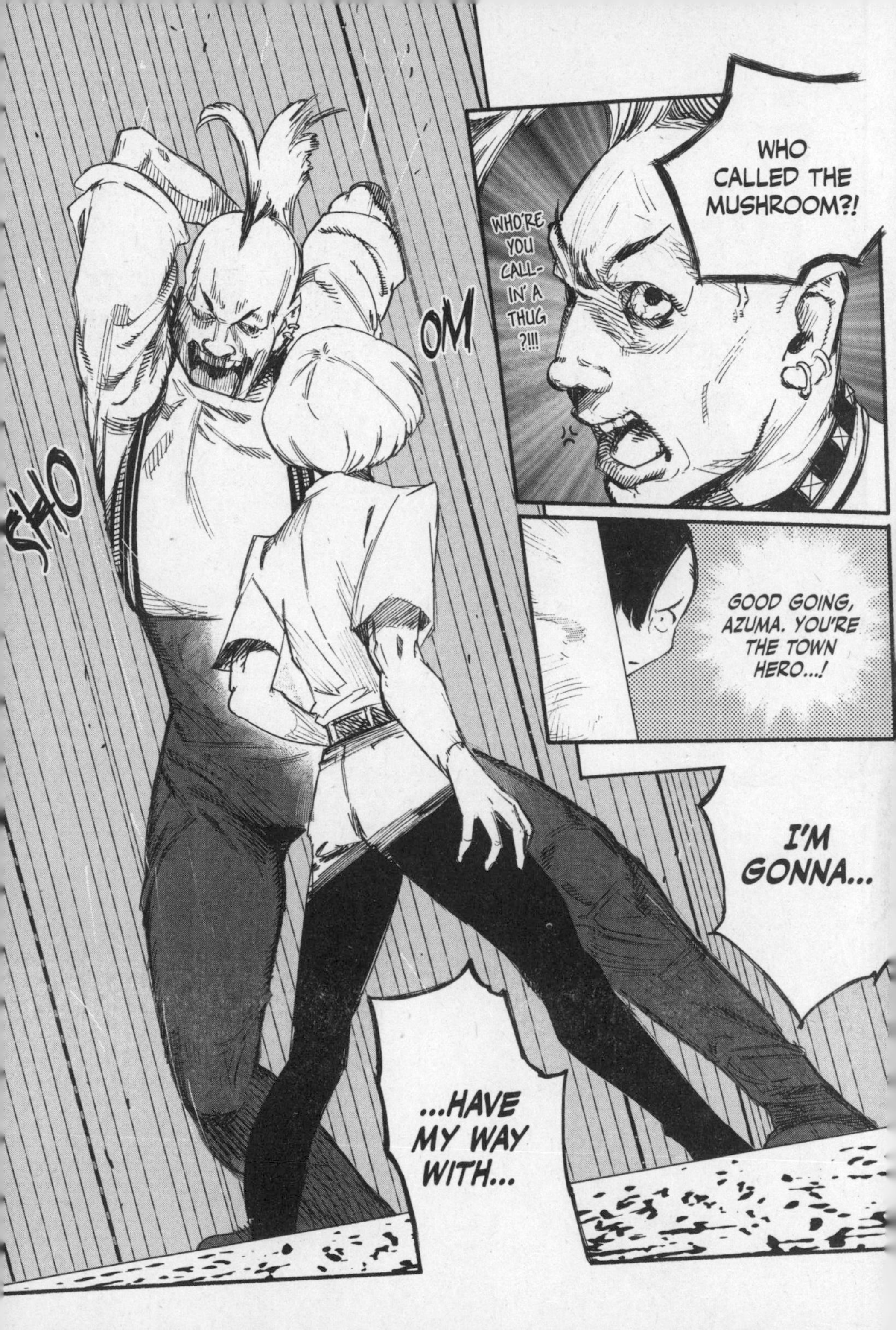
WHO CALLED THE MUSHROOM?!
WHO'RE YOU CALL-IN' A THUG ?!!!
GOOD GOING, AZUMA. YOU'RE THE TOWN HERO...!
OM
SHO
I'M GONNA...
...HAVE MY WAY WITH...

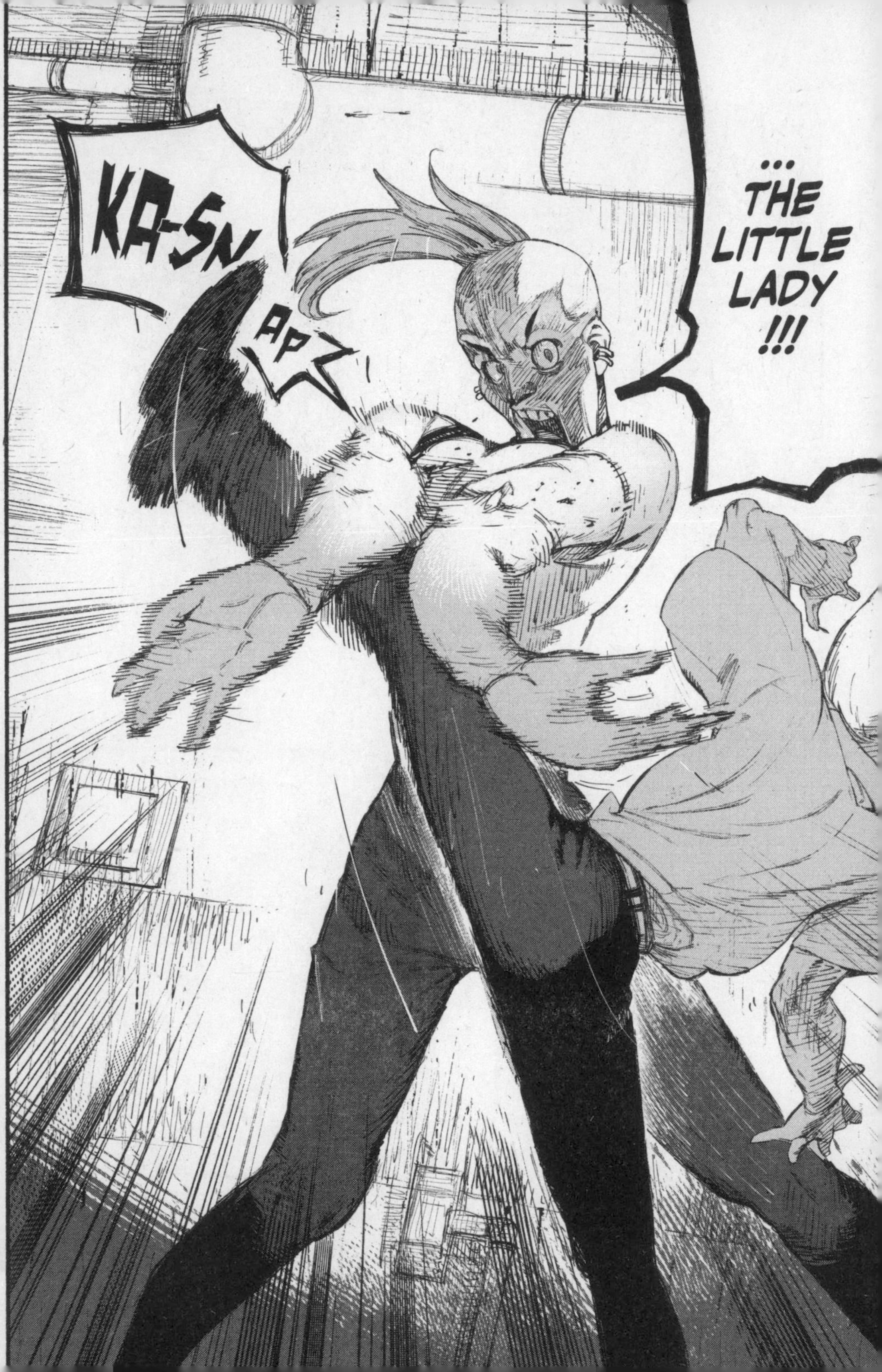
...THE LITTLE LADY!!!
KA-SNAP

AHHH HHHH H HH H H H H H H
AZUMAAA ?!
THAT'S GOING TOO FAR...!
SHUDDER
AHHHHH
NICE KICK ...

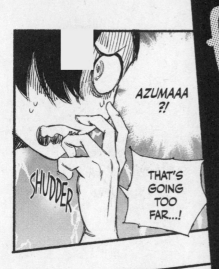

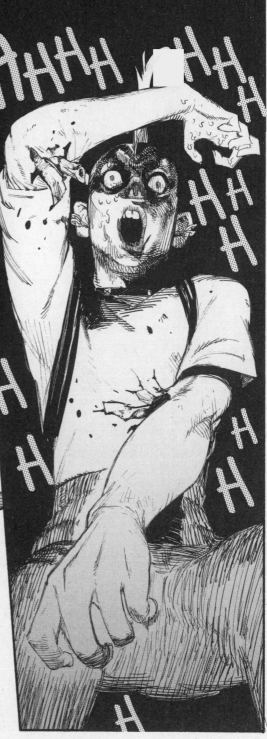

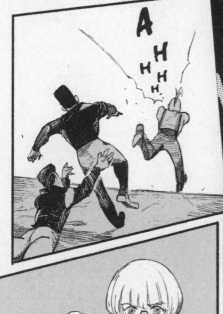

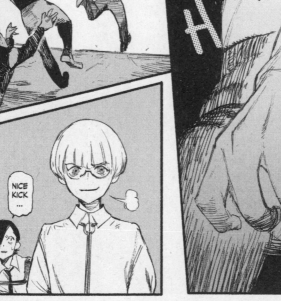

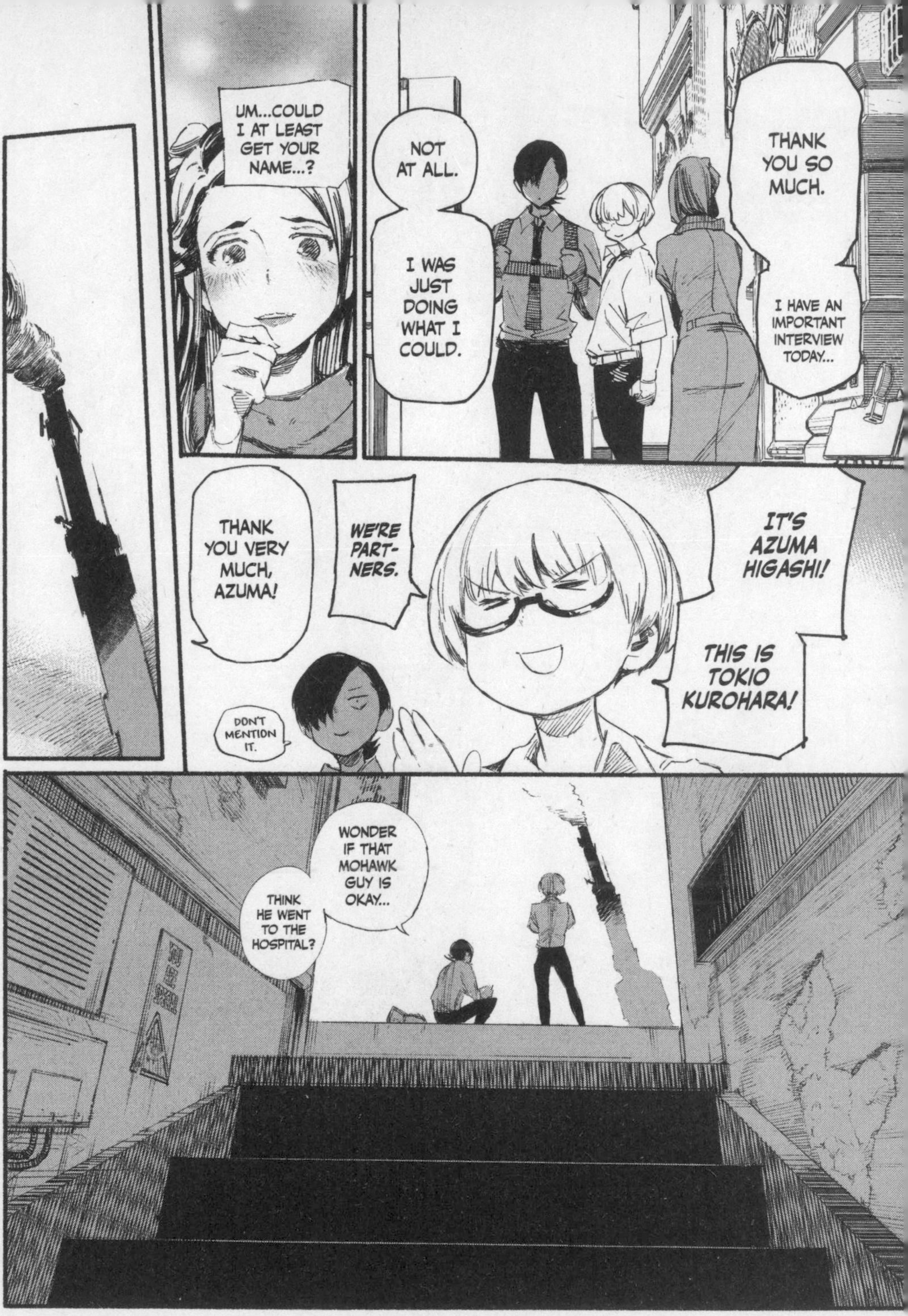
THANK YOU SO MUCH.
I HAVE AN IMPORTANT INTERVIEW TODAY...
NOT AT ALL.
I WAS JUST DOING WHAT I COULD.
UM...COULD I AT LEAST GET YOUR NAME...?
IT'S AZUMA HIGASHI!
THIS IS TOKIO KUROHARA!
WE'RE PARTNERS.
THANK YOU VERY MUCH, AZUMA!
DON'T MENTION IT.
WONDER IF THAT MOHAWK GUY IS OKAY...
THINK HE WENT TO THE HOSPITAL?

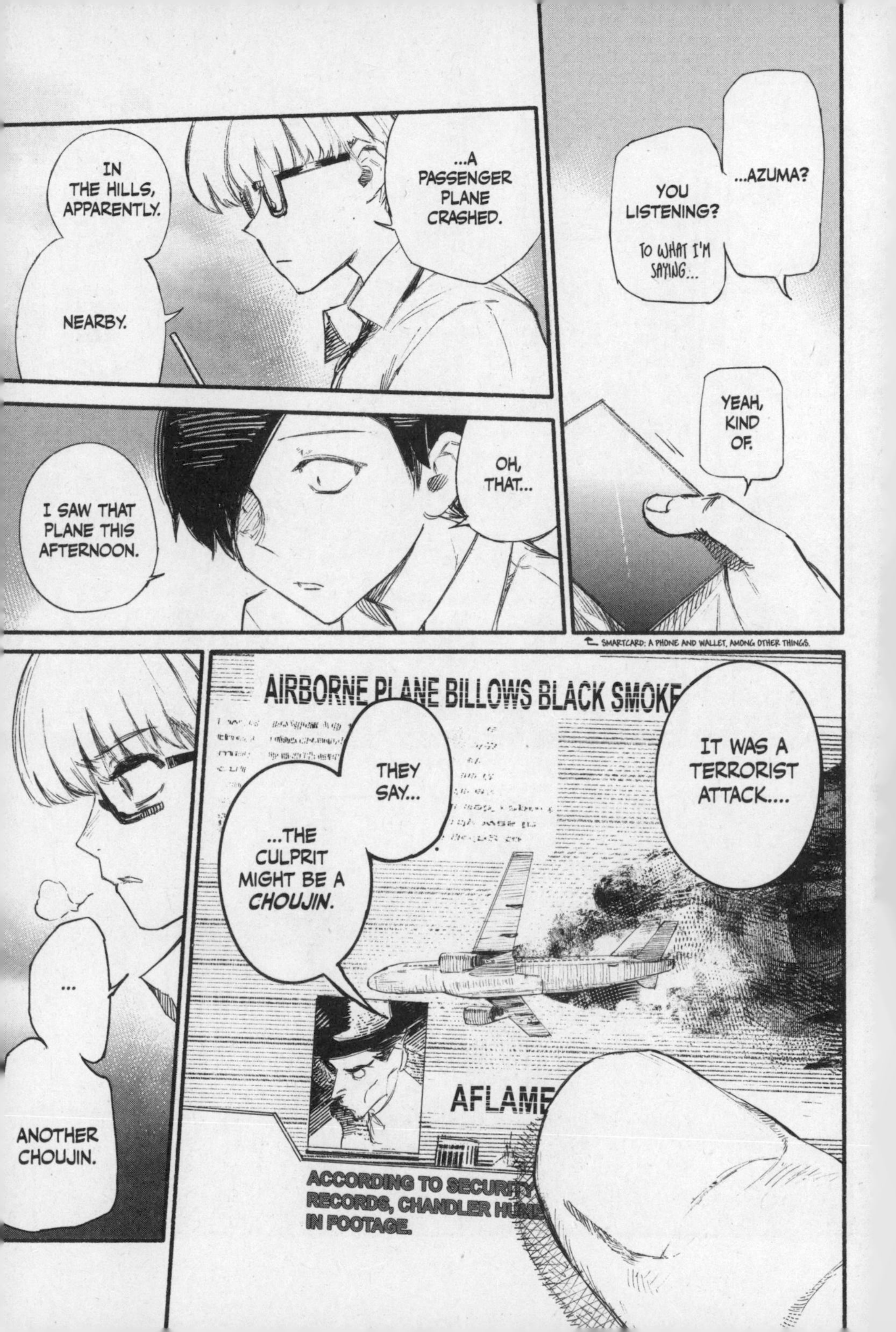

...AZUMA?
YOU LISTENING?
TO WHAT I'M SAYING...
YEAH, KIND OF.
SMARTCARD: A PHONE AND WALLET, AMONG OTHER THINGS.
...A PASSENGER PLANE CRASHED.
IN THE HILLS, APPARENTLY.
NEARBY.
OH, THAT...
I SAW THAT PLANE THIS AFTERNOON.
AIRBORNE PLANE BILLOWS BLACK SMOKE
IT WAS A TERRORIST ATTACK....
THEY SAY...
...THE CULPRIT MIGHT BE A *CHOUJIN.*
AFLAME
ACCORDING TO SECUR
RECORDS, CHANDLER HUN
IN FOOTAGE.
...
ANOTHER CHOUJIN.

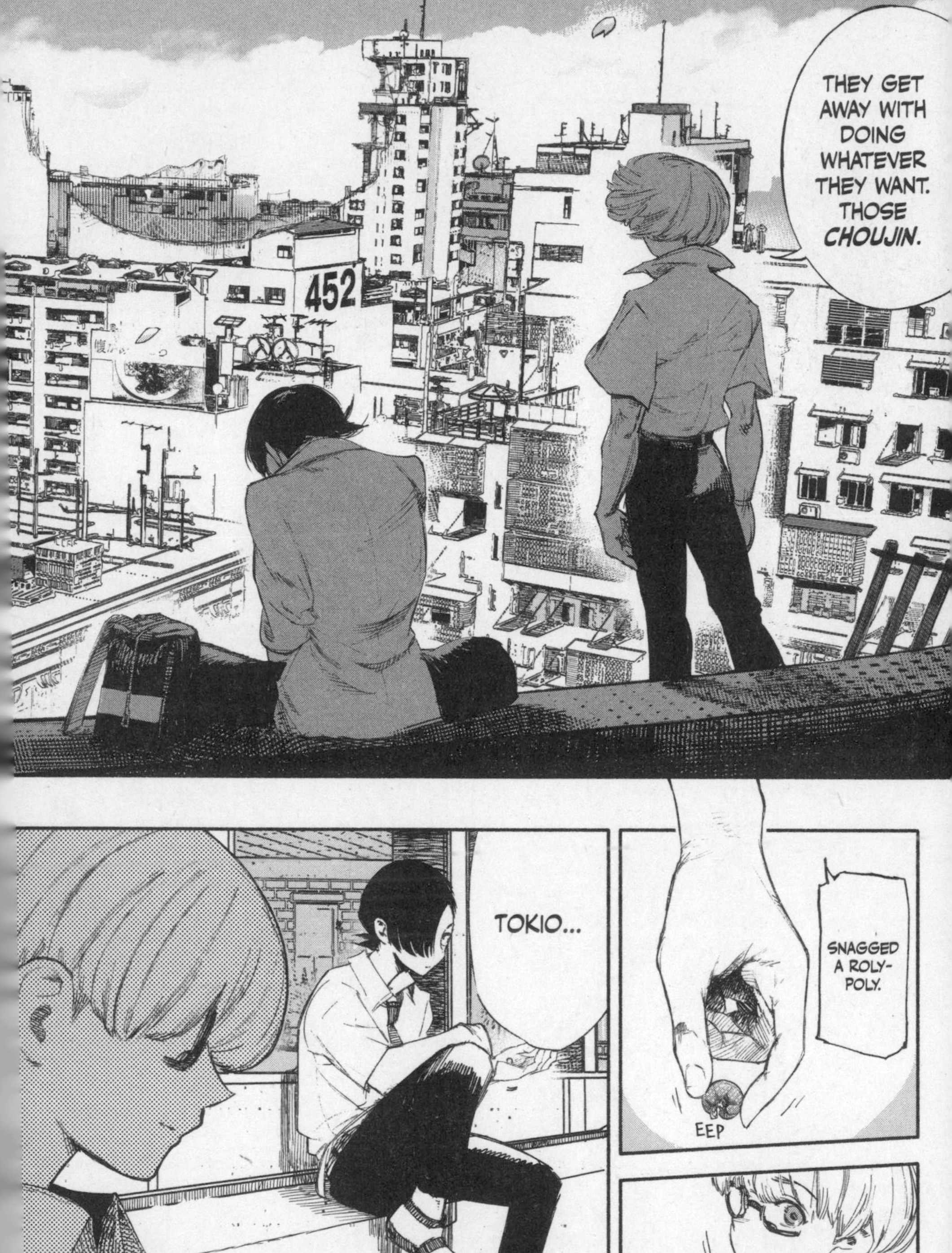
THEY GET AWAY WITH DOING WHATEVER THEY WANT. THOSE *CHOUJIN*.
452
SNAGGED A ROLY-POLY.
EEP
TOKIO...

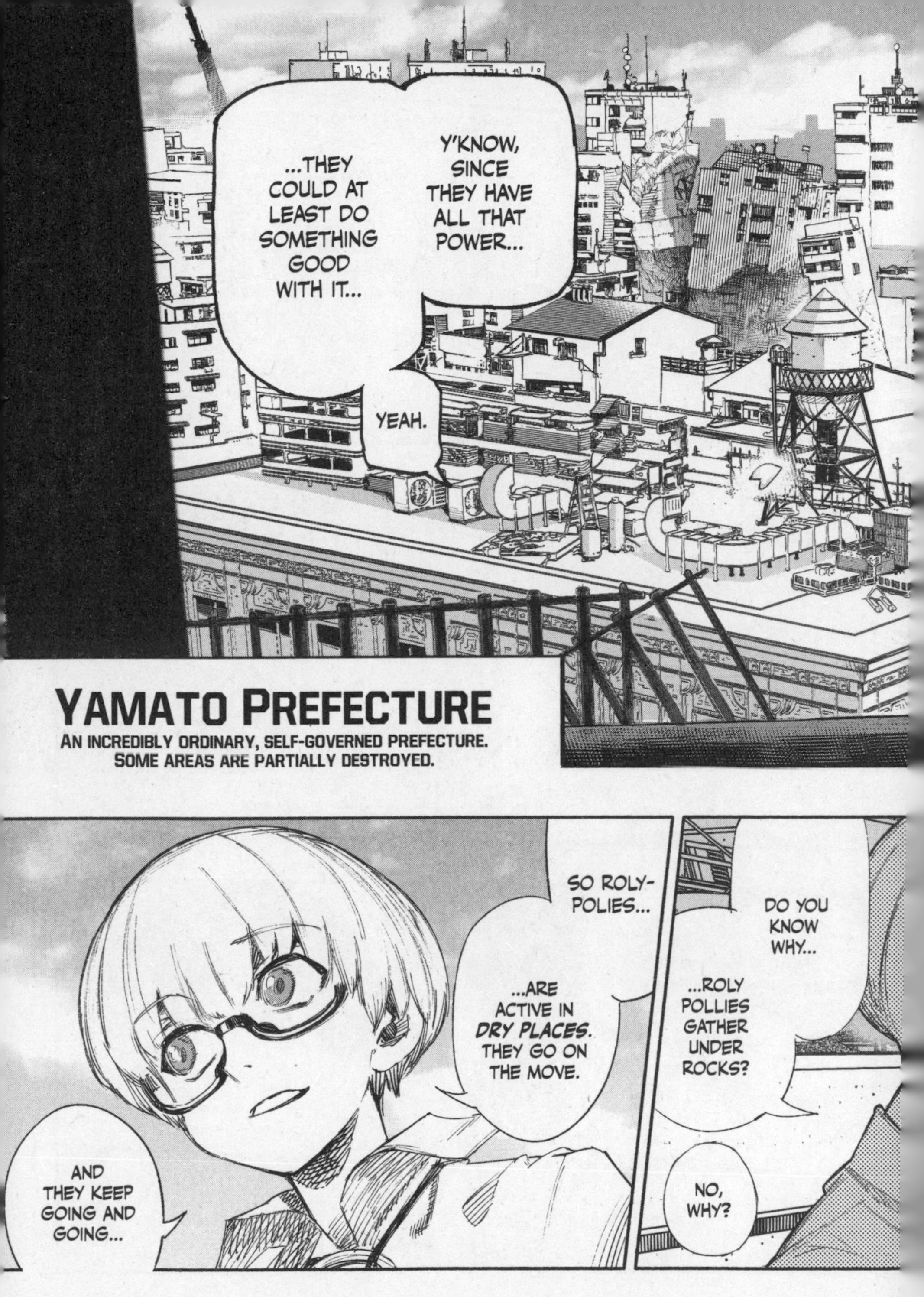
Y'KNOW, SINCE THEY HAVE ALL THAT POWER...
...THEY COULD AT LEAST DO SOMETHING GOOD WITH IT...
YEAH.
YAMATO PREFECTURE
AN INCREDIBLY ORDINARY, SELF-GOVERNED PREFECTURE. SOME AREAS ARE PARTIALLY DESTROYED.
DO YOU KNOW WHY...
...ROLY POLLIES GATHER UNDER ROCKS?
NO, WHY?
SO ROLY-POLIES...
...ARE ACTIVE IN DRY PLACES. THEY GO ON THE MOVE.
AND THEY KEEP GOING AND GOING...

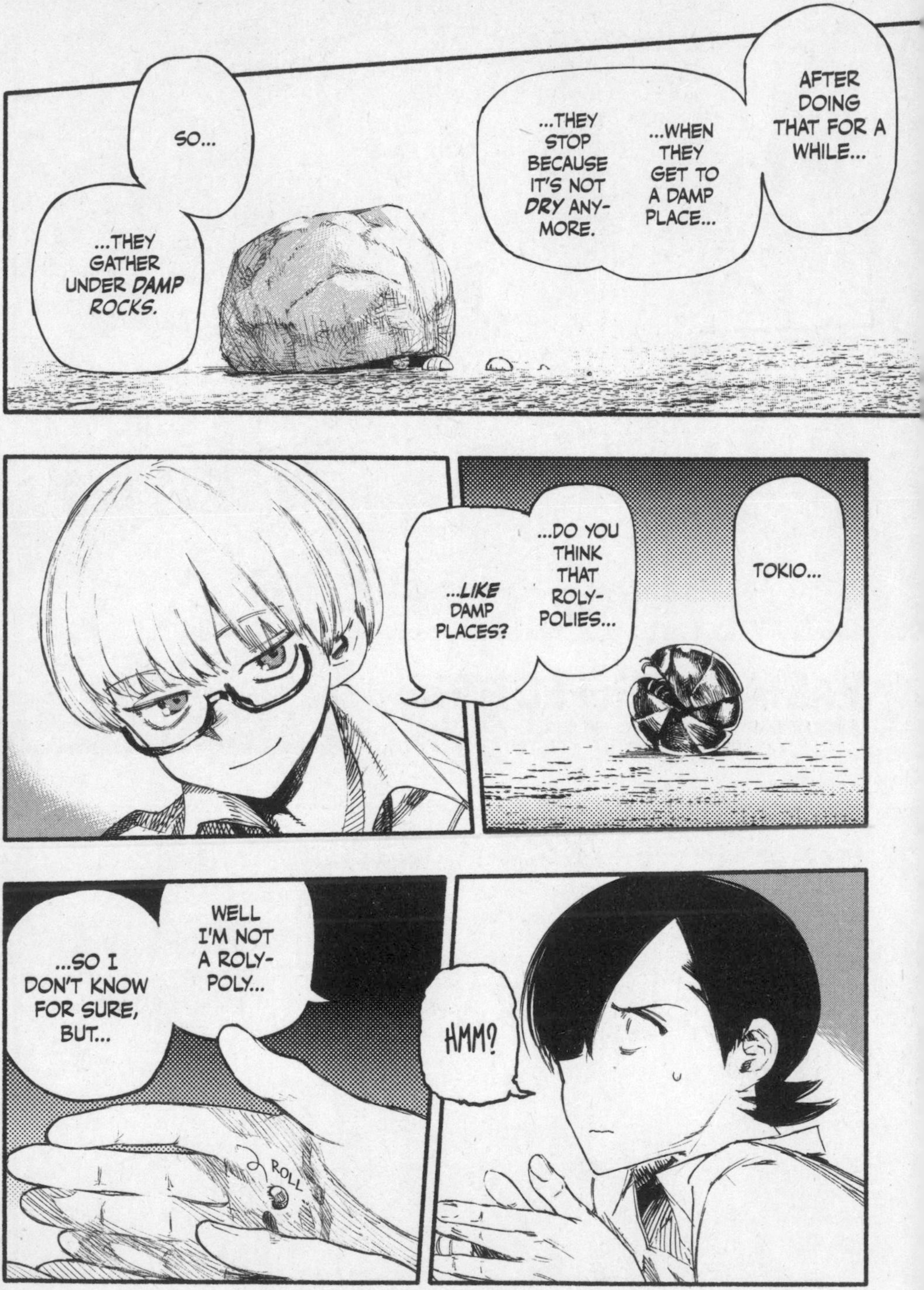
AFTER DOING THAT FOR A WHILE...
...WHEN THEY GET TO A DAMP PLACE...
...THEY STOP BECAUSE IT'S NOT DRY ANYMORE.
SO...
...THEY GATHER UNDER DAMP ROCKS.
TOKIO...
...DO YOU THINK THAT ROLY-POLIES...
...LIKE DAMP PLACES?
HMM?
WELL I'M NOT A ROLY-POLY...
...SO I DON'T KNOW FOR SURE, BUT...
ROLL

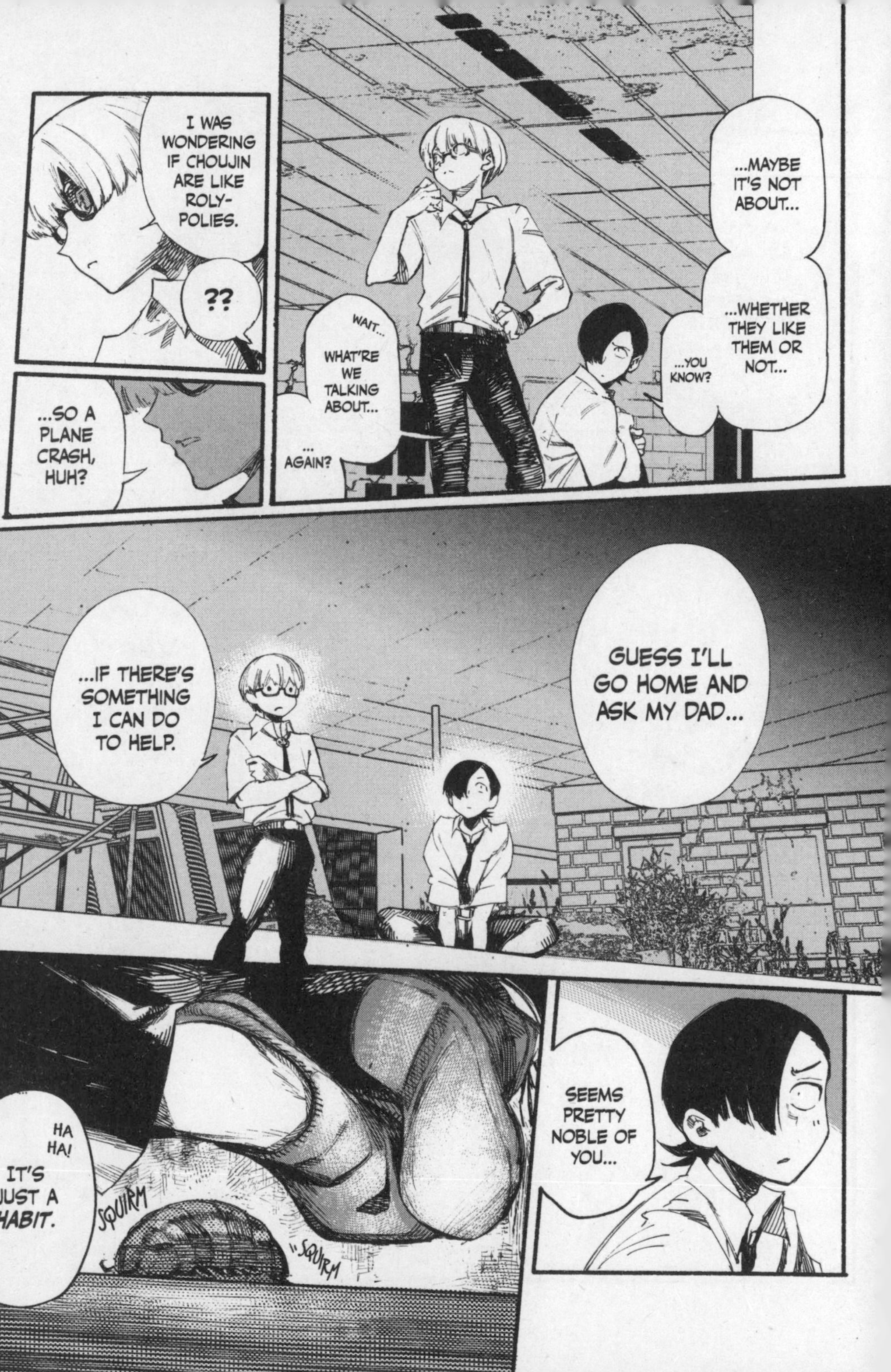
...MAYBE IT'S NOT ABOUT...
...WHETHER THEY LIKE THEM OR NOT...
...YOU KNOW?
WAIT... WHAT'RE WE TALKING ABOUT... ...AGAIN?
I WAS WONDERING IF CHOUJIN ARE LIKE ROLY-POLIES.
??
...SO A PLANE CRASH, HUH?
GUESS I'LL GO HOME AND ASK MY DAD...
...IF THERE'S SOMETHING I CAN DO TO HELP.
SEEMS PRETTY NOBLE OF YOU...
HA HA! IT'S JUST A *HABIT*.
SQUIRM
SQUIRM

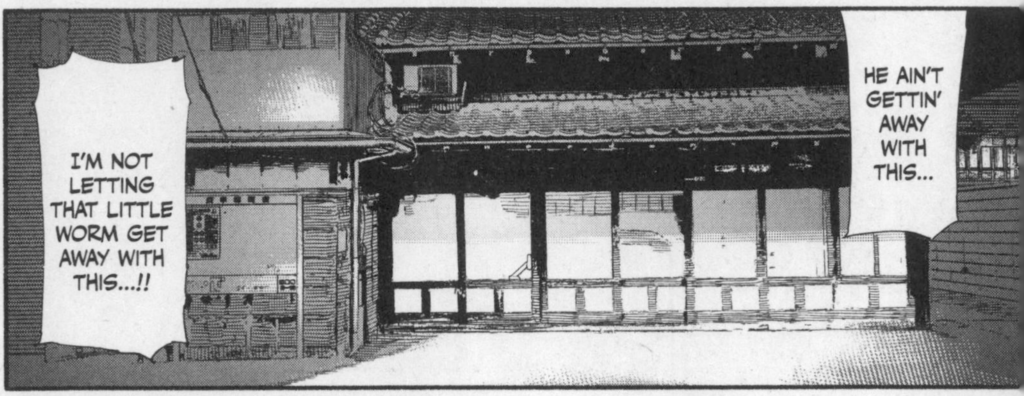
HE AIN'T GETTIN' AWAY WITH THIS...
I'M NOT LETTING THAT LITTLE WORM GET AWAY WITH THIS...!!

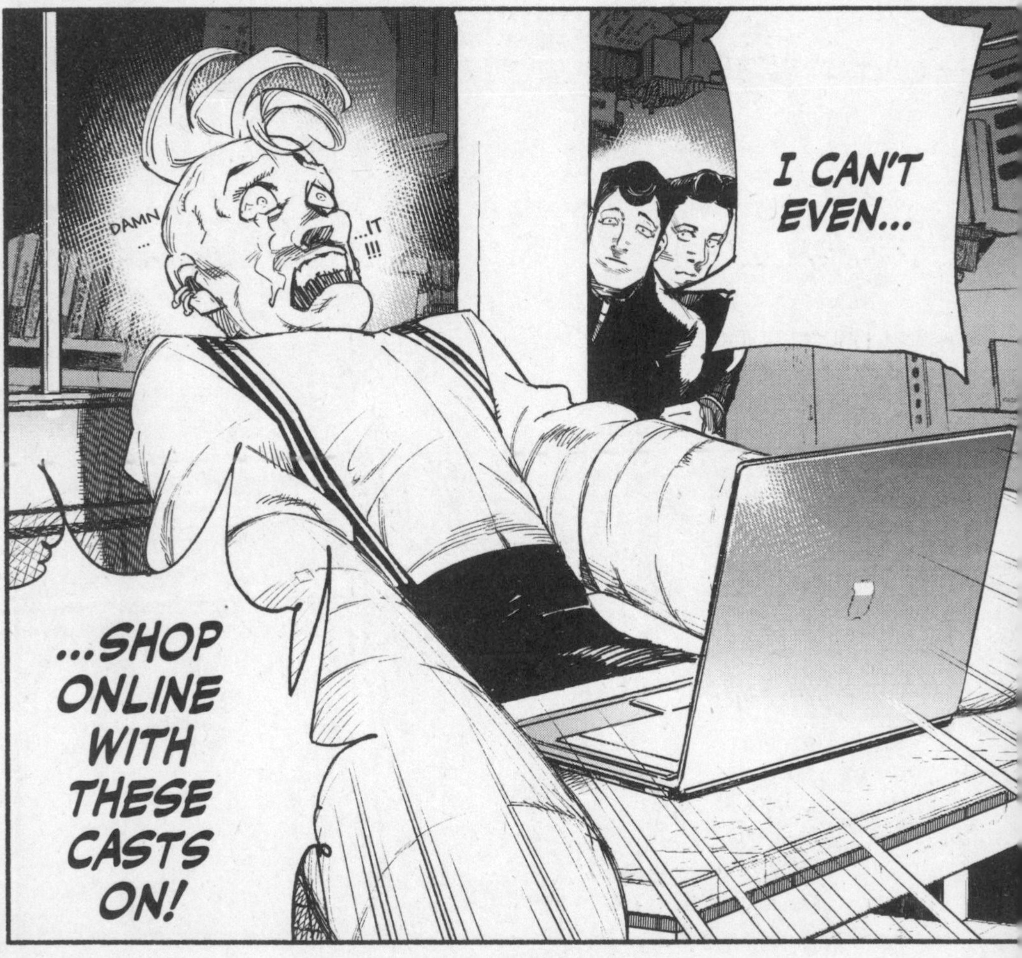
I CAN'T EVEN...
DAMN...
...IT!!!
...SHOP ONLINE WITH THESE CASTS ON!

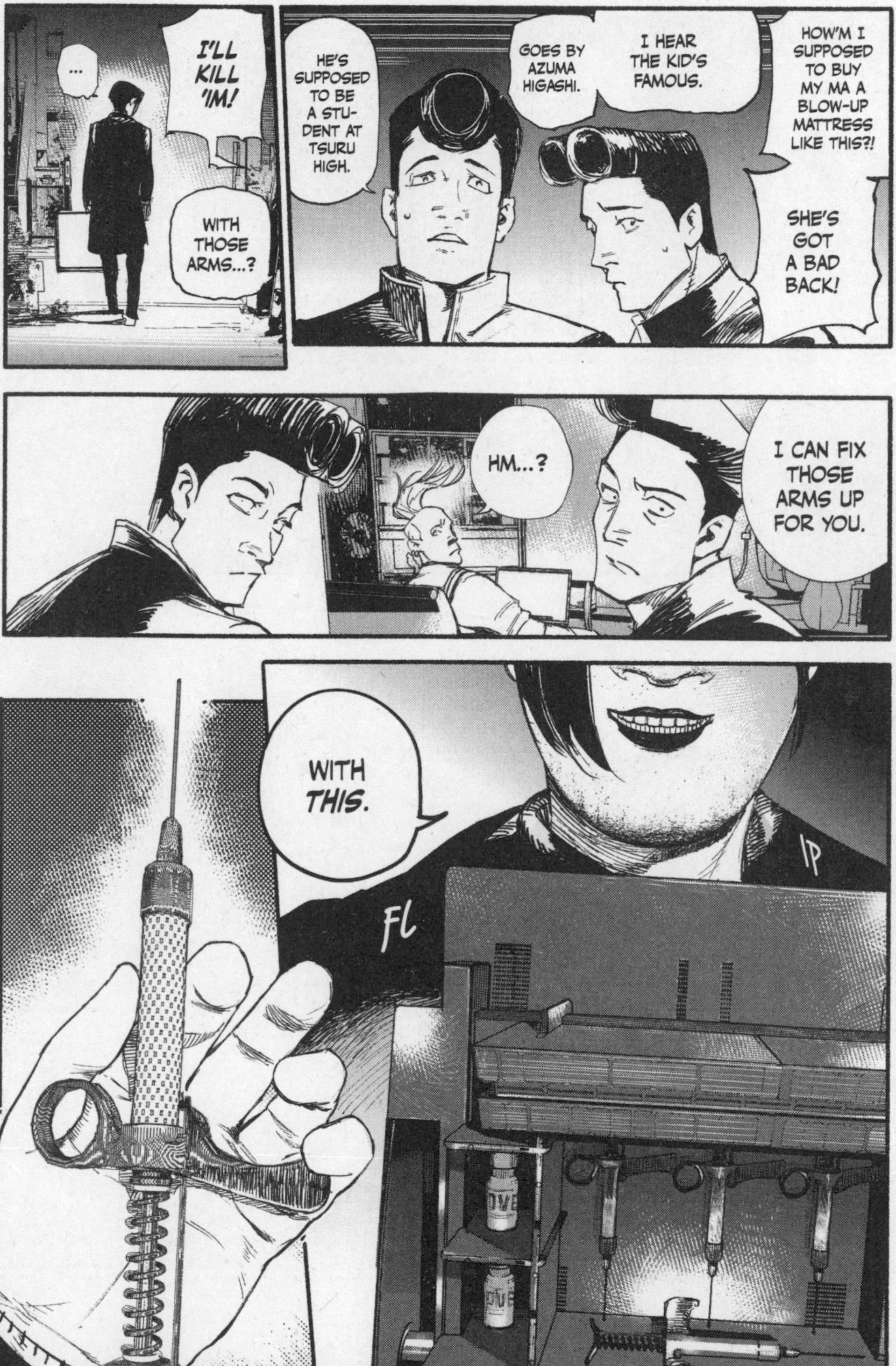
HOW'M I SUPPOSED TO BUY MY MA A BLOW-UP MATTRESS LIKE THIS?!
SHE'S GOT A BAD BACK!
I HEAR THE KID'S FAMOUS.
GOES BY AZUMA HIGASHI.
HE'S SUPPOSED TO BE A STU-DENT AT TSURU HIGH.
I'LL KILL 'IM!
...
WITH THOSE ARMS...?
I CAN FIX THOSE ARMS UP FOR YOU.
HM...?
WITH THIS.

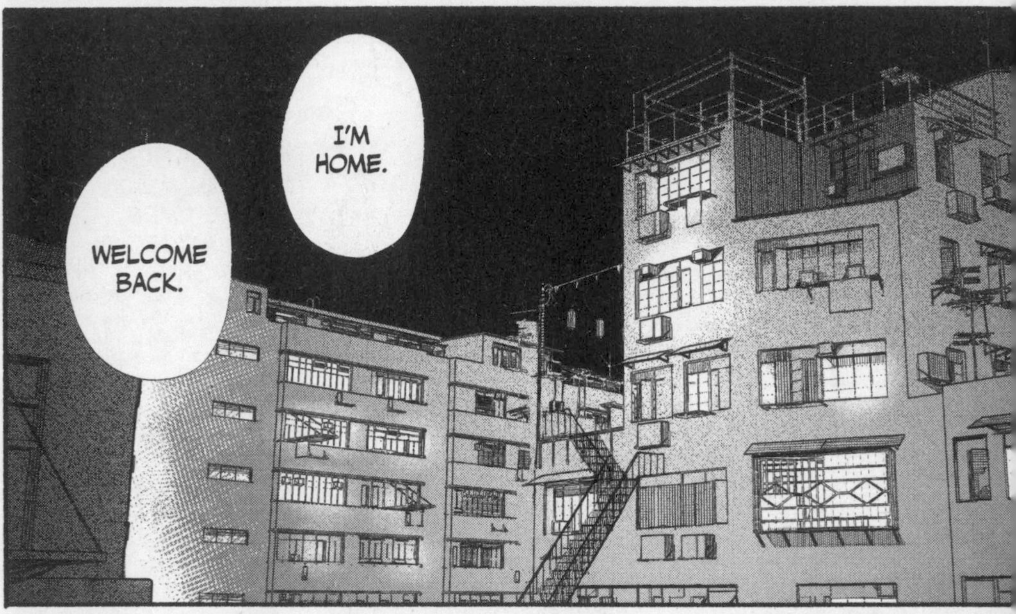
I'M HOME.
WELCOME BACK.

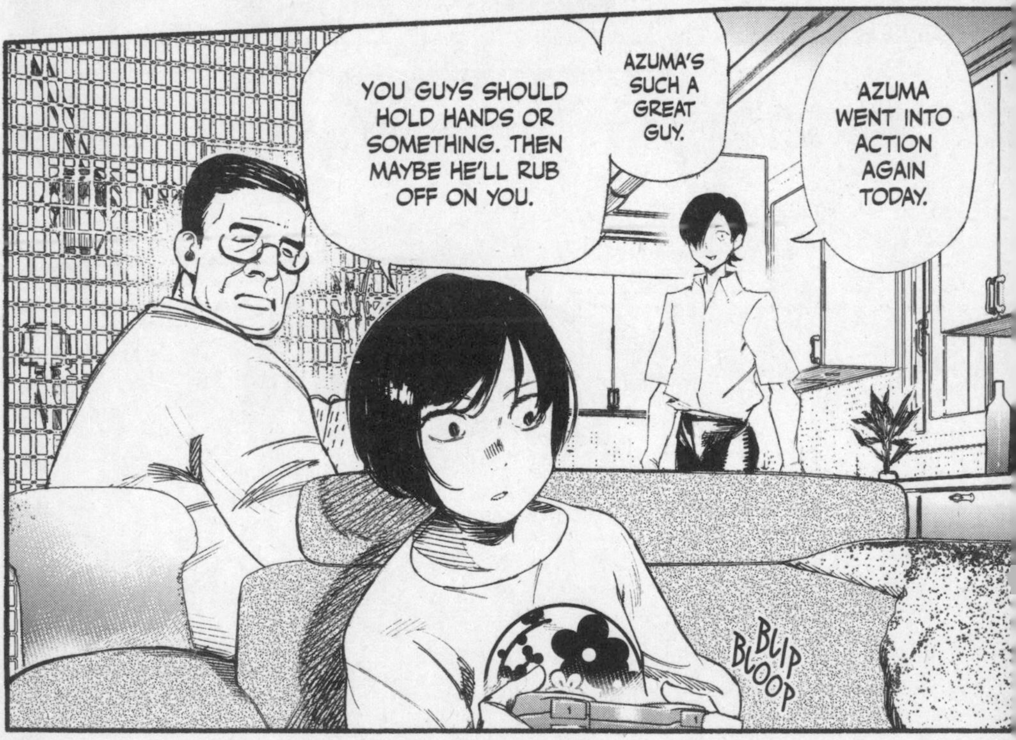
AZUMA WENT INTO ACTION AGAIN TODAY.
AZUMA'S SUCH A GREAT GUY.
YOU GUYS SHOULD HOLD HANDS OR SOMETHING. THEN MAYBE HE'LL RUB OFF ON YOU.
BLIP BLOOP

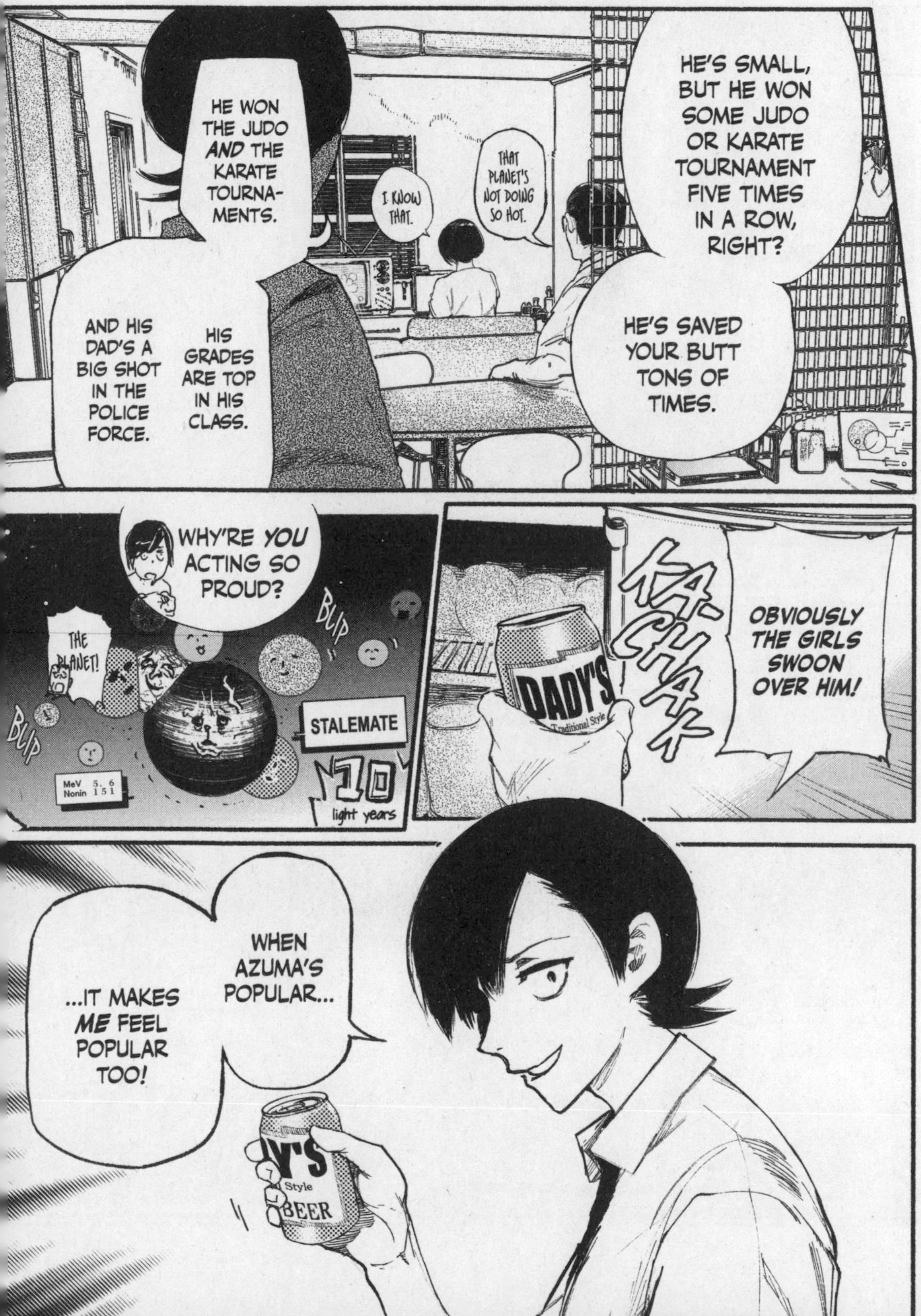
HE'S SMALL, BUT HE WON SOME JUDO OR KARATE TOURNAMENT FIVE TIMES IN A ROW, RIGHT?
HE'S SAVED YOUR BUTT TONS OF TIMES.
THAT PLANET'S NOT DOING SO HOT.
I KNOW THAT.
HE WON THE JUDO *AND* THE KARATE TOURNAMENTS.
HIS GRADES ARE TOP IN HIS CLASS.
AND HIS DAD'S A BIG SHOT IN THE POLICE FORCE.
KA-CHAK
OBVIOUSLY THE GIRLS SWOON OVER HIM!
DADY'S
Traditional Style
WHY'RE *YOU* ACTING SO PROUD?
BLIP
THE PLANET!
STALEMATE
BLIP
MeV 5. 6
Nonin 151
10
light years
WHEN AZUMA'S POPULAR...
...IT MAKES *ME* FEEL POPULAR TOO!
BEER

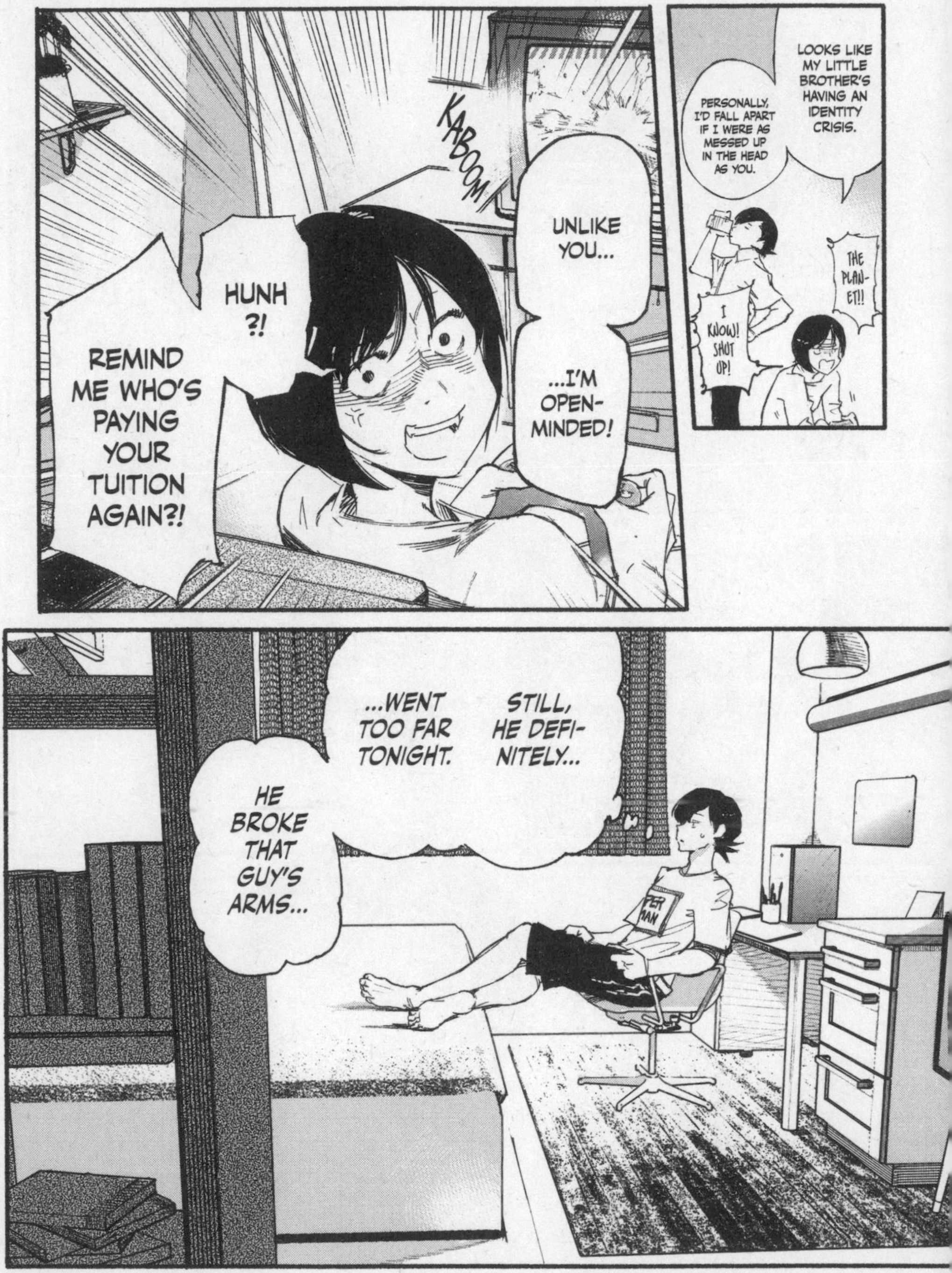
LOOKS LIKE MY LITTLE BROTHER'S HAVING AN IDENTITY CRISIS.
PERSONALLY, I'D FALL APART IF I WERE AS MESSED UP IN THE HEAD AS YOU.
THE PLAN-ET!!
I KNOW! SHUT UP!
UNLIKE YOU...
...I'M OPEN-MINDED!
KABOOM
HUNH ?!
REMIND ME WHO'S PAYING YOUR TUITION AGAIN?!
STILL, HE DEFI-NITELY...
...WENT TOO FAR TONIGHT.
HE BROKE THAT GUY'S ARMS...

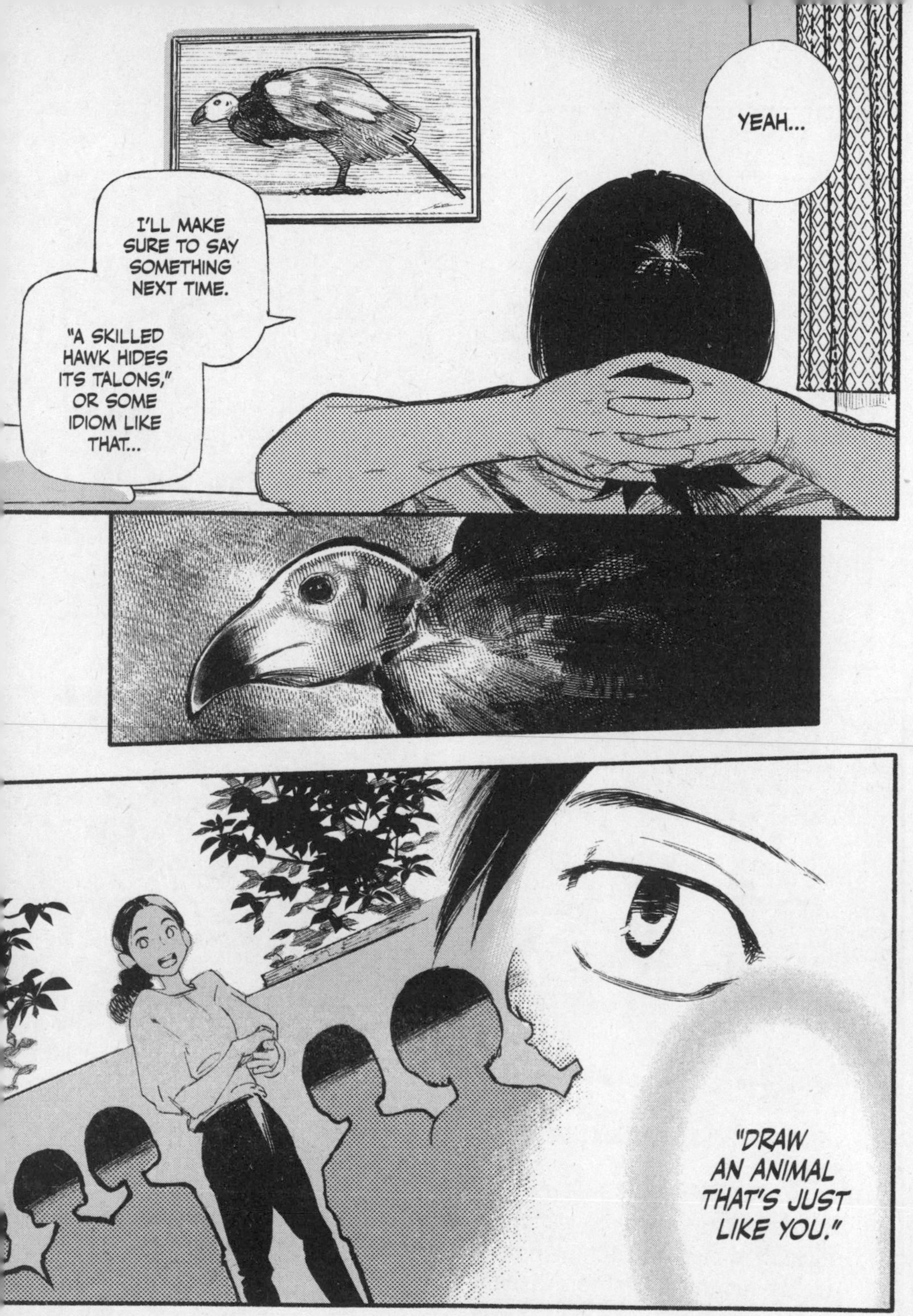
YEAH...
I'LL MAKE SURE TO SAY SOMETHING NEXT TIME.
"A SKILLED HAWK HIDES ITS TALONS," OR SOME IDIOM LIKE THAT...
"DRAW AN ANIMAL THAT'S JUST LIKE YOU."

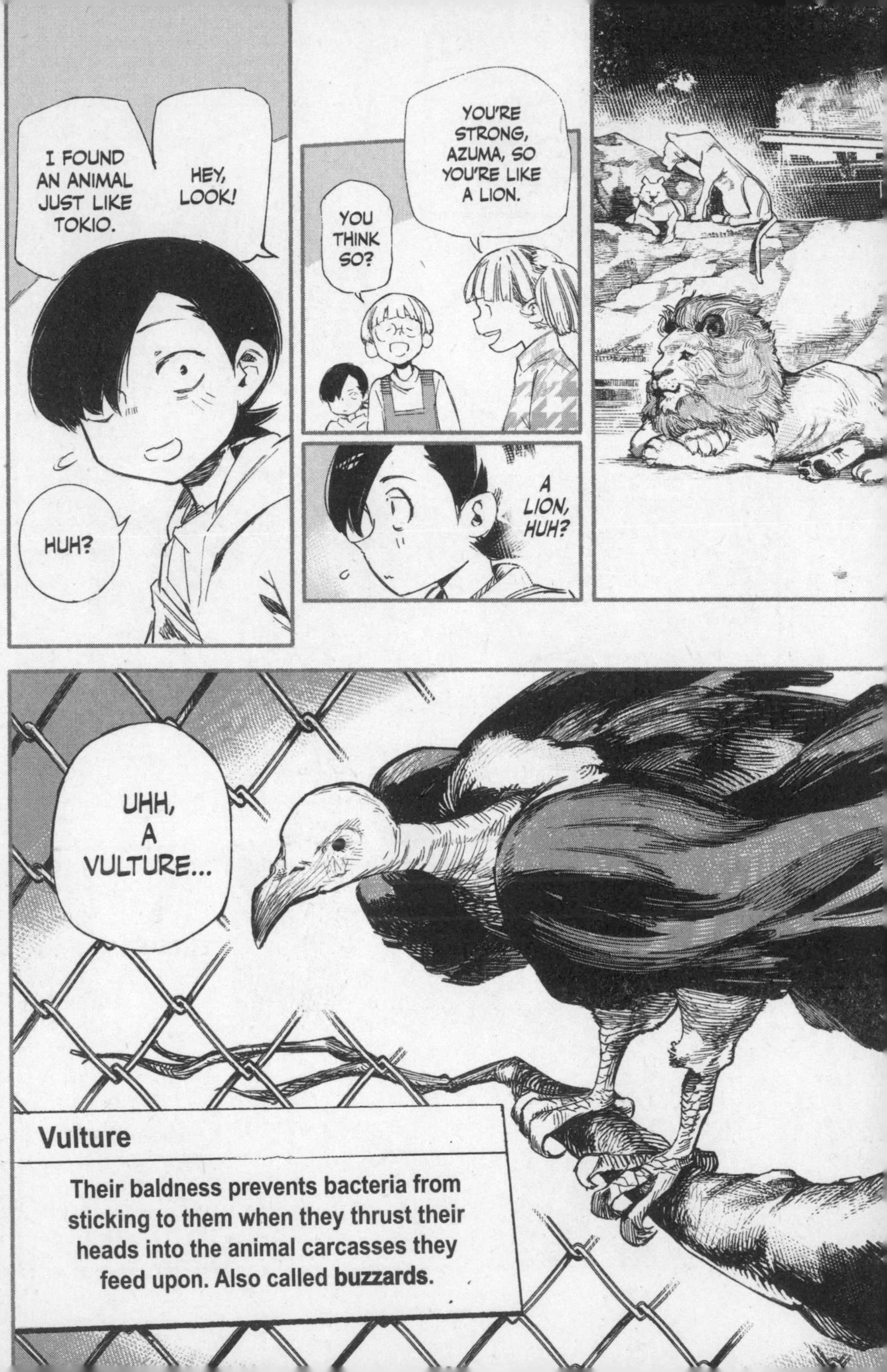
YOU'RE STRONG, AZUMA, SO YOU'RE LIKE A LION.
YOU THINK SO?
A LION, HUH?
HEY, LOOK!
I FOUND AN ANIMAL JUST LIKE TOKIO.
HUH?
UHH, A VULTURE...
Vulture
Their baldness prevents bacteria from sticking to them when they thrust their heads into the animal carcasses they feed upon. Also called buzzards.

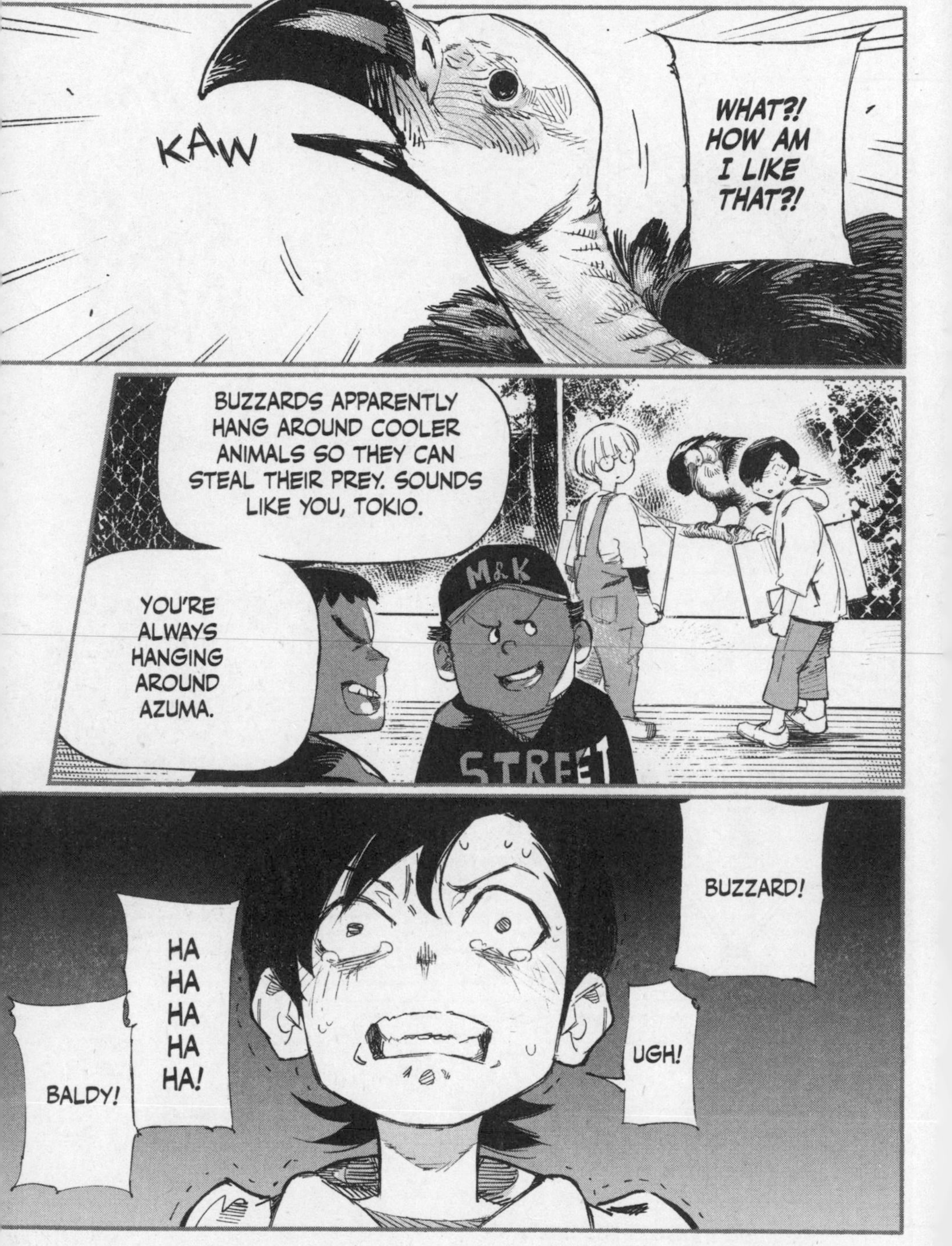
WHAT?! HOW AM I LIKE THAT?!
KAW
BUZZARDS APPARENTLY HANG AROUND COOLER ANIMALS SO THEY CAN STEAL THEIR PREY. SOUNDS LIKE YOU, TOKIO.
YOU'RE ALWAYS HANGING AROUND AZUMA.
M&K
STREET
BUZZARD!
UGH!
HA HA HA HA HA!
BALDY!

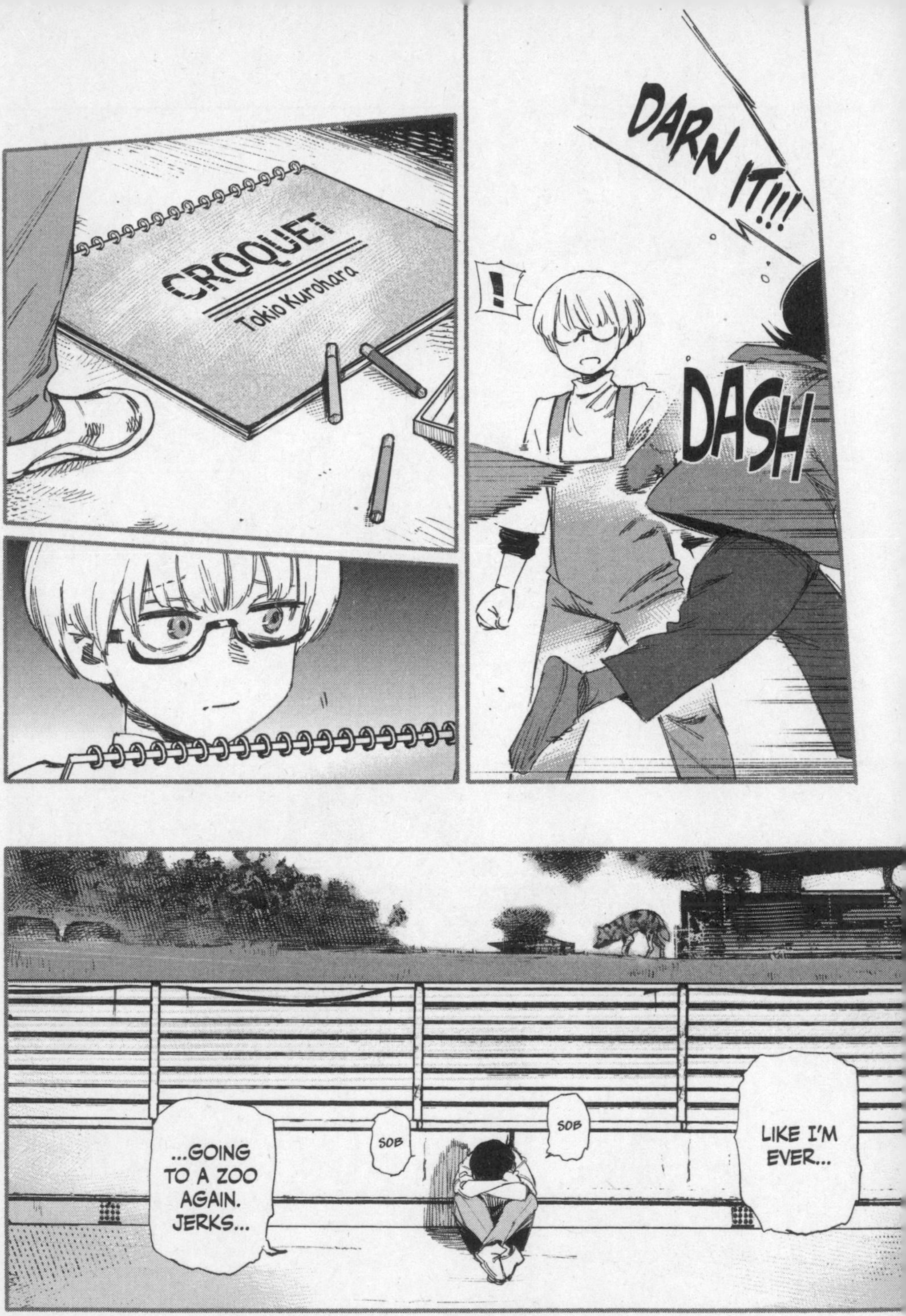
DARN IT!!!
!
DASH
CROQUET
Tokio Kurohara
LIKE I'M EVER...
SOB
SOB
...GOING TO A ZOO AGAIN. JERKS...

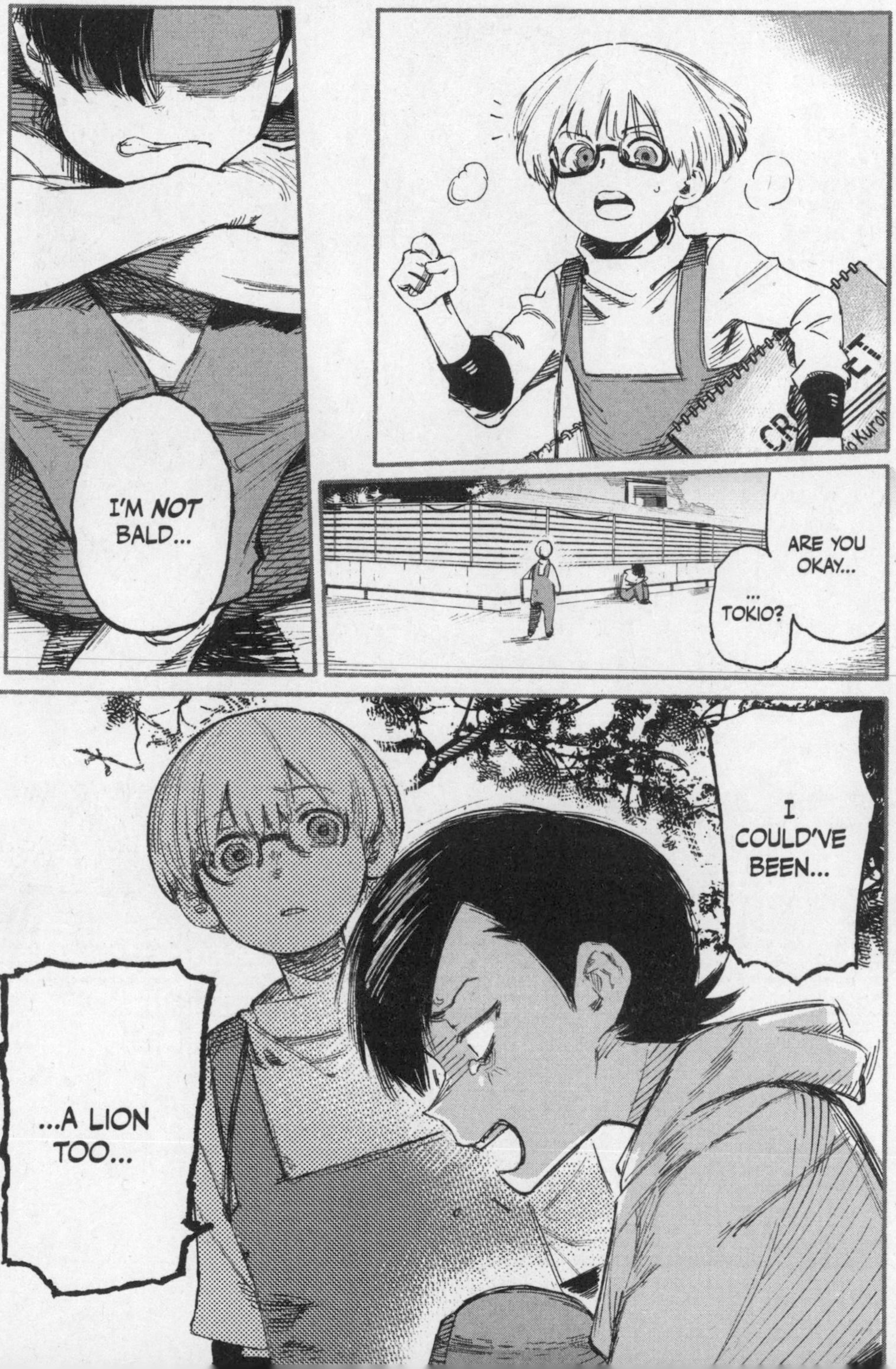
ARE YOU OKAY...
...TOKIO?
I'M *NOT* BALD...
I COULD'VE BEEN...
...A LION TOO...

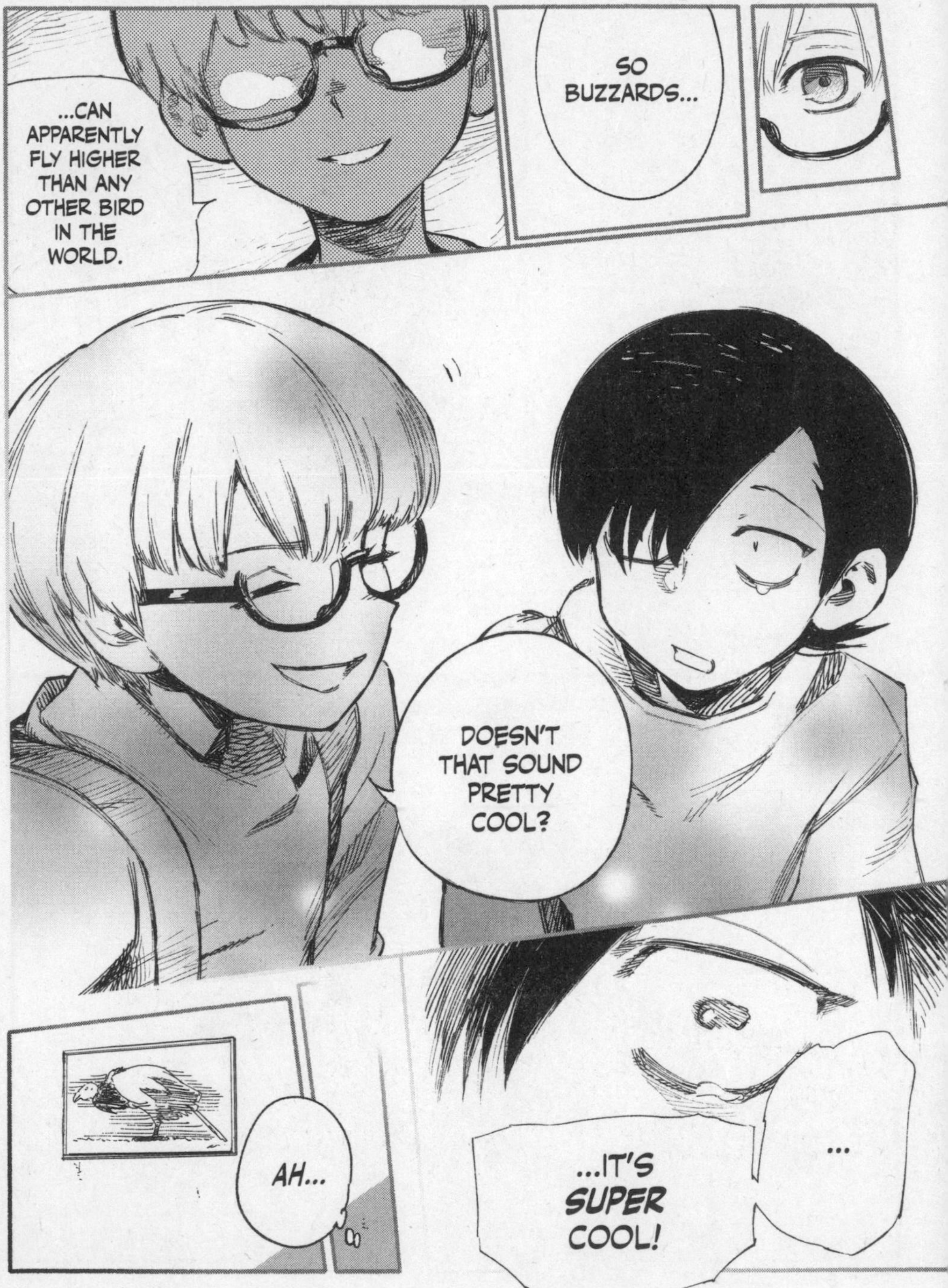
SO BUZZARDS...
...CAN APPARENTLY FLY HIGHER THAN ANY OTHER BIRD IN THE WORLD.
DOESN'T THAT SOUND PRETTY COOL?
...
...IT'S *SUPER* COOL!
AH...

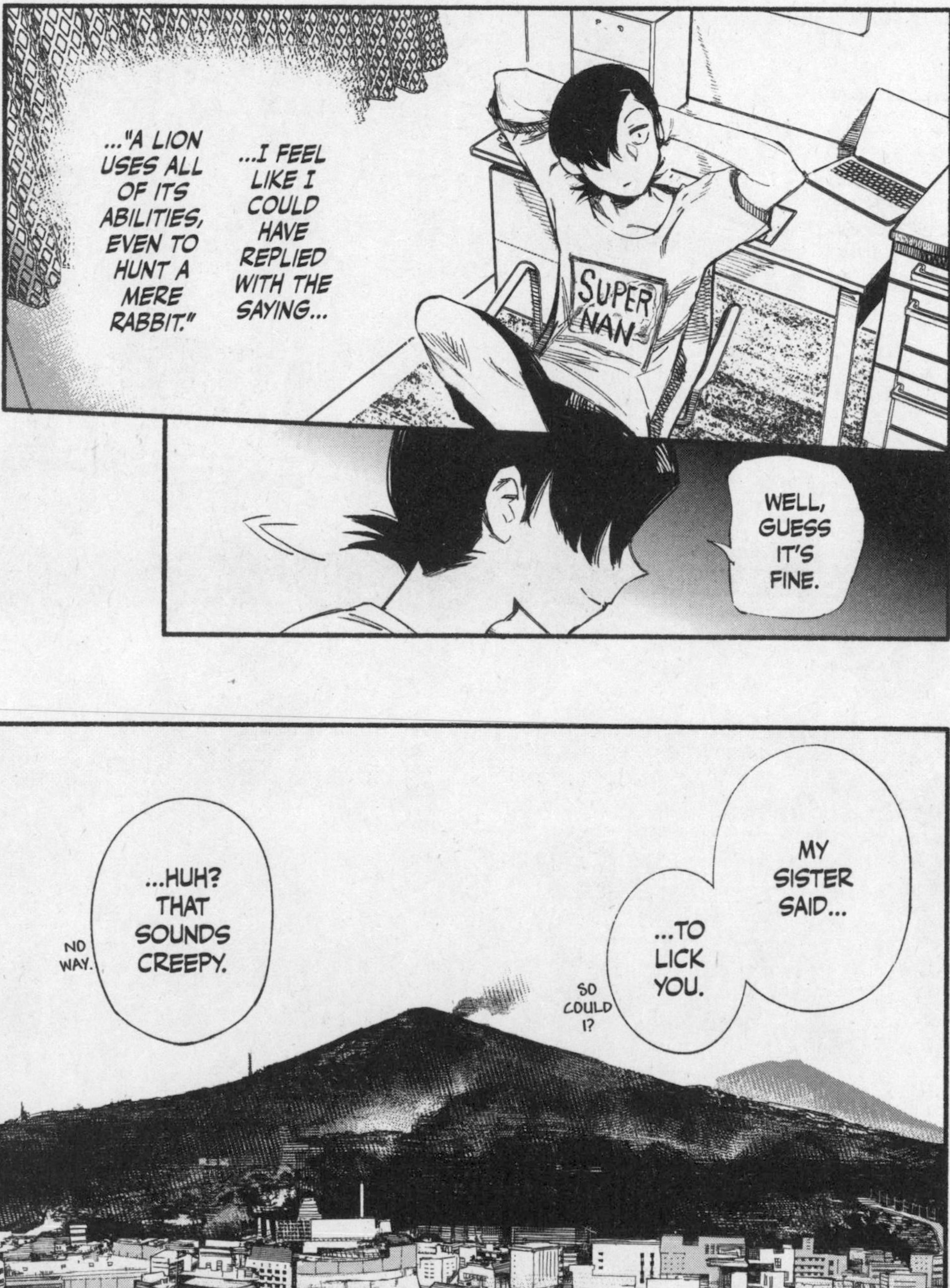
...I FEEL LIKE I COULD HAVE REPLIED WITH THE SAYING...
..."A LION USES ALL OF ITS ABILITIES, EVEN TO HUNT A MERE RABBIT."
SUPER NAN
WELL, GUESS IT'S FINE.
MY SISTER SAID...
...TO LICK YOU.
SO COULD I?
...HUH? THAT SOUNDS CREEPY.
NO WAY.

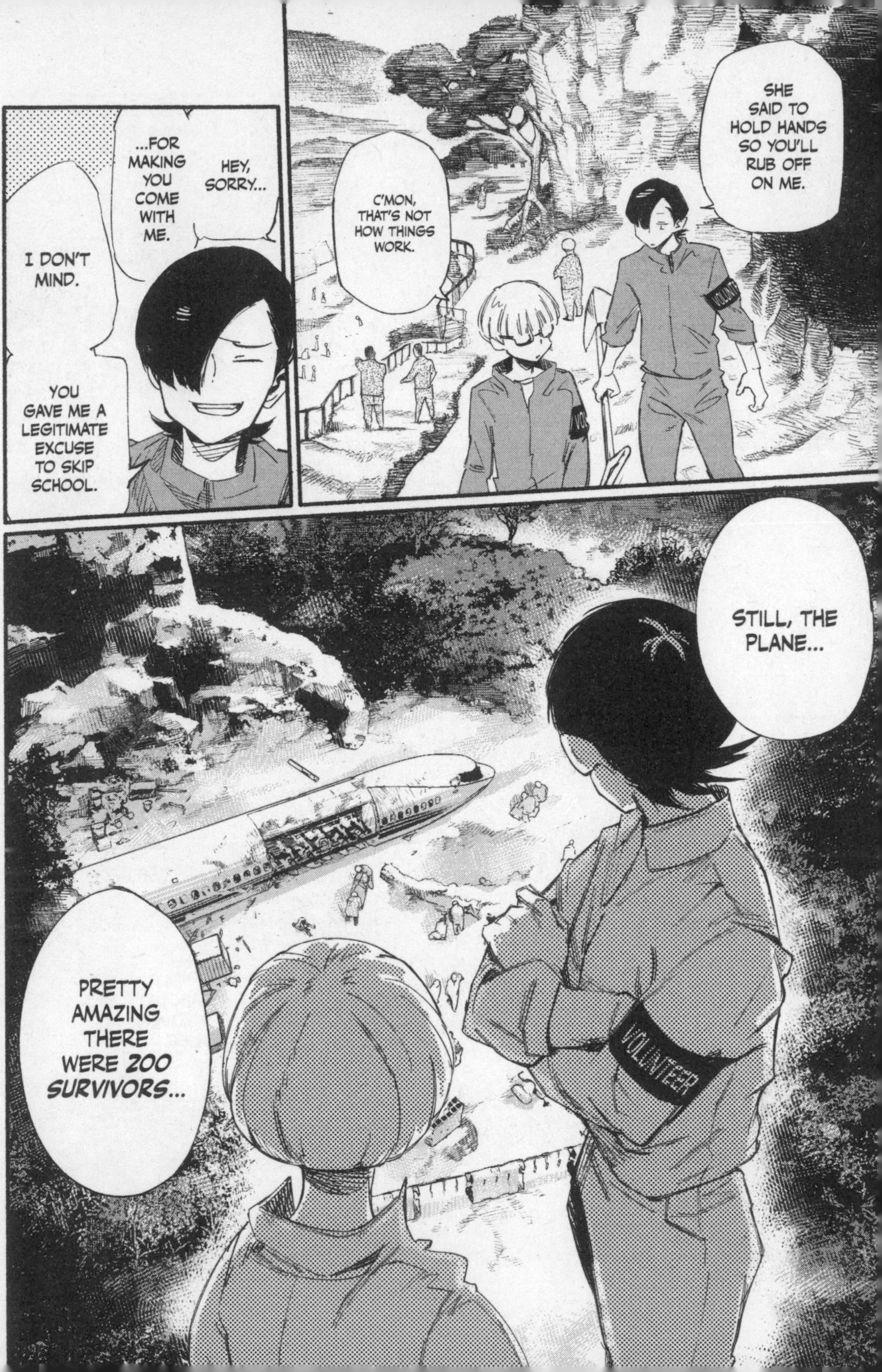
SHE SAID TO HOLD HANDS SO YOU'LL RUB OFF ON ME.
C'MON, THAT'S NOT HOW THINGS WORK.
HEY, SORRY...
...FOR MAKING YOU COME WITH ME.
I DON'T MIND.
YOU GAVE ME A LEGITIMATE EXCUSE TO SKIP SCHOOL.
STILL, THE PLANE...
VOLUNTEER
PRETTY AMAZING THERE WERE *200 SURVIVORS*...

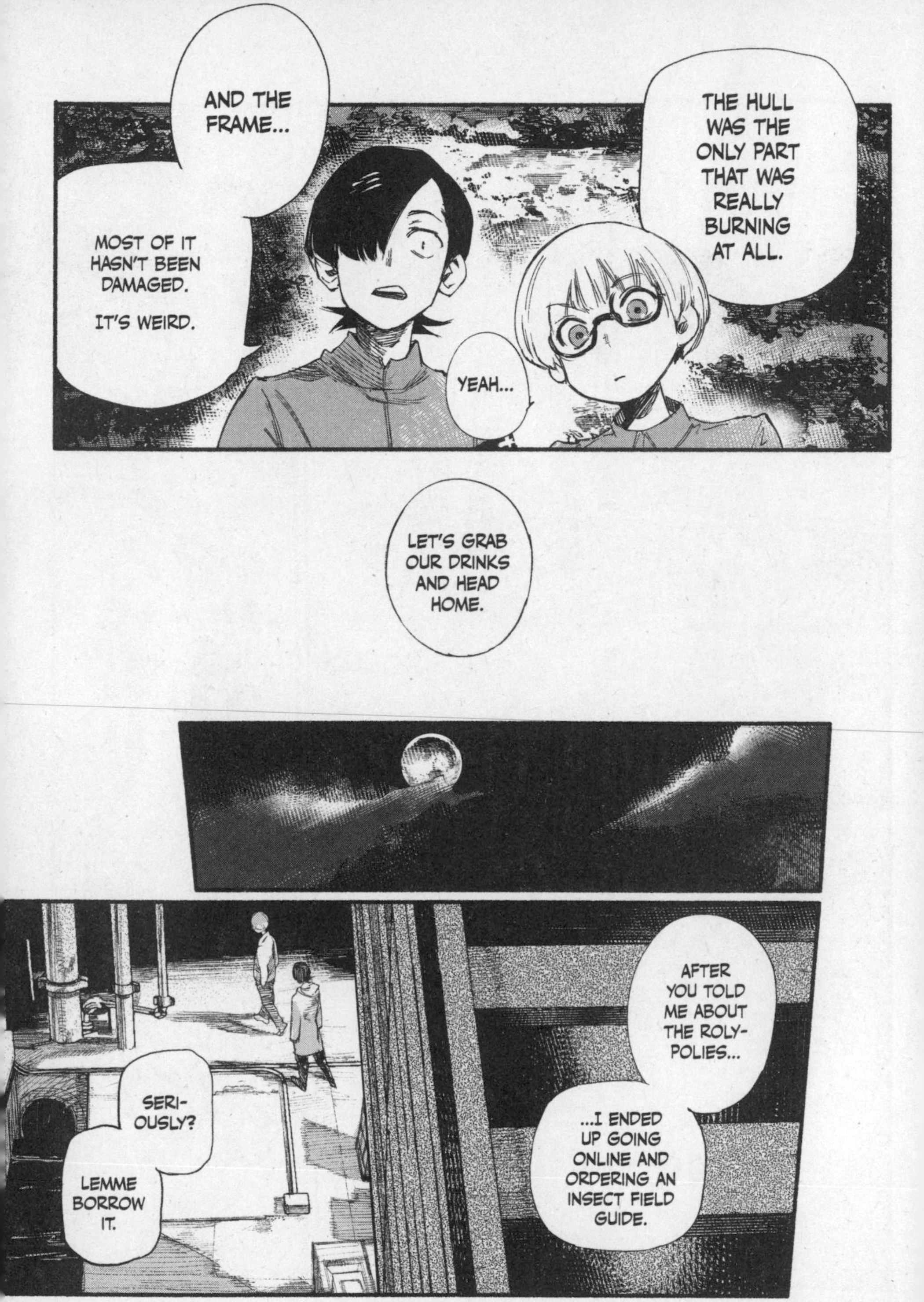
THE HULL WAS THE ONLY PART THAT WAS REALLY BURNING AT ALL.
AND THE FRAME...
MOST OF IT HASN'T BEEN DAMAGED.
IT'S WEIRD.
YEAH...
LET'S GRAB OUR DRINKS AND HEAD HOME.
AFTER YOU TOLD ME ABOUT THE ROLY-POLIES...
...I ENDED UP GOING ONLINE AND ORDERING AN INSECT FIELD GUIDE.
SERI-OUSLY?
LEMME BORROW IT.

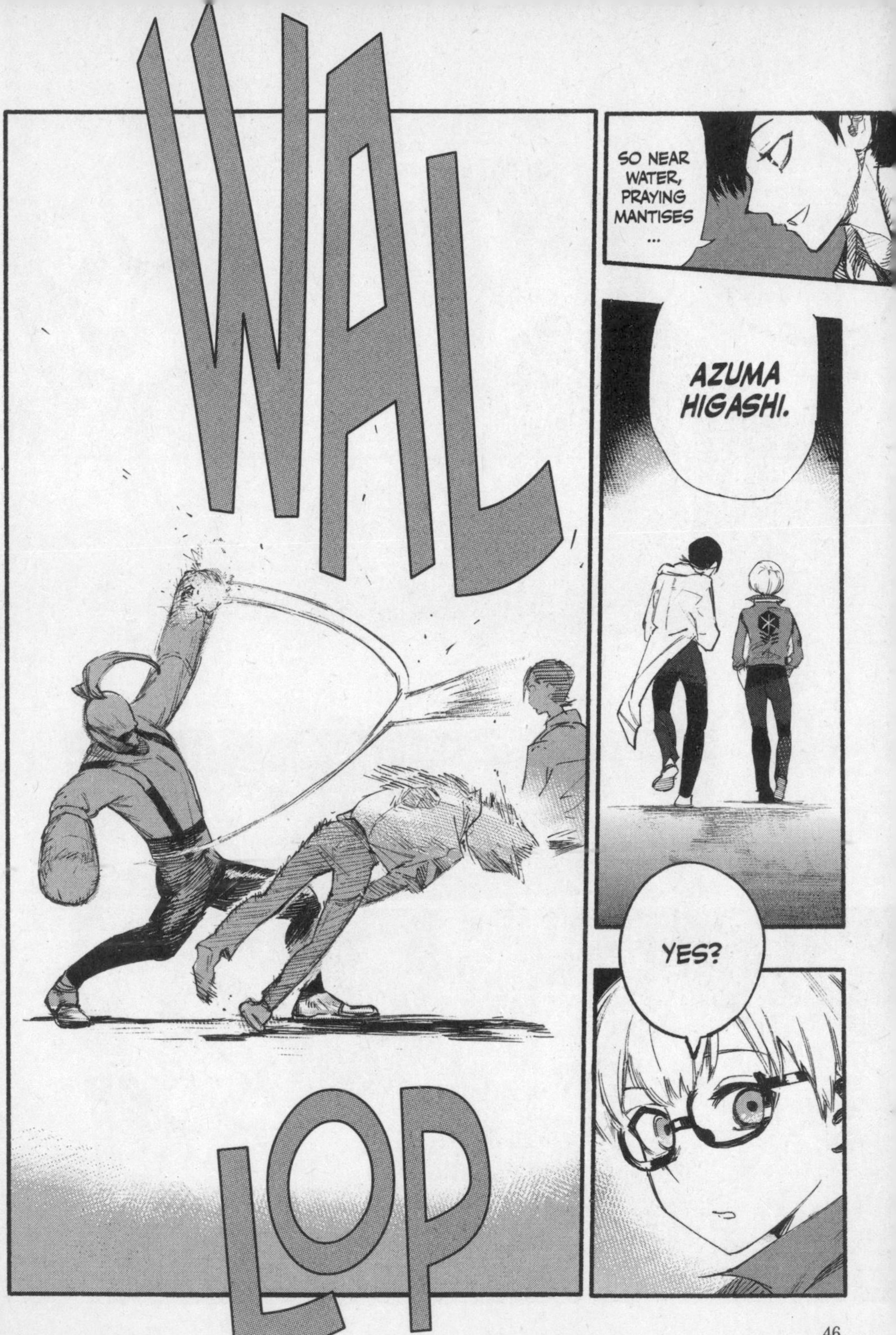
SO NEAR WATER, PRAYING MANTISES ...
AZUMA HIGASHI.
YES?
WALLOP

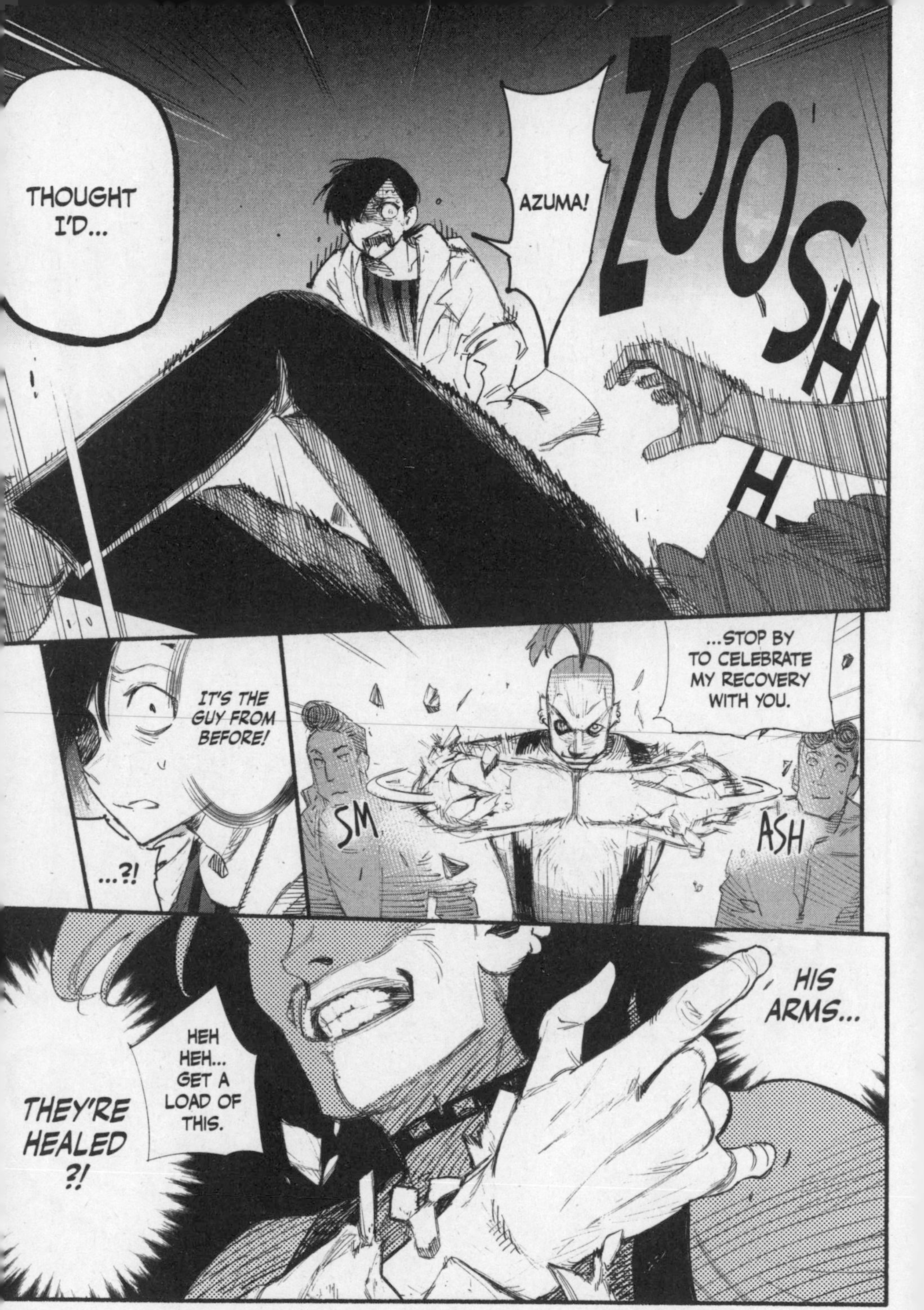
ZOOSH
H
AZUMA!
THOUGHT I'D...
!
...STOP BY TO CELEBRATE MY RECOVERY WITH YOU.
SM
ASH
IT'S THE GUY FROM BEFORE!
...?!
HIS ARMS...
HEH HEH... GET A LOAD OF THIS.
THEY'RE HEALED ?!

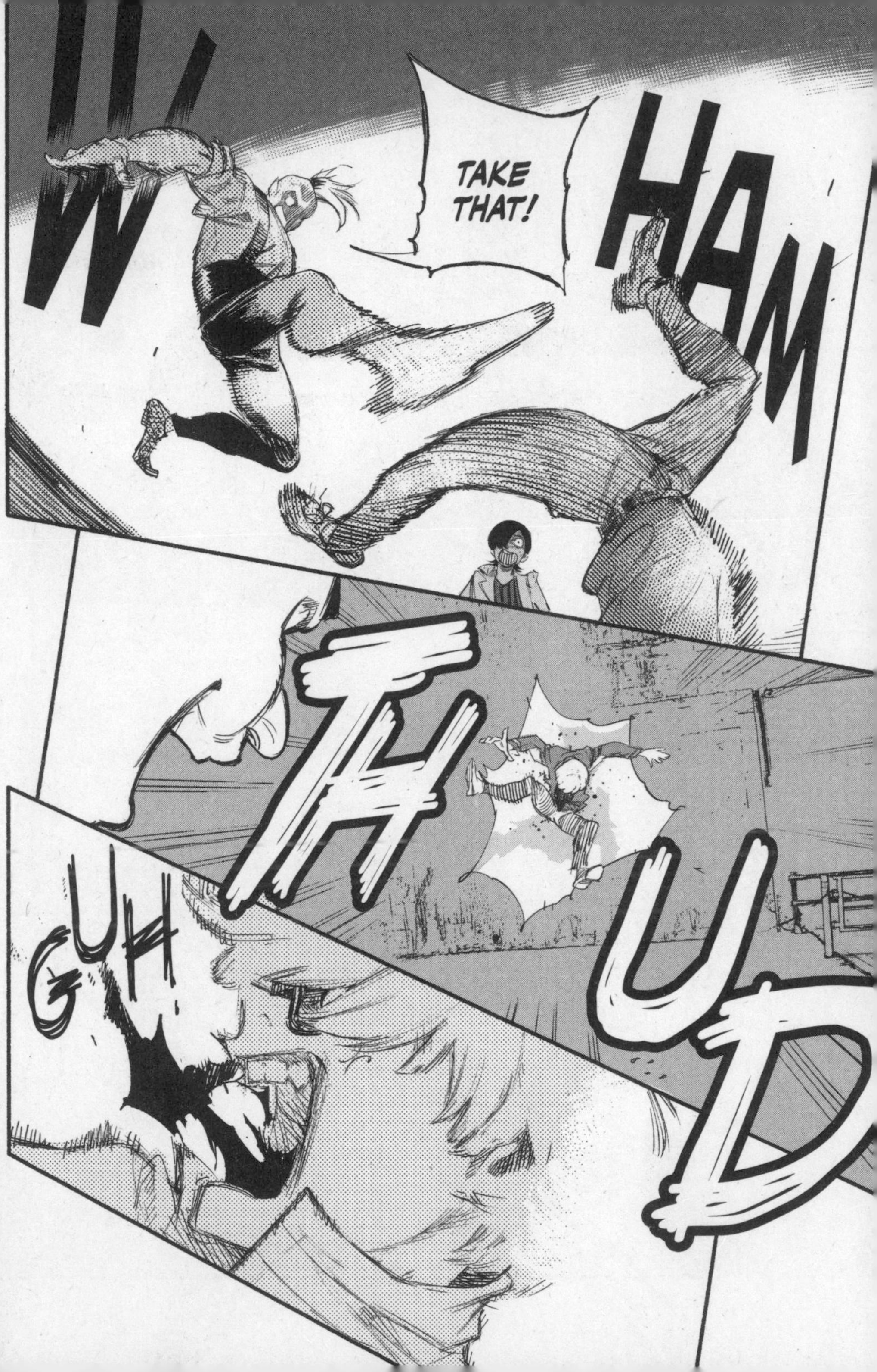
WHAM
TAKE THAT!
THUD
GUH

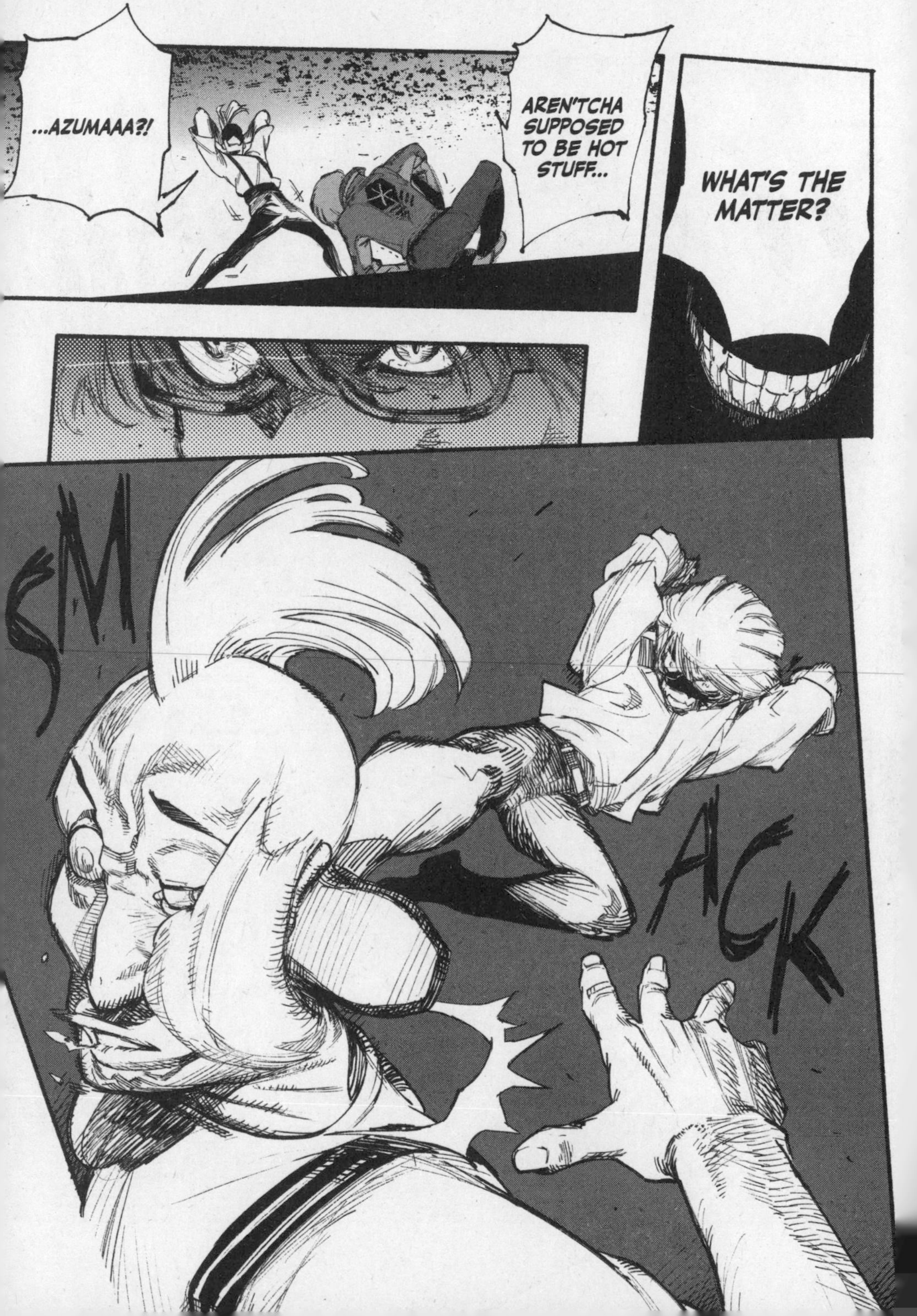
WHAT'S THE MATTER?
AREN'TCHA SUPPOSED TO BE HOT STUFF...
...AZUMAAA?!
SMACK

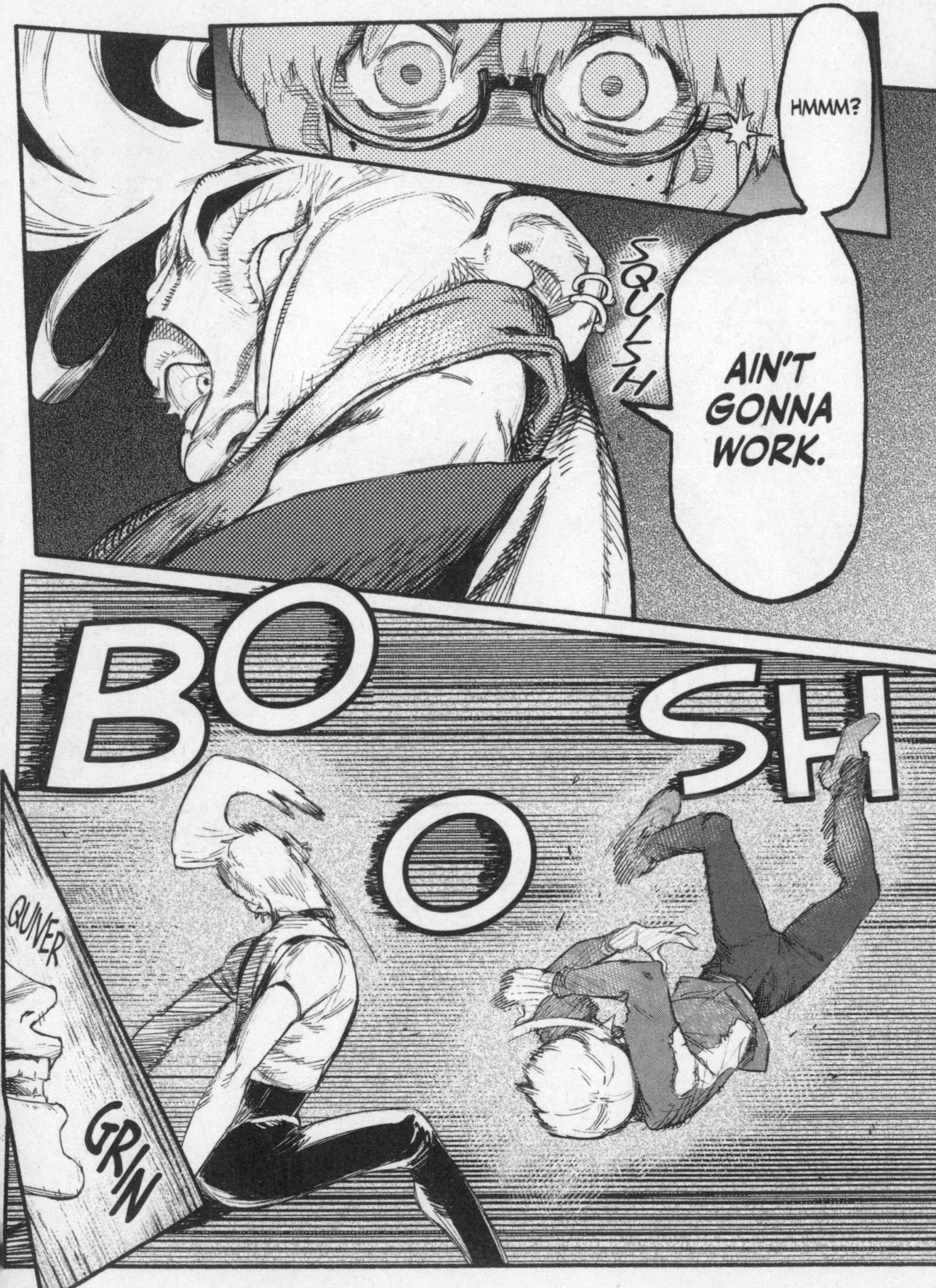
HMMM?
AIN'T GONNA WORK.
SQUISH
BOOSH
QUIVER
GRIN

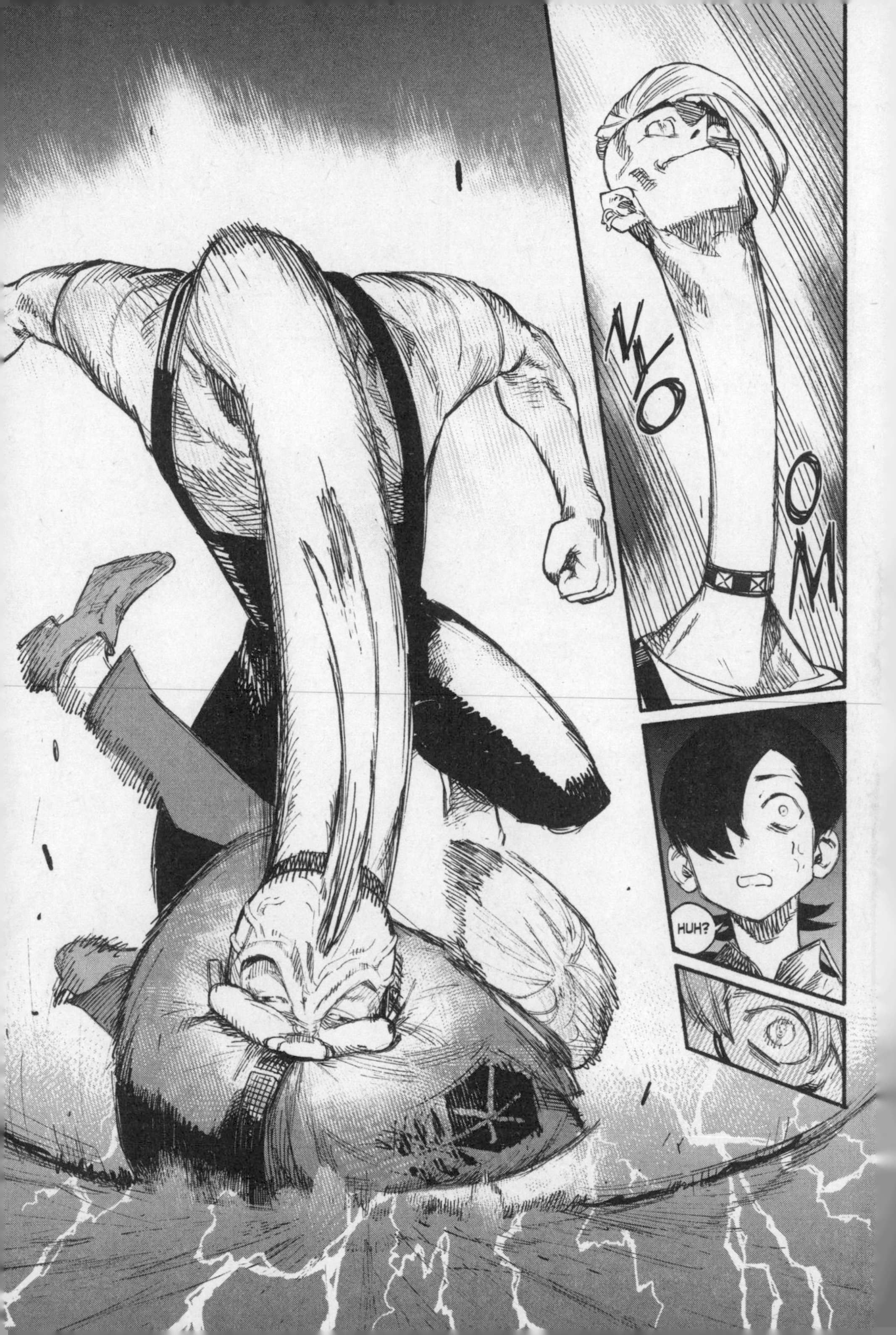
NYOOOM
HUH?

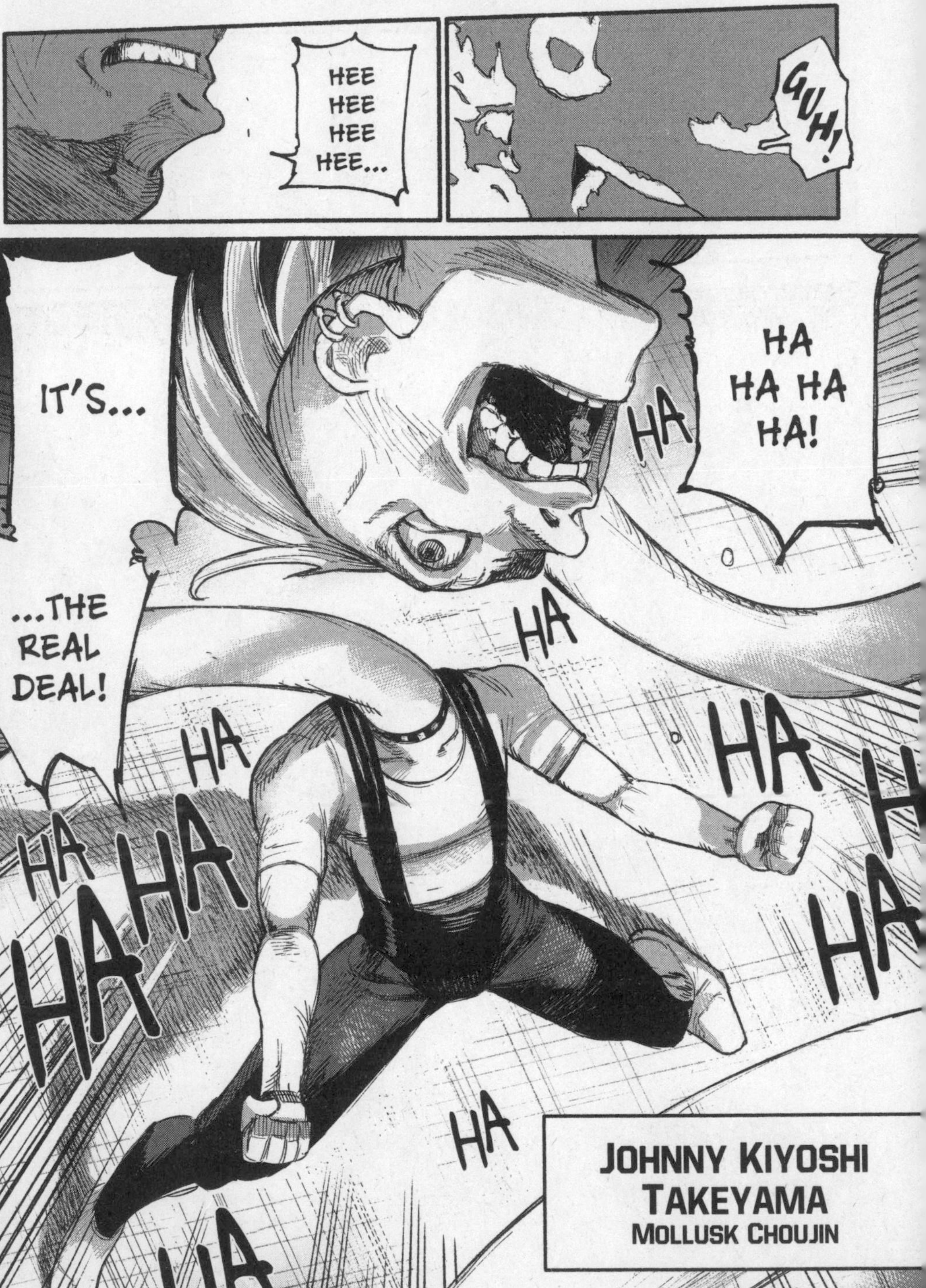
GUH!
HEE HEE HEE HEE...
HA HA HA HA!
HA
IT'S...
...THE REAL DEAL!
HA
HA
HA
HA HA HA
HA
JOHNNY KIYOSHI TAKEYAMA
MOLLUSK CHOUJIN
HA

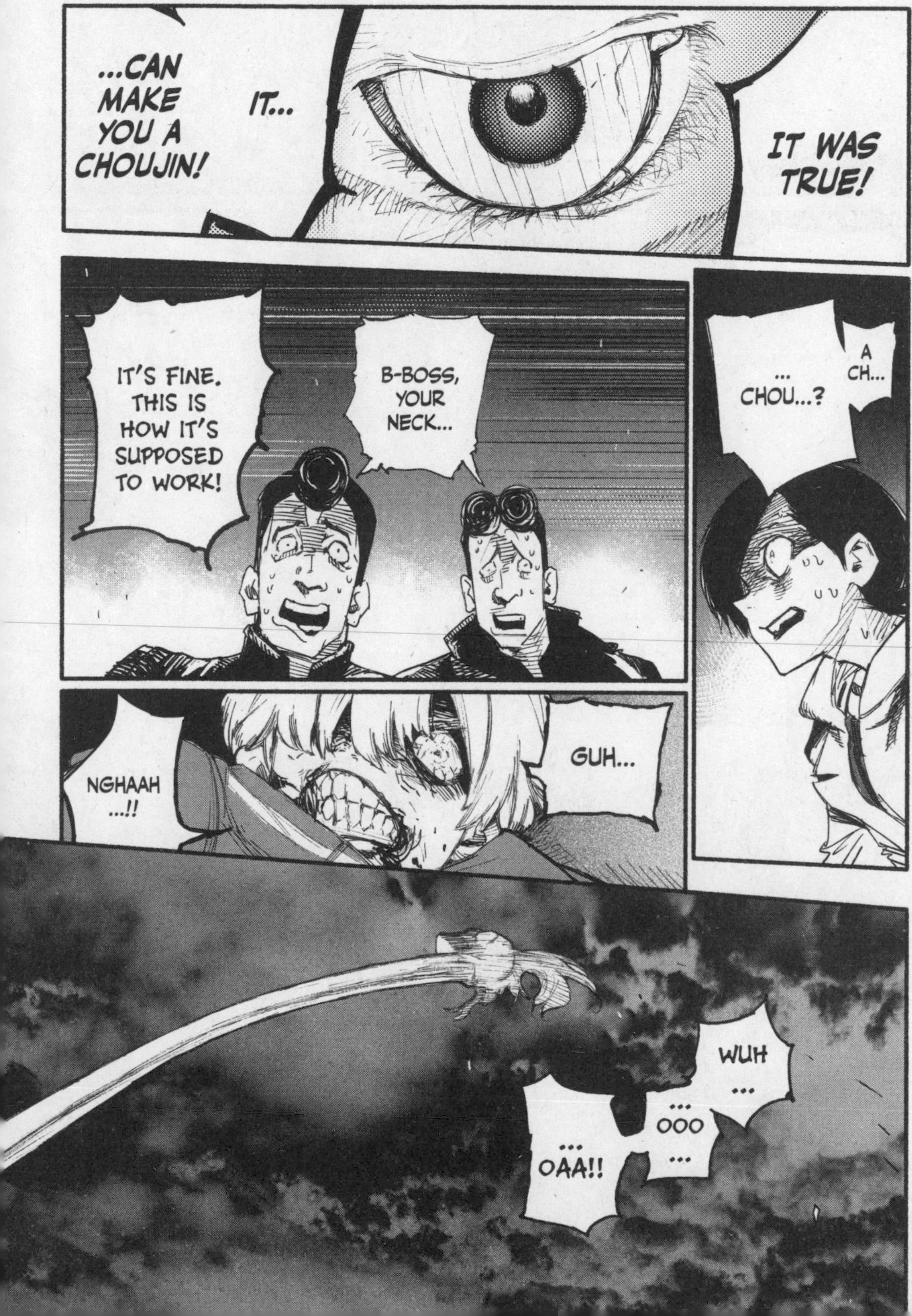
IT WAS TRUE!
IT...
...CAN MAKE YOU A CHOUJIN!
A CH...
... CHOU...?
B-BOSS, YOUR NECK...
IT'S FINE. THIS IS HOW IT'S SUPPOSED TO WORK!
GUH...
NGHAAH ...!!
WUH ...
... OOO ...
... OAA!!

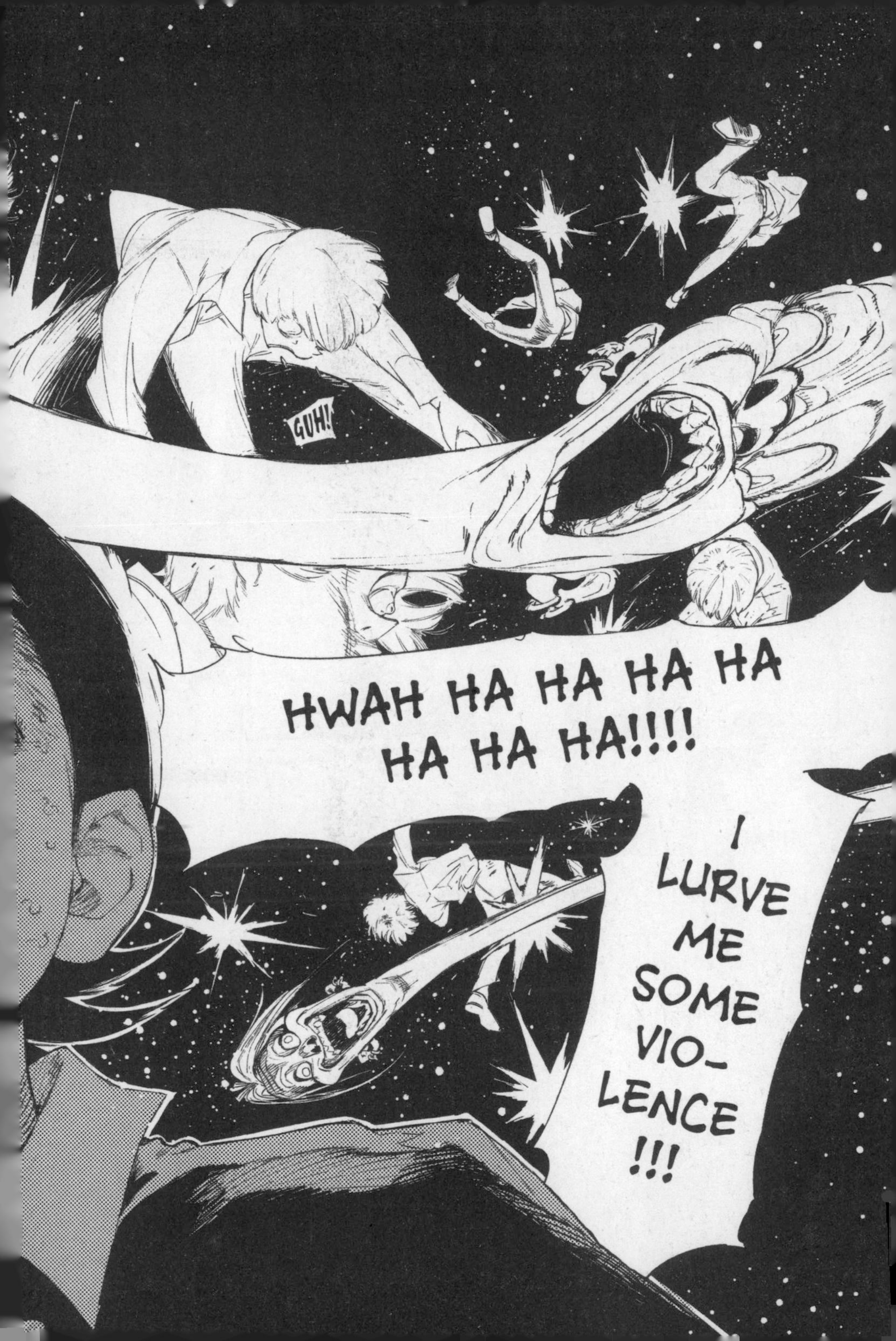
GUH!
HWAH HA HA HA HA HA HA HA!!!!
I LURVE ME SOME VIO-LENCE!!!

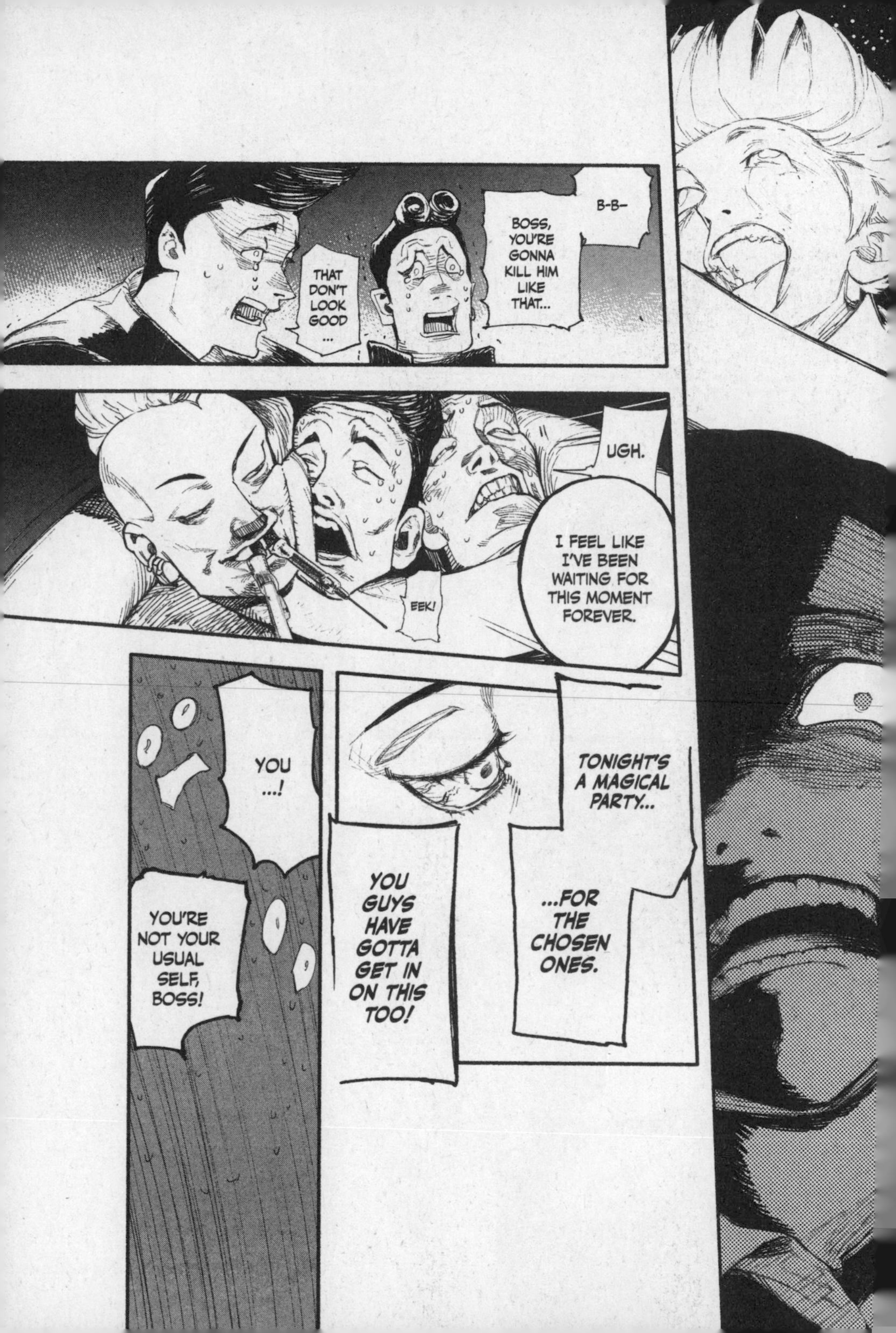
B-B-
BOSS, YOU'RE GONNA KILL HIM LIKE THAT...
THAT DON'T LOOK GOOD ...
UGH.
I FEEL LIKE I'VE BEEN WAITING FOR THIS MOMENT FOREVER.
EEK!
TONIGHT'S A MAGICAL PARTY...
...FOR THE CHOSEN ONES.
YOU GUYS HAVE GOTTA GET IN ON THIS TOO!
YOU ...!
YOU'RE NOT YOUR USUAL SELF, BOSS!

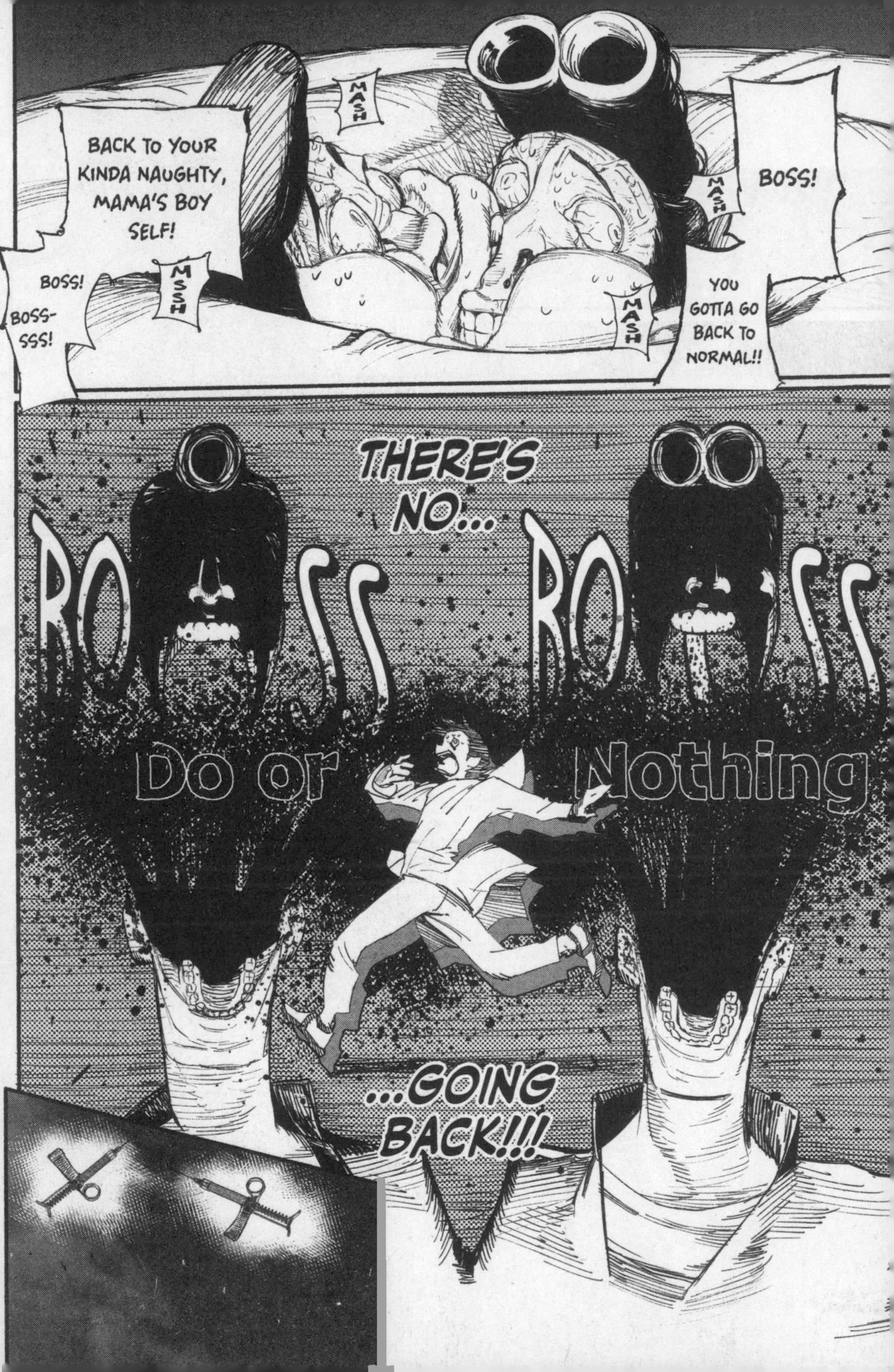
BOSS!
YOU GOTTA GO BACK TO NORMAL!!
MASH
MASH
MASH
BACK TO YOUR KINDA NAUGHTY, MAMA'S BOY SELF!
MSSH
BOSS!
BOSS-SSS!
THERE'S NO...
Do or Nothing
...GOING BACK!!!

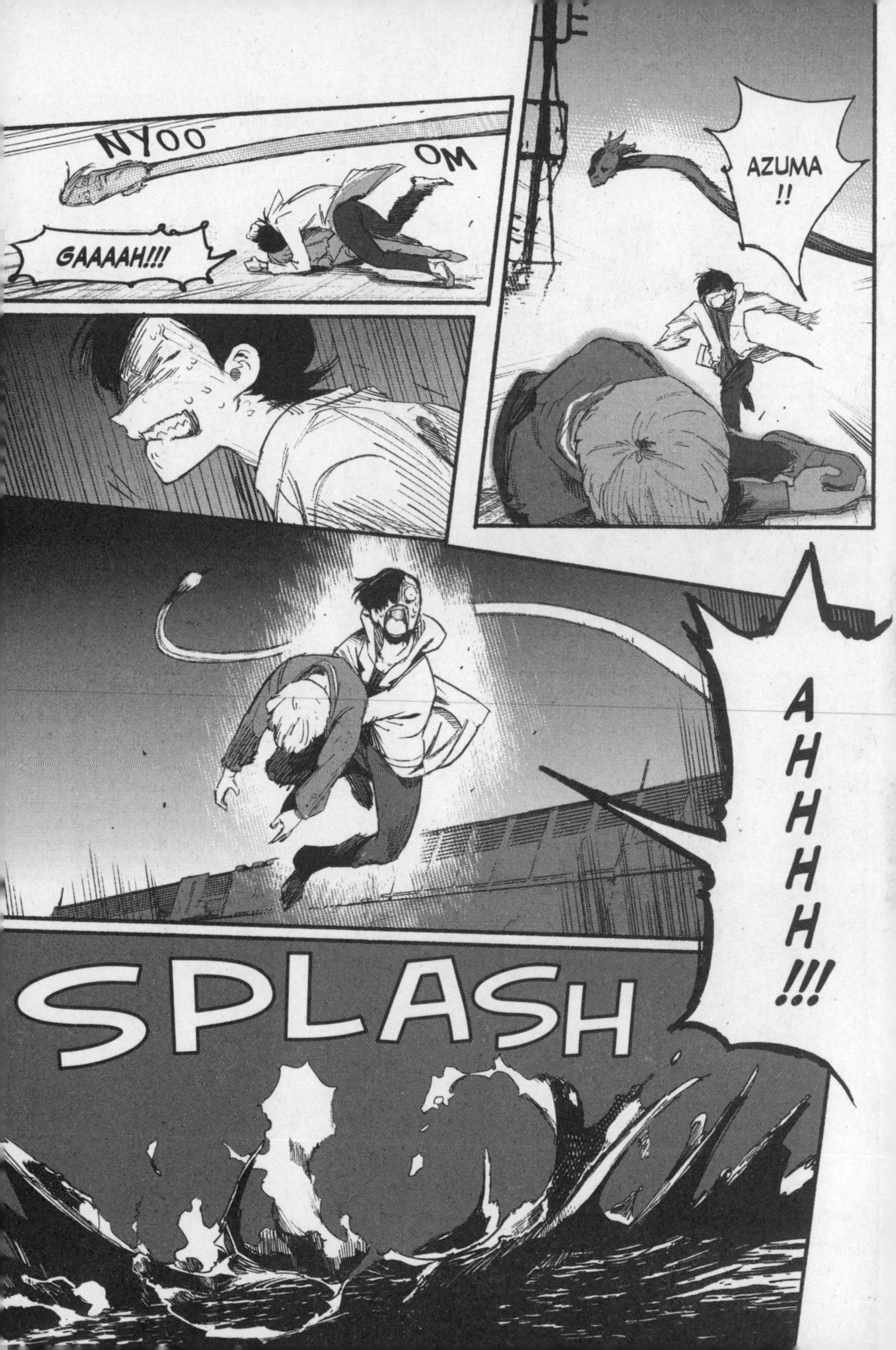
AZUMA !!
NYOO OM
GAAAAH!!!
AHHHHH!!!
SPLASH

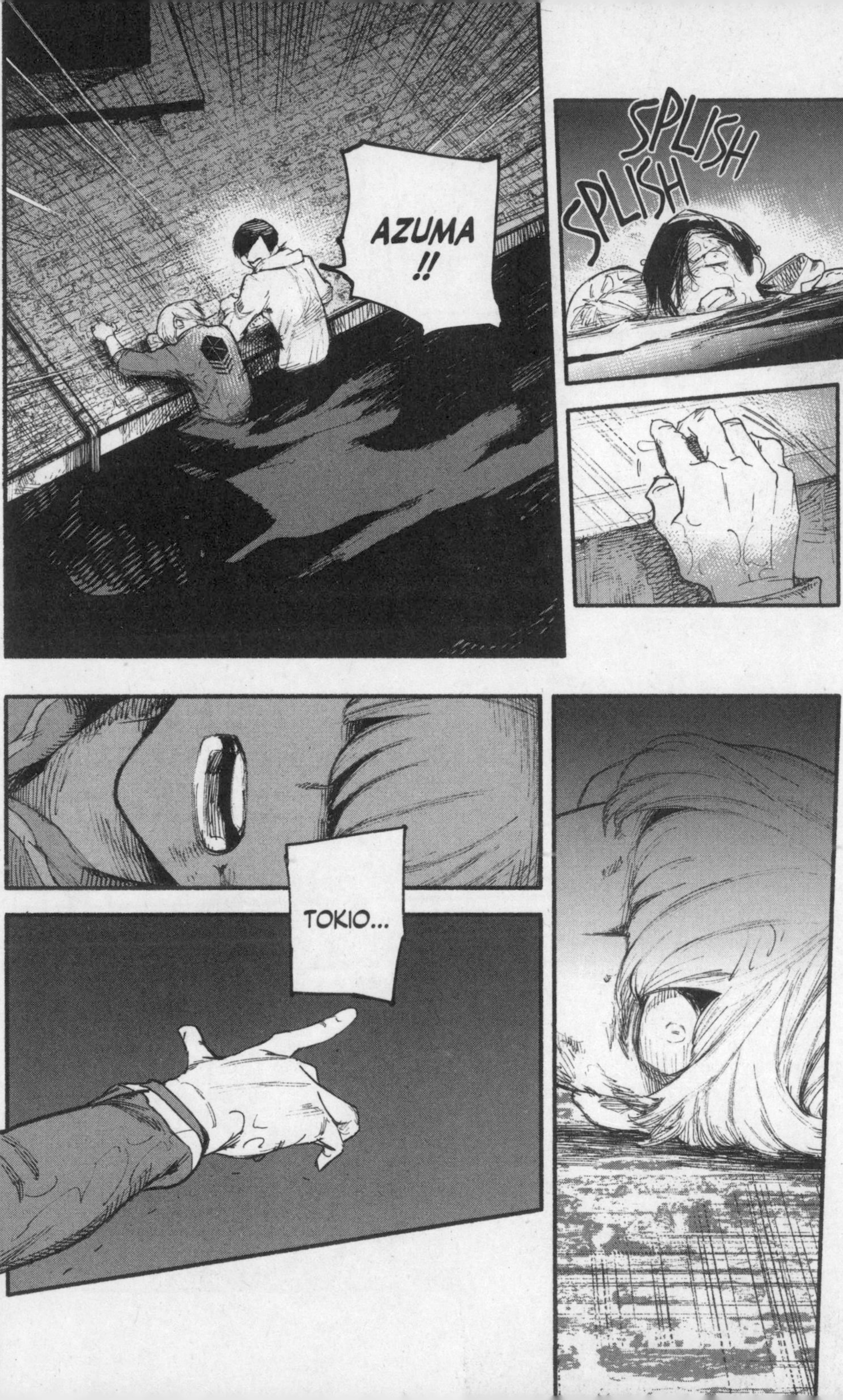
SPLISH SPLISH
AZUMA !!
TOKIO...

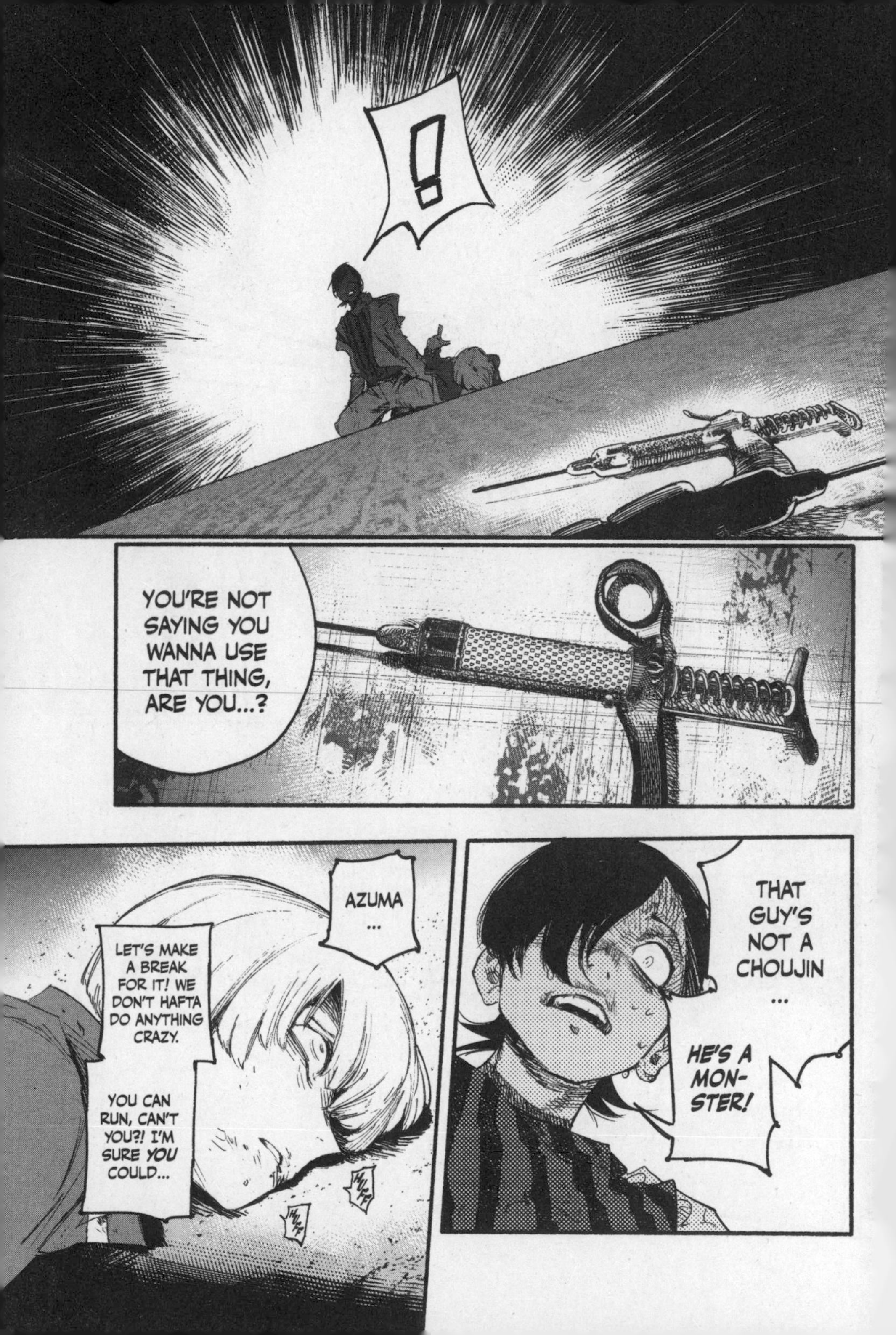
!
YOU'RE NOT SAYING YOU WANNA USE THAT THING, ARE YOU...?
THAT GUY'S NOT A CHOUJIN ...
HE'S A MON-STER!
AZUMA ...
LET'S MAKE A BREAK FOR IT! WE DON'T HAFTA DO ANYTHING CRAZY.
YOU CAN RUN, CAN'T YOU?! I'M SURE YOU COULD...
HUFF
HUFF

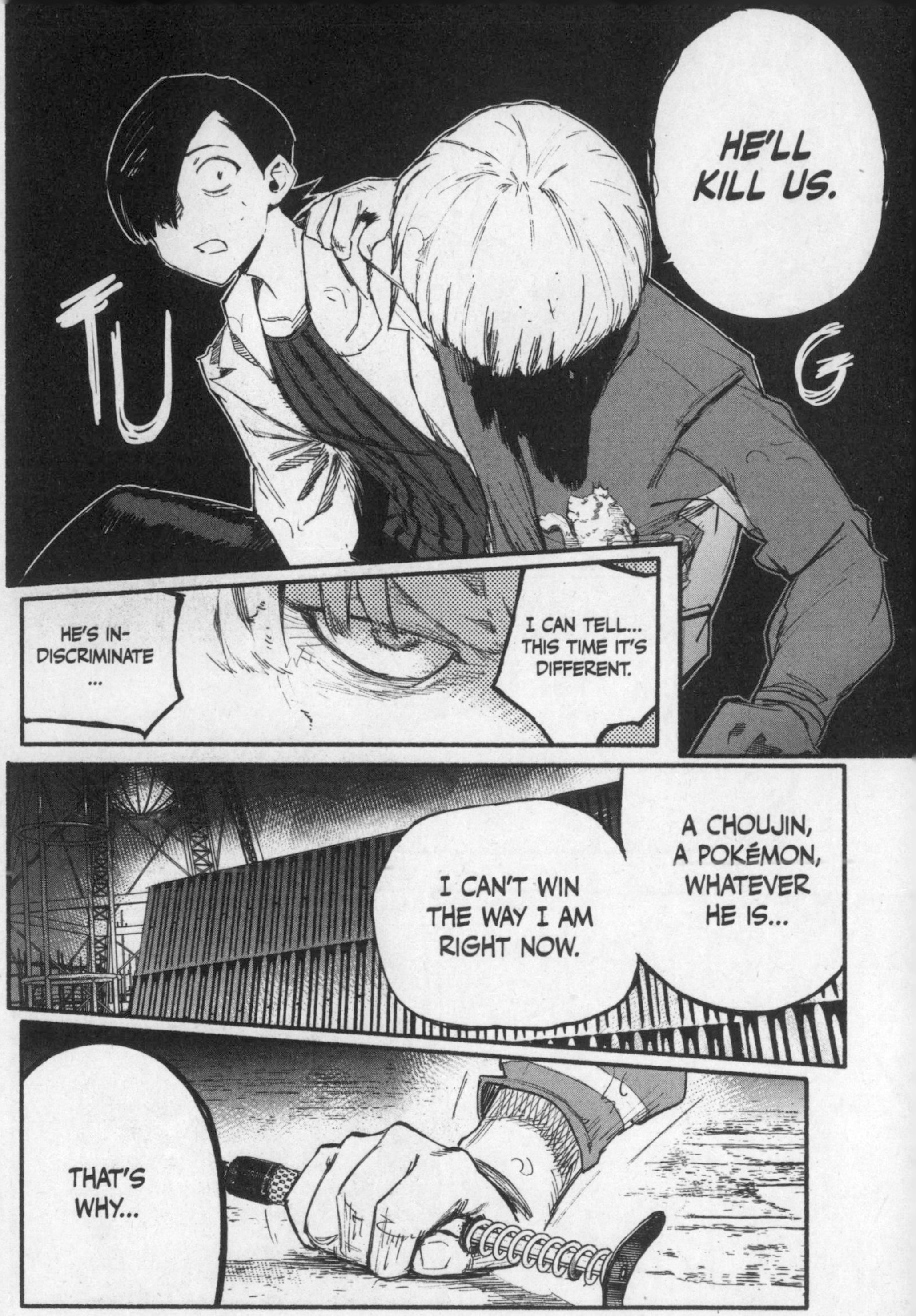
HE'LL KILL US.
TUG
I CAN TELL... THIS TIME IT'S DIFFERENT.
HE'S IN-DISCRIMINATE ...
A CHOUJIN, A POKÉMON, WHATEVER HE IS...
I CAN'T WIN THE WAY I AM RIGHT NOW.
THAT'S WHY...

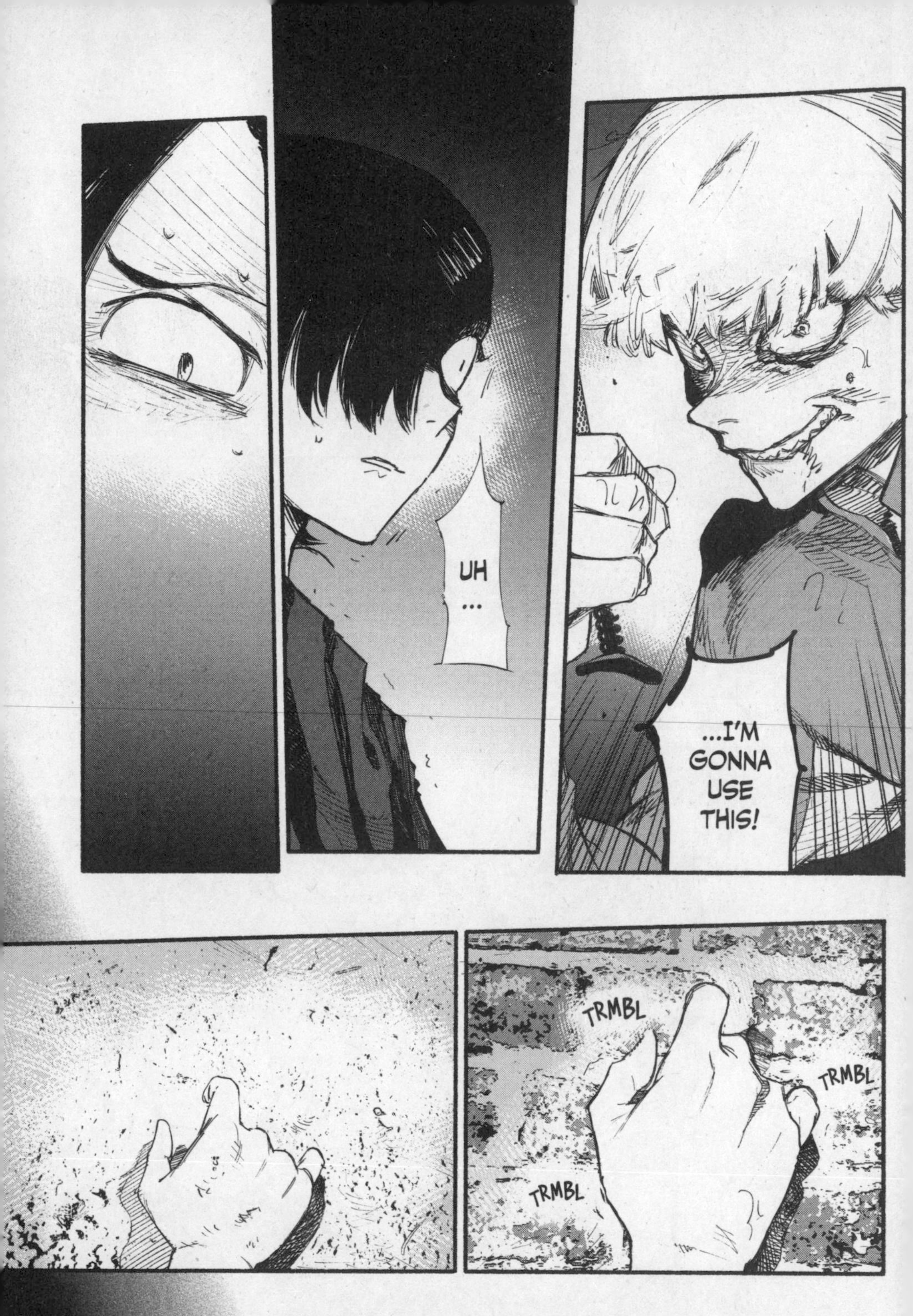
...I'M GONNA USE THIS!
UH ...
TRMBL
TRMBL
TRMBL

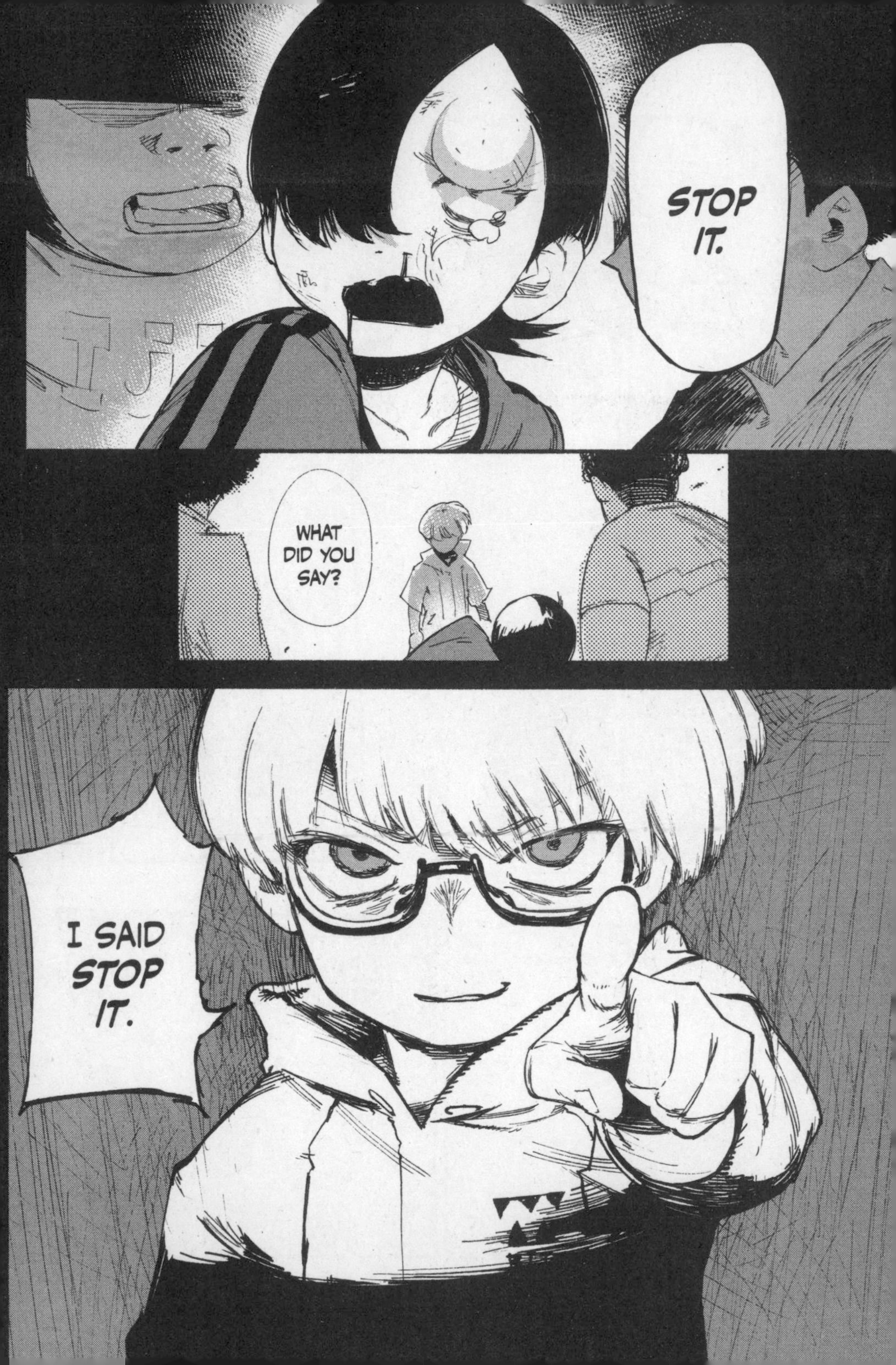
STOP IT.
WHAT DID YOU SAY?
I SAID STOP IT.

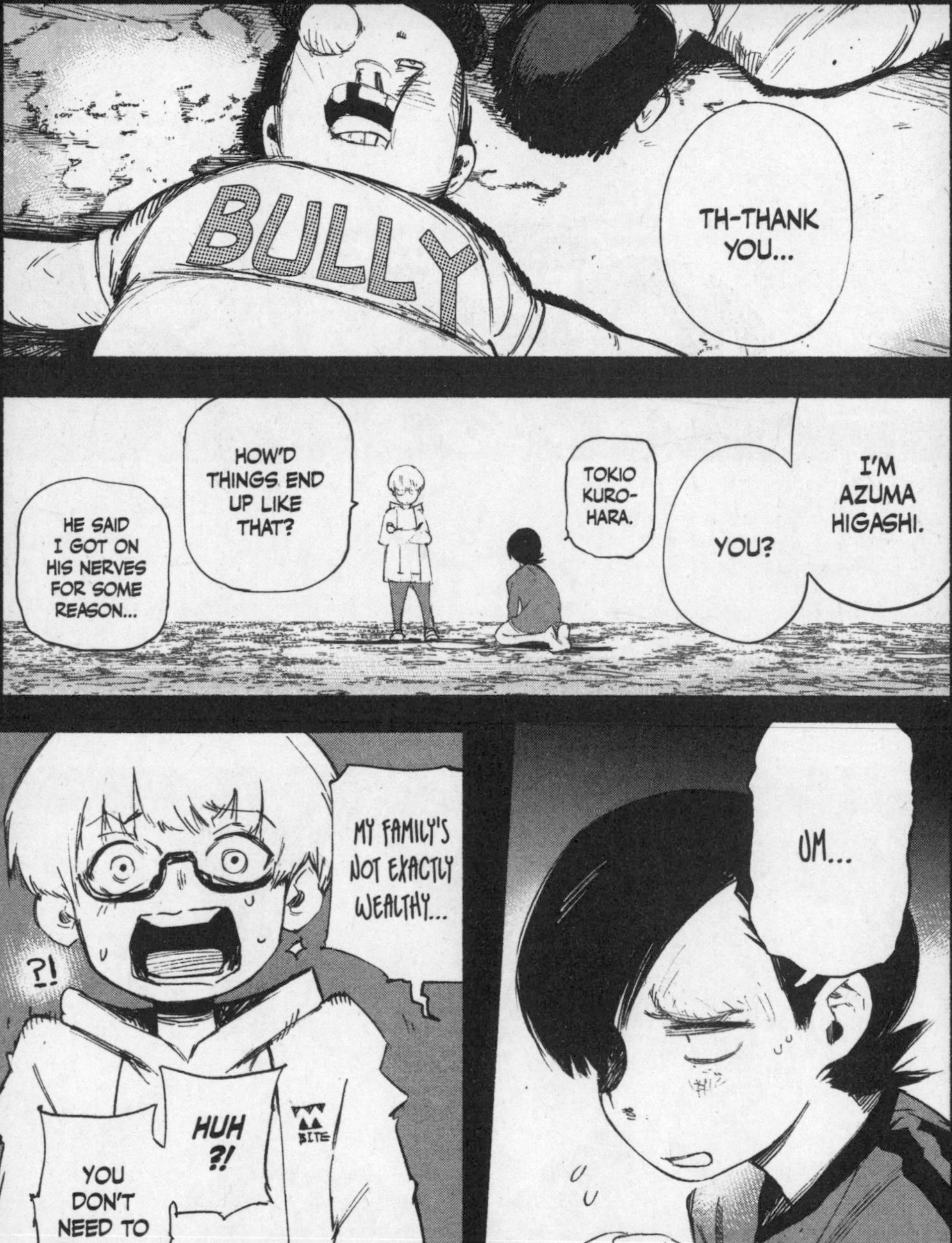
BULLY
TH-THANK YOU...
I'M AZUMA HIGASHI.
YOU?
TOKIO KURO-HARA.
HOW'D THINGS END UP LIKE THAT?
HE SAID I GOT ON HIS NERVES FOR SOME REASON...
UM...
MY FAMILY'S NOT EXACTLY WEALTHY...
?!
BITE
HUH ?!
YOU DON'T NEED TO PAY ME...

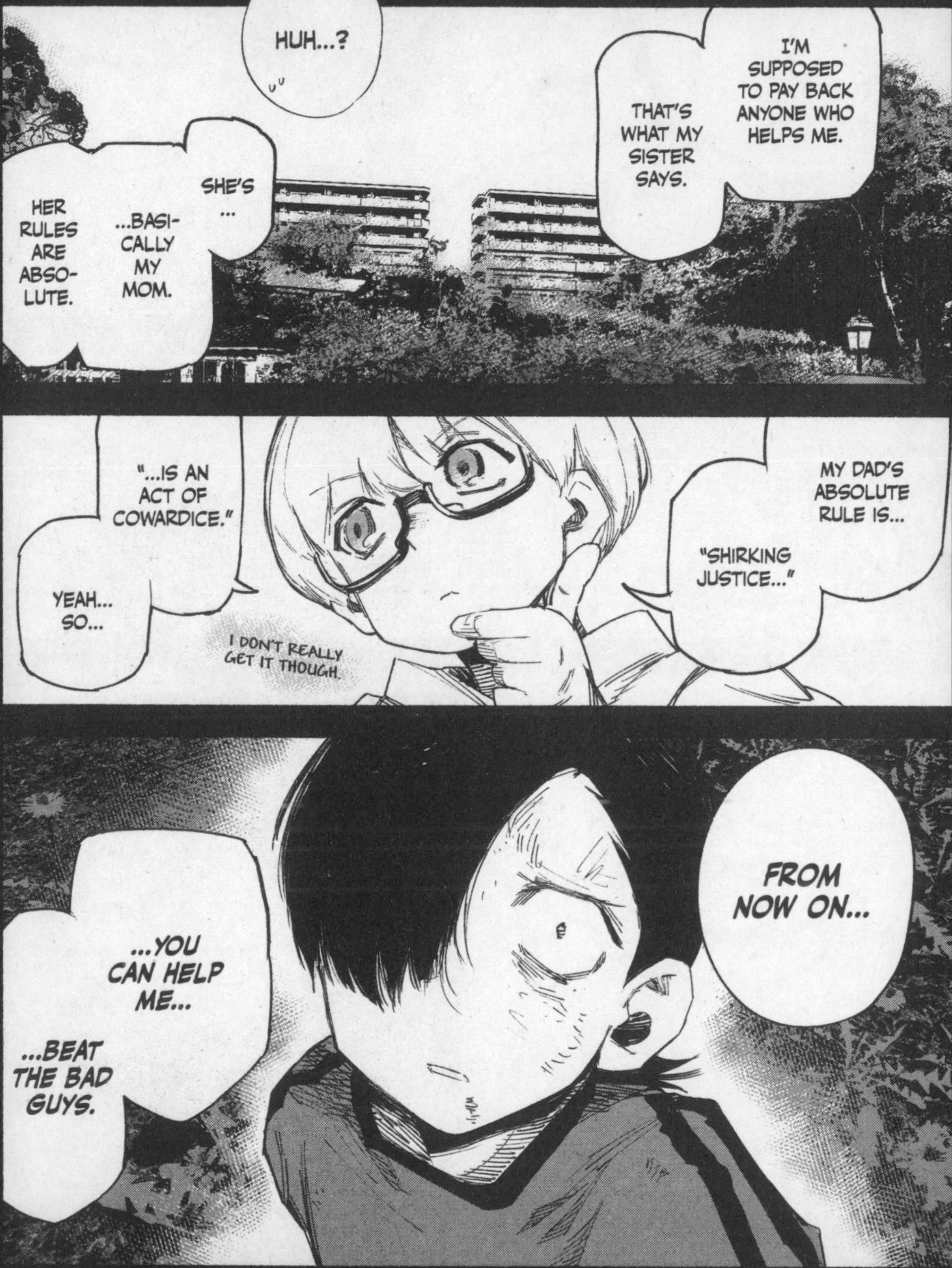
I'M SUPPOSED TO PAY BACK ANYONE WHO HELPS ME.
THAT'S WHAT MY SISTER SAYS.
HUH...?
SHE'S...
...BASICALLY MY MOM.
HER RULES ARE ABSOLUTE.
MY DAD'S ABSOLUTE RULE IS...
"SHIRKING JUSTICE..."
"...IS AN ACT OF COWARDICE."
YEAH... SO...
I DON'T REALLY GET IT THOUGH.
FROM NOW ON...
...YOU CAN HELP ME...
...BEAT THE BAD GUYS.

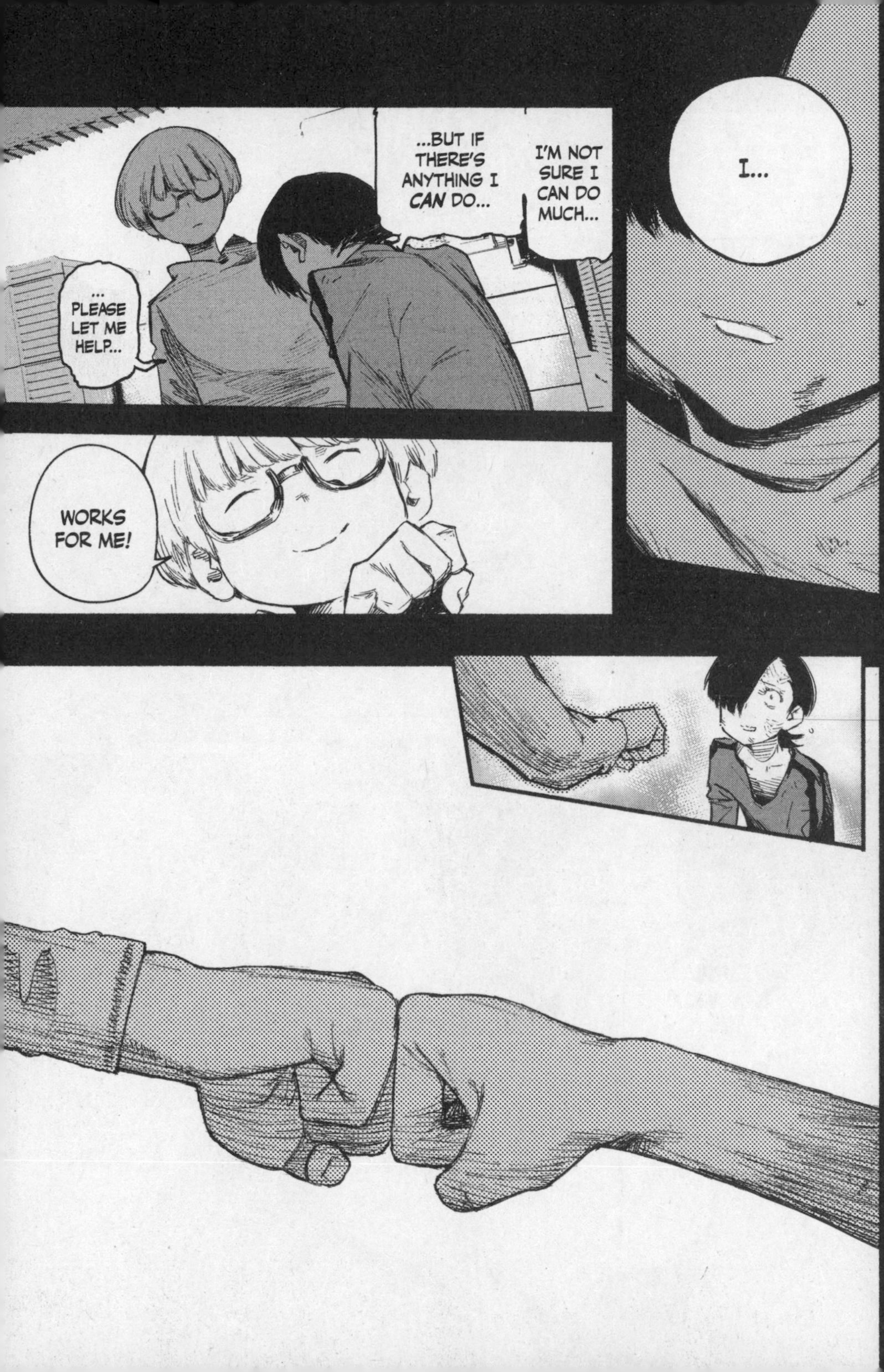
I...
I'M NOT SURE I CAN DO MUCH...
...BUT IF THERE'S ANYTHING I *CAN* DO...
... PLEASE LET ME HELP...
WORKS FOR ME!

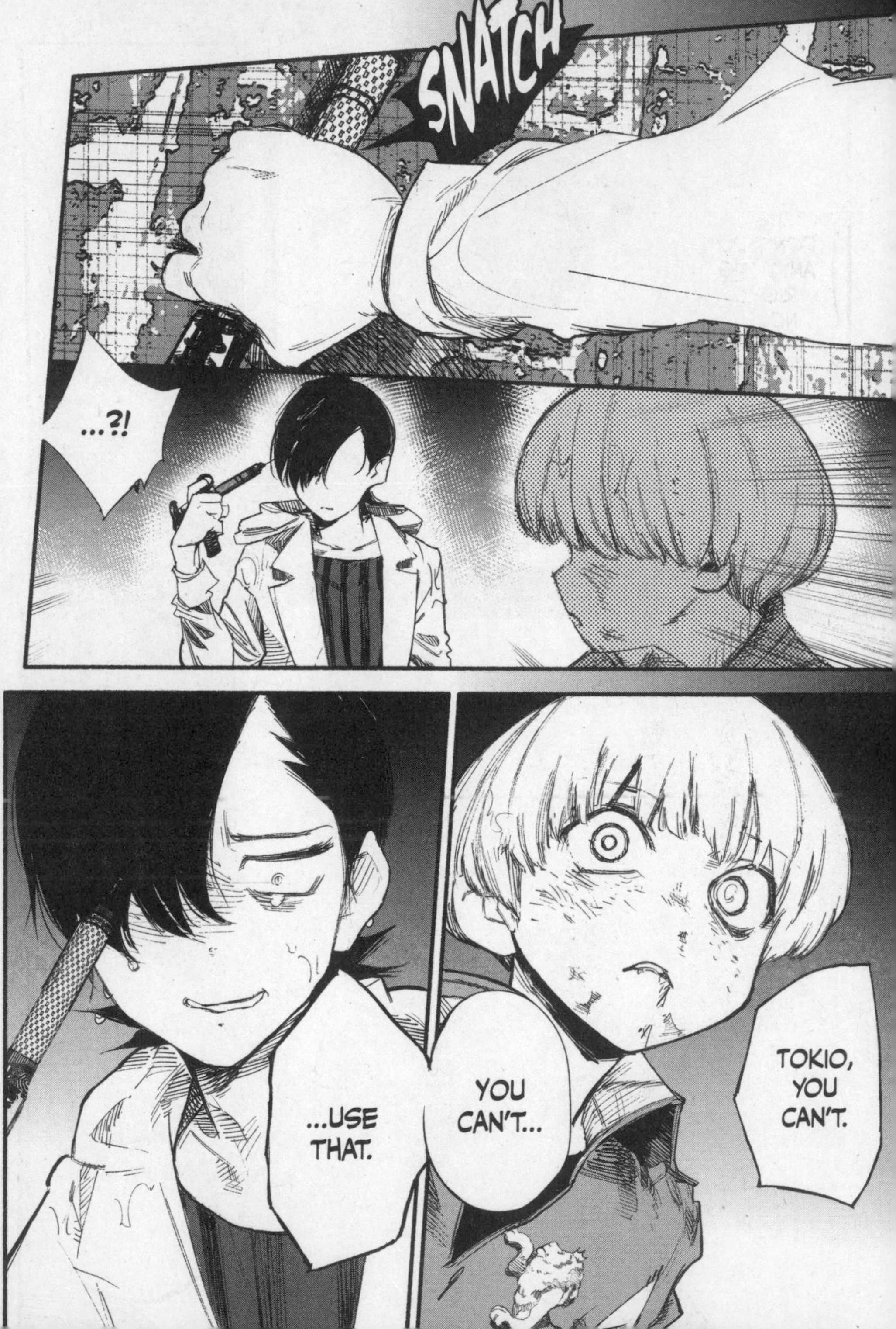
SNATCH
...?!
TOKIO, YOU CAN'T.
YOU CAN'T...
...USE THAT.

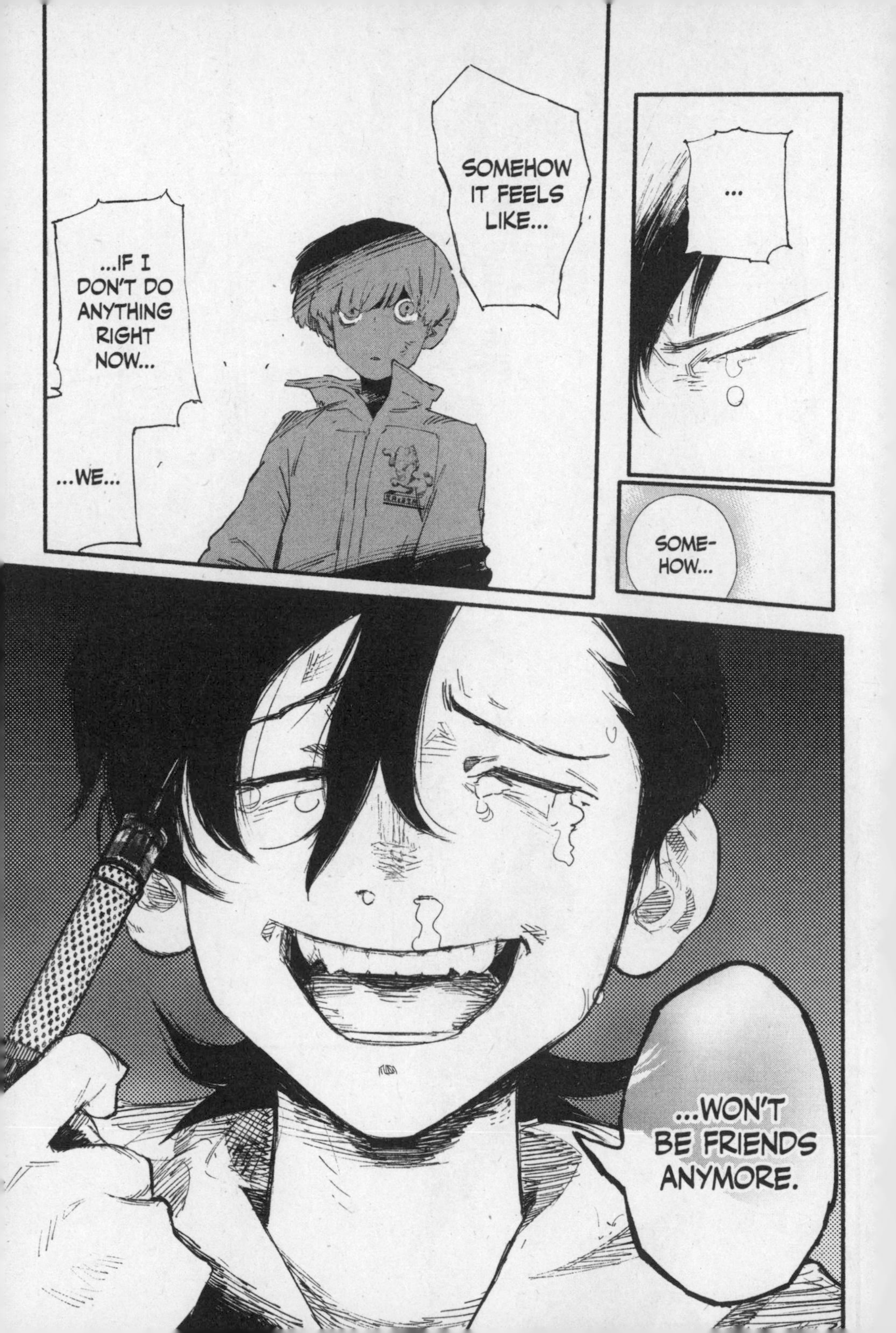
...
SOME-HOW...
SOMEHOW IT FEELS LIKE...
...IF I DON'T DO ANYTHING RIGHT NOW...
...WE...
...WON'T BE FRIENDS ANYMORE.

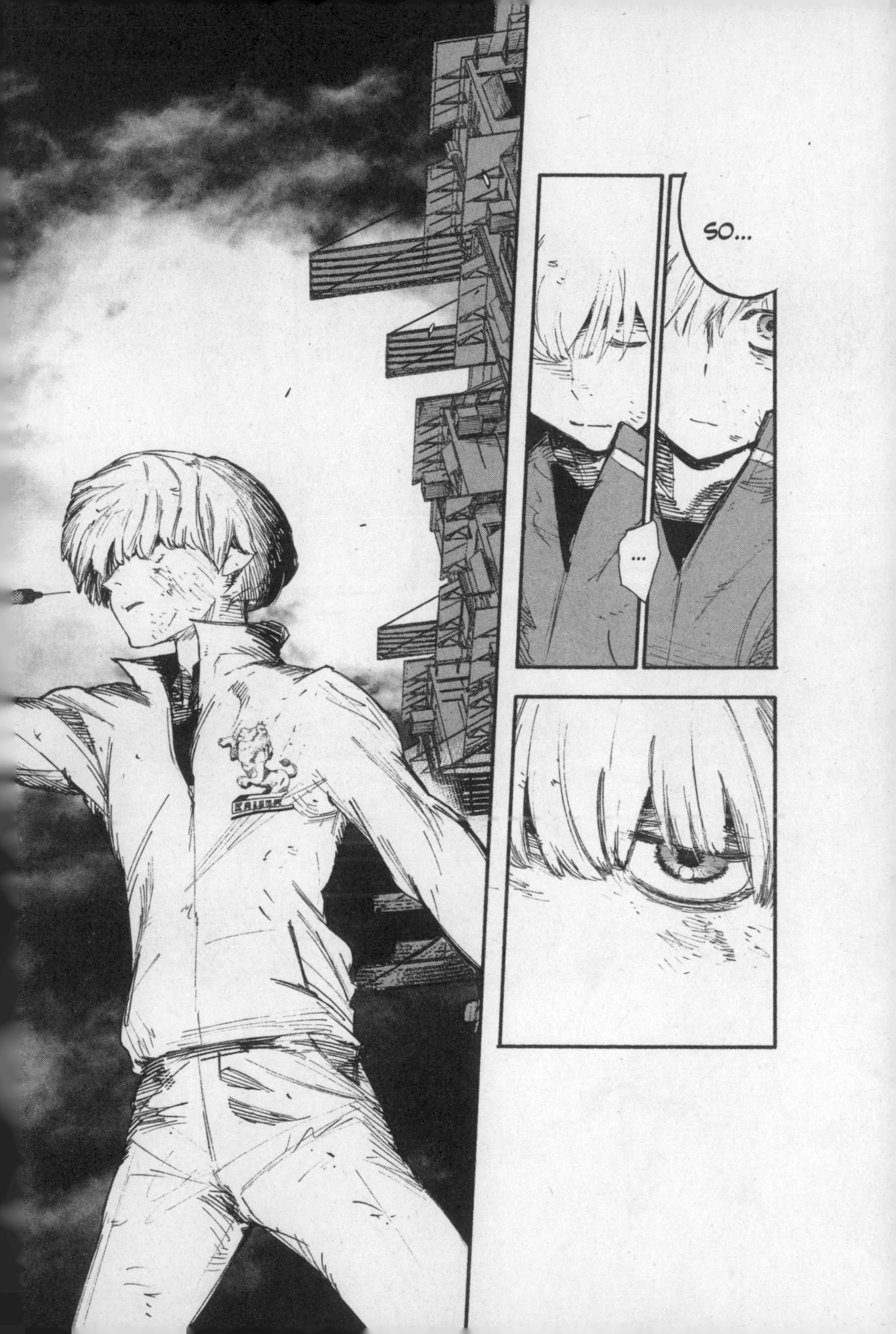
SO...
...

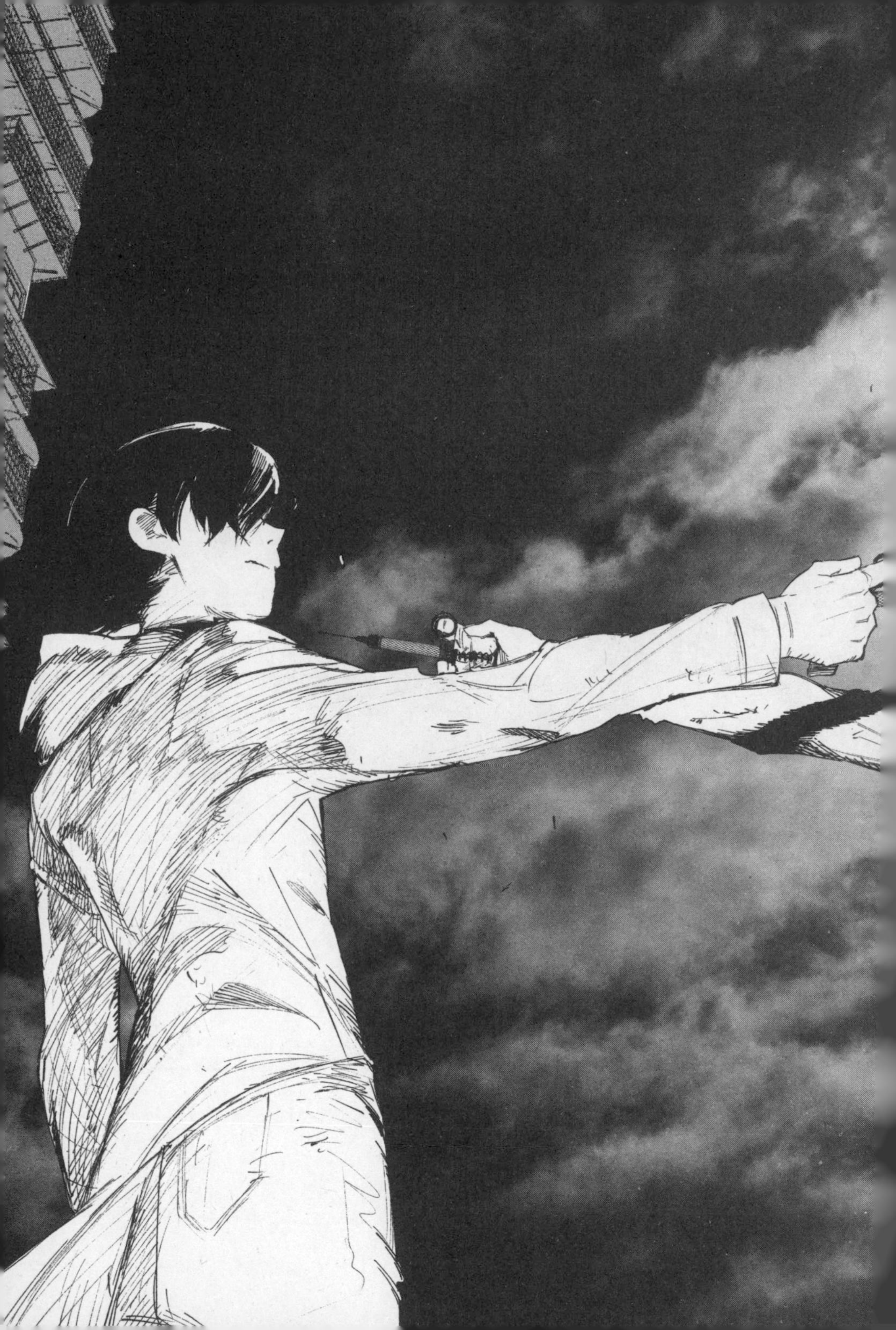

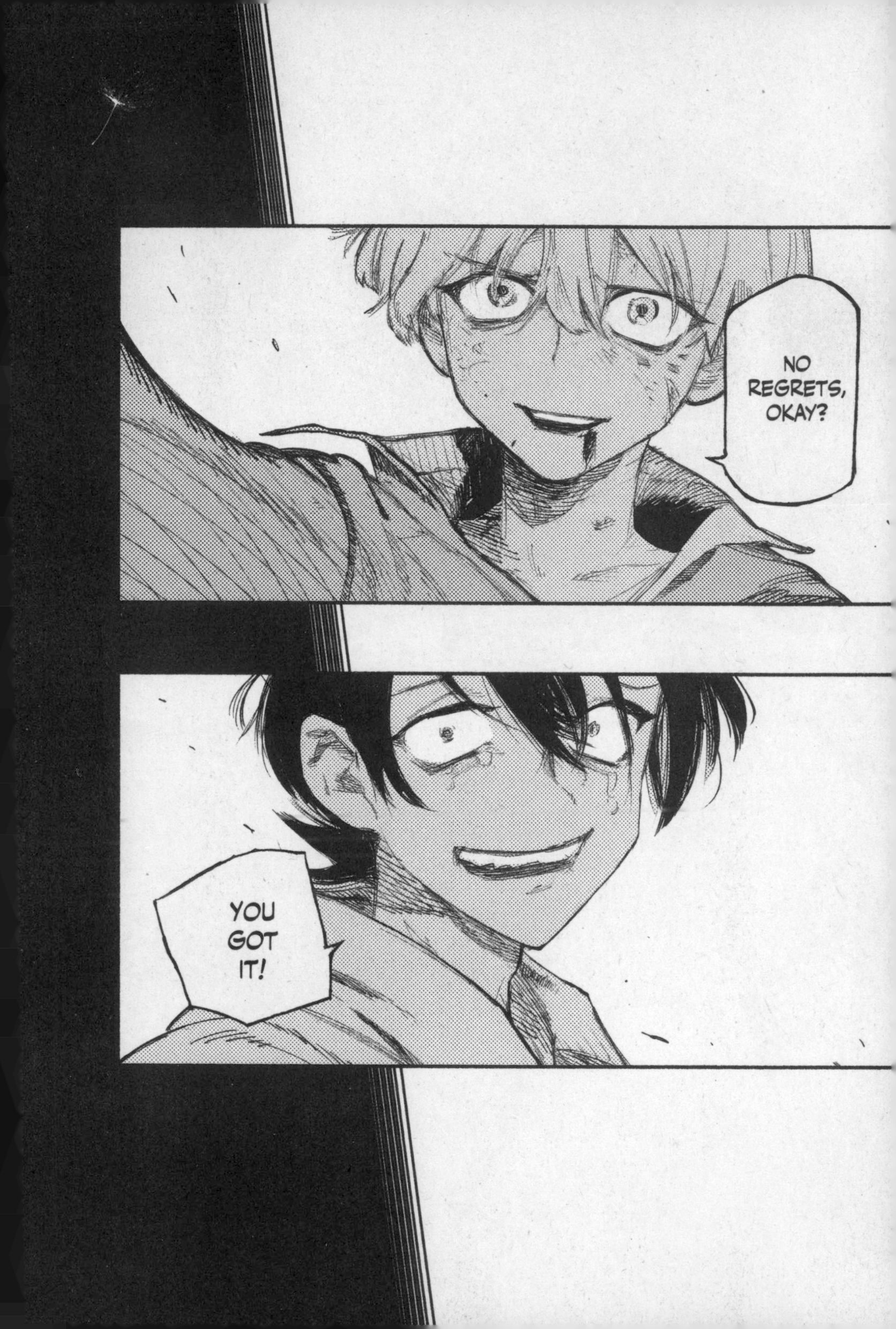
NO REGRETS, OKAY?
YOU GOT IT!

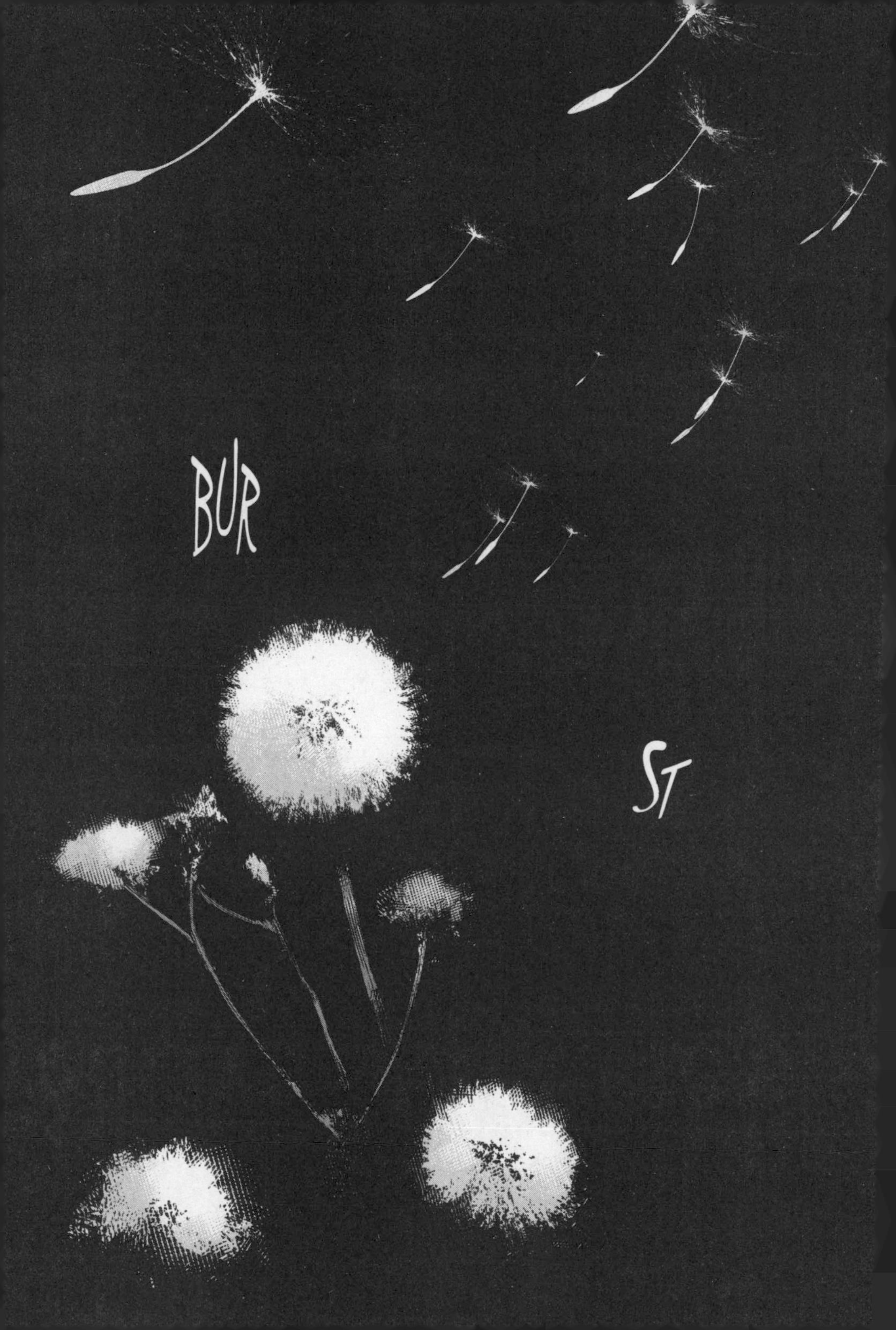
BUR
ST

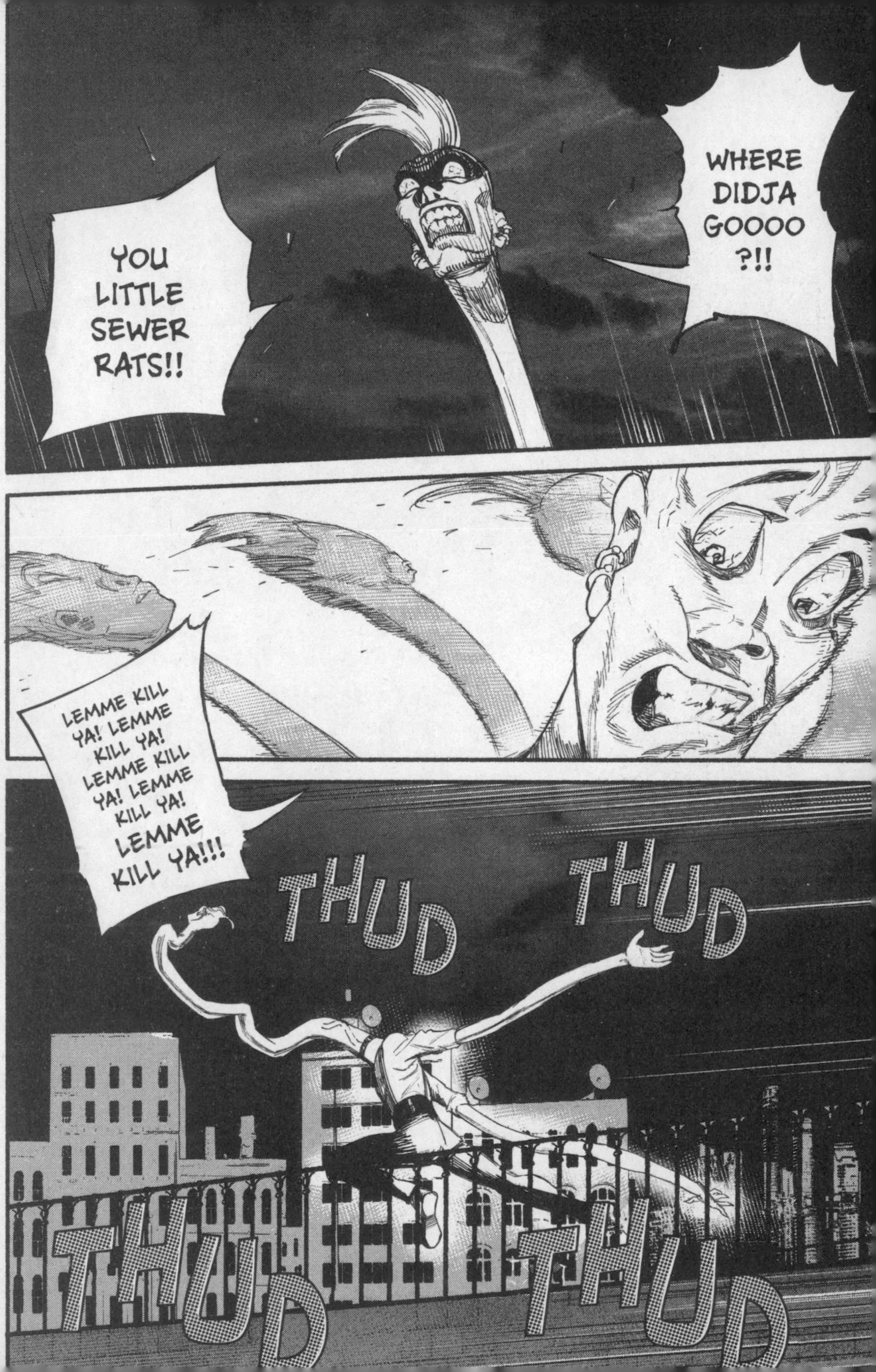
WHERE DIDJA GOOOO ?!!
YOU LITTLE SEWER RATS!!
LEMME KILL YA! LEMME KILL YA! LEMME KILL YA! LEMME KILL YA! LEMME KILL YA!!!
THUD THUD
THUD THUD

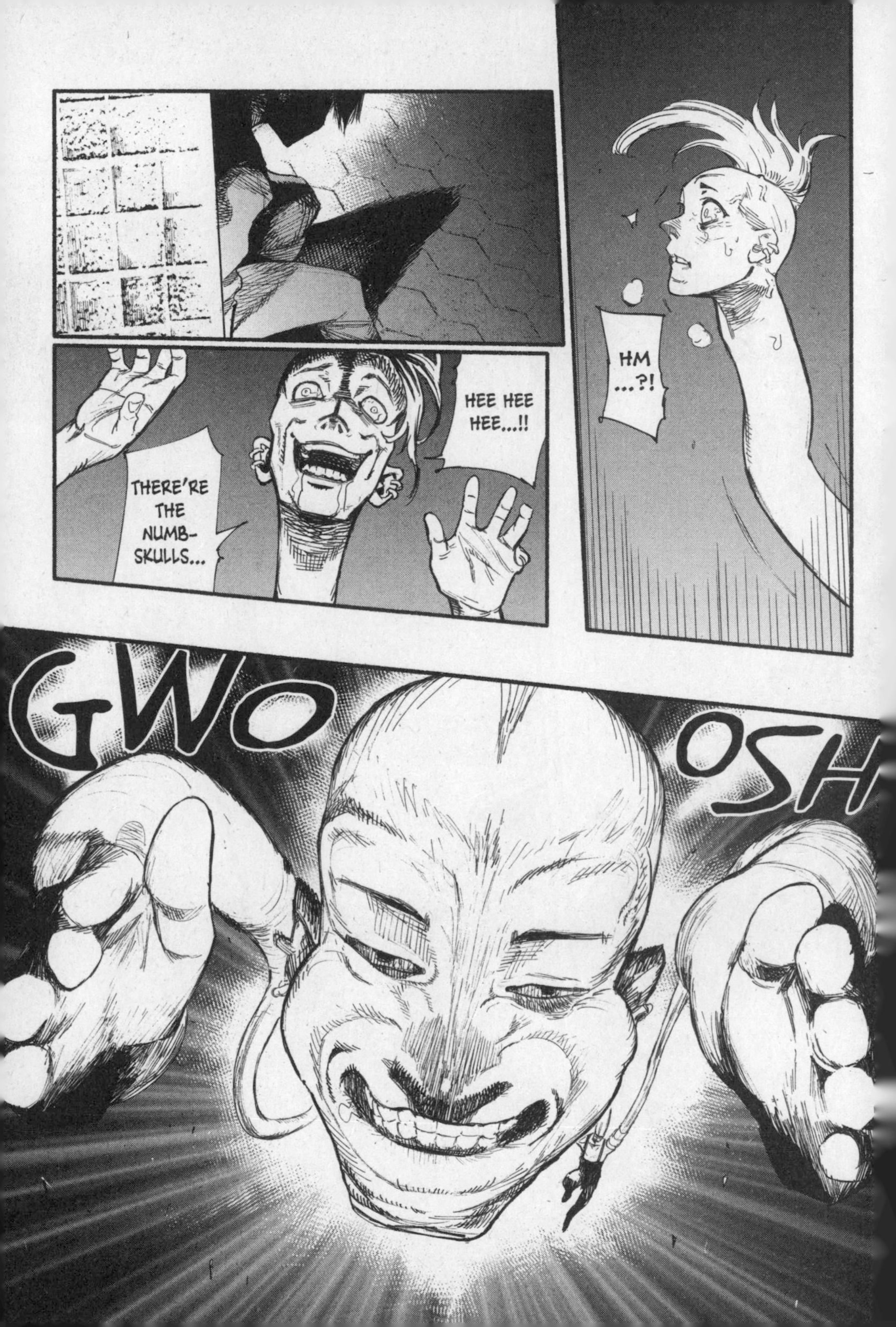
HM ...?!
HEE HEE HEE...!!
THERE'RE THE NUMBSKULLS...
GWOOSH

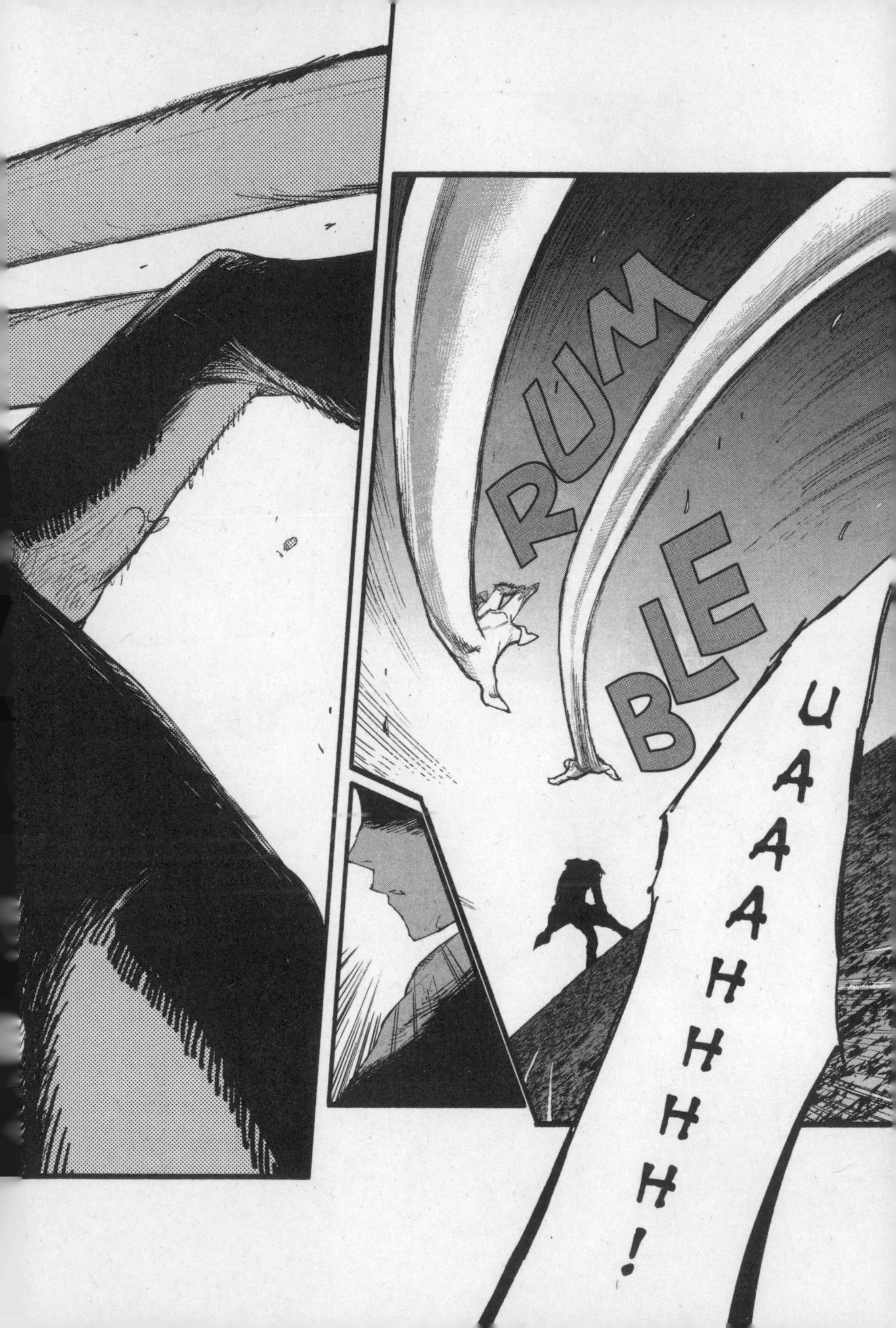
RUMBLE
UAAAAHHHHH!

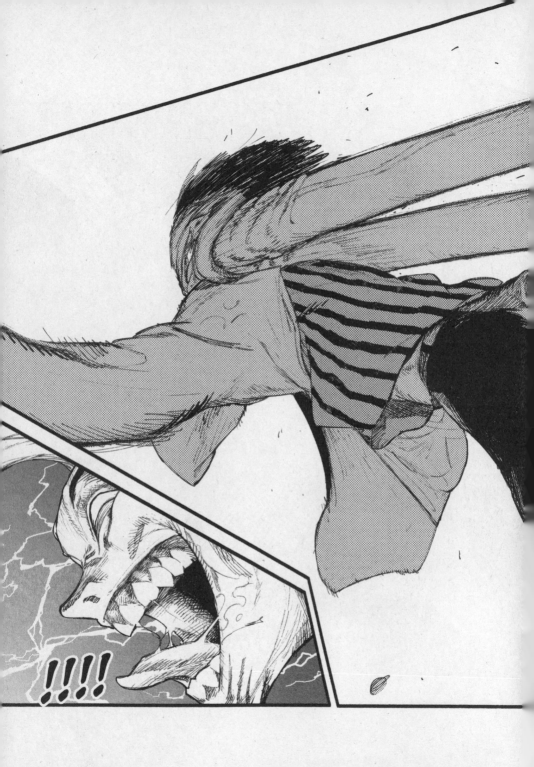

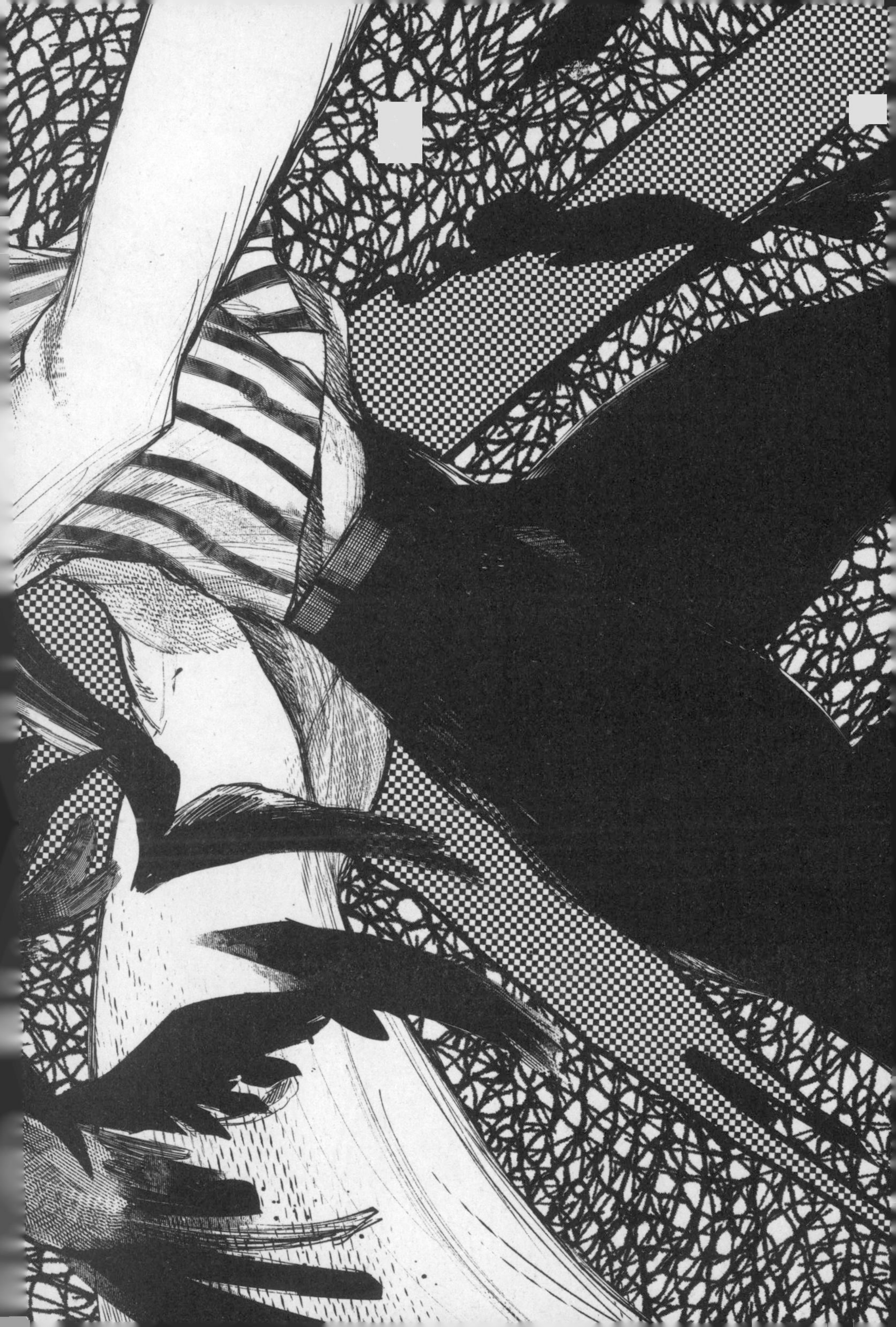

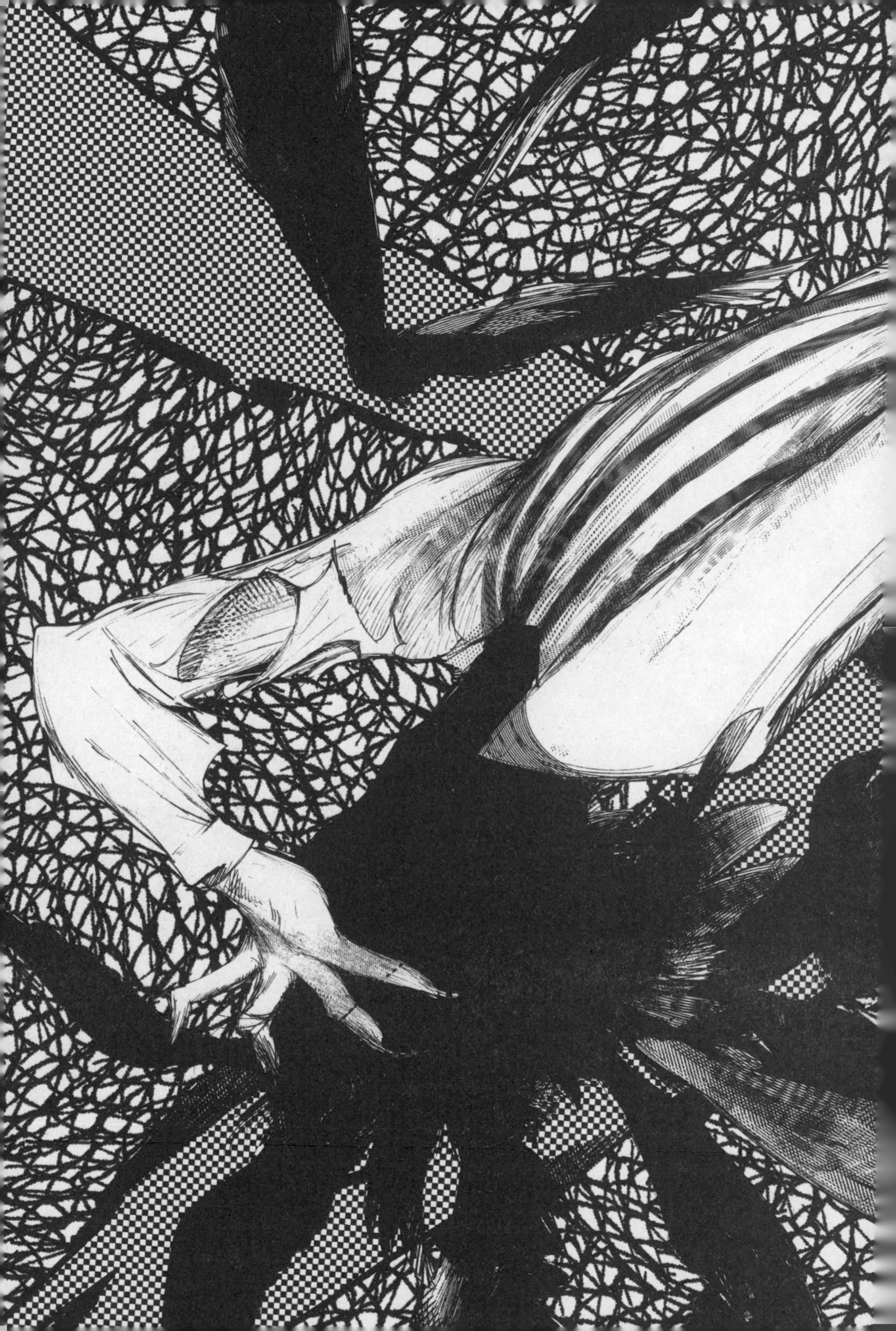

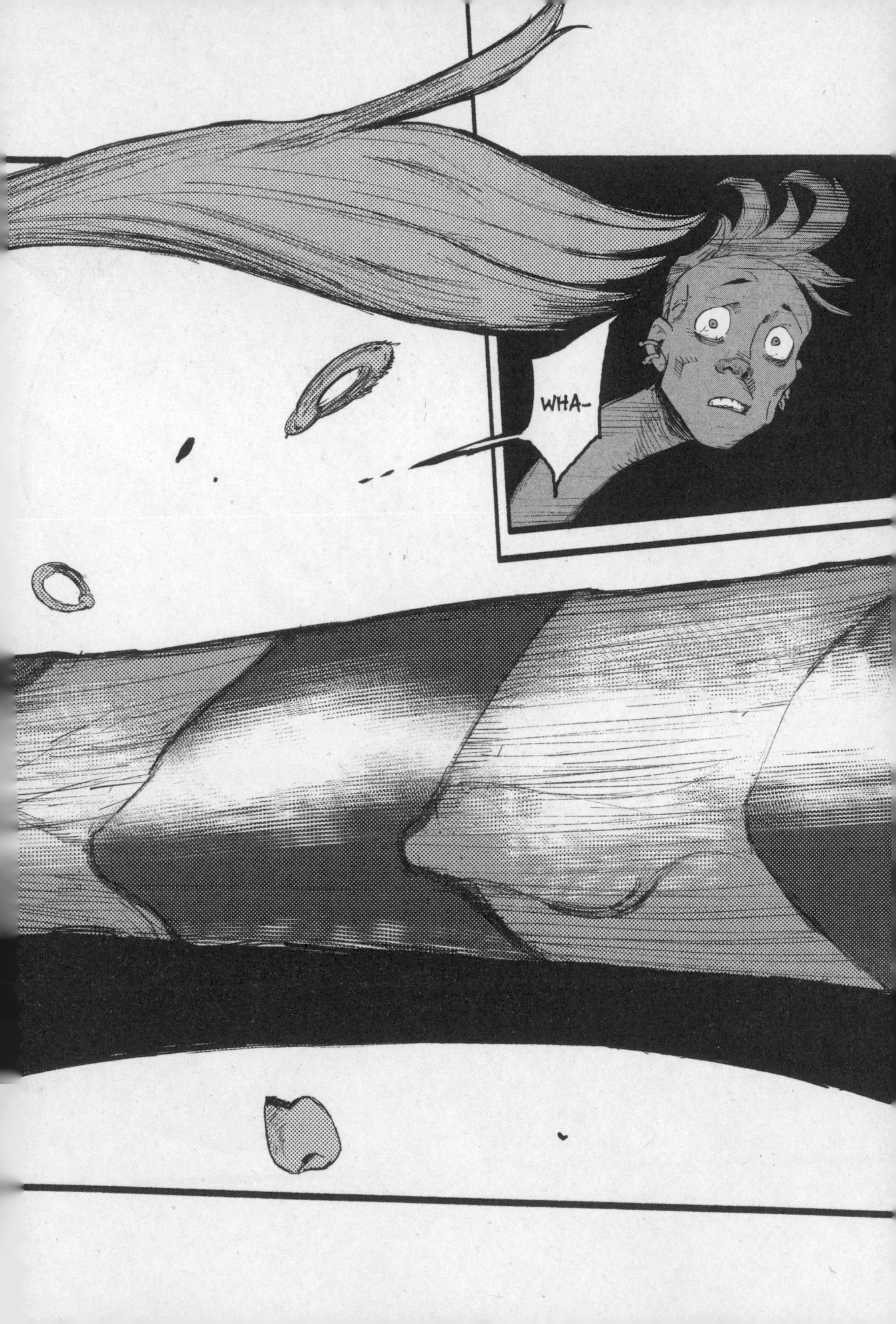
WHA-

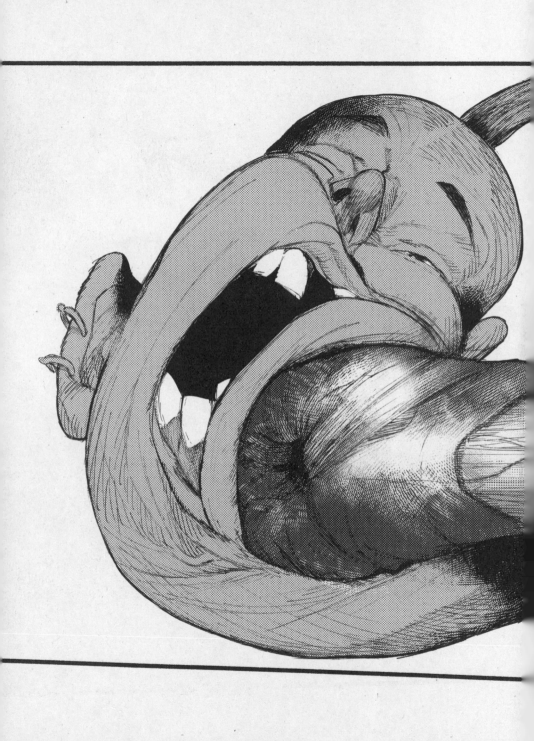

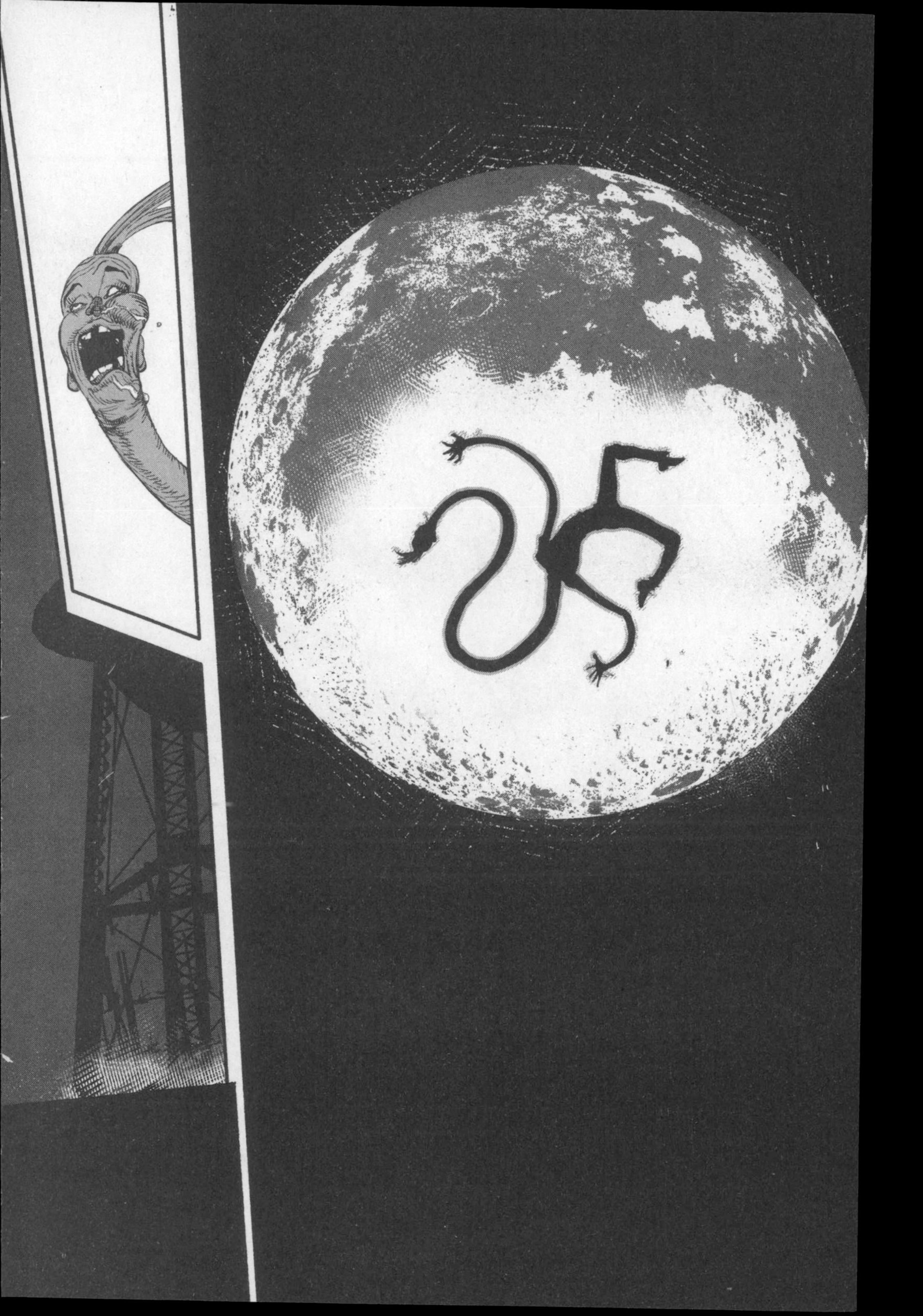

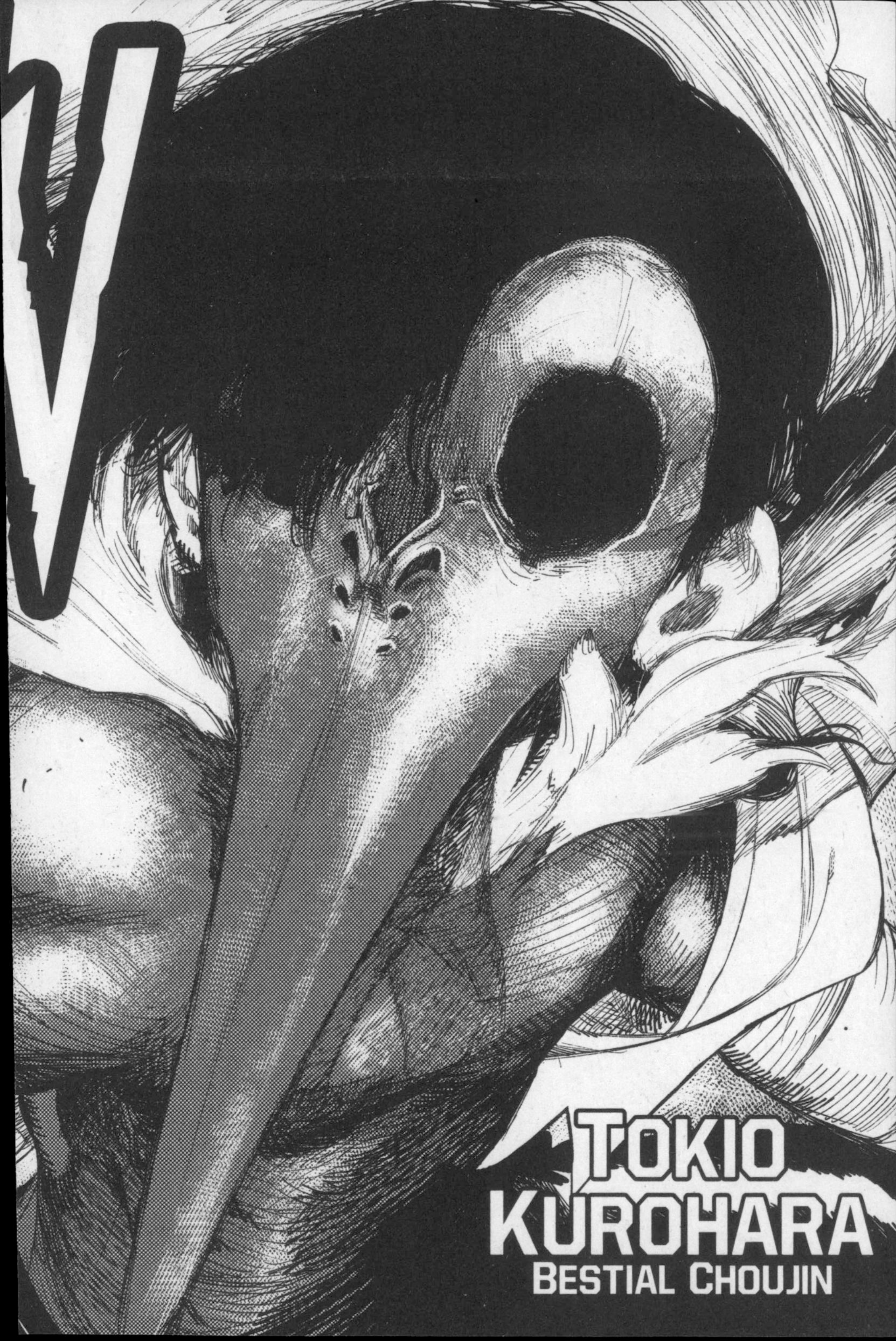
TOKIO
KUROHARA
BESTIAL CHOUJIN

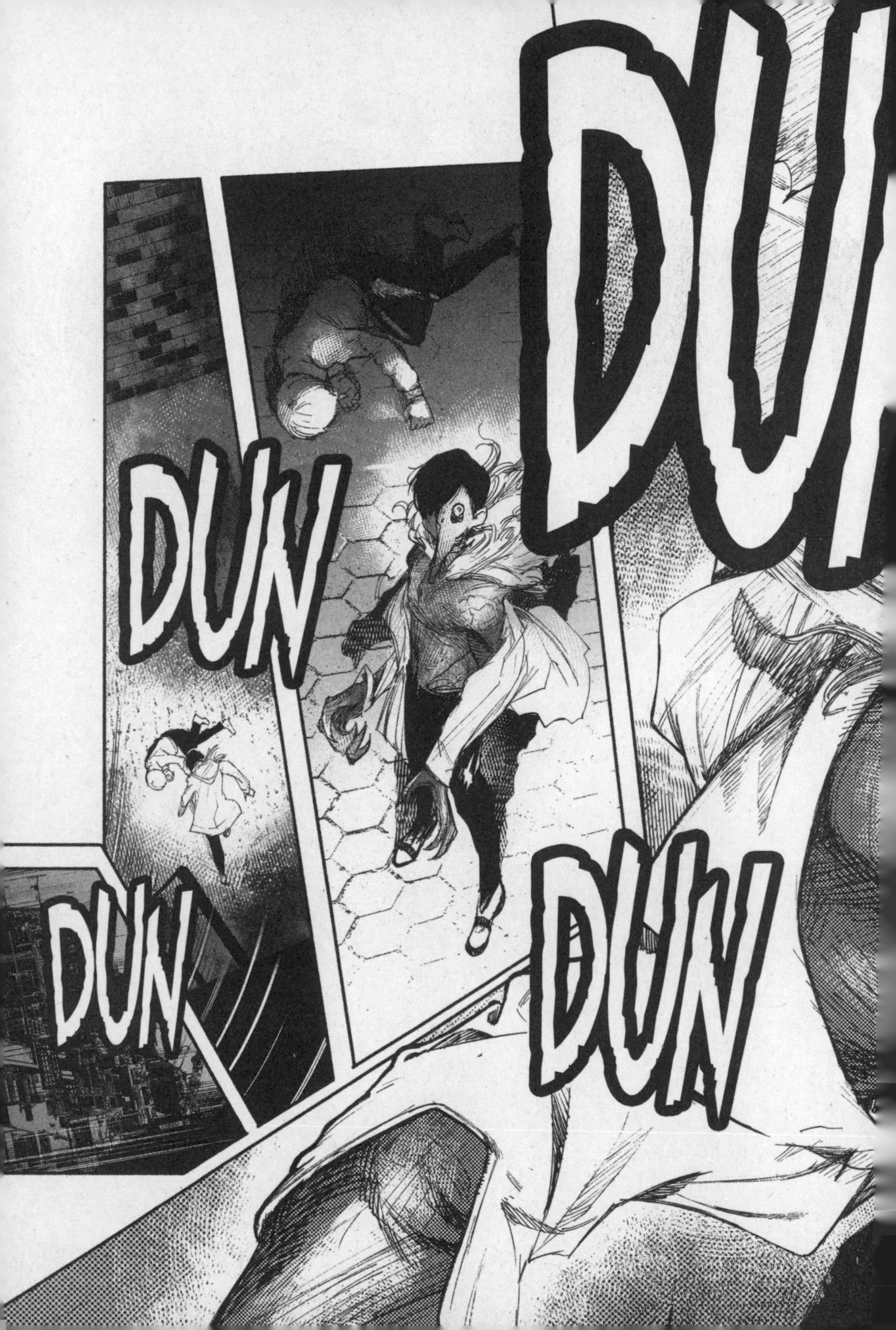
DU
DUN
DUN
DUN

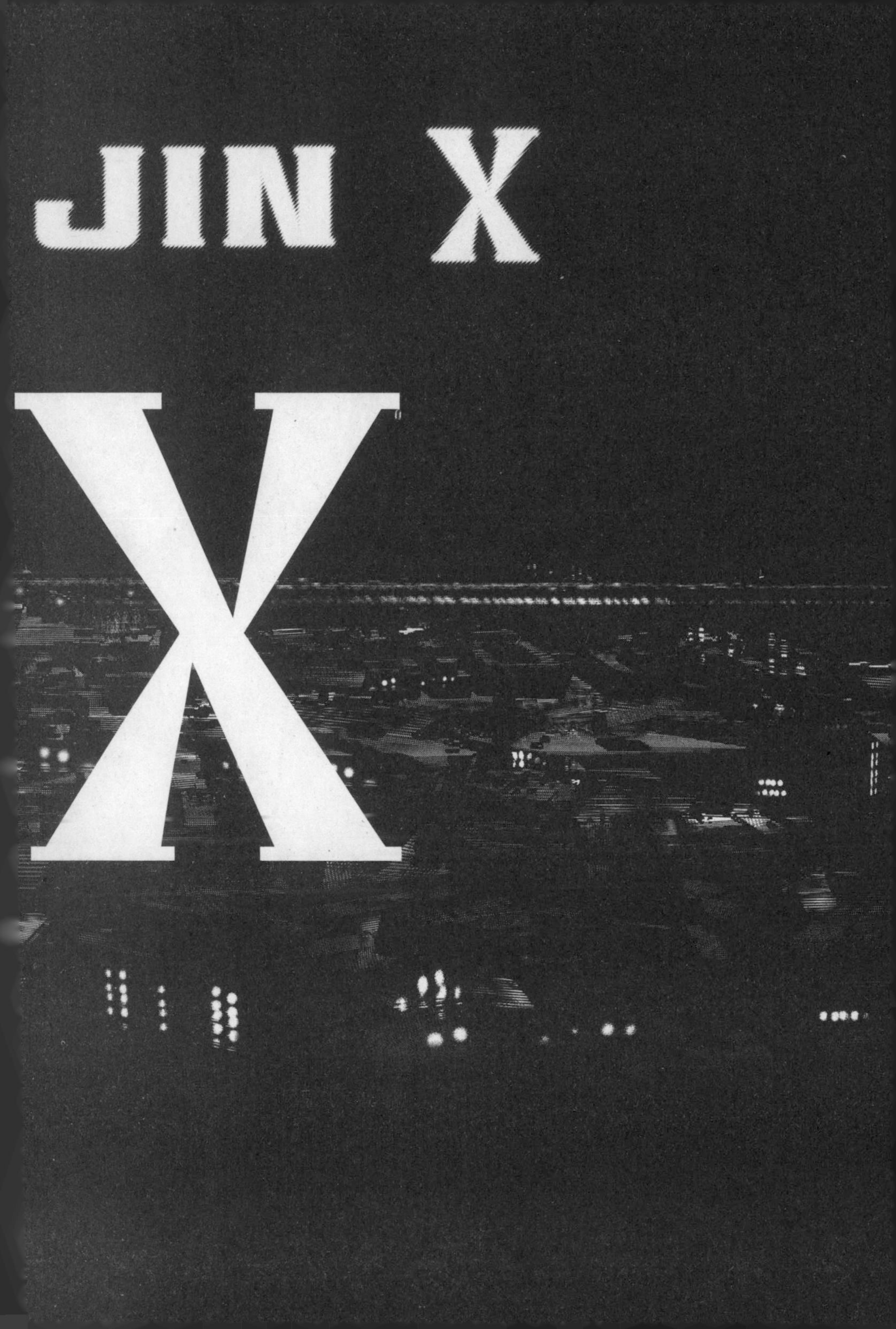
JIN X
X

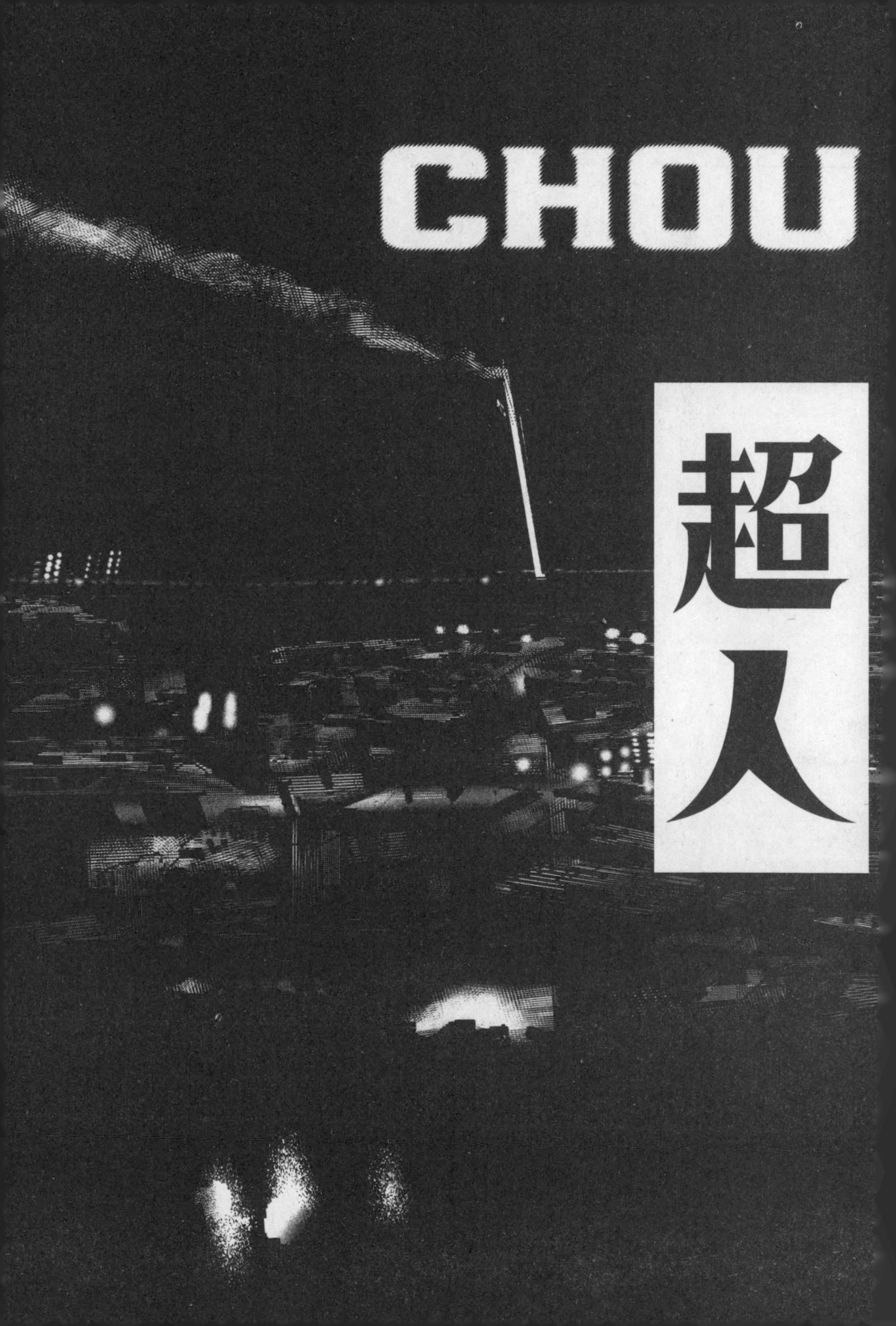
CHOU
超人

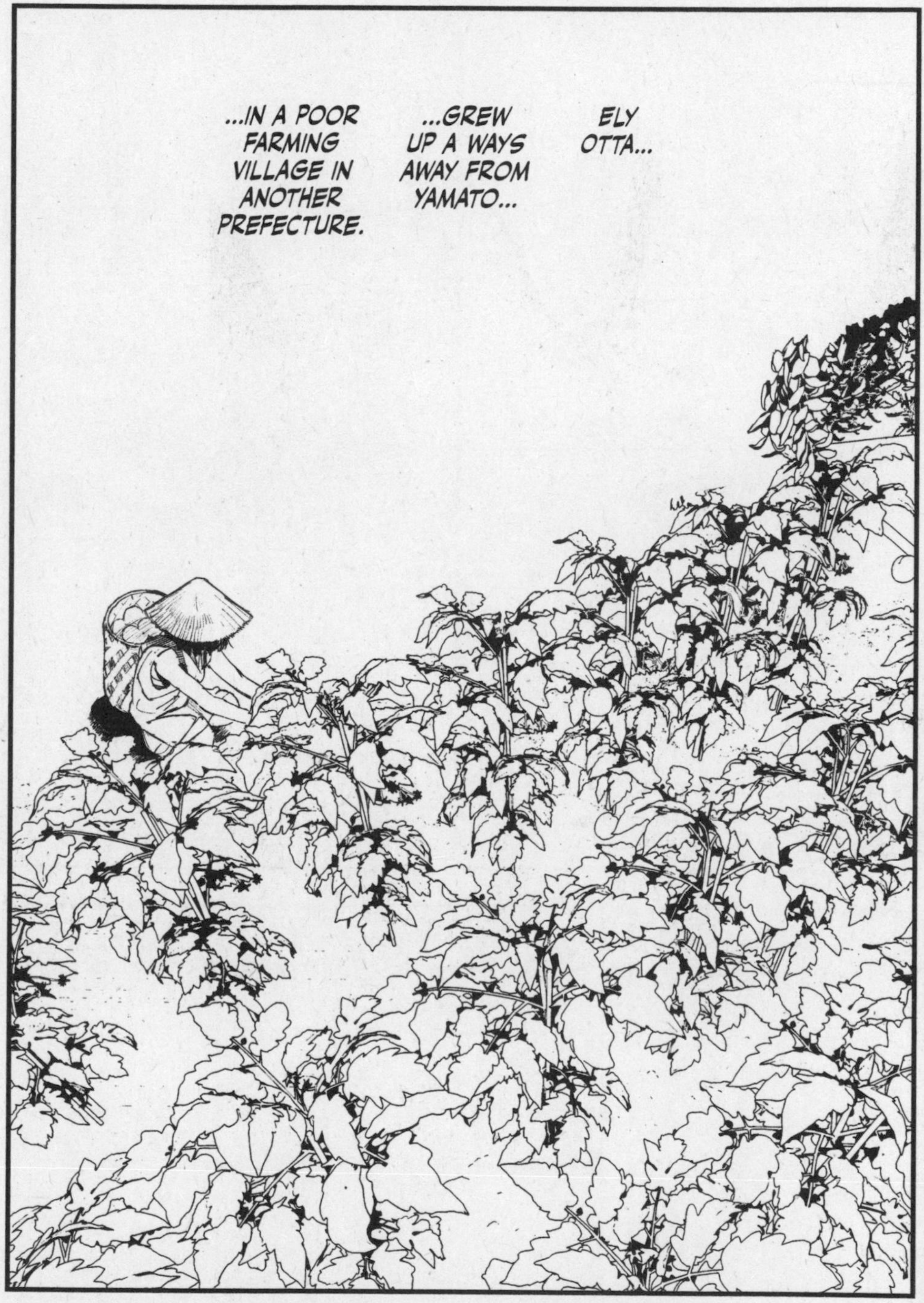
ELY OTTA...
...GREW UP A WAYS AWAY FROM YAMATO...
...IN A POOR FARMING VILLAGE IN ANOTHER PREFECTURE.

Chapter 2: Uncrossed Paths! The Two Choujin

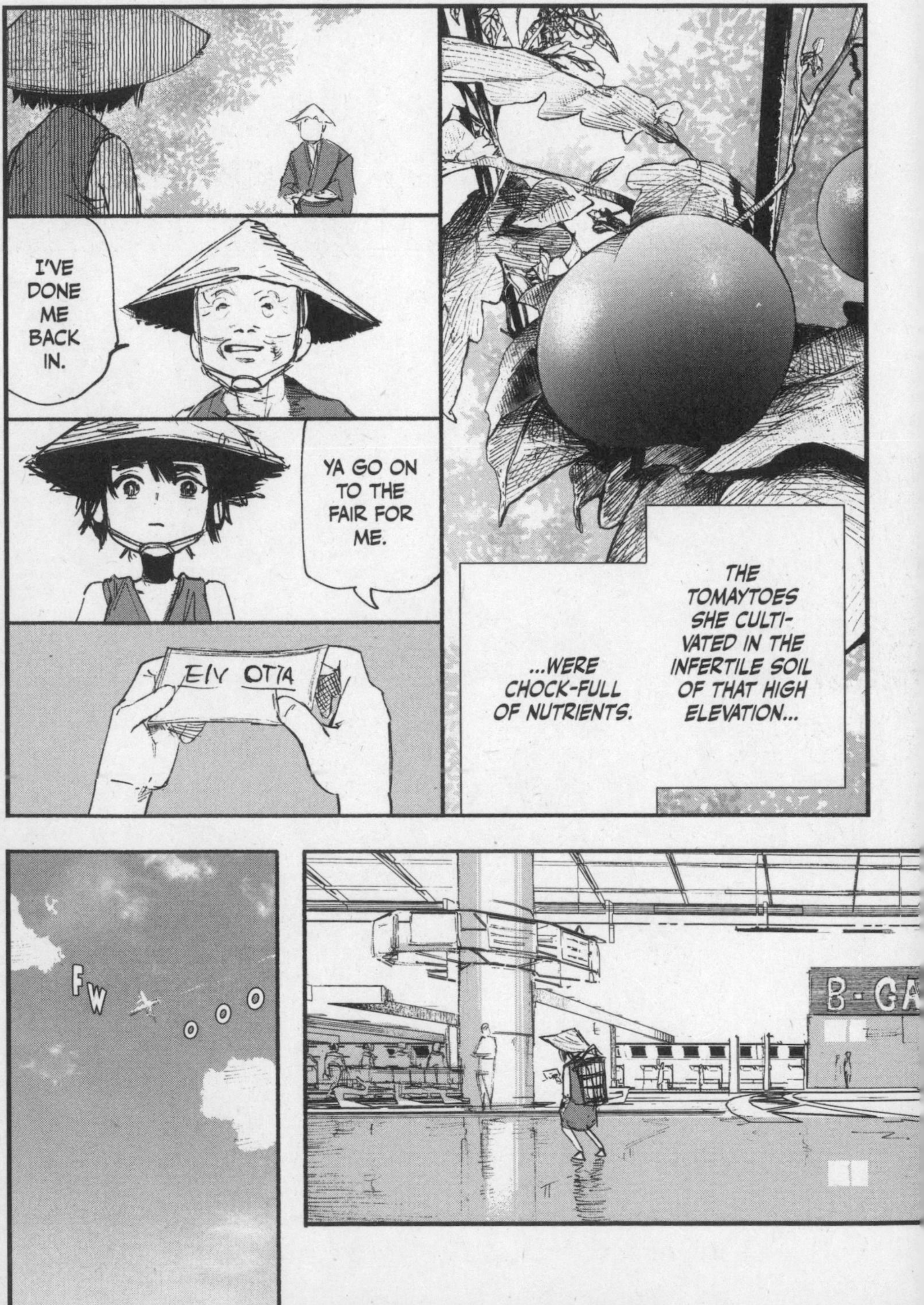
THE TOMAYTOES SHE CULTIVATED IN THE INFERTILE SOIL OF THAT HIGH ELEVATION...
...WERE CHOCK-FULL OF NUTRIENTS.
I'VE DONE ME BACK IN.
YA GO ON TO THE FAIR FOR ME.
B-GA
FWOOOO

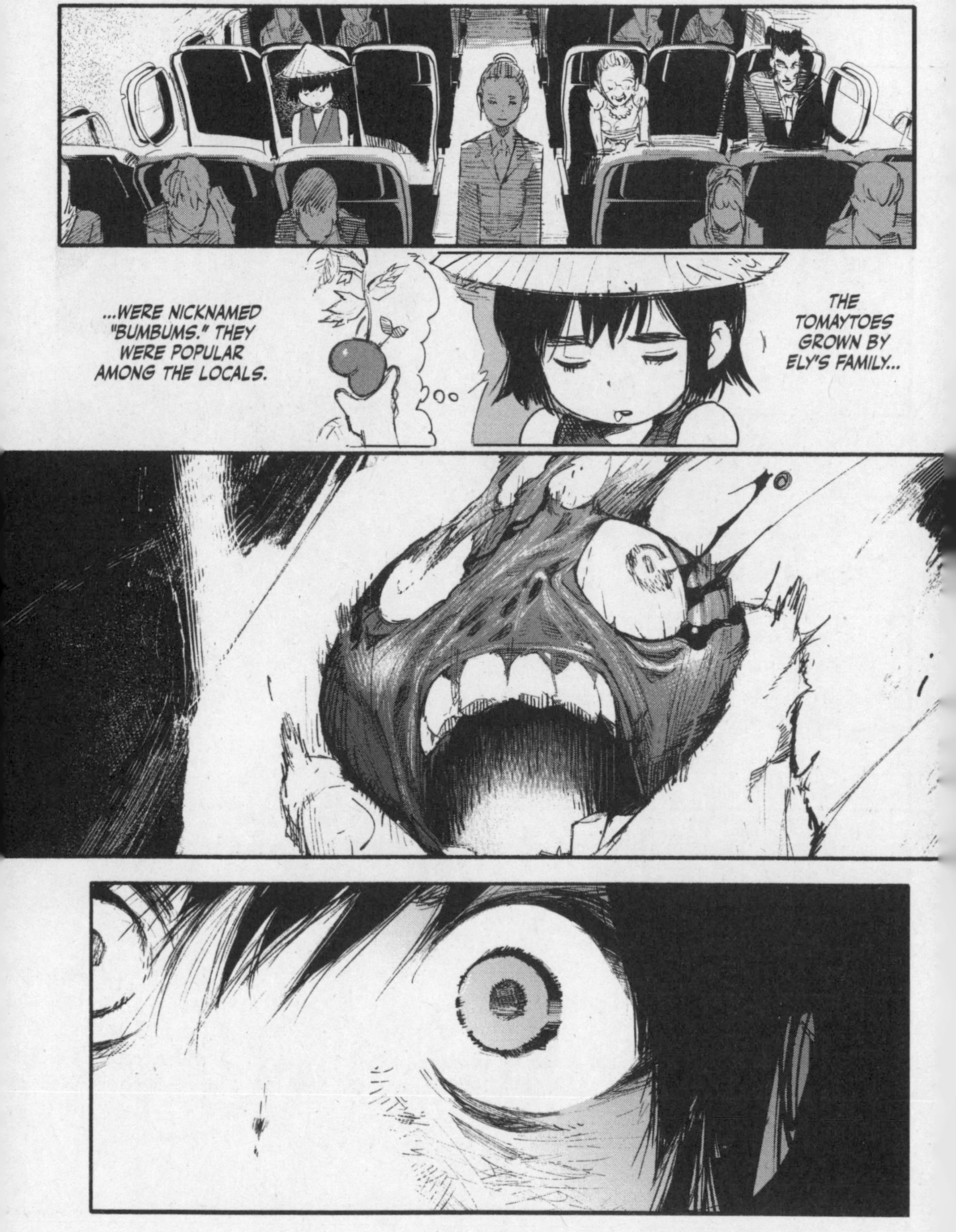
THE TOMAYTOES GROWN BY ELY'S FAMILY...
...WERE NICKNAMED "BUMBUMS." THEY WERE POPULAR AMONG THE LOCALS.

Chapter 2: Uncrossed Paths! The Two Choujin

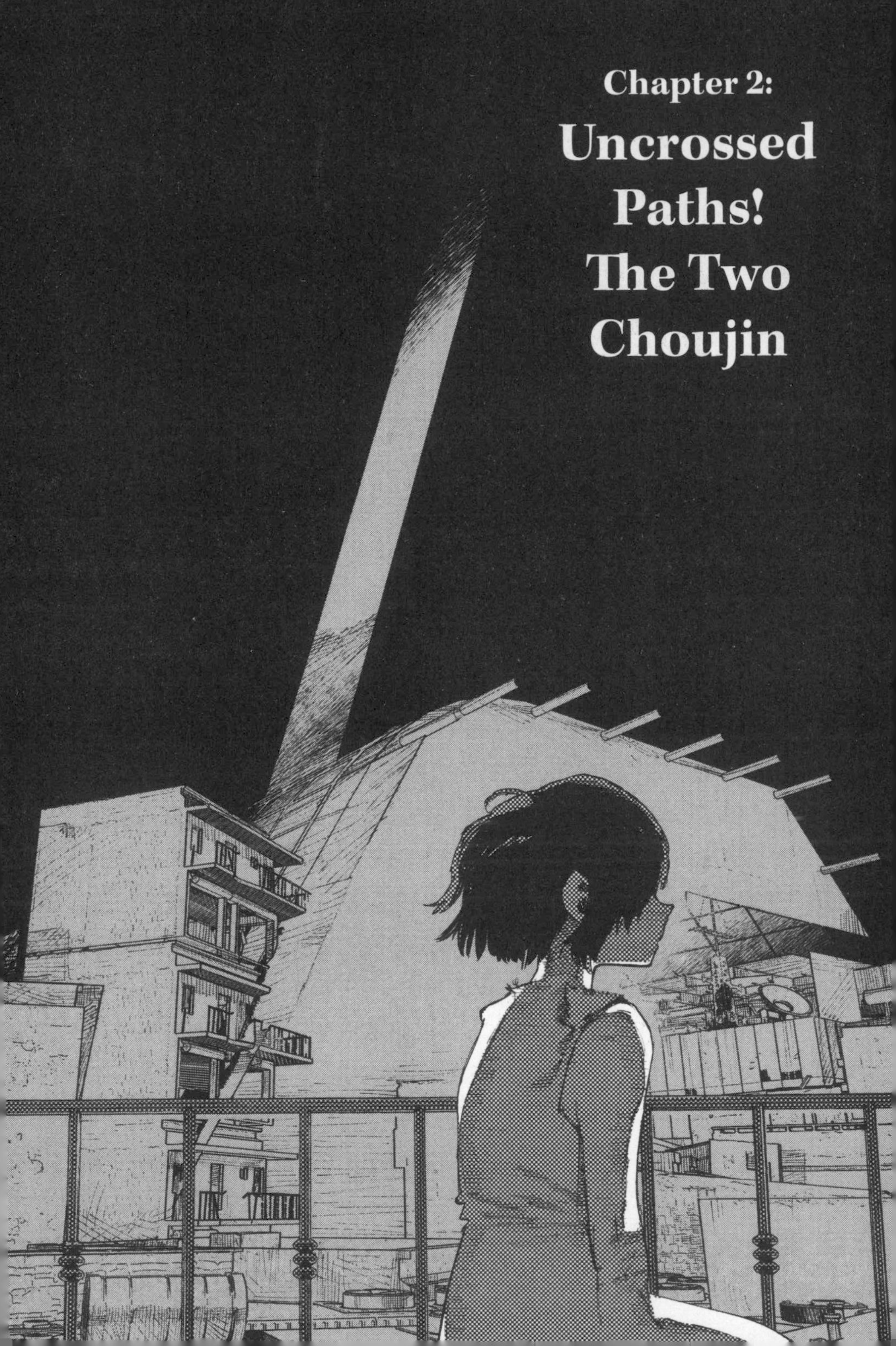

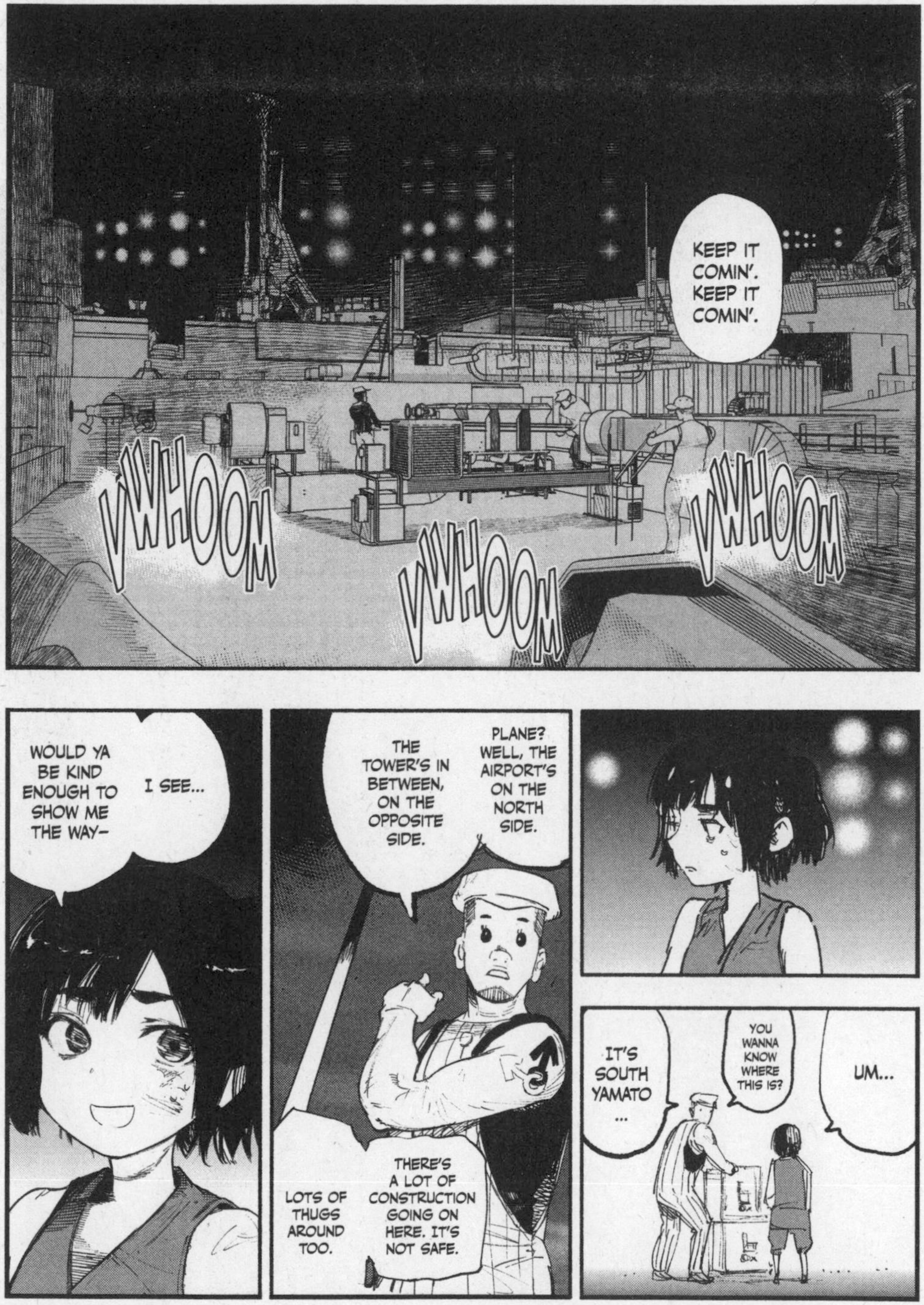
KEEP IT COMIN'. KEEP IT COMIN'.
VWHOOM
VWHOOM
VWHOOM
UM...
YOU WANNA KNOW WHERE THIS IS?
IT'S SOUTH YAMATO ...
PLANE? WELL, THE AIRPORT'S ON THE NORTH SIDE.
THE TOWER'S IN BETWEEN, ON THE OPPOSITE SIDE.
THERE'S A LOT OF CONSTRUCTION GOING ON HERE. IT'S NOT SAFE.
LOTS OF THUGS AROUND TOO.
I SEE...
WOULD YA BE KIND ENOUGH TO SHOW ME THE WAY–

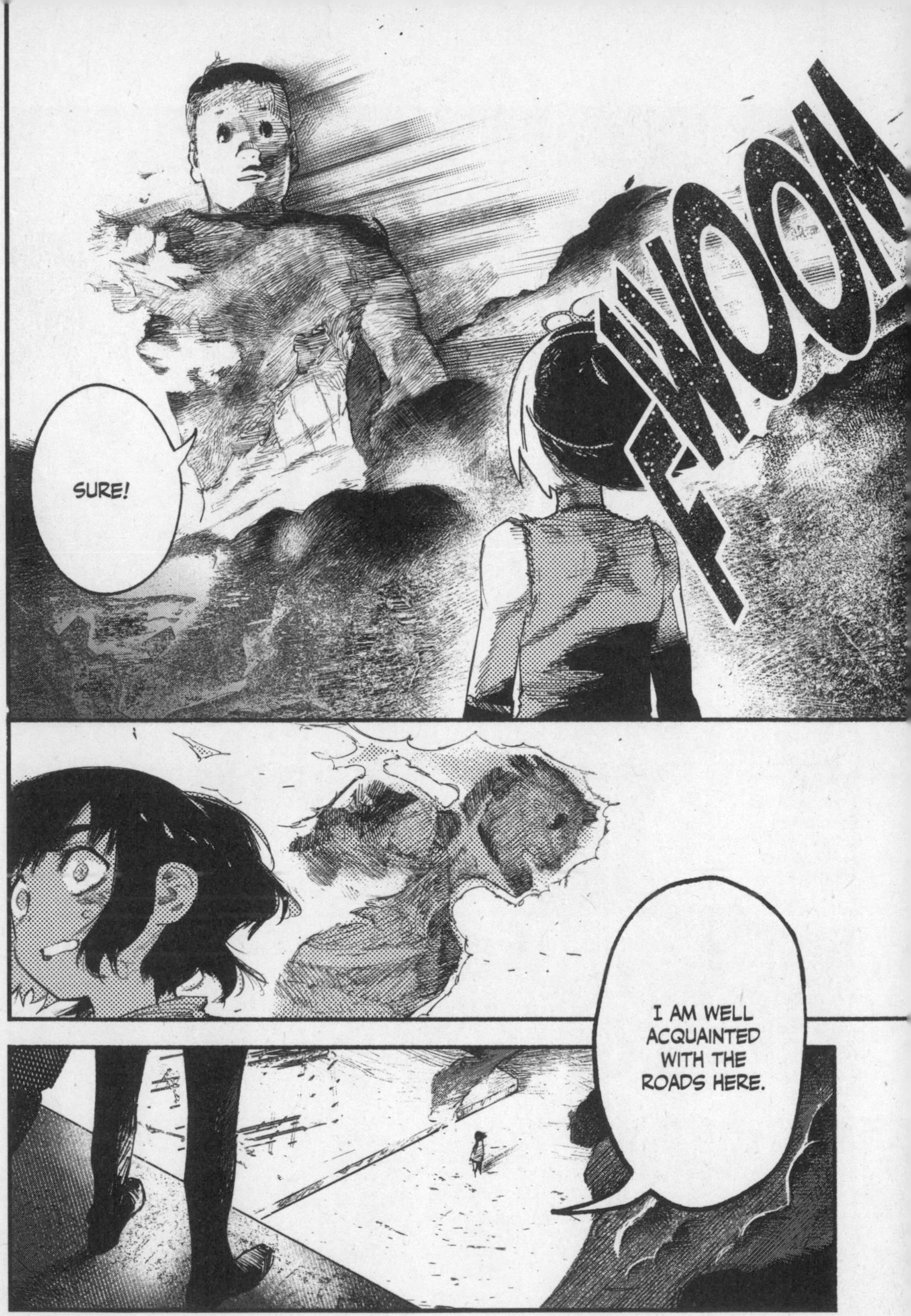
FWOOM
SURE!
I AM WELL ACQUAINTED WITH THE ROADS HERE.

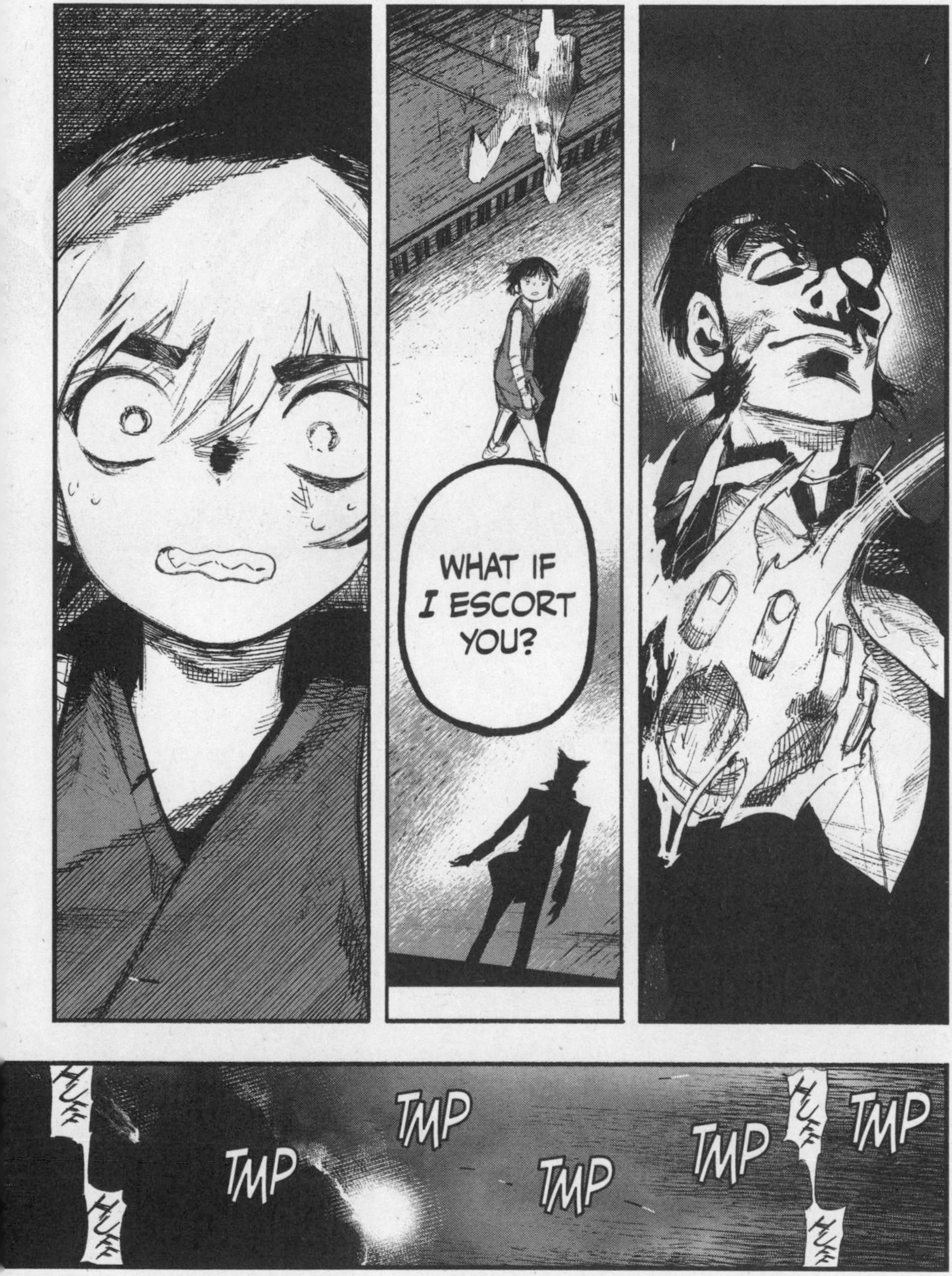
WHAT IF I ESCORT YOU?
TMP
HUFF
HUFF
TMP
TMP
TMP
TMP
HUFF
HUFF

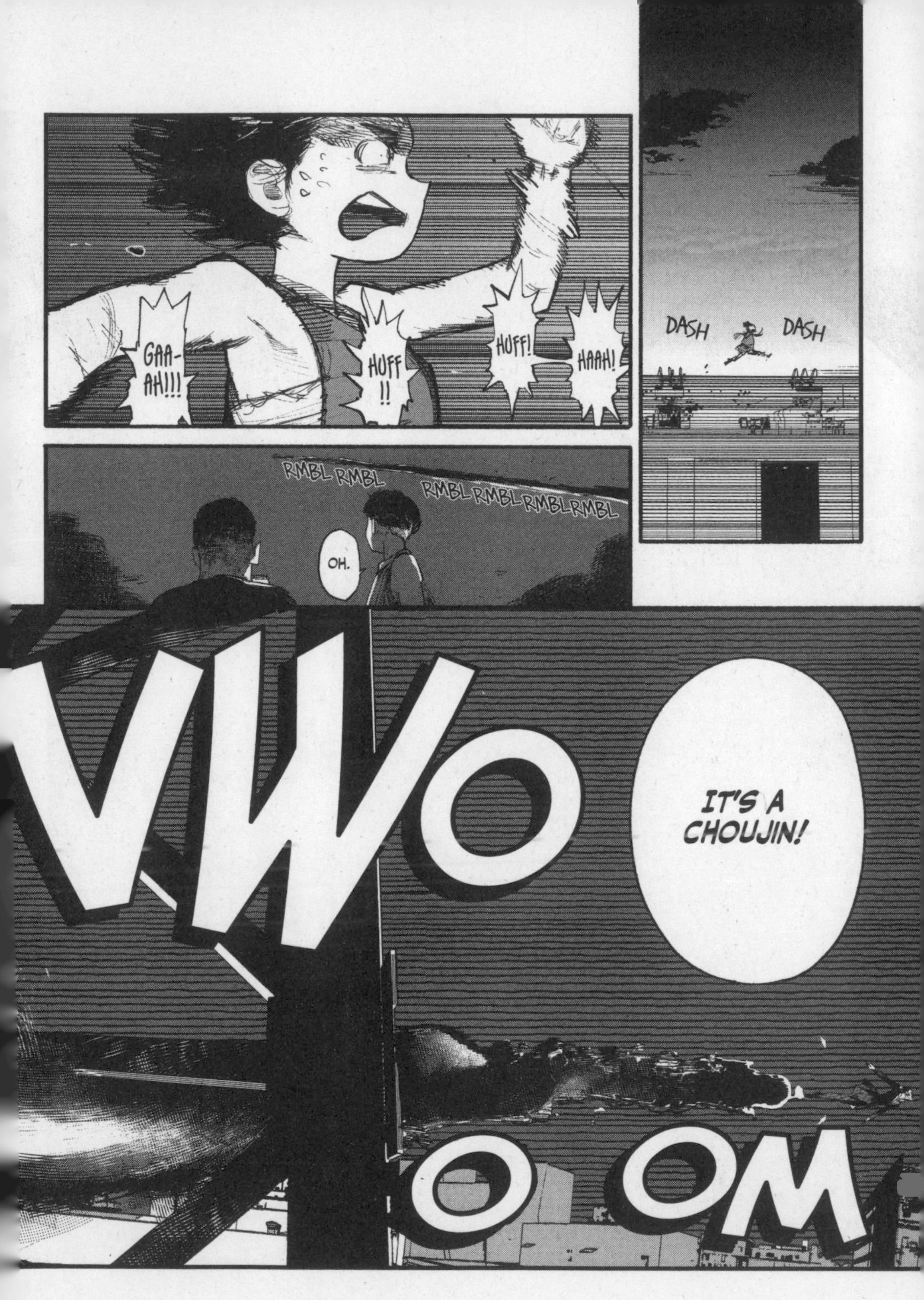
DASH
DASH
HAAH!
HUFF!
HUFF !!
GAA-AH!!!
RMBL RMBL
RMBL RMBL RMBL RMBL
OH.
IT'S A CHOUJIN!
VWOOOM

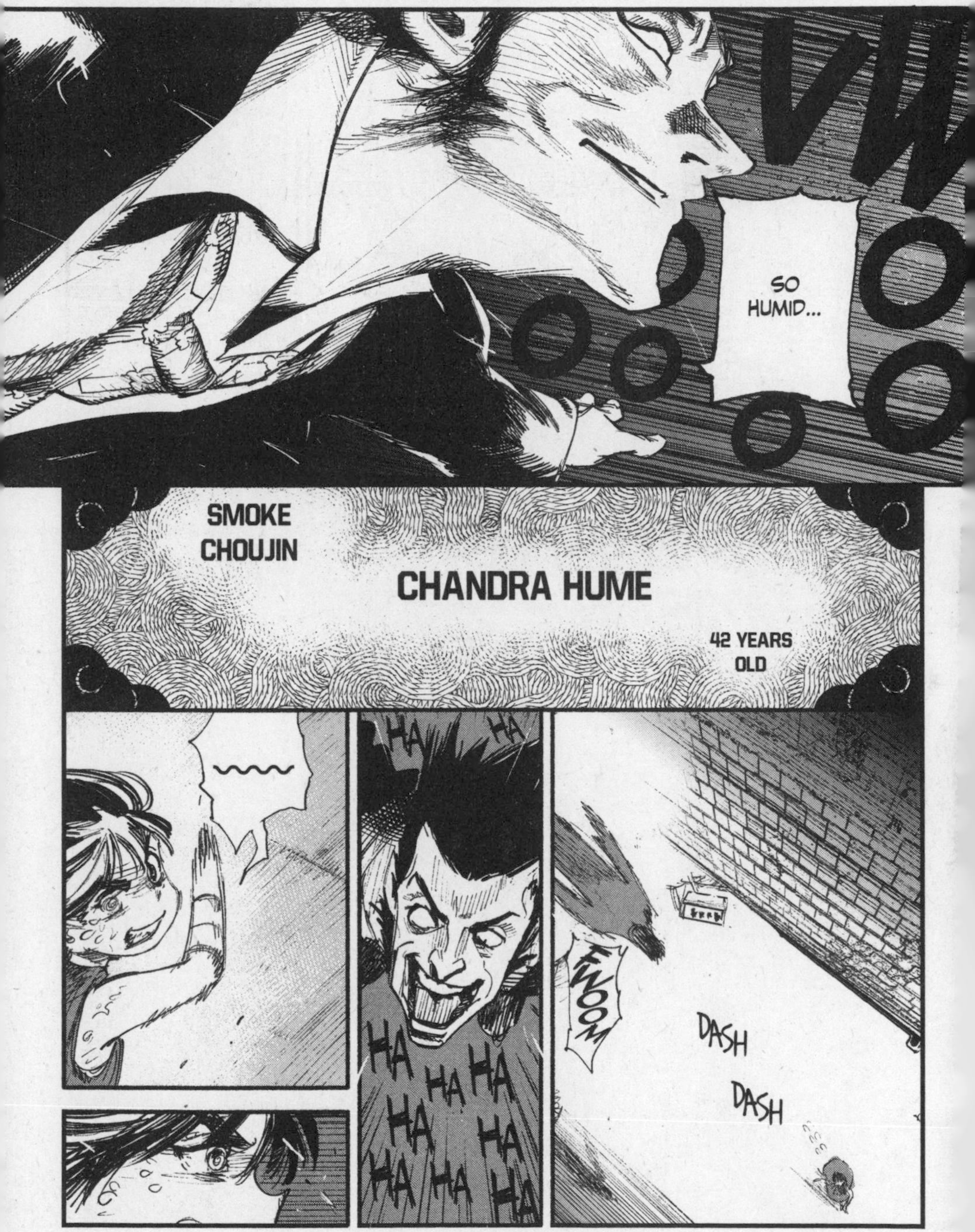
VWOOOOOO
SO HUMID...
SMOKE CHOUJIN
CHANDRA HUME
42 YEARS OLD
FWOOM
DASH
DASH
HA HA
HA HA HA HA HA HA HA HA HA HA HA

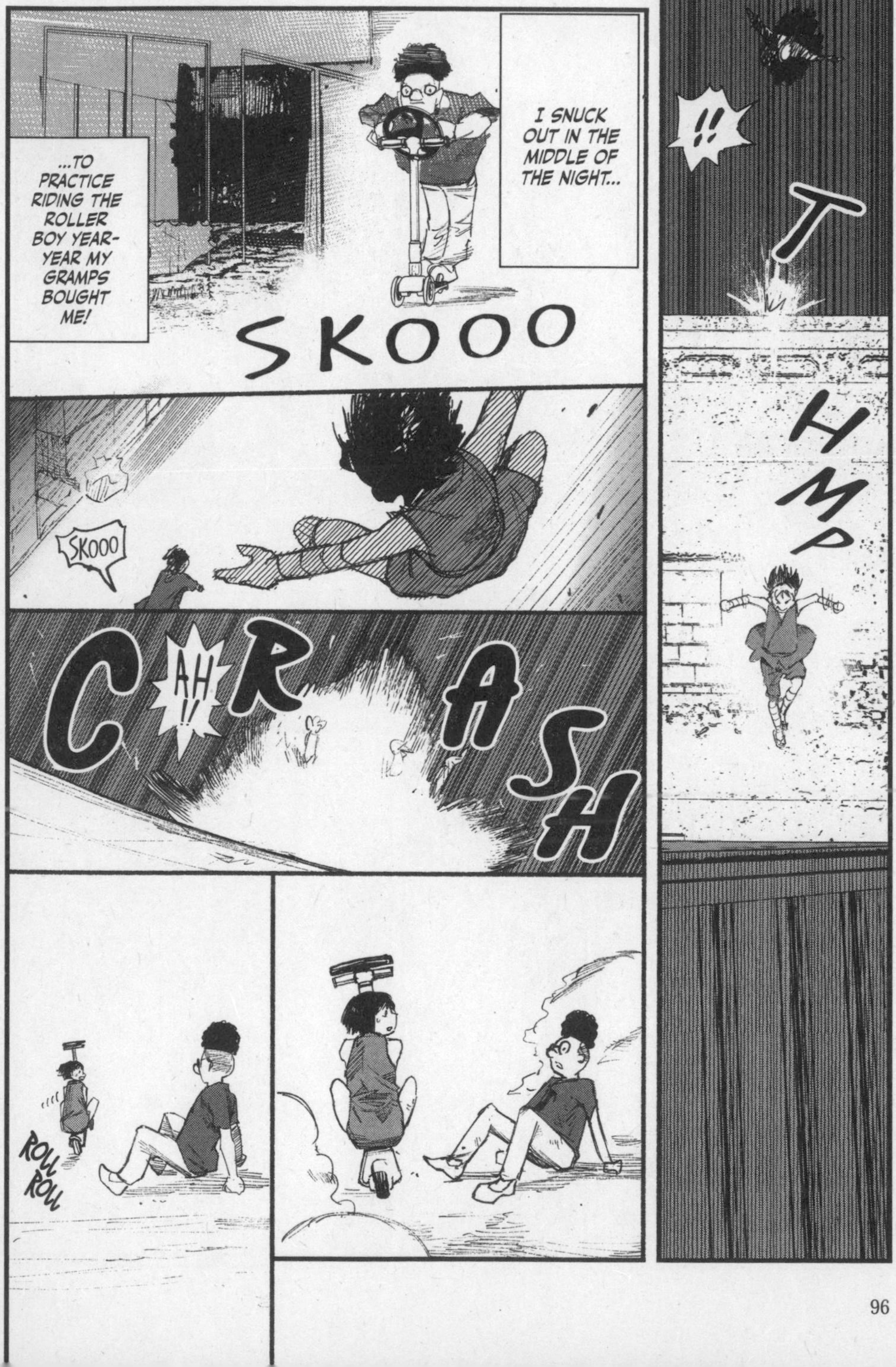
!!
THUMP
I SNUCK OUT IN THE MIDDLE OF THE NIGHT...
...TO PRACTICE RIDING THE ROLLER BOY YEAR-YEAR MY GRAMPS BOUGHT ME!
SKOOO
SKOOO
CRASH
AH!!
ROLL ROLL

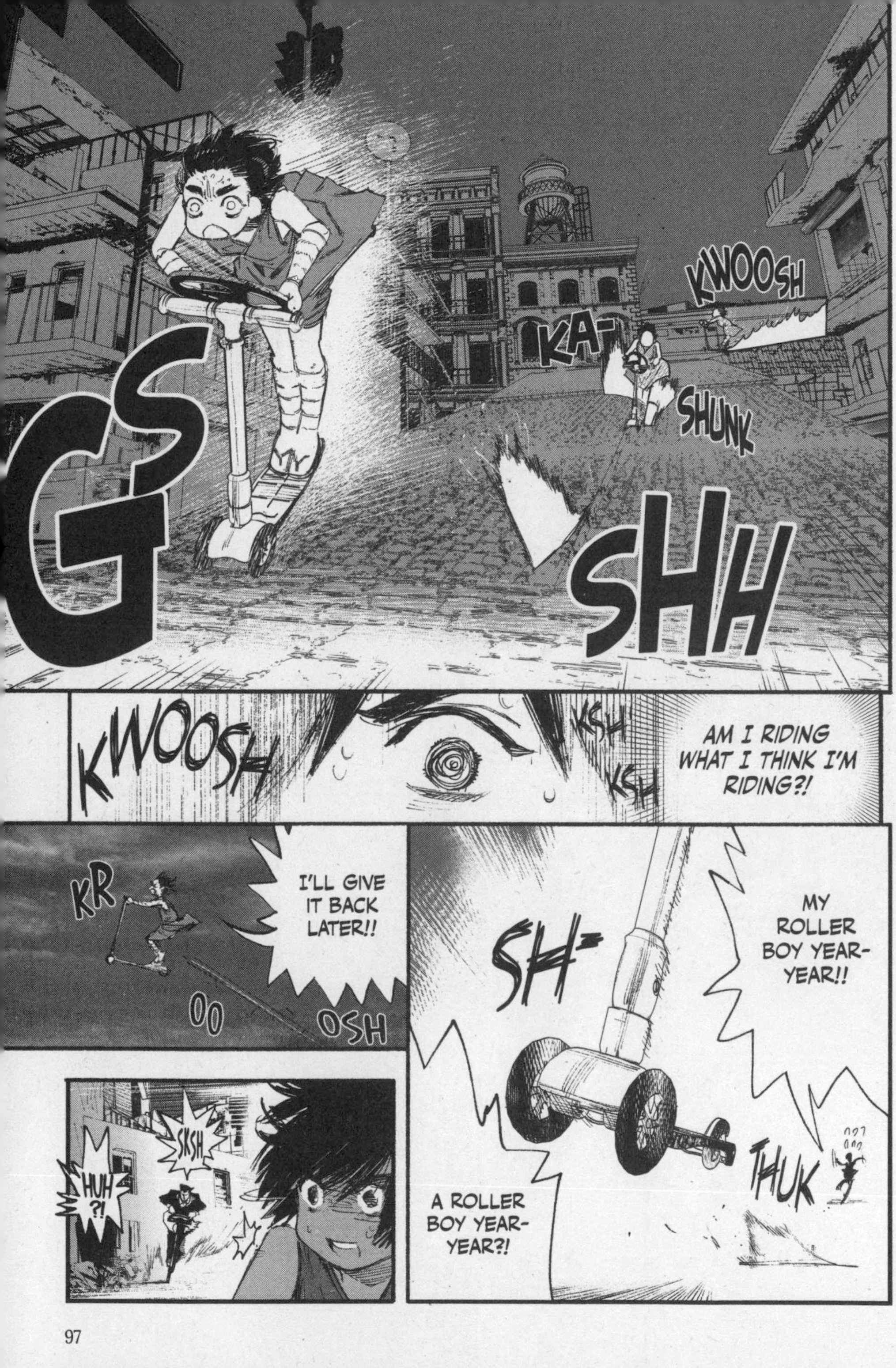
KWOOSH
KA-
SHUNK
GS
SHH
AM I RIDING WHAT I THINK I'M RIDING?!
KSH
KSH
KWOOSH
MY ROLLER BOY YEAR-YEAR!!
SH-
THUK
A ROLLER BOY YEAR-YEAR?!
I'LL GIVE IT BACK LATER!!
KR
OO
OSH
SKSH
HUH ?!

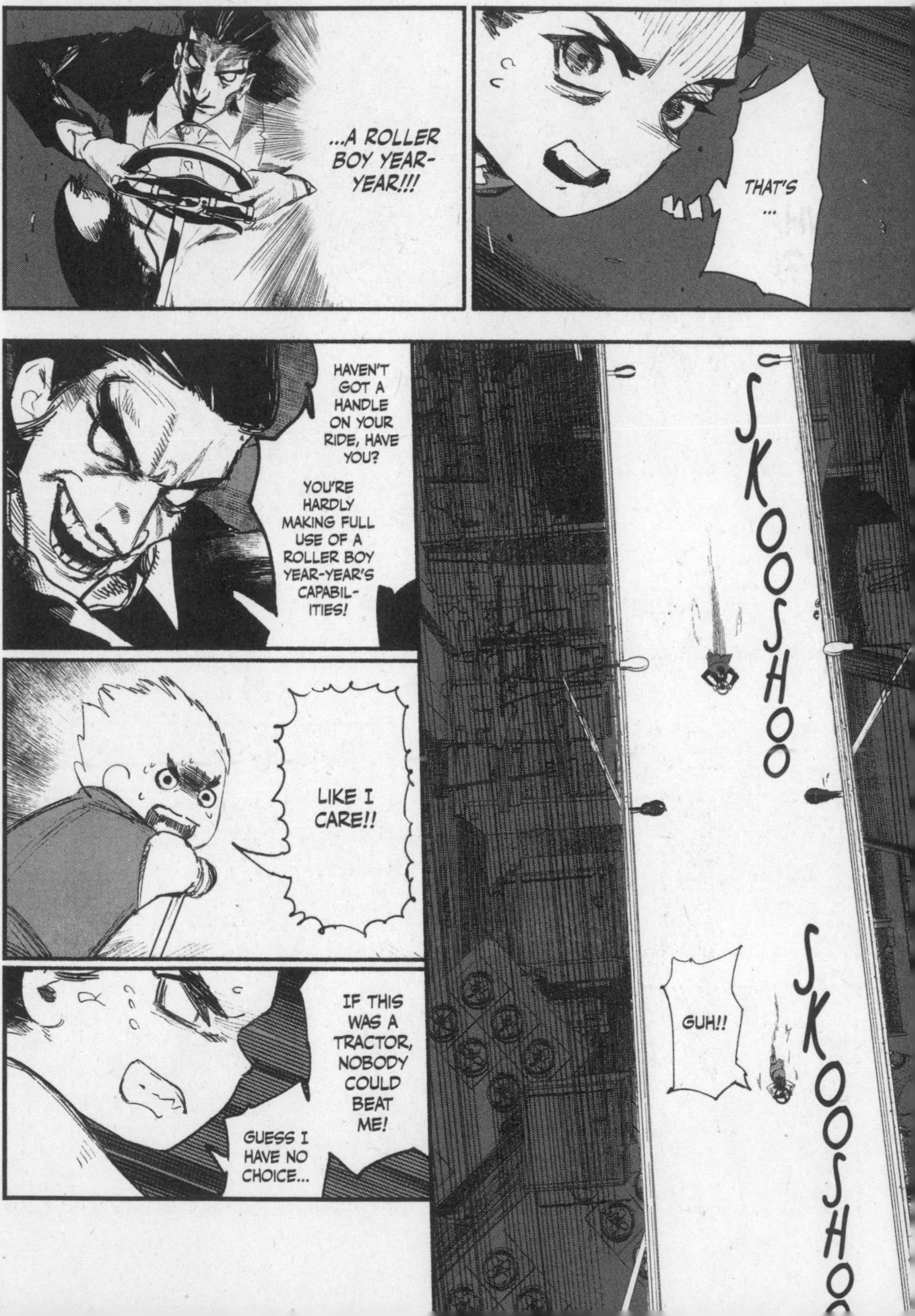
THAT'S ...
...A ROLLER BOY YEAR-YEAR!!!
SKOOSHOO
GUH!!
SKOOSHOO
HAVEN'T GOT A HANDLE ON YOUR RIDE, HAVE YOU?
YOU'RE HARDLY MAKING FULL USE OF A ROLLER BOY YEAR-YEAR'S CAPABIL-ITIES!
LIKE I CARE!!
IF THIS WAS A TRACTOR, NOBODY COULD BEAT ME!
GUESS I HAVE NO CHOICE...

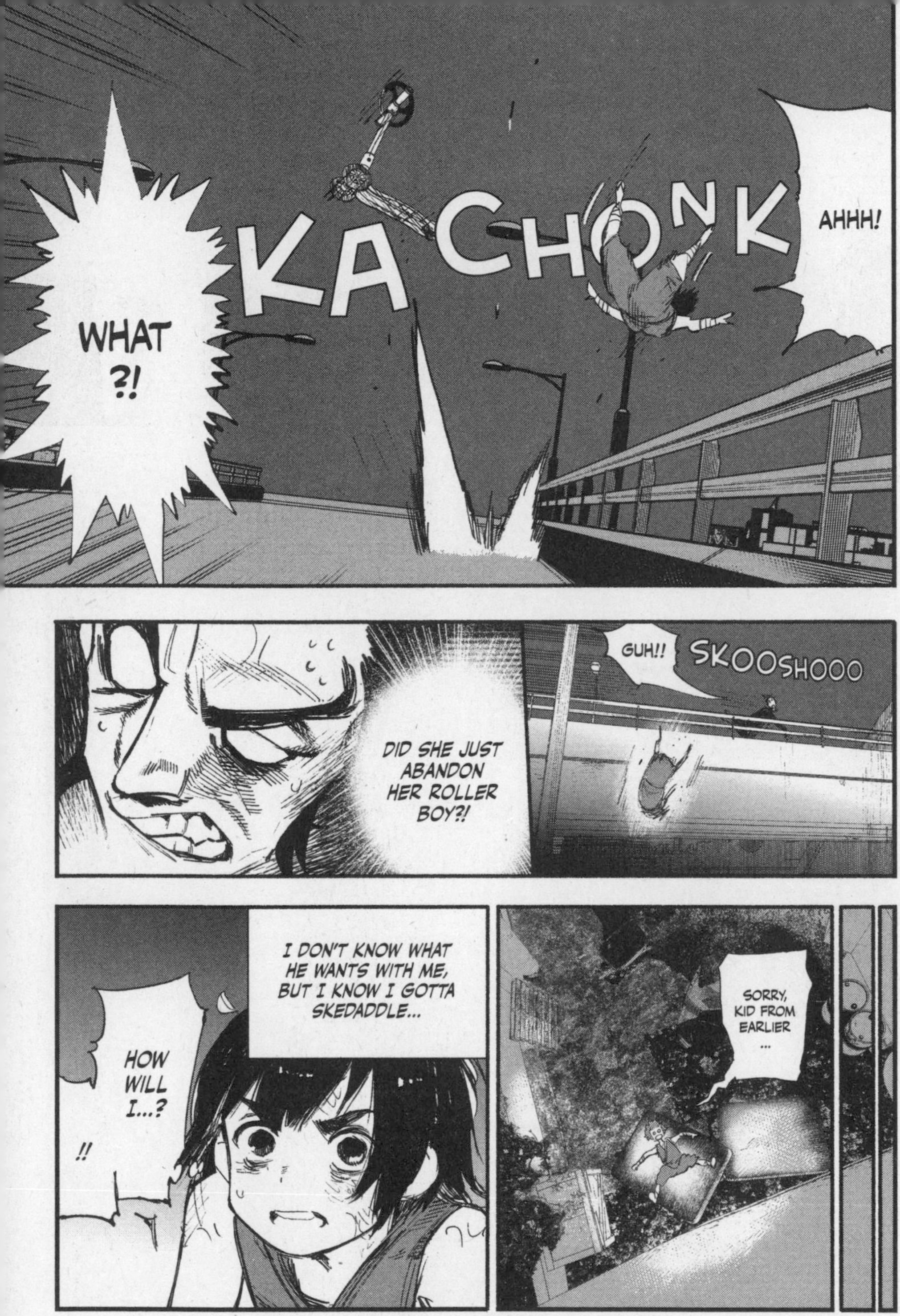
AHHH!
KACHONK
WHAT?!
SKOOSHOOO
GUH!!
DID SHE JUST ABANDON HER ROLLER BOY?!
SORRY, KID FROM EARLIER ...
I DON'T KNOW WHAT HE WANTS WITH ME, BUT I KNOW I GOTTA SKEDADDLE...
HOW WILL I...?
!!

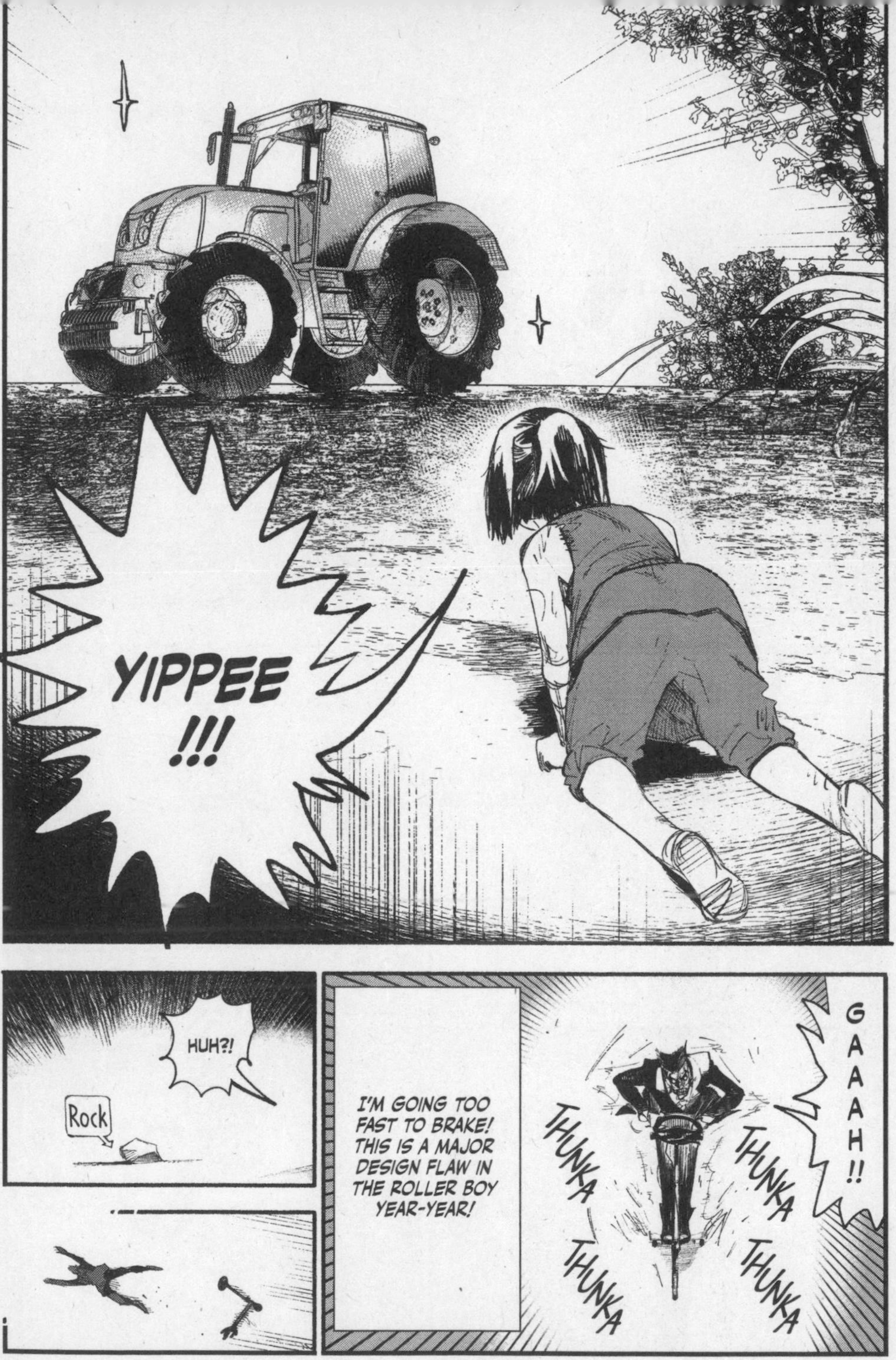
YIPPEE !!!
GAAAH!!
THUNKA THUNKA
I'M GOING TOO FAST TO BRAKE! THIS IS A MAJOR DESIGN FLAW IN THE ROLLER BOY YEAR-YEAR!
THUNKA THUNKA
HUH?!
Rock

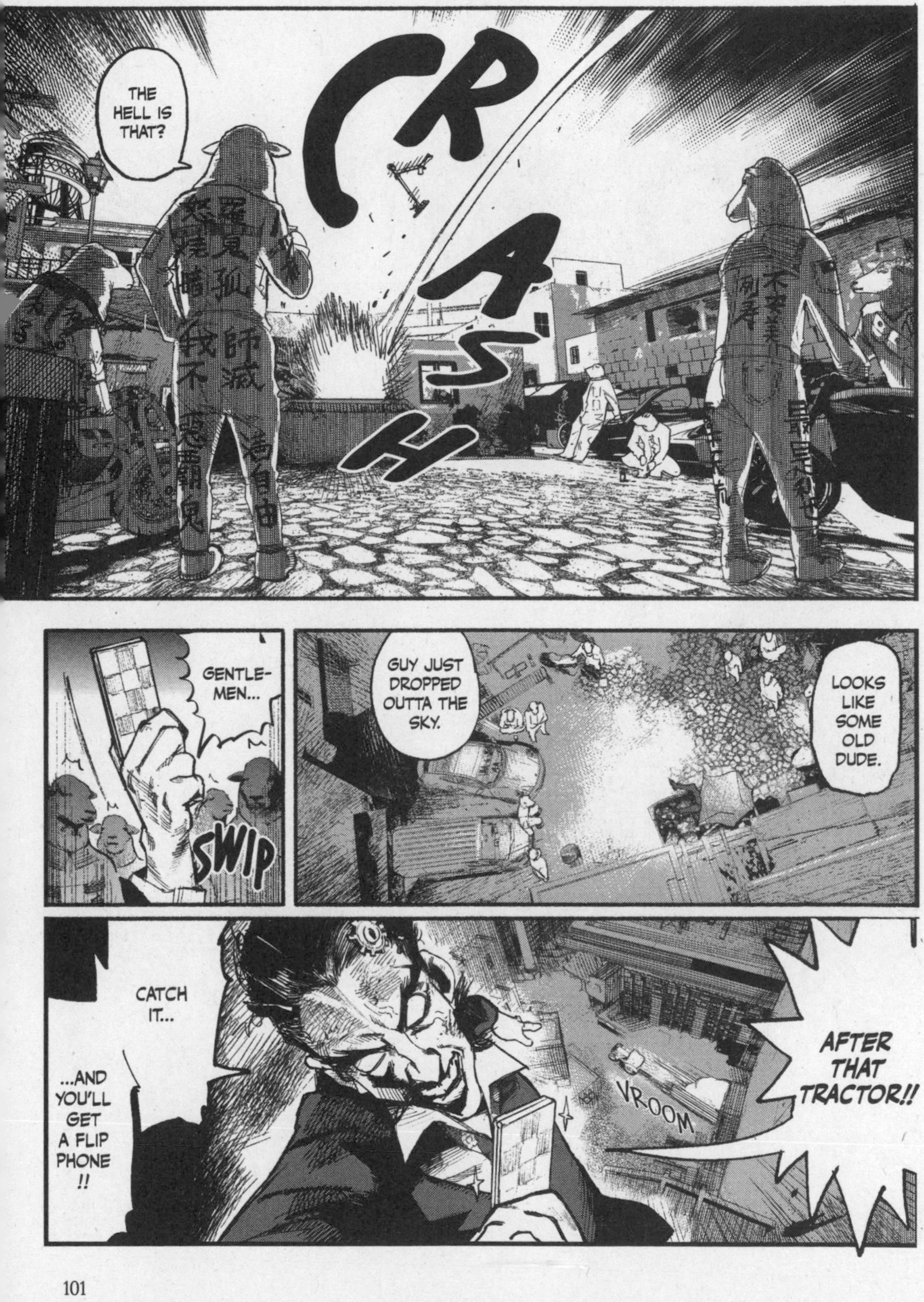
CRASH
THE HELL IS THAT?
LOOKS LIKE SOME OLD DUDE.
GUY JUST DROPPED OUTTA THE SKY.
GENTLE-MEN...
SWIP
AFTER THAT TRACTOR!!
VROOM
CATCH IT...
...AND YOU'LL GET A FLIP PHONE !!

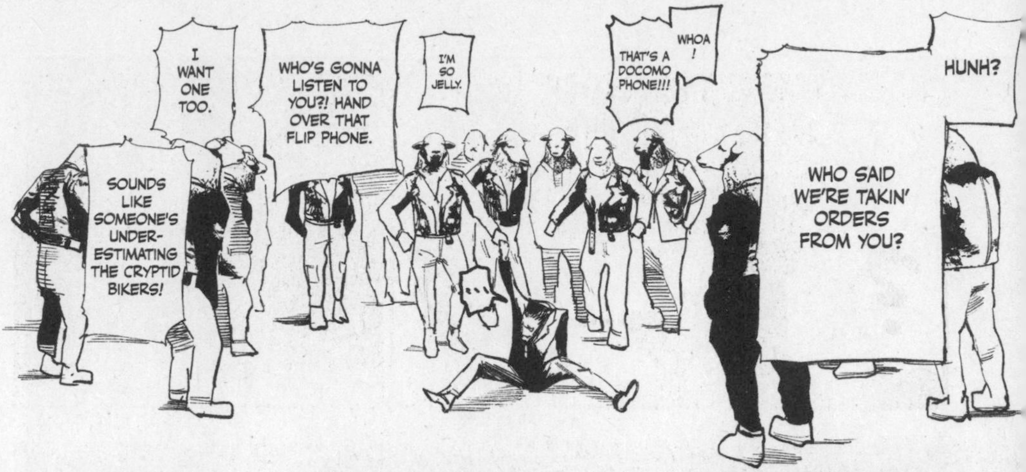
HUNH?
WHO SAID WE'RE TAKIN' ORDERS FROM YOU?
WHOA!
THAT'S A DOCOMO PHONE!!!
I'M SO JELLY.
...
WHO'S GONNA LISTEN TO YOU?! HAND OVER THAT FLIP PHONE.
I WANT ONE TOO.
SOUNDS LIKE SOMEONE'S UNDER-ESTIMATING THE CRYPTID BIKERS!
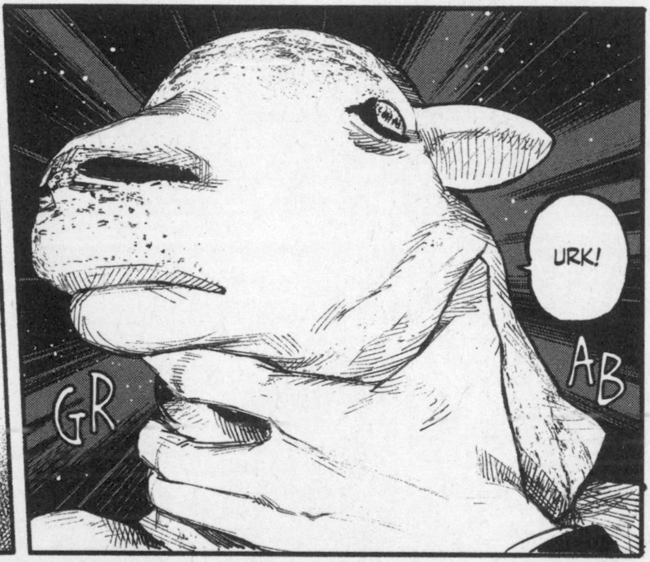
URK!
GR
AB
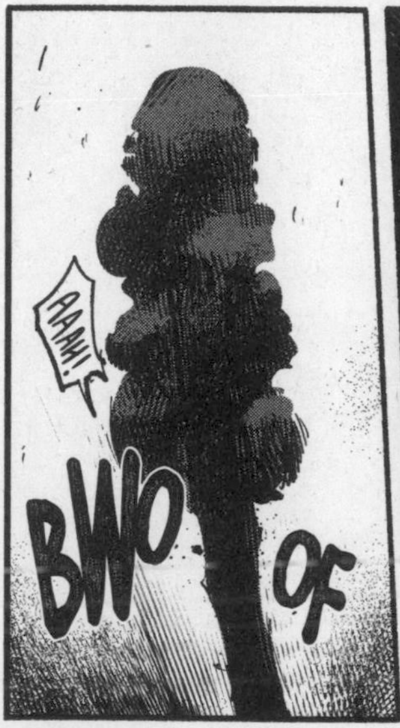
AAAH!
BWOOF
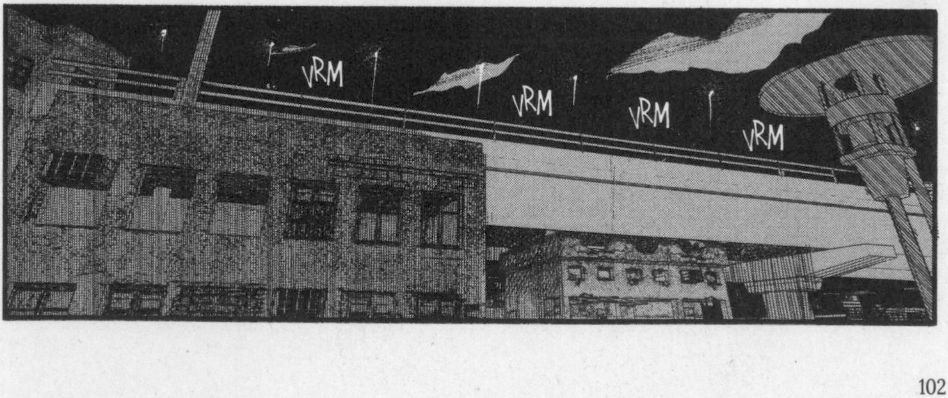
VRM
VRM
VRM
VRM

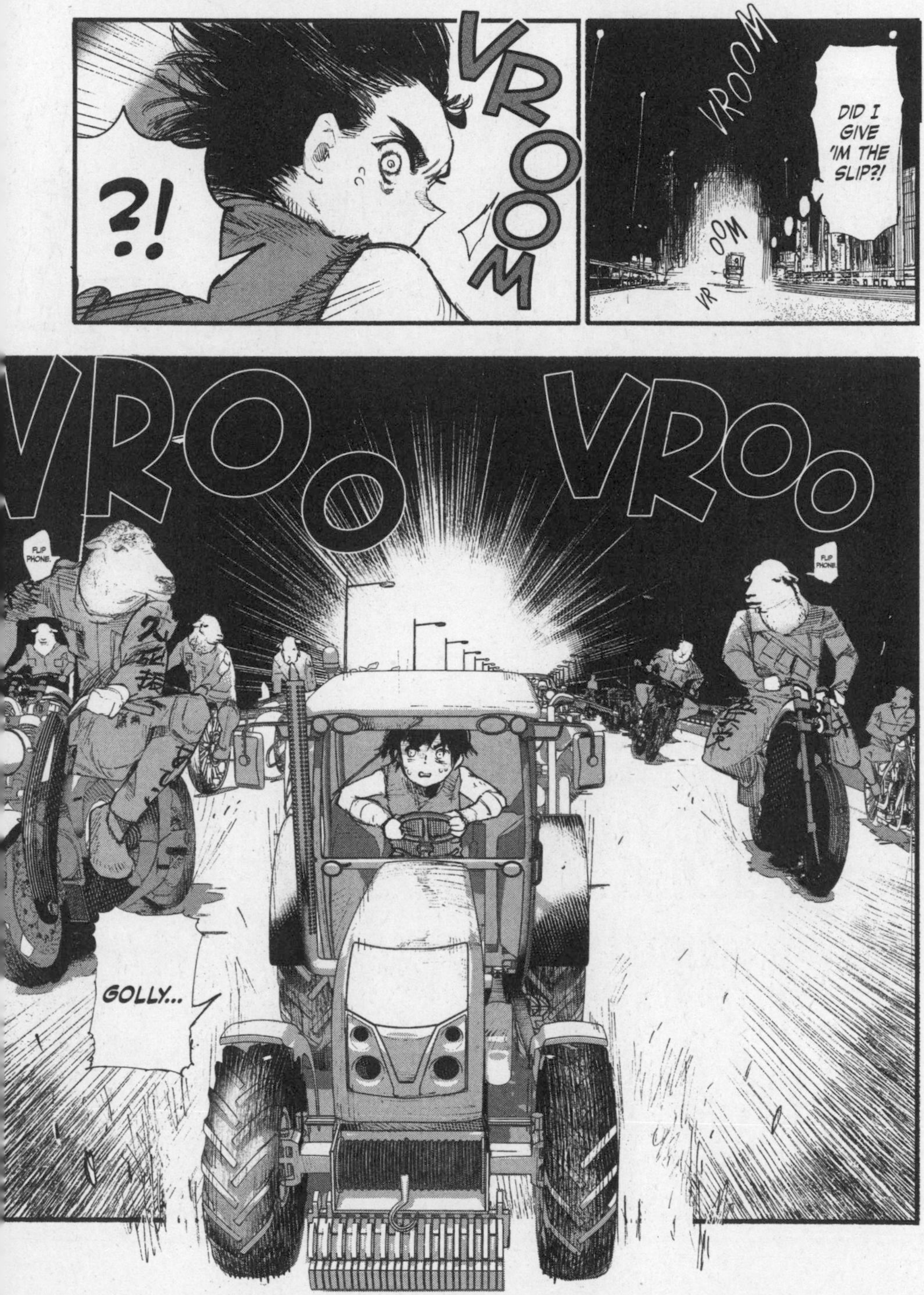
VROOM
DID I GIVE 'IM THE SLIP?!
VR
OOM
VROOM
?!
VROO
FLIP PHONE.
VROO
FLIP PHONE.
GOLLY...

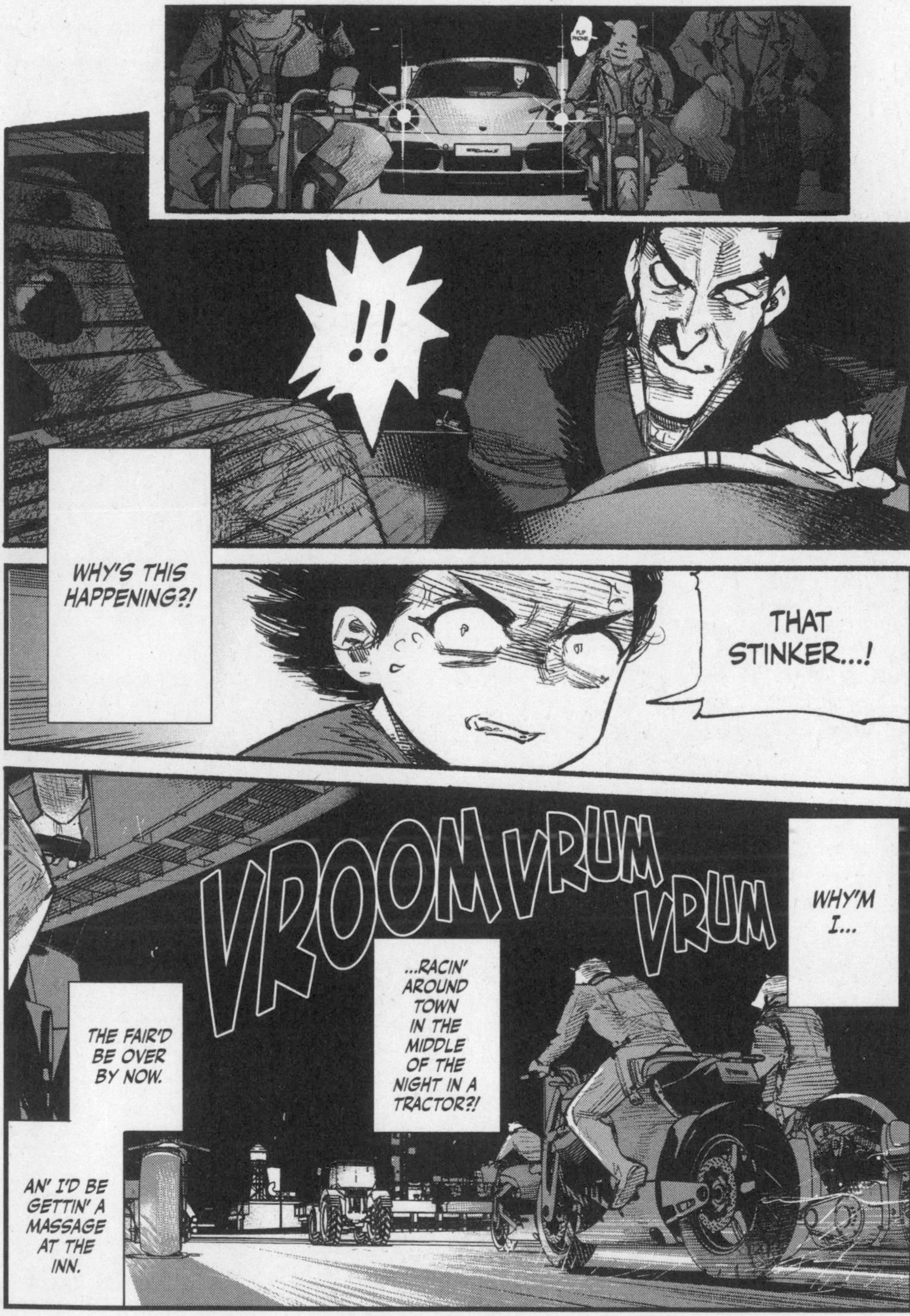
FLIP PHONE
!!
THAT STINKER...!
WHY'S THIS HAPPENING?!
WHY'M I...
VROOM
VRUM
VRUM
...RACIN' AROUND TOWN IN THE MIDDLE OF THE NIGHT IN A TRACTOR?!
THE FAIR'D BE OVER BY NOW.
AN' I'D BE GETTIN' A MASSAGE AT THE INN.

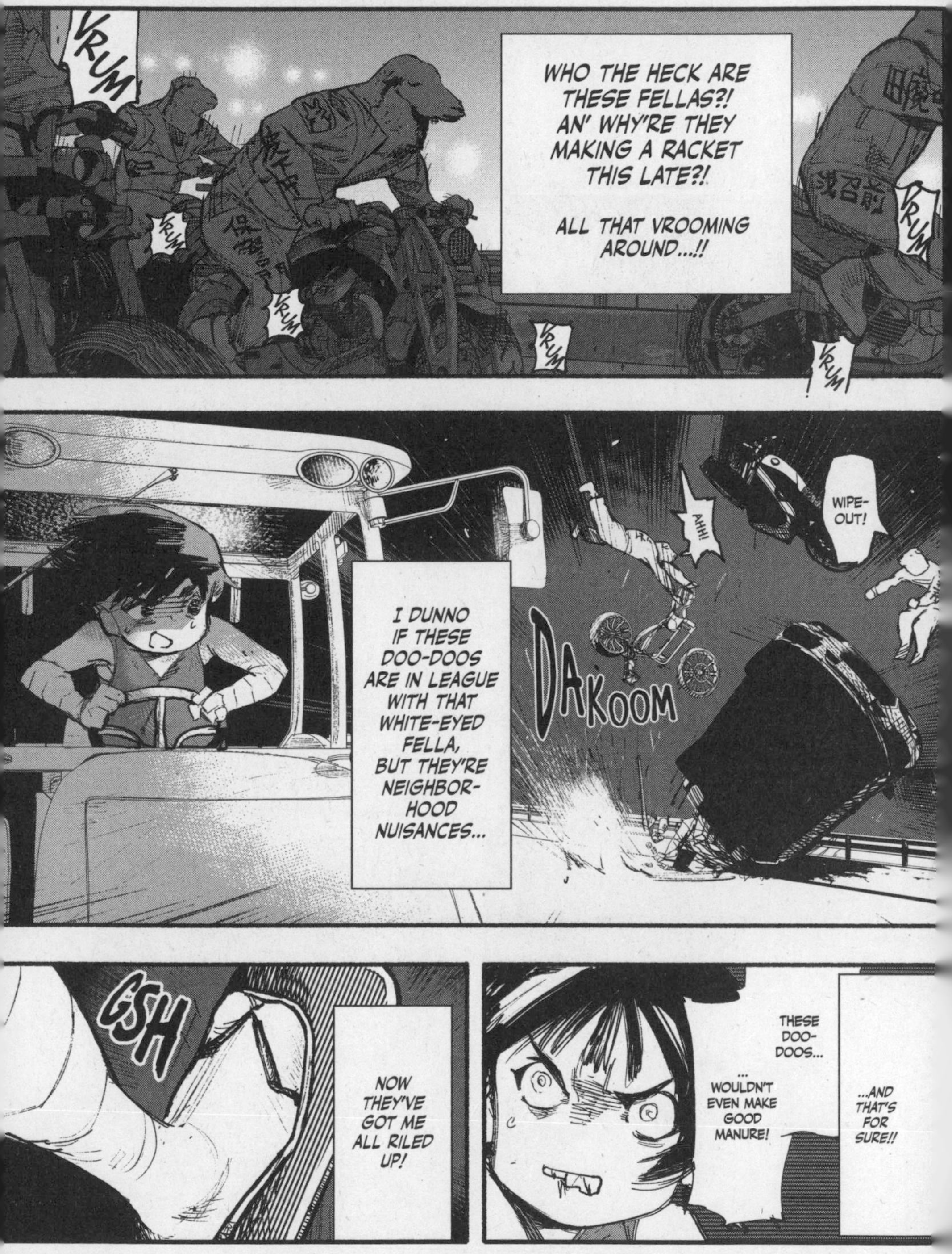
VRUM
WHO THE HECK ARE THESE FELLAS?! AN' WHY'RE THEY MAKING A RACKET THIS LATE?!
ALL THAT VROOMING AROUND...!!
VRUM
VRUM
VRUM
VRUM
VRUM
VRUM
WIPE-OUT!
AHH!!
I DUNNO IF THESE DOO-DOOS ARE IN LEAGUE WITH THAT WHITE-EYED FELLA, BUT THEY'RE NEIGHBOR-HOOD NUISANCES...
DAKOOM
THESE DOO-DOOS...
...WOULDN'T EVEN MAKE GOOD MANURE!
...AND THAT'S FOR SURE!!
NOW THEY'VE GOT ME ALL RILED UP!
CSH

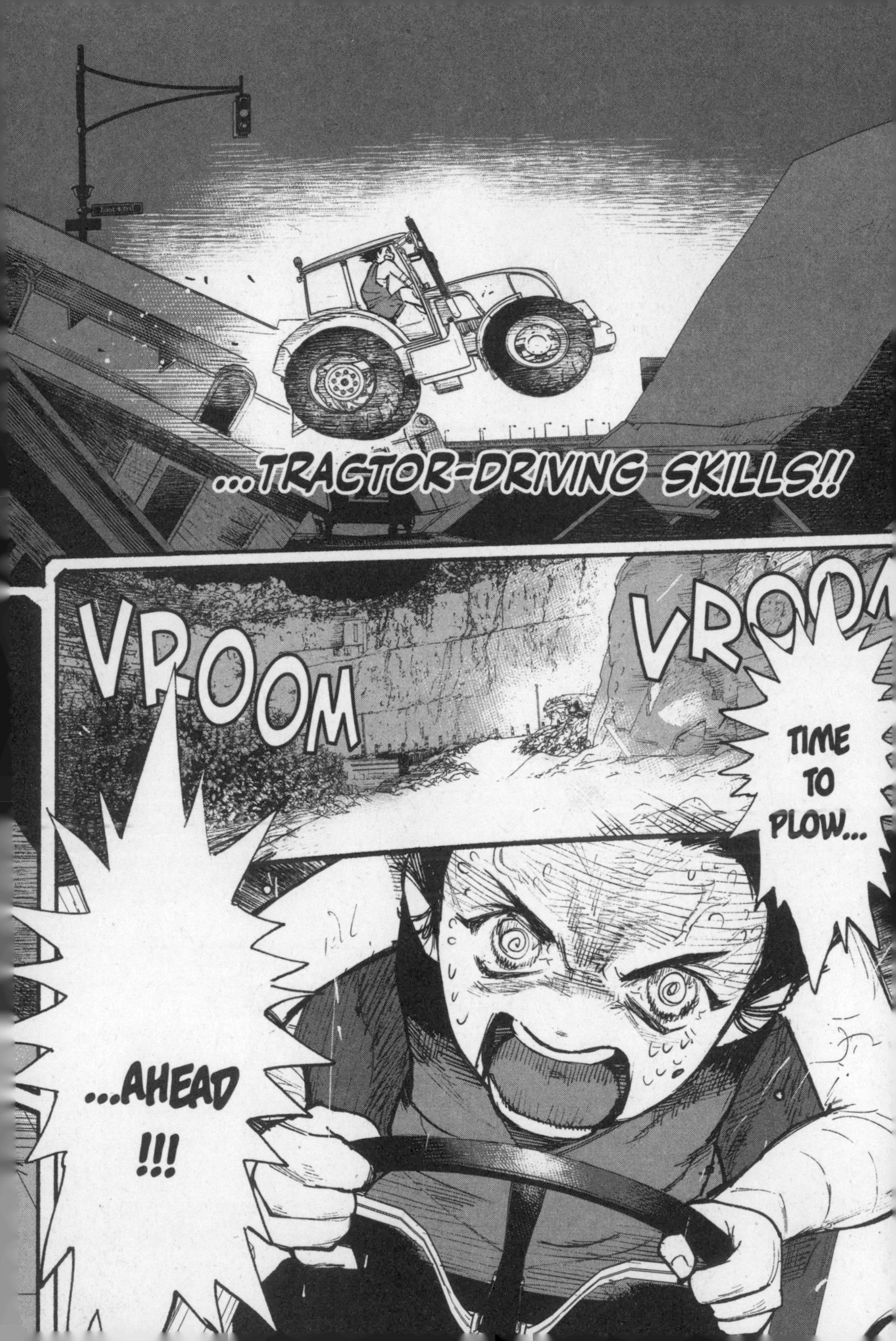
...TRACTOR-DRIVING SKILLS!!
VROO
VROOM
TIME TO PLOW...
...AHEAD !!!

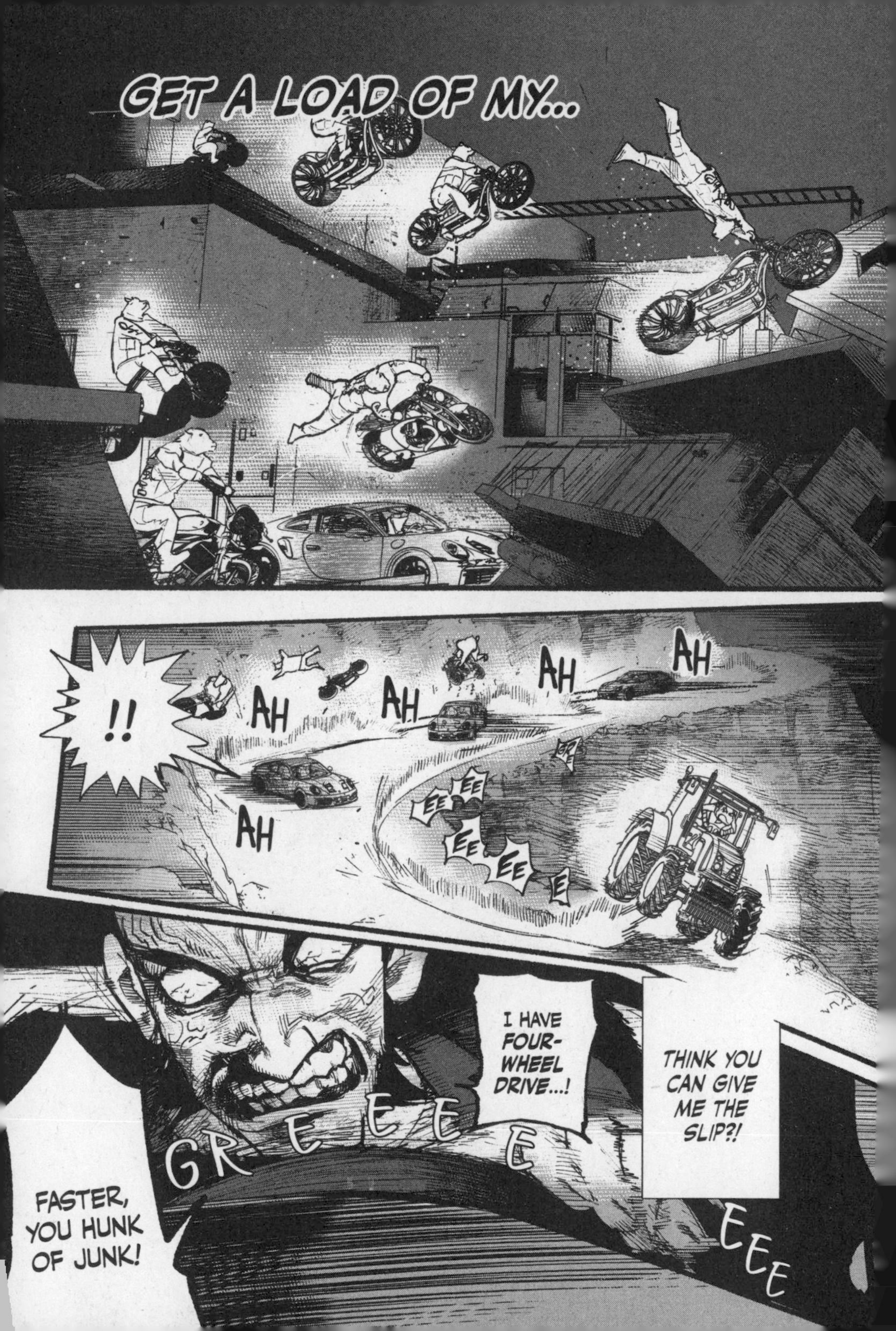
GET A LOAD OF MY...
AH
AH
AH
AH
!!
AH
EE EE EE EE EE E
THINK YOU CAN GIVE ME THE SLIP?!
I HAVE FOUR-WHEEL DRIVE...!
GREEEEE
EEE
FASTER, YOU HUNK OF JUNK!

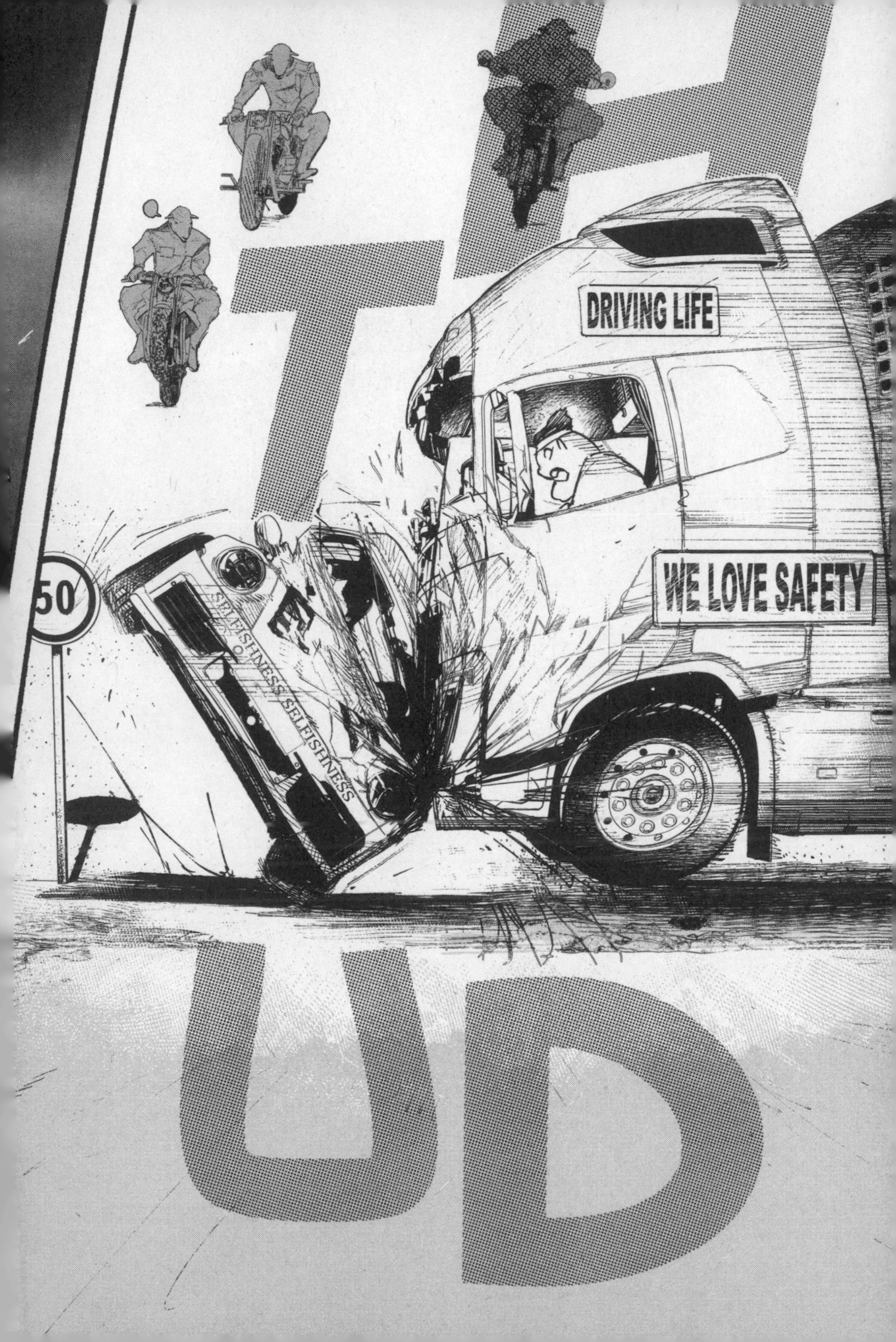

THUD
DRIVING LIFE
WE LOVE SAFETY
50
SELFISHNESS SELFISHNESS SELFISHNESS

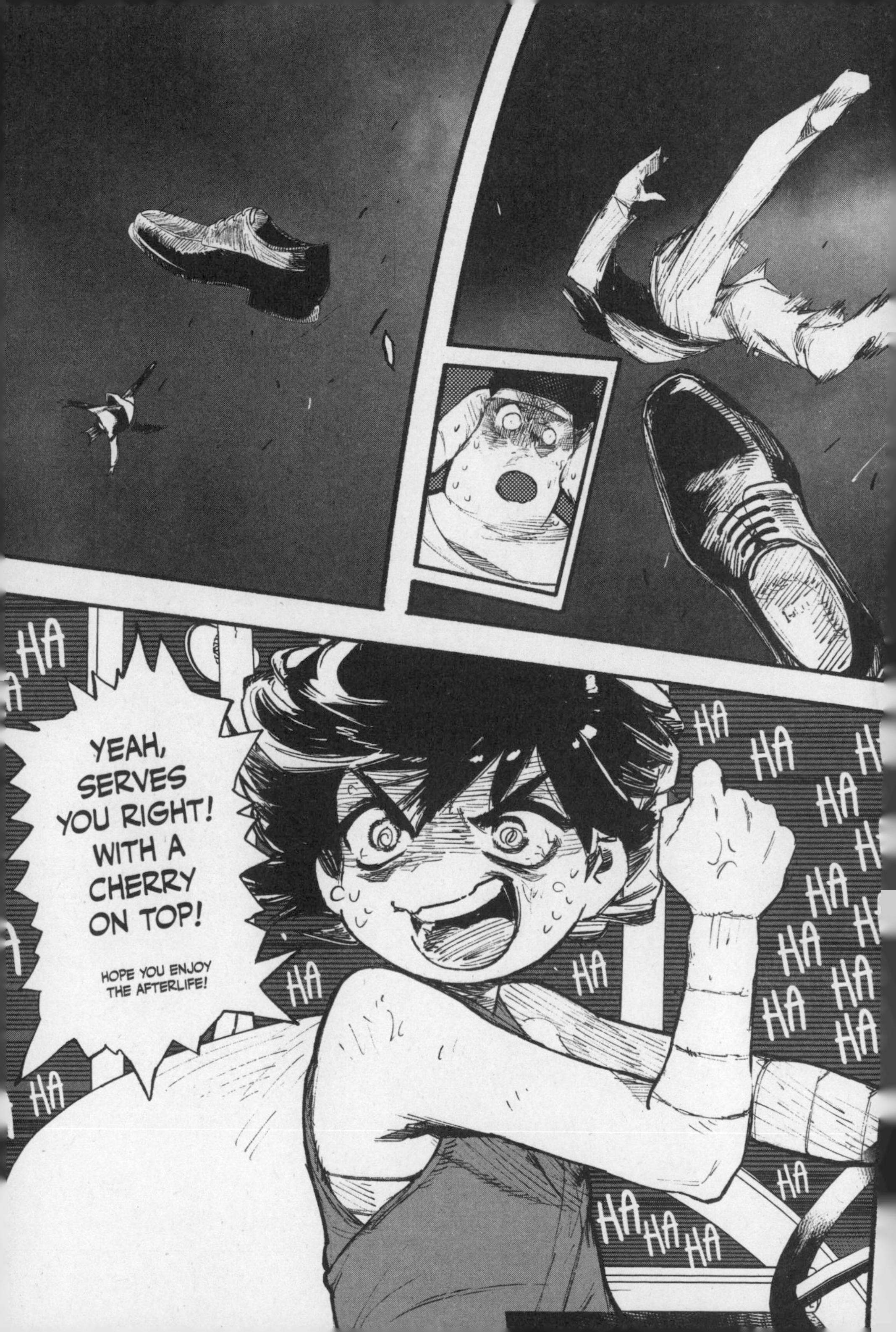
YEAH, SERVES YOU RIGHT! WITH A CHERRY ON TOP!
HOPE YOU ENJOY THE AFTERLIFE!
HA HA HA HA HA HA HA HA HA HA
HA HA HA
HA
HA
HA
HA HA HA

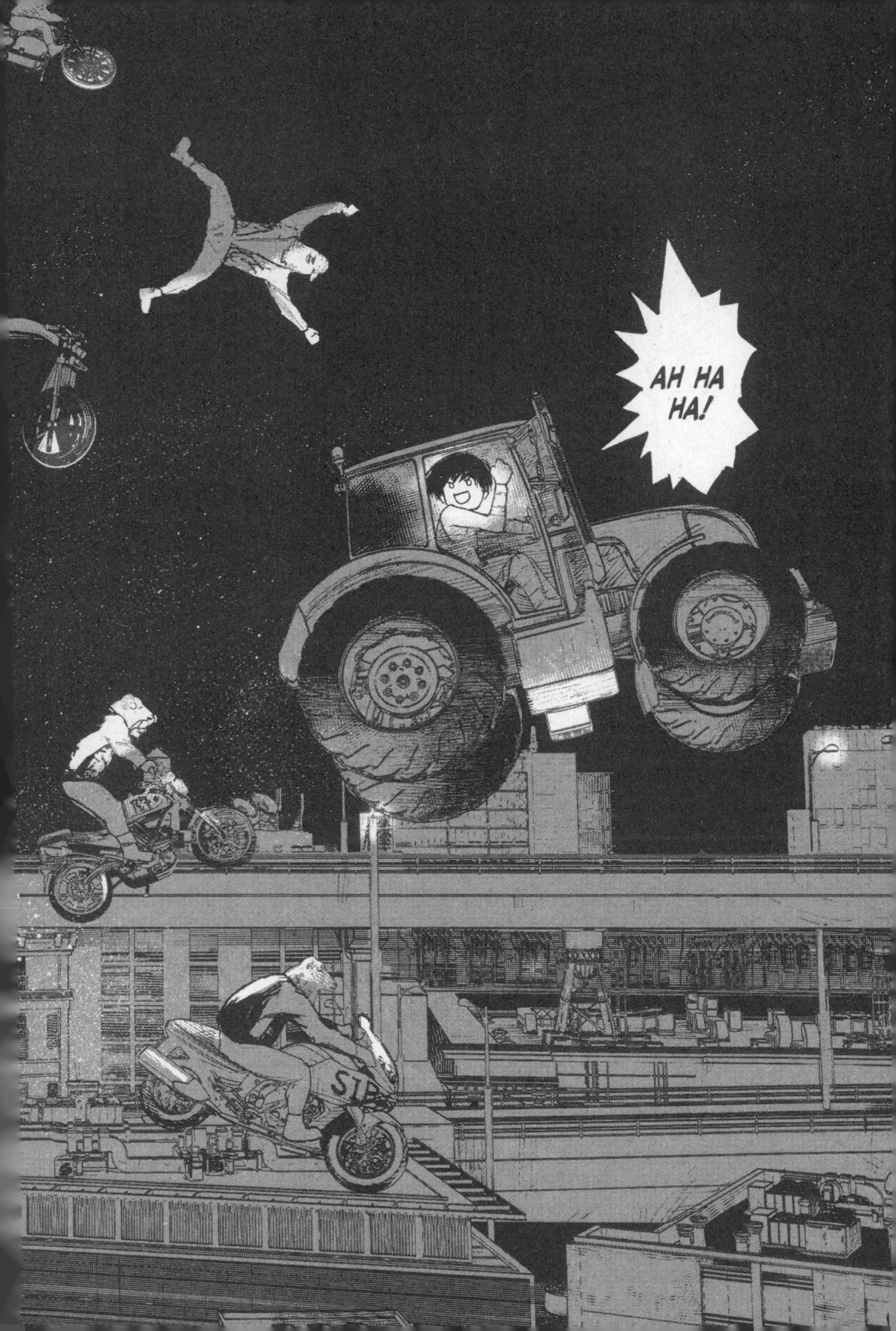
AH HA HA!

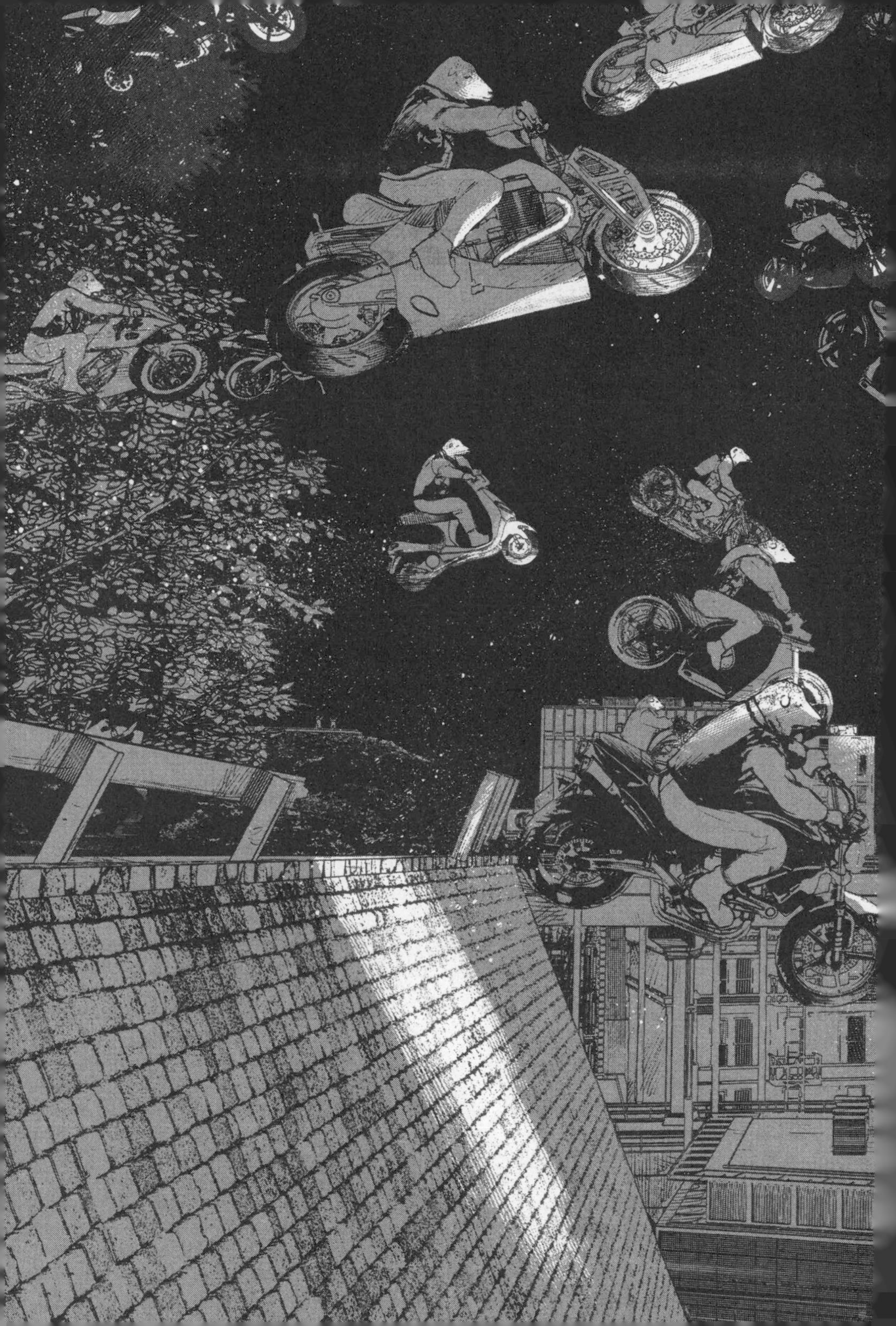

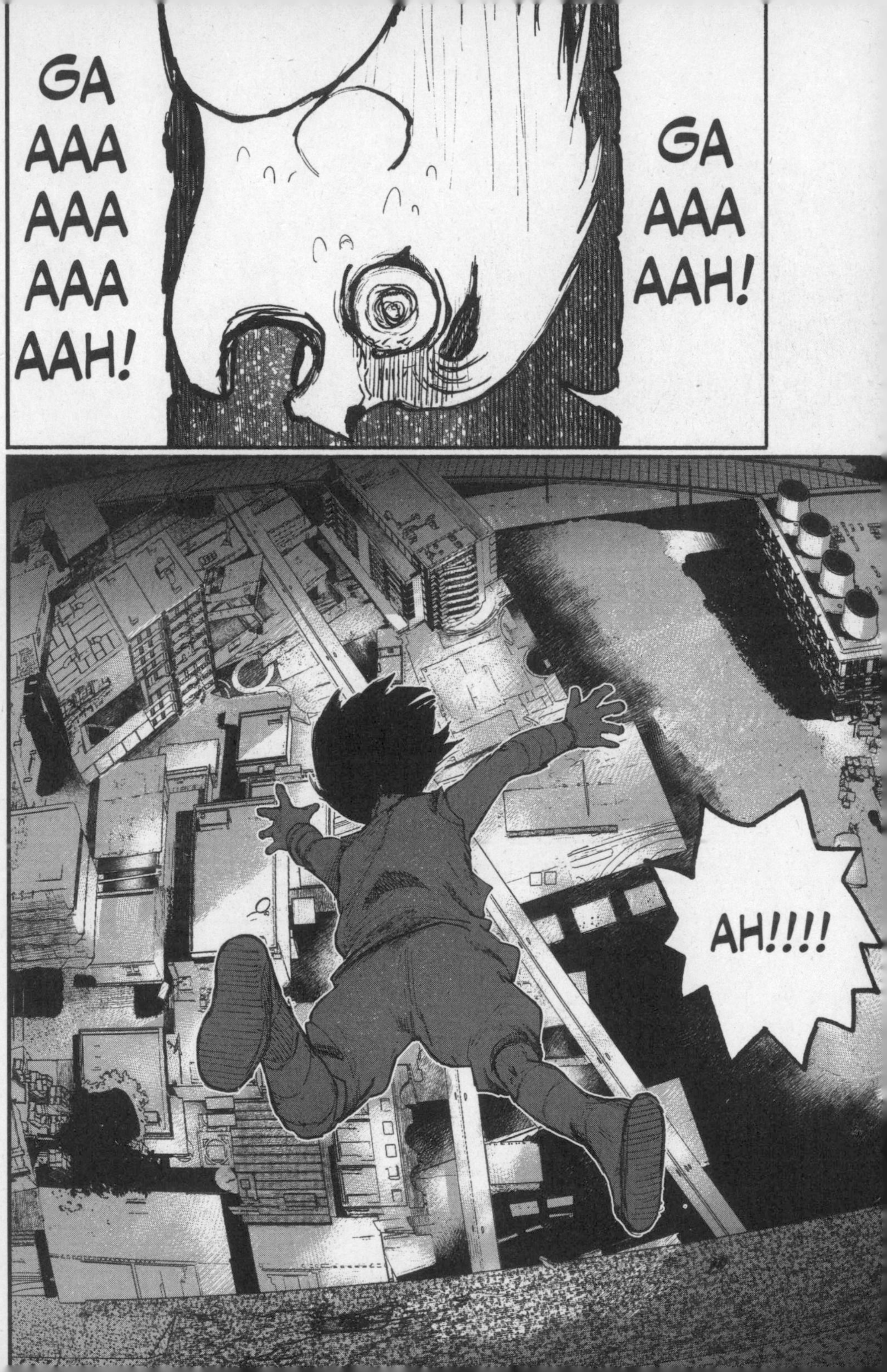
GA AAA AAAH!
GA AAA AAA AAA AAH!
AH!!!!

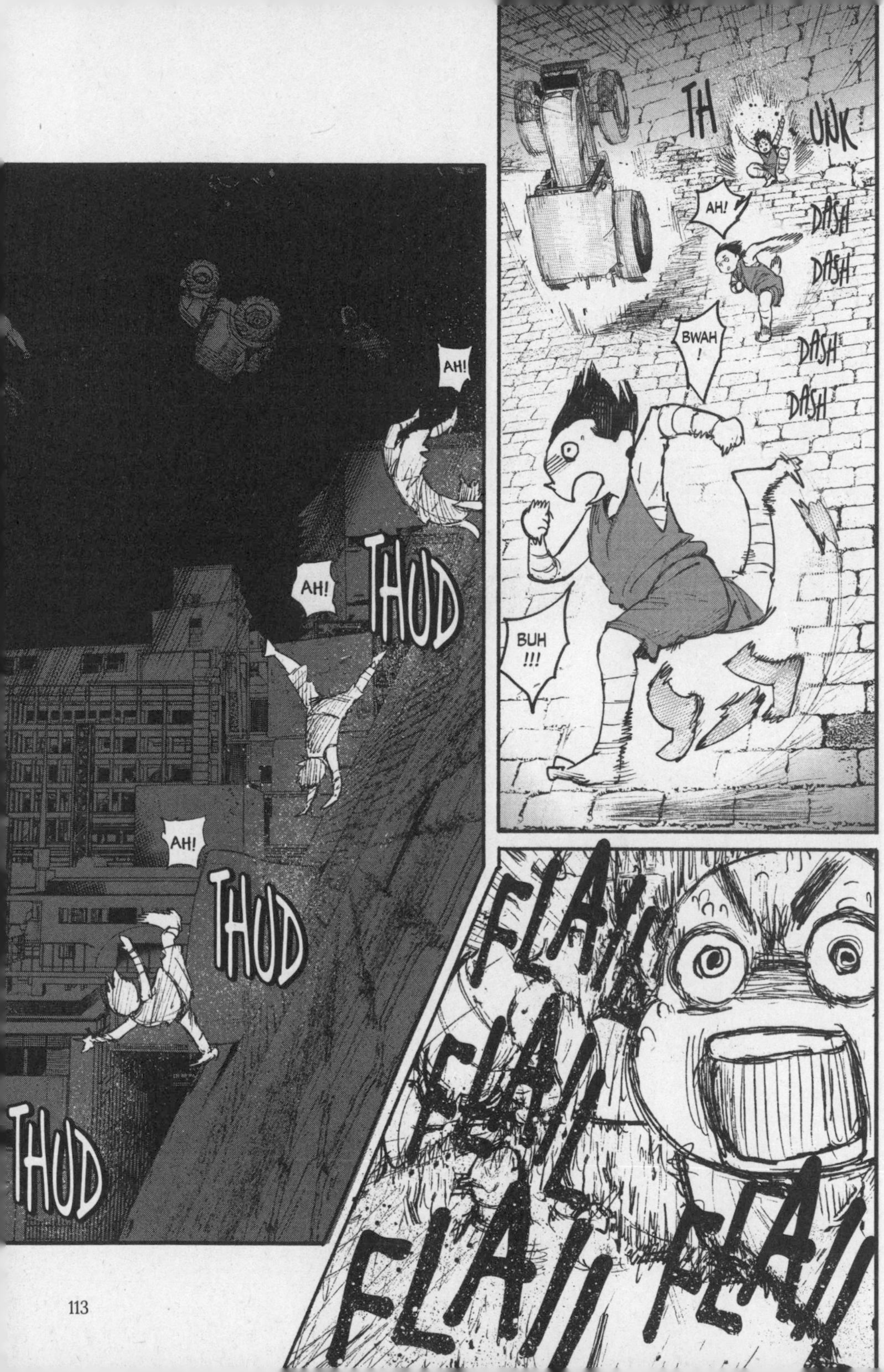
TH UNK
AH!
DASH
DASH
DASH
DASH
BWAH!
BUH!!!
FLAIL
FLAIL
FLAIL
FLAIL
AH!
AH!
THUD
AH!
THUD
THUD

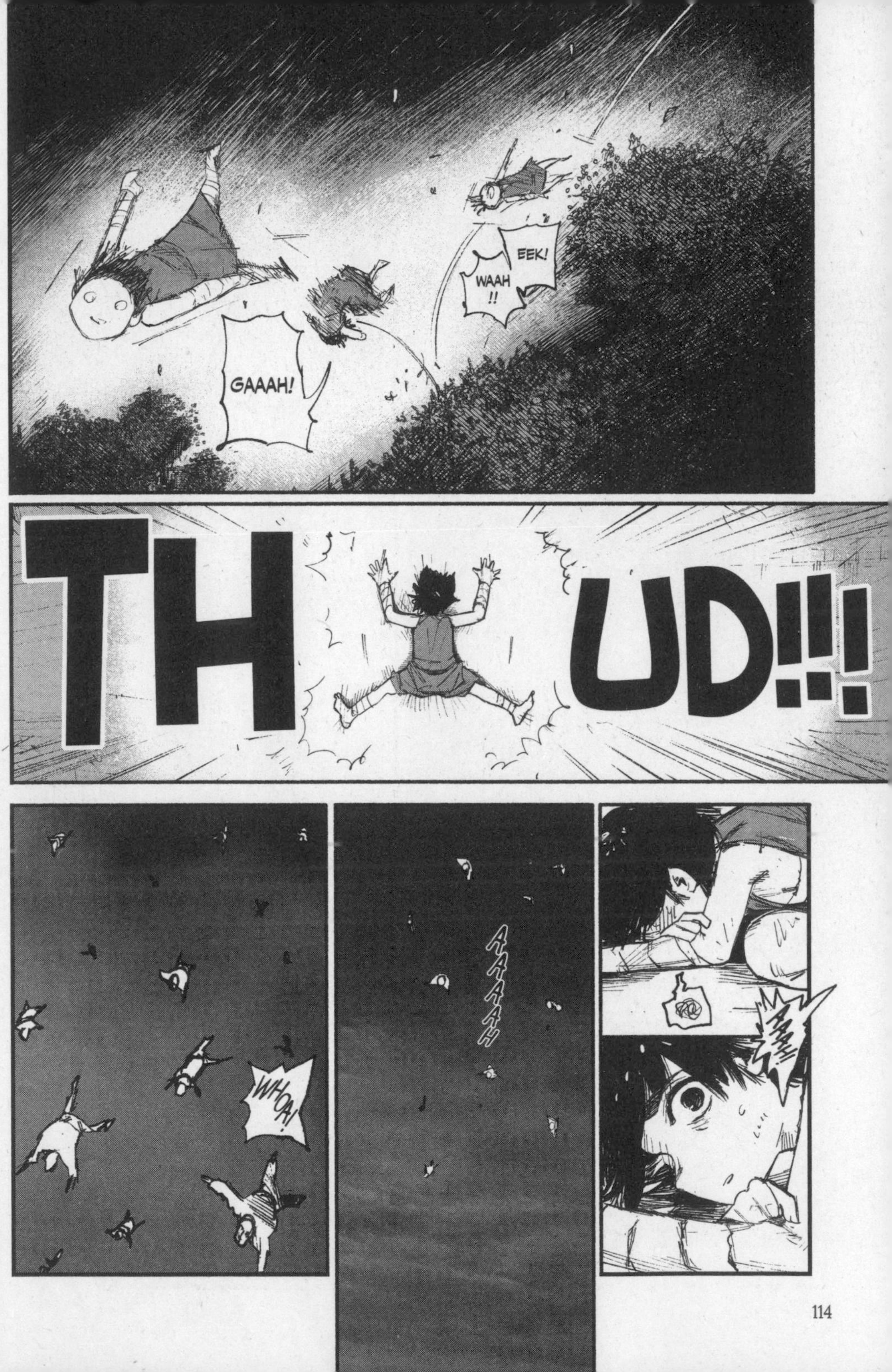
EEK!
WAAH !!
GAAAH!
TH UD!!!
AAAH!!
AAAAAAH
WHOA!

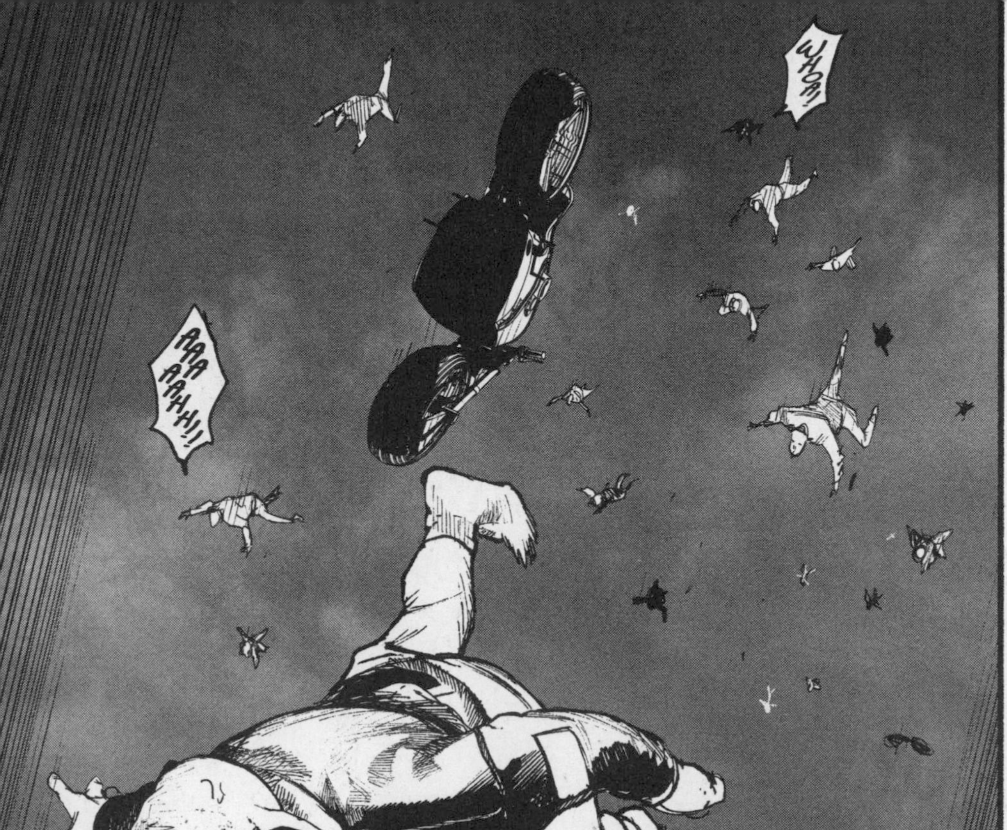
WHOM!
AAAAAAH!!!
EEP!
AAAAH...!!!

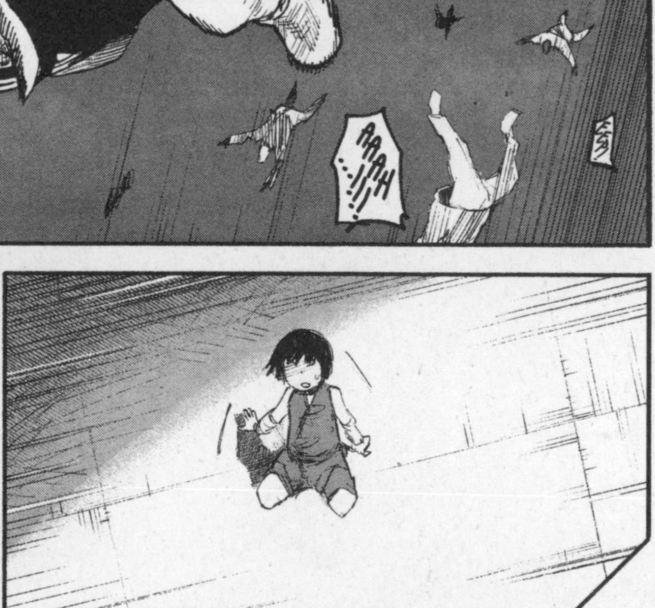

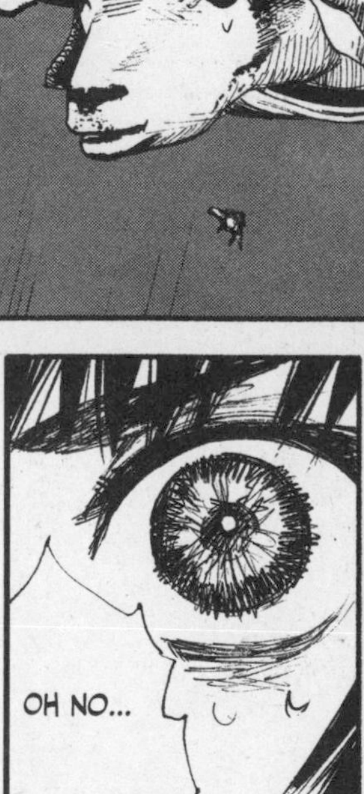
OH NO...

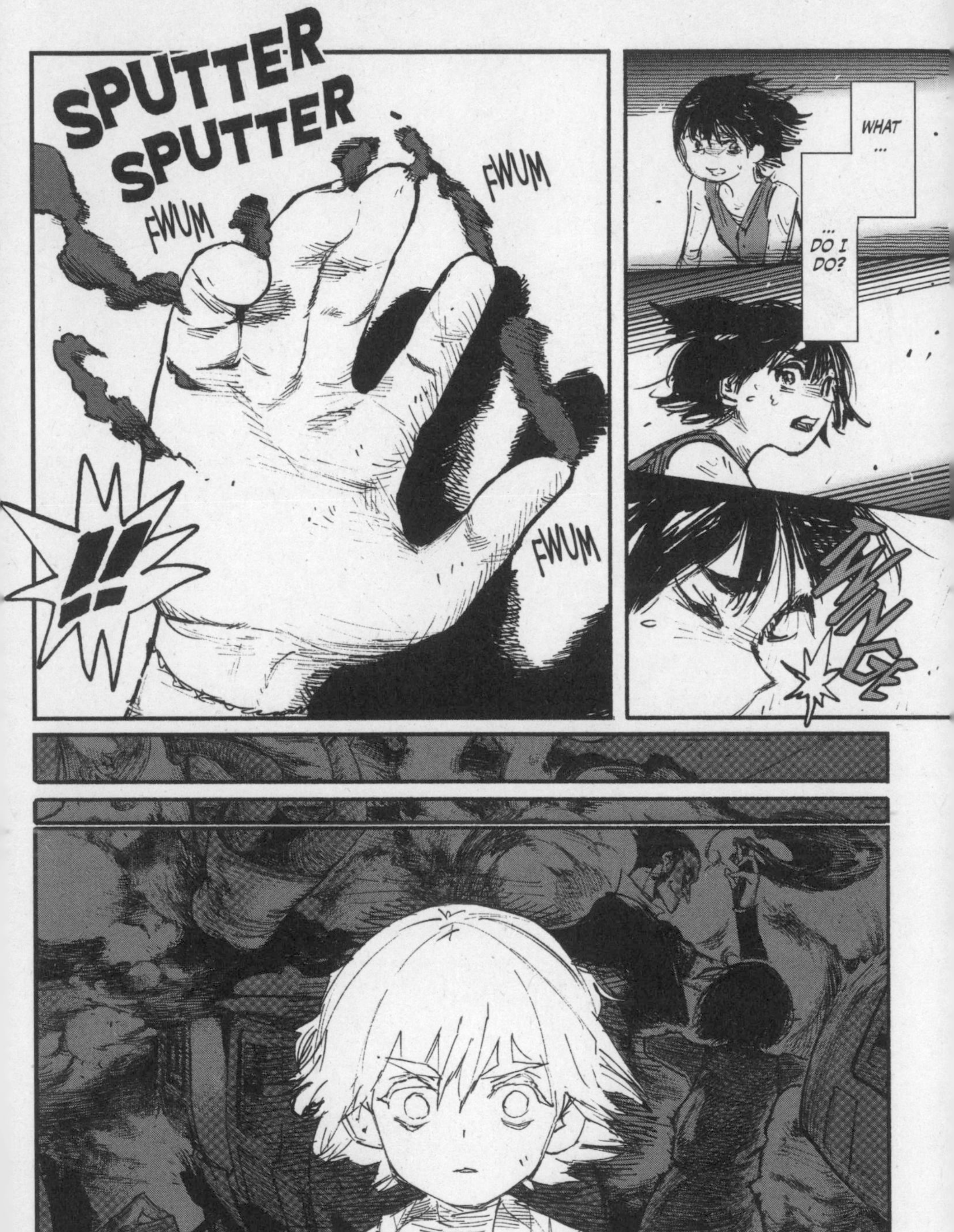
WHAT ...
... DO I DO?
TWINGE
SPUTTER SPUTTER
FWUM
FWUM
FWUM
!!

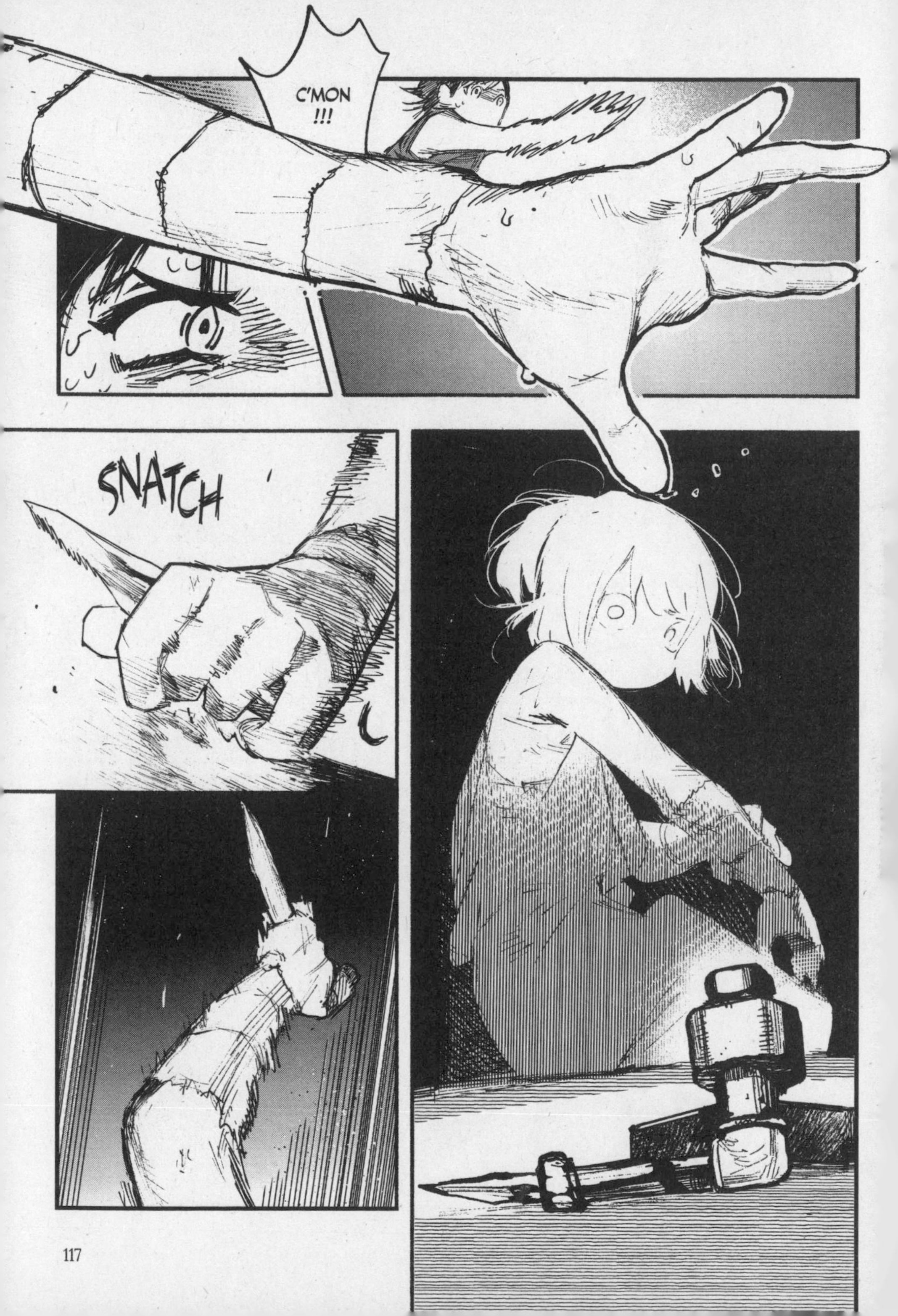
C'MON !!!
SNATCH

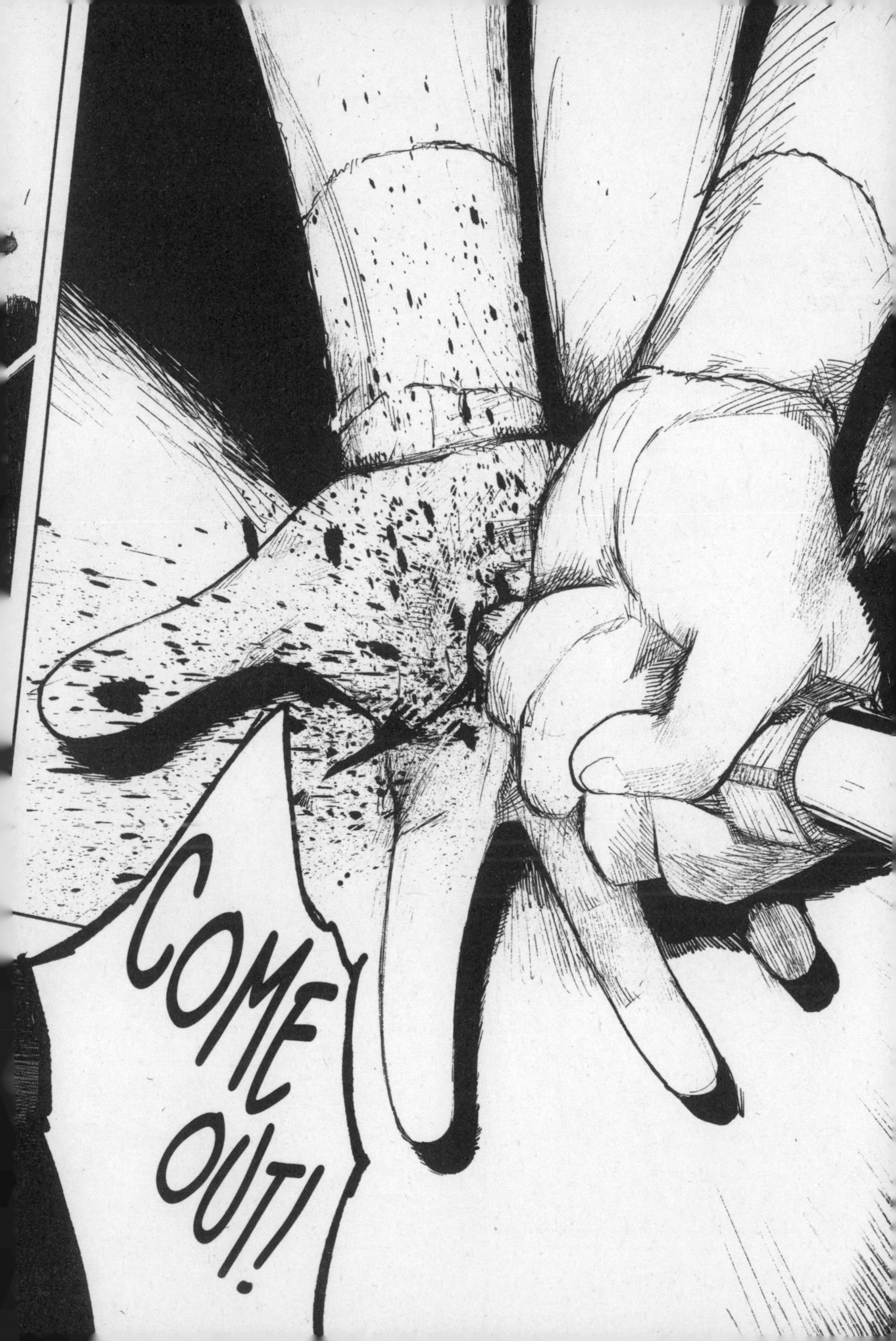
COME OUT!!

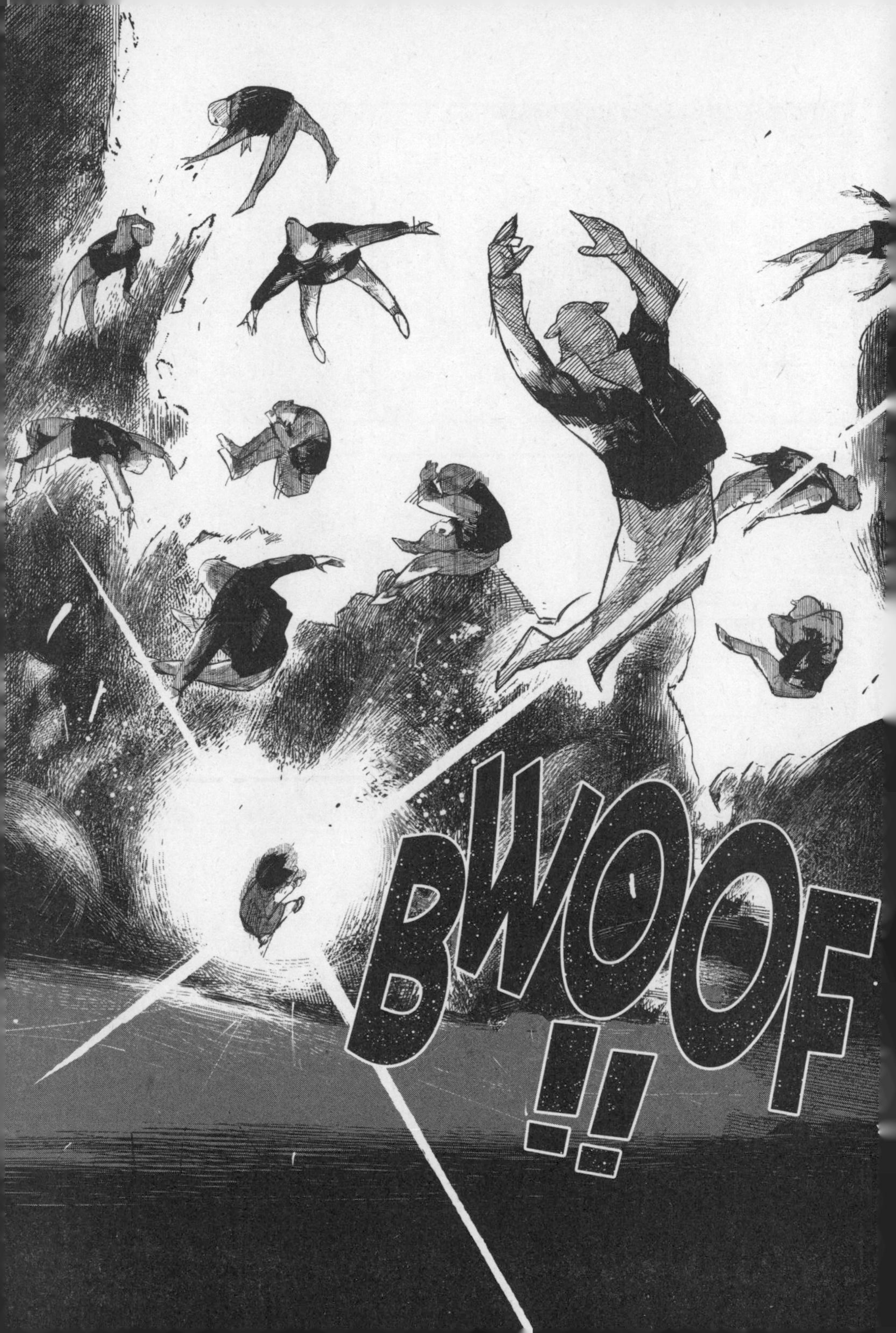
BWOOF!!

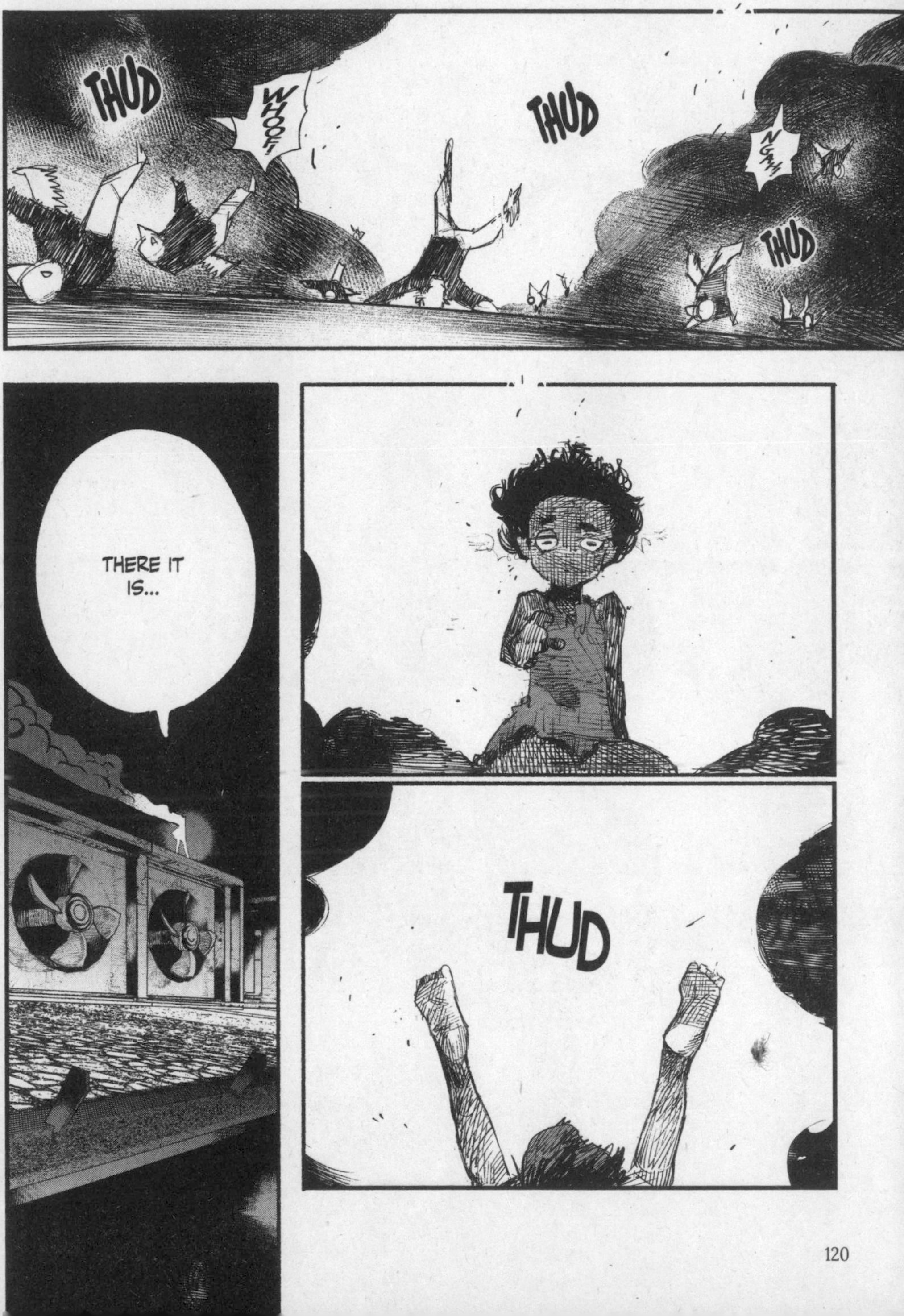
NGAH!
THUD
THUD
WHOOF!
THUD
THUD
THERE IT IS...

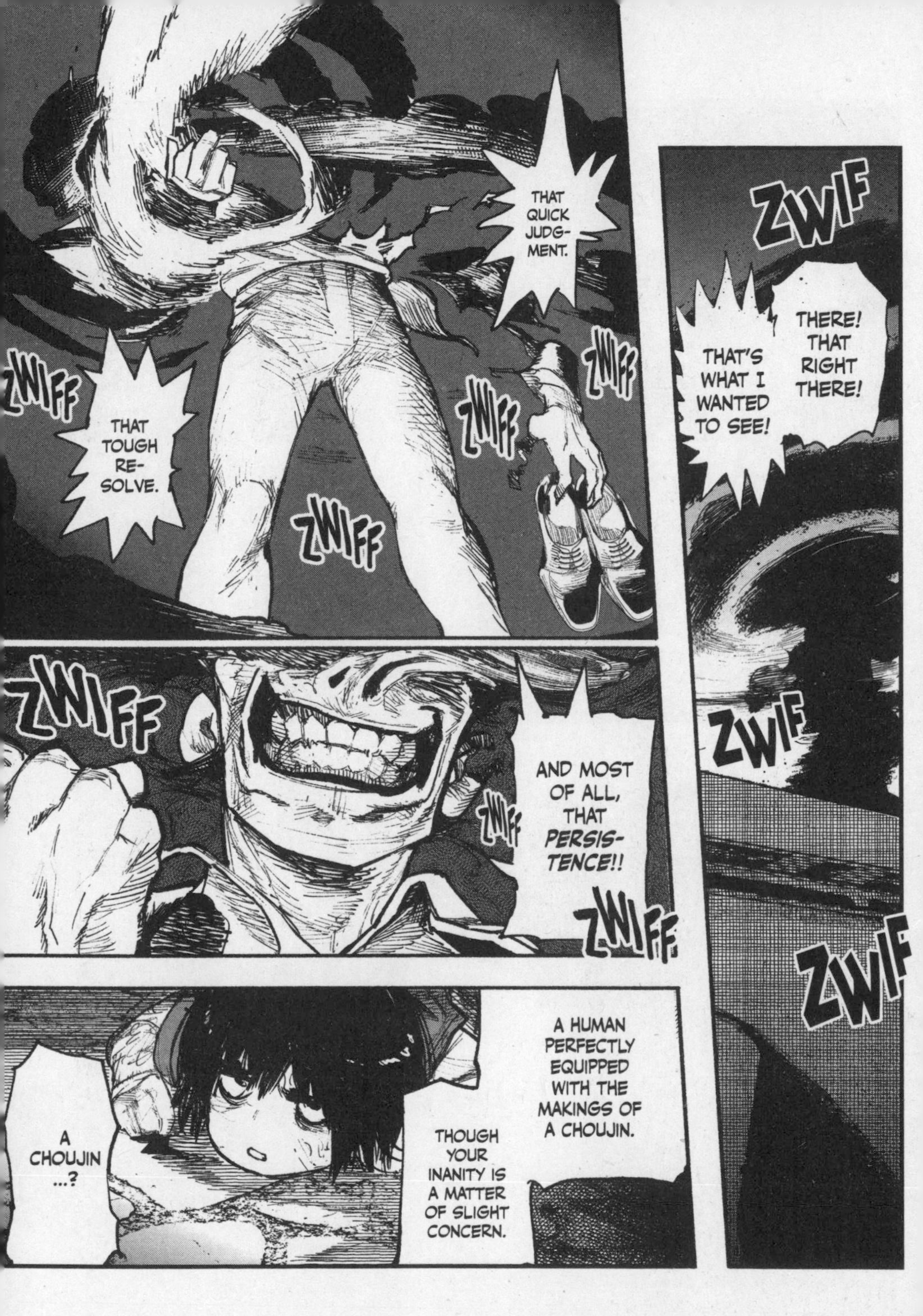
ZWIF
THERE! THAT RIGHT THERE!
THAT'S WHAT I WANTED TO SEE!
ZWIF
ZWIF
THAT QUICK JUDG- MENT.
ZWIFF
ZWIFF
THAT TOUGH RE- SOLVE.
ZWIFF
ZWIFF
ZWIFF
AND MOST OF ALL, THAT *PERSIS- TENCE!!*
ZWIFF
ZWIFF
A HUMAN PERFECTLY EQUIPPED WITH THE MAKINGS OF A CHOUJIN.
THOUGH YOUR INANITY IS A MATTER OF SLIGHT CONCERN.
A CHOUJIN ...?

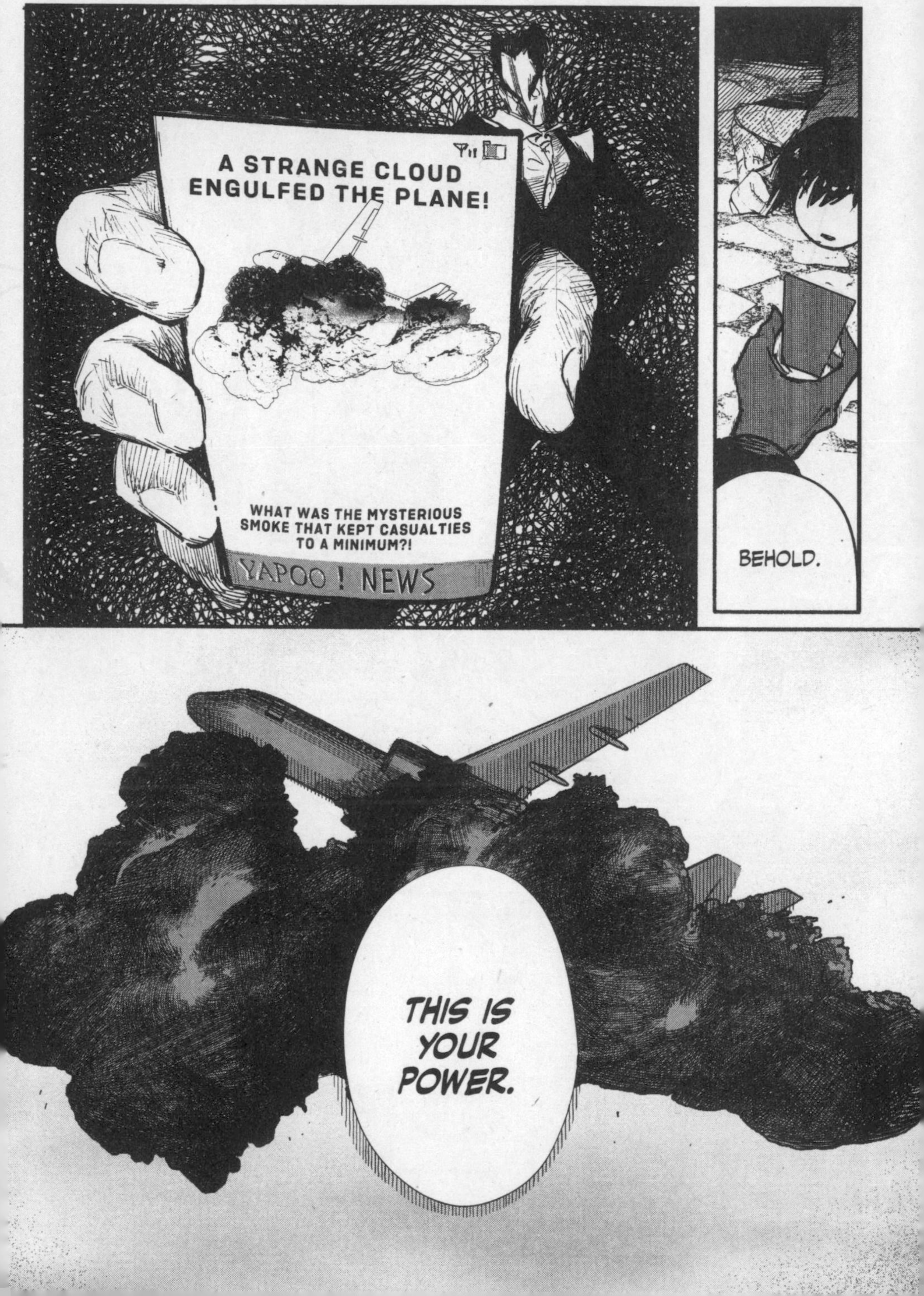
BEHOLD.
A STRANGE CLOUD ENGULFED THE PLANE!
WHAT WAS THE MYSTERIOUS SMOKE THAT KEPT CASUALTIES TO A MINIMUM?!
YAPOO ! NEWS
THIS IS YOUR POWER.

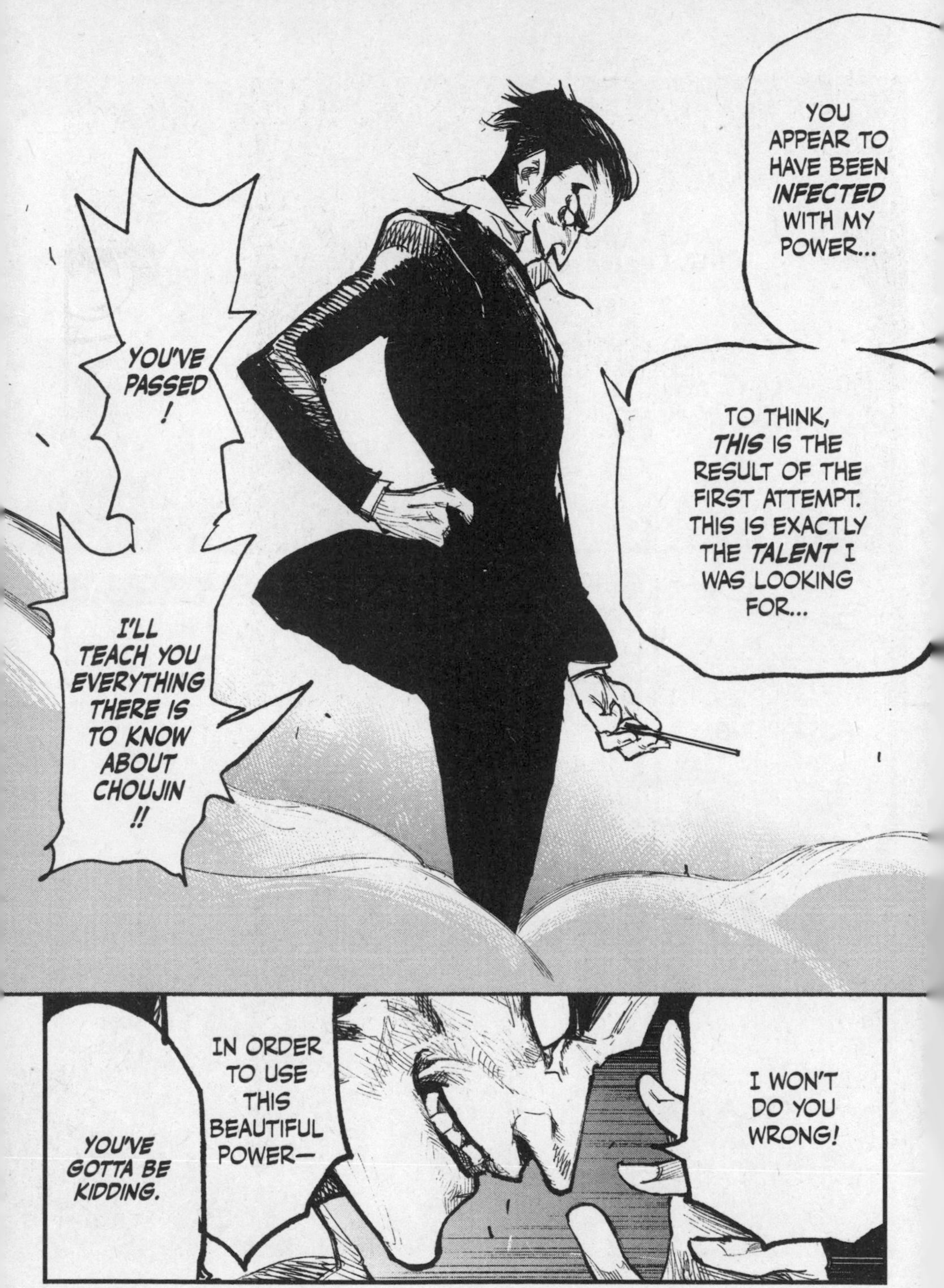
YOU APPEAR TO HAVE BEEN INFECTED WITH MY POWER...
TO THINK, THIS IS THE RESULT OF THE FIRST ATTEMPT. THIS IS EXACTLY THE TALENT I WAS LOOKING FOR...
YOU'VE PASSED!
I'LL TEACH YOU EVERYTHING THERE IS TO KNOW ABOUT CHOUJIN!!
I WON'T DO YOU WRONG!
IN ORDER TO USE THIS BEAUTIFUL POWER—
YOU'VE GOTTA BE KIDDING.

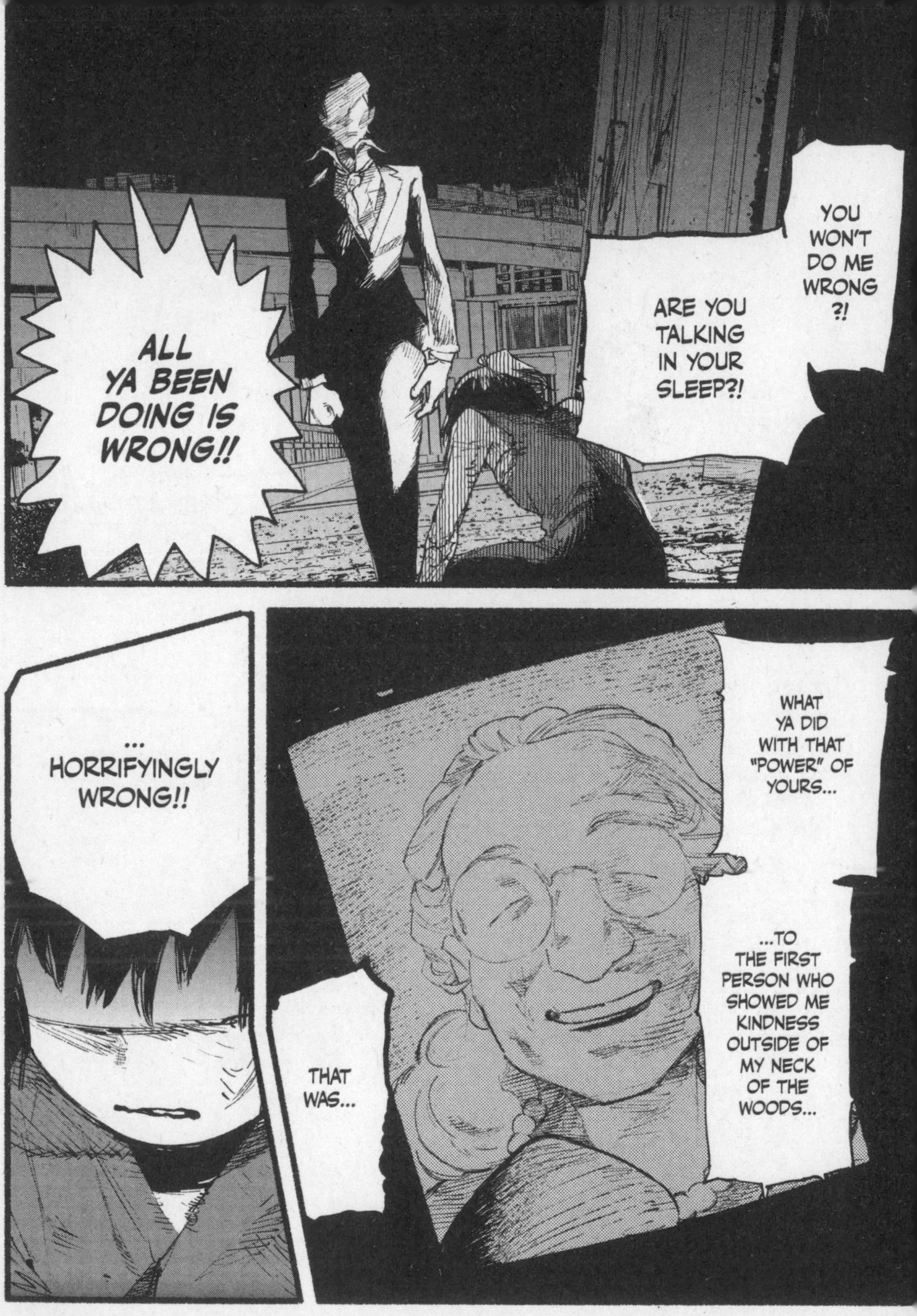
YOU WON'T DO ME WRONG?!
ARE YOU TALKING IN YOUR SLEEP?!
ALL YA BEEN DOING IS WRONG!!
WHAT YA DID WITH THAT "POWER" OF YOURS...
...TO THE FIRST PERSON WHO SHOWED ME KINDNESS OUTSIDE OF MY NECK OF THE WOODS...
THAT WAS...
... HORRIFYINGLY WRONG!!

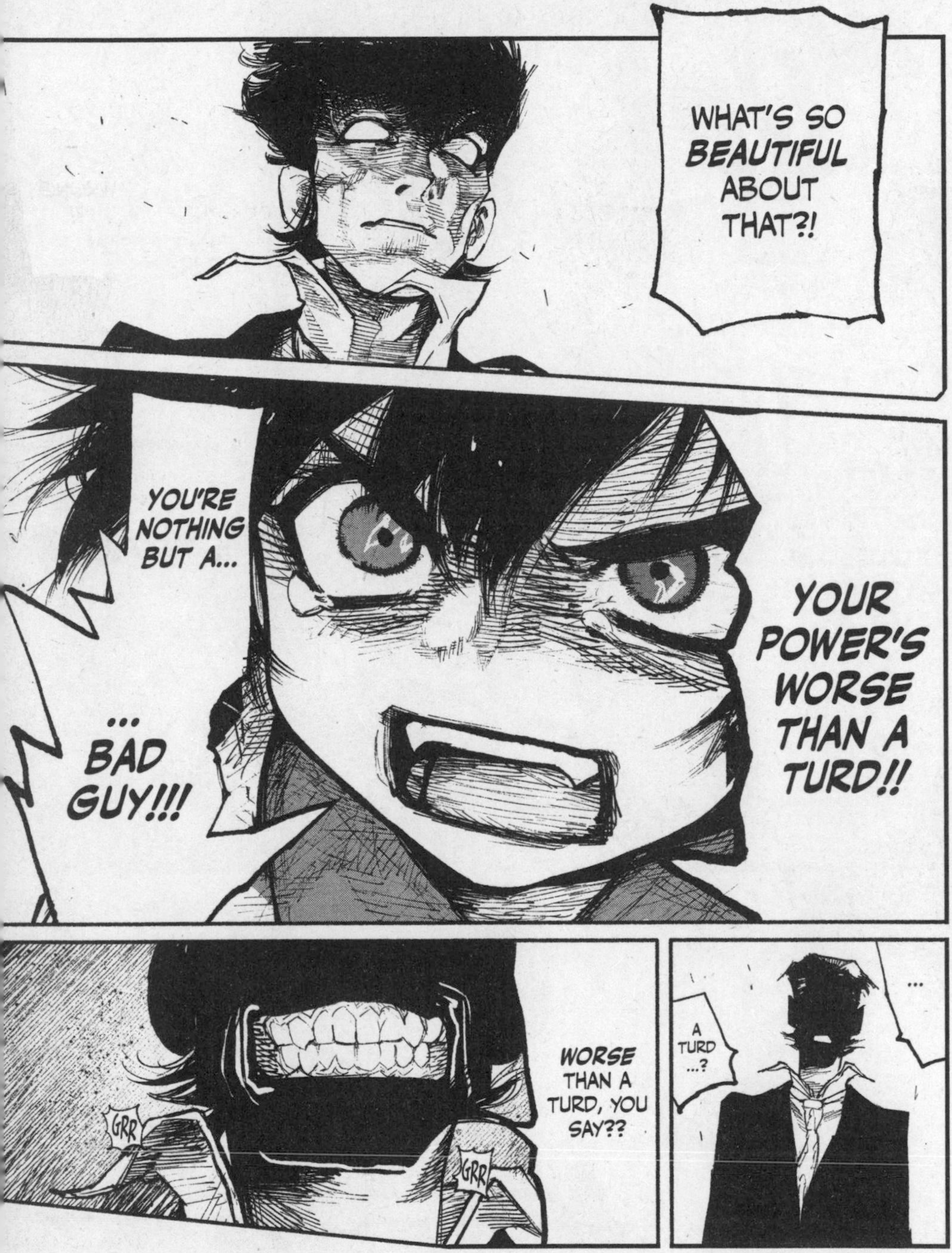
WHAT'S SO BEAUTIFUL ABOUT THAT?!
YOUR POWER'S WORSE THAN A TURD!!
YOU'RE NOTHING BUT A...
... BAD GUY!!!
...
A TURD ...?
WORSE THAN A TURD, YOU SAY??
GRR
GRR

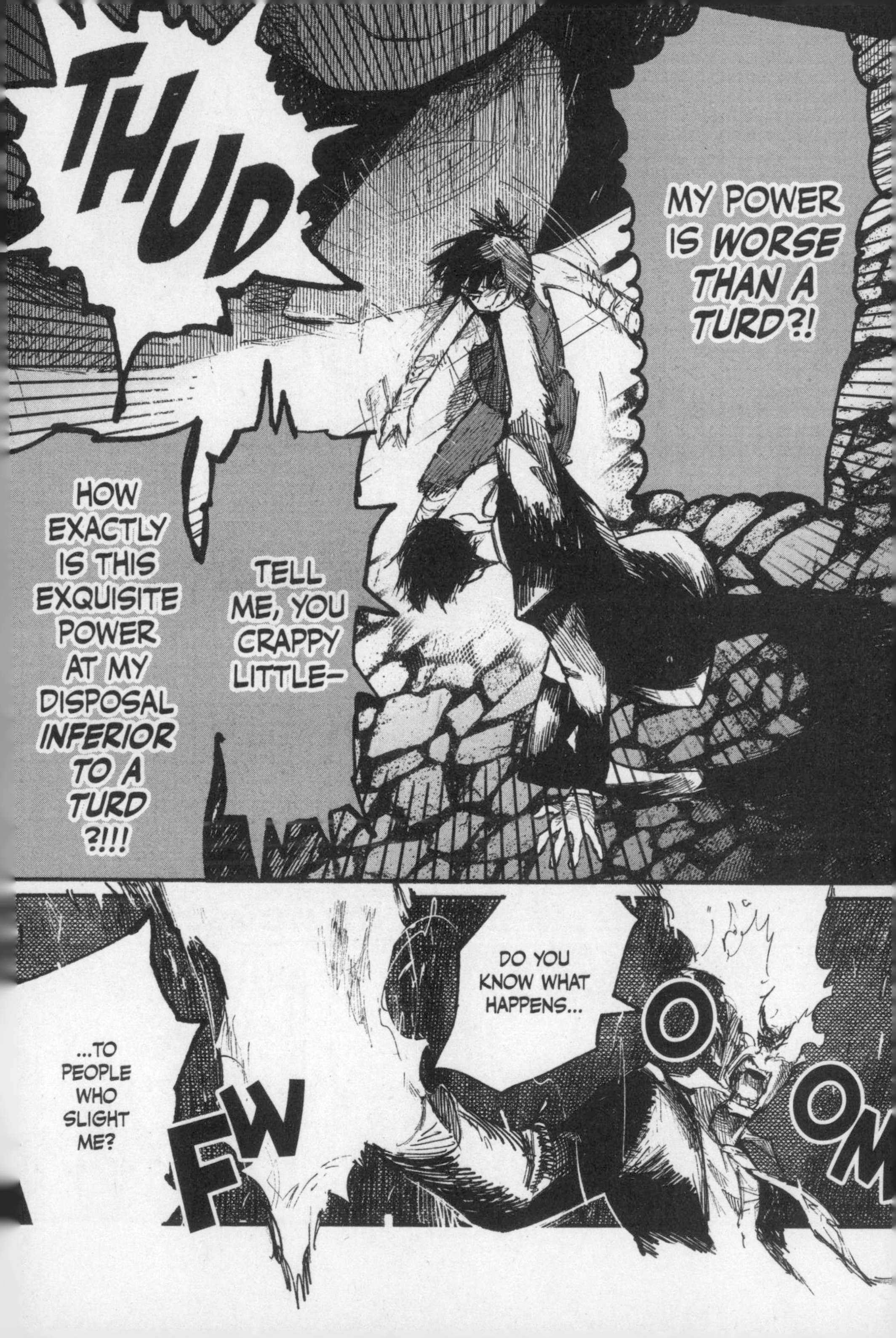
MY POWER IS WORSE THAN A TURD?!
THUD
TELL ME, YOU CRAPPY LITTLE-
HOW EXACTLY IS THIS EXQUISITE POWER AT MY DISPOSAL INFERIOR TO A TURD ?!!!
DO YOU KNOW WHAT HAPPENS...
FWOOM
...TO PEOPLE WHO SLIGHT ME?

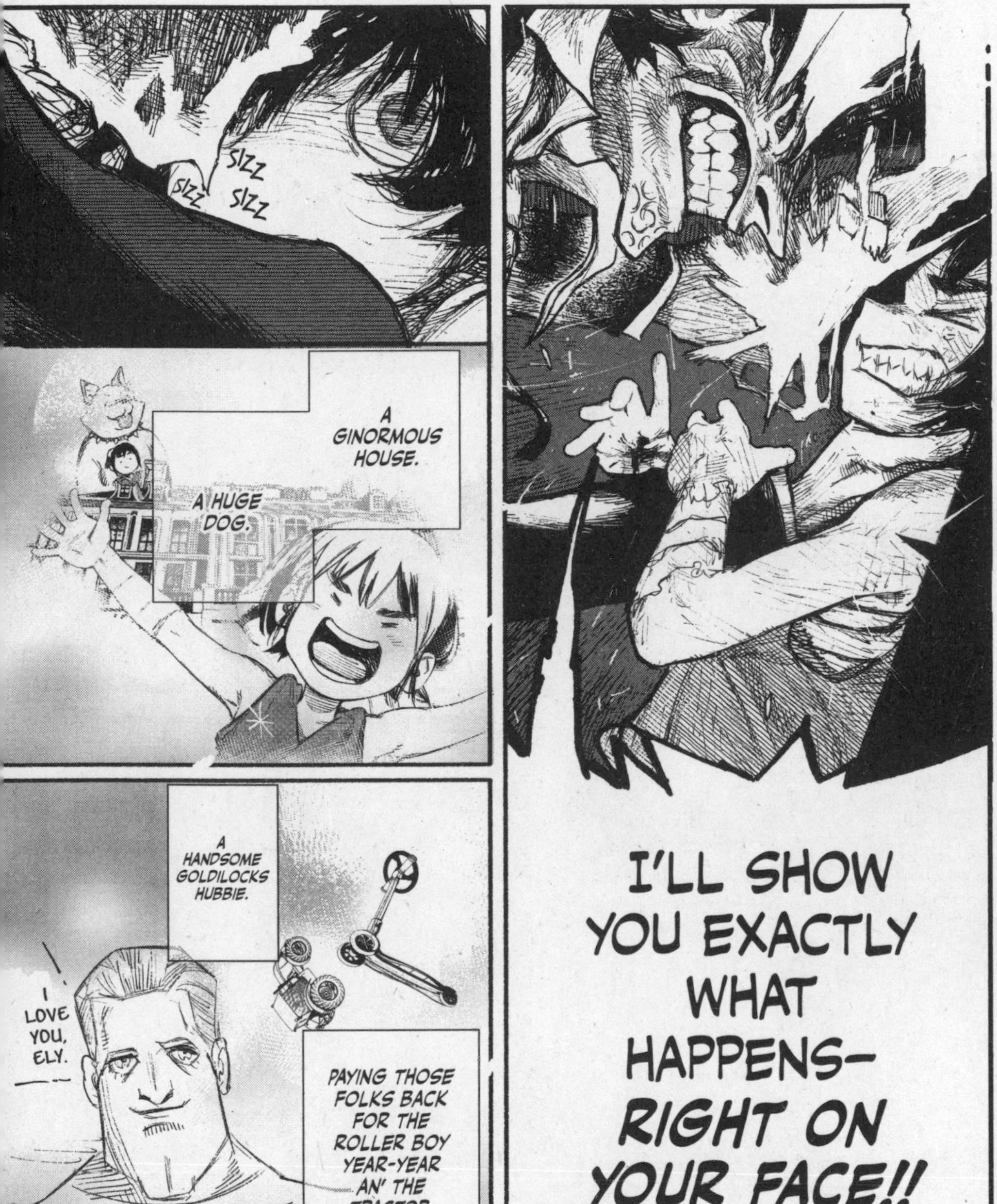
I'LL SHOW YOU EXACTLY WHAT HAPPENS— RIGHT ON YOUR FACE!!
SIZZ
SIZZ
SIZZ
A GINORMOUS HOUSE.
A HUGE DOG.
A HANDSOME GOLDILOCKS HUBBIE.
I LOVE YOU, ELY.
PAYING THOSE FOLKS BACK FOR THE ROLLER BOY YEAR-YEAR AN' THE TRACTOR.

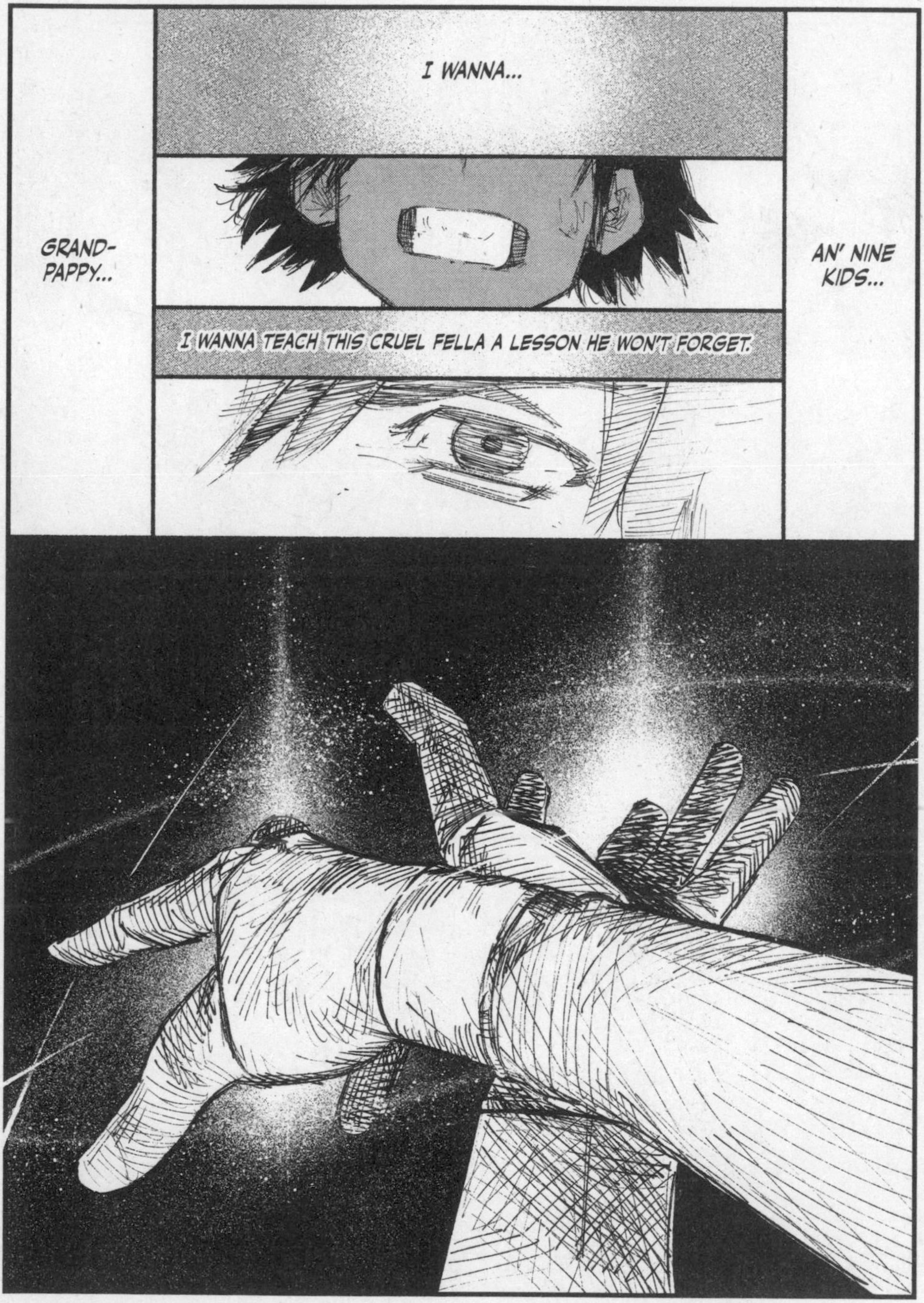
AN' NINE KIDS...
I WANNA...
I WANNA TEACH THIS CRUEL FELLA A LESSON HE WON'T FORGET.
GRAND-PAPPY...

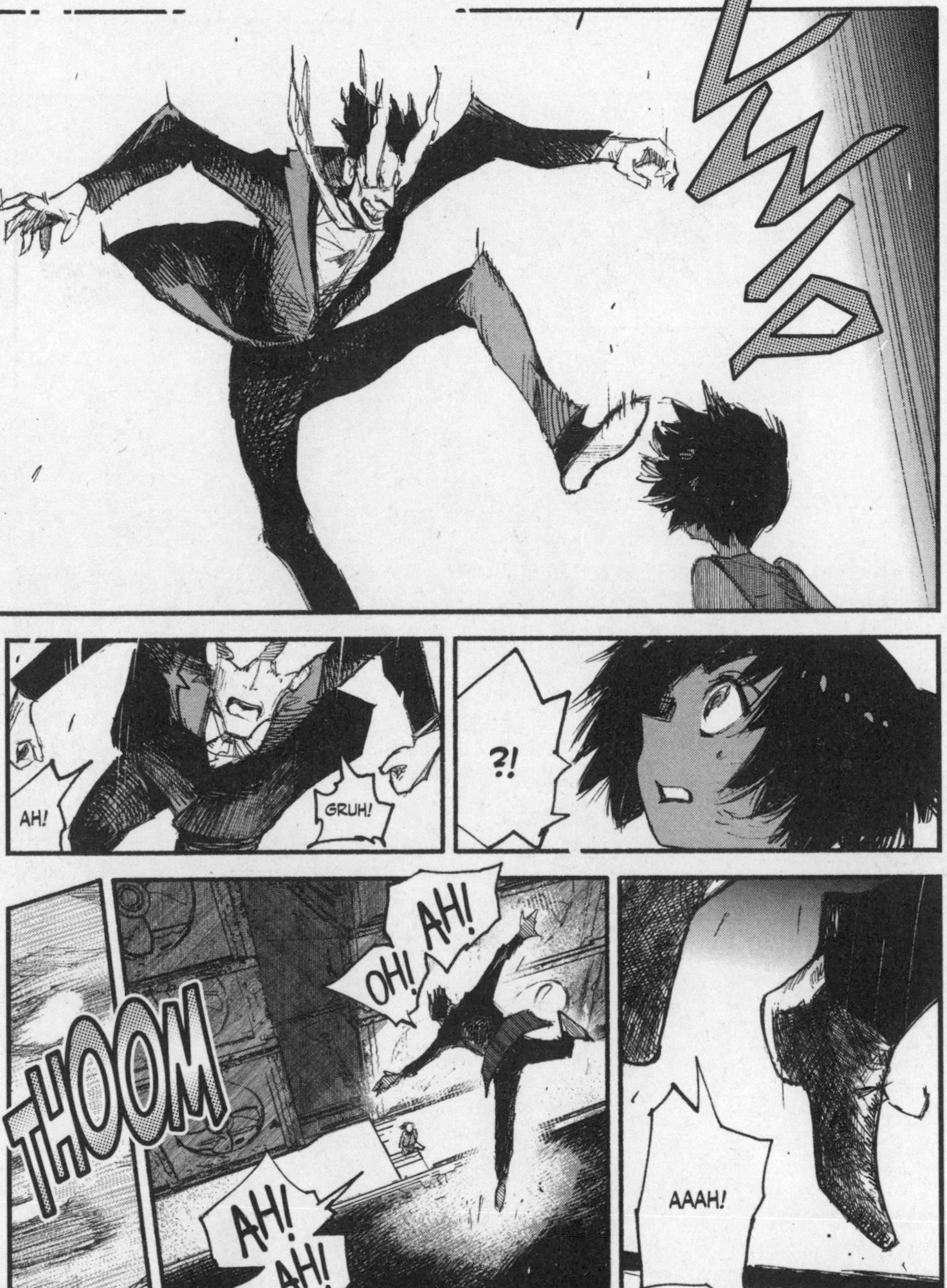
VWIP
?!
GRUH!
AH!
AAAH!
AH!
OH!
THOOM
AH! AH!

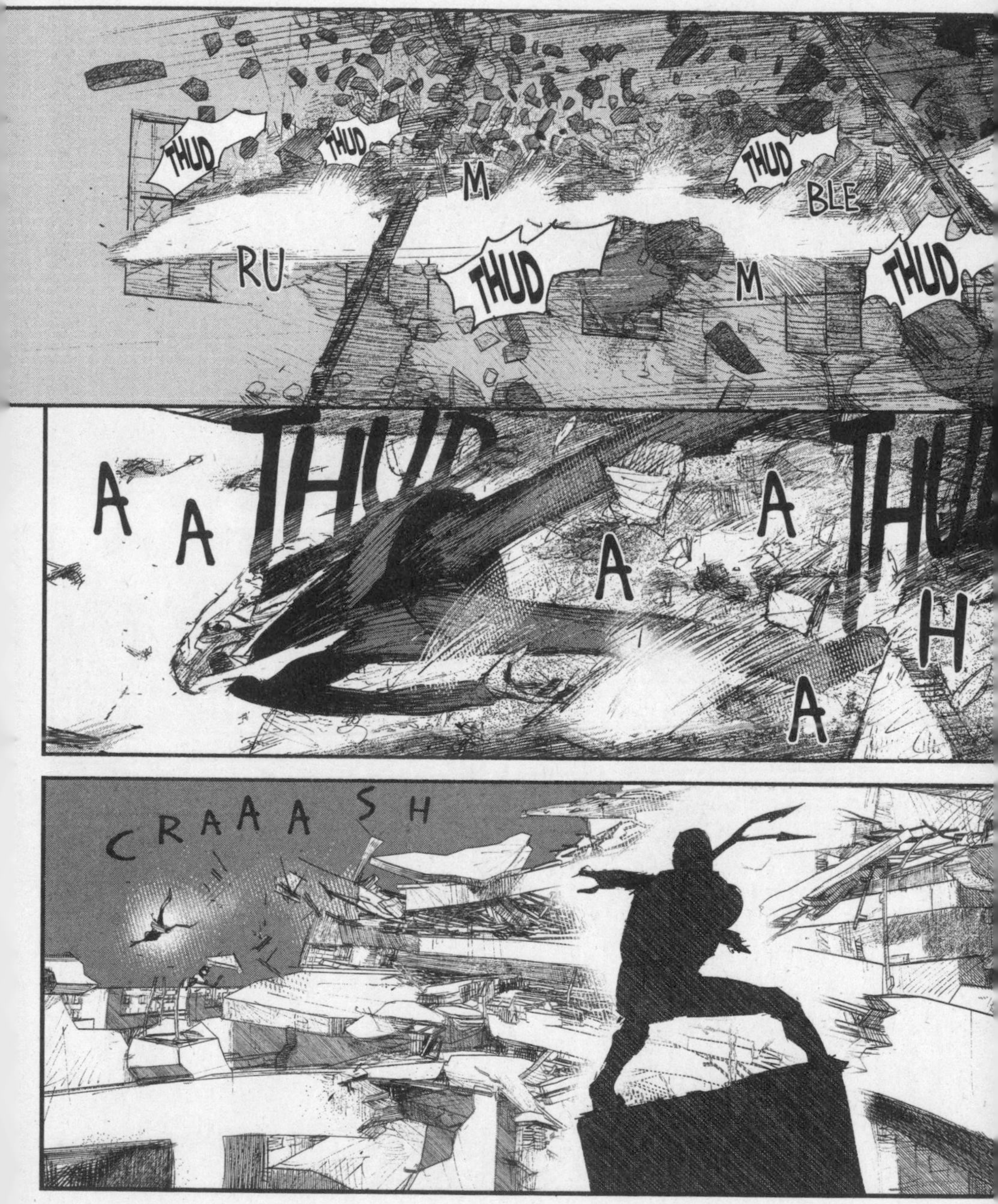
THUD
THUD
THUD
THUD
THUD
RU M M BLE
THUD
THUD
A A A A A A H
CRAAASH

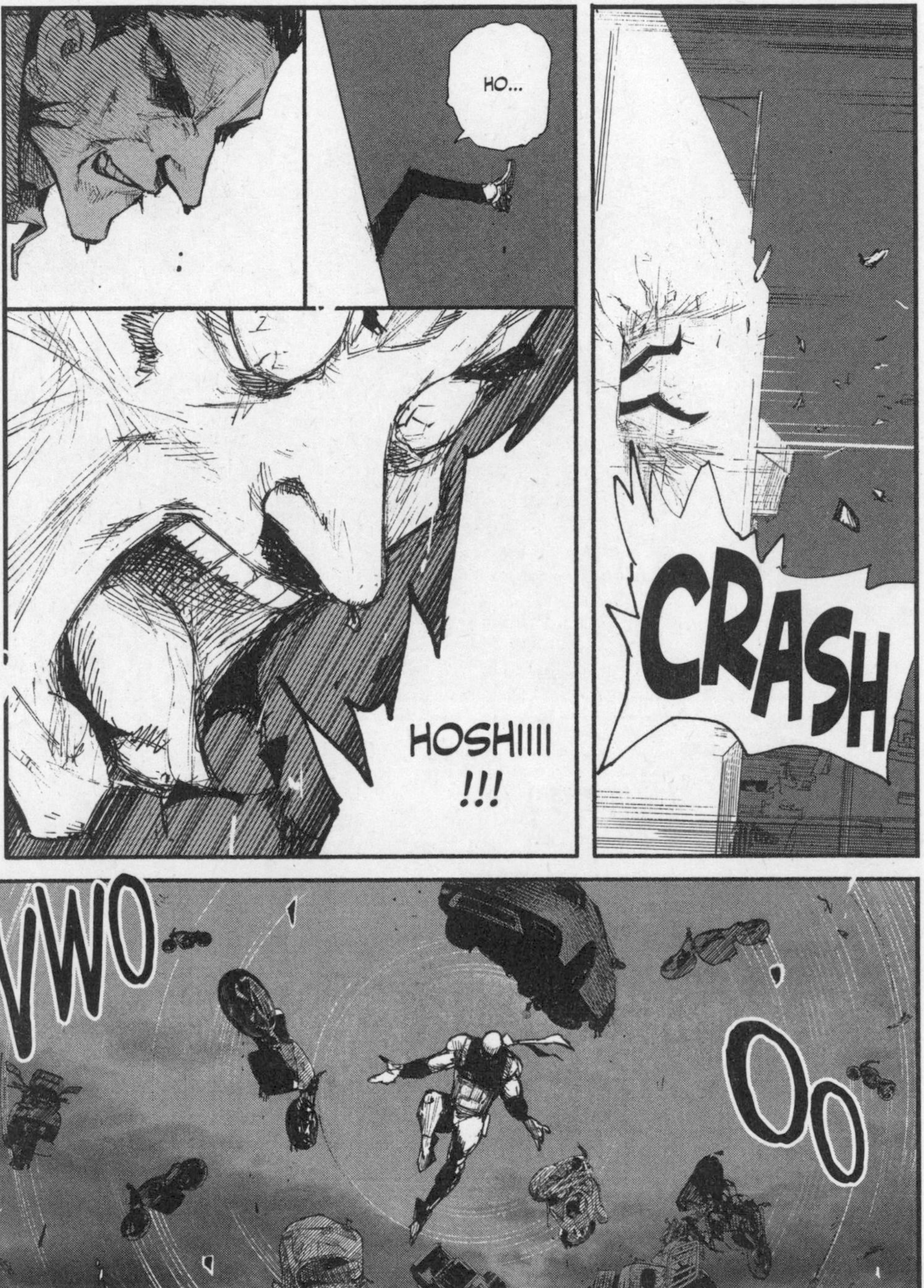
CRASH
HO...
HOSHIIIII!!!
VWOOO

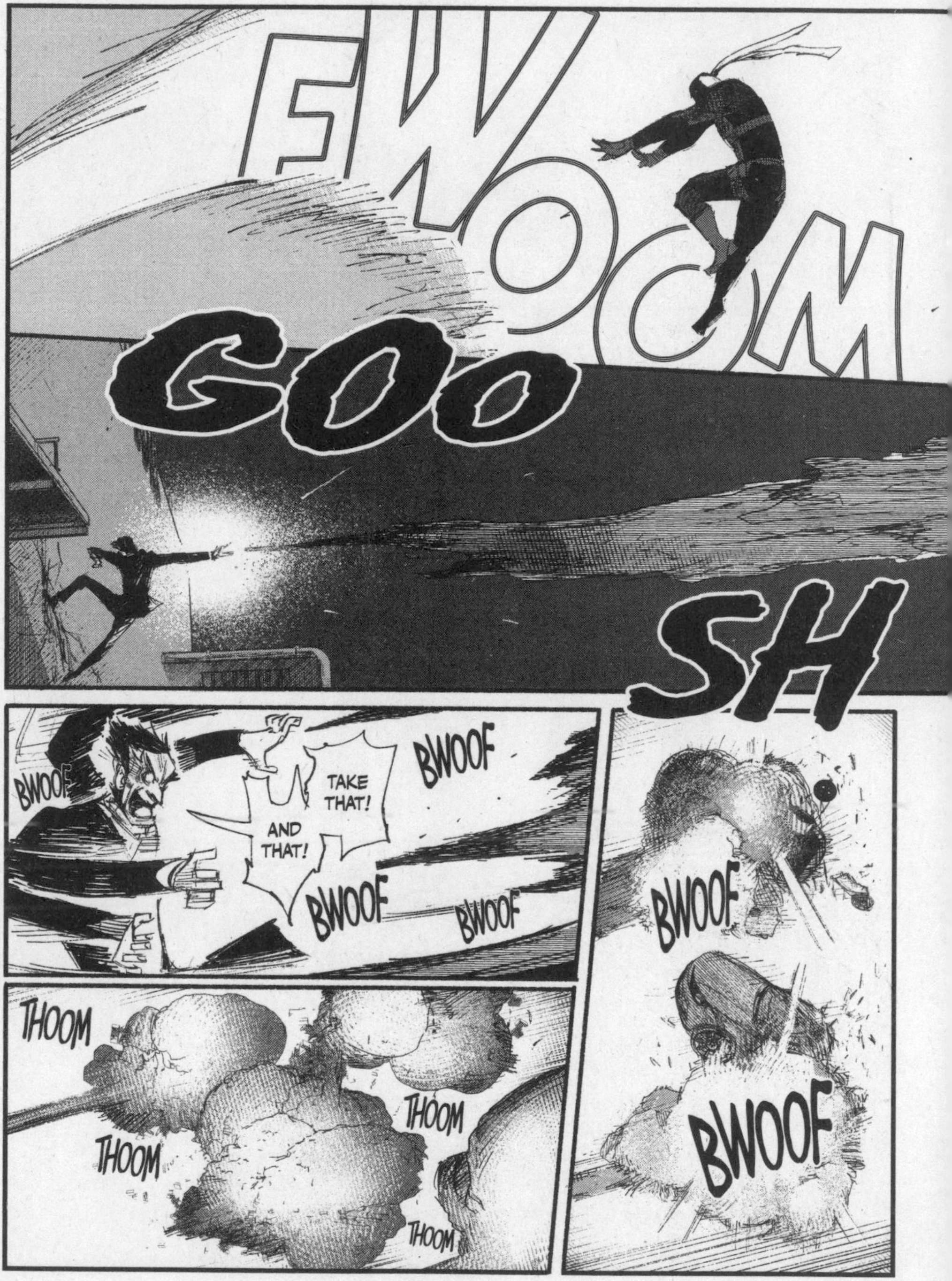
EWOOM
GOOSH
BWOOF
BWOOF
BWOOF
TAKE THAT!
AND THAT!
BWOOF
BWOOF
BWOOF
THOOM
THOOM
THOOM
THOOM

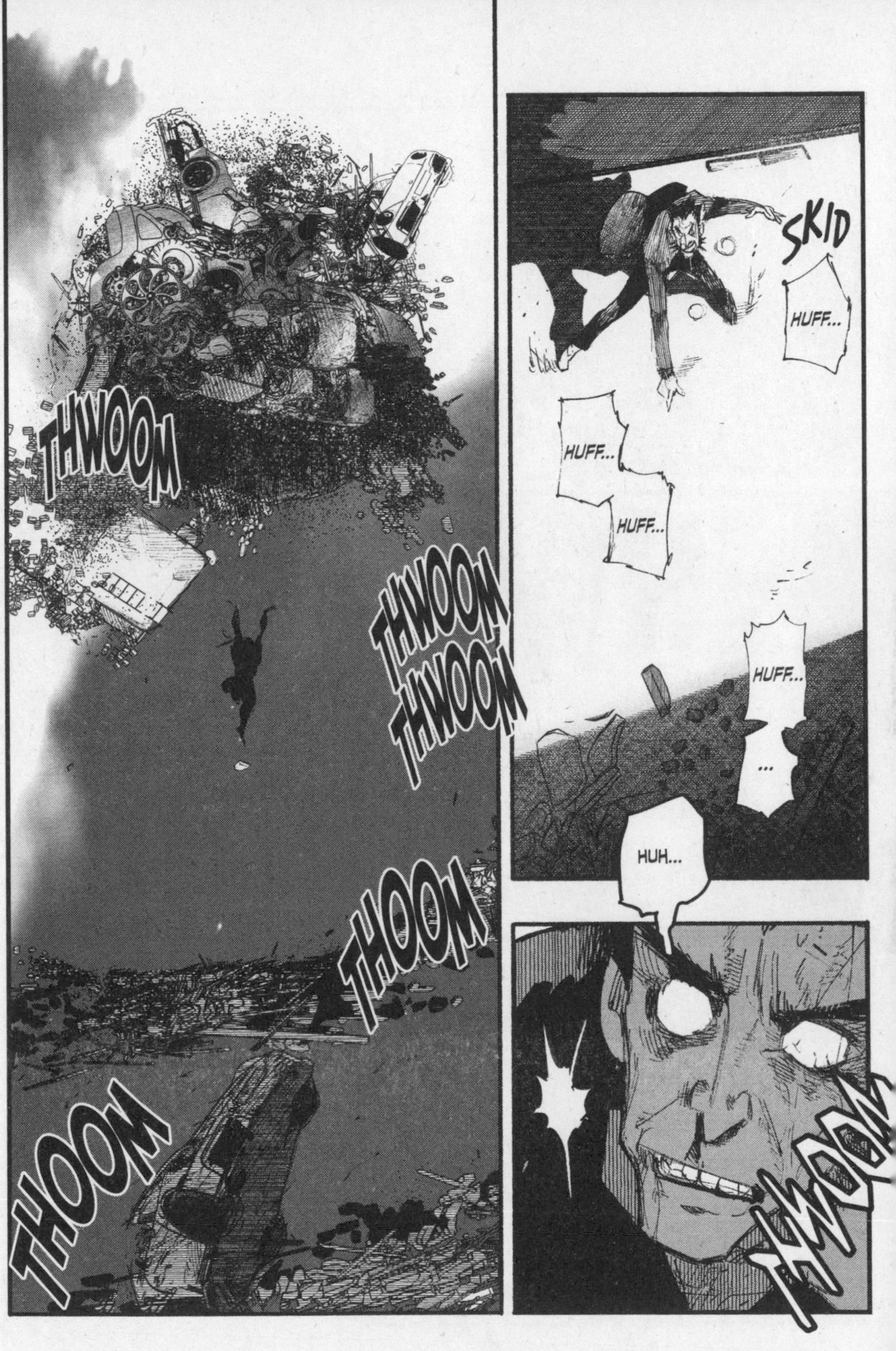
SKID
HUFF...
HUFF...
HUFF...
HUFF...
...
HUH...
THWOOM
THWOOM
THWOOM
THWOOM
THOOM
THOOM

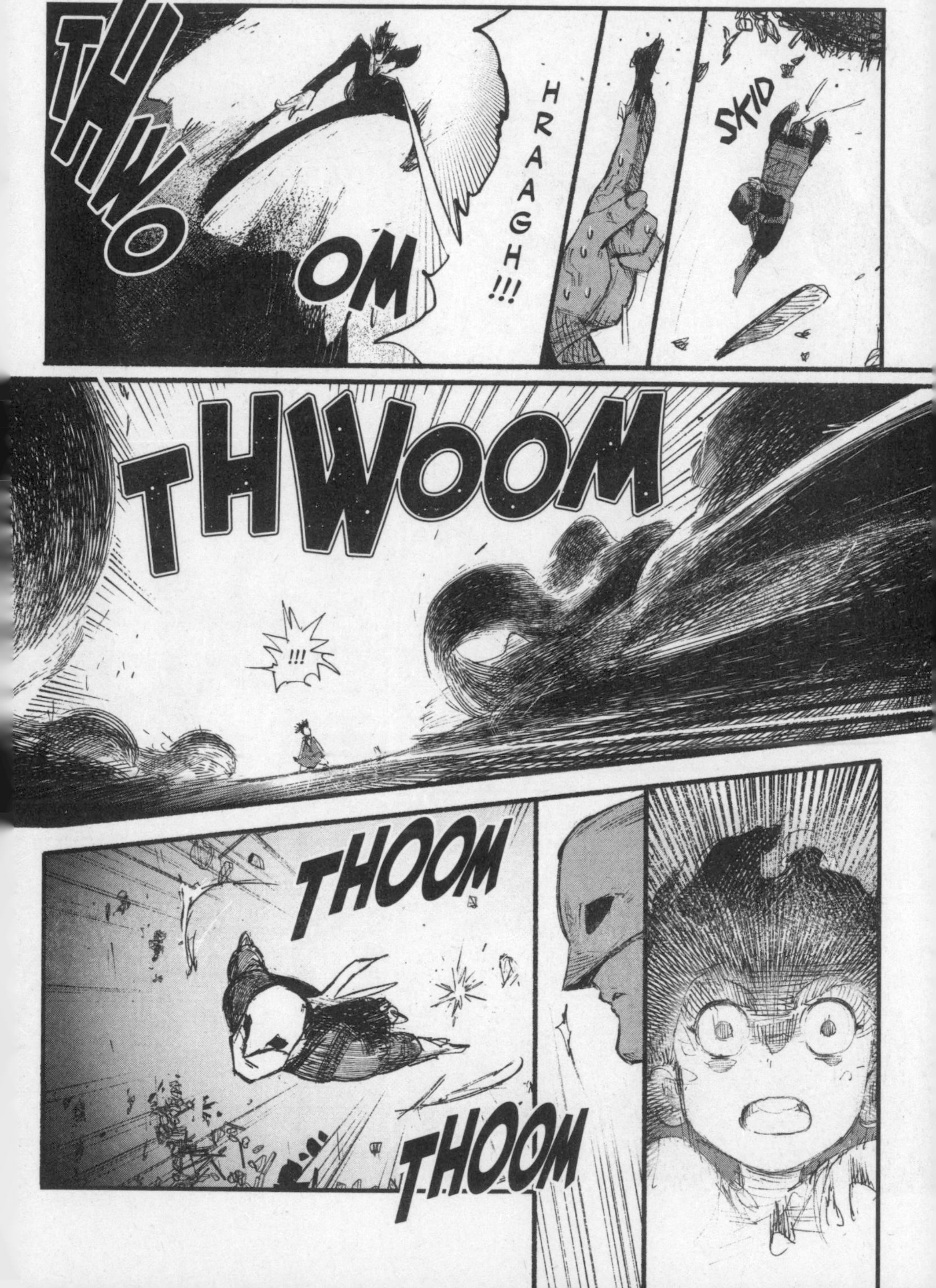
SKID
HRAAGH!!!
THWOOM
THWOOM
!!!
THOOM
THOOM

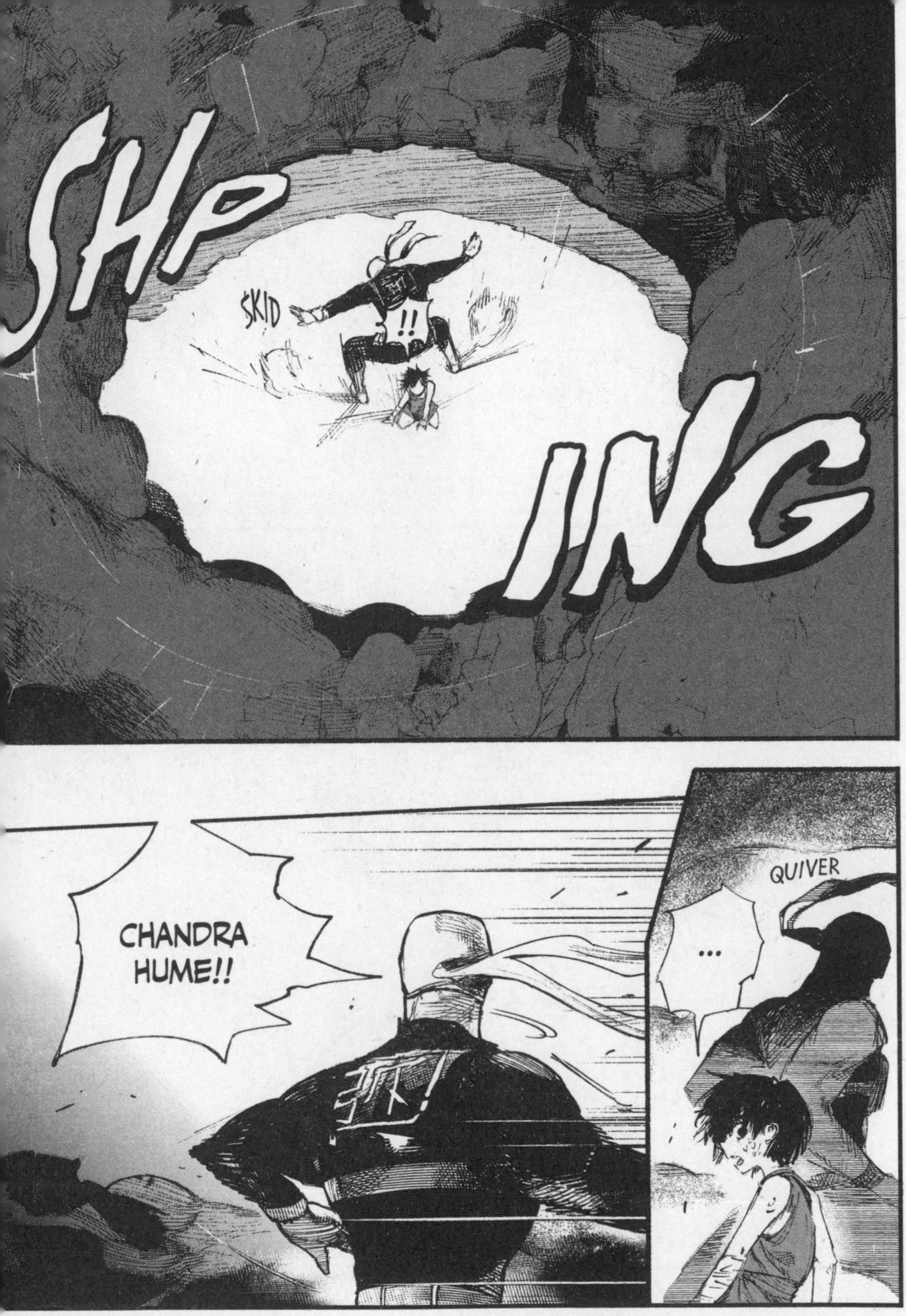
SHP
ING
SKID
!!
QUIVER
...
CHANDRA HUME!!

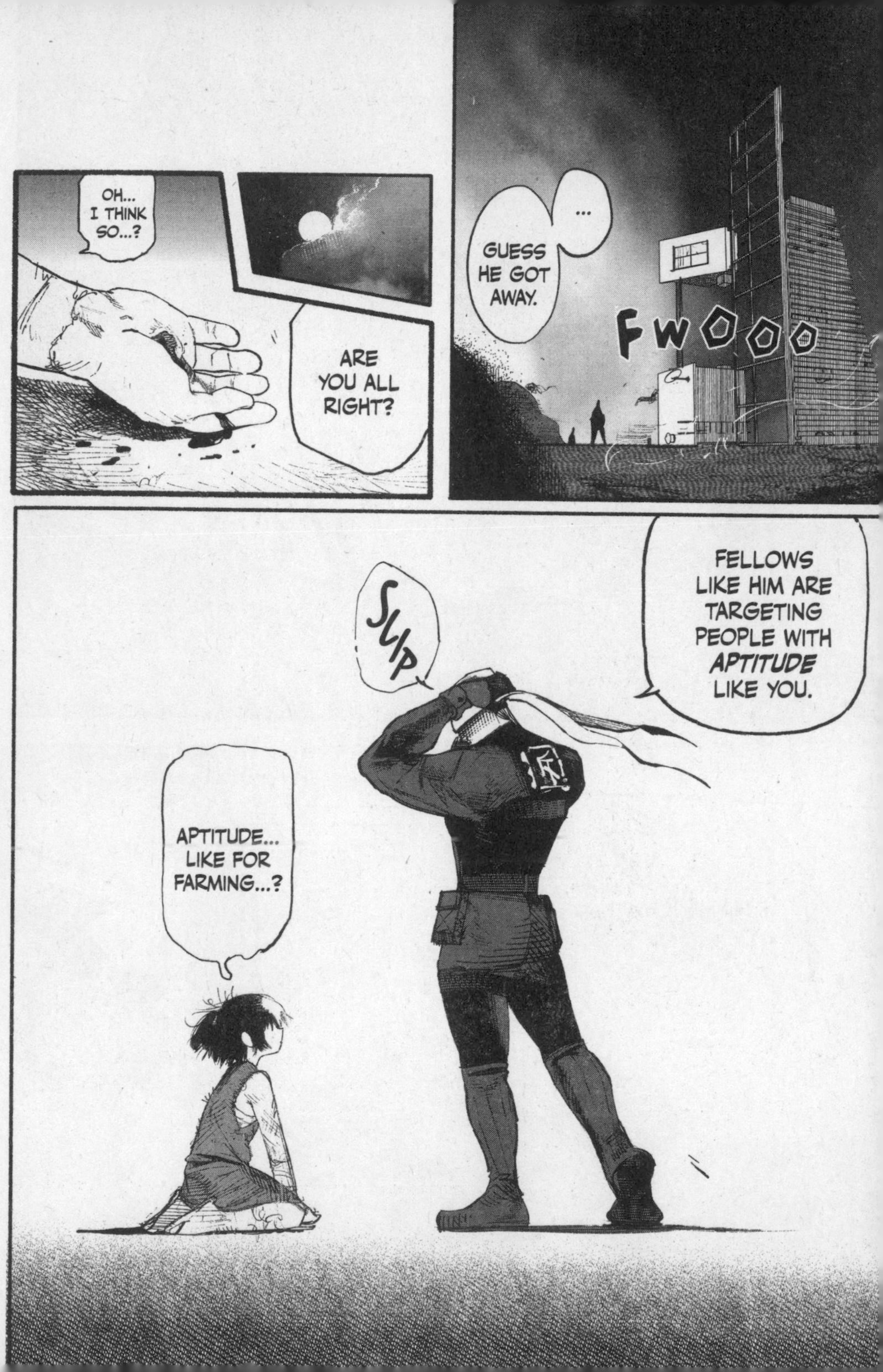
...
GUESS HE GOT AWAY.
FWOOO
ARE YOU ALL RIGHT?
OH... I THINK SO...?
FELLOWS LIKE HIM ARE TARGETING PEOPLE WITH *APTITUDE* LIKE YOU.
SLIP
APTITUDE... LIKE FOR FARMING...?

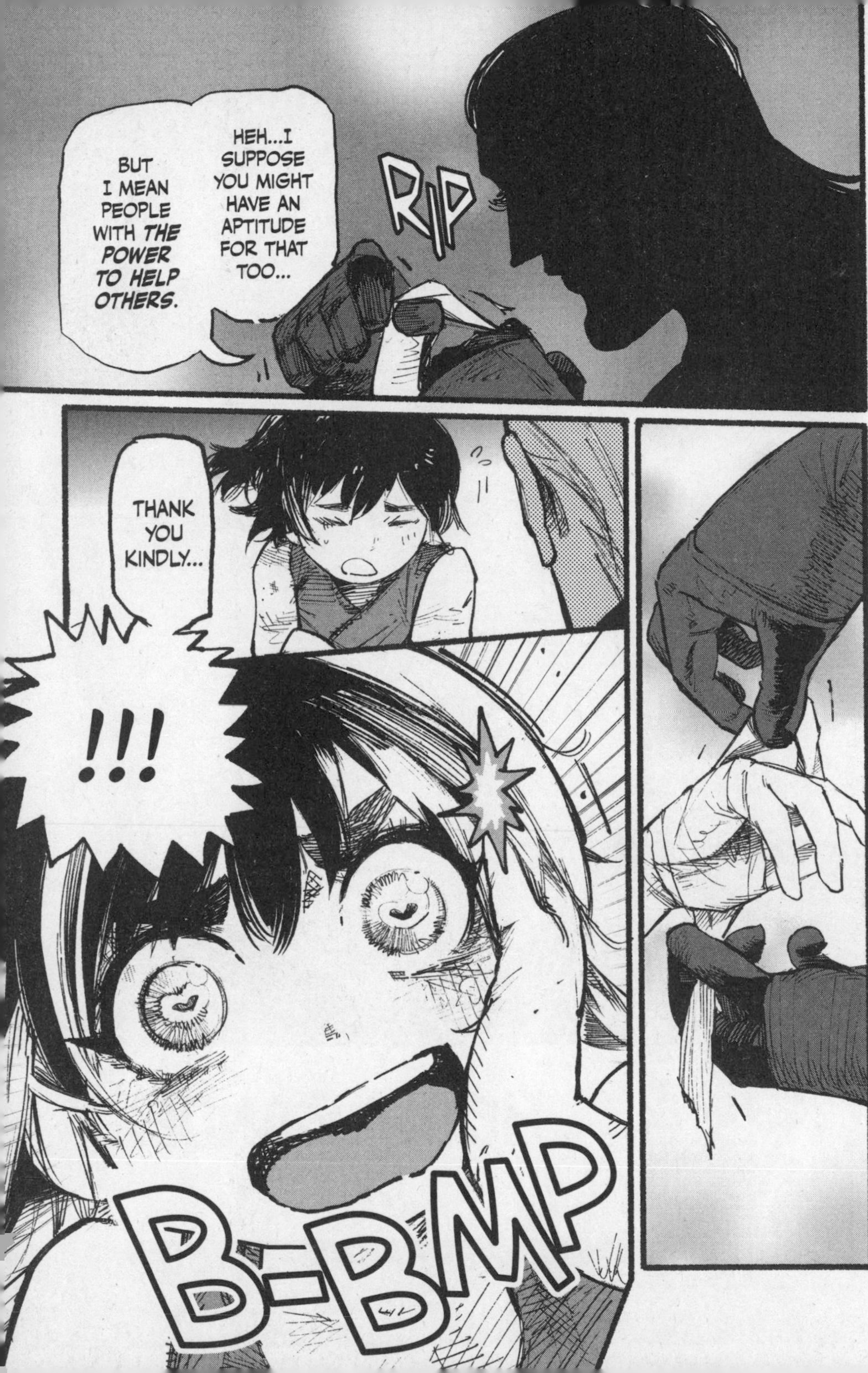
RIP
HEH...I SUPPOSE YOU MIGHT HAVE AN APTITUDE FOR THAT TOO...
BUT I MEAN PEOPLE WITH *THE POWER TO HELP OTHERS.*
THANK YOU KINDLY...
!!!
B-BMP

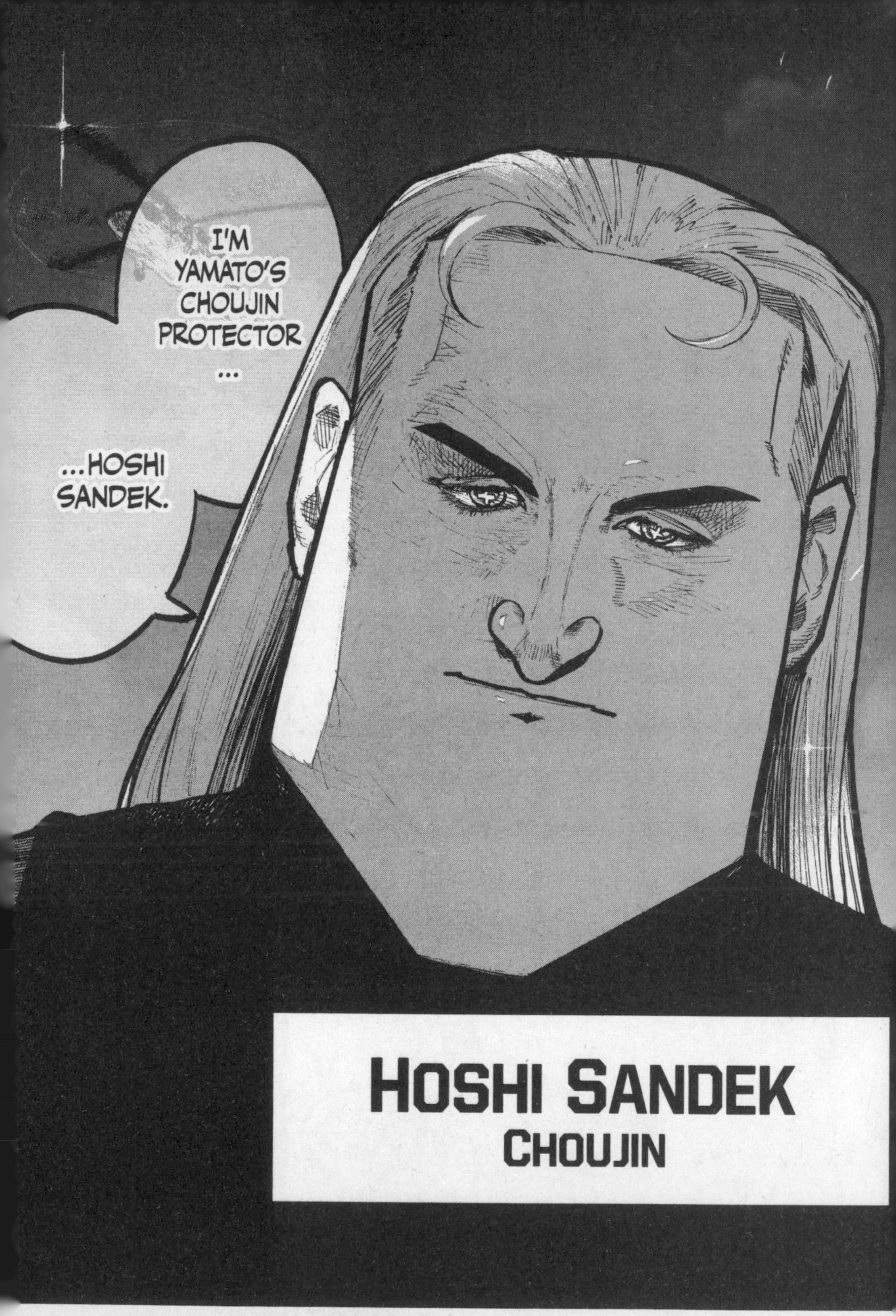
I'M YAMATO'S CHOUJIN PROTECTOR ...
...HOSHI SANDEK.
HOSHI SANDEK
CHOUJIN

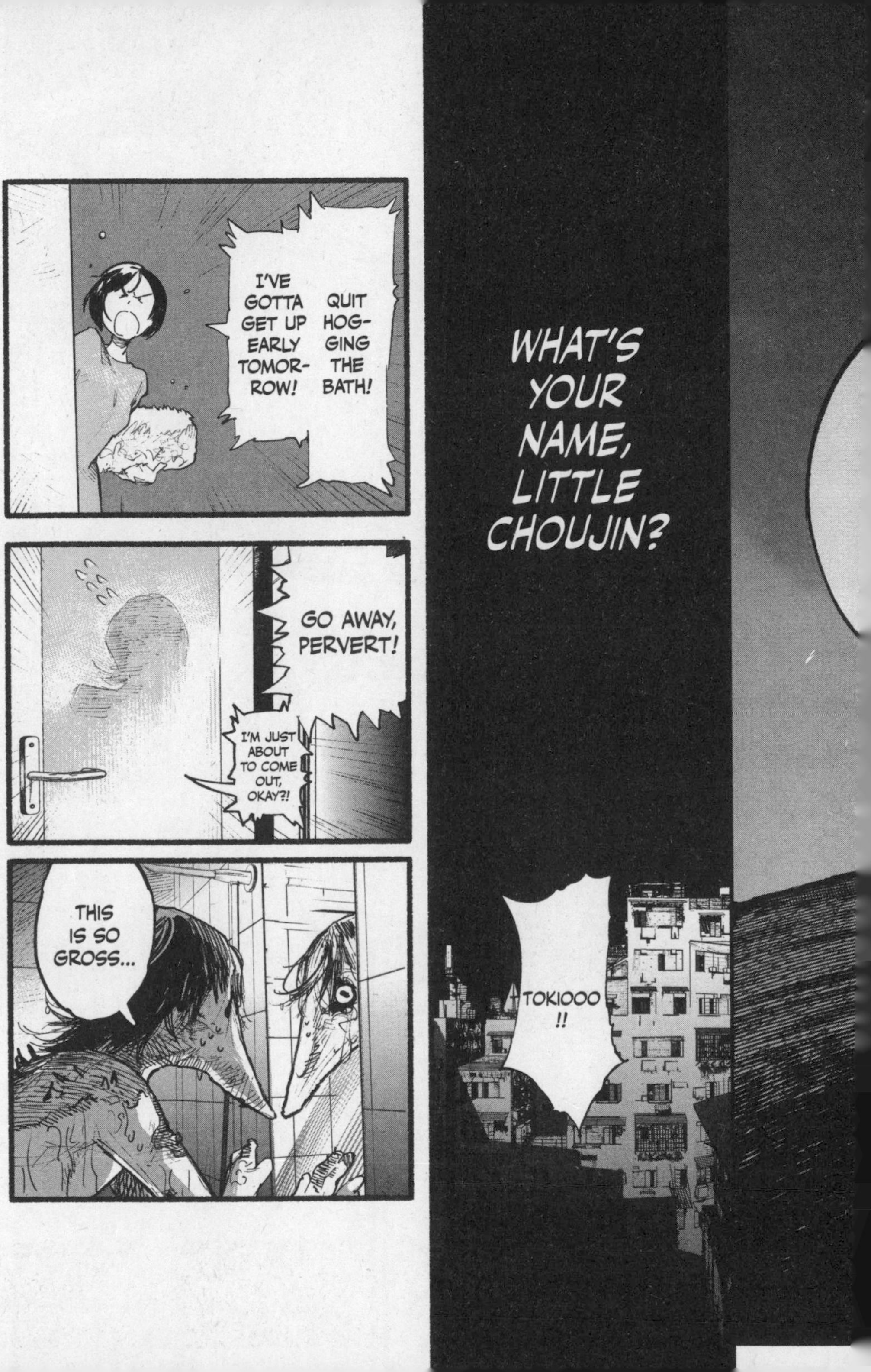
WHAT'S YOUR NAME, LITTLE CHOUJIN?
TOKIOOO !!
QUIT HOG-GING THE BATH!
I'VE GOTTA GET UP EARLY TOMOR-ROW!
GO AWAY, PERVERT!
I'M JUST ABOUT TO COME OUT, OKAY?!
THIS IS SO GROSS...

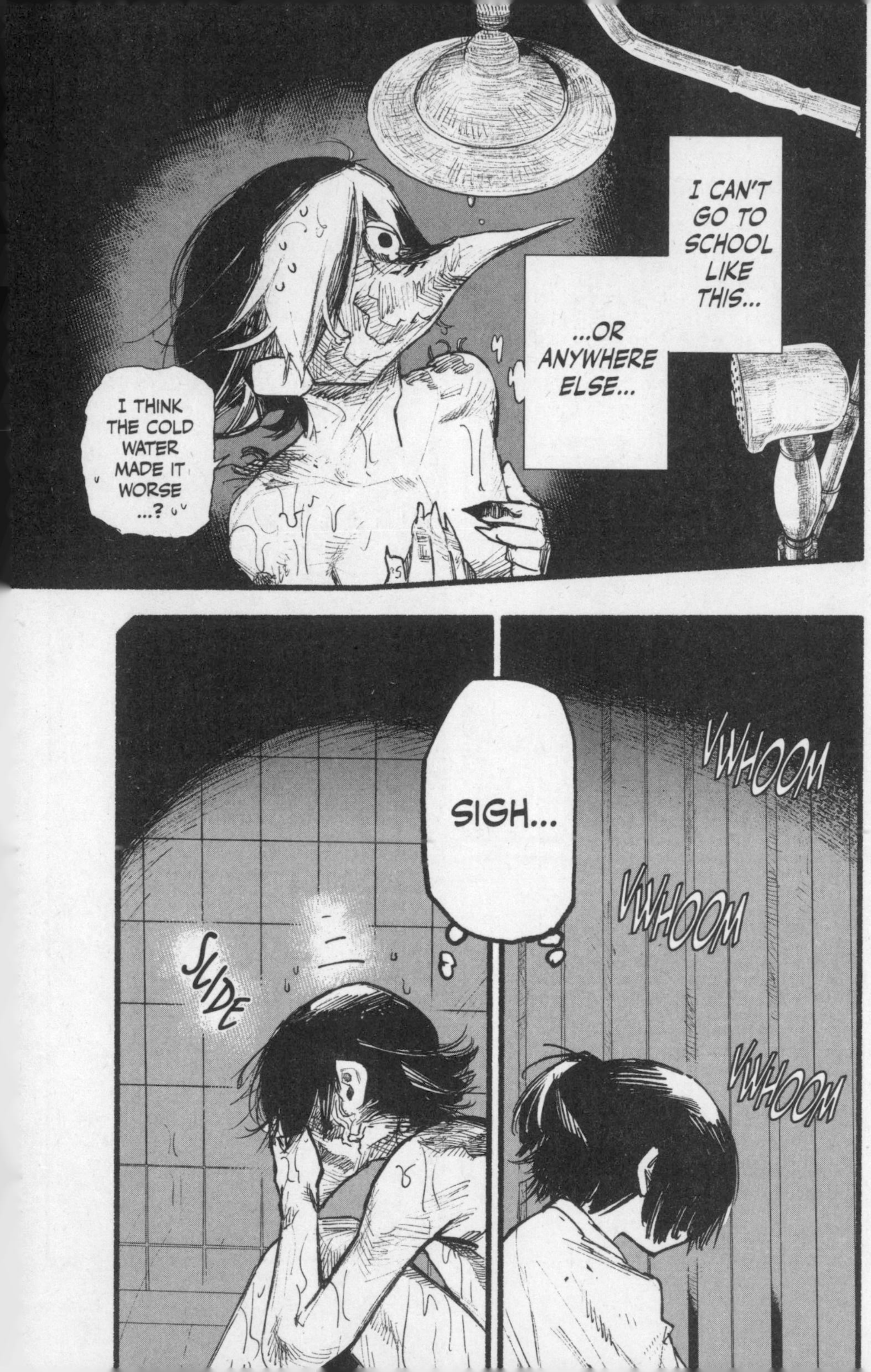
I CAN'T GO TO SCHOOL LIKE THIS...
...OR ANYWHERE ELSE...
I THINK THE COLD WATER MADE IT WORSE ...?
VWHOOM
VWHOOM
VWHOOM
SIGH...
SLIDE

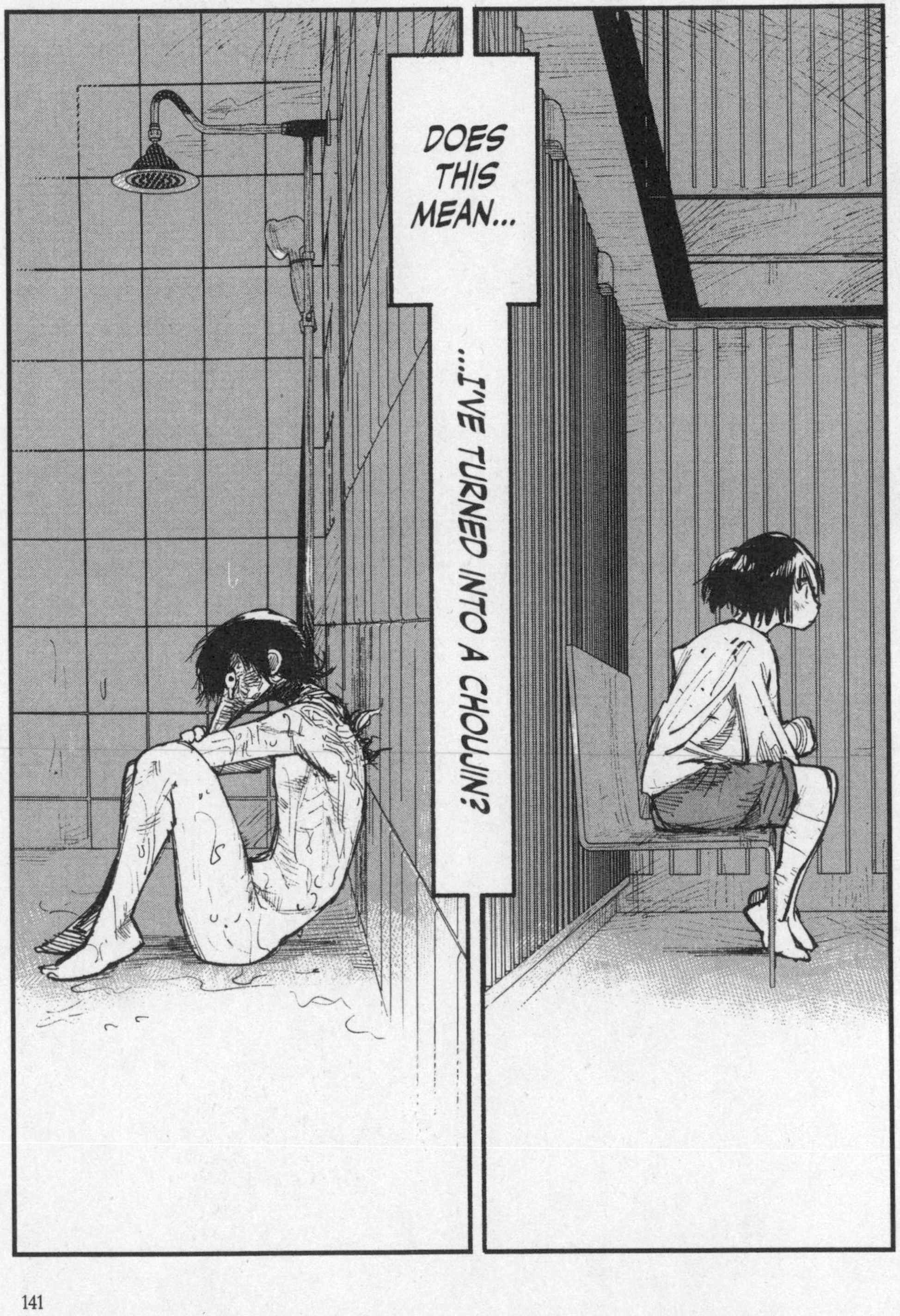
DOES THIS MEAN...
...I'VE TURNED INTO A CHOUJIN?

CHOUJIN X

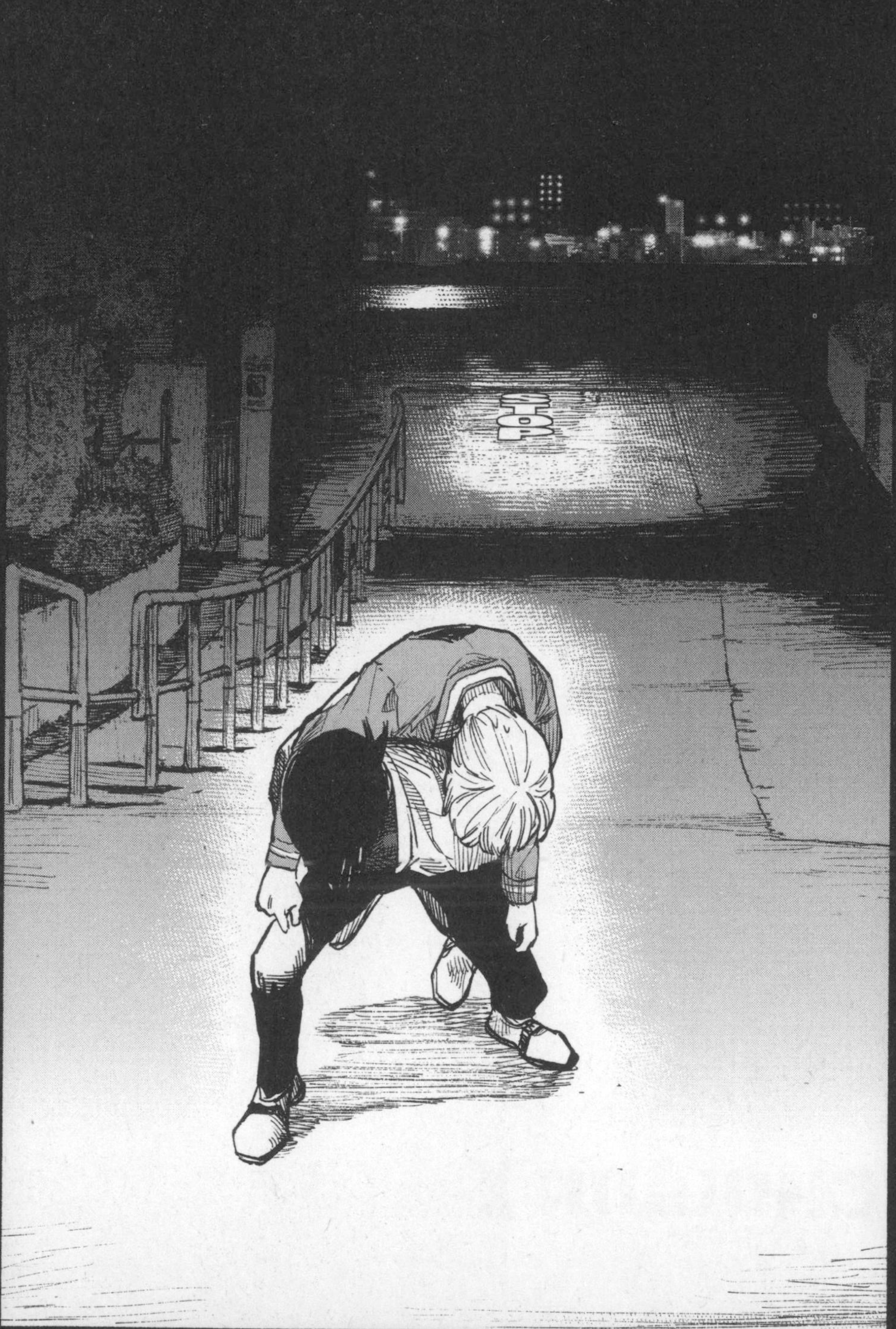
STOP

Chapter 3: stand by the west

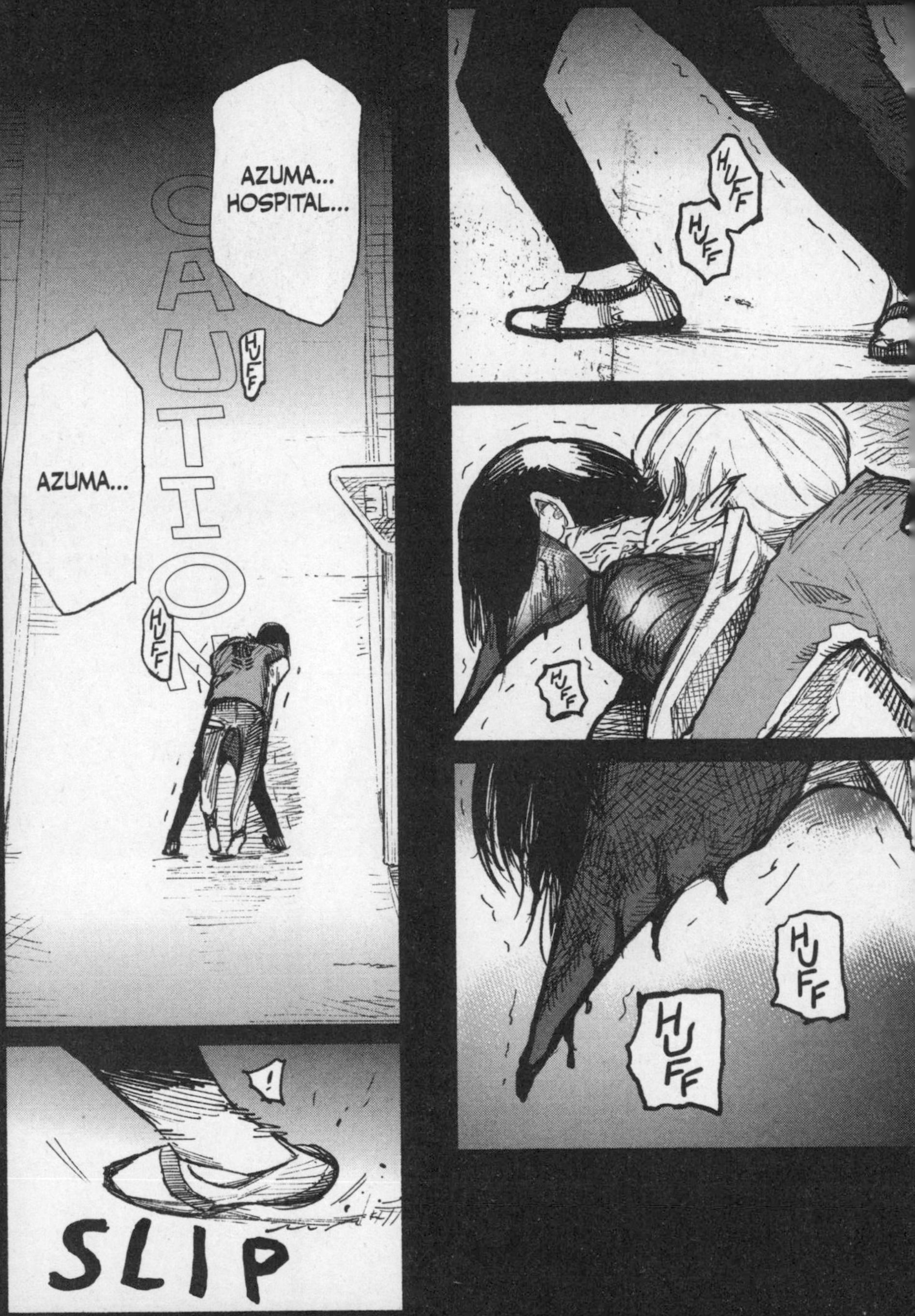
HUFF
HUFF
HUFF
HUFF
HUFF
AZUMA... HOSPITAL...
CAUTION
HUFF
AZUMA...
HUFF
!
SLIP

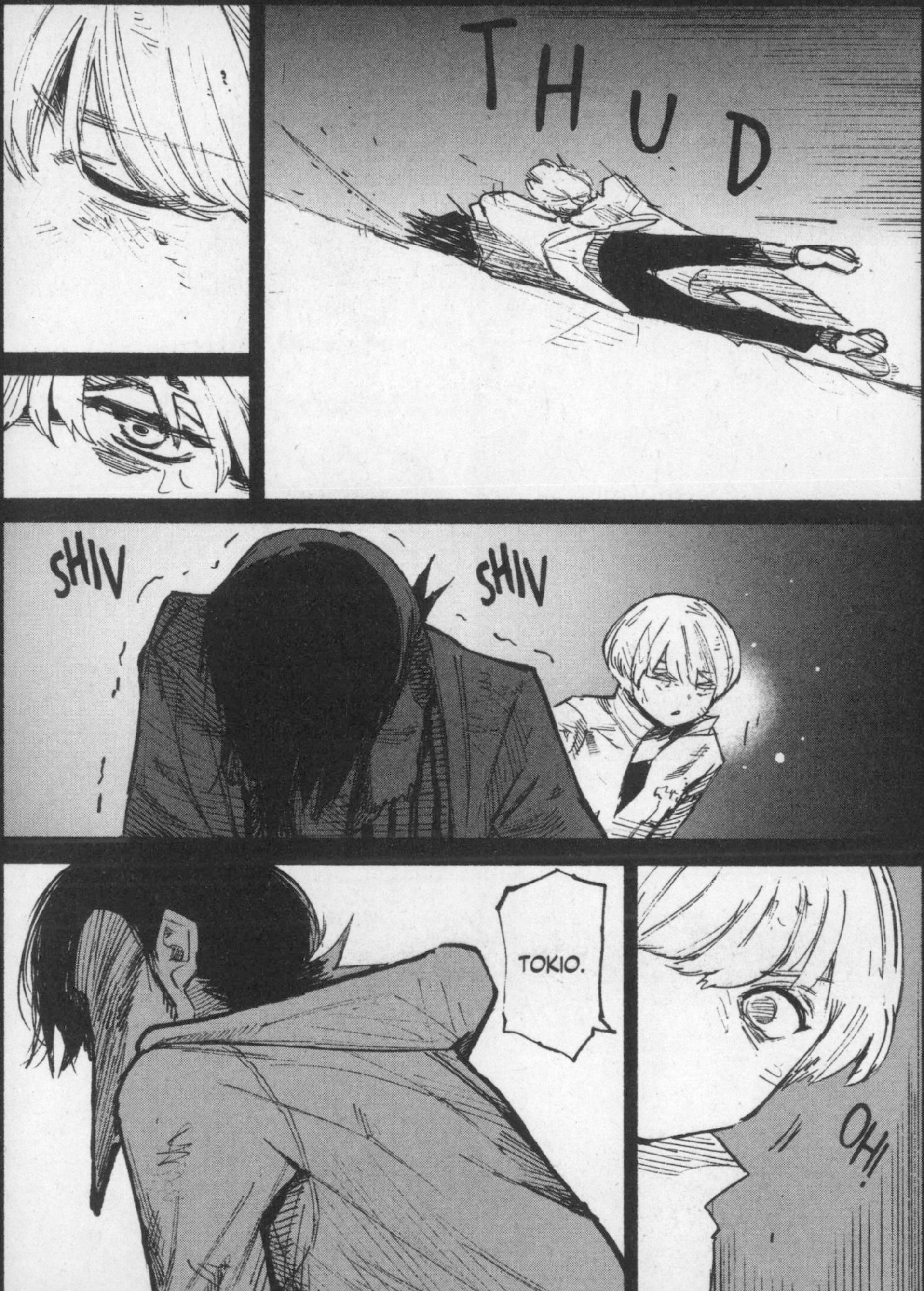
THUD
SHIV
SHIV
OH!
TOKIO.

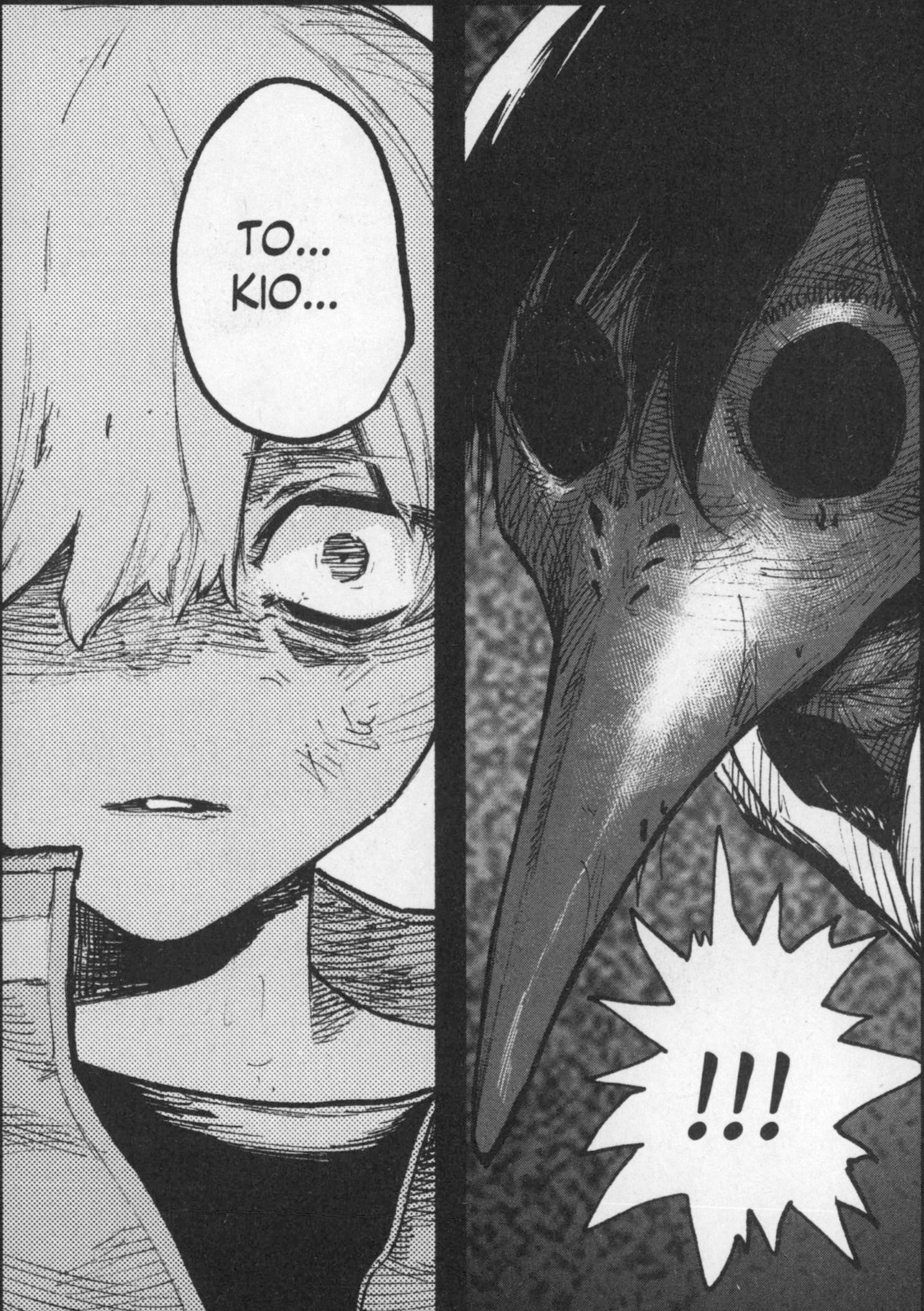
!!!
TO... KIO...

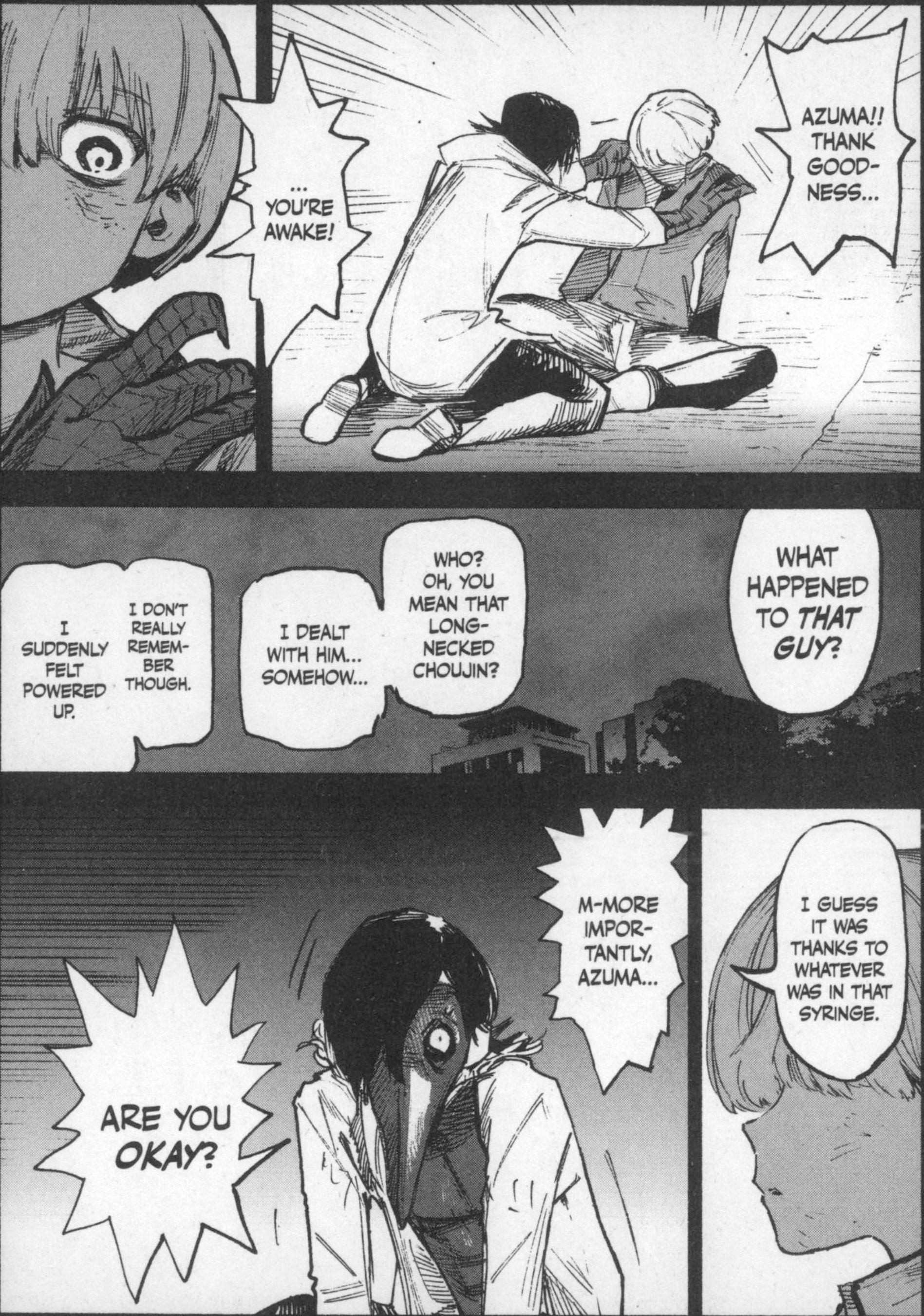
AZUMA!! THANK GOOD-NESS...
... YOU'RE AWAKE!
WHAT HAPPENED TO *THAT* GUY?
WHO? OH, YOU MEAN THAT LONG-NECKED CHOUJIN?
I DEALT WITH HIM... SOMEHOW...
I DON'T REALLY REMEM-BER THOUGH.
I SUDDENLY FELT POWERED UP.
I GUESS IT WAS THANKS TO WHATEVER WAS IN THAT SYRINGE.
M-MORE IMPOR-TANTLY, AZUMA...
ARE YOU *OKAY*?

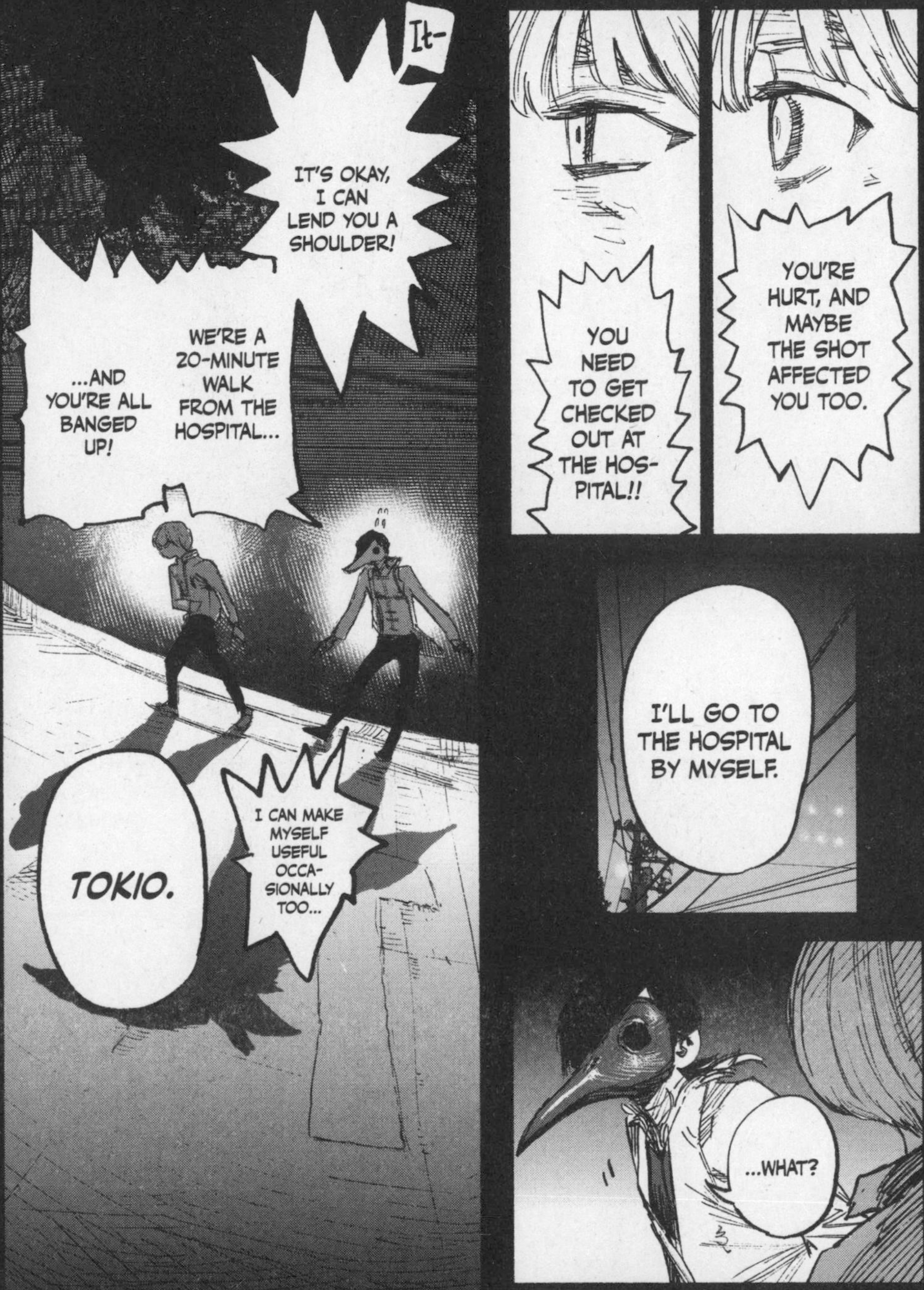
YOU'RE HURT, AND MAYBE THE SHOT AFFECTED YOU TOO.
YOU NEED TO GET CHECKED OUT AT THE HOS-PITAL!!
I'LL GO TO THE HOSPITAL BY MYSELF.
...WHAT?
It-
IT'S OKAY, I CAN LEND YOU A SHOULDER!
WE'RE A 20-MINUTE WALK FROM THE HOSPITAL...
...AND YOU'RE ALL BANGED UP!
I CAN MAKE MYSELF USEFUL OCCA-SIONALLY TOO...
TOKIO.

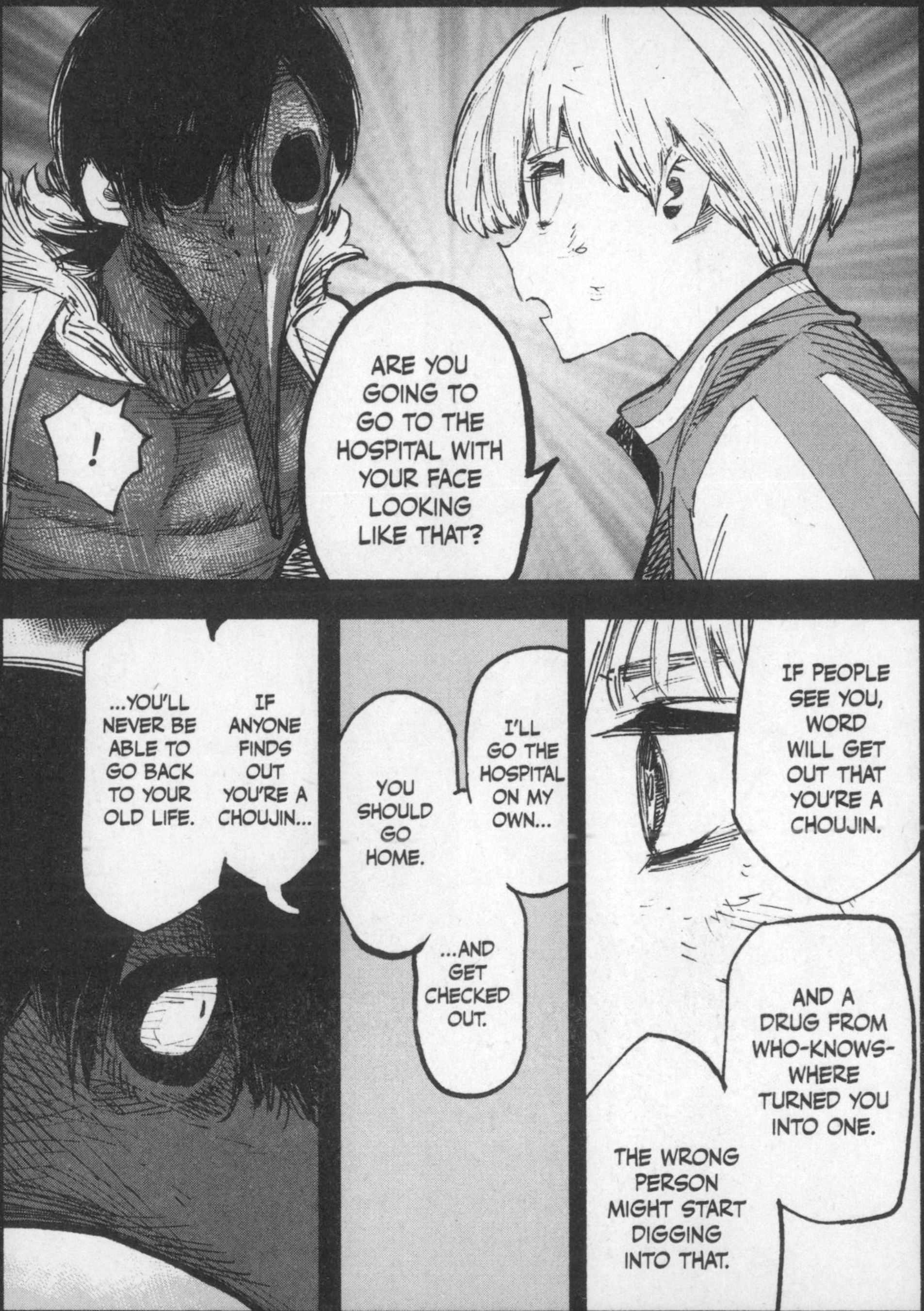
ARE YOU GOING TO GO TO THE HOSPITAL WITH YOUR FACE LOOKING LIKE THAT?
!
IF PEOPLE SEE YOU, WORD WILL GET OUT THAT YOU'RE A CHOUJIN.
AND A DRUG FROM WHO-KNOWS-WHERE TURNED YOU INTO ONE.
THE WRONG PERSON MIGHT START DIGGING INTO THAT.
I'LL GO THE HOSPITAL ON MY OWN...
YOU SHOULD GO HOME.
...AND GET CHECKED OUT.
IF ANYONE FINDS OUT YOU'RE A CHOUJIN...
...YOU'LL NEVER BE ABLE TO GO BACK TO YOUR OLD LIFE.

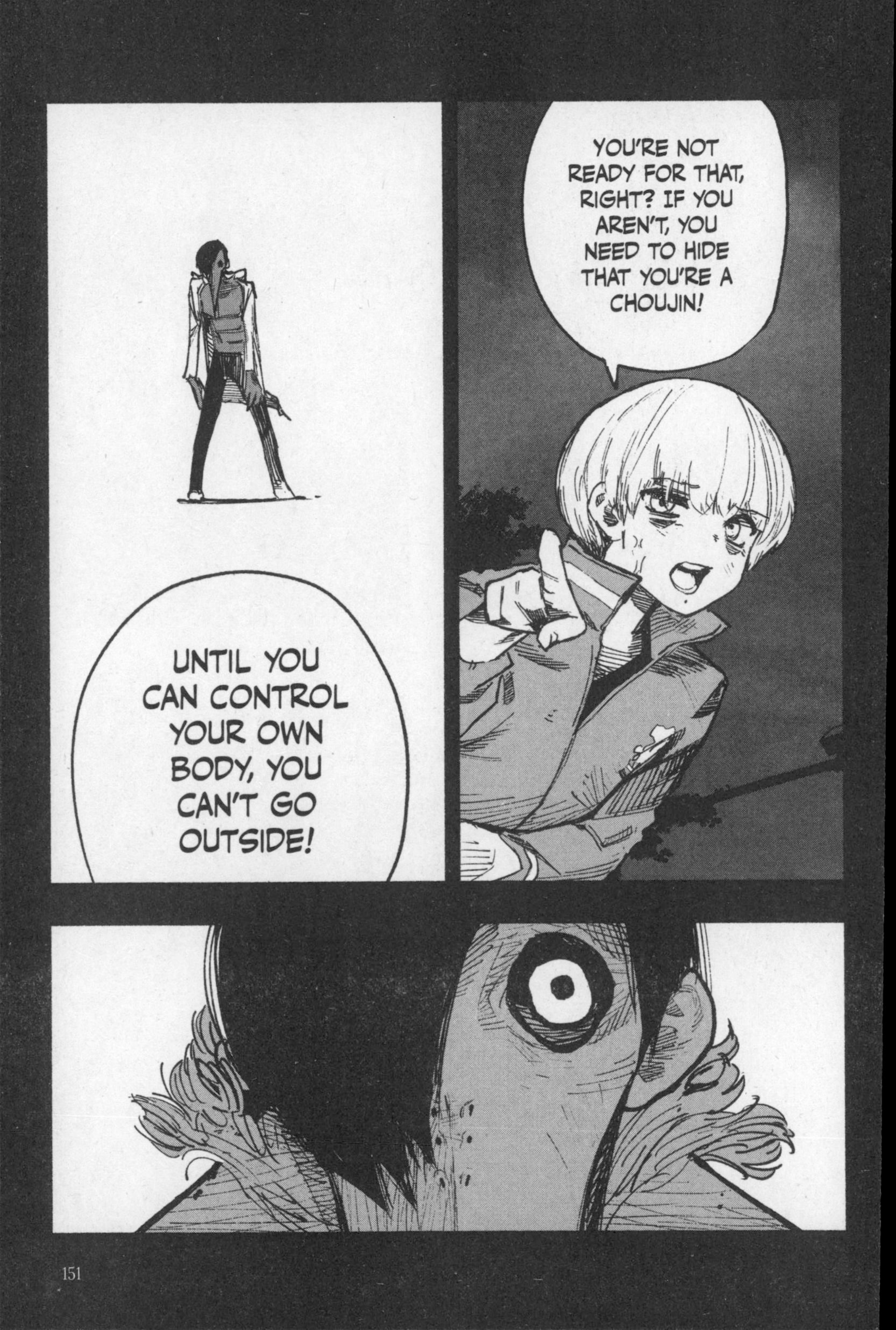
YOU'RE NOT READY FOR THAT, RIGHT? IF YOU AREN'T, YOU NEED TO HIDE THAT YOU'RE A CHOUJIN!
UNTIL YOU CAN CONTROL YOUR OWN BODY, YOU CAN'T GO OUTSIDE!

Chapter 3: stand by the west

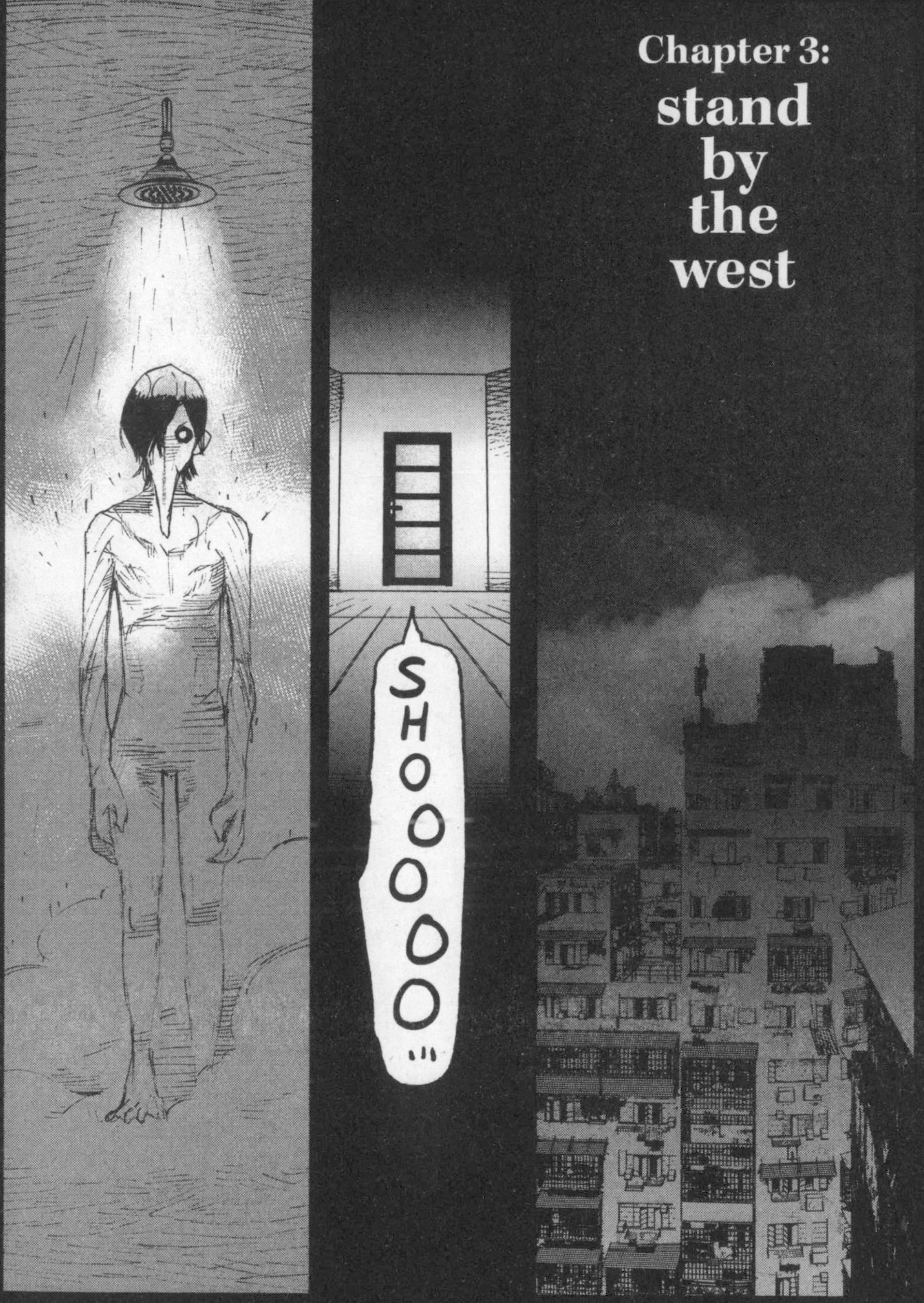
SHOOOOO...

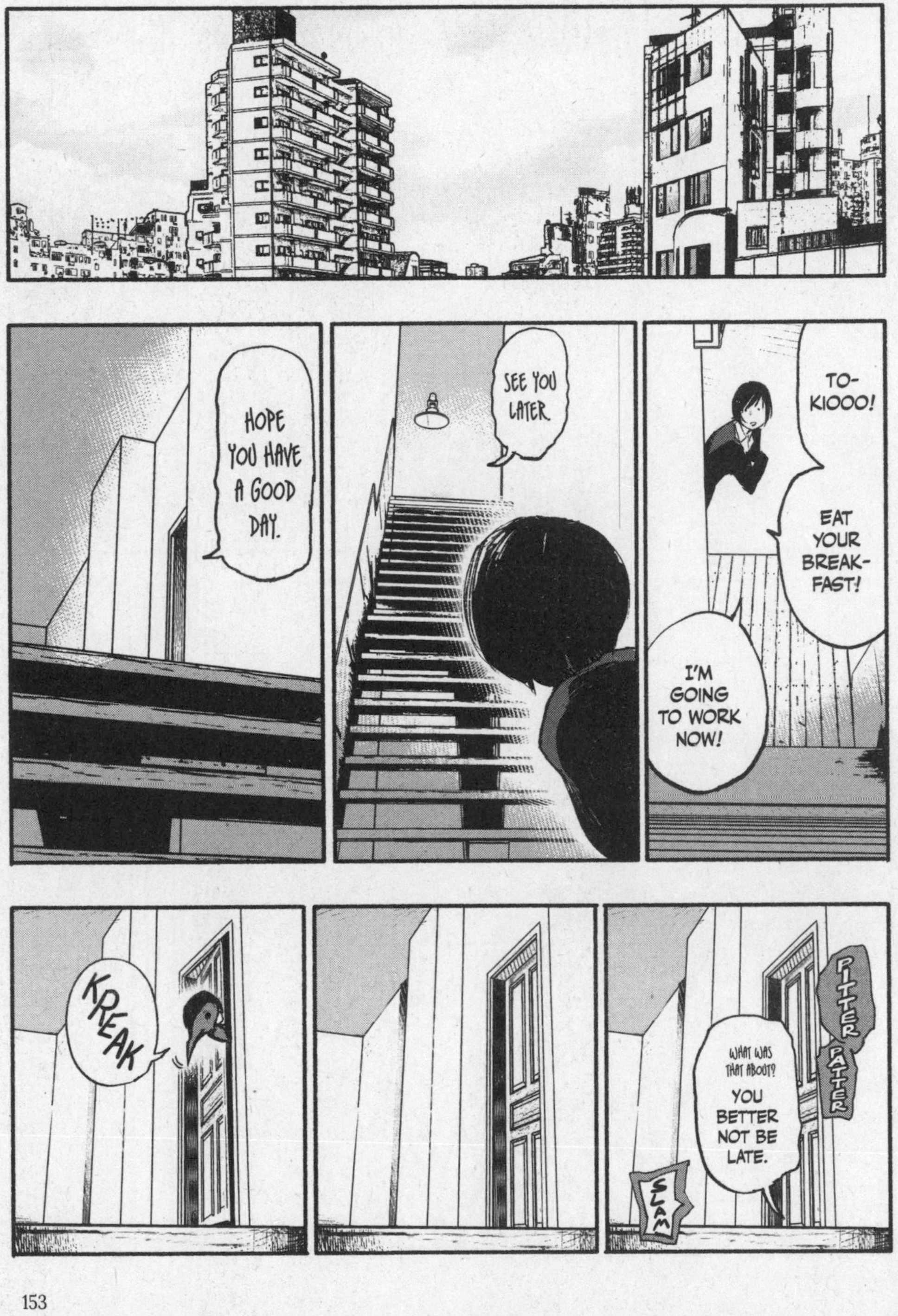
TO-KIOOO!
EAT YOUR BREAK-FAST!
I'M GOING TO WORK NOW!
SEE YOU LATER.
HOPE YOU HAVE A GOOD DAY.
PITTER PATTER
WHAT WAS THAT ABOUT? YOU BETTER NOT BE LATE.
SLAM
KREAK

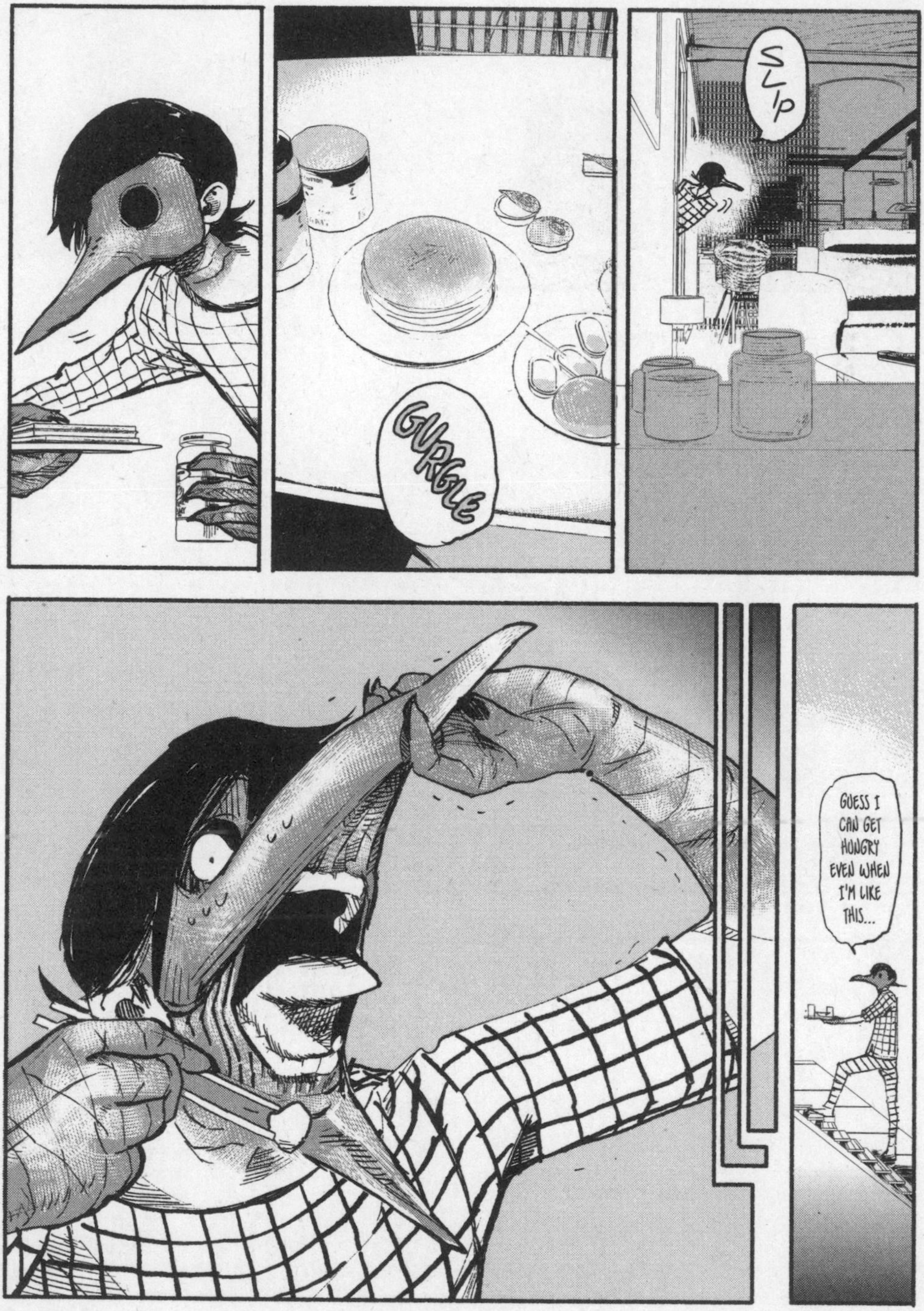
SLIP
GURGLE
GUESS I CAN GET HUNGRY EVEN WHEN I'M LIKE THIS...

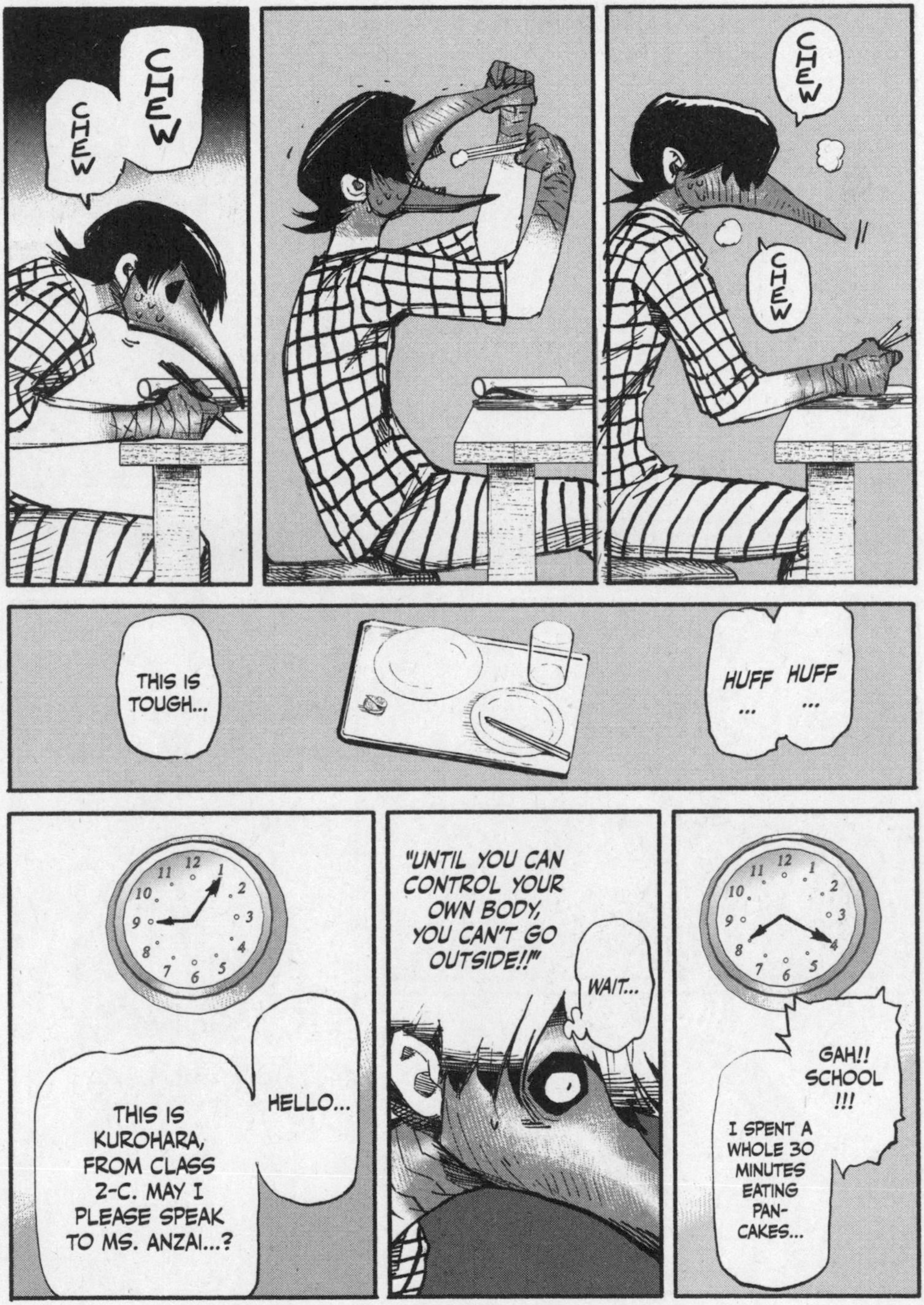
CHEW
CHEW
CHEW
CHEW
HUFF ... HUFF ...
THIS IS TOUGH...
GAH!! SCHOOL !!!
I SPENT A WHOLE 30 MINUTES EATING PAN-CAKES...
"UNTIL YOU CAN CONTROL YOUR OWN BODY, YOU CAN'T GO OUTSIDE!!"
WAIT...
HELLO...
THIS IS KUROHARA, FROM CLASS 2-C. MAY I PLEASE SPEAK TO MS. ANZAI...?

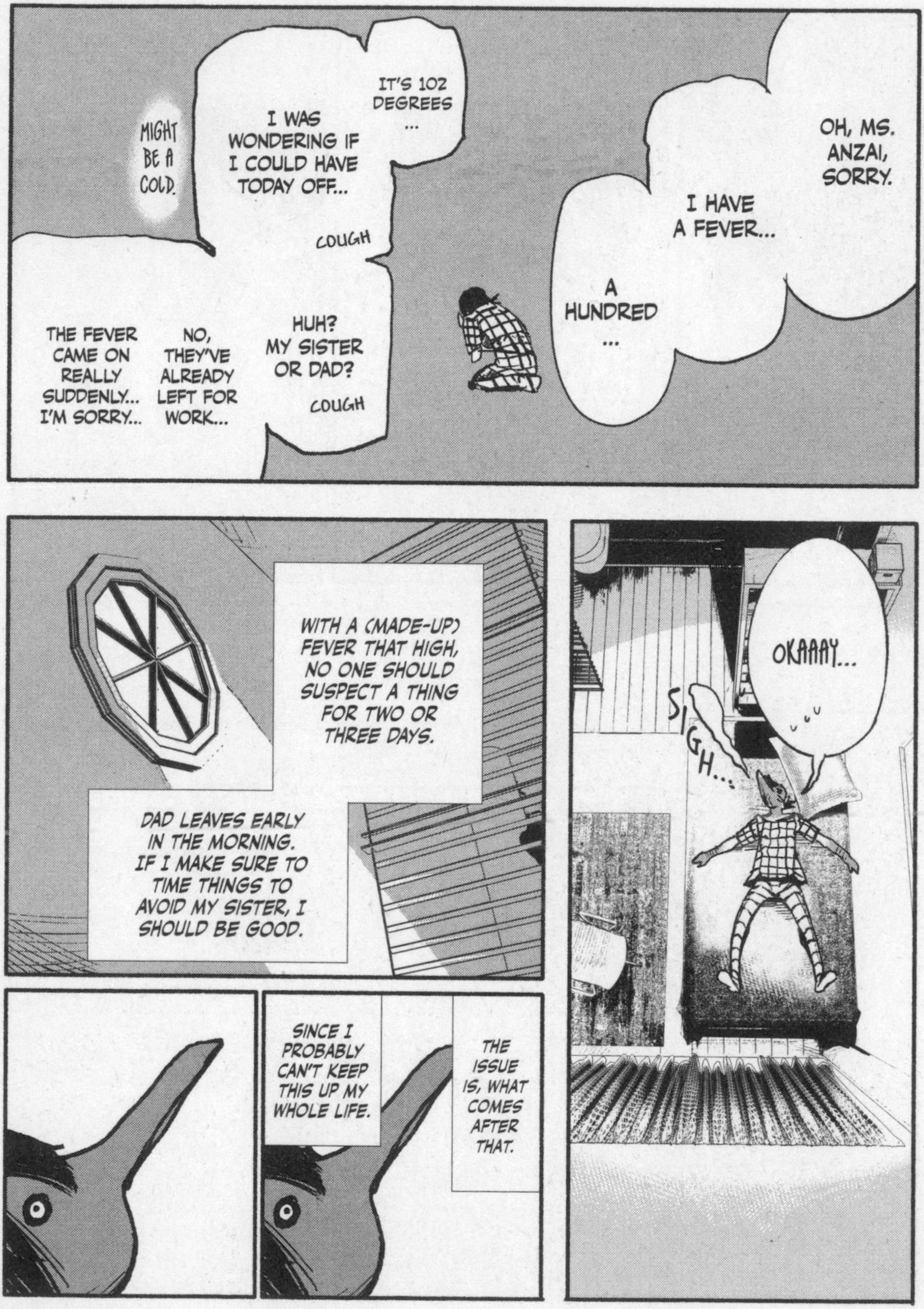
OH, MS. ANZAI, SORRY.
I HAVE A FEVER...
A HUNDRED ...
IT'S 102 DEGREES ...
I WAS WONDERING IF I COULD HAVE TODAY OFF...
MIGHT BE A COLD.
COUGH
HUH? MY SISTER OR DAD?
COUGH
NO, THEY'VE ALREADY LEFT FOR WORK...
THE FEVER CAME ON REALLY SUDDENLY... I'M SORRY...
OKAAAY...
SIGH...
WITH A (MADE-UP) FEVER THAT HIGH, NO ONE SHOULD SUSPECT A THING FOR TWO OR THREE DAYS.
DAD LEAVES EARLY IN THE MORNING. IF I MAKE SURE TO TIME THINGS TO AVOID MY SISTER, I SHOULD BE GOOD.
THE ISSUE IS, WHAT COMES AFTER THAT.
SINCE I PROBABLY CAN'T KEEP THIS UP MY WHOLE LIFE.

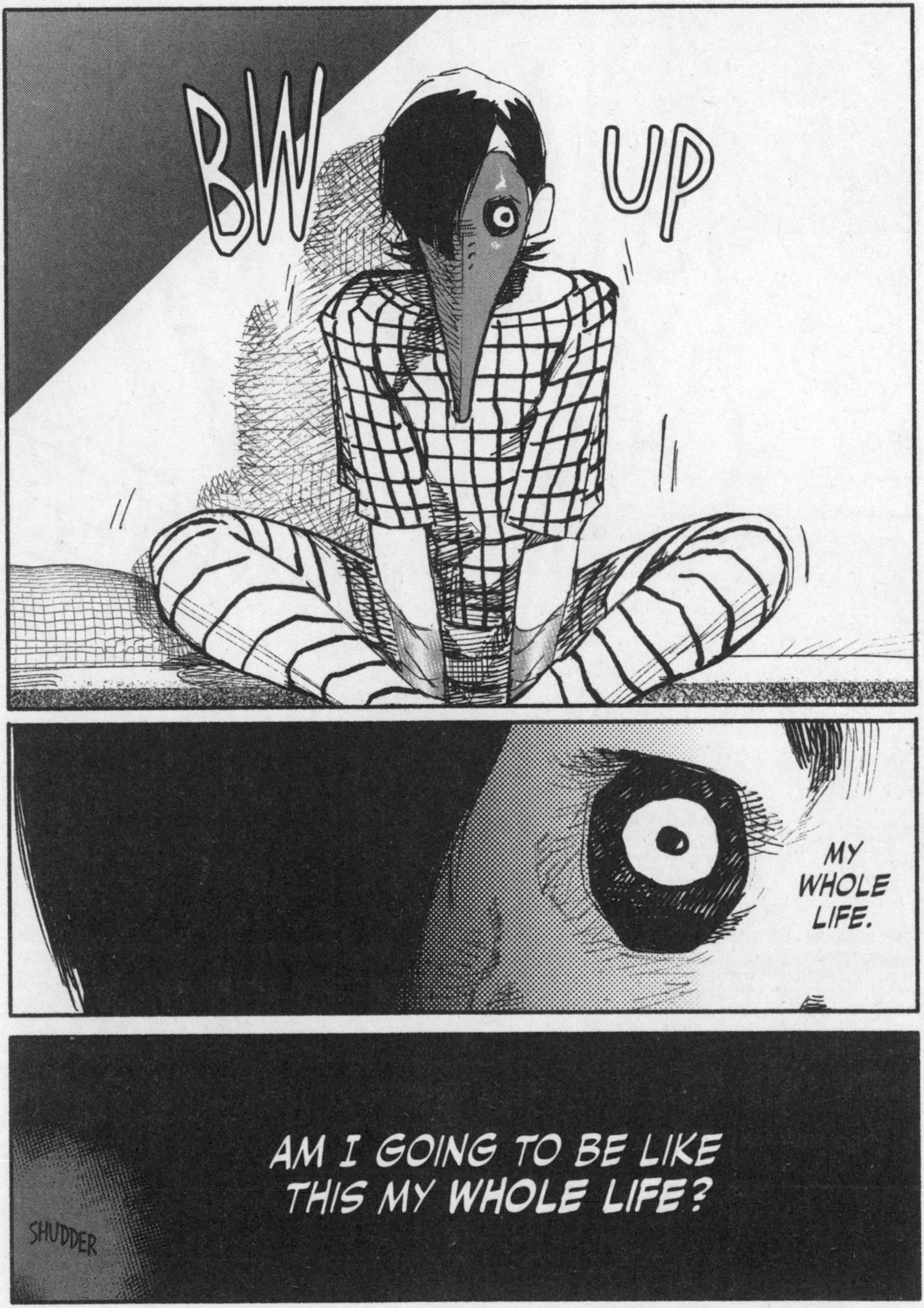
BW
UP
MY WHOLE LIFE.
AM I GOING TO BE LIKE THIS MY WHOLE LIFE?
SHUDDER

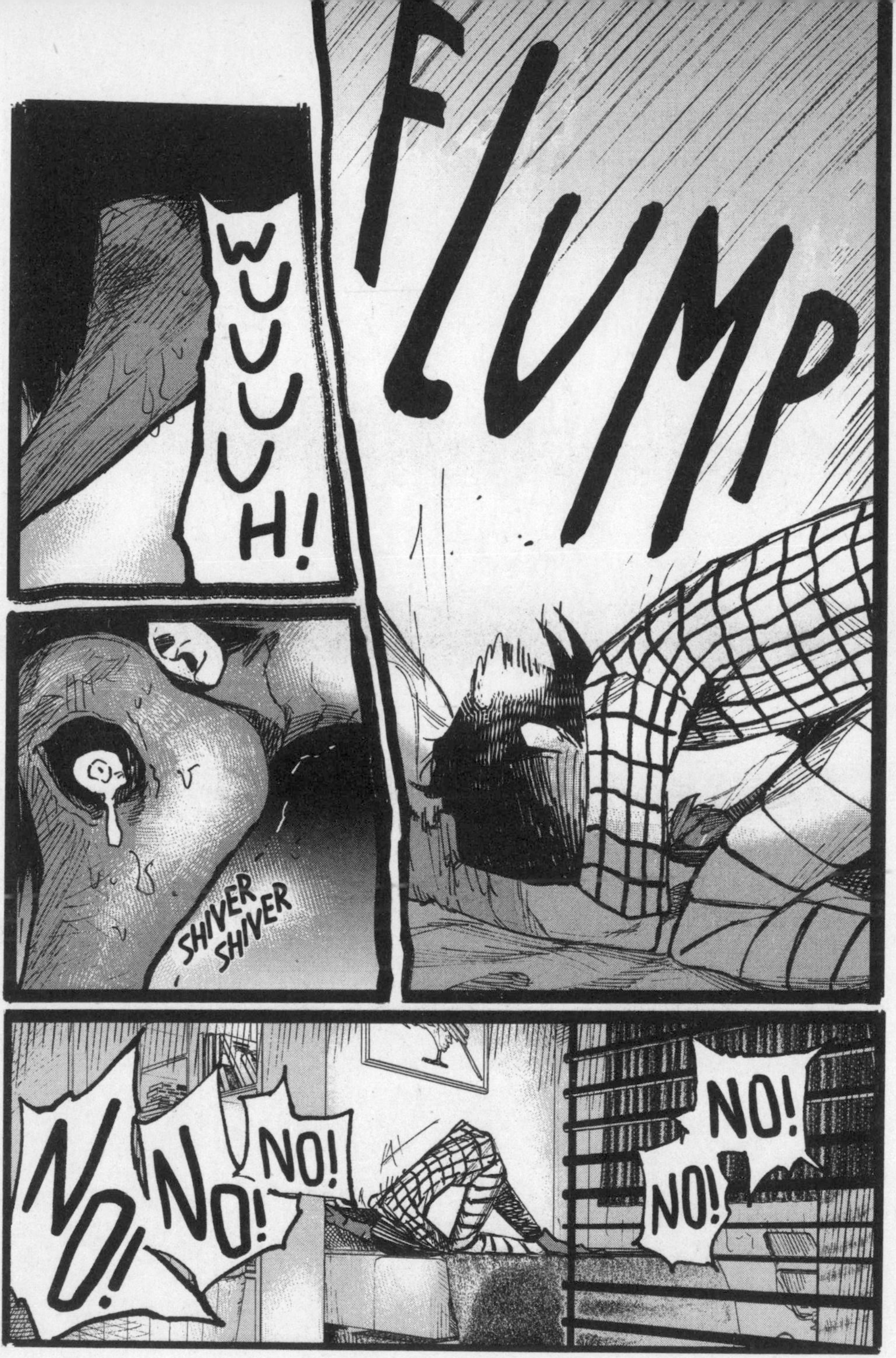
FLUMP
WUUUUUH!
SHIVER SHIVER
NO!
NO!
NO!
NO NO!
NO!

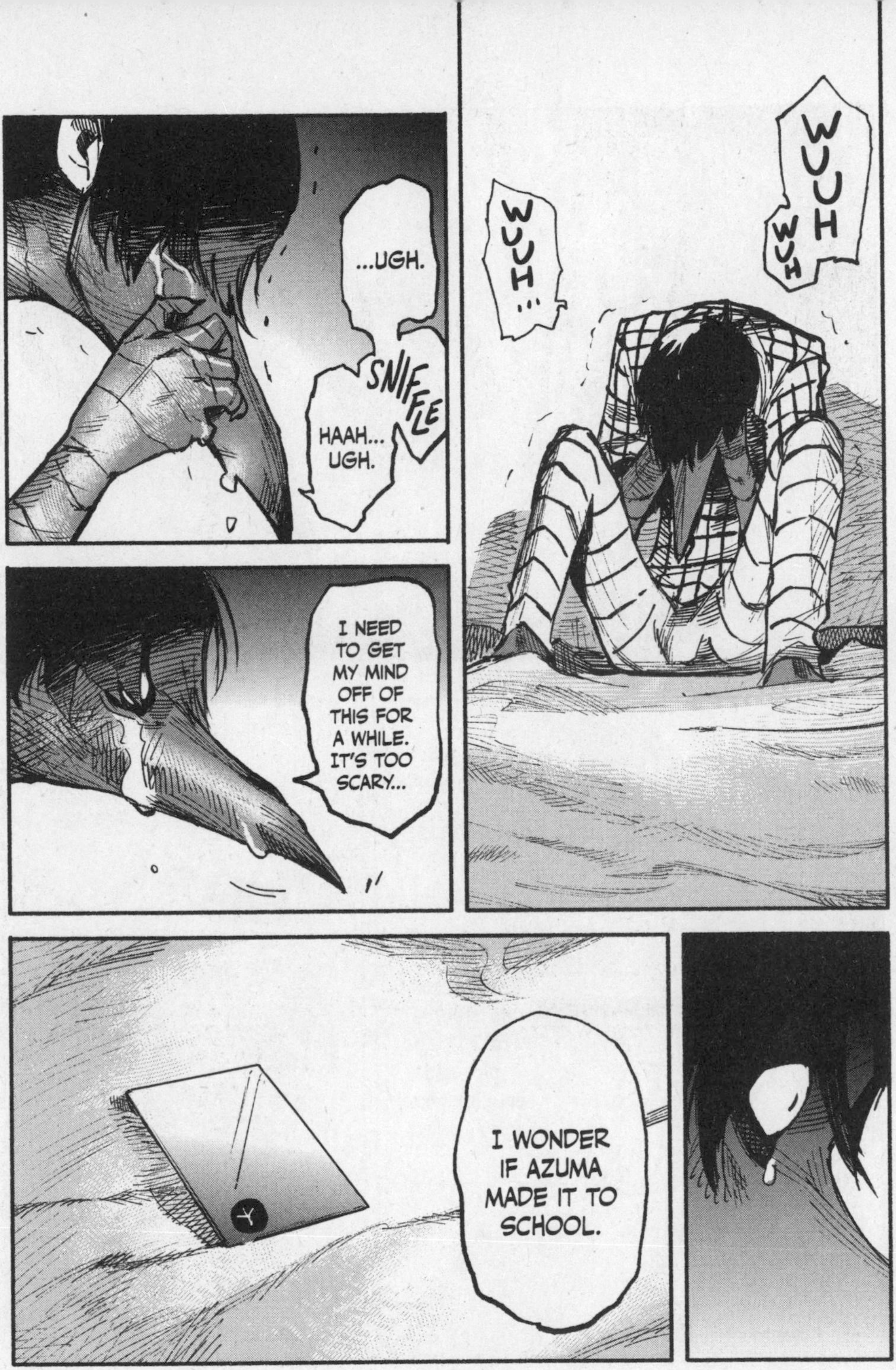
WUUH
WUH
WUUH...
...UGH.
SNIFFLE
HAAH... UGH.
I NEED TO GET MY MIND OFF OF THIS FOR A WHILE. IT'S TOO SCARY...
I WONDER IF AZUMA MADE IT TO SCHOOL.

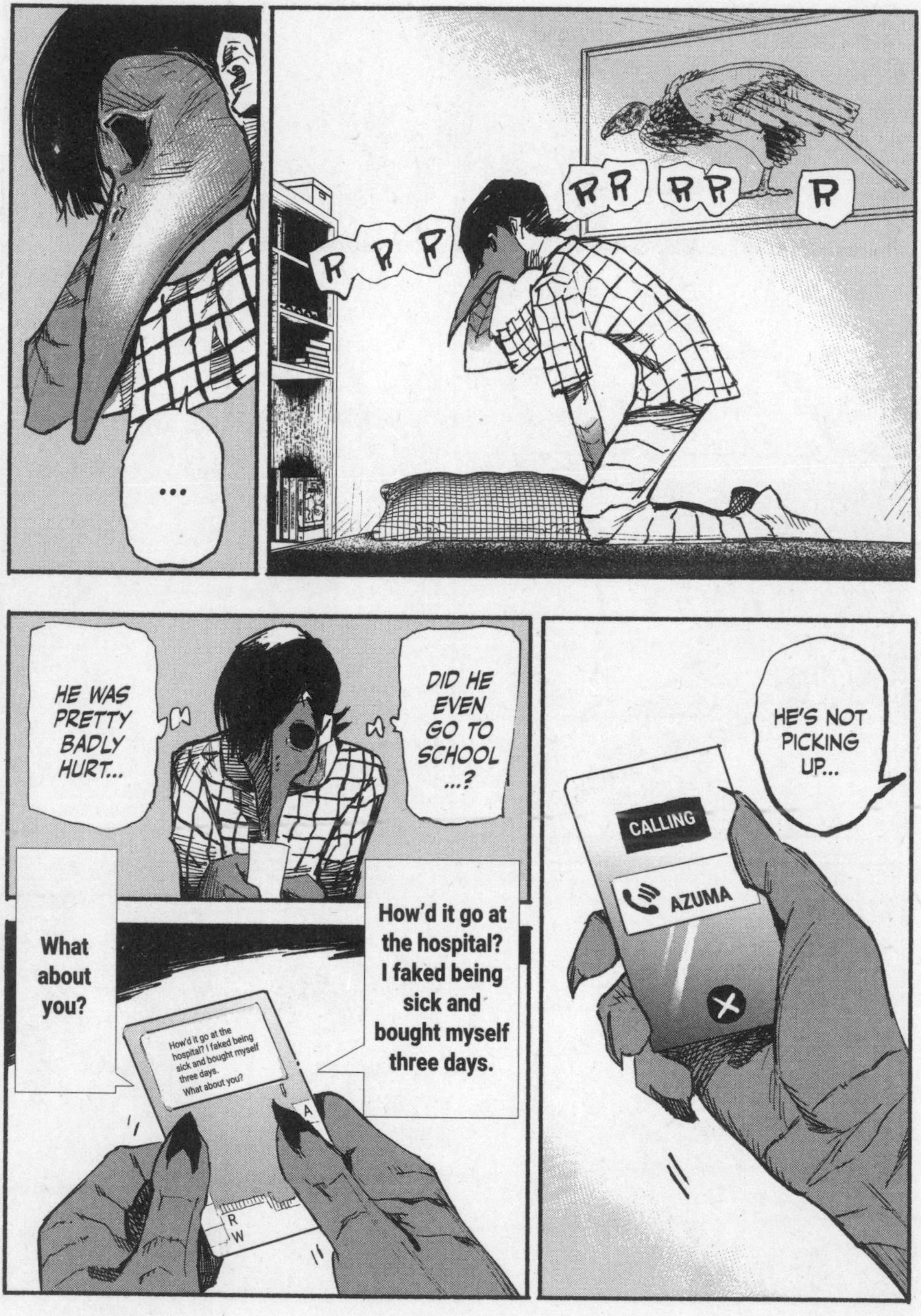
R
RR
RR
RRR
...
HE'S NOT PICKING UP...
CALLING
AZUMA
DID HE EVEN GO TO SCHOOL ...?
HE WAS PRETTY BADLY HURT...
How'd it go at the hospital? I faked being sick and bought myself three days.
How'd it go at the hospital? I faked being sick and bought myself three days. What about you?
What about you?

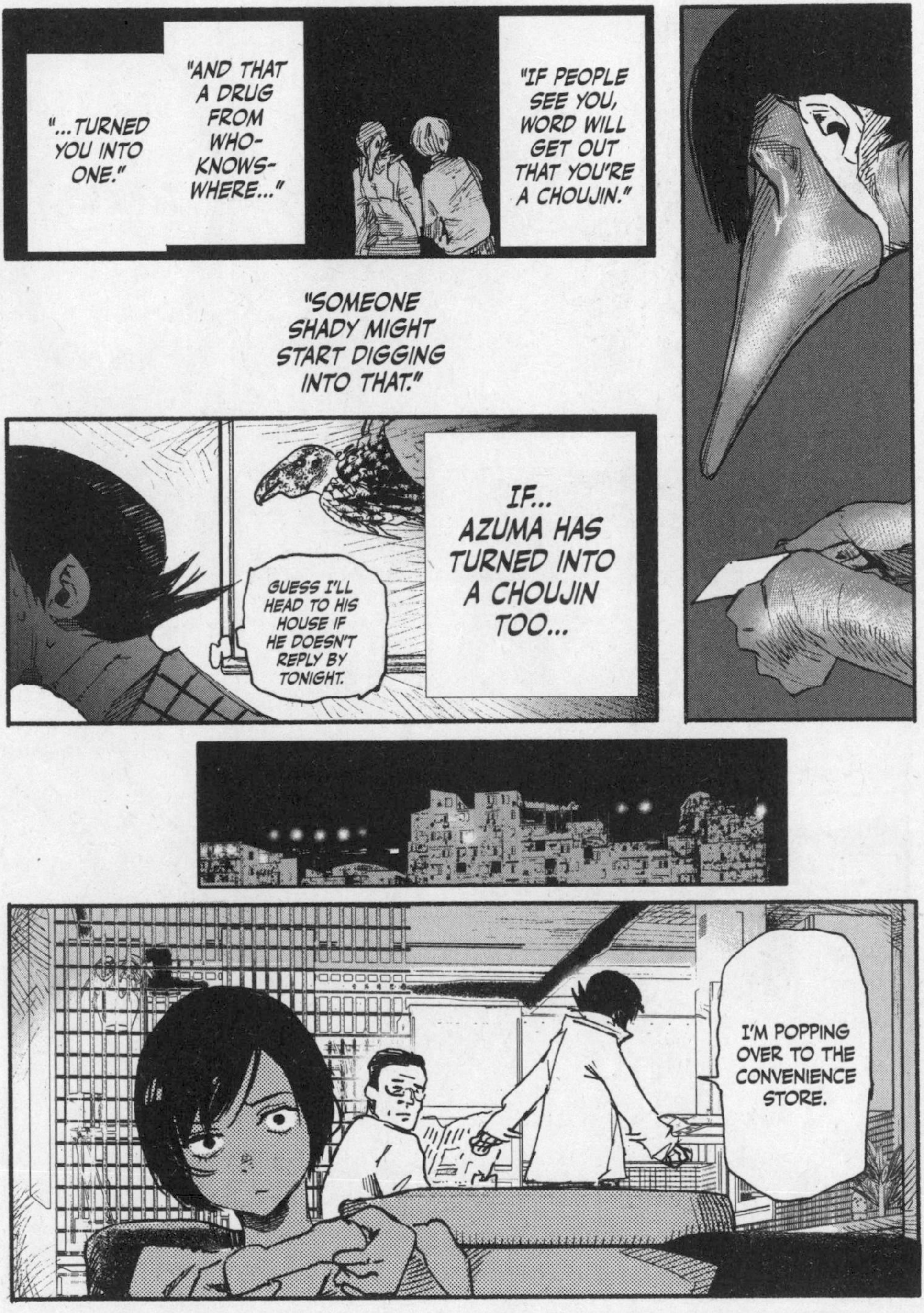

"IF PEOPLE SEE YOU, WORD WILL GET OUT THAT YOU'RE A CHOUJIN."
"AND THAT A DRUG FROM WHO-KNOWS-WHERE..."
"...TURNED YOU INTO ONE."
"SOMEONE SHADY MIGHT START DIGGING INTO THAT."
IF... AZUMA HAS TURNED INTO A CHOUJIN TOO...
GUESS I'LL HEAD TO HIS HOUSE IF HE DOESN'T REPLY BY TONIGHT.
I'M POPPING OVER TO THE CONVENIENCE STORE.

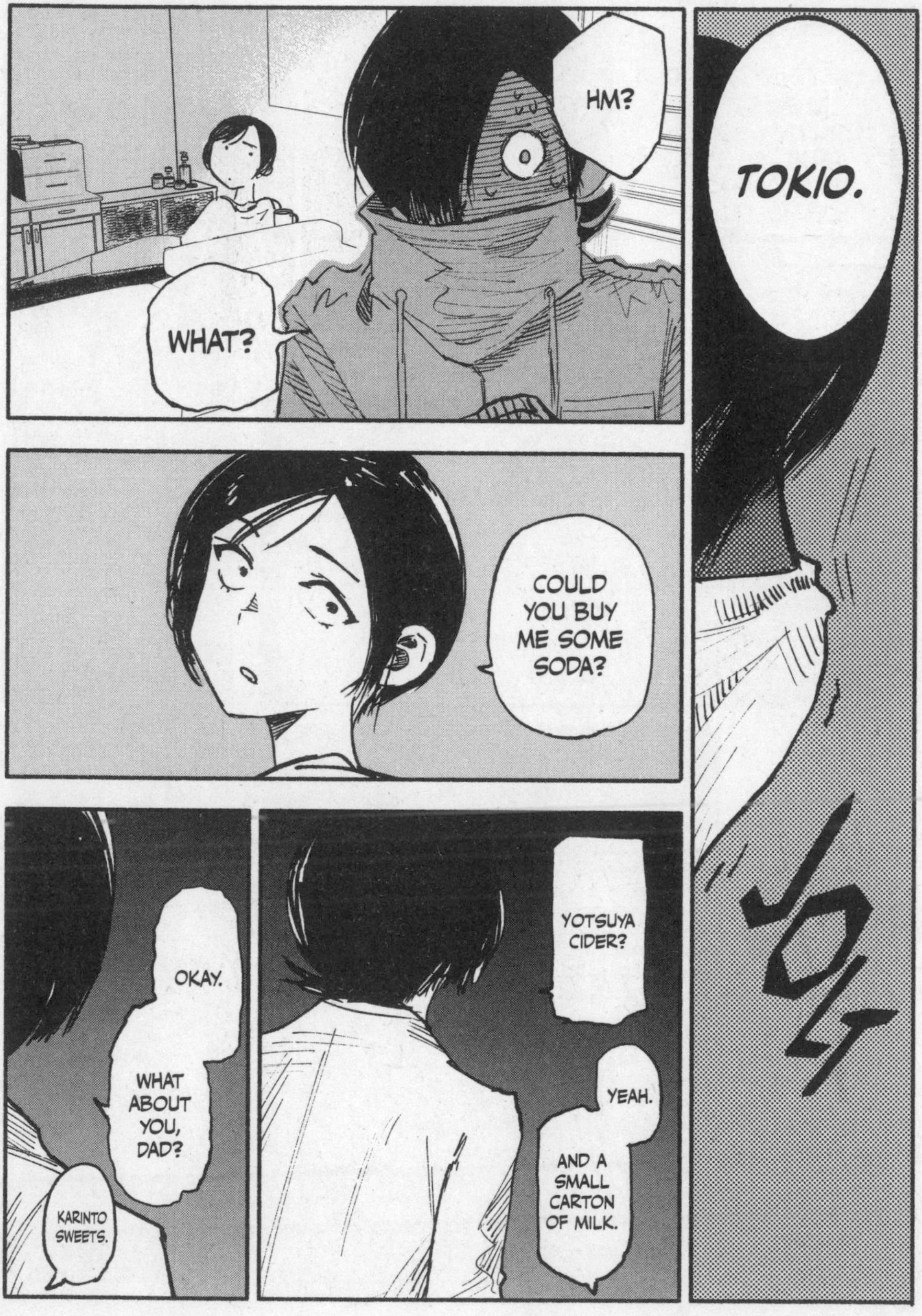
TOKIO.
JOLT
HM?
WHAT?
COULD YOU BUY ME SOME SODA?
YOTSUYA CIDER?
YEAH.
AND A SMALL CARTON OF MILK.
OKAY.
WHAT ABOUT YOU, DAD?
KARINTO SWEETS.

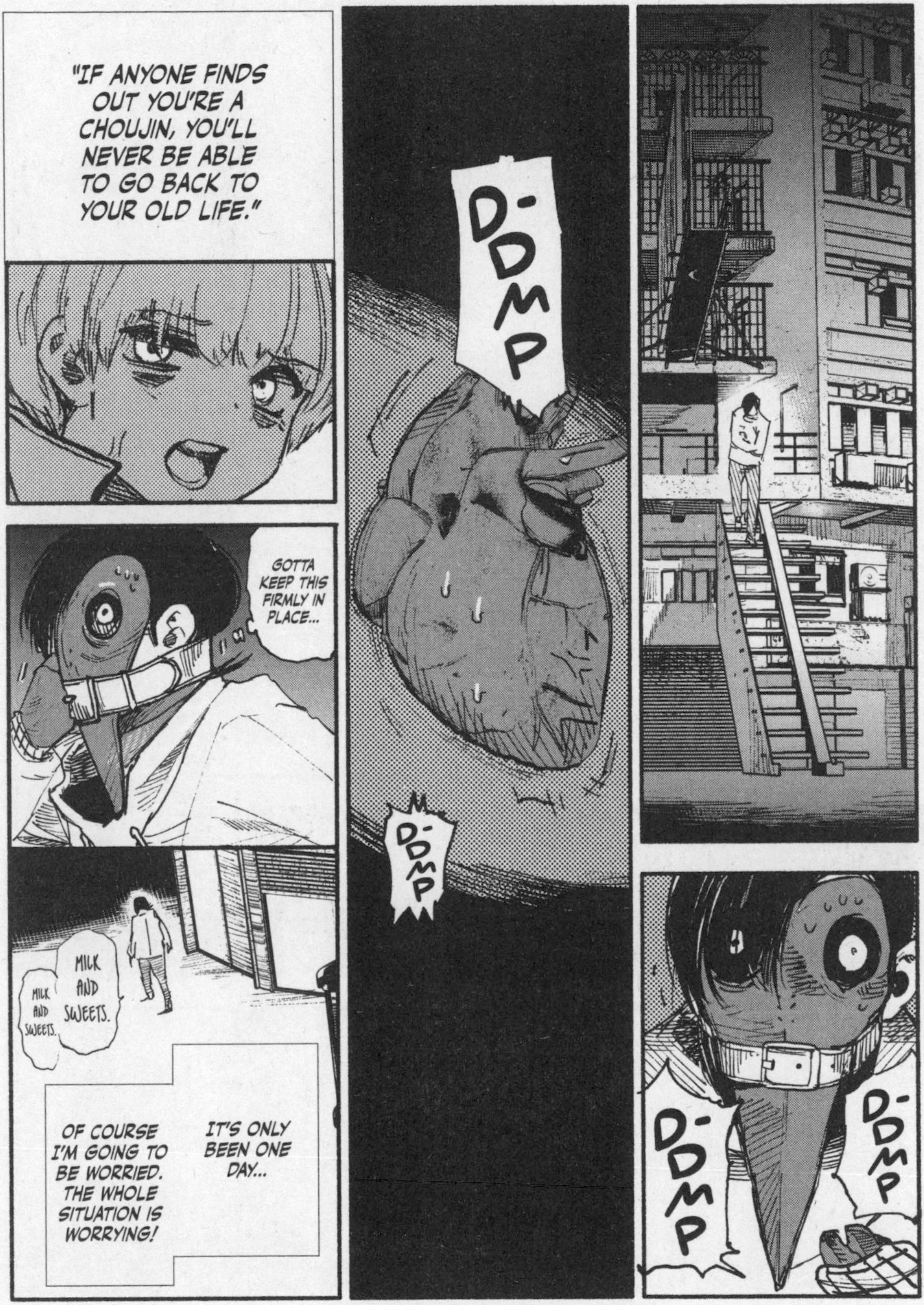
D-DMP
D-DMP
D-DMP
D-DMP
"IF ANYONE FINDS OUT YOU'RE A CHOUJIN, YOU'LL NEVER BE ABLE TO GO BACK TO YOUR OLD LIFE."
GOTTA KEEP THIS FIRMLY IN PLACE...
MILK AND SWEETS.
MILK AND SWEETS.
IT'S ONLY BEEN ONE DAY...
OF COURSE I'M GOING TO BE WORRIED. THE WHOLE SITUATION IS WORRYING!

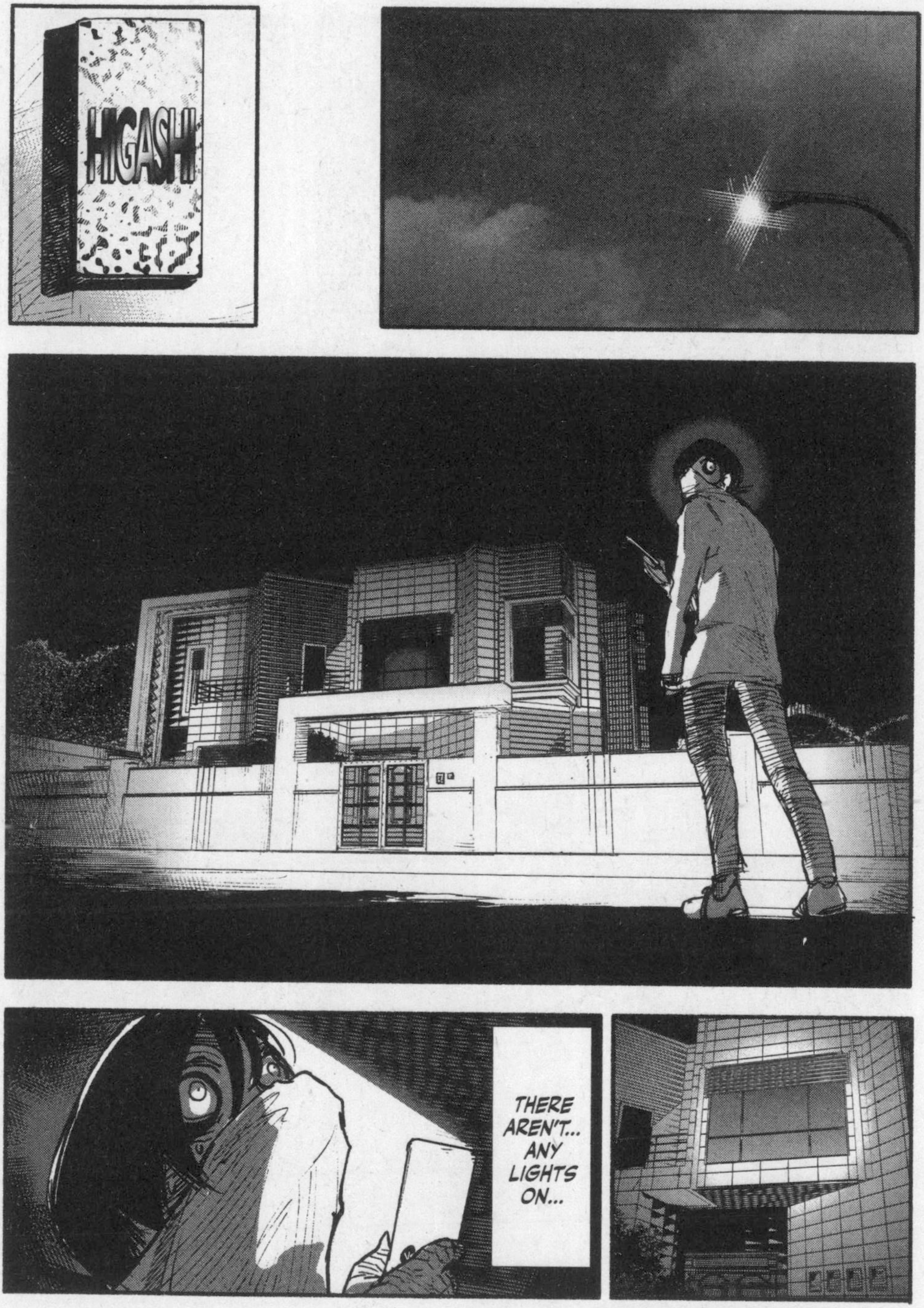
HIGASHI
THERE AREN'T... ANY LIGHTS ON...

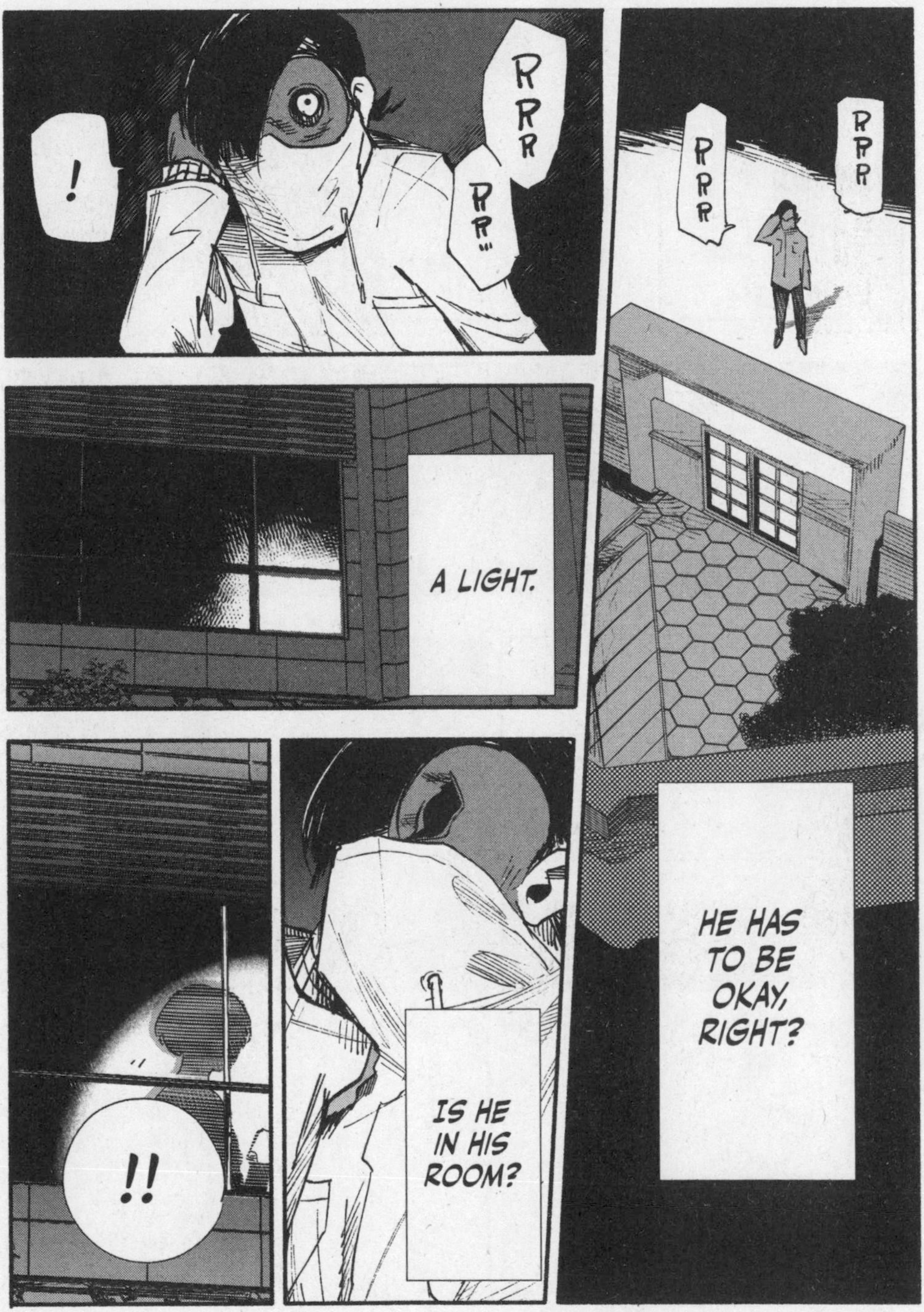
RRR
RRR
HE HAS TO BE OKAY, RIGHT?
RRR
RR...
!
A LIGHT.
IS HE IN HIS ROOM?
!!

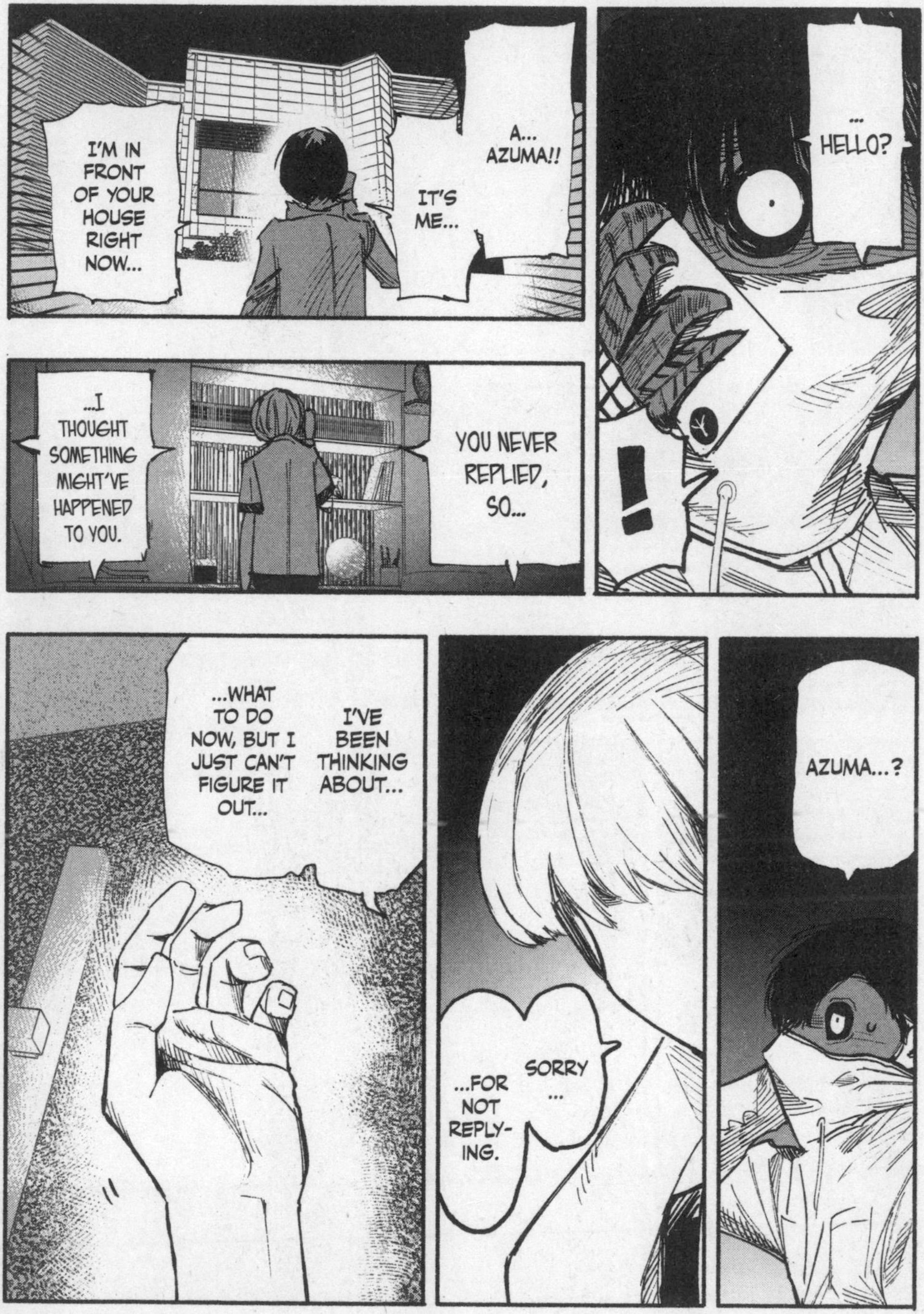
... HELLO?
!
A... AZUMA!!
IT'S ME...
I'M IN FRONT OF YOUR HOUSE RIGHT NOW...
YOU NEVER REPLIED, SO...
...I THOUGHT SOMETHING MIGHT'VE HAPPENED TO YOU.
AZUMA...?
SORRY...
...FOR NOT REPLY-ING.
I'VE BEEN THINKING ABOUT...
...WHAT TO DO NOW, BUT I JUST CAN'T FIGURE IT OUT...

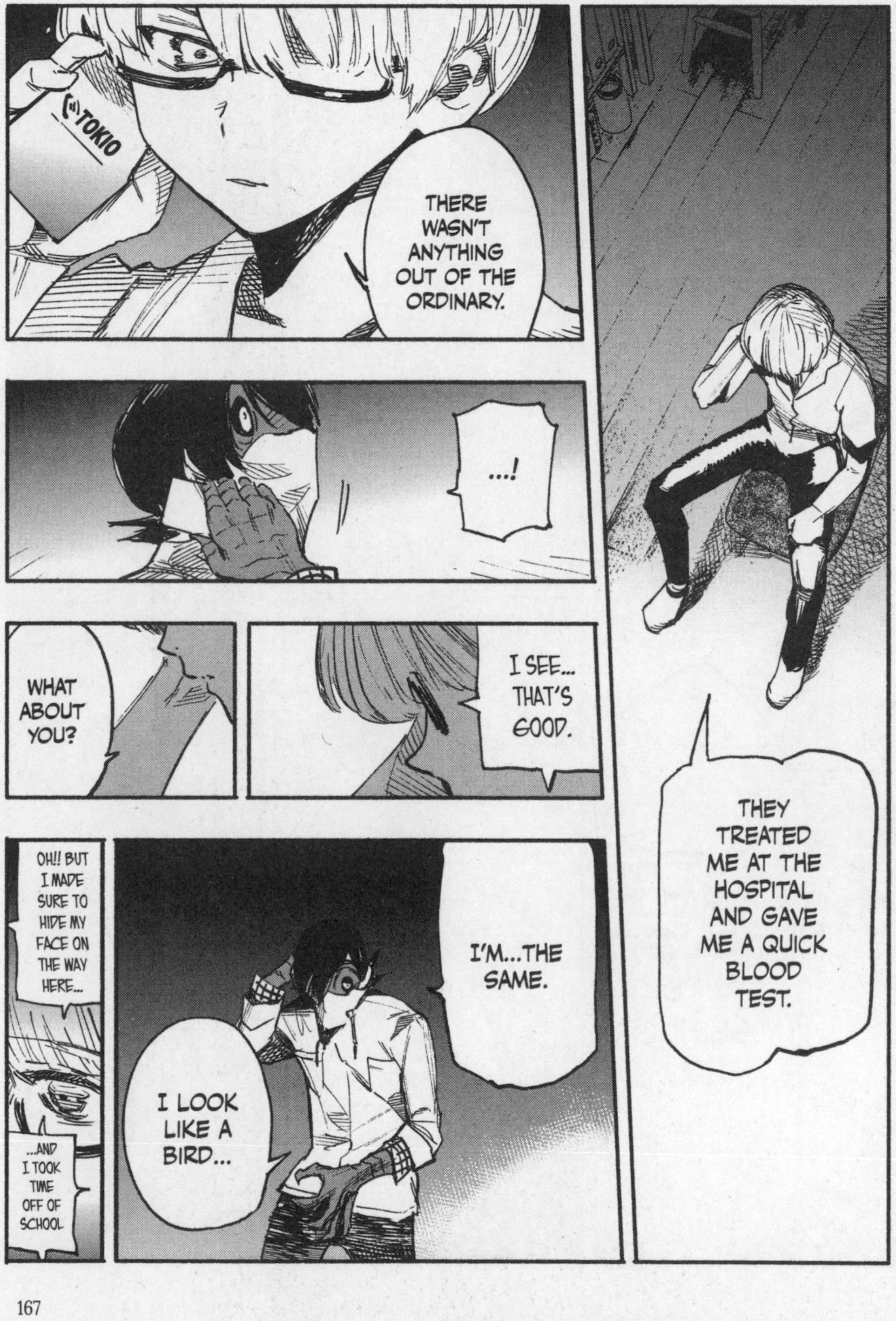
THEY TREATED ME AT THE HOSPITAL AND GAVE ME A QUICK BLOOD TEST.
THERE WASN'T ANYTHING OUT OF THE ORDINARY.
TOKIO
...!
I SEE... THAT'S GOOD.
WHAT ABOUT YOU?
I'M...THE SAME.
I LOOK LIKE A BIRD...
OH!! BUT I MADE SURE TO HIDE MY FACE ON THE WAY HERE...
...AND I TOOK TIME OFF OF SCHOOL

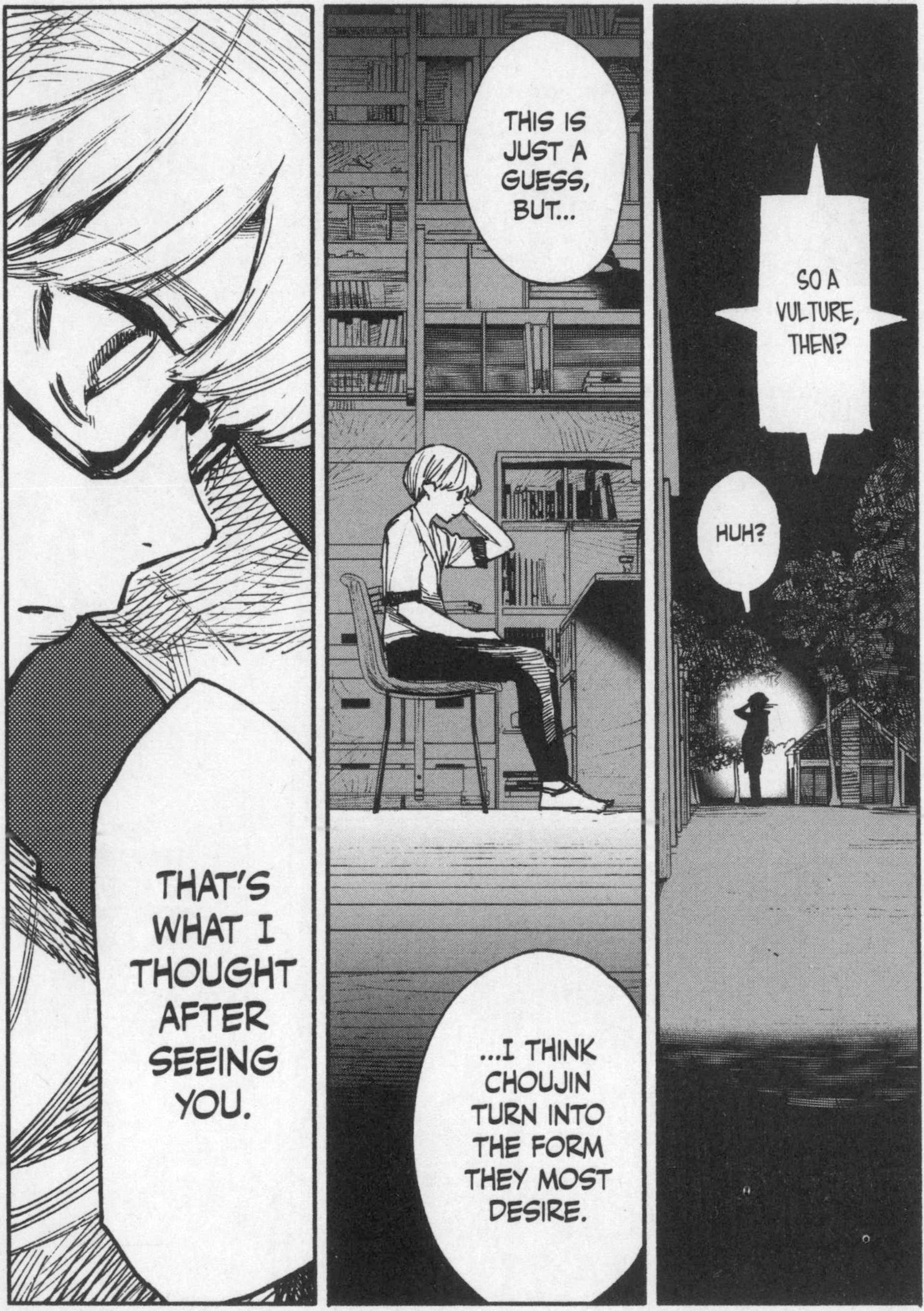
SO A VULTURE, THEN?
HUH?
THIS IS JUST A GUESS, BUT...
...I THINK CHOUJIN TURN INTO THE FORM THEY MOST DESIRE.
THAT'S WHAT I THOUGHT AFTER SEEING YOU.

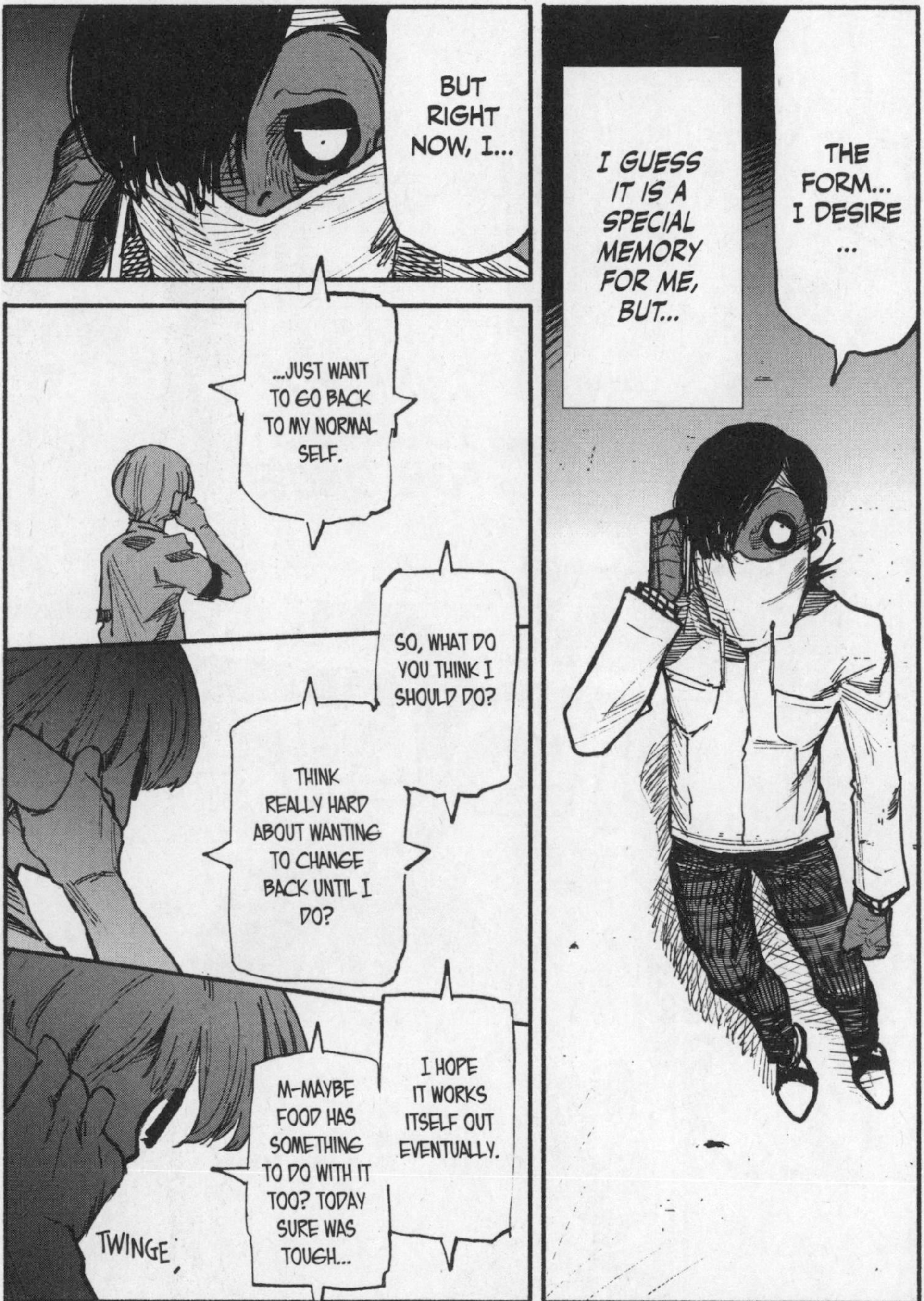
THE FORM... I DESIRE ...
I GUESS IT IS A SPECIAL MEMORY FOR ME, BUT...
BUT RIGHT NOW, I...
...JUST WANT TO GO BACK TO MY NORMAL SELF.
SO, WHAT DO YOU THINK I SHOULD DO?
THINK REALLY HARD ABOUT WANTING TO CHANGE BACK UNTIL I DO?
I HOPE IT WORKS ITSELF OUT EVENTUALLY.
M-MAYBE FOOD HAS SOMETHING TO DO WITH IT TOO? TODAY SURE WAS TOUGH...
TWINGE

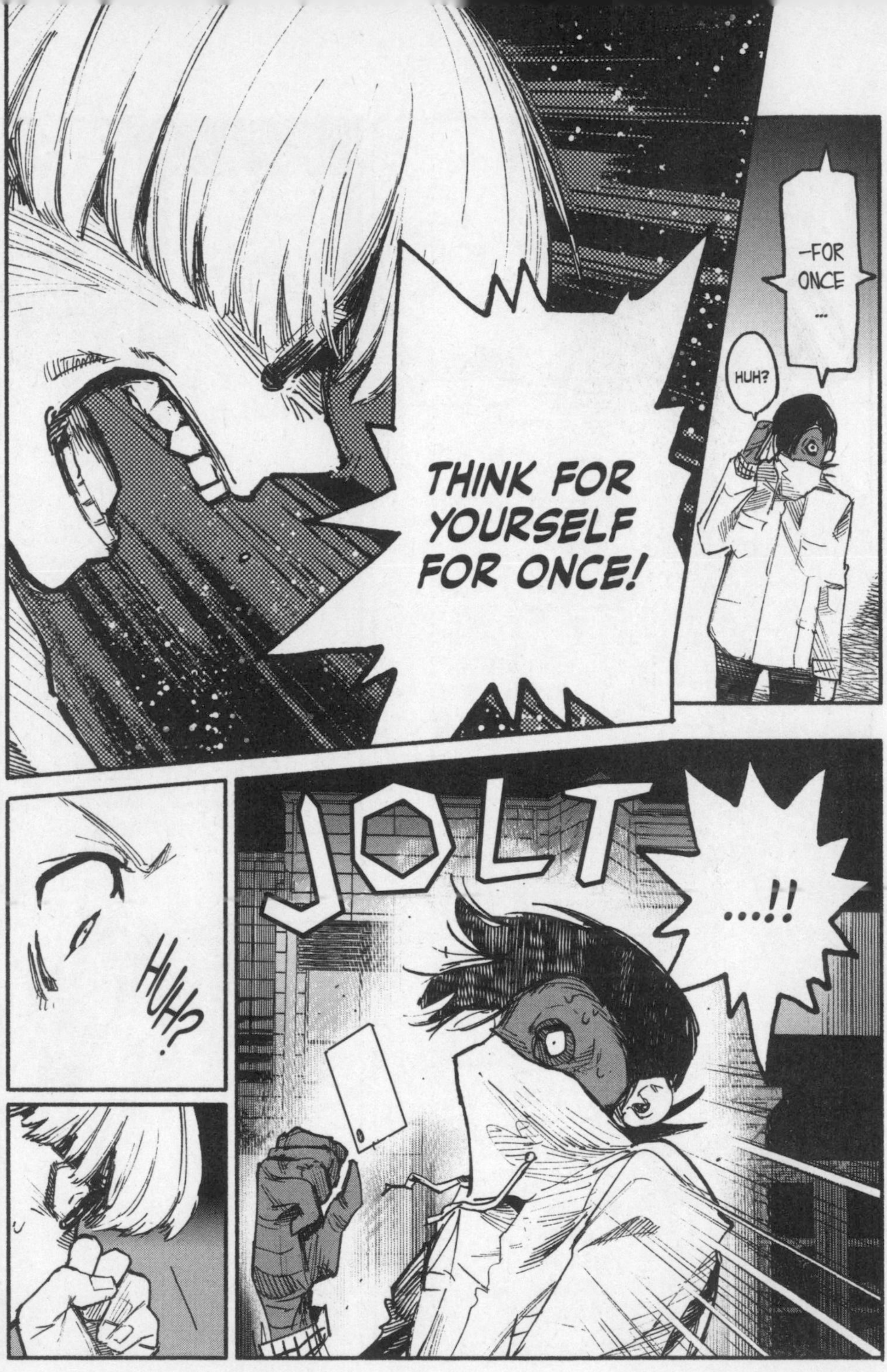
—FOR ONCE ...
HUH?
THINK FOR YOURSELF FOR ONCE!
JOLT
...!!
HUH?

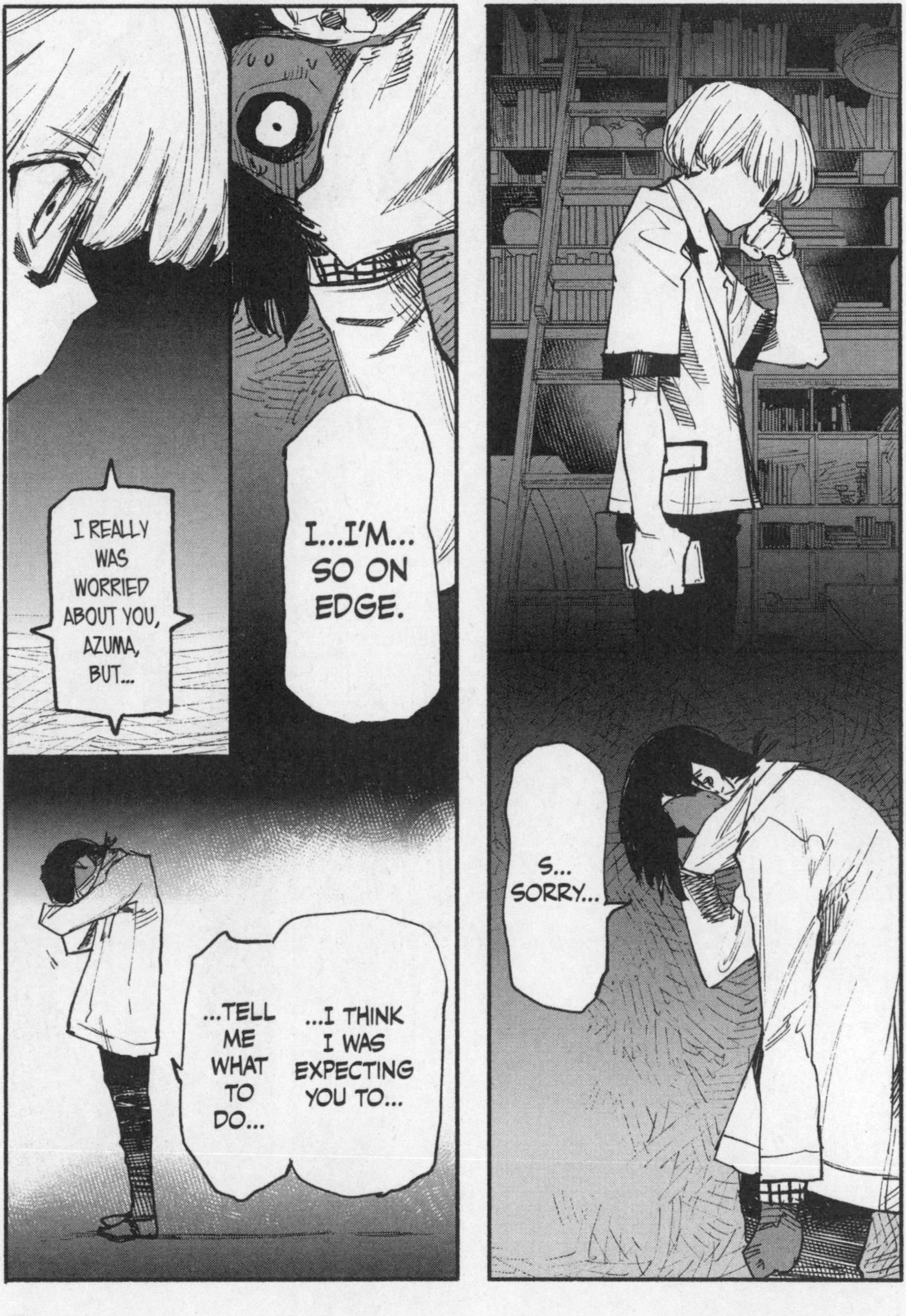
S... SORRY...
I...I'M... SO ON EDGE.
I REALLY WAS WORRIED ABOUT YOU, AZUMA, BUT...
...I THINK I WAS EXPECTING YOU TO...
...TELL ME WHAT TO DO...

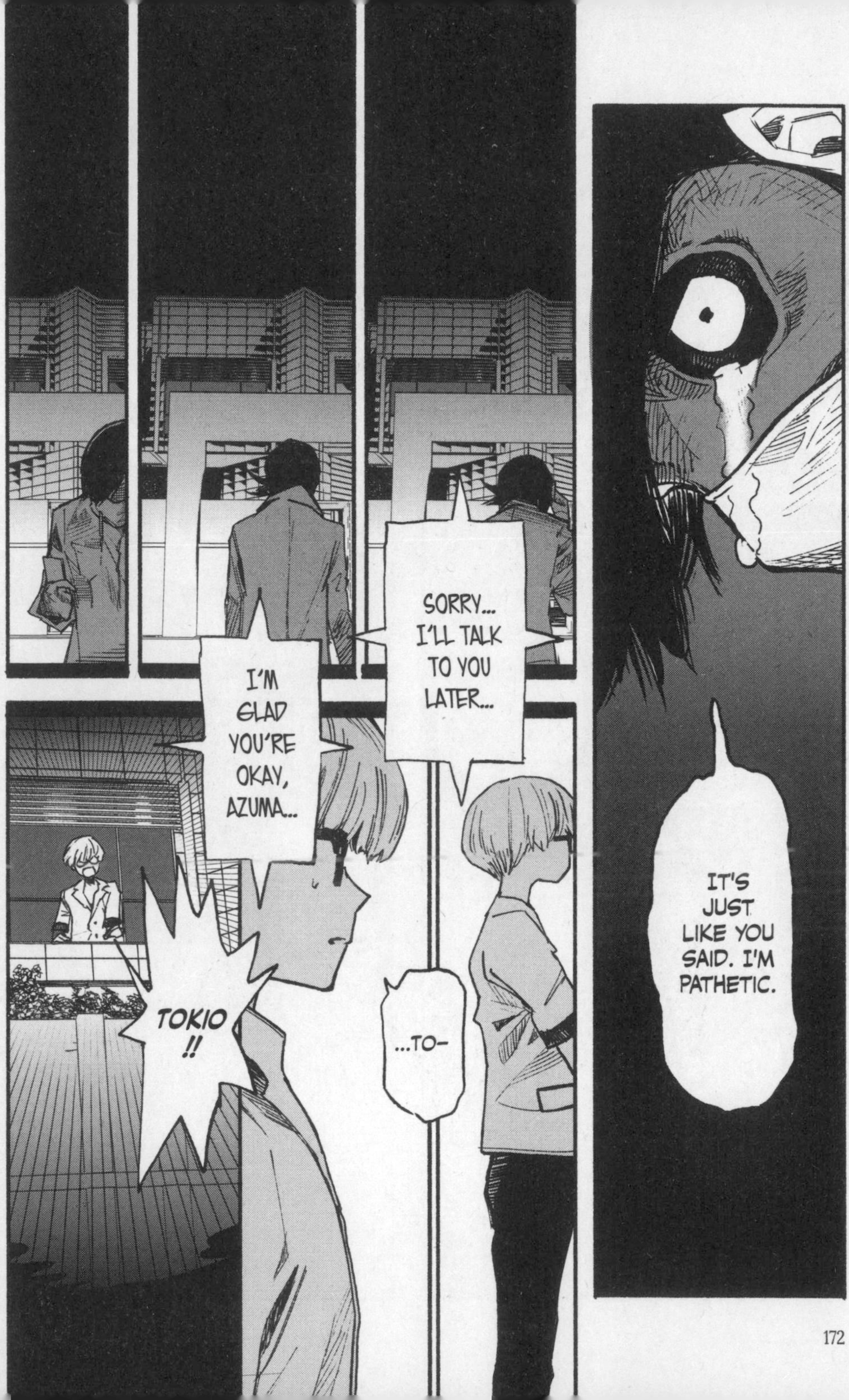
IT'S JUST LIKE YOU SAID. I'M PATHETIC.
SORRY... I'LL TALK TO YOU LATER...
I'M GLAD YOU'RE OKAY, AZUMA...
...TO-
TOKIO!!

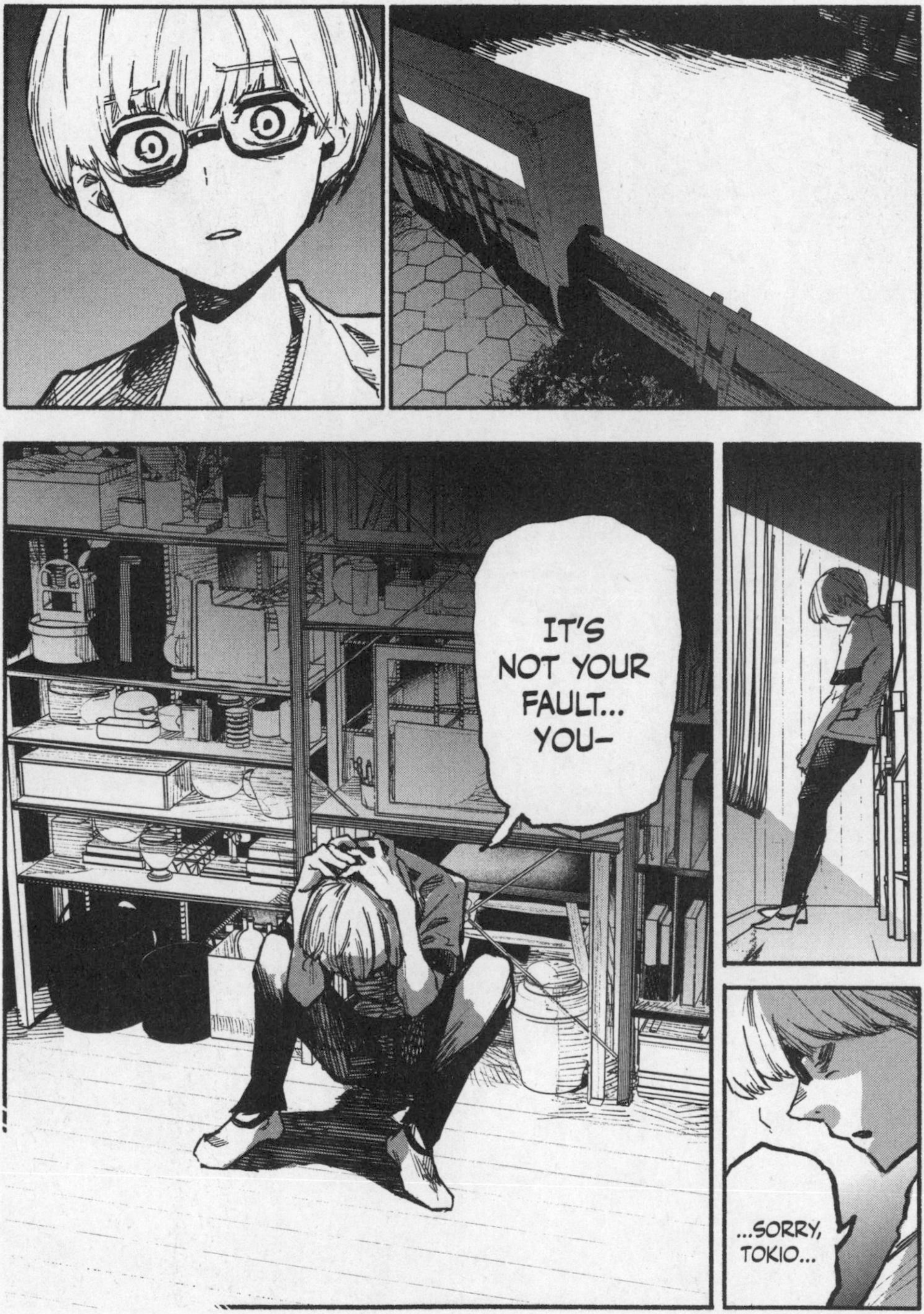
IT'S NOT YOUR FAULT... YOU-
...SORRY, TOKIO...

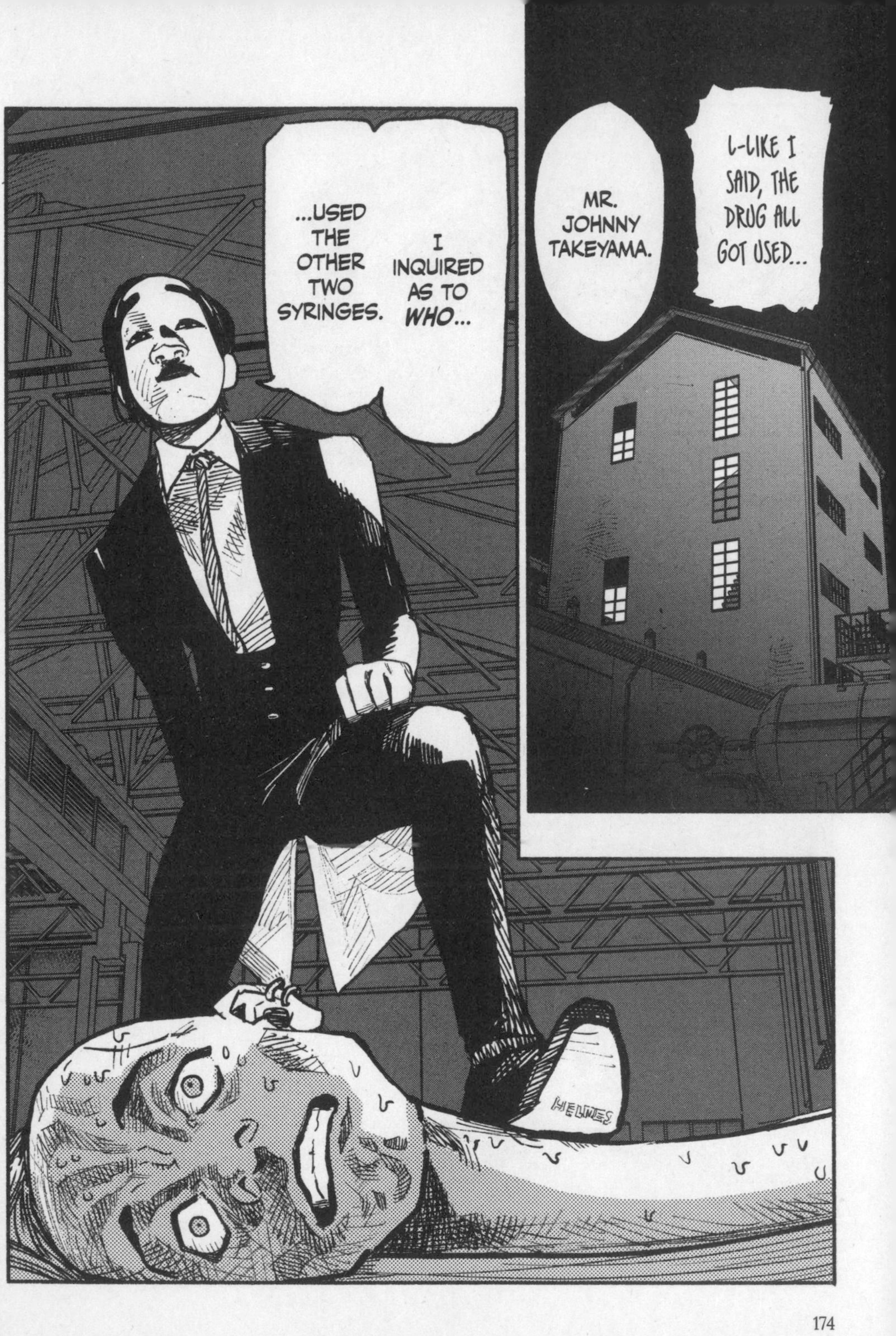
L-LIKE I SAID, THE DRUG ALL GOT USED...
MR. JOHNNY TAKEYAMA.
I INQUIRED AS TO *WHO*...
...USED THE OTHER TWO SYRINGES.

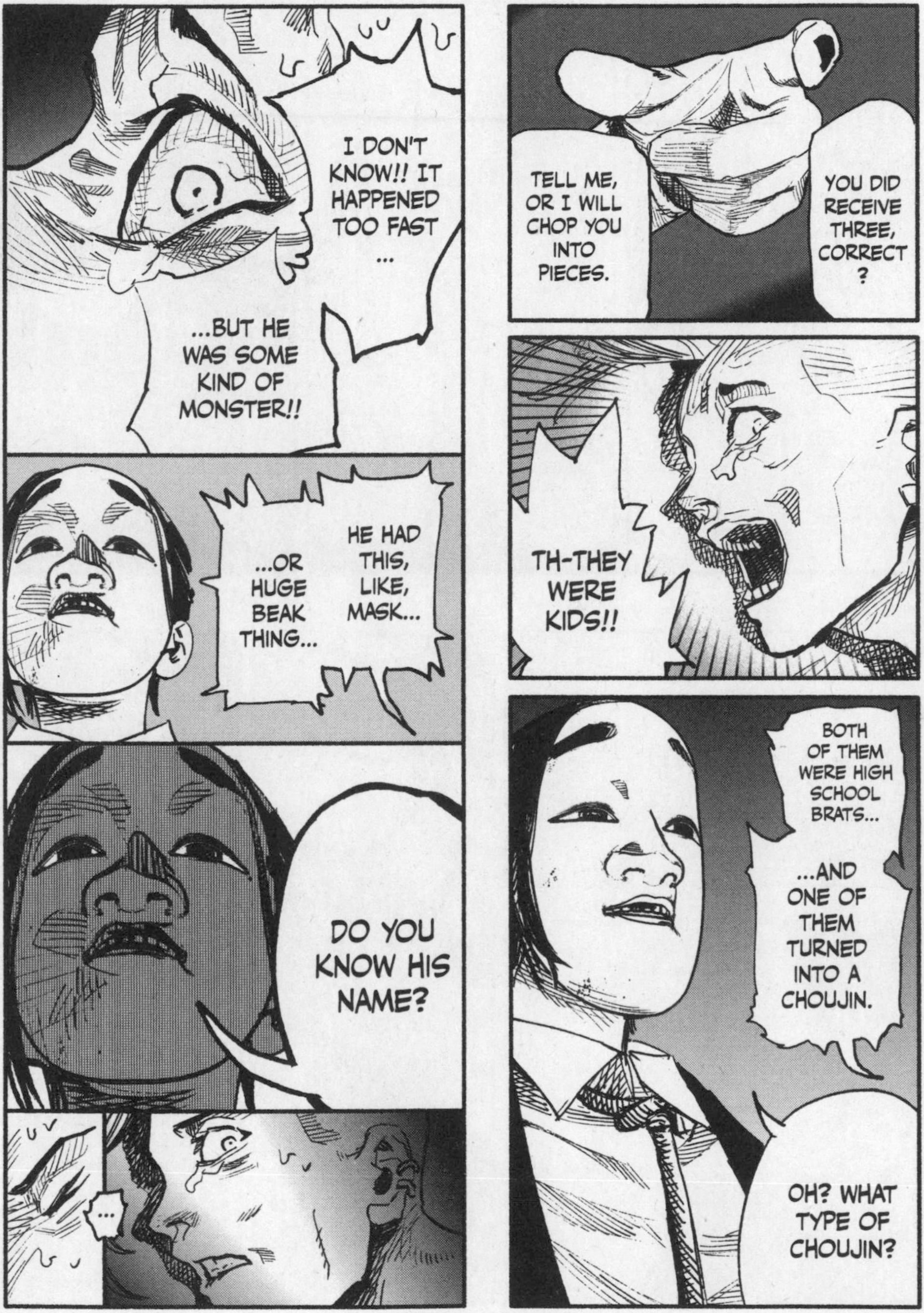
YOU DID RECEIVE THREE, CORRECT?
TELL ME, OR I WILL CHOP YOU INTO PIECES.
TH-THEY WERE KIDS!!
BOTH OF THEM WERE HIGH SCHOOL BRATS...
...AND ONE OF THEM TURNED INTO A CHOUJIN.
OH? WHAT TYPE OF CHOUJIN?
I DON'T KNOW!! IT HAPPENED TOO FAST ...
...BUT HE WAS SOME KIND OF MONSTER!!
HE HAD THIS, LIKE, MASK...
...OR HUGE BEAK THING...
DO YOU KNOW HIS NAME?
...

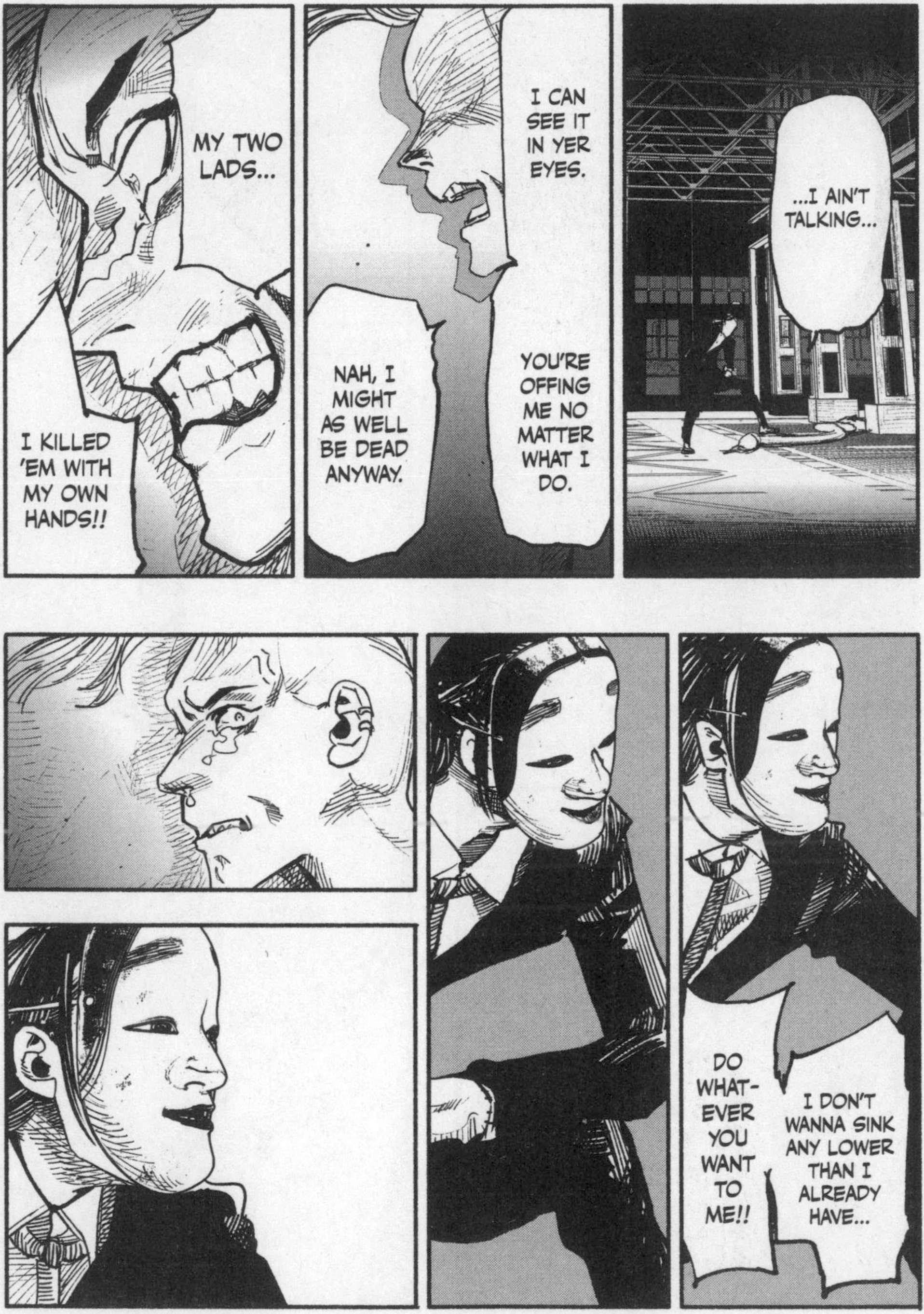
...I AIN'T TALKING...
I CAN SEE IT IN YER EYES.
YOU'RE OFFING ME NO MATTER WHAT I DO.
NAH, I MIGHT AS WELL BE DEAD ANYWAY.
MY TWO LADS...
I KILLED 'EM WITH MY OWN HANDS!!
I DON'T WANNA SINK ANY LOWER THAN I ALREADY HAVE...
DO WHAT-EVER YOU WANT TO ME!!

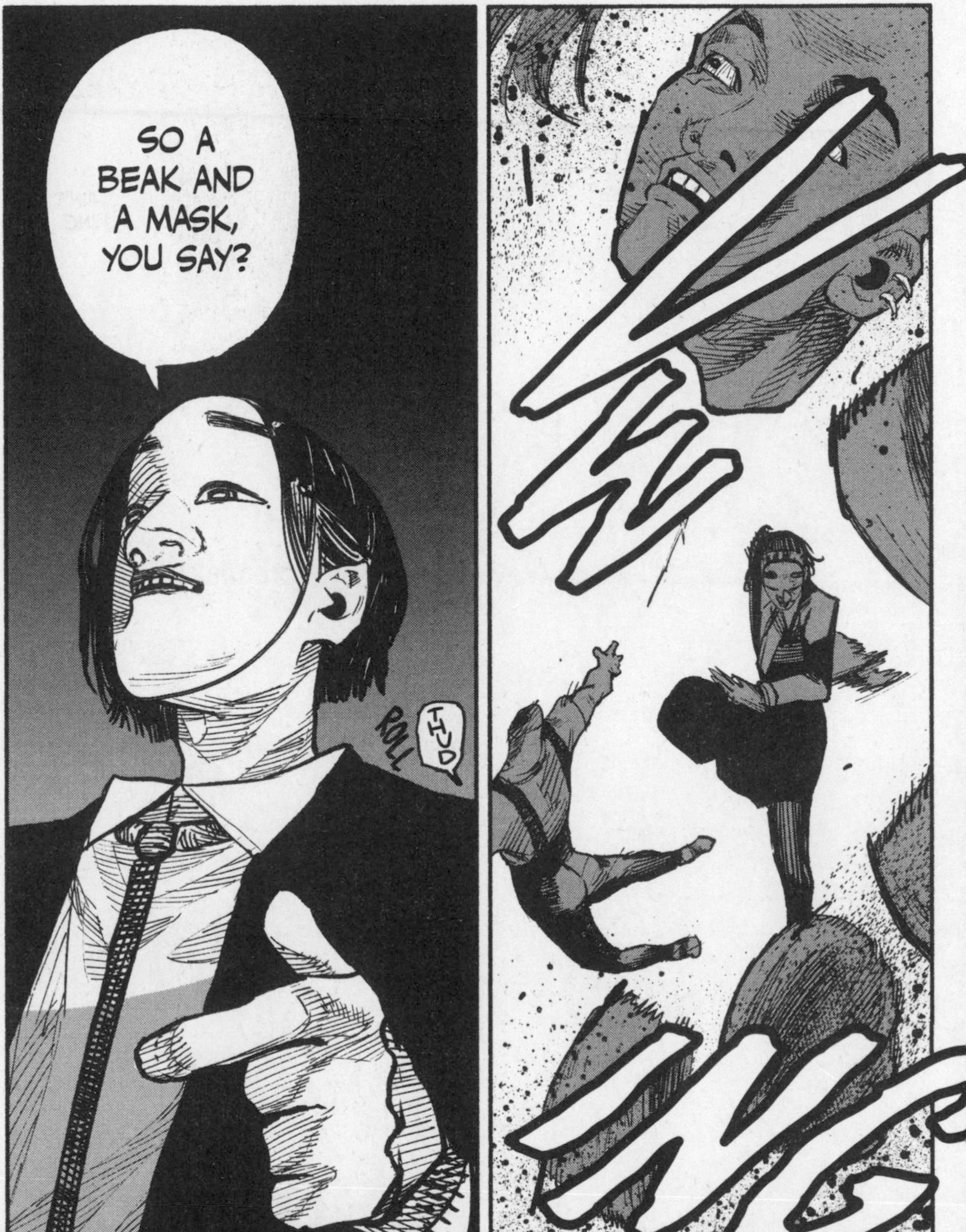
ING
SO A BEAK AND A MASK, YOU SAY?
THUD
ROLL

CHOUJIN X

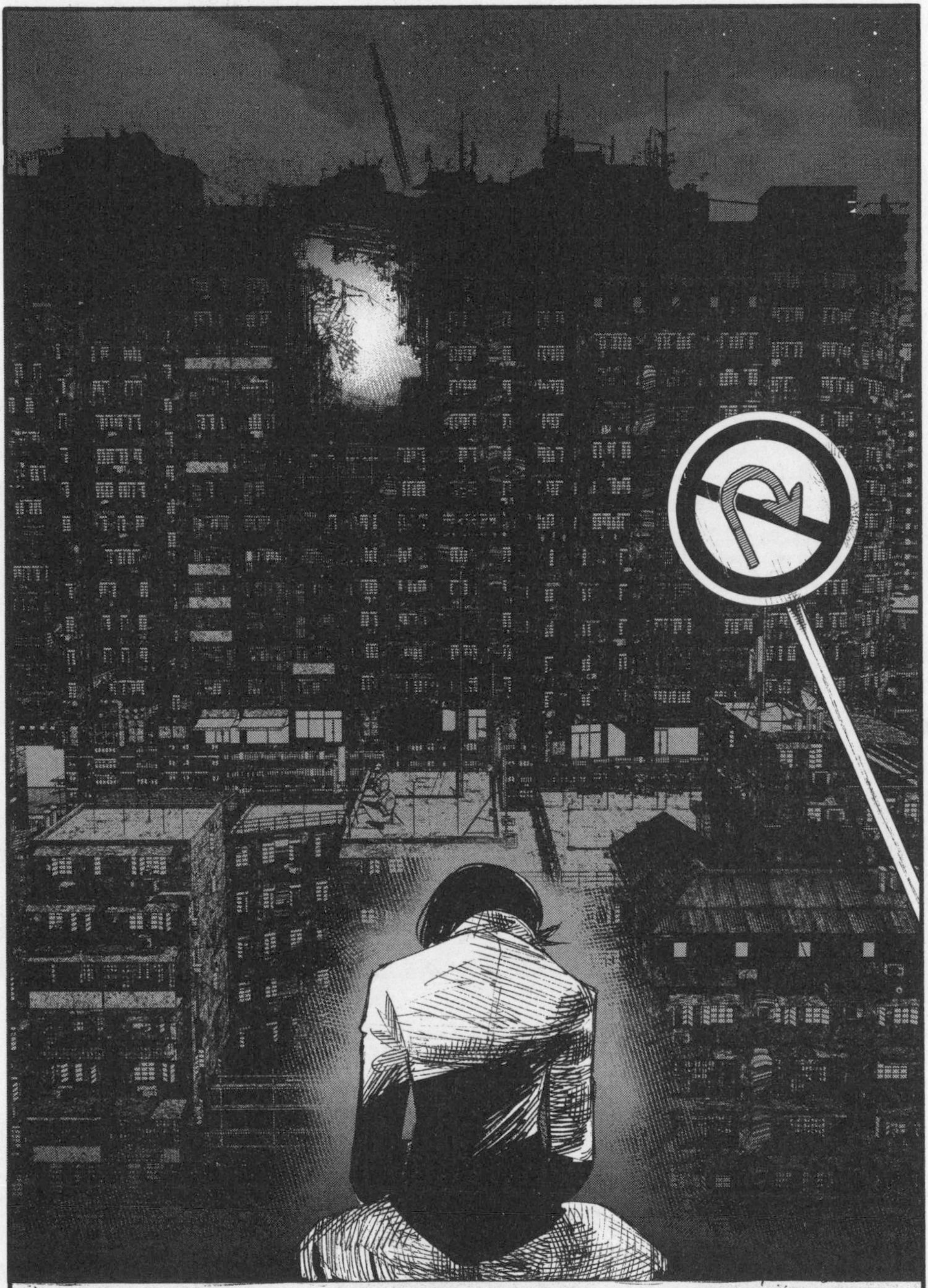

Chapter 4: June 14/innocent world

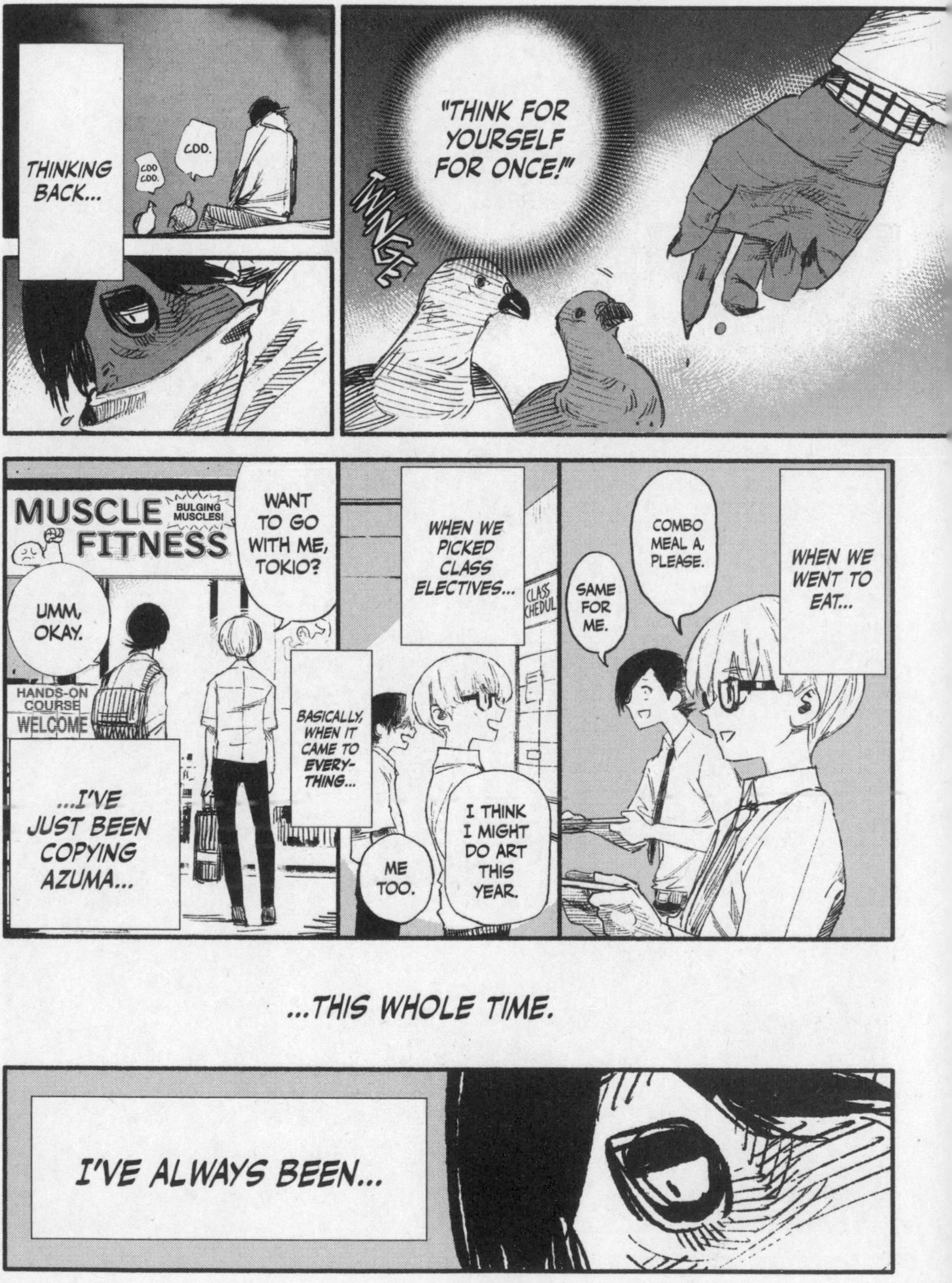
"THINK FOR YOURSELF FOR ONCE!"
TWINGE
THINKING BACK...
COO.
COO COO.
WHEN WE WENT TO EAT...
COMBO MEAL A, PLEASE.
SAME FOR ME.
WHEN WE PICKED CLASS ELECTIVES...
BASICALLY, WHEN IT CAME TO EVERYTHING...
I THINK I MIGHT DO ART THIS YEAR.
ME TOO.
WANT TO GO WITH ME, TOKIO?
MUSCLE FITNESS
BULGING MUSCLES!
UMM, OKAY.
HANDS-ON COURSE
WELCOME
...I'VE JUST BEEN COPYING AZUMA...
...THIS WHOLE TIME.
I'VE ALWAYS BEEN...

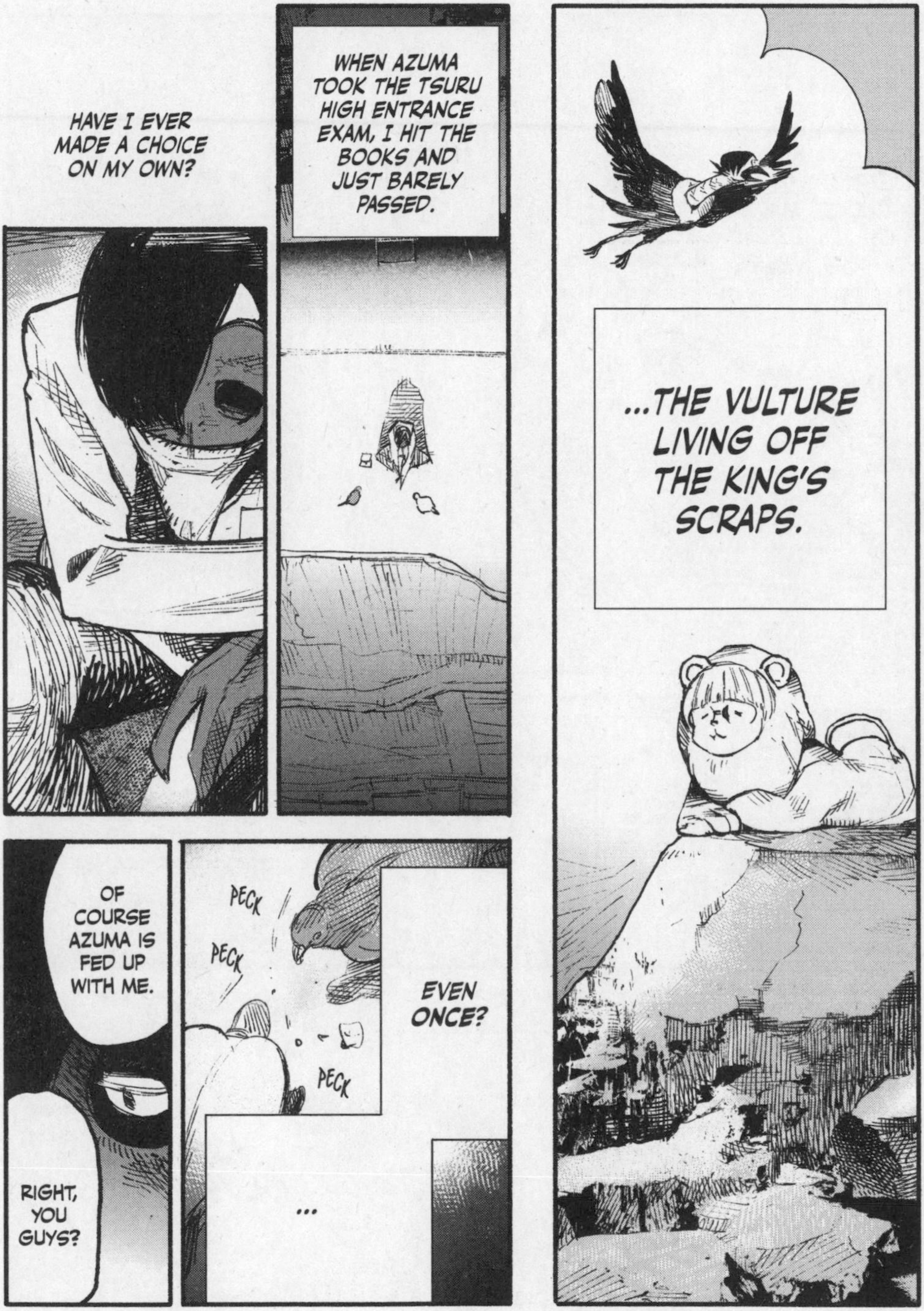
...THE VULTURE LIVING OFF THE KING'S SCRAPS.
WHEN AZUMA TOOK THE TSURU HIGH ENTRANCE EXAM, I HIT THE BOOKS AND JUST BARELY PASSED.
HAVE I EVER MADE A CHOICE ON MY OWN?
PECK
PECK
EVEN ONCE?
PECK
...
OF COURSE AZUMA IS FED UP WITH ME.
RIGHT, YOU GUYS?

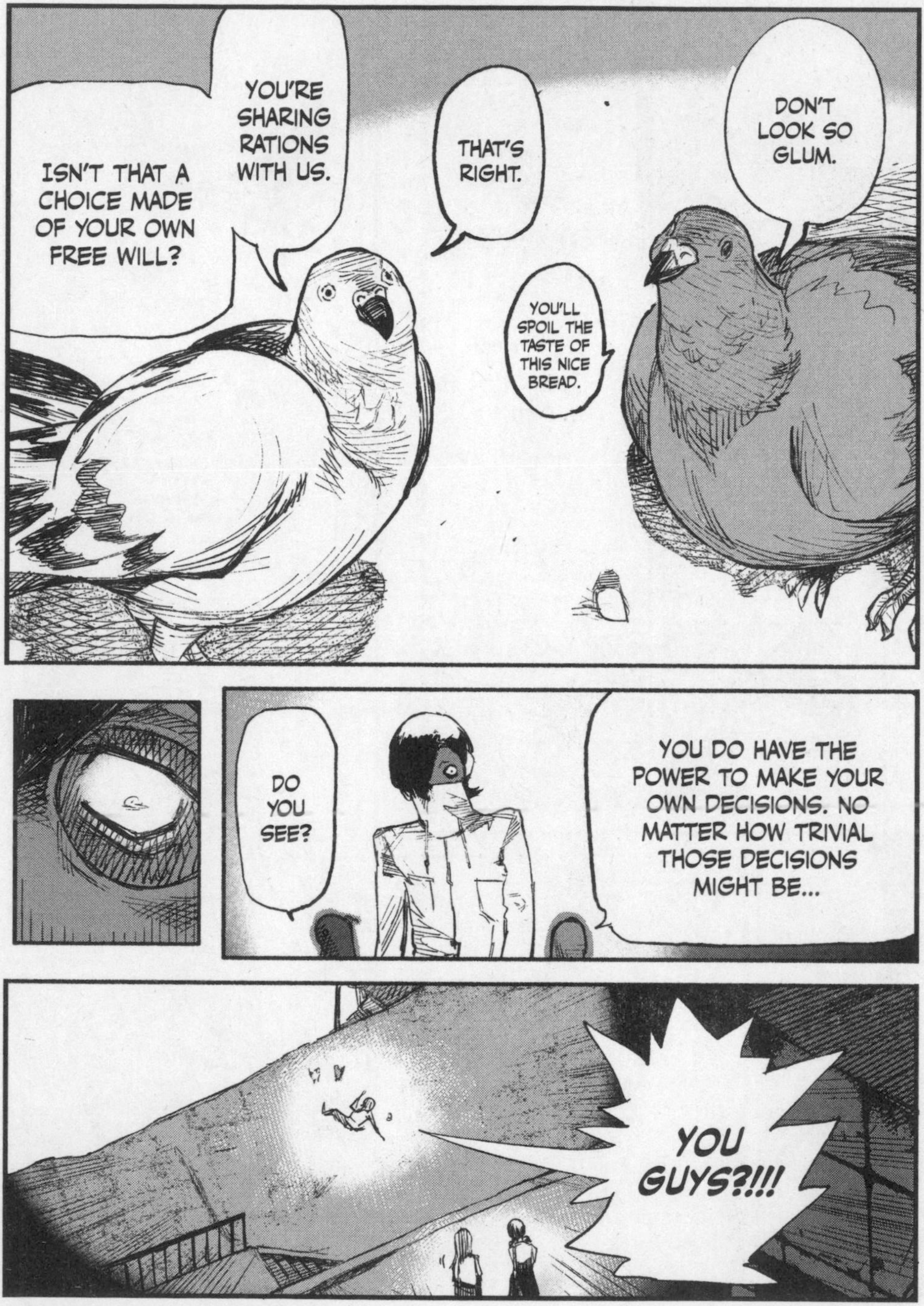
DON'T LOOK SO GLUM.
YOU'LL SPOIL THE TASTE OF THIS NICE BREAD.
THAT'S RIGHT.
YOU'RE SHARING RATIONS WITH US.
ISN'T THAT A CHOICE MADE OF YOUR OWN FREE WILL?
YOU DO HAVE THE POWER TO MAKE YOUR OWN DECISIONS. NO MATTER HOW TRIVIAL THOSE DECISIONS MIGHT BE...
DO YOU SEE?
YOU GUYS?!!!

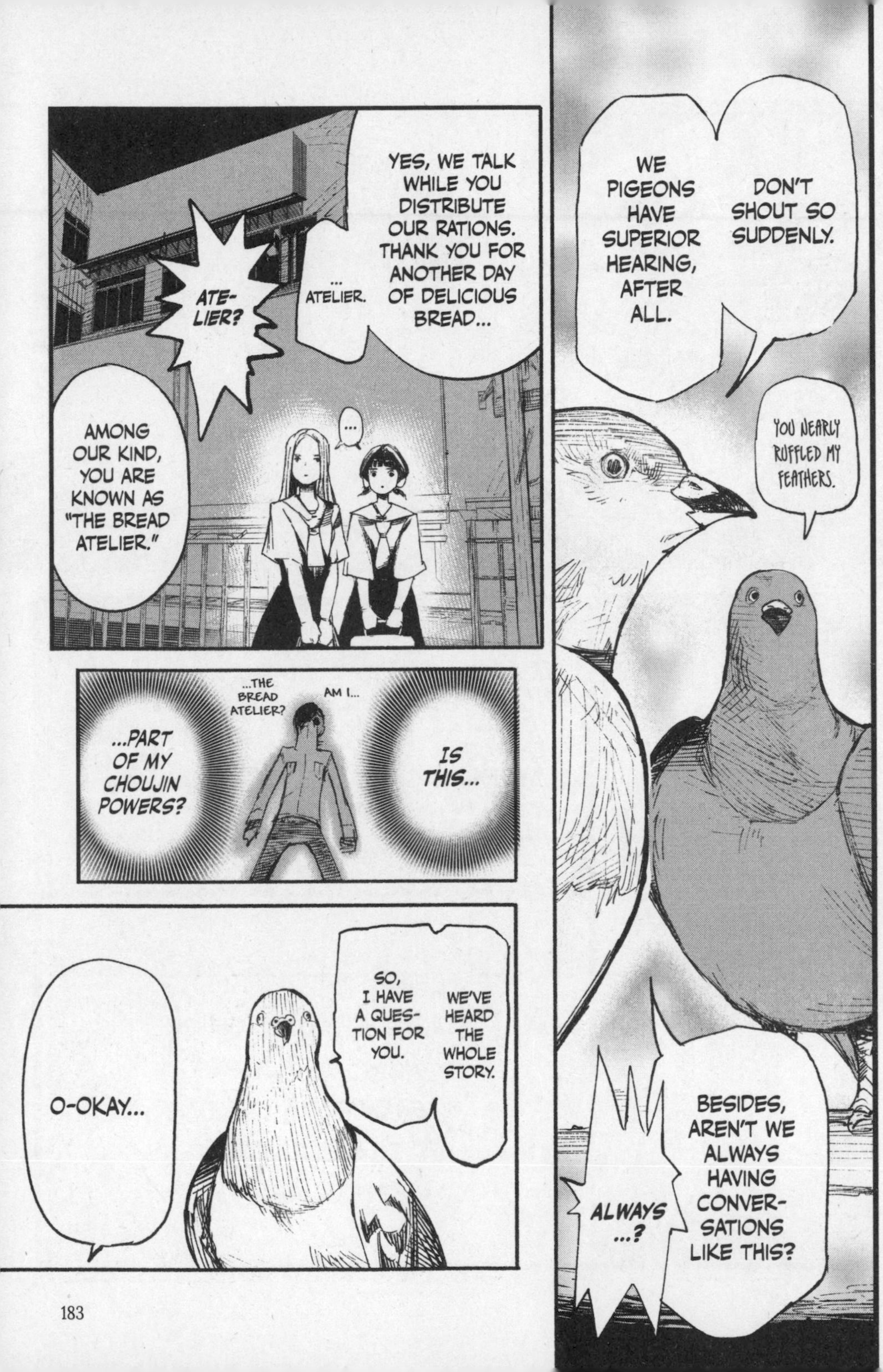
DON'T SHOUT SO SUDDENLY.
WE PIGEONS HAVE SUPERIOR HEARING, AFTER ALL.
YOU NEARLY RUFFLED MY FEATHERS.
BESIDES, AREN'T WE ALWAYS HAVING CONVERSATIONS LIKE THIS?
ALWAYS ...?
YES, WE TALK WHILE YOU DISTRIBUTE OUR RATIONS. THANK YOU FOR ANOTHER DAY OF DELICIOUS BREAD...
... ATELIER.
ATE-LIER?
...
AMONG OUR KIND, YOU ARE KNOWN AS "THE BREAD ATELIER."
AM I...
...THE BREAD ATELIER?
IS THIS...
...PART OF MY CHOUJIN POWERS?
WE'VE HEARD THE WHOLE STORY.
SO, I HAVE A QUESTION FOR YOU.
O-OKAY...

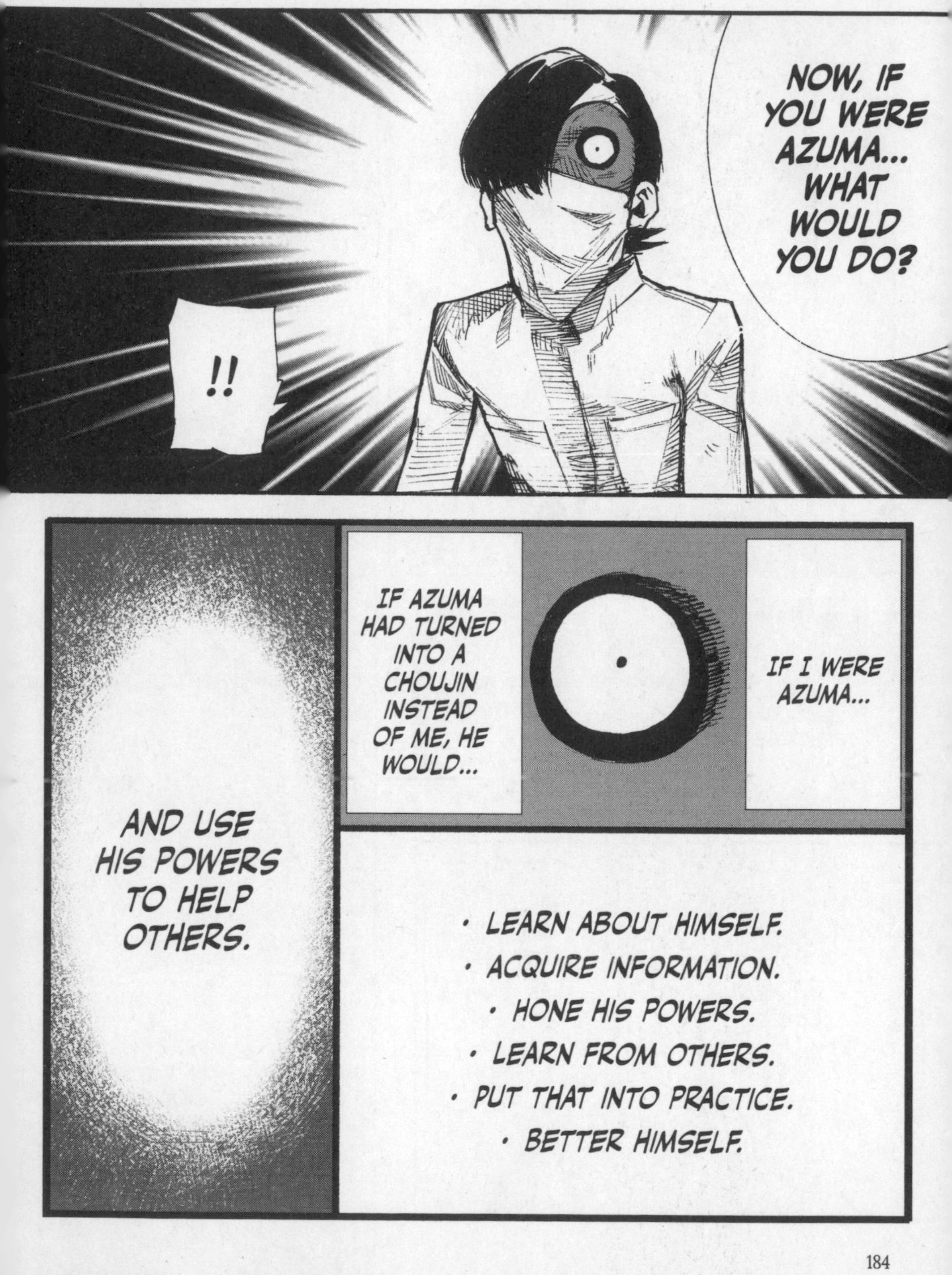
NOW, IF YOU WERE AZUMA... WHAT WOULD YOU DO?
!!
IF I WERE AZUMA...
IF AZUMA HAD TURNED INTO A CHOUJIN INSTEAD OF ME, HE WOULD...
• LEARN ABOUT HIMSELF.
• ACQUIRE INFORMATION.
• HONE HIS POWERS.
• LEARN FROM OTHERS.
• PUT THAT INTO PRACTICE.
• BETTER HIMSELF.
AND USE HIS POWERS TO HELP OTHERS.

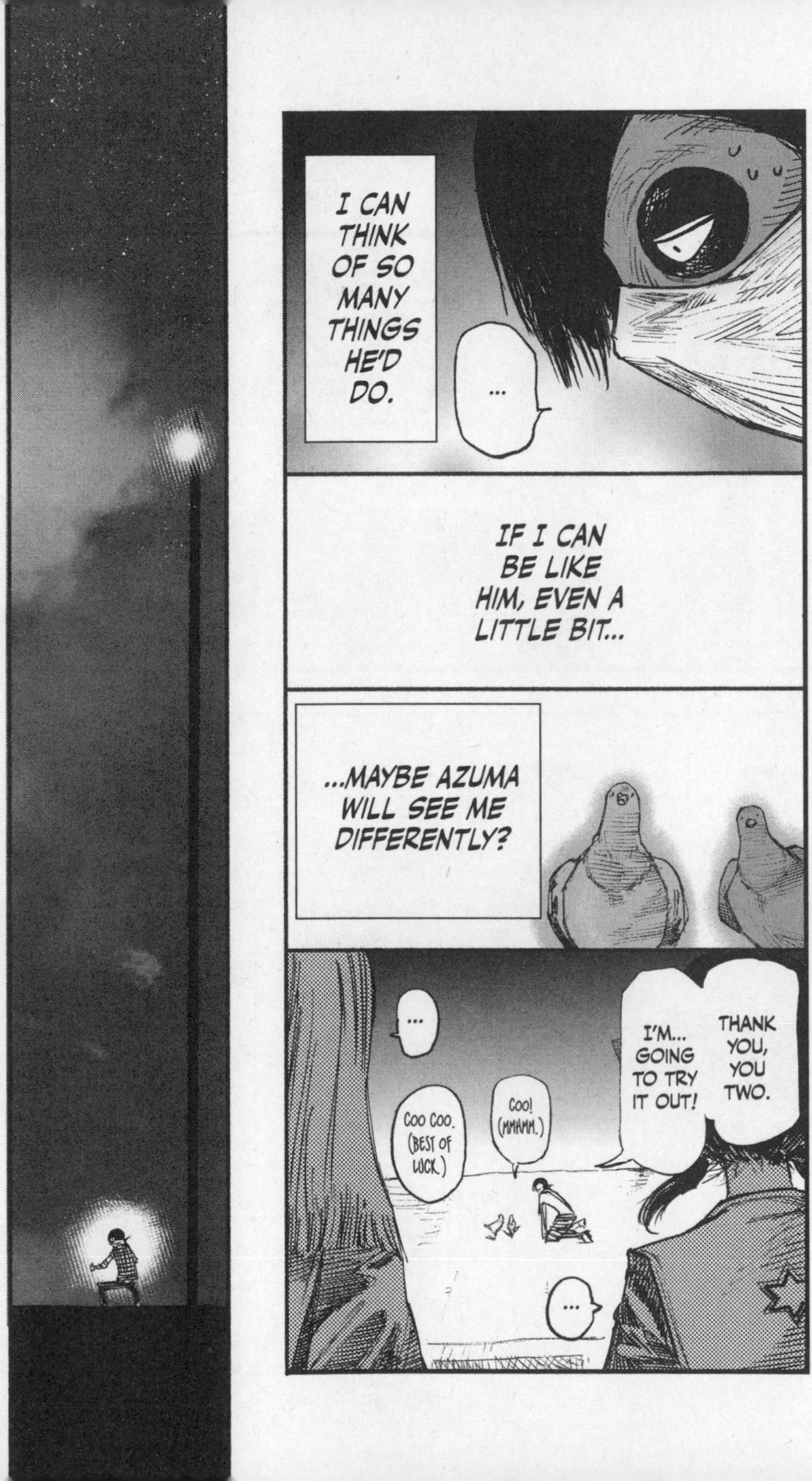
I CAN THINK OF SO MANY THINGS HE'D DO.
...
IF I CAN BE LIKE HIM, EVEN A LITTLE BIT...
...MAYBE AZUMA WILL SEE ME DIFFERENTLY?
THANK YOU, YOU TWO.
I'M... GOING TO TRY IT OUT!
...
COO! (MMHMM.)
COO COO. (BEST OF LUCK.)
...

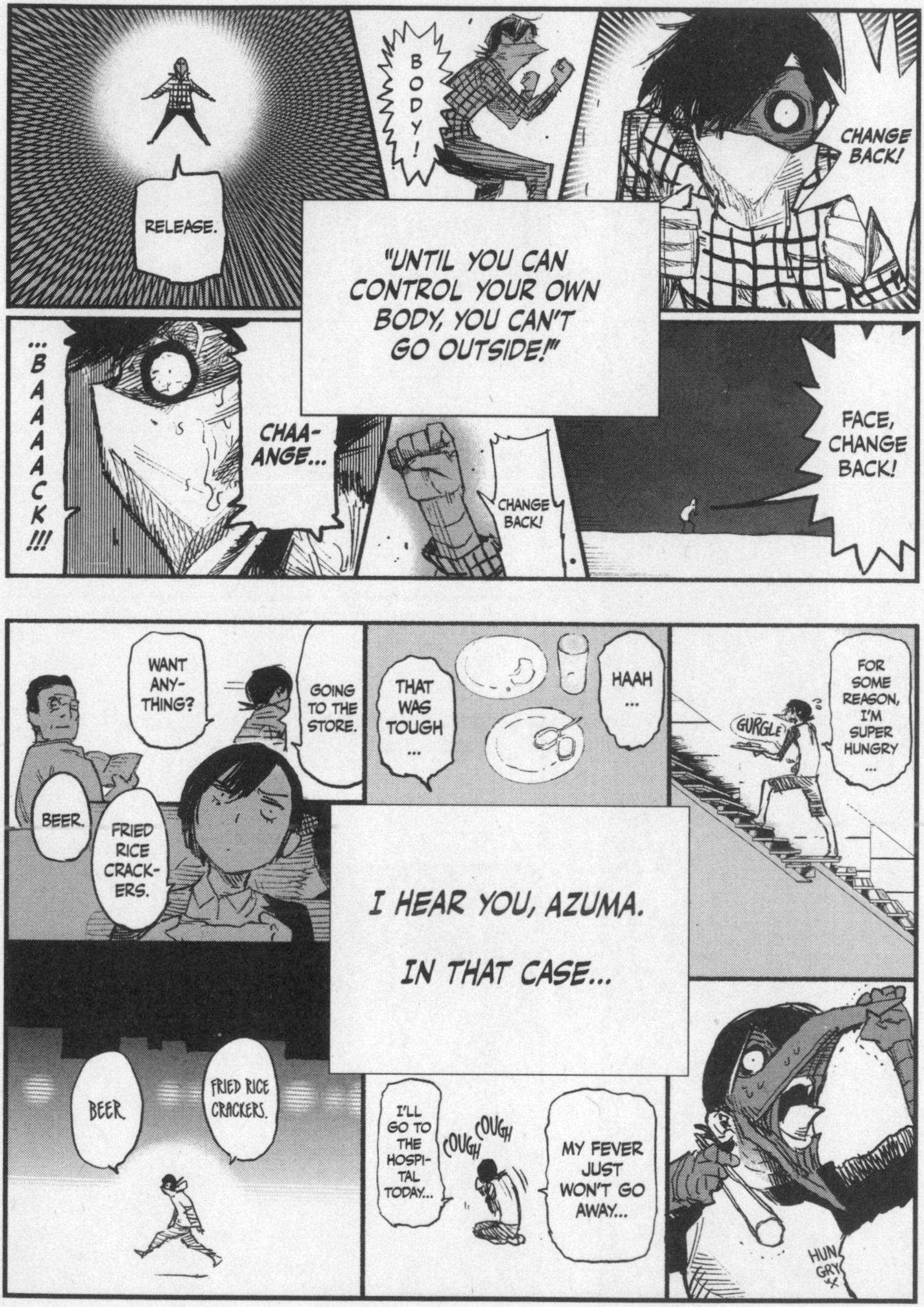
CHANGE BACK!
BODY!
RELEASE.
"UNTIL YOU CAN CONTROL YOUR OWN BODY, YOU CAN'T GO OUTSIDE!"
FACE, CHANGE BACK!
CHANGE BACK!
CHAAA-ANGE...
...BAAAAACK!!!
FOR SOME REASON, I'M SUPER HUNGRY ...
GURGLE
HAAH ...
THAT WAS TOUGH ...
GOING TO THE STORE.
WANT ANYTHING?
FRIED RICE CRACKERS.
BEER.
I HEAR YOU, AZUMA.
IN THAT CASE...
HUNGRY
MY FEVER JUST WON'T GO AWAY...
COUGH COUGH
I'LL GO TO THE HOSPITAL TODAY...
FRIED RICE CRACKERS.
BEER.

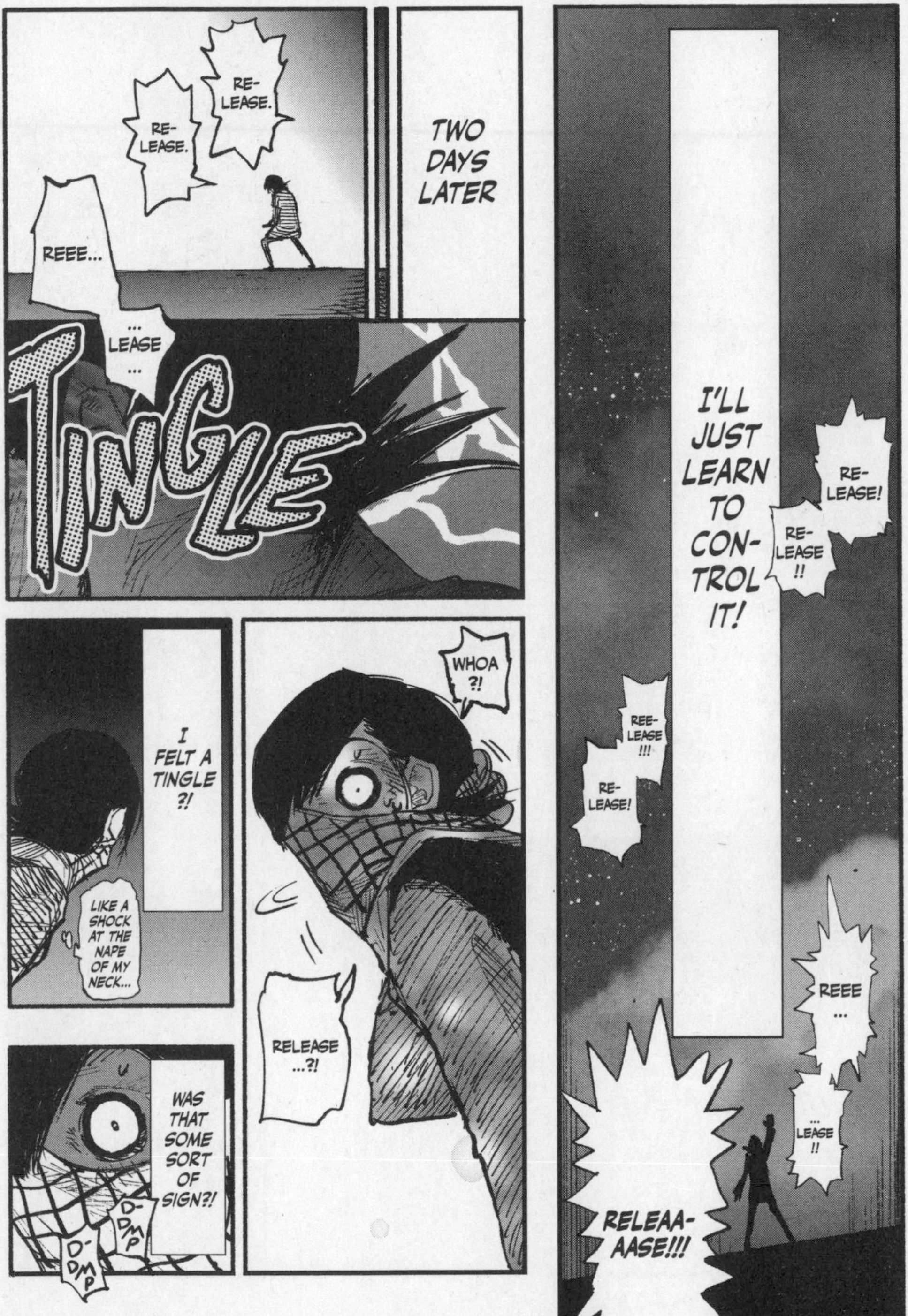
I'LL JUST LEARN TO CONTROL IT!
RE-LEASE!
RE-LEASE!!
REE-LEASE!!!
RE-LEASE!
REEE...
...LEASE!!
RELEAA-AASE!!!
TWO DAYS LATER
RE-LEASE.
RE-LEASE.
REEE...
...LEASE...
TINGLE
WHOA?!
RELEASE...?!
I FELT A TINGLE?!
LIKE A SHOCK AT THE NAPE OF MY NECK...
WAS THAT SOME SORT OF SIGN?!
D-DMP
D-DMP

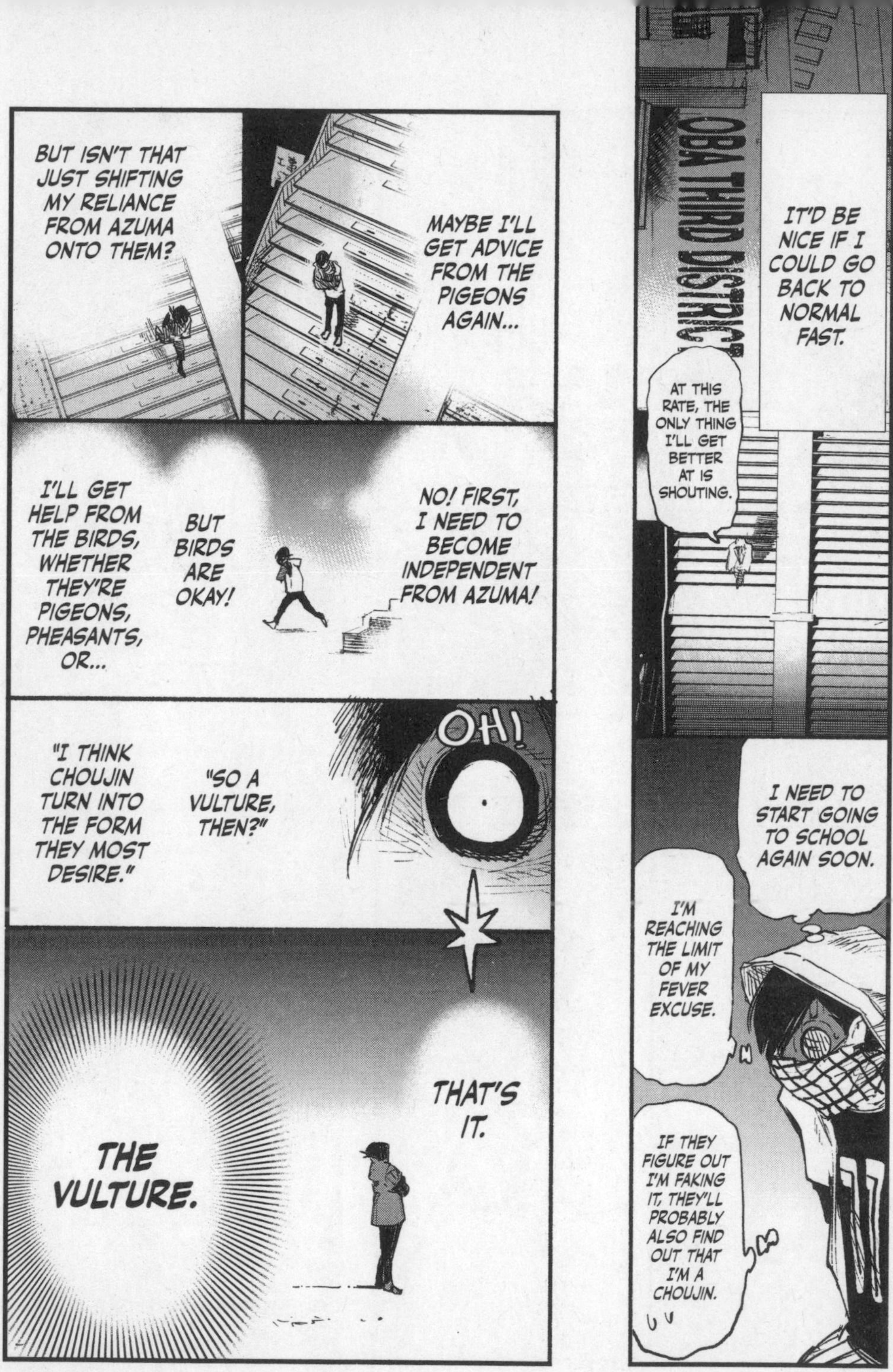
OBA THIRD DISTRICT
IT'D BE NICE IF I COULD GO BACK TO NORMAL FAST.
AT THIS RATE, THE ONLY THING I'LL GET BETTER AT IS SHOUTING.
I NEED TO START GOING TO SCHOOL AGAIN SOON.
I'M REACHING THE LIMIT OF MY FEVER EXCUSE.
IF THEY FIGURE OUT I'M FAKING IT, THEY'LL PROBABLY ALSO FIND OUT THAT I'M A CHOUJIN.
MAYBE I'LL GET ADVICE FROM THE PIGEONS AGAIN...
BUT ISN'T THAT JUST SHIFTING MY RELIANCE FROM AZUMA ONTO THEM?
NO! FIRST, I NEED TO BECOME INDEPENDENT FROM AZUMA!
BUT BIRDS ARE OKAY!
I'LL GET HELP FROM THE BIRDS, WHETHER THEY'RE PIGEONS, PHEASANTS, OR...
OH!
"SO A VULTURE, THEN?"
"I THINK CHOUJIN TURN INTO THE FORM THEY MOST DESIRE."
THAT'S IT.
THE VULTURE.

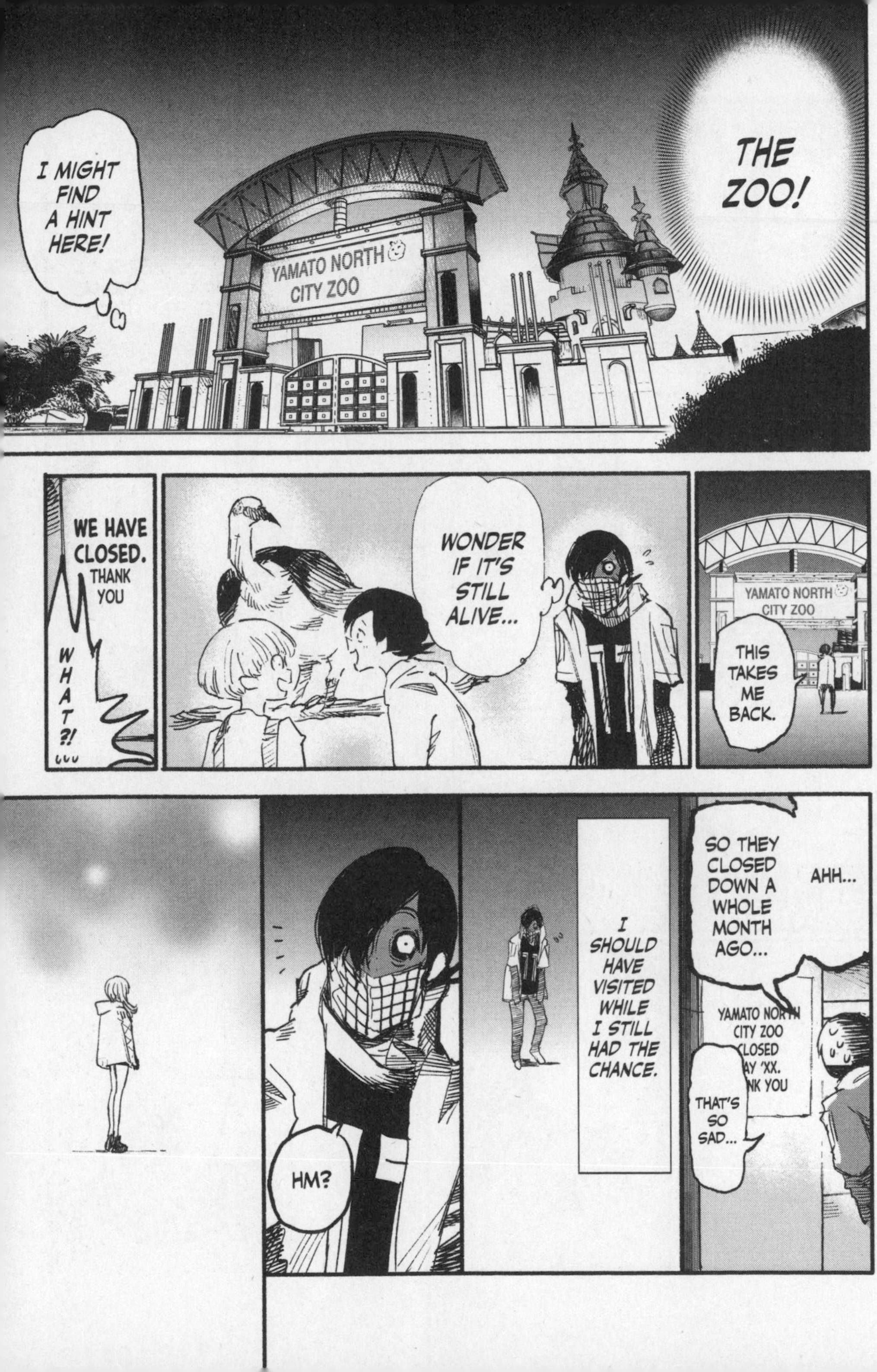
THE ZOO!
I MIGHT FIND A HINT HERE!
YAMATO NORTH CITY ZOO
YAMATO NORTH CITY ZOO
THIS TAKES ME BACK.
WONDER IF IT'S STILL ALIVE...
WE HAVE CLOSED. THANK YOU
WHAT?!
AHH...
SO THEY CLOSED DOWN A WHOLE MONTH AGO...
YAMATO NORTH CITY ZOO CLOSED
THAT'S SO SAD...
I SHOULD HAVE VISITED WHILE I STILL HAD THE CHANCE.
HM?

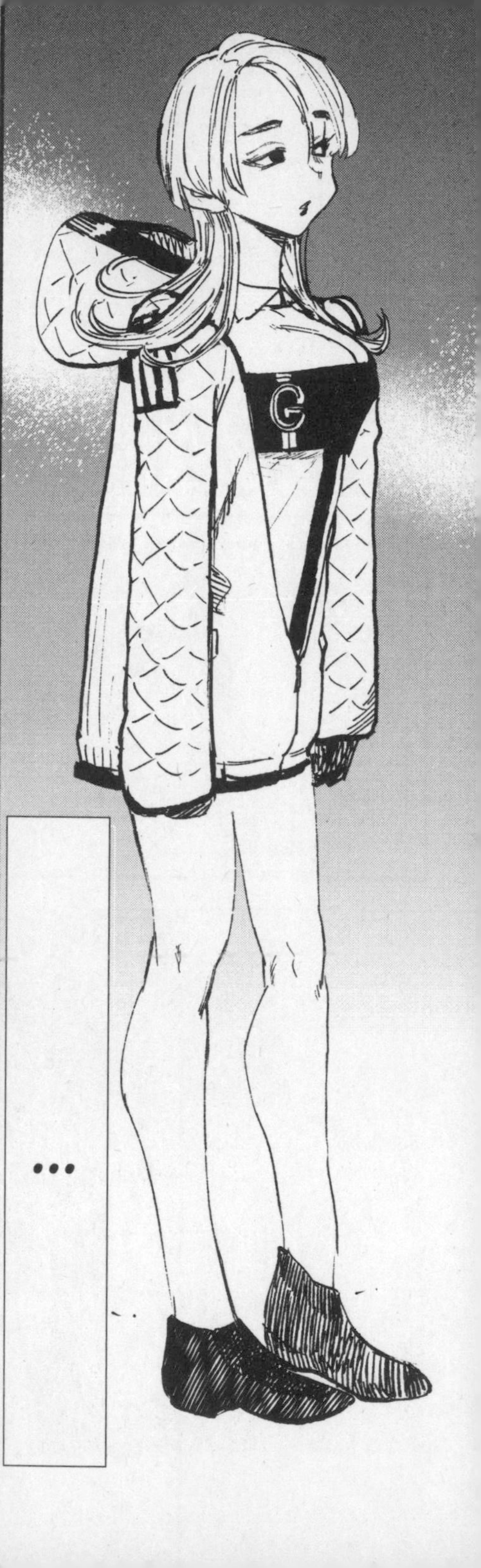
...

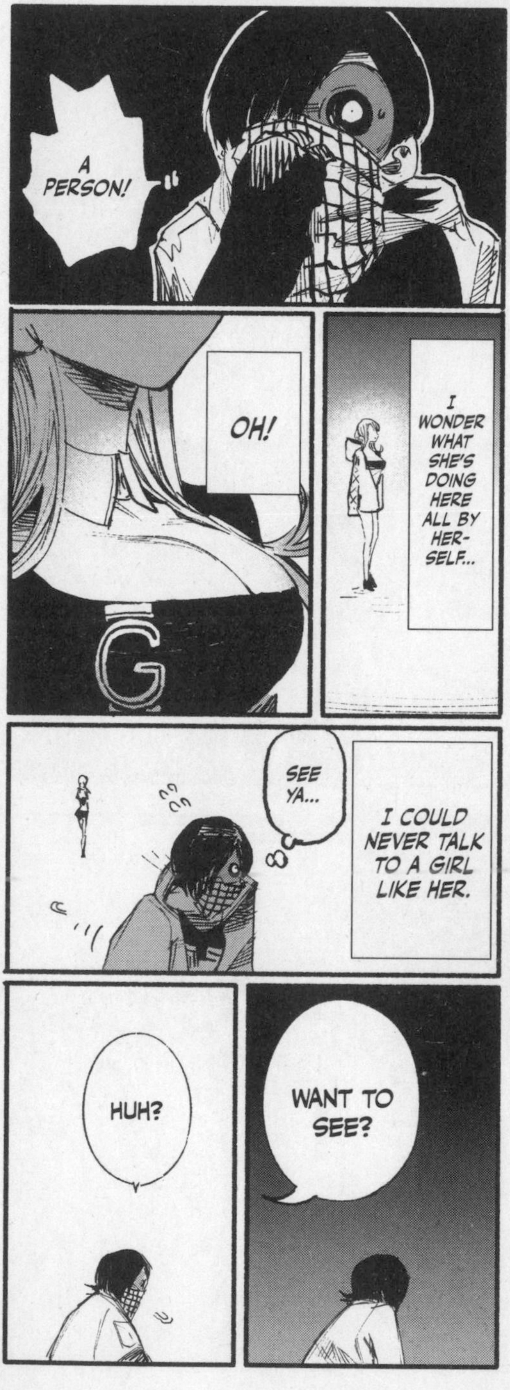
A PERSON!
I WONDER WHAT SHE'S DOING HERE ALL BY HER-SELF...
OH!
I COULD NEVER TALK TO A GIRL LIKE HER.
SEE YA...
WANT TO SEE?
HUH?

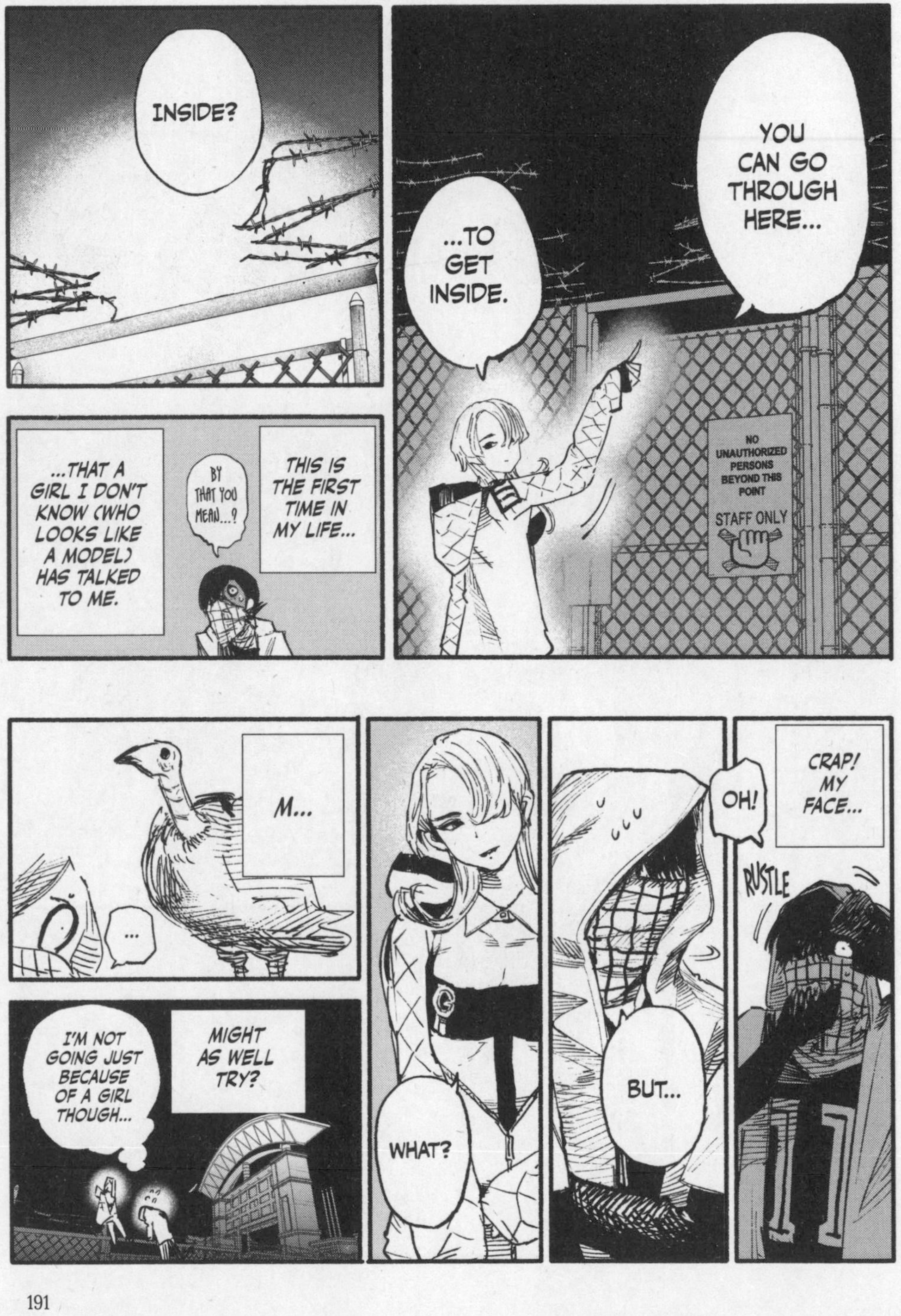
YOU CAN GO THROUGH HERE...
...TO GET INSIDE.
NO UNAUTHORIZED PERSONS BEYOND THIS POINT
STAFF ONLY
INSIDE?
THIS IS THE FIRST TIME IN MY LIFE...
BY THAT YOU MEAN...?
...THAT A GIRL I DON'T KNOW (WHO LOOKS LIKE A MODEL) HAS TALKED TO ME.
OH!
CRAP! MY FACE...
RUSTLE
BUT...
WHAT?
M...
...
MIGHT AS WELL TRY?
I'M NOT GOING JUST BECAUSE OF A GIRL THOUGH...

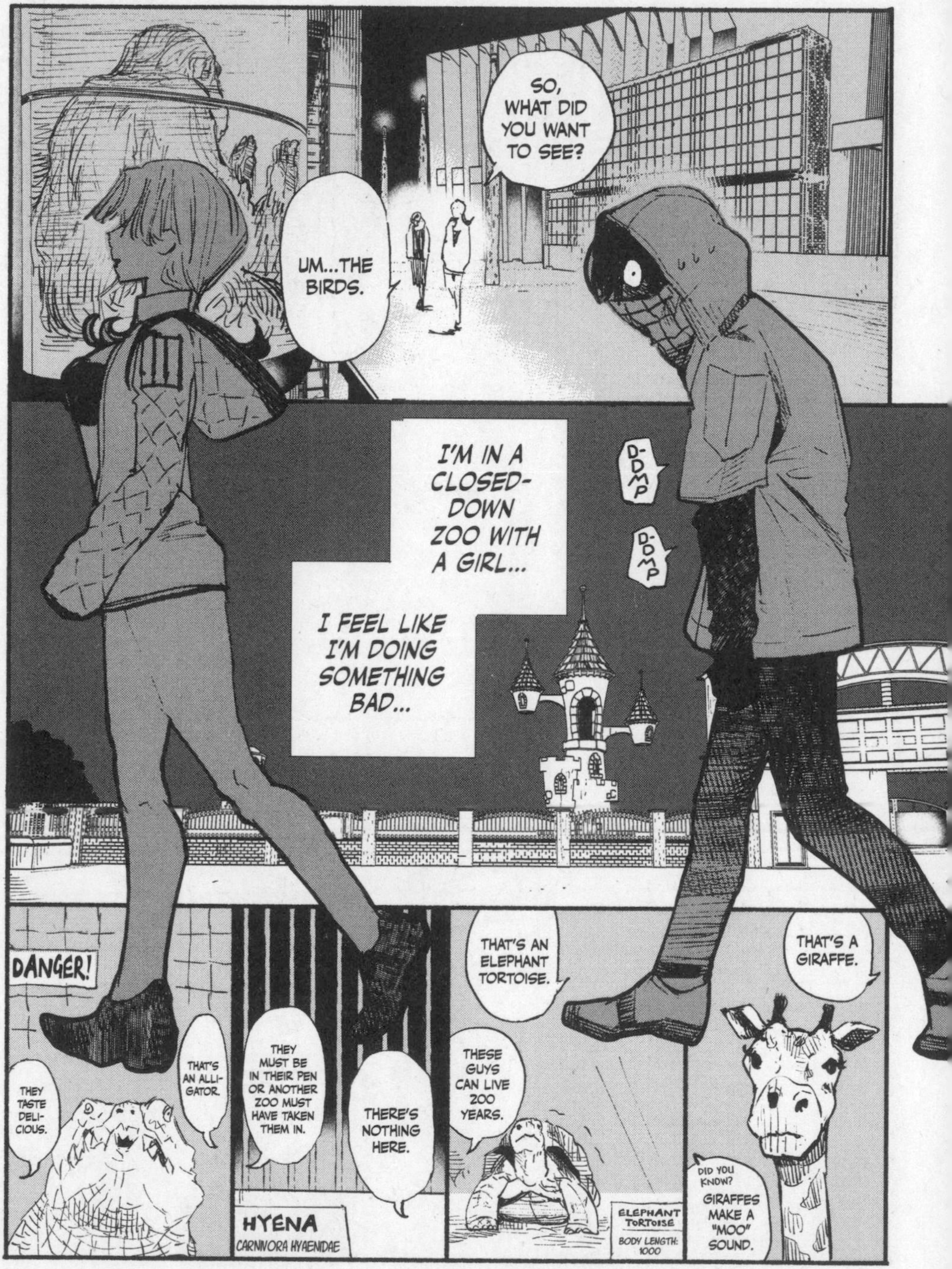
SO, WHAT DID YOU WANT TO SEE?
UM...THE BIRDS.
D-DMP
D-DMP
I'M IN A CLOSED-DOWN ZOO WITH A GIRL...
I FEEL LIKE I'M DOING SOMETHING BAD...
THAT'S A GIRAFFE.
DID YOU KNOW?
GIRAFFES MAKE A "MOO" SOUND.
THAT'S AN ELEPHANT TORTOISE.
THESE GUYS CAN LIVE 200 YEARS.
ELEPHANT TORTOISE
BODY LENGTH: 1000
THERE'S NOTHING HERE.
THEY MUST BE IN THEIR PEN OR ANOTHER ZOO MUST HAVE TAKEN THEM IN.
HYENA
CARNIVORA HYAENIDAE
DANGER!
THAT'S AN ALLIGATOR.
THEY TASTE DELICIOUS.

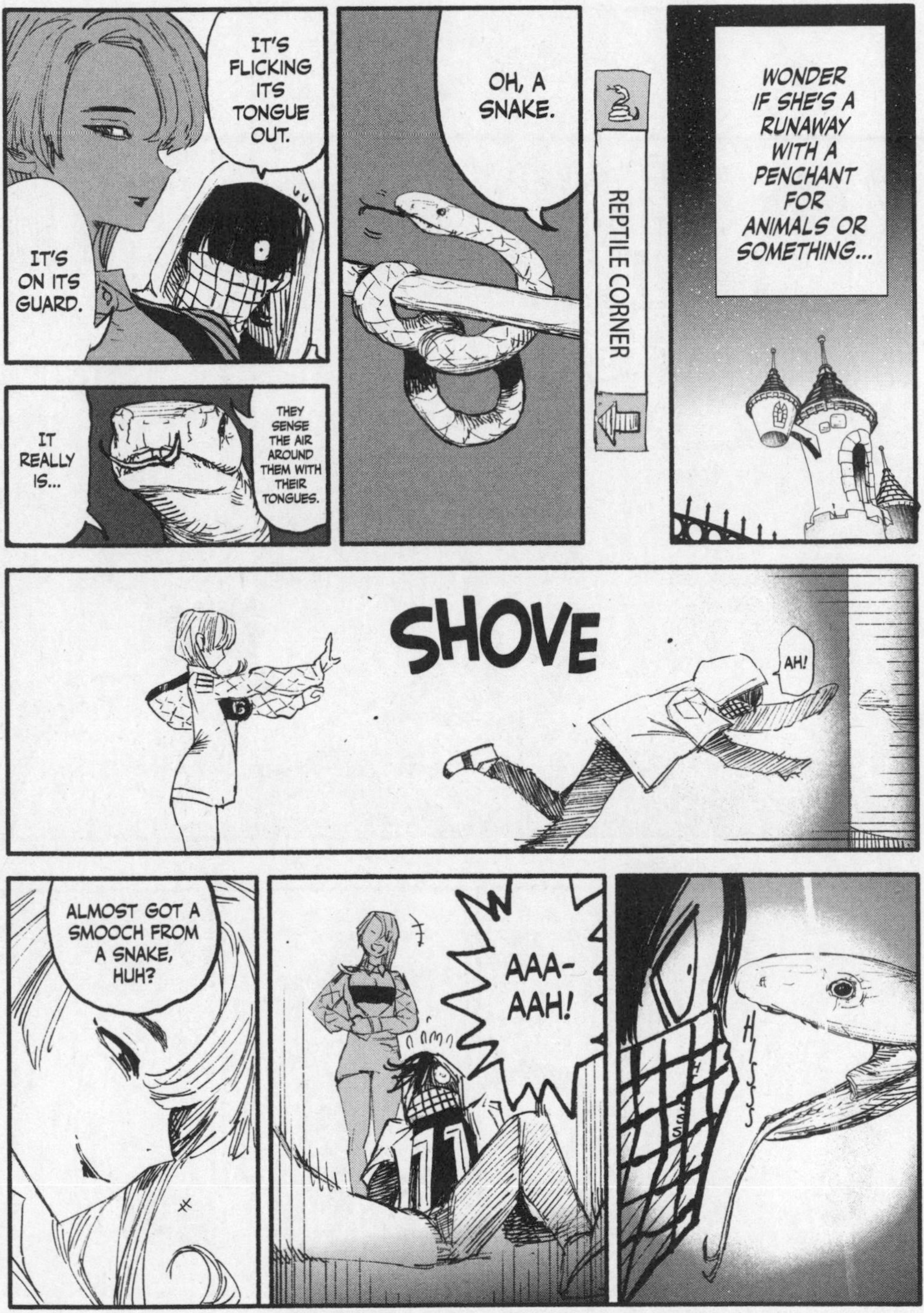
WONDER IF SHE'S A RUNAWAY WITH A PENCHANT FOR ANIMALS OR SOMETHING...
OH, A SNAKE.
REPTILE CORNER
IT'S FLICKING ITS TONGUE OUT.
IT'S ON ITS GUARD.
THEY SENSE THE AIR AROUND THEM WITH THEIR TONGUES.
IT REALLY IS...
SHOVE
AH!
AAA-AAH!
ALMOST GOT A SMOOCH FROM A SNAKE, HUH?

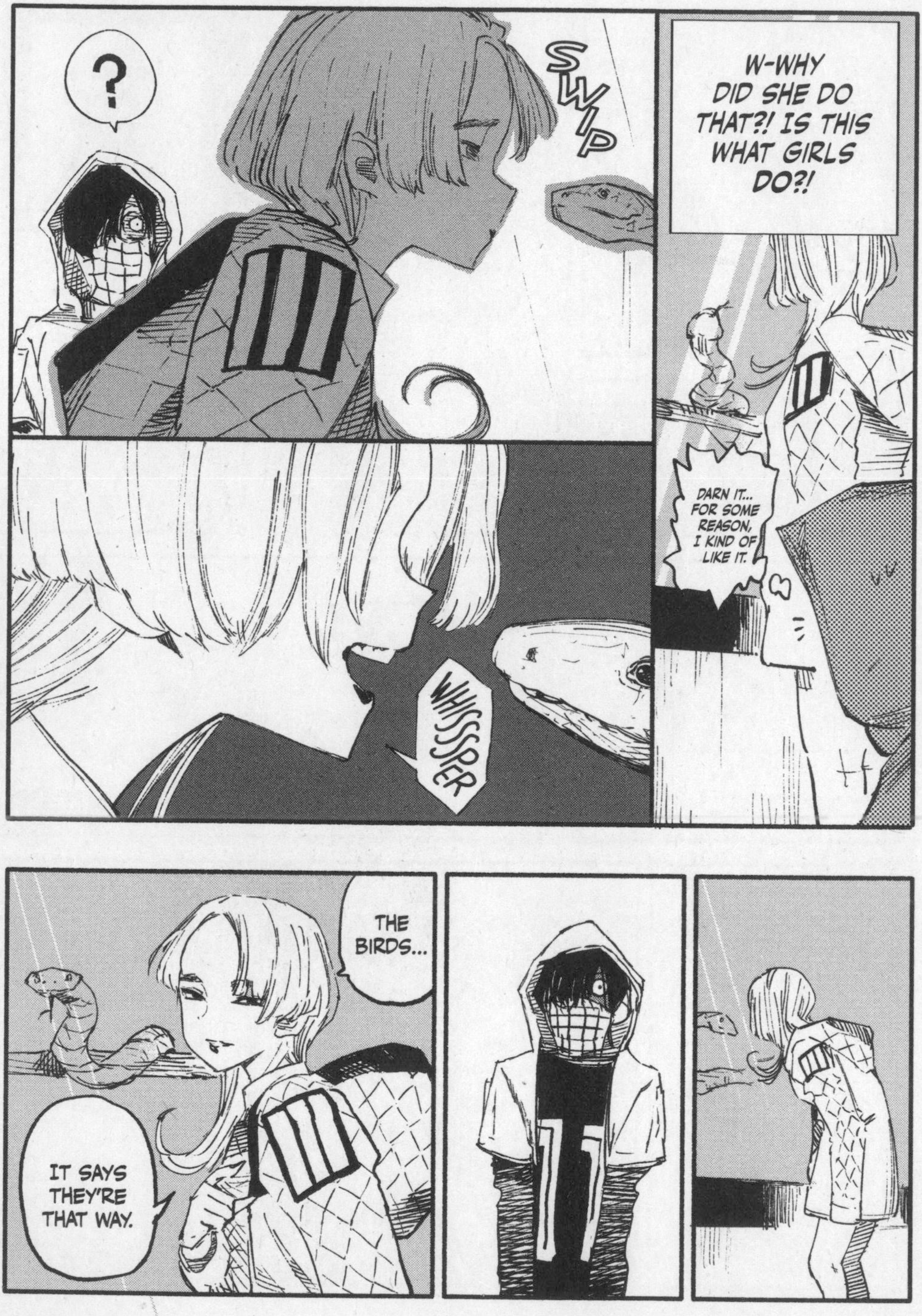
W-WHY DID SHE DO THAT?! IS THIS WHAT GIRLS DO?!
DARN IT... FOR SOME REASON, I KIND OF LIKE IT.
SWIP
?
WHISSSPER
THE BIRDS...
IT SAYS THEY'RE THAT WAY.

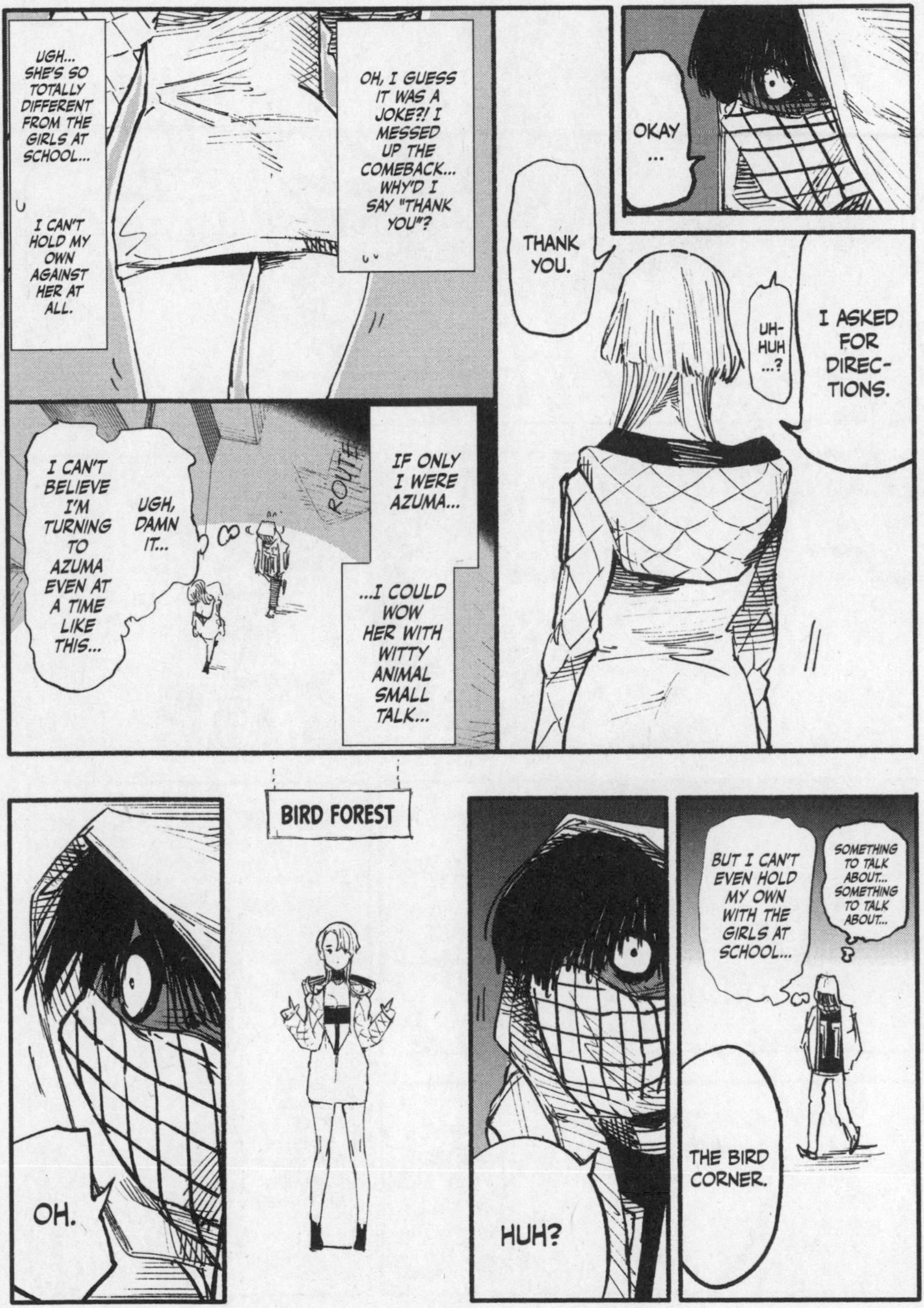
OKAY ...
I ASKED FOR DIREC-TIONS.
UH-HUH ...?
THANK YOU.
OH, I GUESS IT WAS A JOKE?! I MESSED UP THE COMEBACK... WHY'D I SAY "THANK YOU"?
UGH... SHE'S SO TOTALLY DIFFERENT FROM THE GIRLS AT SCHOOL...
I CAN'T HOLD MY OWN AGAINST HER AT ALL.
IF ONLY I WERE AZUMA...
...I COULD WOW HER WITH WITTY ANIMAL SMALL TALK...
ROUTE
UGH, DAMN IT...
I CAN'T BELIEVE I'M TURNING TO AZUMA EVEN AT A TIME LIKE THIS...
SOMETHING TO TALK ABOUT... SOMETHING TO TALK ABOUT...
BUT I CAN'T EVEN HOLD MY OWN WITH THE GIRLS AT SCHOOL...
THE BIRD CORNER.
HUH?
BIRD FOREST
OH.

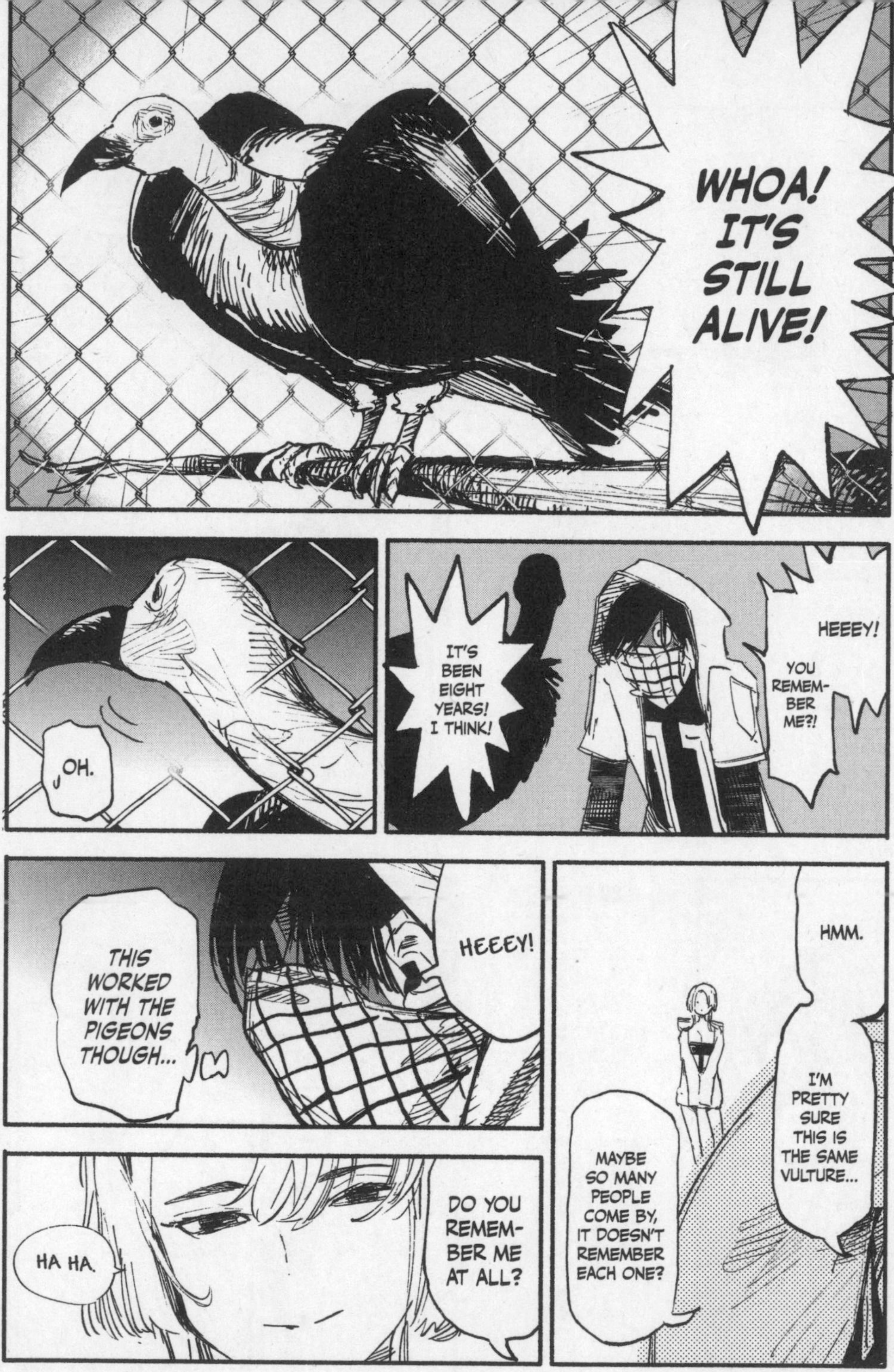
WHOA! IT'S STILL ALIVE!
HEEEY!
YOU REMEMBER ME?!
IT'S BEEN EIGHT YEARS! I THINK!
OH.
HMM.
I'M PRETTY SURE THIS IS THE SAME VULTURE...
MAYBE SO MANY PEOPLE COME BY, IT DOESN'T REMEMBER EACH ONE?
HEEEY!
THIS WORKED WITH THE PIGEONS THOUGH...
DO YOU REMEMBER ME AT ALL?
HA HA.

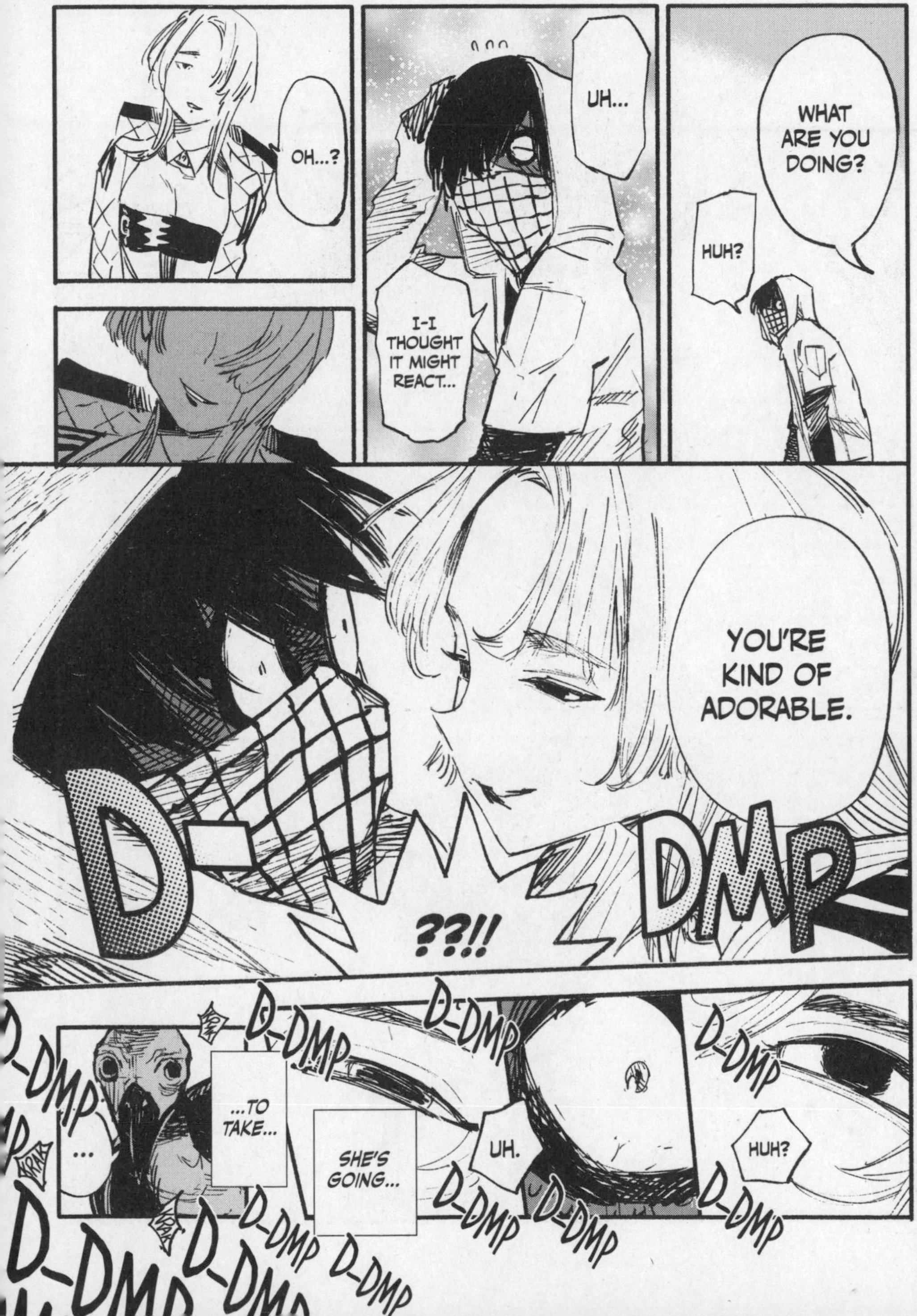
WHAT ARE YOU DOING?
HUH?
UH...
I-I THOUGHT IT MIGHT REACT...
OH...?
YOU'RE KIND OF ADORABLE.
D-DMP
??!!
HUH?
D-DMP
D-DMP
UH.
D-DMP
D-DMP
SHE'S GOING...
...TO TAKE...
D-DMP
D-DMP
...
D-DMP
D-DMP
D-DMP

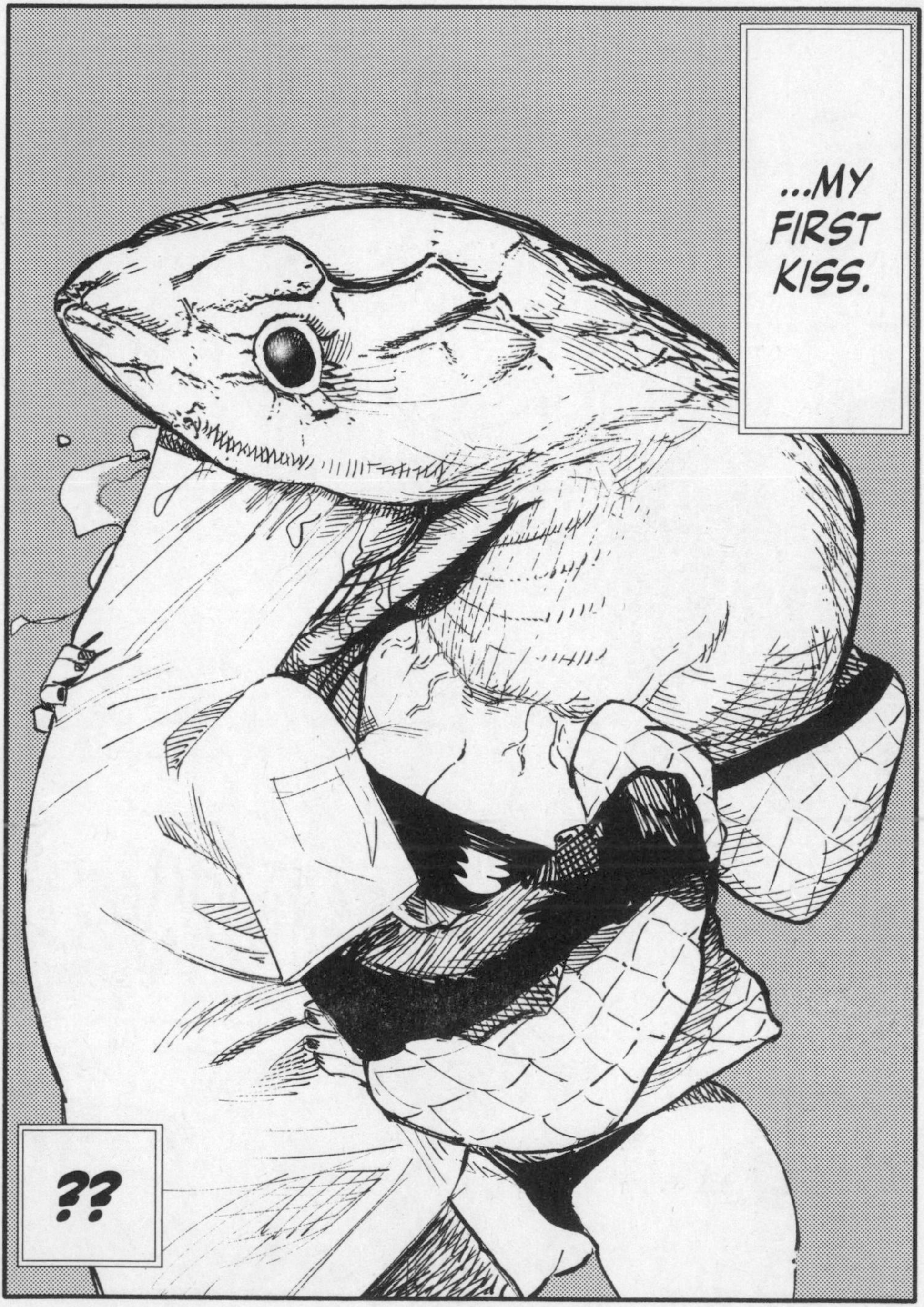
...MY FIRST KISS.
??

CHOUJIN X

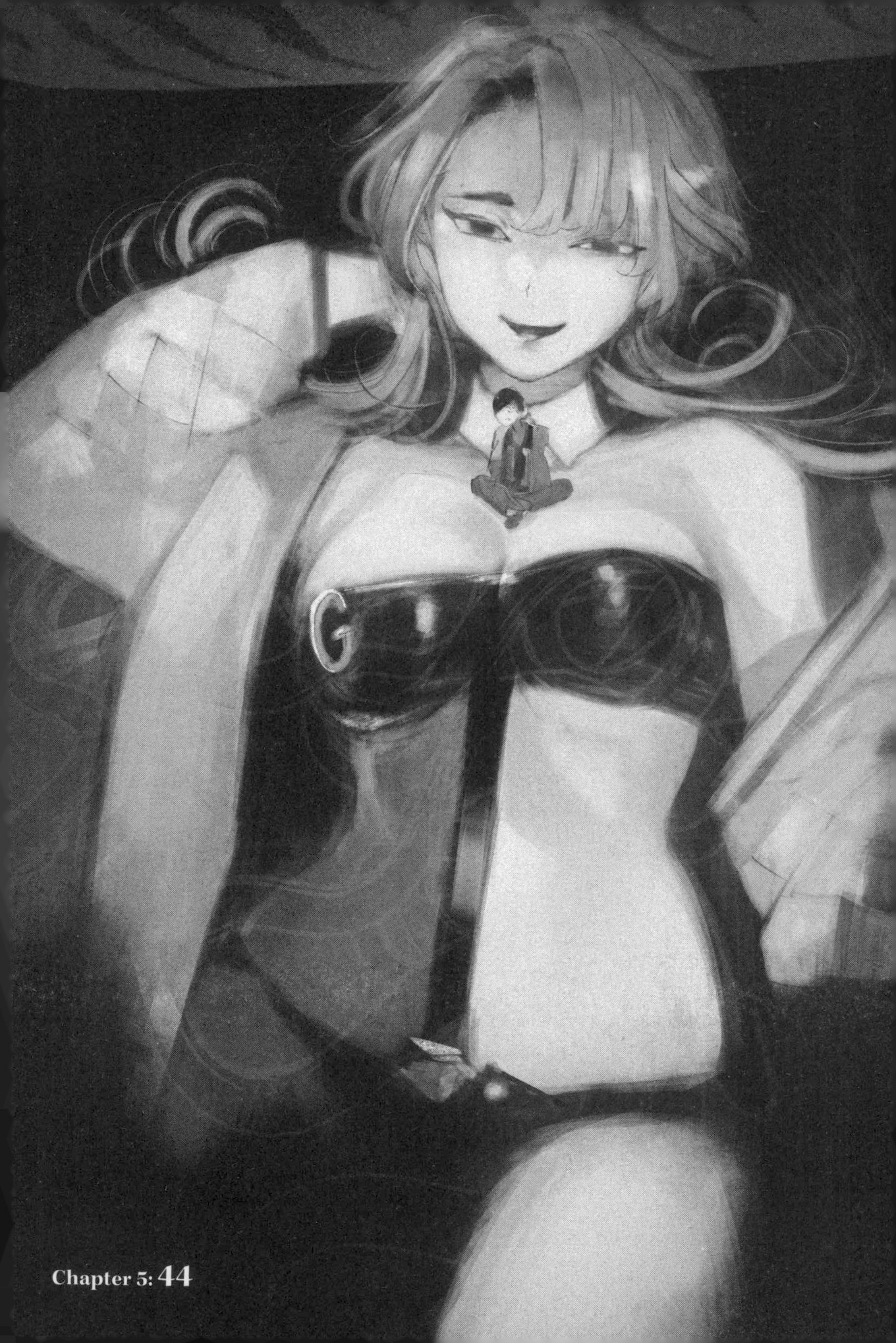

Chapter 5: 44

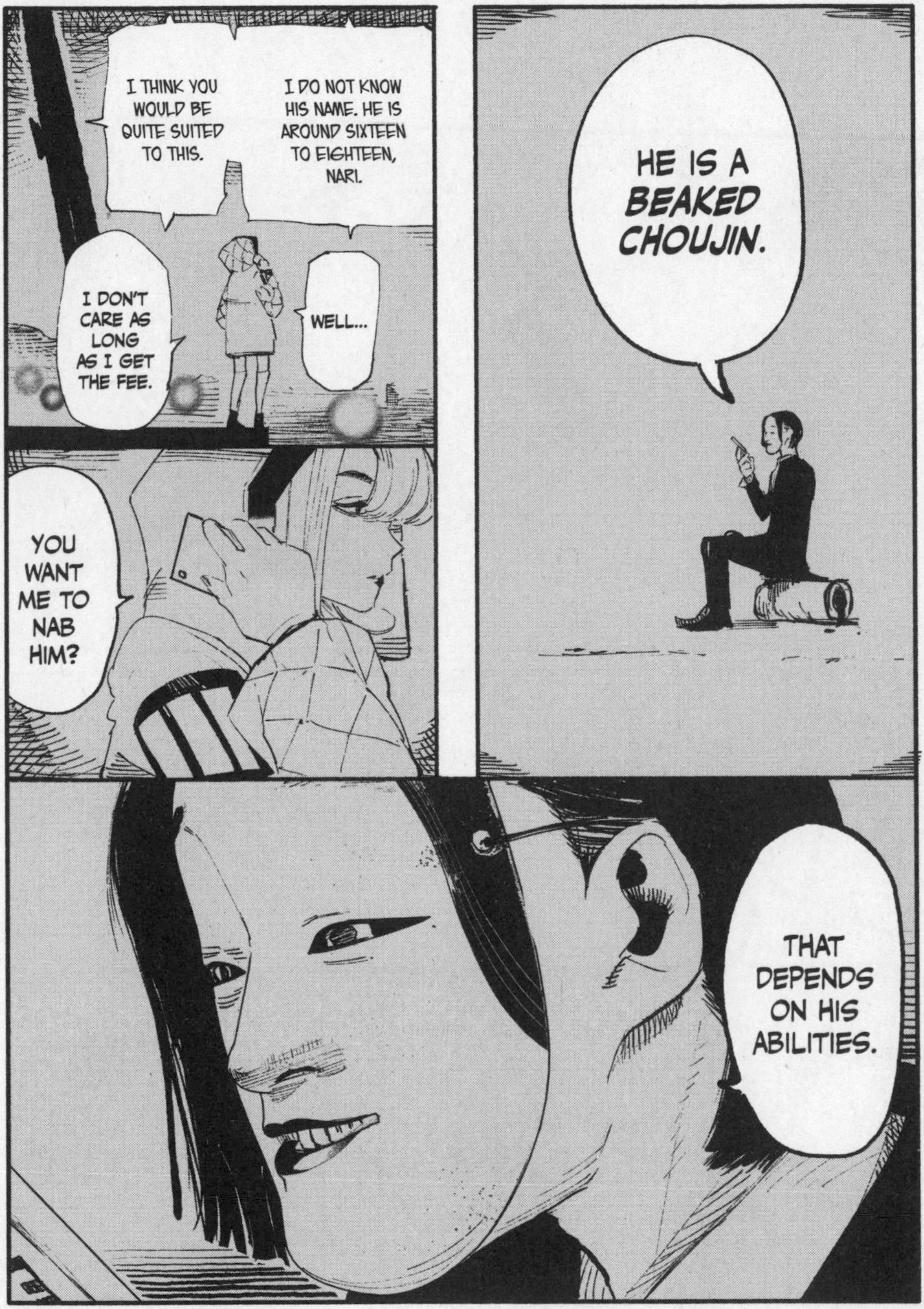
HE IS A BEAKED CHOUJIN.
I DO NOT KNOW HIS NAME. HE IS AROUND SIXTEEN TO EIGHTEEN, NARI.
I THINK YOU WOULD BE QUITE SUITED TO THIS.
WELL...
I DON'T CARE AS LONG AS I GET THE FEE.
YOU WANT ME TO NAB HIM?
THAT DEPENDS ON HIS ABILITIES.

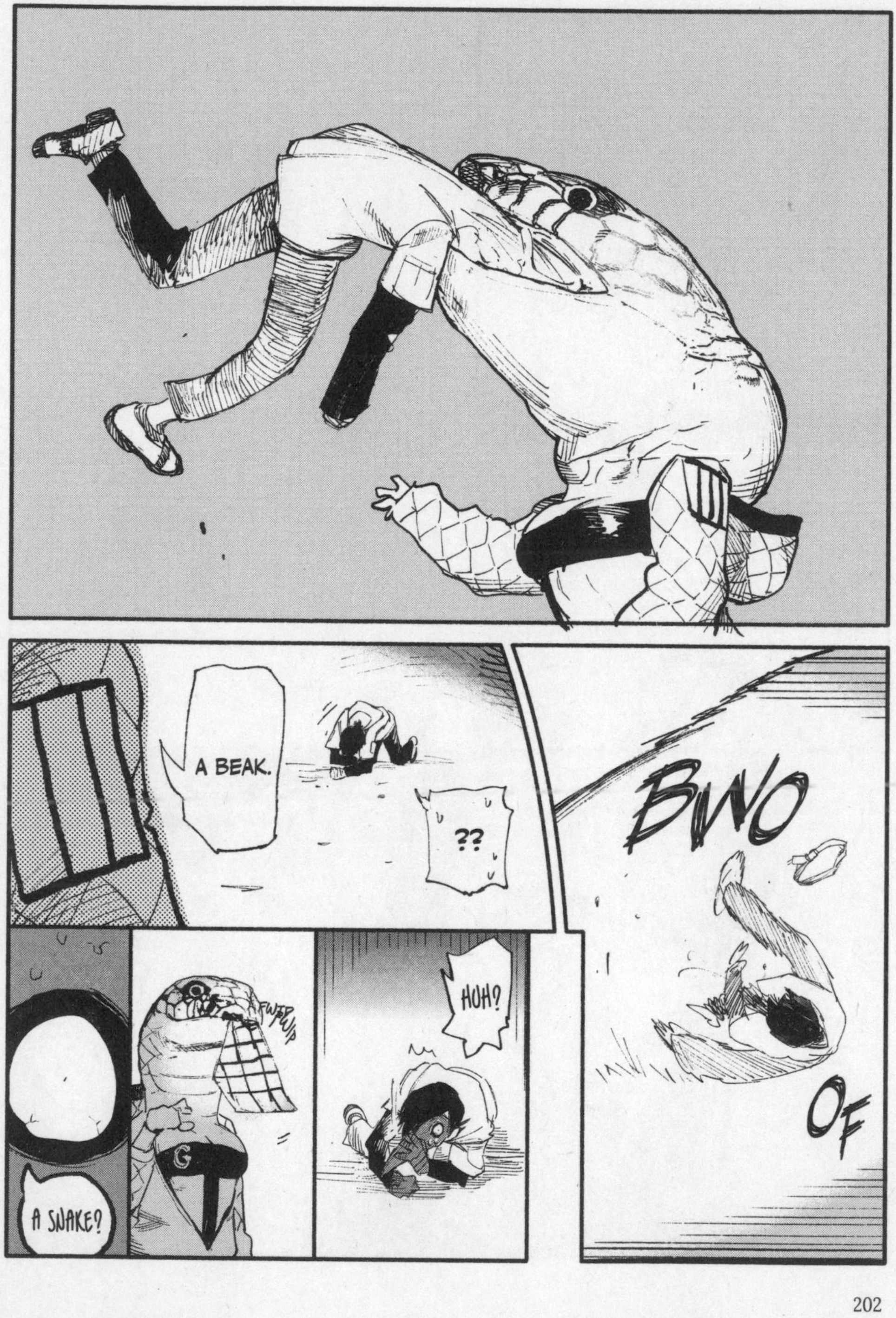
BWO
OF
??
A BEAK.
HUH?
A SNAKE?

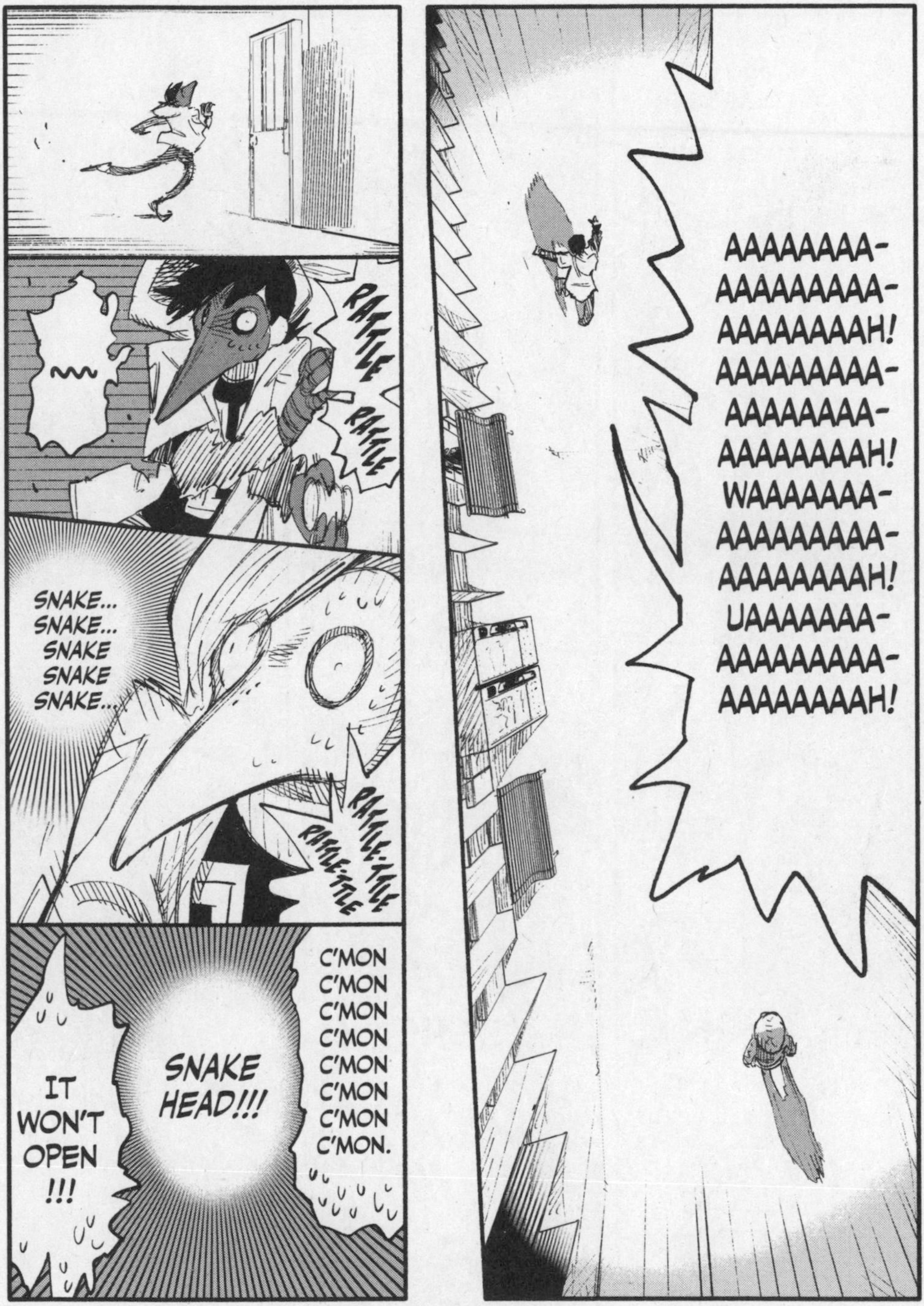
AAAAAAAA-
AAAAAAAAA-
AAAAAAAAH!
AAAAAAAAAA-
AAAAAAAAA-
AAAAAAAAAH!
WAAAAAAA-
AAAAAAAAAA-
AAAAAAAAAH!
UAAAAAAA-
AAAAAAAAAA-
AAAAAAAAAH!
RATTLE
RATTLE
~~~
SNAKE... SNAKE... SNAKE SNAKE SNAKE...
RATTLE-TTLE
RATTLE-TTLE
C'MON C'MON C'MON C'MON C'MON C'MON C'MON C'MON.
SNAKE HEAD!!!
IT WON'T OPEN !!!
~~~

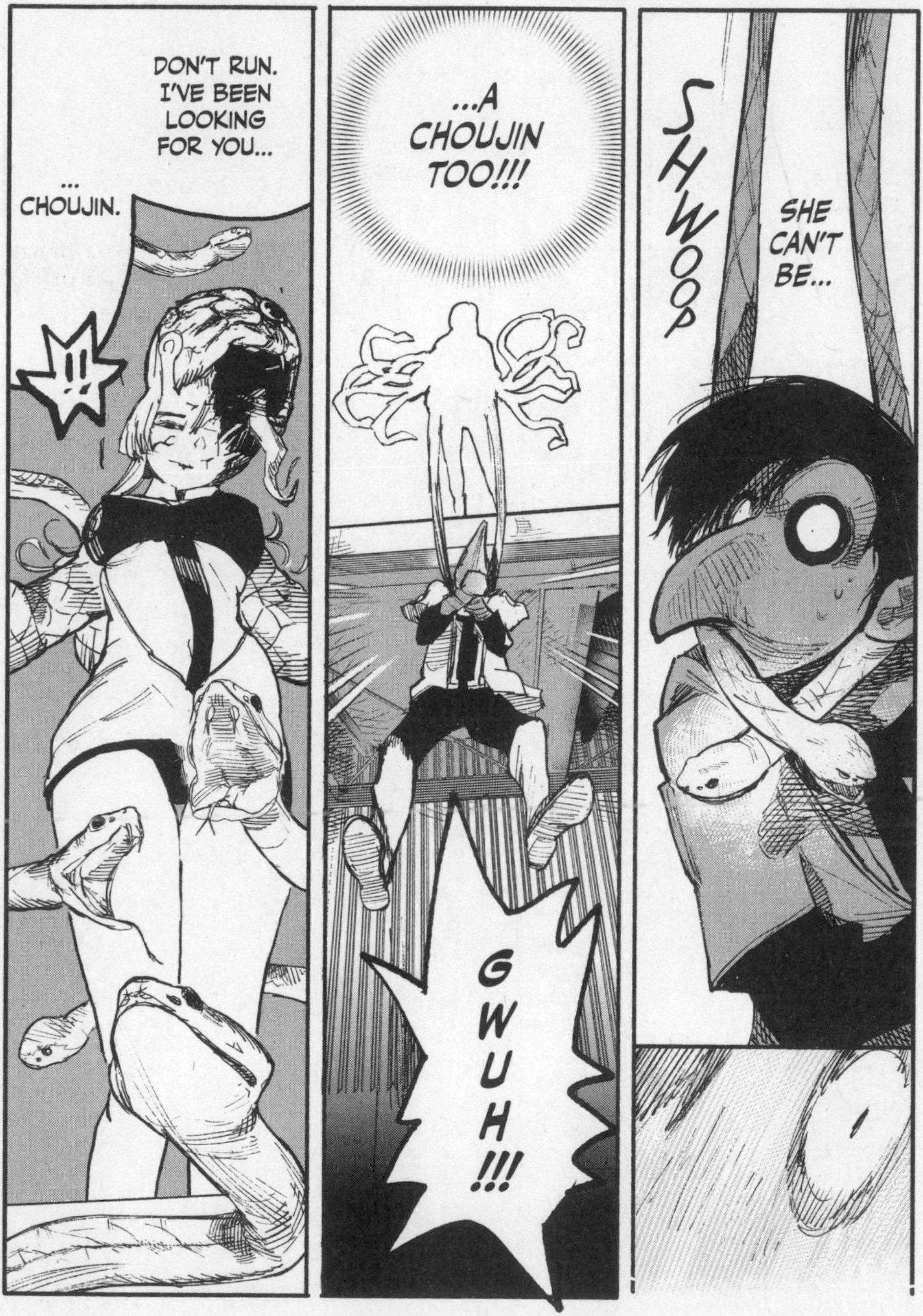
SHWOOP
SHE CAN'T BE...
...A CHOUJIN TOO!!!
GWUH!!!
DON'T RUN. I'VE BEEN LOOKING FOR YOU...
... CHOUJIN.
!!

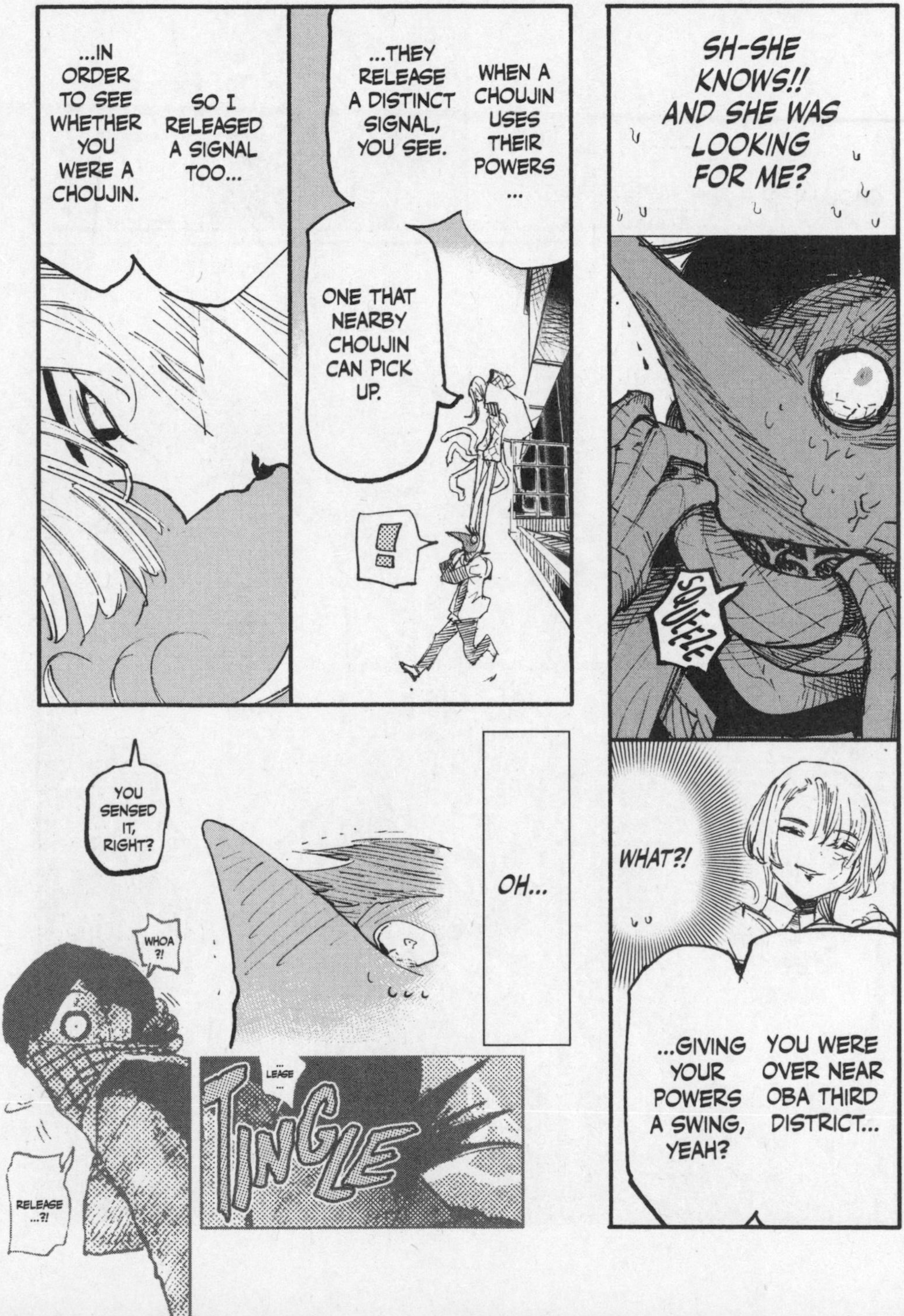
SH-SHE KNOWS!! AND SHE WAS LOOKING FOR ME?
SQUEEZE
WHEN A CHOUJIN USES THEIR POWERS ...
...THEY RELEASE A DISTINCT SIGNAL, YOU SEE.
ONE THAT NEARBY CHOUJIN CAN PICK UP.
!!
SO I RELEASED A SIGNAL TOO...
...IN ORDER TO SEE WHETHER YOU WERE A CHOUJIN.
WHAT?!
YOU WERE OVER NEAR OBA THIRD DISTRICT...
...GIVING YOUR POWERS A SWING, YEAH?
OH...
YOU SENSED IT, RIGHT?
WHOA ?!
...LEASE...
TINGLE
RELEASE ...?!

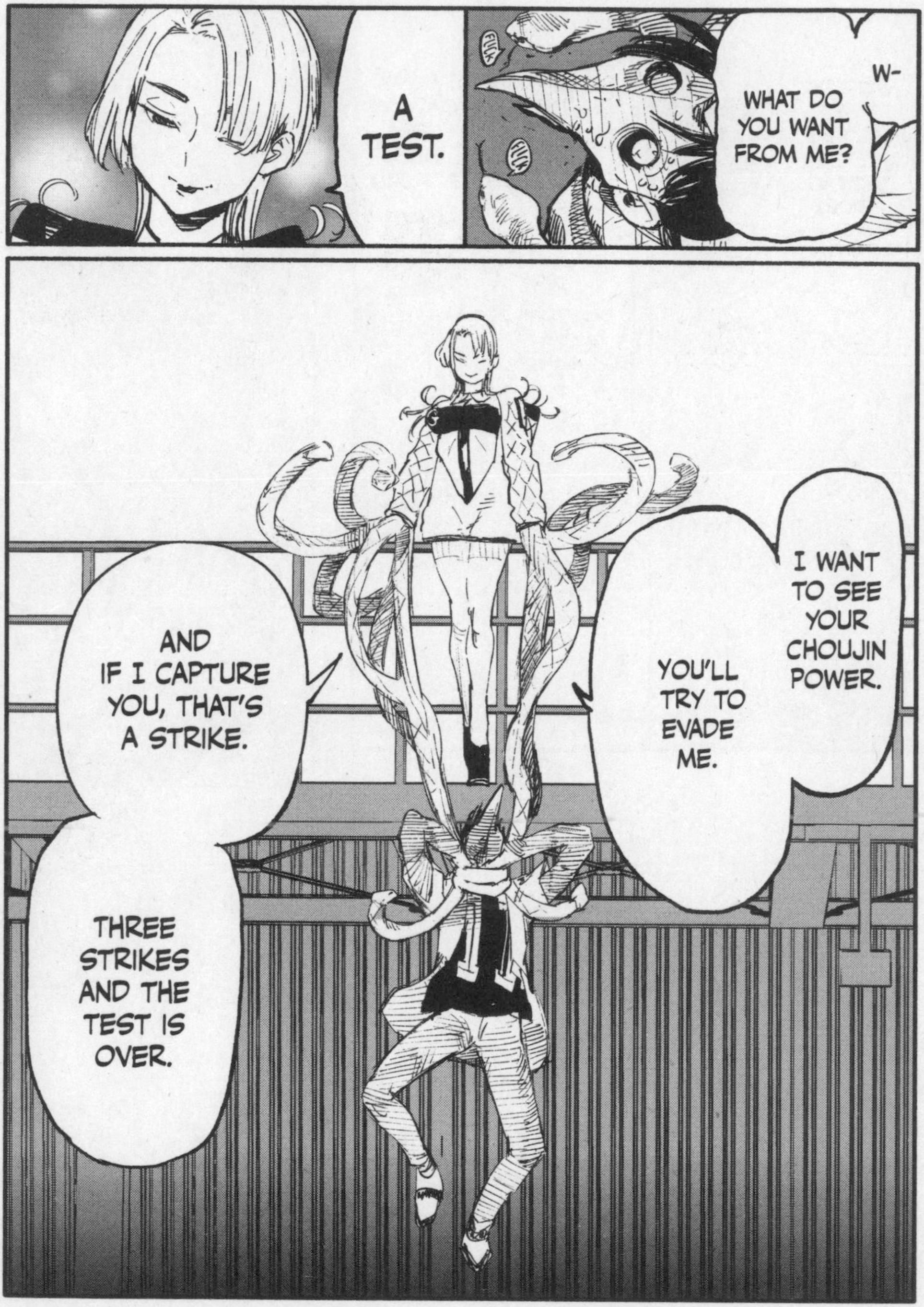
FUCK
FUCK
W-
WHAT DO YOU WANT FROM ME?
A TEST.
I WANT TO SEE YOUR CHOUJIN POWER.
YOU'LL TRY TO EVADE ME.
AND IF I CAPTURE YOU, THAT'S A STRIKE.
THREE STRIKES AND THE TEST IS OVER.

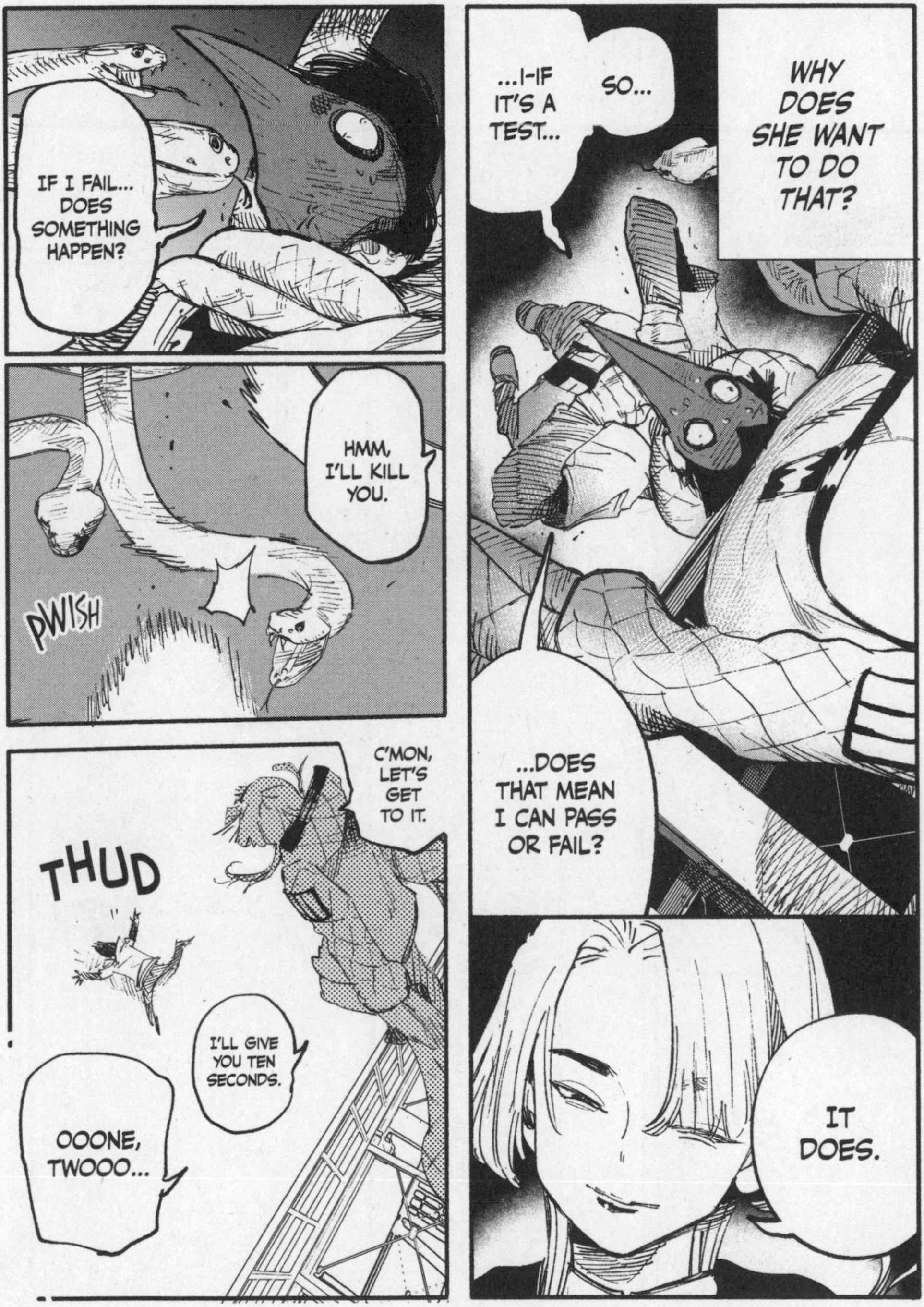
WHY DOES SHE WANT TO DO THAT?
SO...
...I-IF IT'S A TEST...
...DOES THAT MEAN I CAN PASS OR FAIL?
IT DOES.
IF I FAIL... DOES SOMETHING HAPPEN?
HMM, I'LL KILL YOU.
PWISH
C'MON, LET'S GET TO IT.
THUD
I'LL GIVE YOU TEN SECONDS.
OOONE, TWOOO...

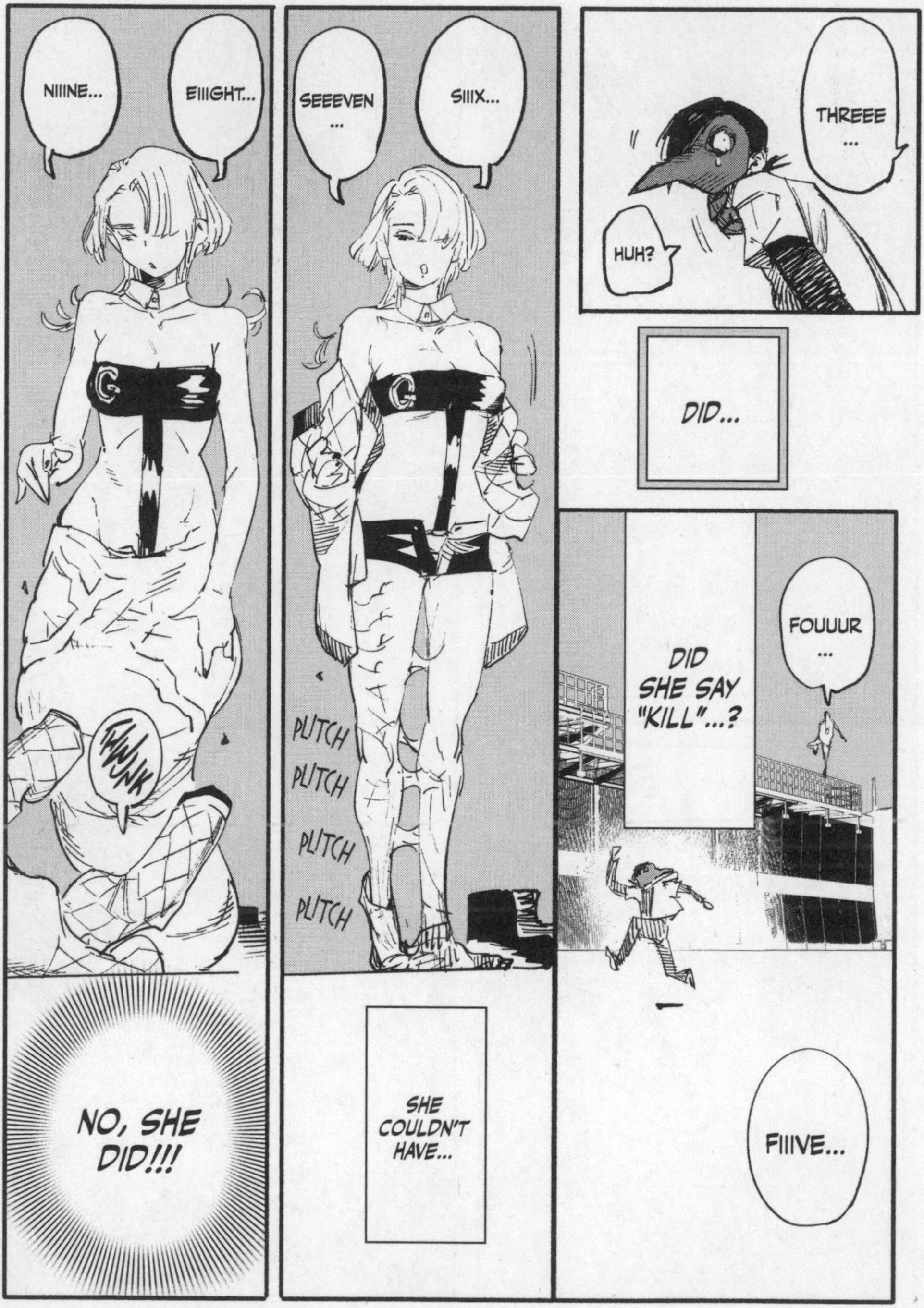
THREEE ...
HUH?
DID...
FOUUUR ...
DID SHE SAY "KILL"...?
FIIIVE...
SIIIX...
SEEEVEN ...
PLITCH
PLITCH
PLITCH
PLITCH
SHE COULDN'T HAVE...
EIIIGHT...
NIIINE...
TWUNK
NO, SHE DID!!!

Chapter 5: 44

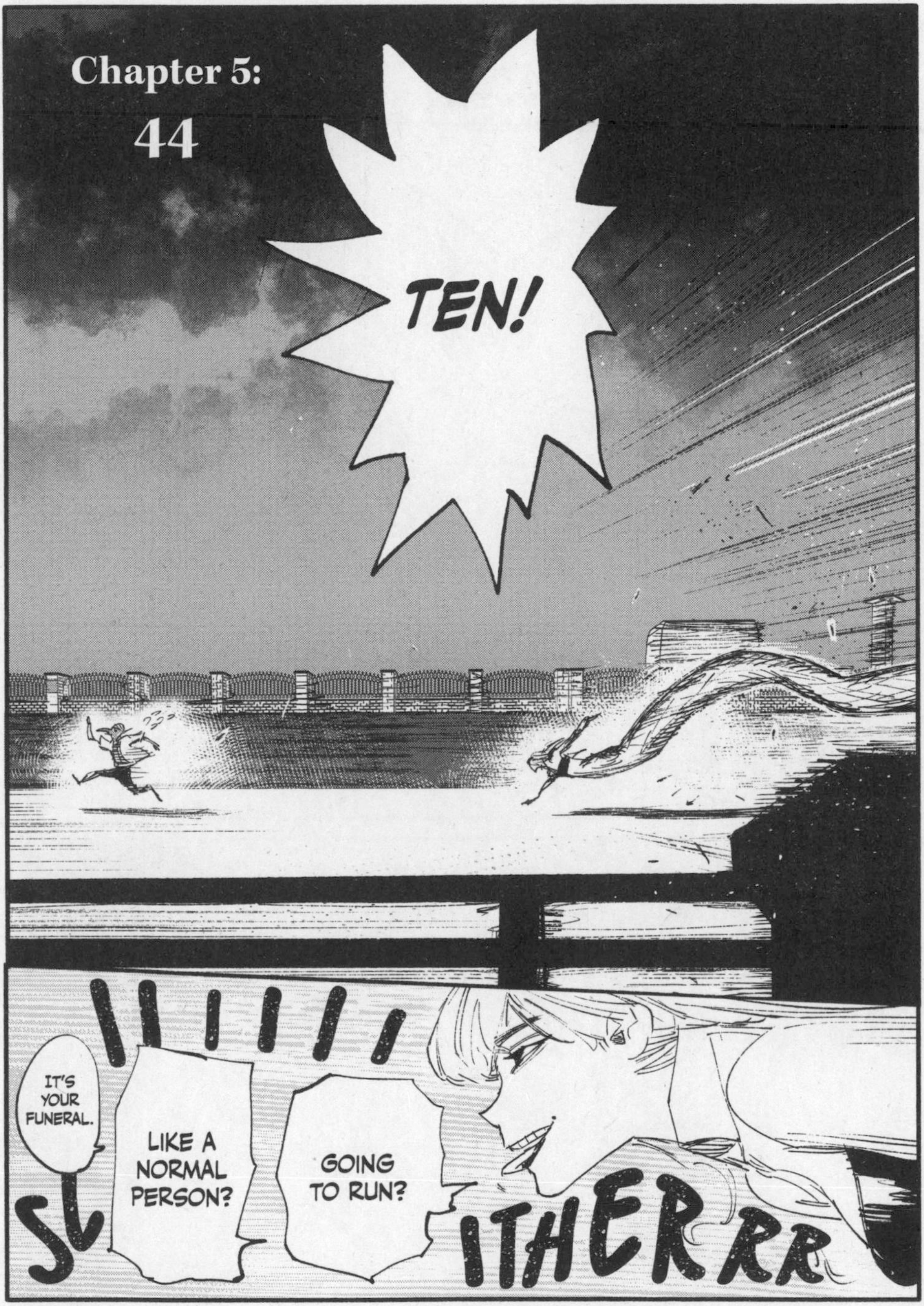
TEN!
GOING TO RUN?
LIKE A NORMAL PERSON?
IT'S YOUR FUNERAL.
SLITHERRR

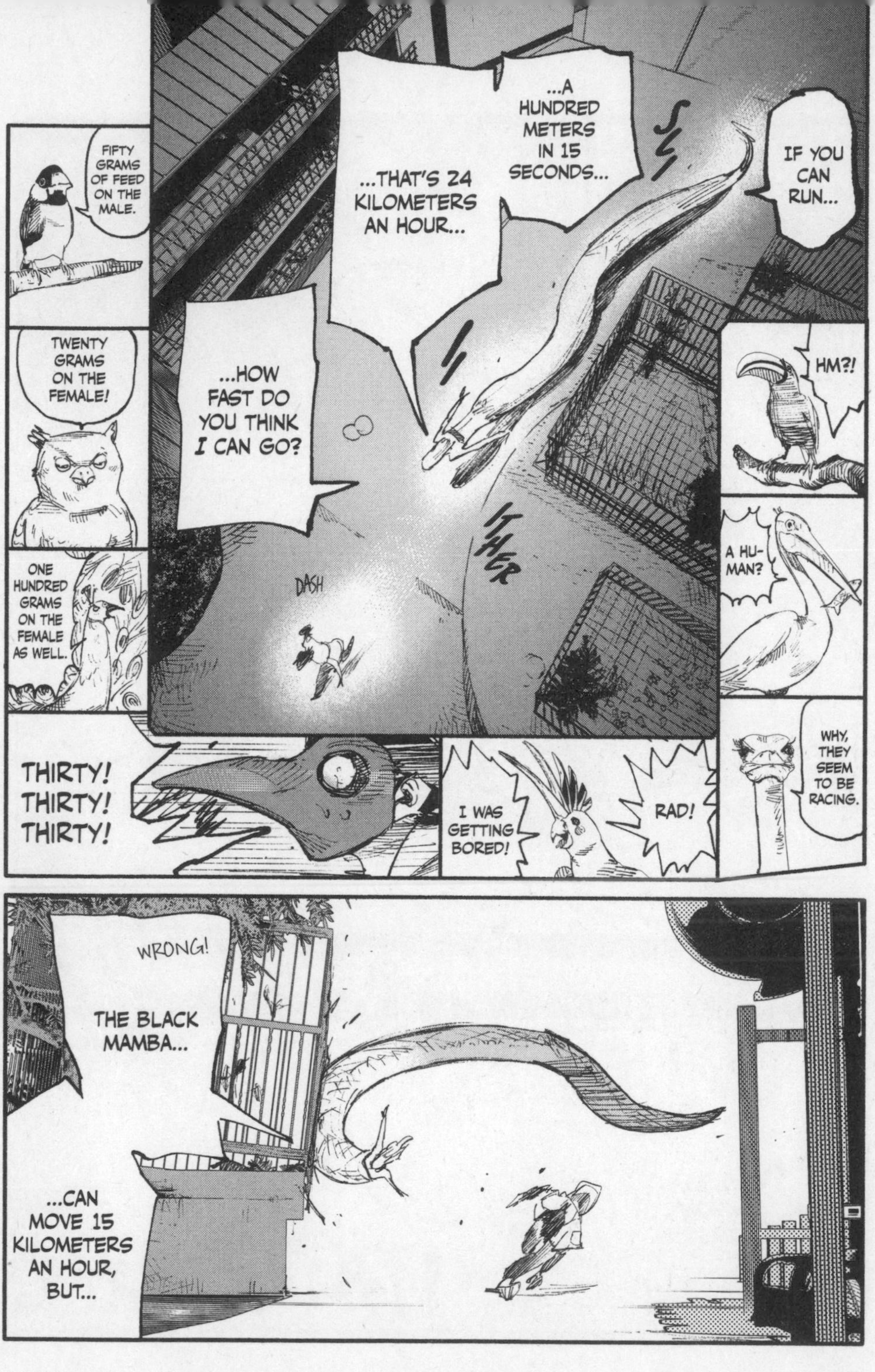

IF YOU CAN RUN...
...A HUNDRED METERS IN 15 SECONDS...
...THAT'S 24 KILOMETERS AN HOUR...
...HOW FAST DO YOU THINK I CAN GO?
DASH
HM?!
A HU-MAN?
FIFTY GRAMS OF FEED ON THE MALE.
TWENTY GRAMS ON THE FEMALE!
ONE HUNDRED GRAMS ON THE FEMALE AS WELL.
WHY, THEY SEEM TO BE RACING.
RAD!
I WAS GETTING BORED!
THIRTY! THIRTY! THIRTY!
WRONG!
THE BLACK MAMBA...
...CAN MOVE 15 KILOMETERS AN HOUR, BUT...

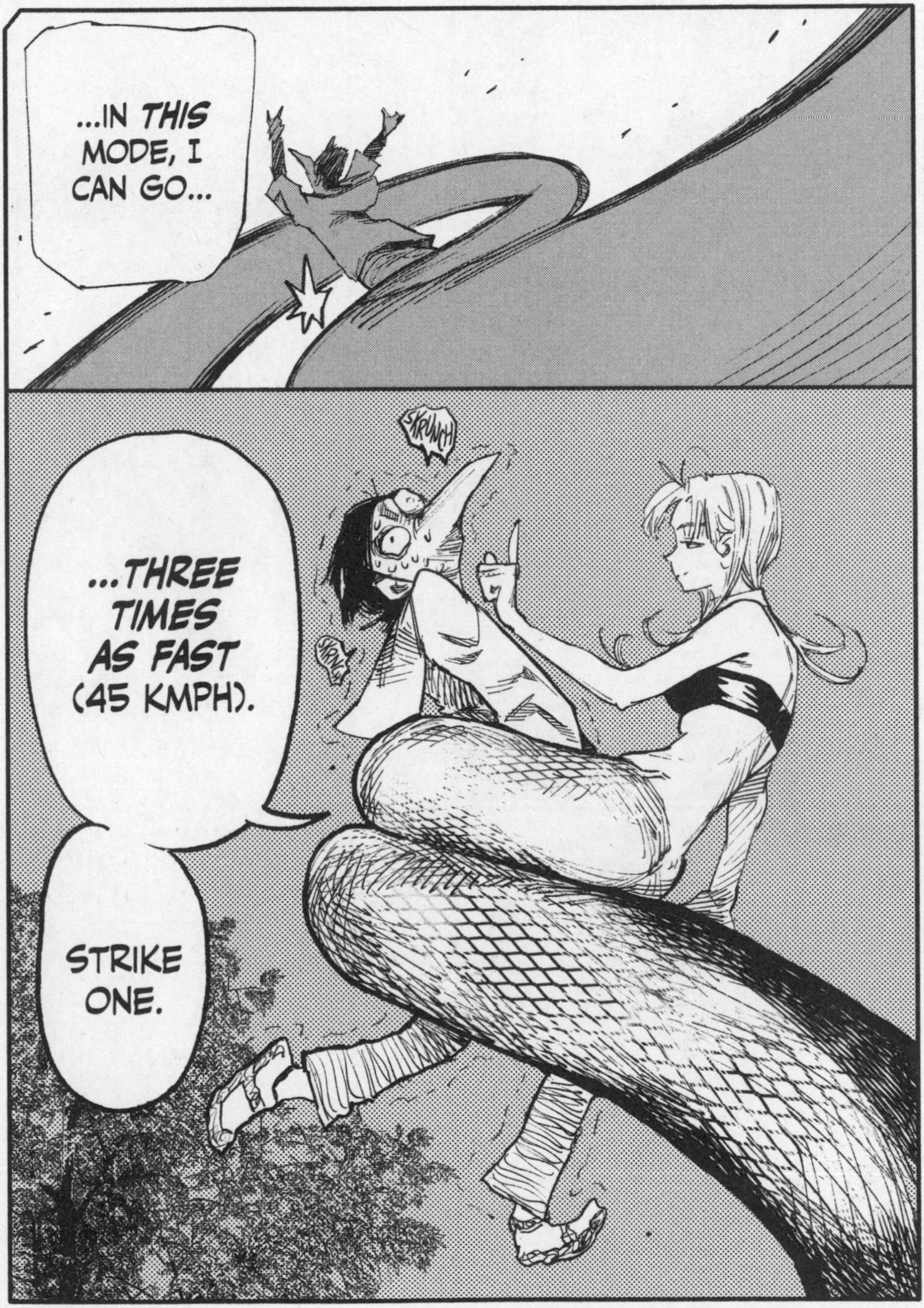
...IN *THIS* MODE, I CAN GO...
SKRUNCH
...*THREE TIMES AS FAST* (45 KMPH).
STRIKE ONE.

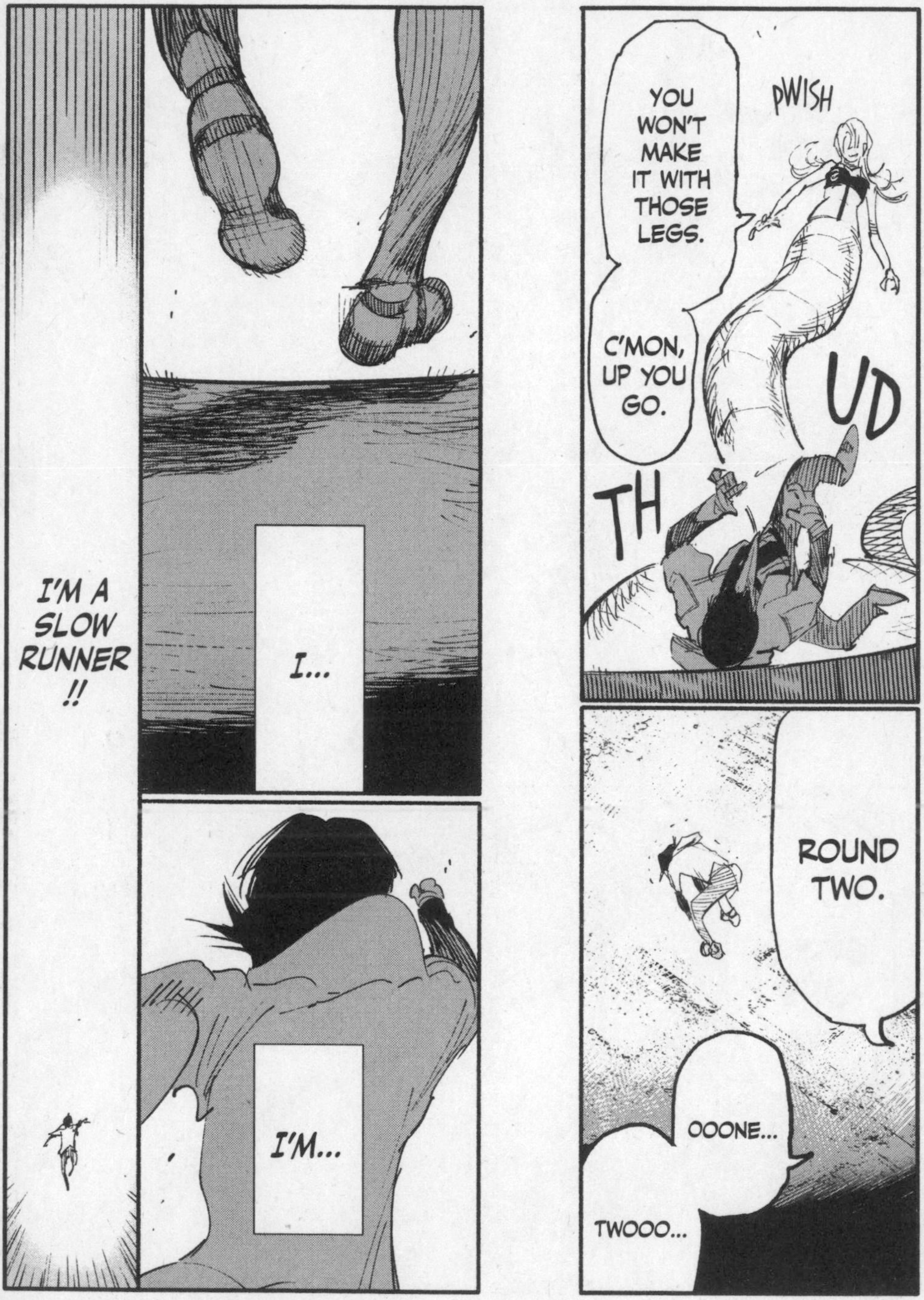
YOU WON'T MAKE IT WITH THOSE LEGS.
PWISH
C'MON, UP YOU GO.
UD
TH
ROUND TWO.
OOONE...
TWOOO...
I...
I'M...
I'M A SLOW RUNNER !!

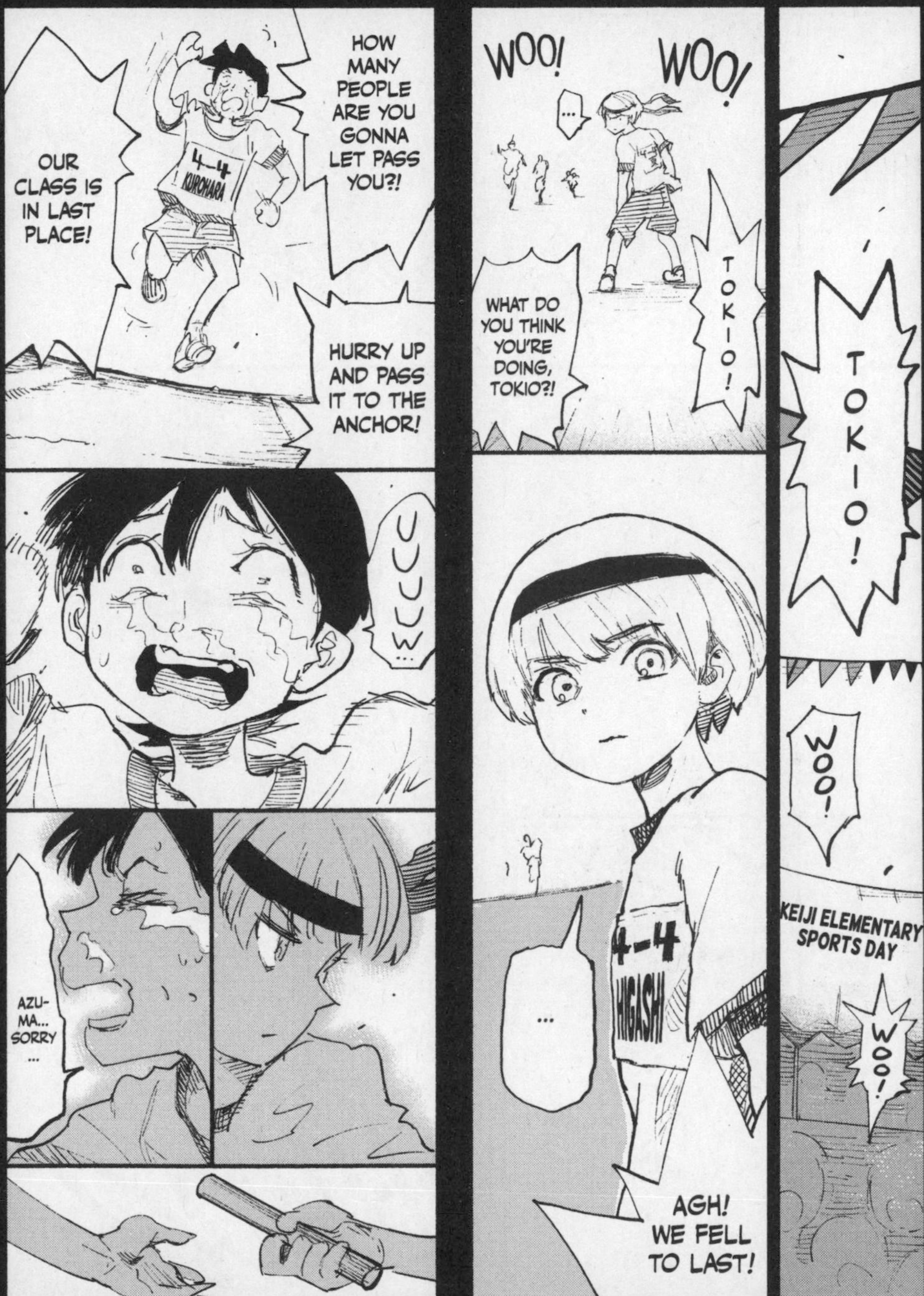
TOKIO!
WOO!
KEIJI ELEMENTARY SPORTS DAY
WOO!
WOO!
WOO!
...
TOKIO!
WHAT DO YOU THINK YOU'RE DOING, TOKIO?!
HOW MANY PEOPLE ARE YOU GONNA LET PASS YOU?!
4-4 KUROHARA
OUR CLASS IS IN LAST PLACE!
HURRY UP AND PASS IT TO THE ANCHOR!
AGH! WE FELL TO LAST!
4-4 HIGASHI
...
UUUUW...
AZUMA... SORRY...

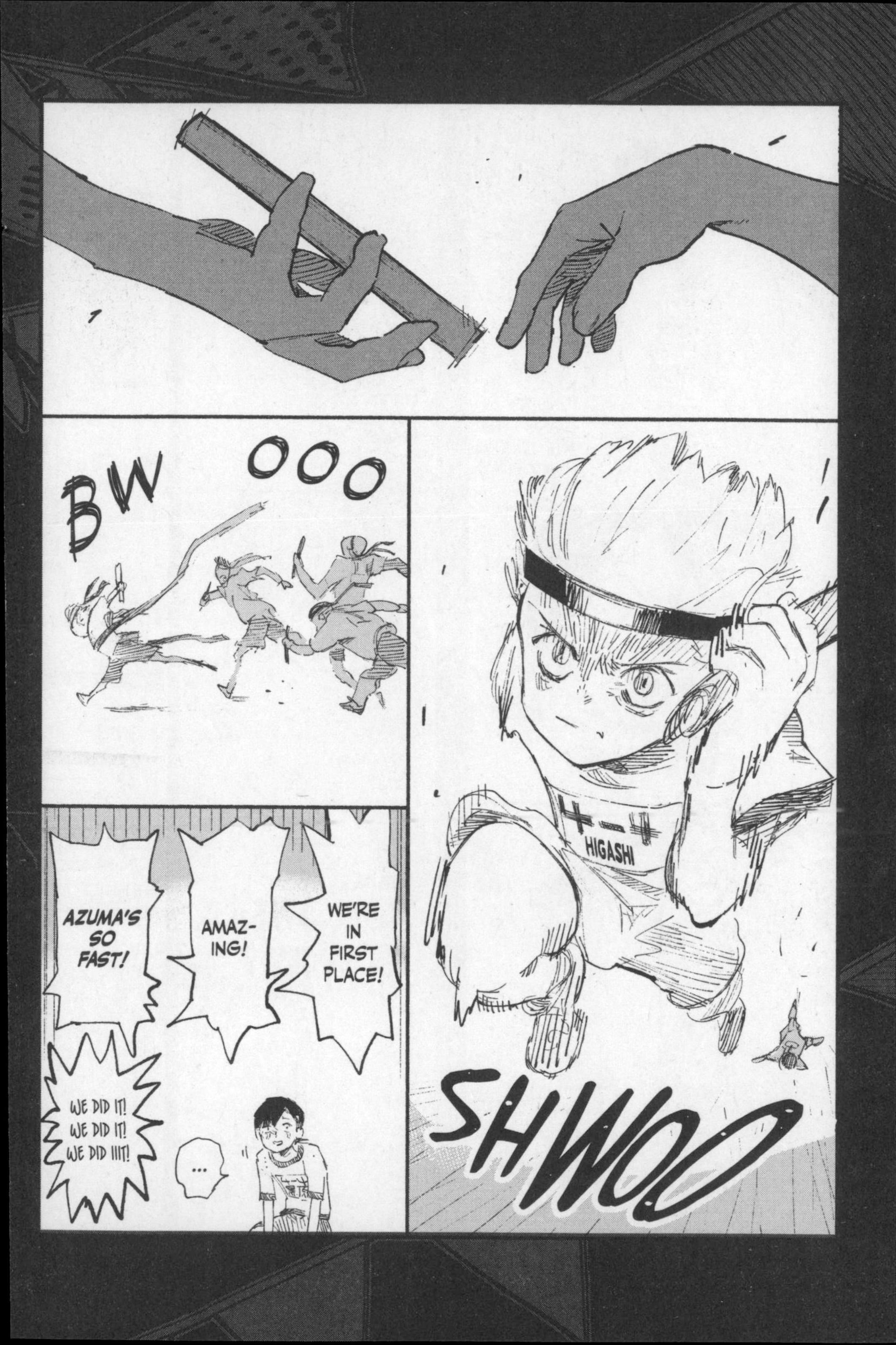
HIGASHI
SHWOO
BWOOO
WE'RE IN FIRST PLACE!
AMAZING!
AZUMA'S SO FAST!
WE DID IT! WE DID IT! WE DID IIIT!
...

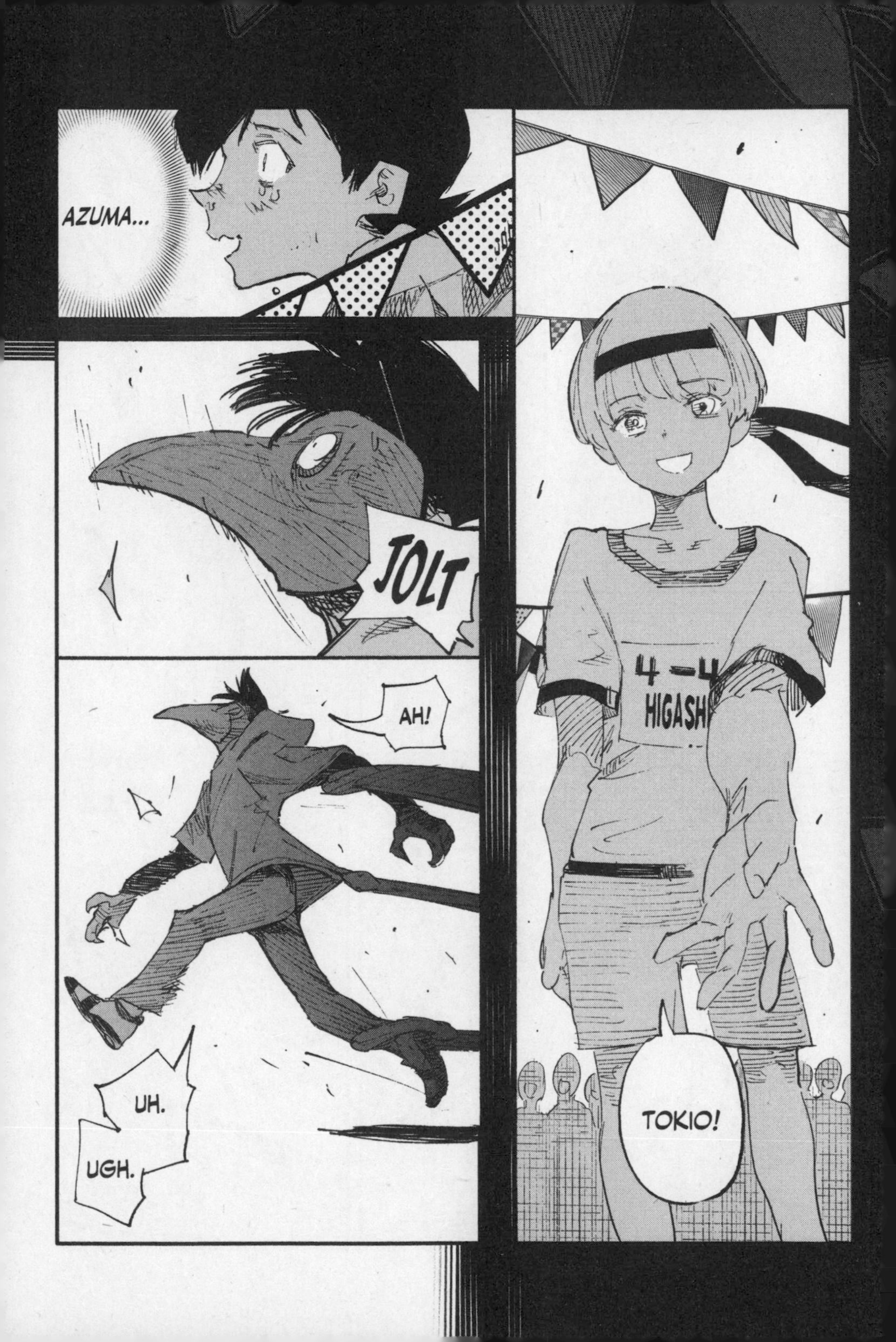
4-4
HIGASH
TOKIO!
AZUMA...
JOLT
AH!
UH.
UGH.

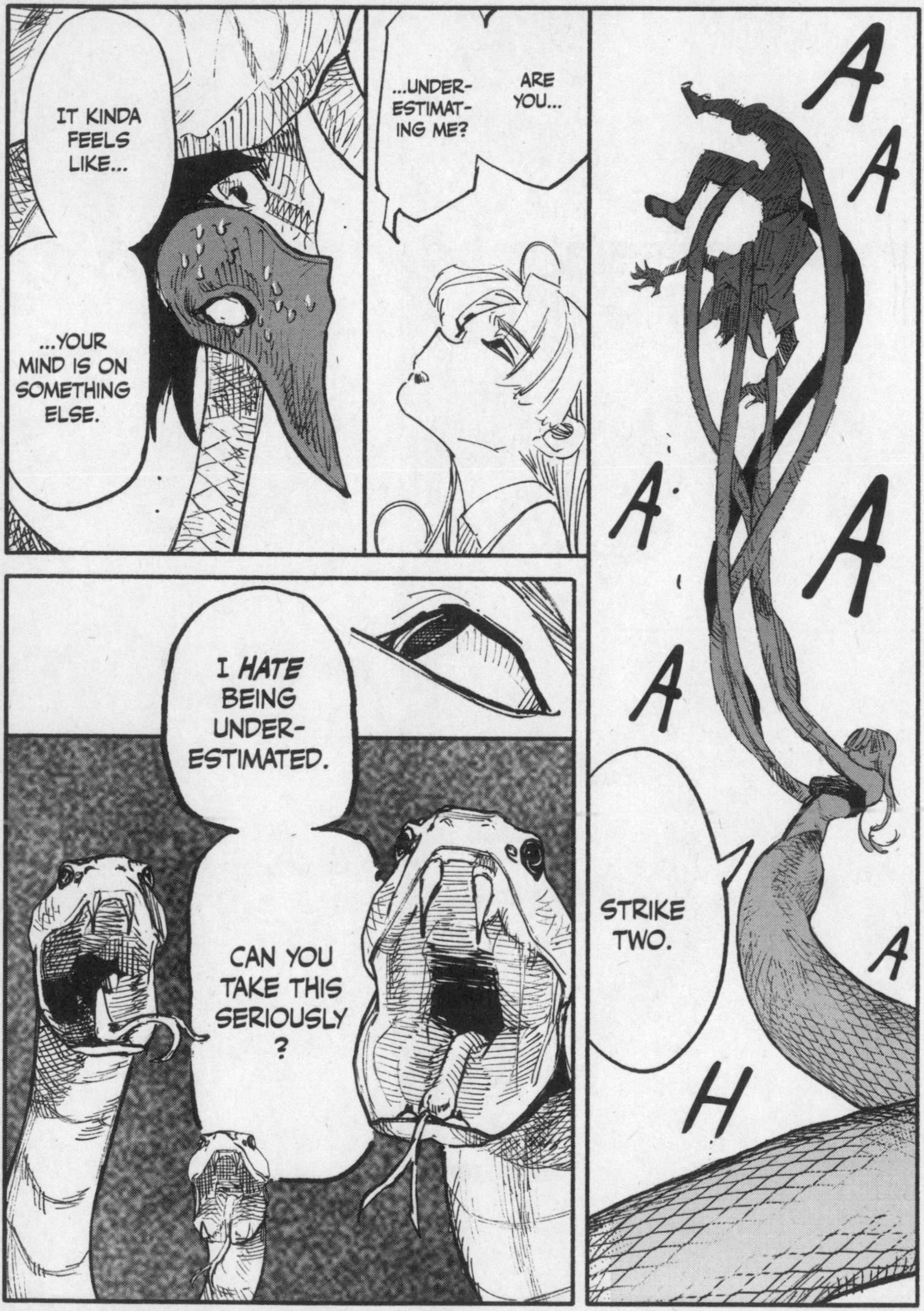
AAAAAAAAH
STRIKE TWO.
ARE YOU...
...UNDERESTIMATING ME?
IT KINDA FEELS LIKE...
...YOUR MIND IS ON SOMETHING ELSE.
I *HATE* BEING UNDERESTIMATED.
CAN YOU TAKE THIS SERIOUSLY?

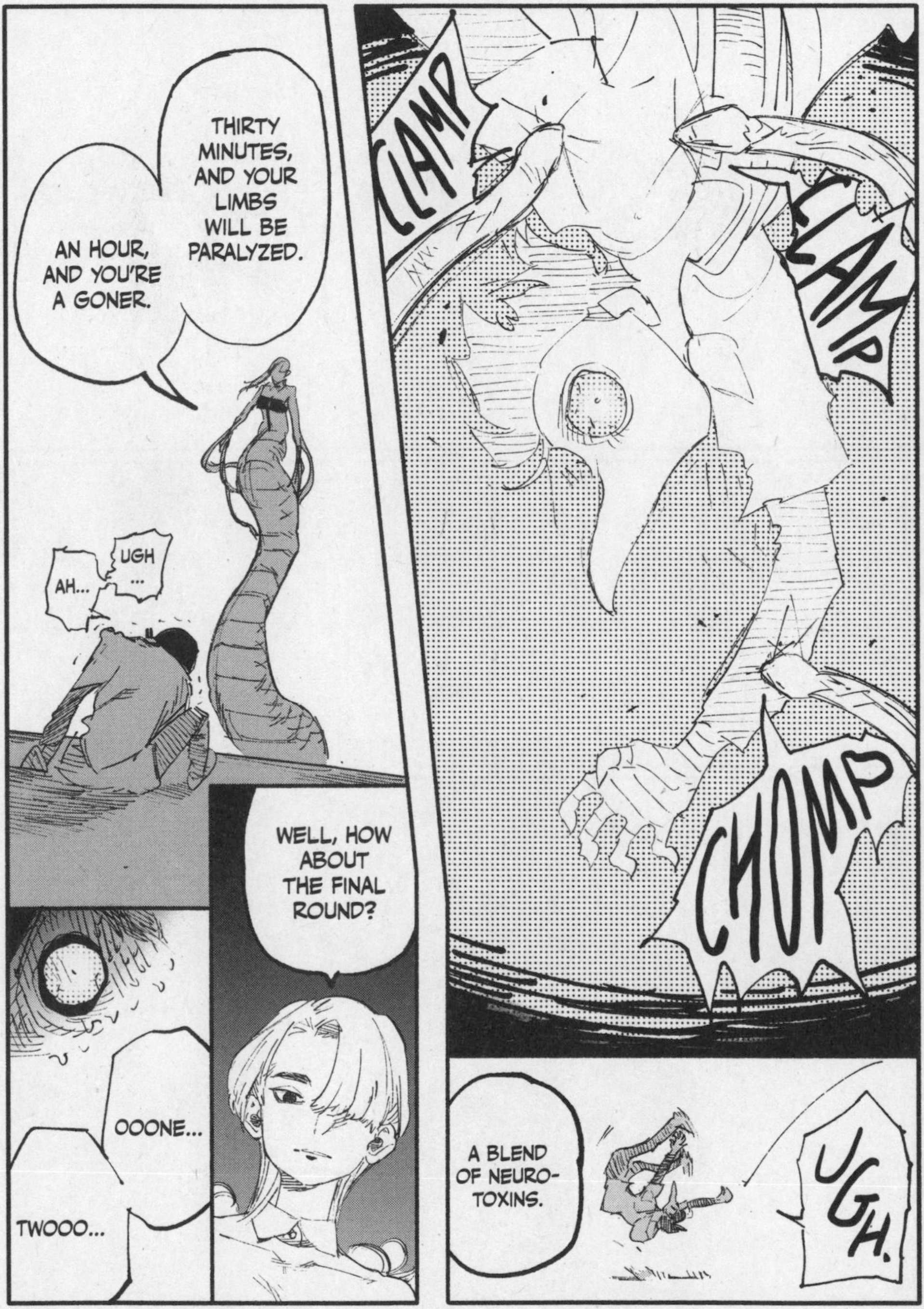
CLAMP
CLAMP
CHOMP
UGH.
A BLEND OF NEURO-TOXINS.
THIRTY MINUTES, AND YOUR LIMBS WILL BE PARALYZED.
AN HOUR, AND YOU'RE A GONER.
UGH...
AH...
WELL, HOW ABOUT THE FINAL ROUND?
OOONE...
TWOOO...

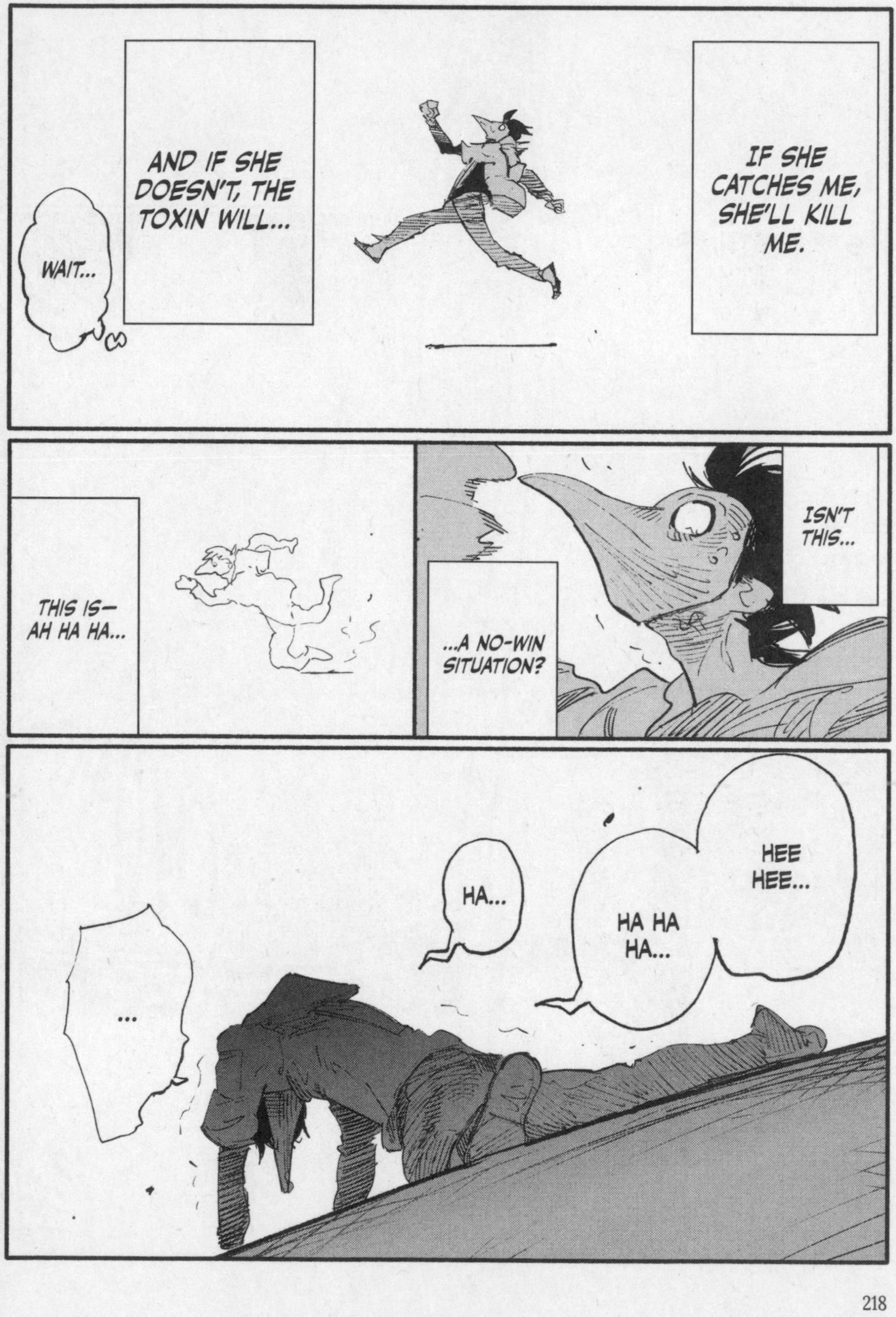
IF SHE CATCHES ME, SHE'LL KILL ME.
AND IF SHE DOESN'T, THE TOXIN WILL...
WAIT...
ISN'T THIS...
...A NO-WIN SITUATION?
THIS IS— AH HA HA...
HEE HEE...
HA HA HA...
HA...
...

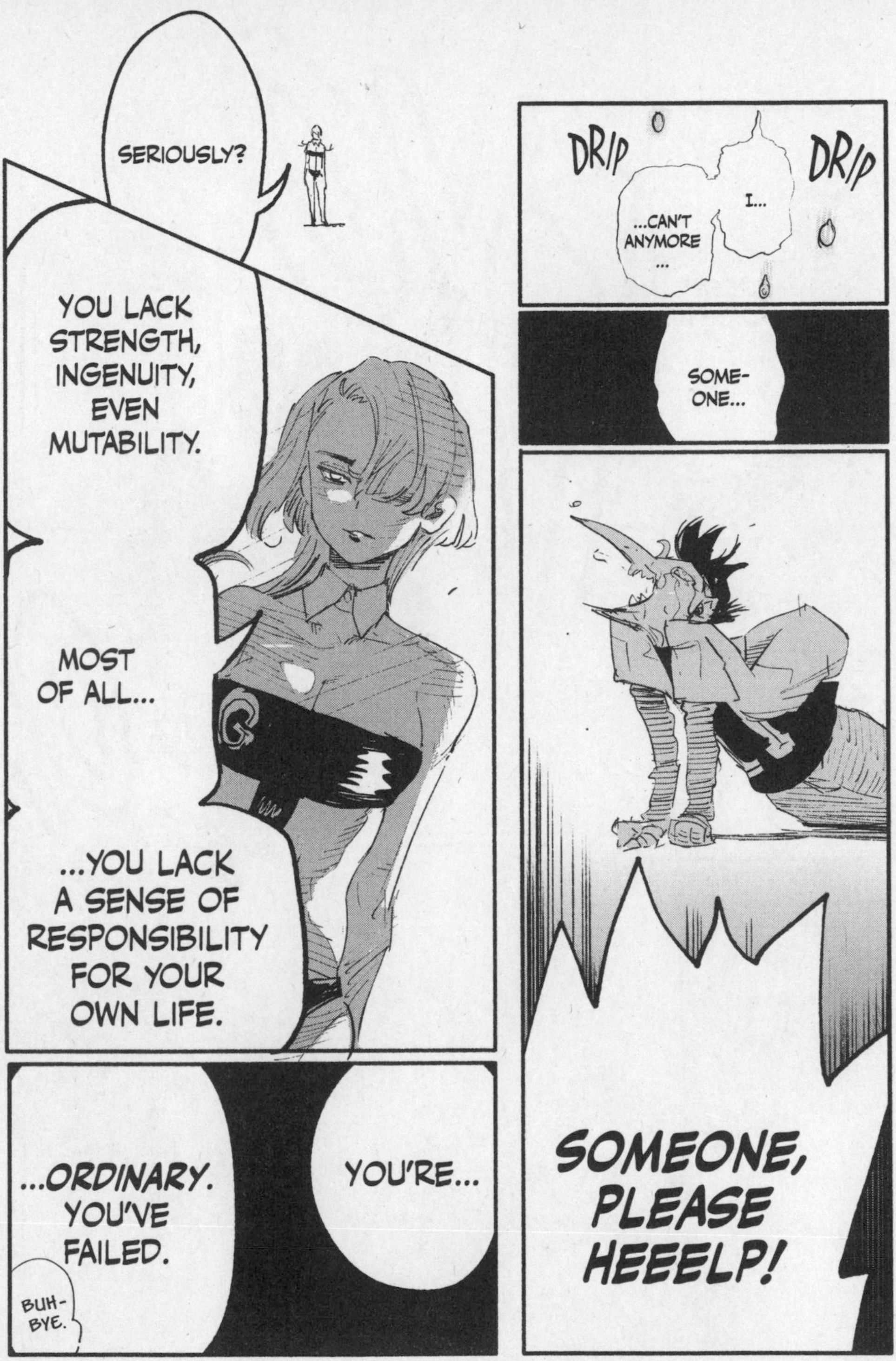
DRIP
I...
...CAN'T ANYMORE ...
DRIP
SOME-ONE...
SOMEONE, PLEASE HEEELP!
SERIOUSLY?
YOU LACK STRENGTH, INGENUITY, EVEN MUTABILITY.
MOST OF ALL...
...YOU LACK A SENSE OF RESPONSIBILITY FOR YOUR OWN LIFE.
YOU'RE...
...ORDINARY. YOU'VE FAILED.
BUH-BYE.

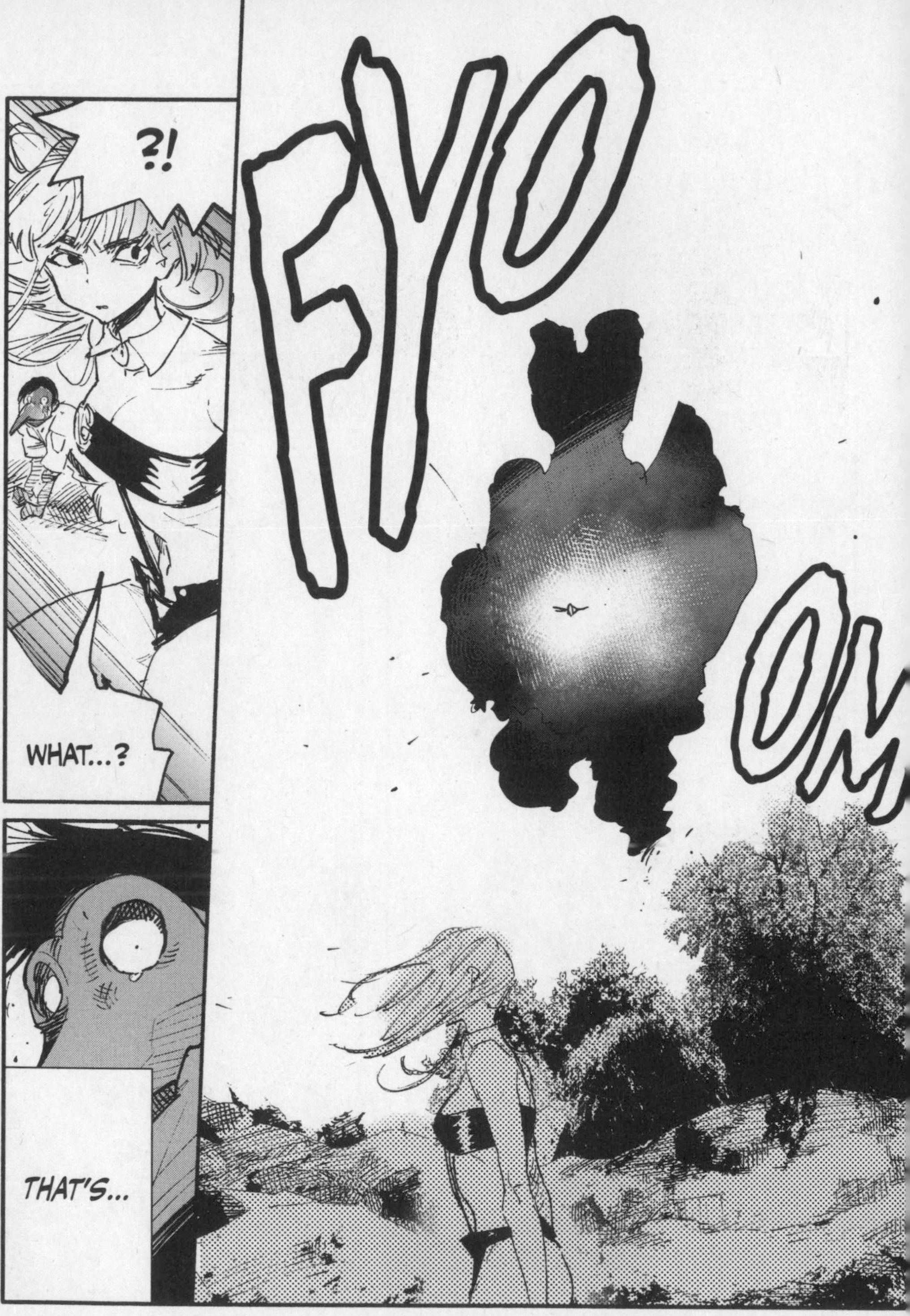
FYO
OM
?!
WHAT...?
THAT'S...

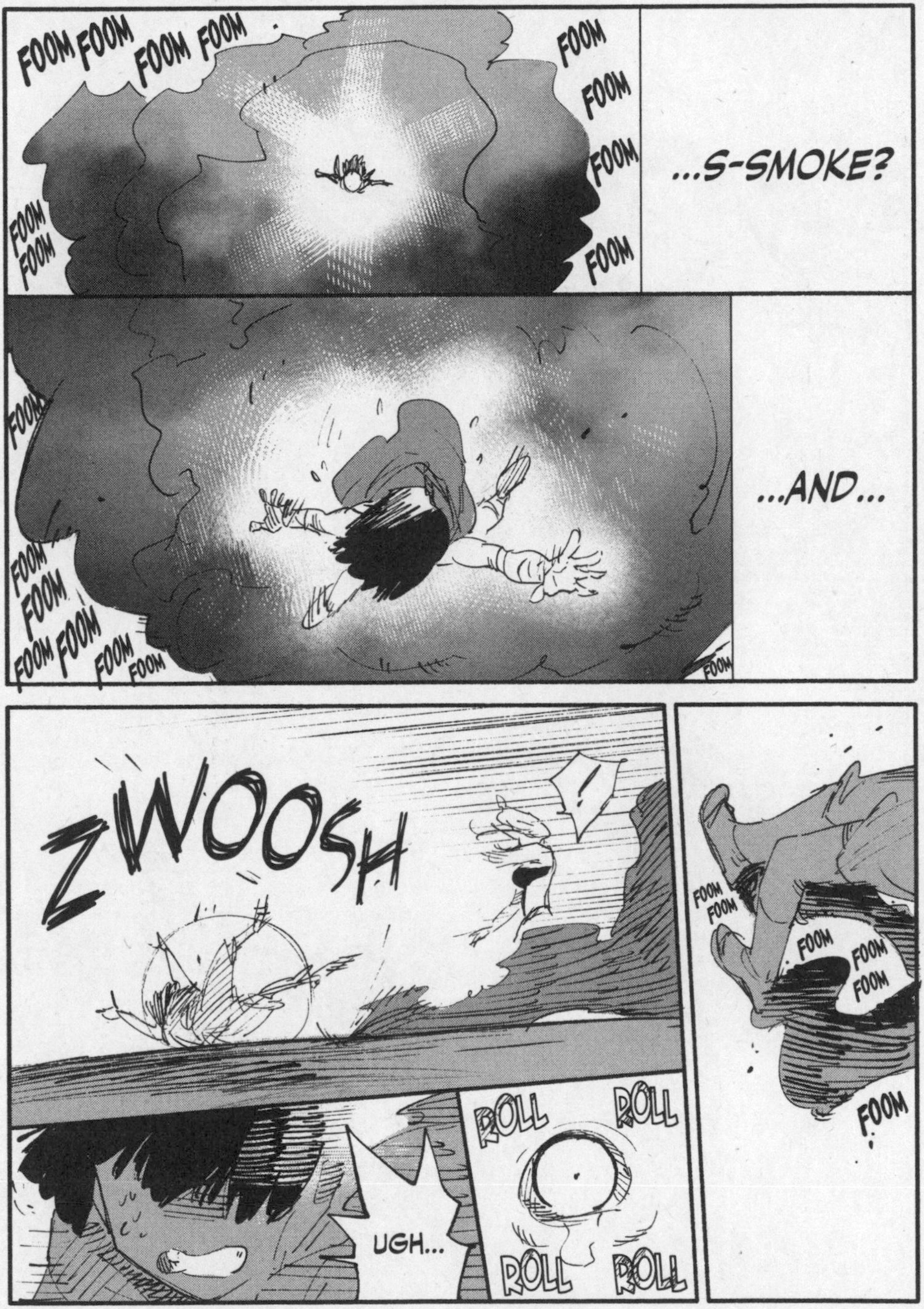
...S-SMOKE?
FOOM FOOM FOOM FOOM
FOOM FOOM FOOM FOOM
FOOM FOOM
...AND...
FOOM
FOOM FOOM FOOM FOOM FOOM FOOM
FOOM
FOOM FOOM
FOOM
FOOM FOOM
FOOM
FOOM
ZWOOSH
!
ROLL ROLL ROLL ROLL
UGH...

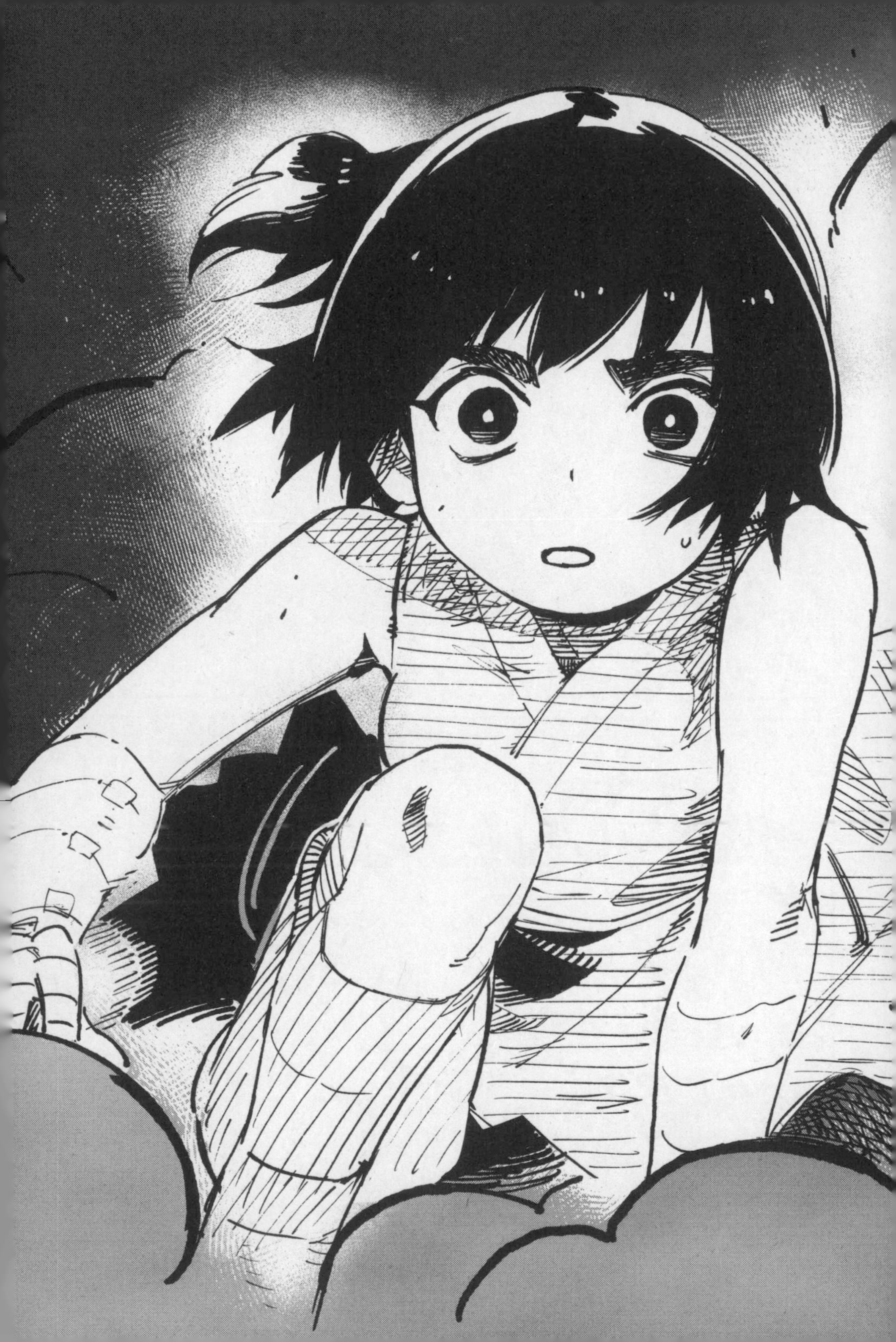

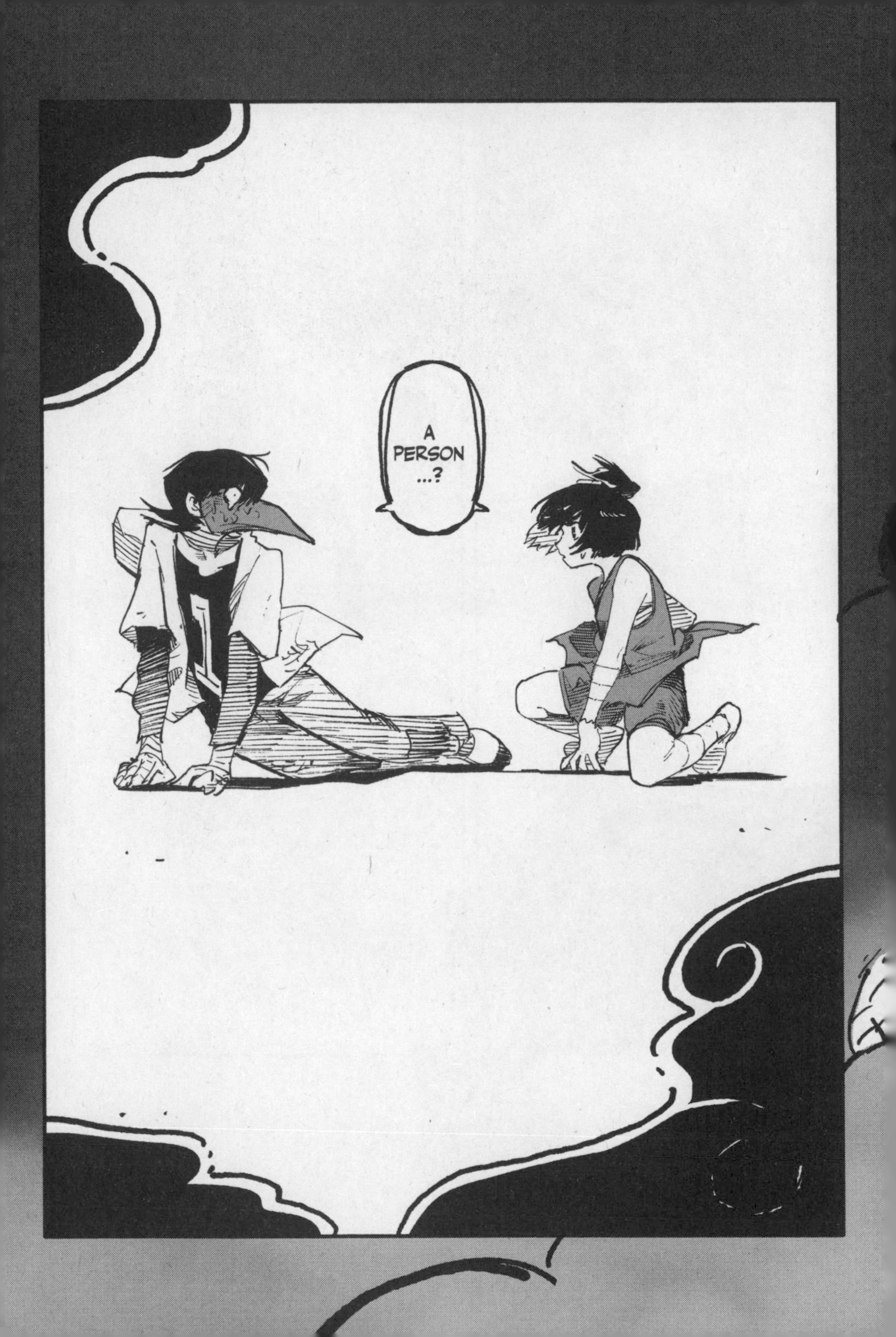
A PERSON ...?

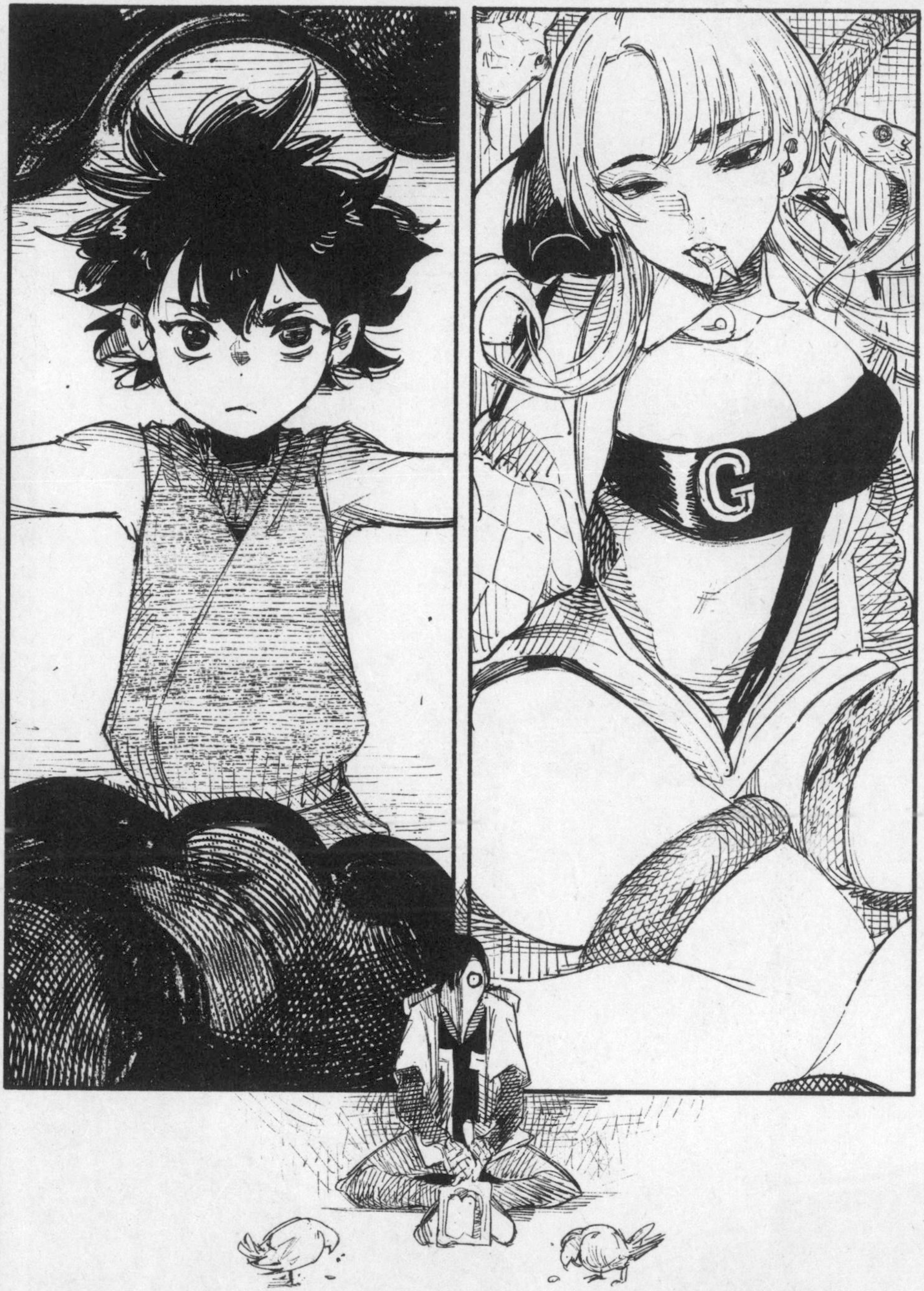
G

Chapter 6: FIRST APOSTASY

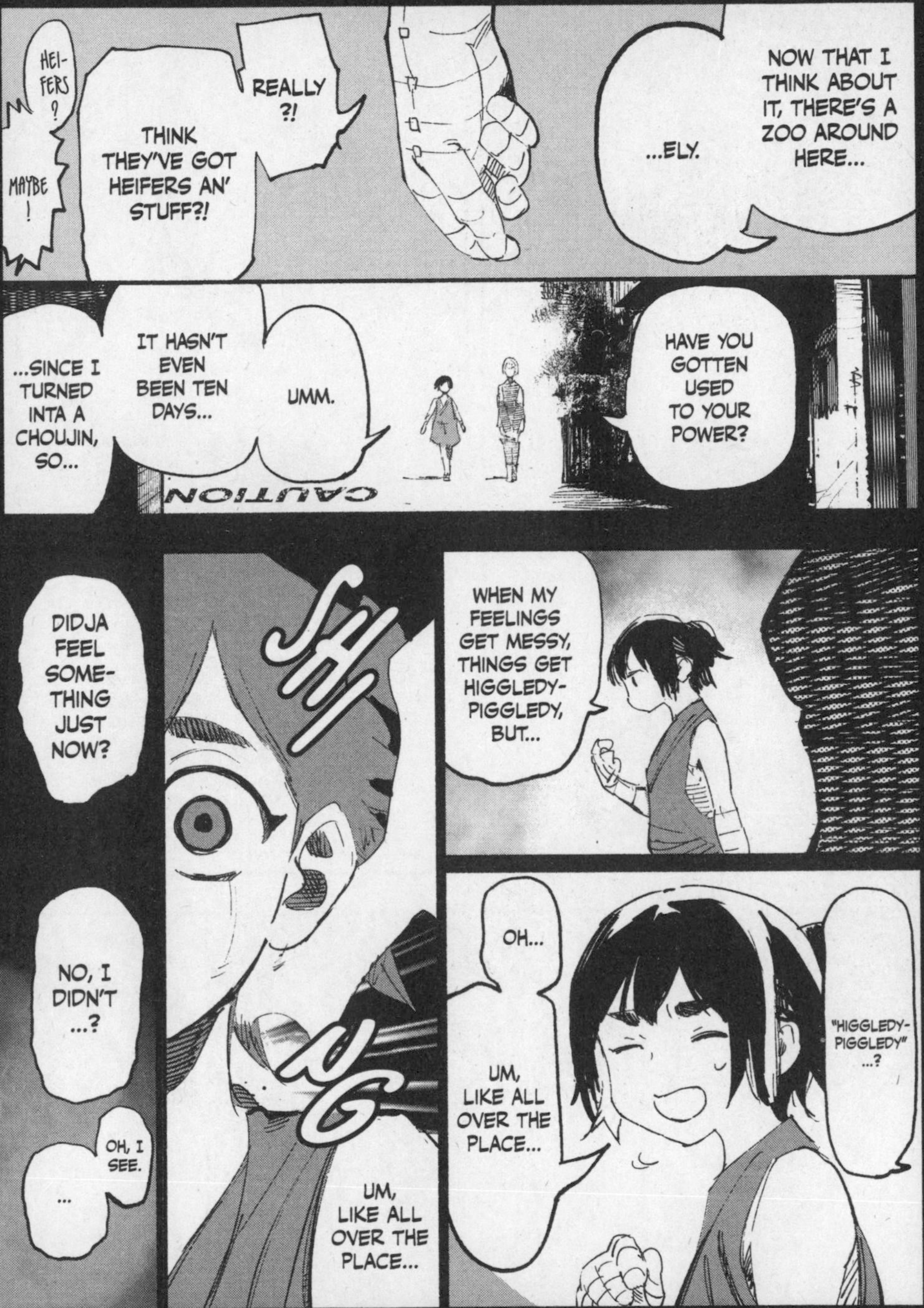
NOW THAT I THINK ABOUT IT, THERE'S A ZOO AROUND HERE...
...ELY.
REALLY ?!
THINK THEY'VE GOT HEIFERS AN' STUFF?!
HEI-FERS ?
MAYBE !
HAVE YOU GOTTEN USED TO YOUR POWER?
UMM.
IT HASN'T EVEN BEEN TEN DAYS...
...SINCE I TURNED INTA A CHOUJIN, SO...
WHEN MY FEELINGS GET MESSY, THINGS GET HIGGLEDY-PIGGLEDY, BUT...
"HIGGLEDY-PIGGLEDY" ...?
OH...
UM, LIKE ALL OVER THE PLACE...
UM, LIKE ALL OVER THE PLACE...
SHING
DIDJA FEEL SOME-THING JUST NOW?
NO, I DIDN'T ...?
OH, I SEE.
...

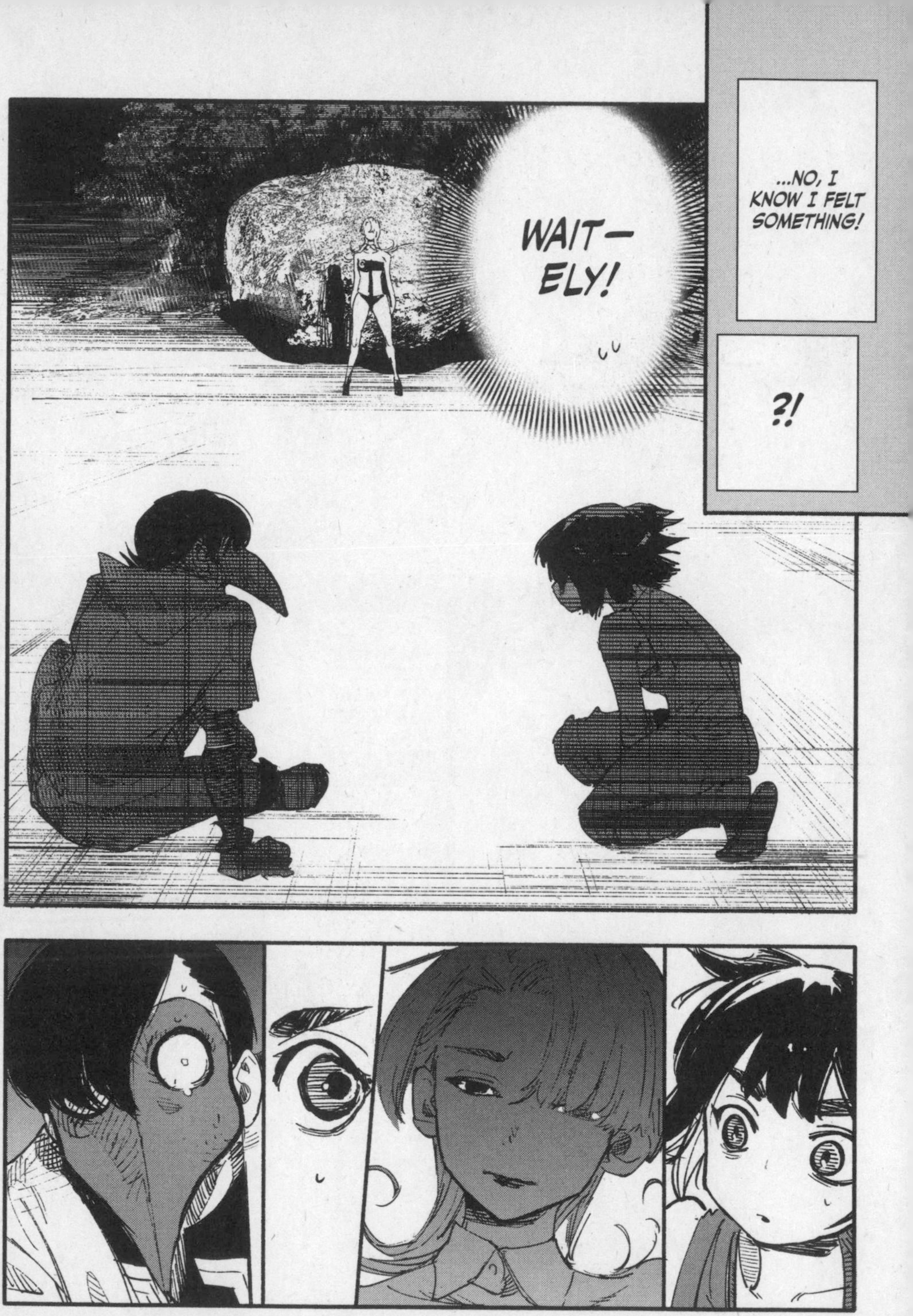
...NO, I KNOW I FELT SOMETHING!
?!
WAIT— ELY!

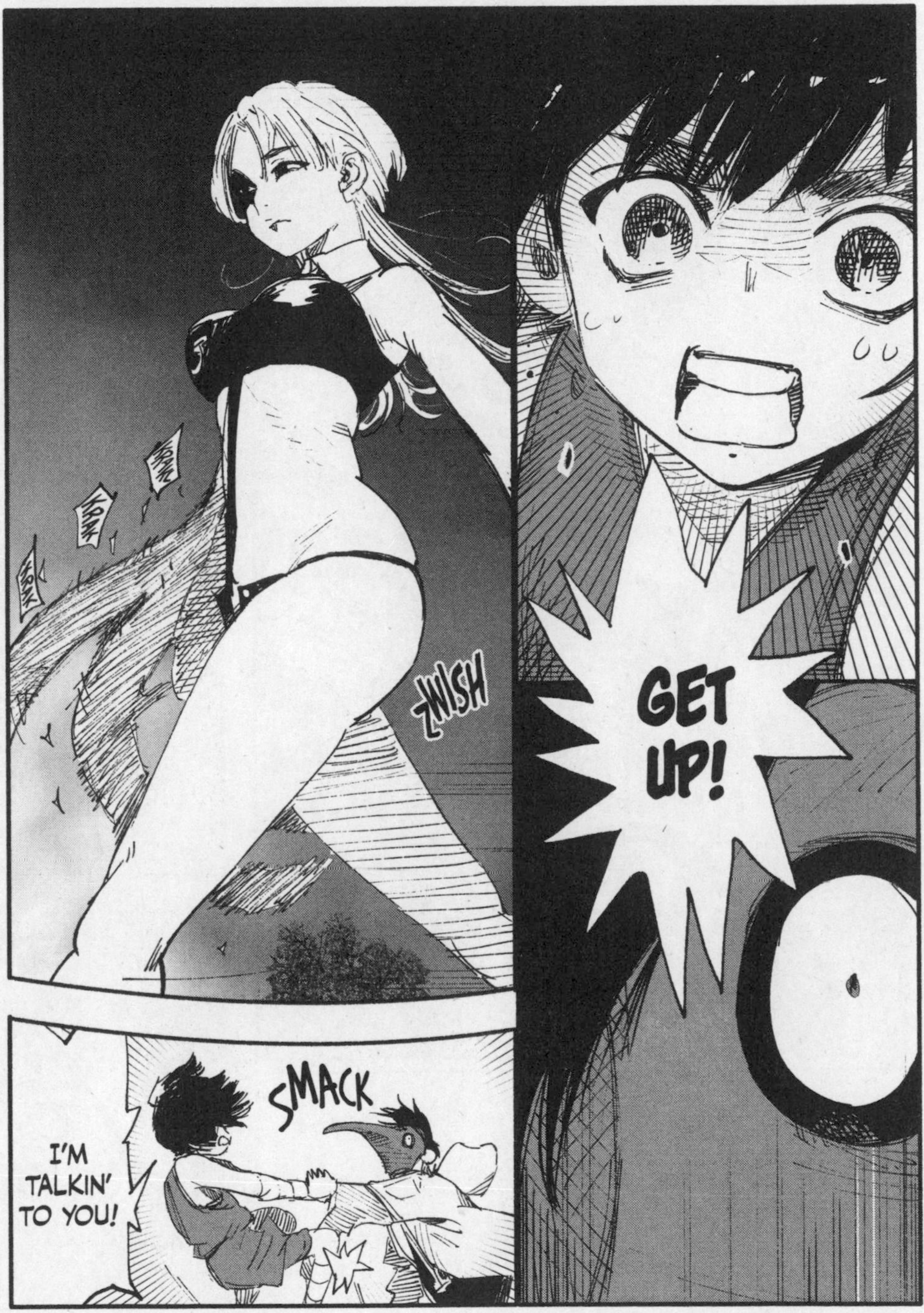
GET UP!
KRAK
KRAK
KRAK
ZWISH
SMACK
I'M TALKIN' TO YOU!

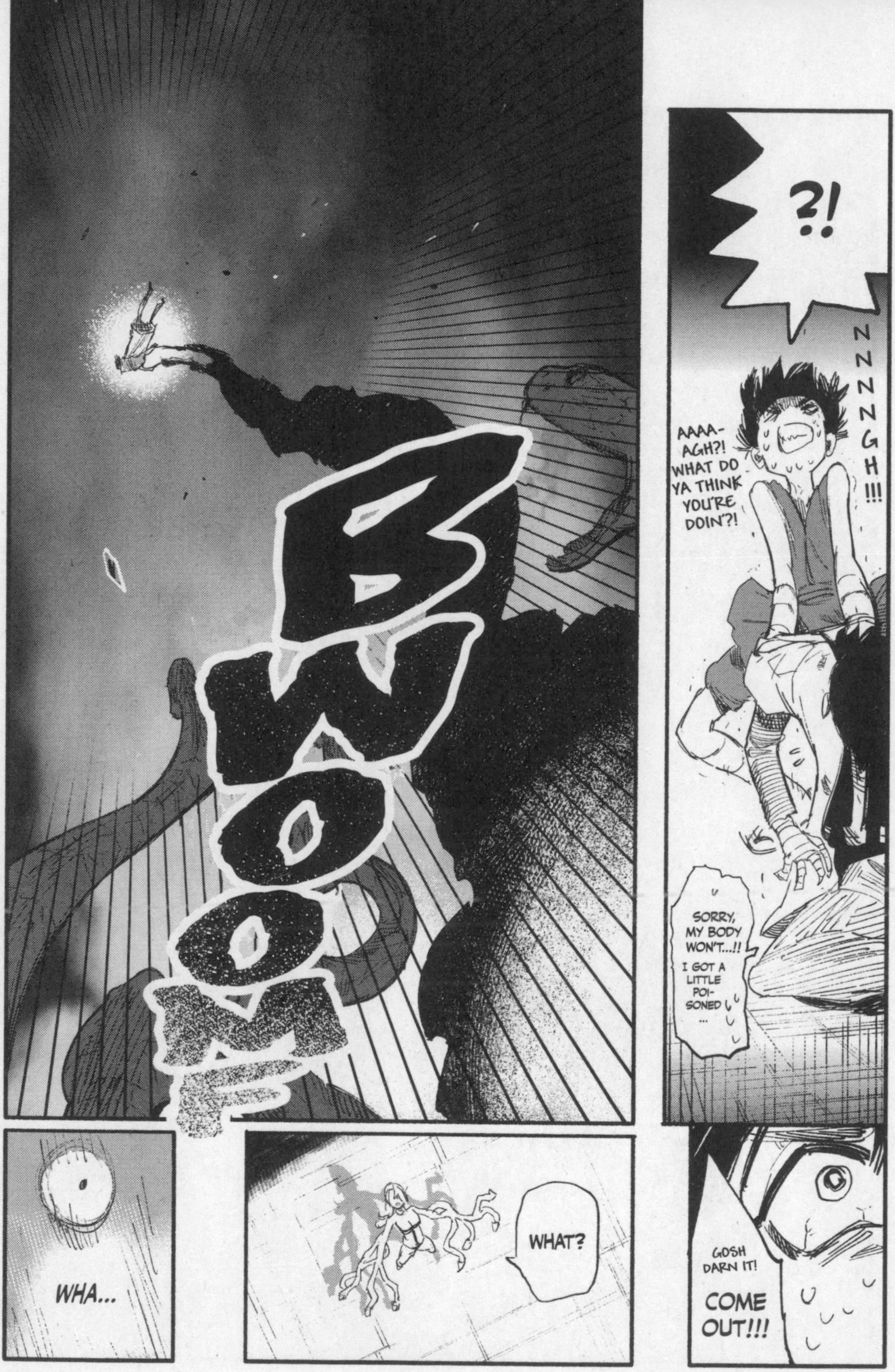
?!
NNNNGH!!!
AAAA-AGH?! WHAT DO YA THINK YOU'RE DOIN'?!
SORRY, MY BODY WON'T...!!
I GOT A LITTLE POI-SONED...
BWOOM
GOSH DARN IT!
COME OUT!!!
WHAT?
WHA...

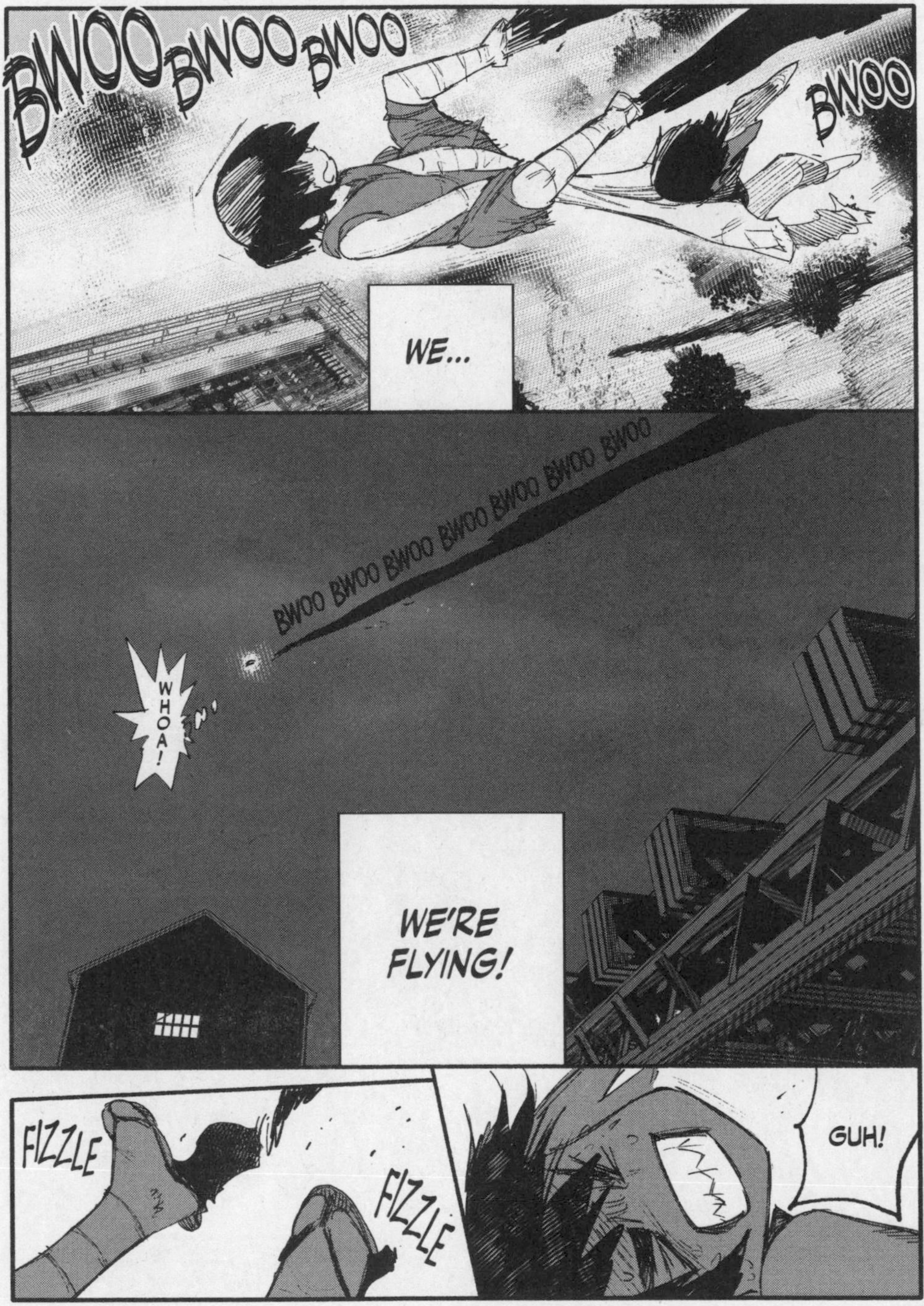
BWOO
BWOO BWOO BWOO
WE...
BWOO BWOO BWOO BWOO BWOO BWOO BWOO BWOO
WHOA!
WE'RE FLYING!
GUH!
FIZZLE
FIZZLE

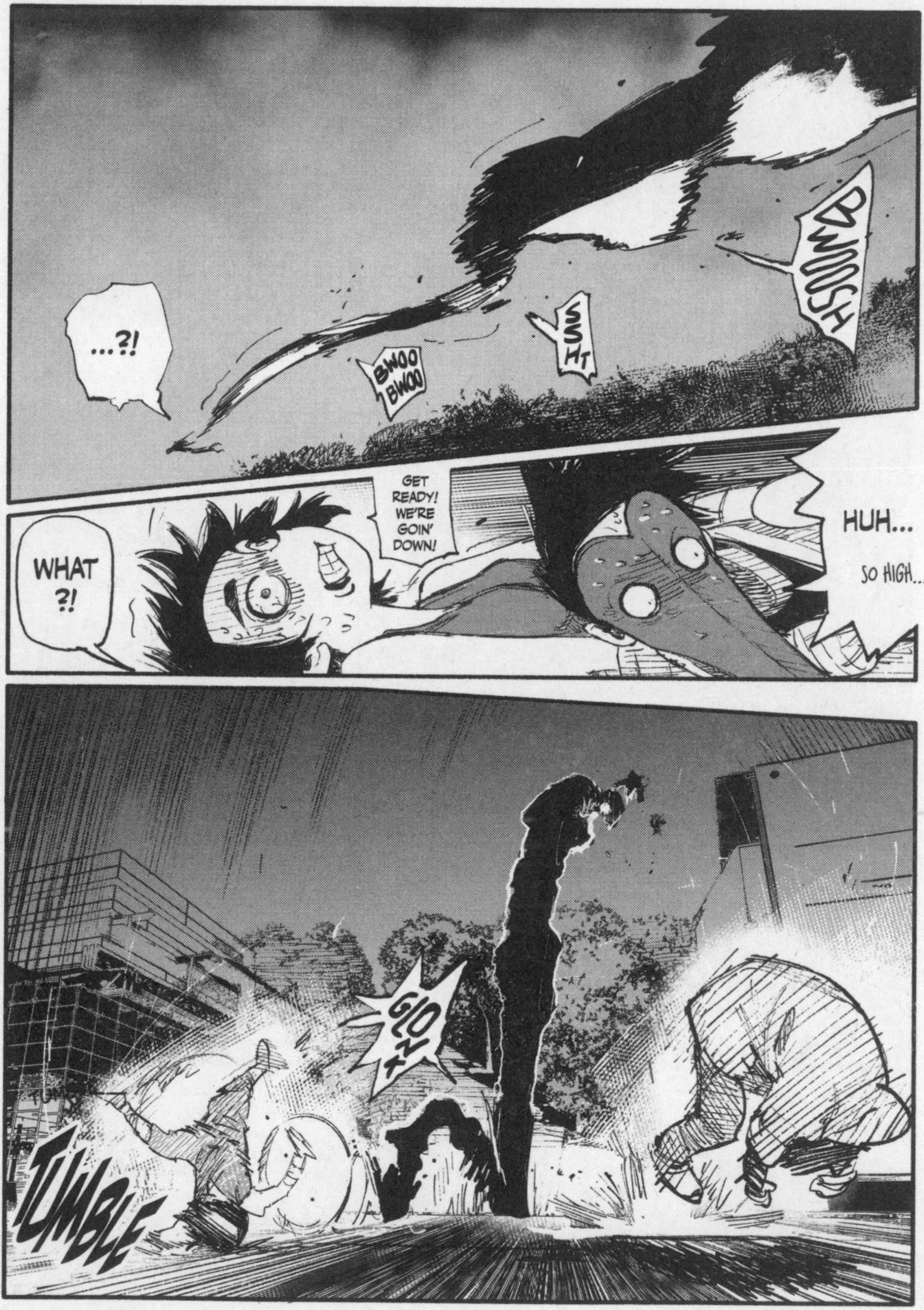
BWOOSH
SSHT
BWOO BWOO
...?!
HUH...
SO HIGH...
GET READY! WE'RE GOIN' DOWN!
WHAT ?!
GIONK
TUMBLE

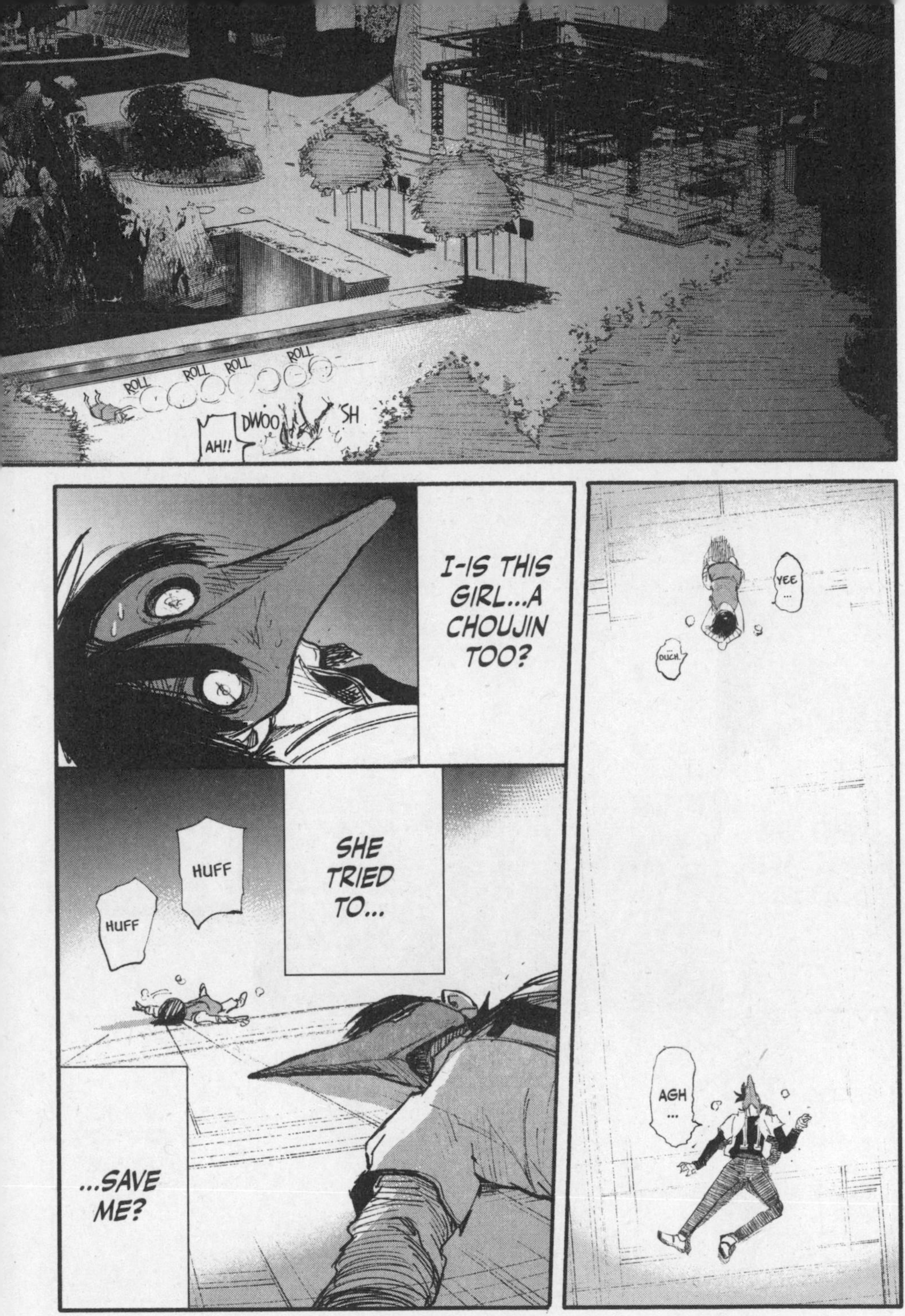

ROLL
ROLL
ROLL
ROLL
DWOO'SH
AH!!
YEE...
...OUCH.
AGH...
I-IS THIS GIRL...A CHOUJIN TOO?
SHE TRIED TO...
HUFF
HUFF
...SAVE ME?

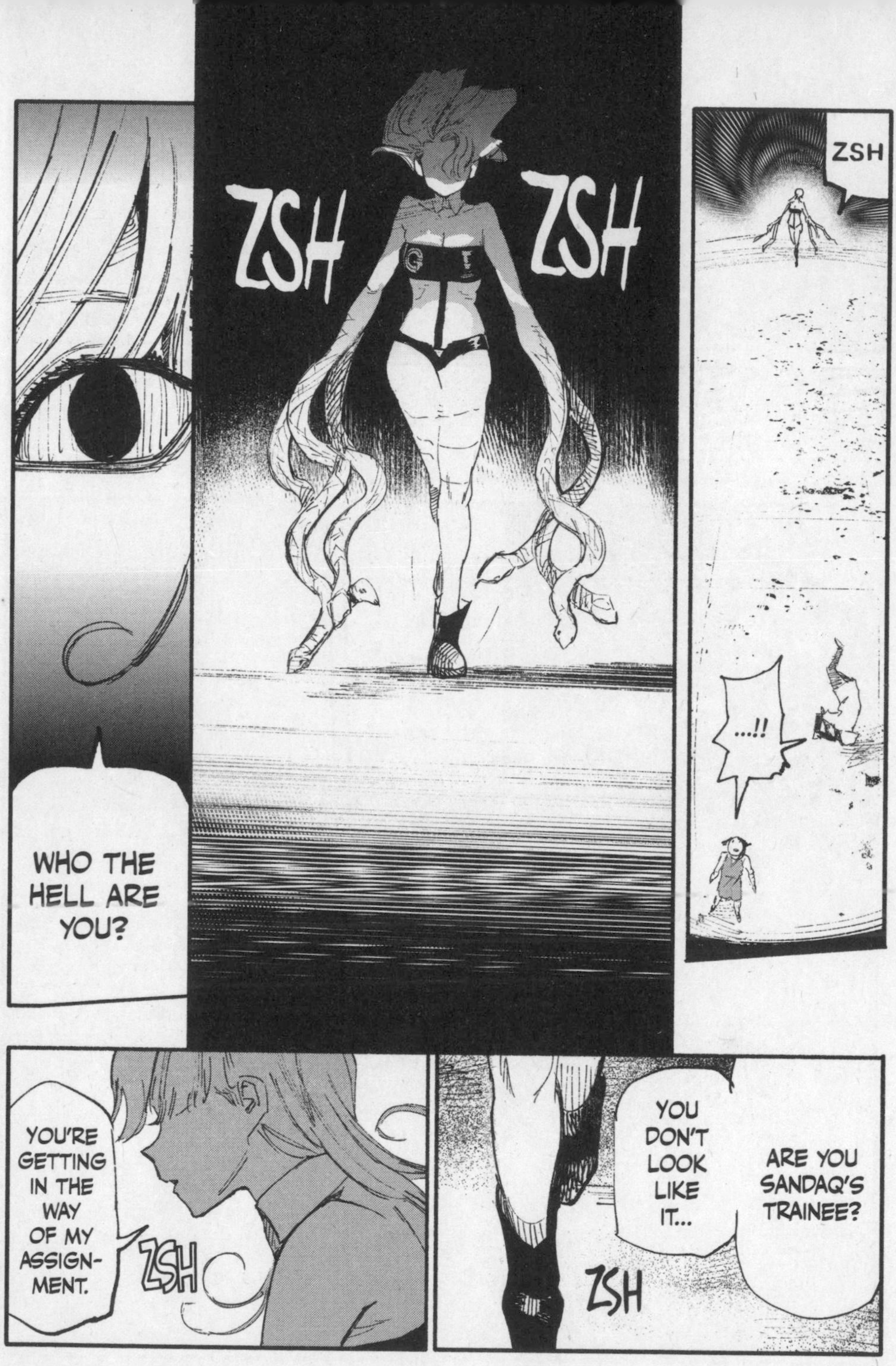
ZSH
...!!
ZSH ZSH
WHO THE HELL ARE YOU?
ARE YOU SANDAQ'S TRAINEE?
YOU DON'T LOOK LIKE IT...
ZSH
YOU'RE GETTING IN THE WAY OF MY ASSIGNMENT.
ZSH

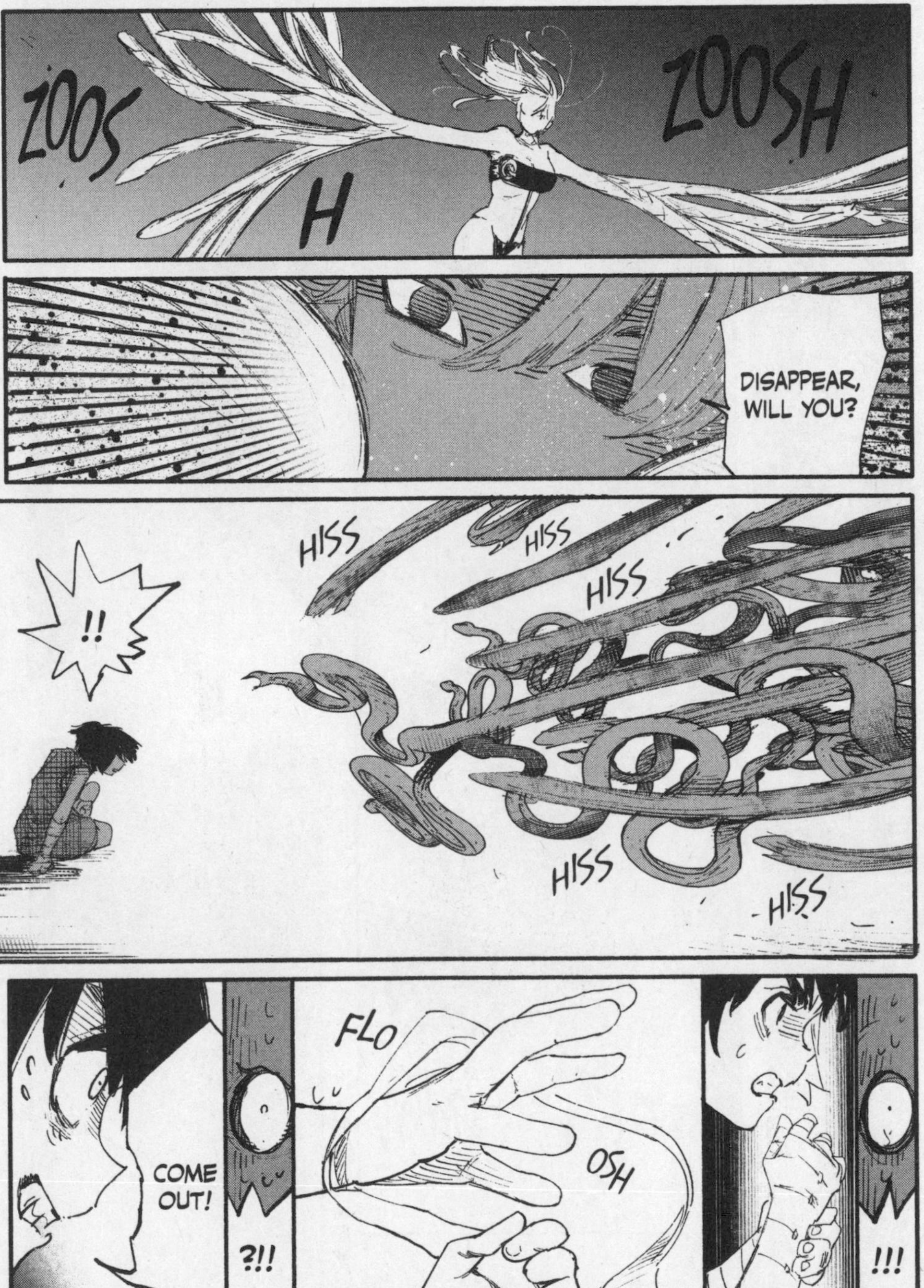
ZOOSH
ZOOS
H
DISAPPEAR, WILL YOU?
HISS
HISS
HISS
HISS
HISS
HISS
!!
!!!
FLO
OSH
?!!
COME OUT!

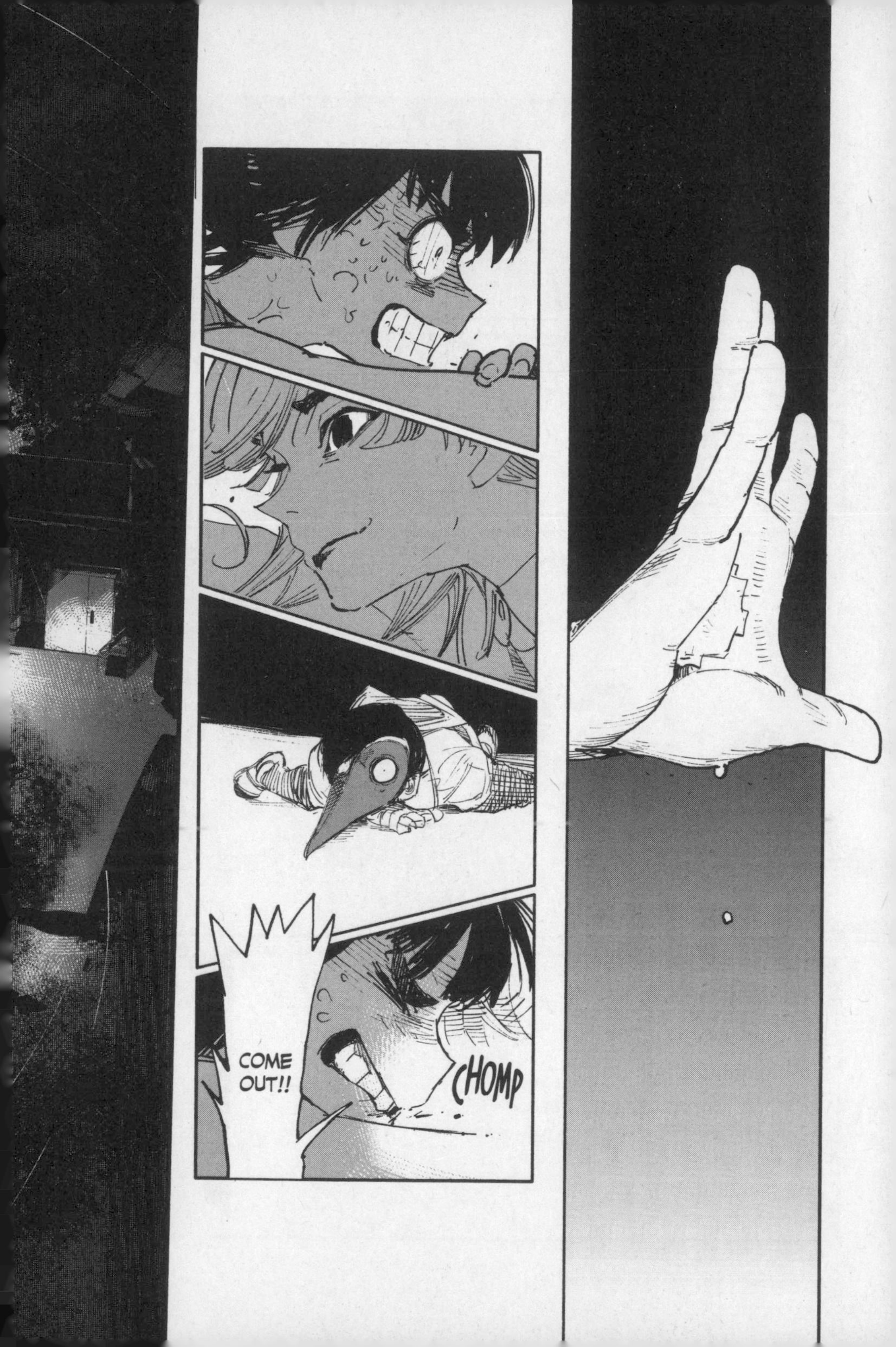
COME OUT!!
CHOMP

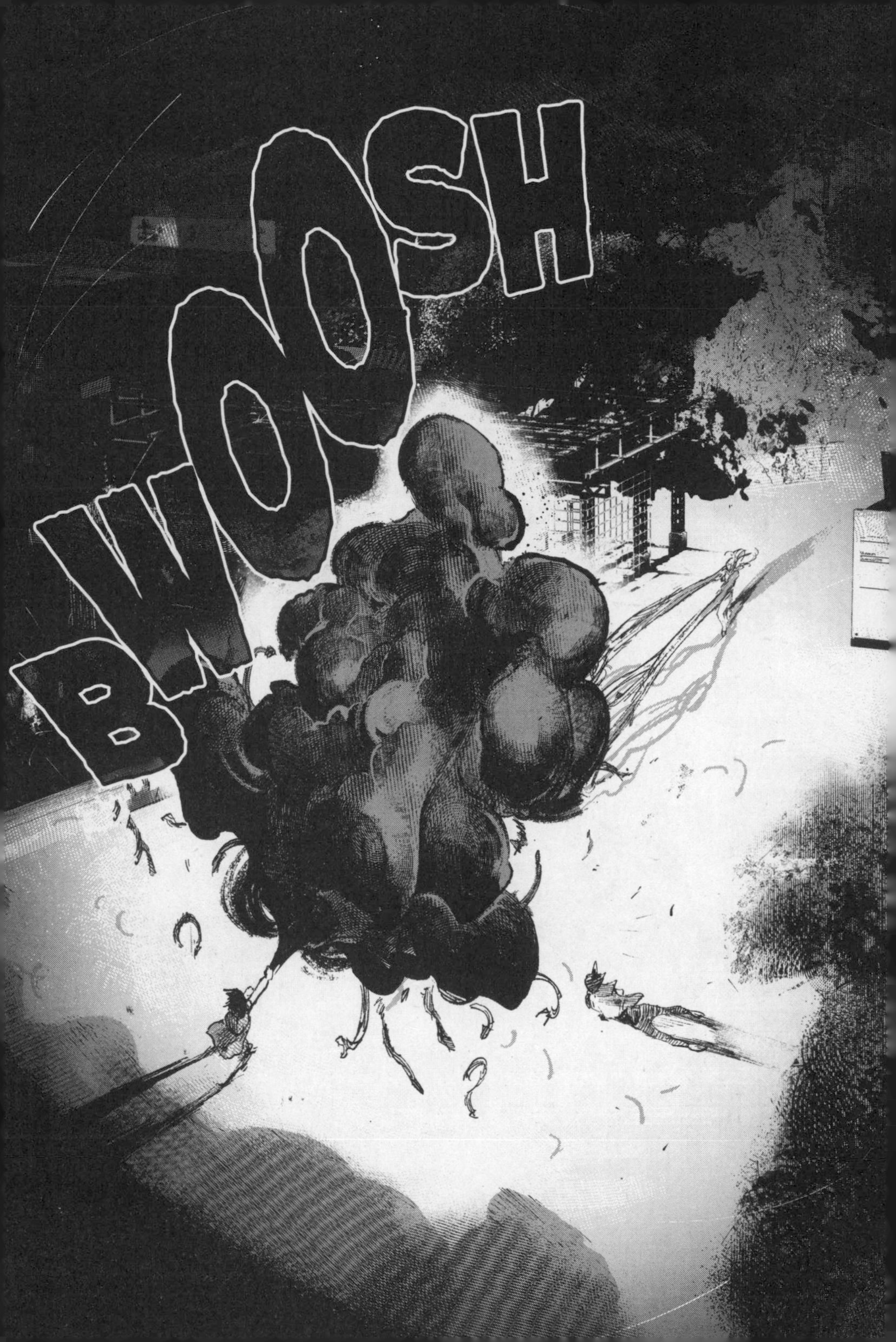
BWOOSH

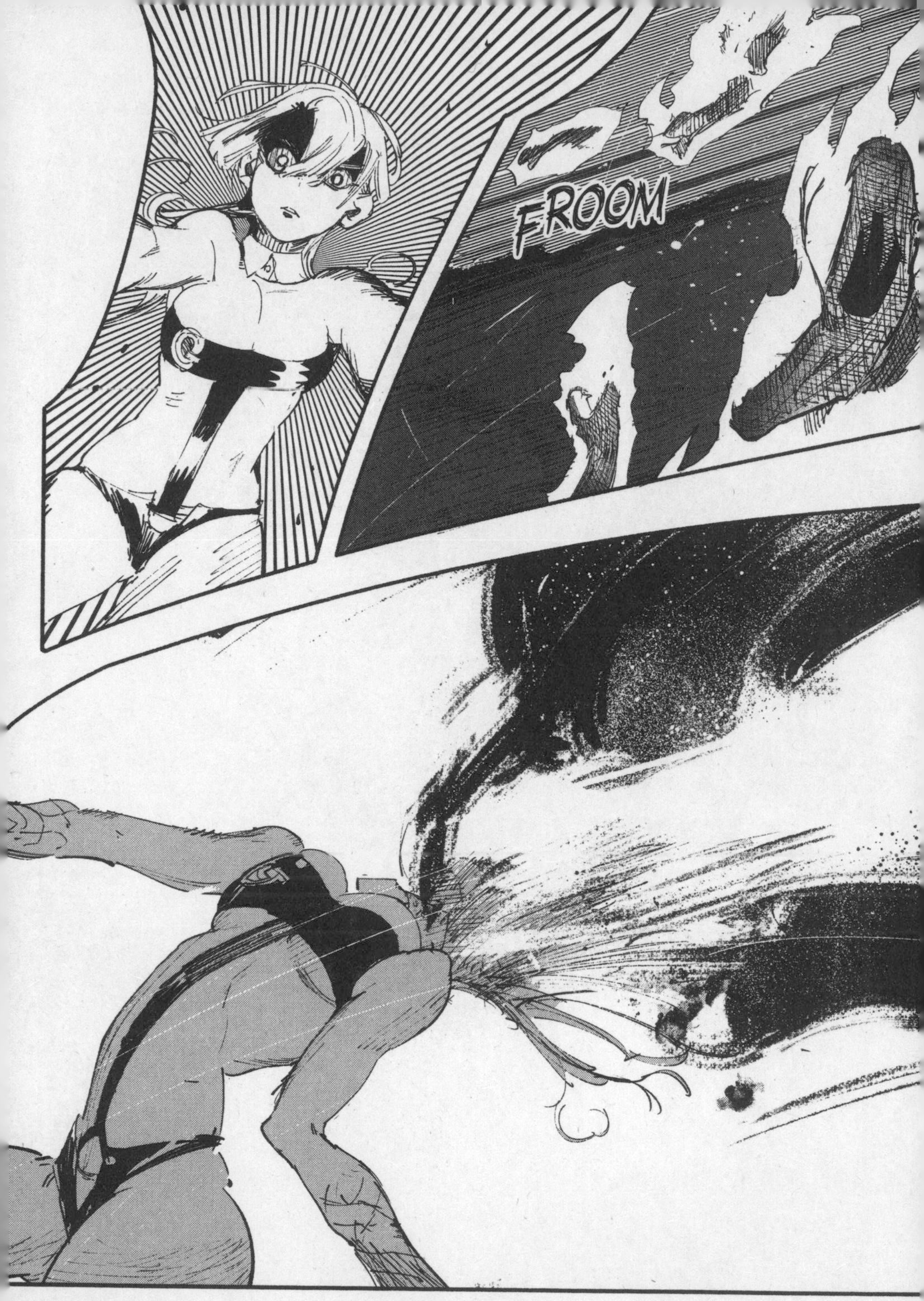
FROOM

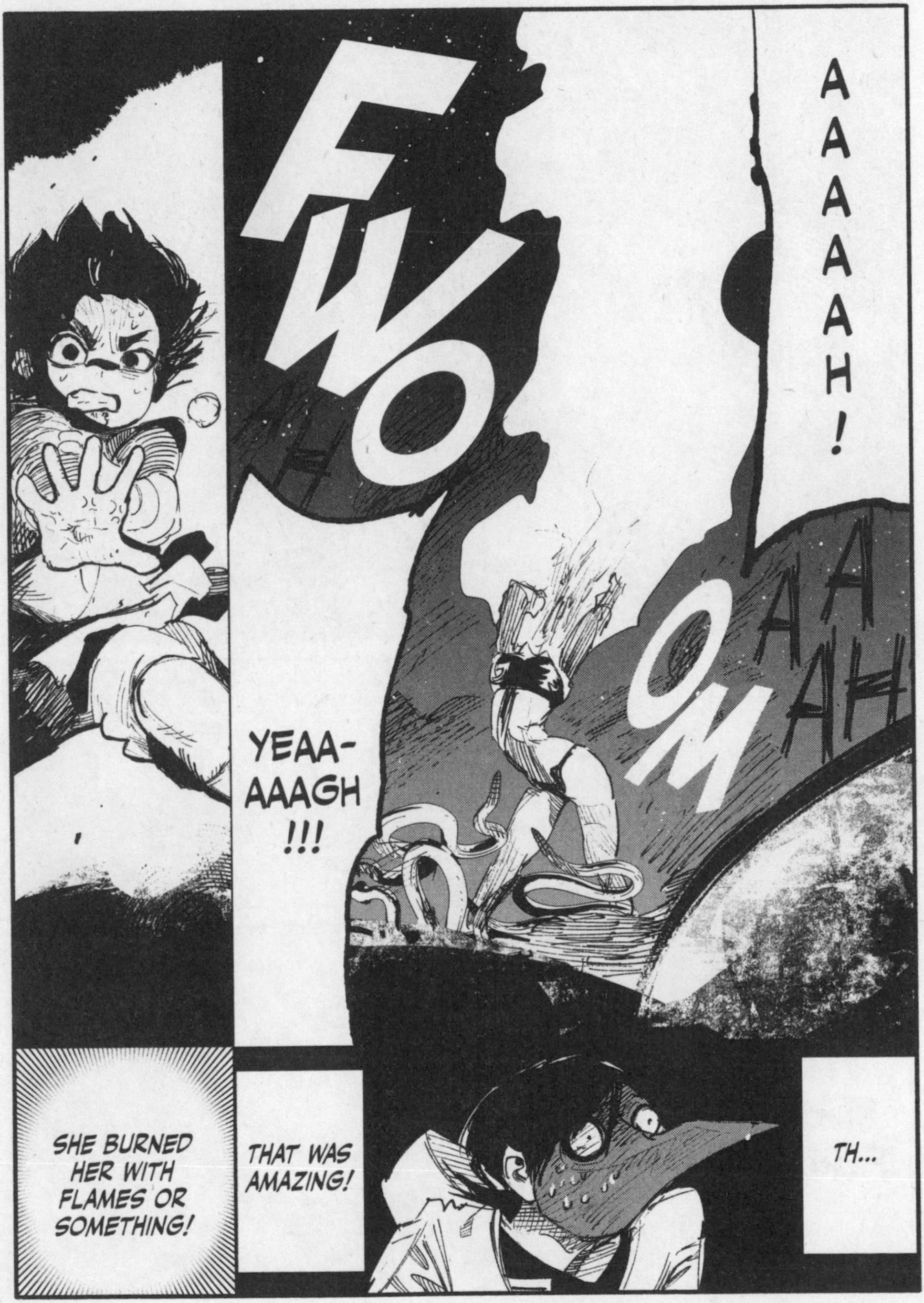

AAAAAH!
FWOOM
AAAAAH
YEAAAAAGH!!!
TH...
THAT WAS AMAZING!
SHE BURNED HER WITH FLAMES OR SOMETHING!

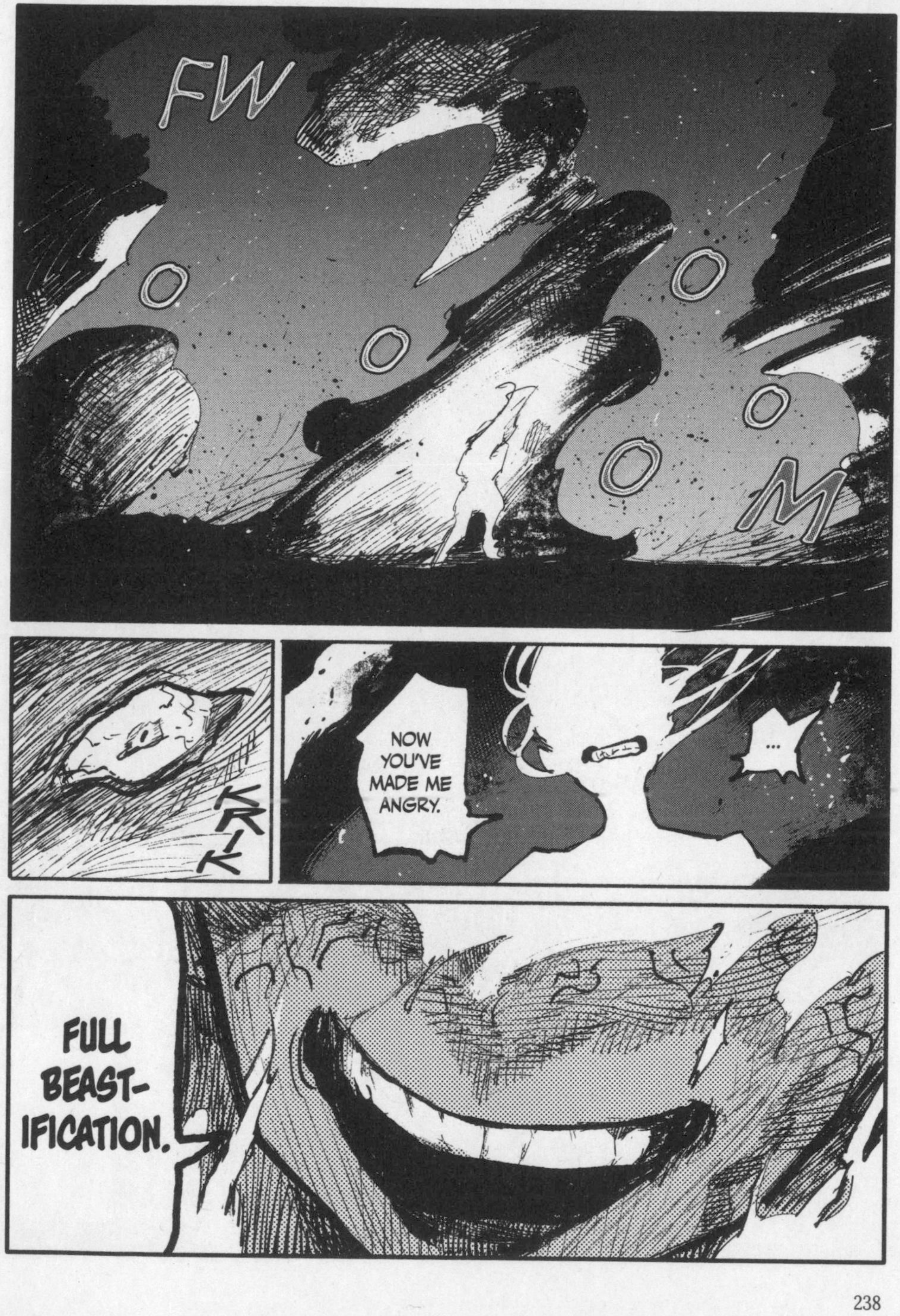
FWOOOOOOM
NOW YOU'VE MADE ME ANGRY.
...
KRIK
FULL BEAST-IFICATION.

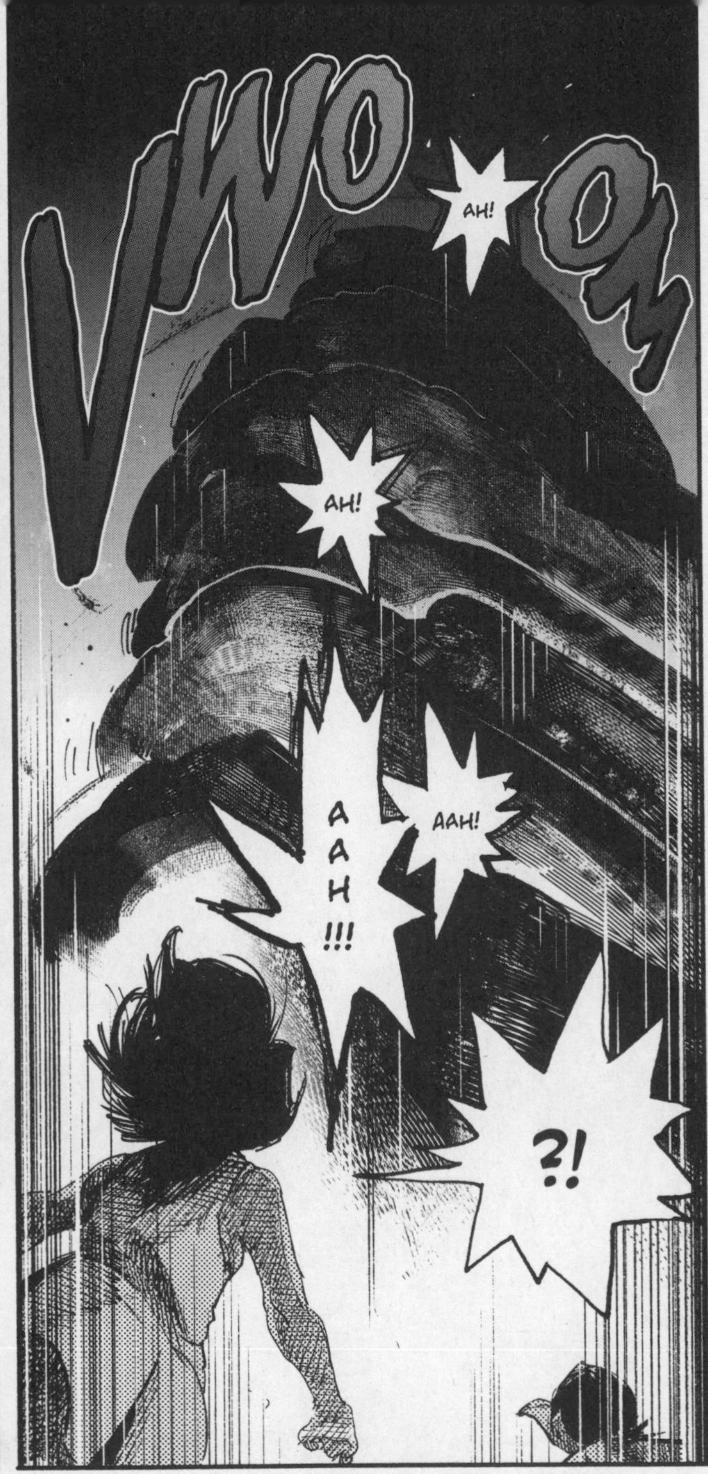
VWOOM
AH!
AH!
AAH!
AAH!!!
?!
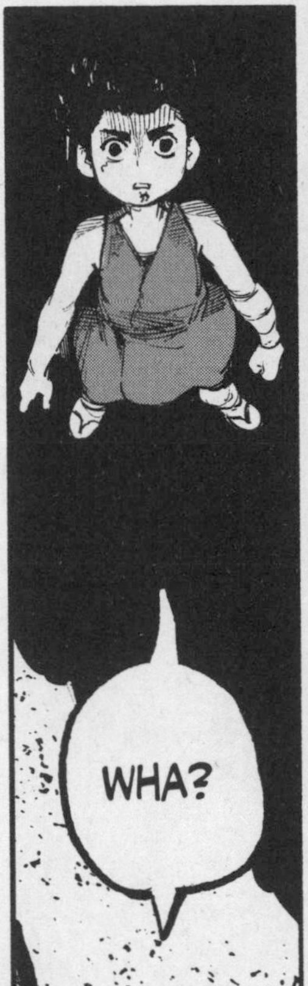
WHA?

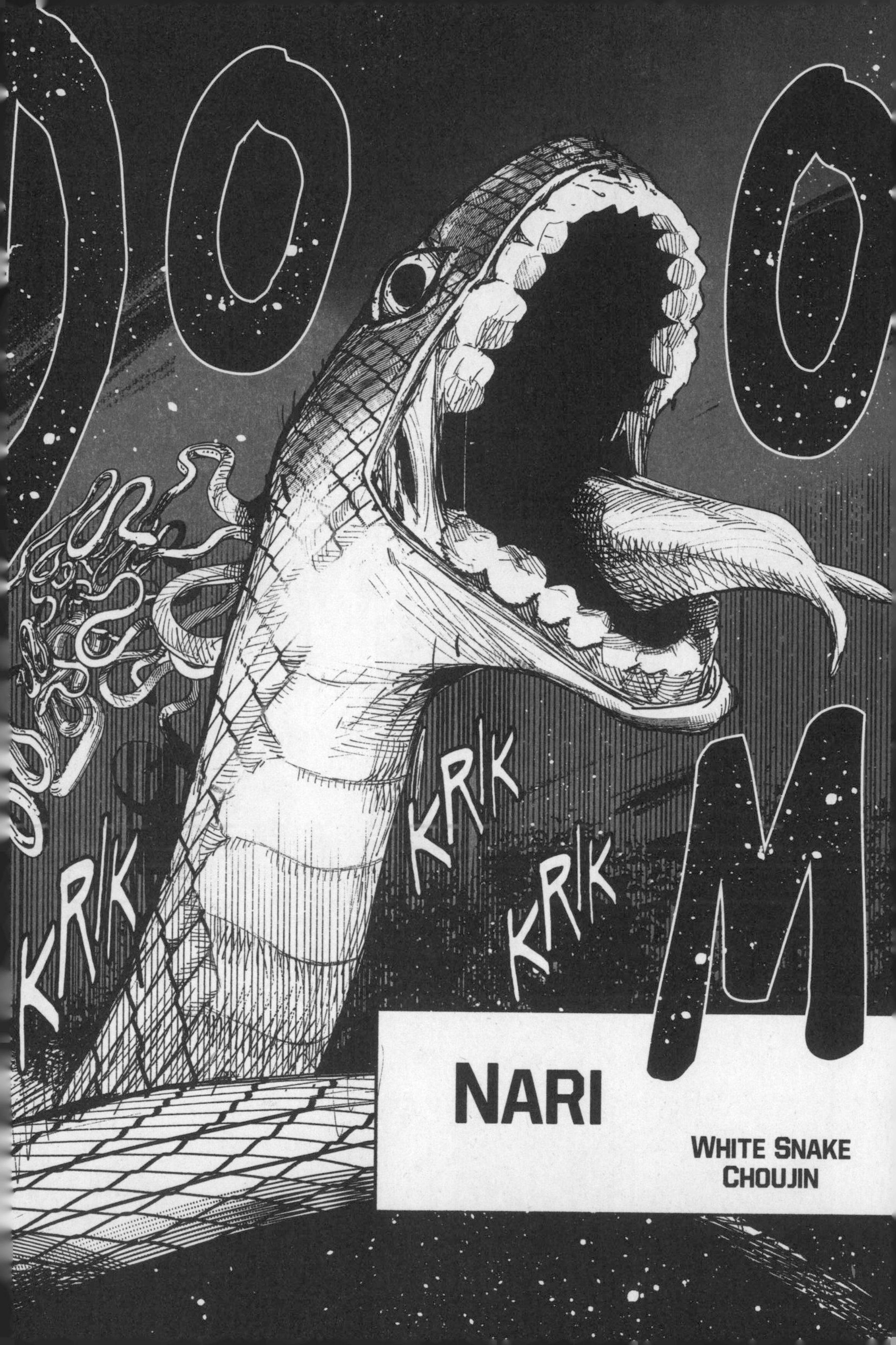
DOOOM
KRIK KRIK KRIK
NARI
WHITE SNAKE CHOUJIN

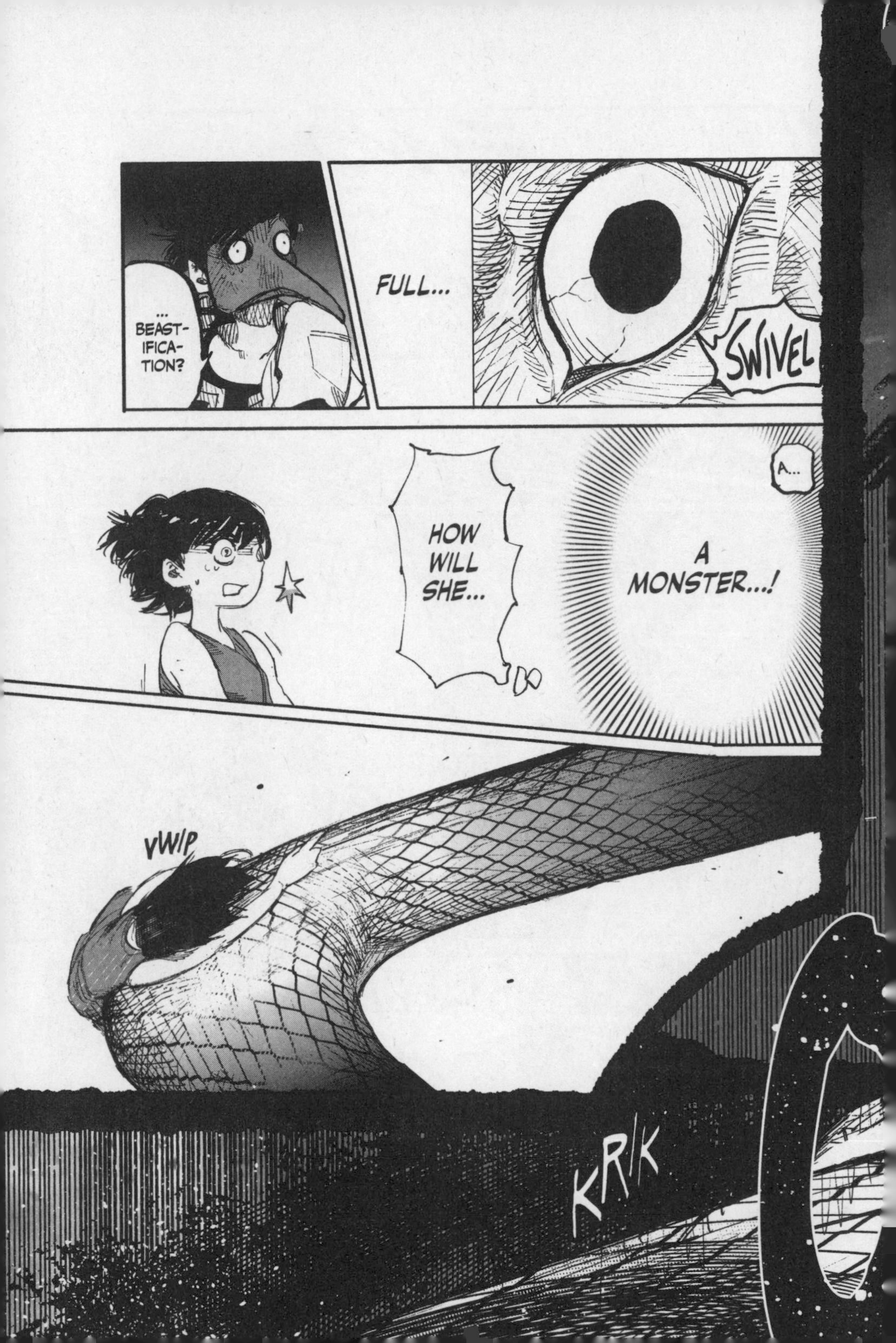
SWIVEL
FULL...
... BEAST-IFICATION?
A...
A MONSTER...!
HOW WILL SHE...
VWIP
KRIK

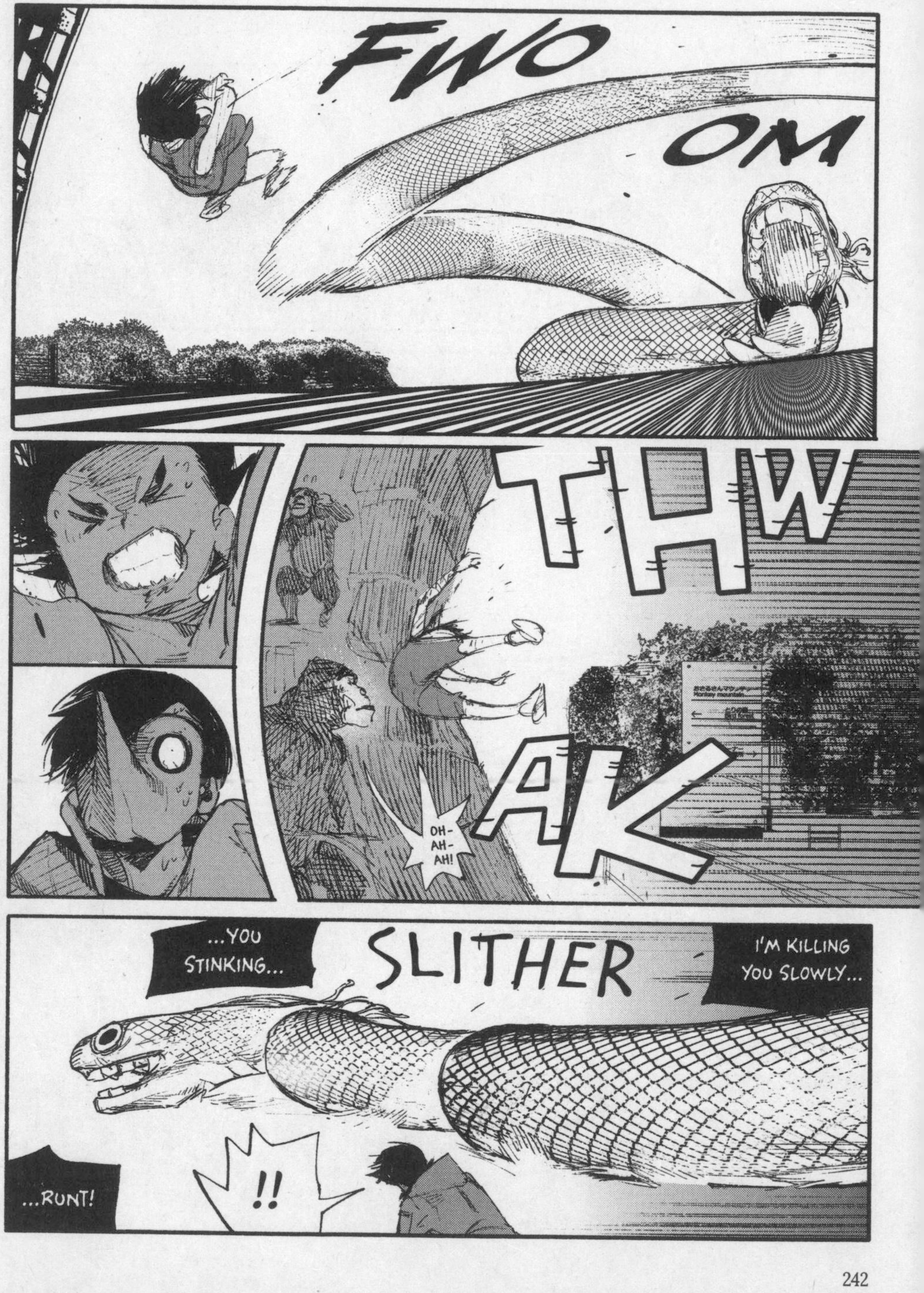
FWO
OM
THW
AK
OH-AH-AH!
I'M KILLING YOU SLOWLY...
SLITHER
...YOU STINKING...
!!
...RUNT!

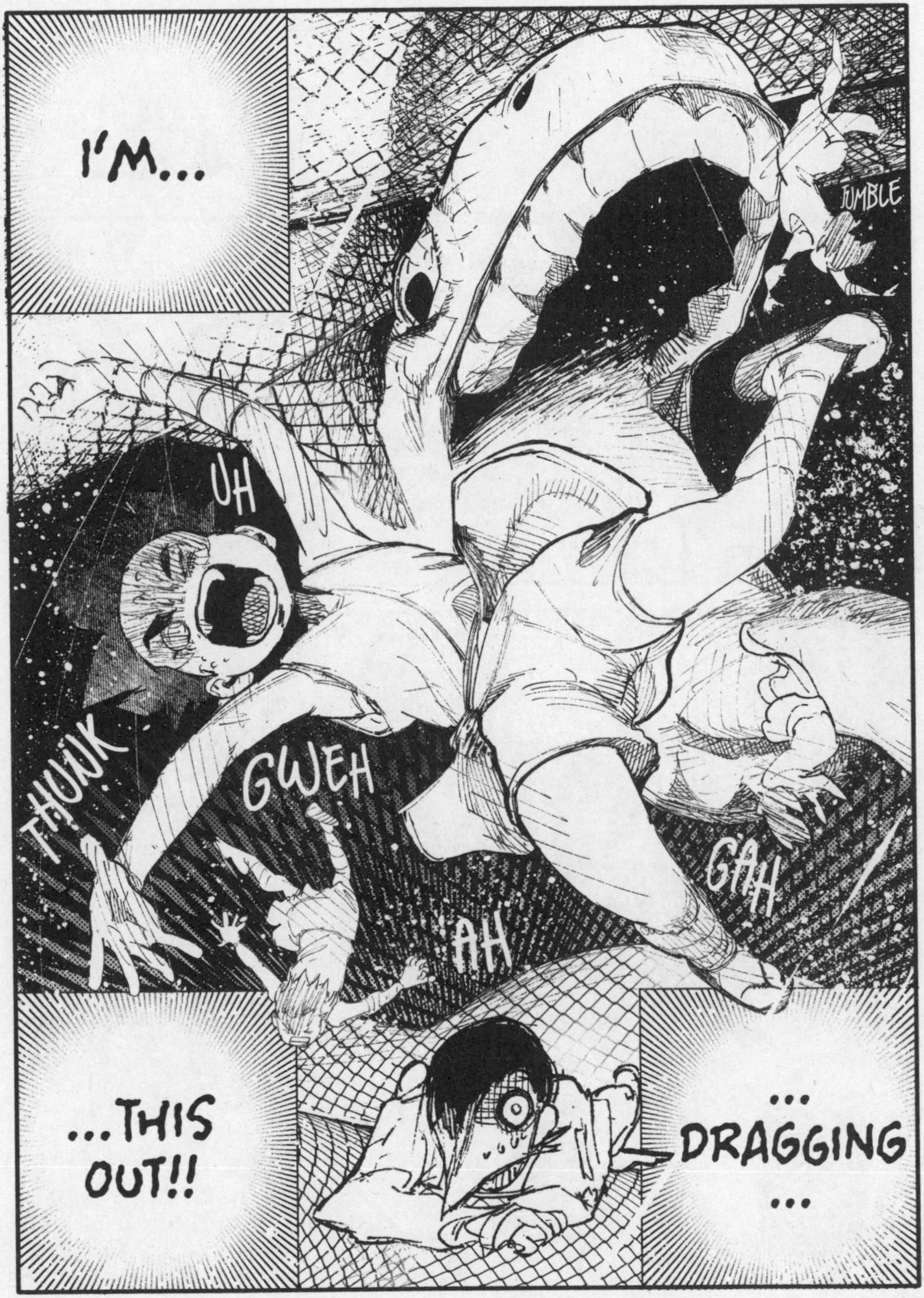
JUMBLE
UH
GAH
AH
GWEH
THUNK
I'M...
...
DRAGGING
...
...THIS
OUT!!

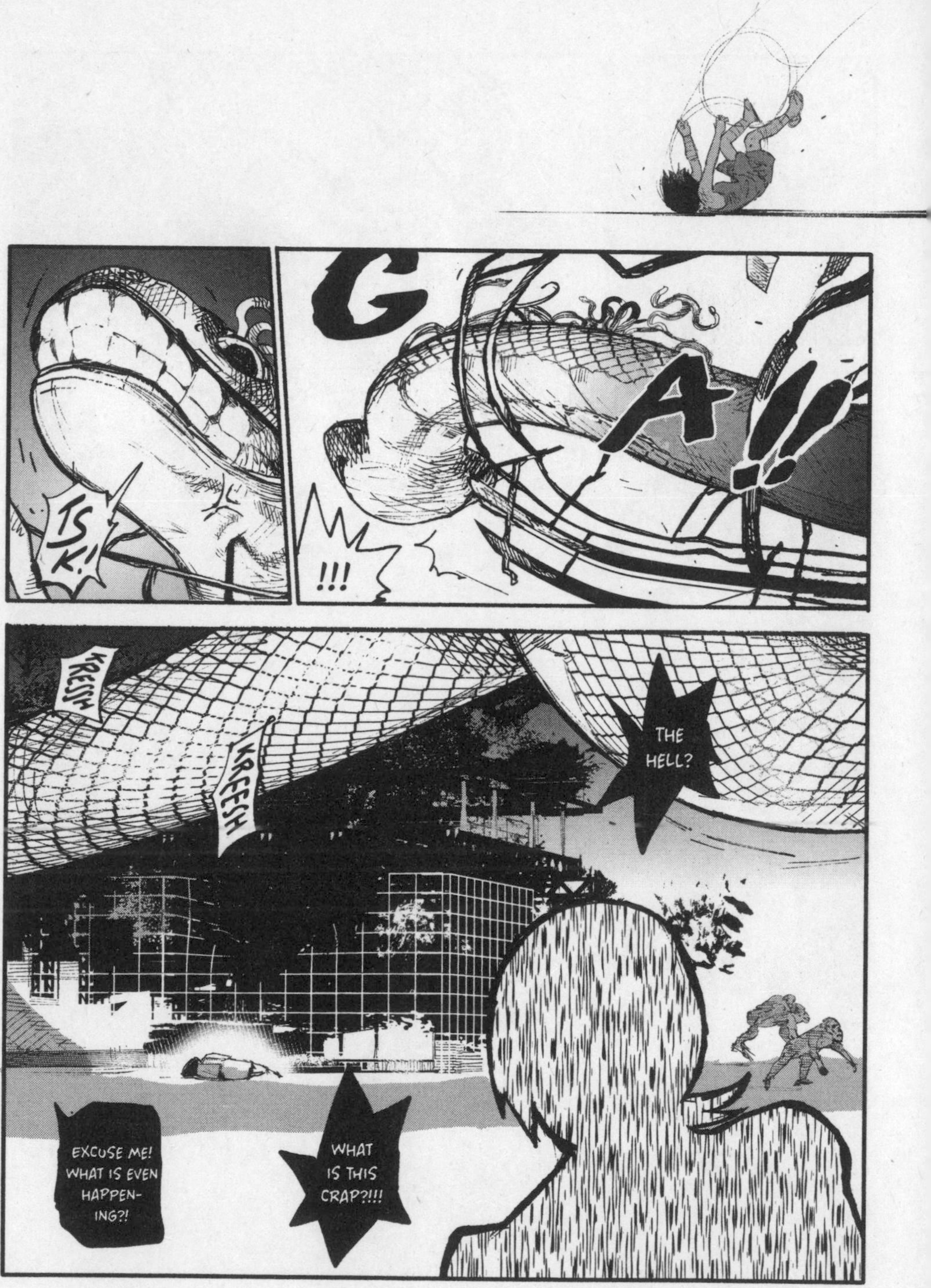
GA!!
!!!
TSK!
THE HELL?
KREEESH
KRESSH
WHAT IS THIS CRAP?!!!
EXCUSE ME! WHAT IS EVEN HAPPEN-ING?!

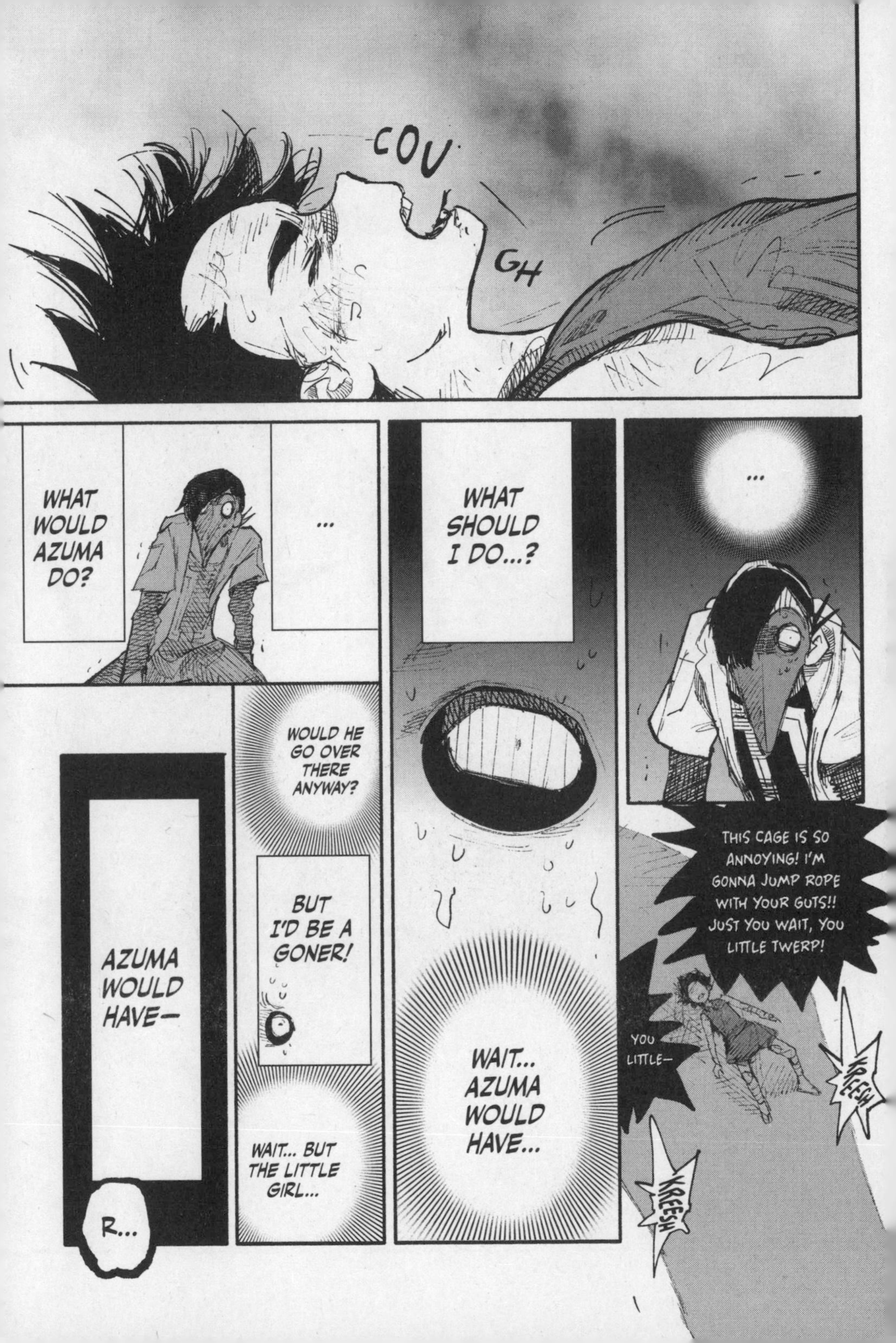
COU
GH
...
THIS CAGE IS SO ANNOYING! I'M GONNA JUMP ROPE WITH YOUR GUTS!! JUST YOU WAIT, YOU LITTLE TWERP!
YOU LITTLE—
KREESH
KREESH
WHAT SHOULD I DO...?
WAIT... AZUMA WOULD HAVE...
...
WHAT WOULD AZUMA DO?
WOULD HE GO OVER THERE ANYWAY?
BUT I'D BE A GONER!
WAIT... BUT THE LITTLE GIRL...
AZUMA WOULD HAVE—
R...

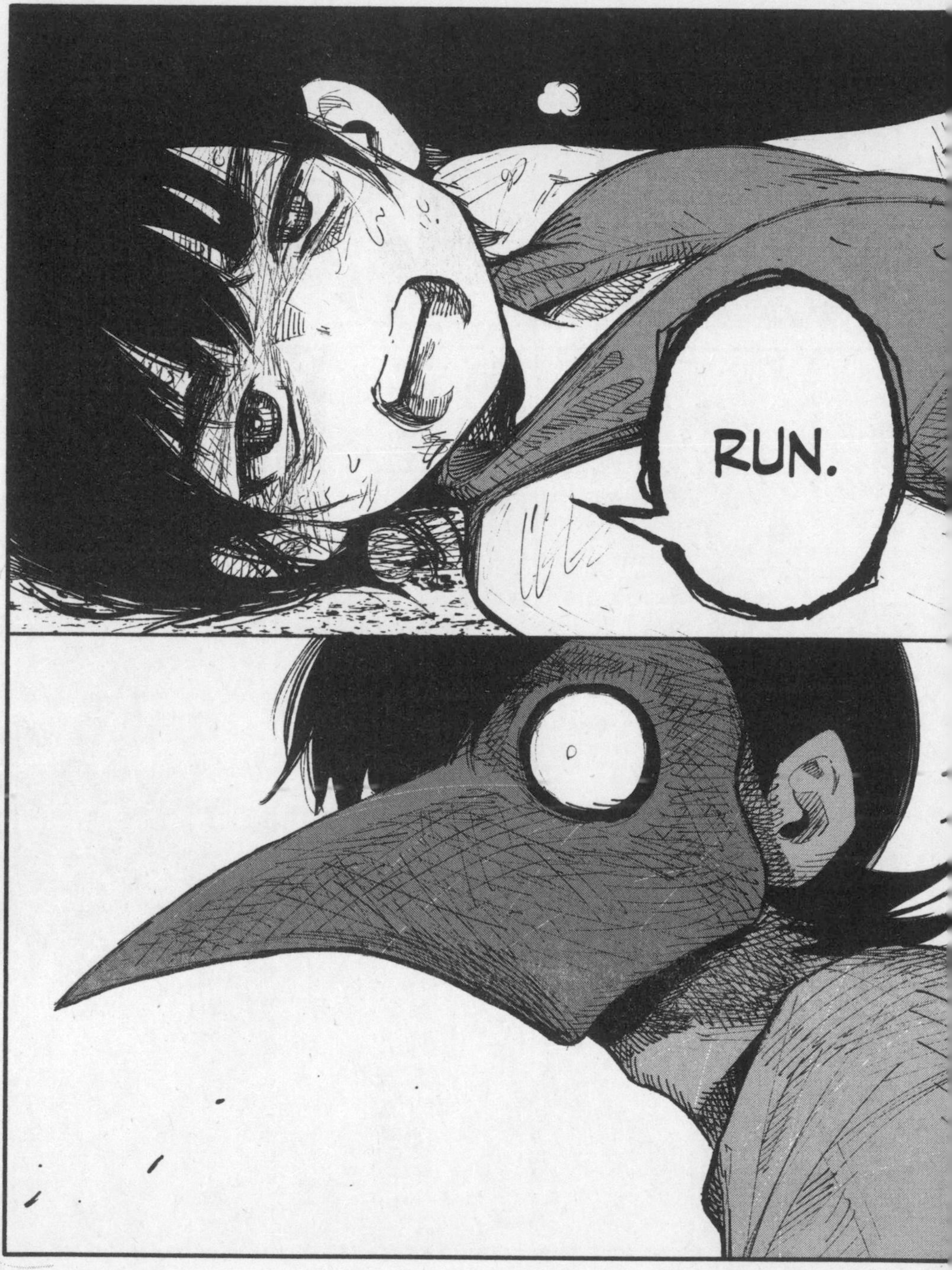
RUN.

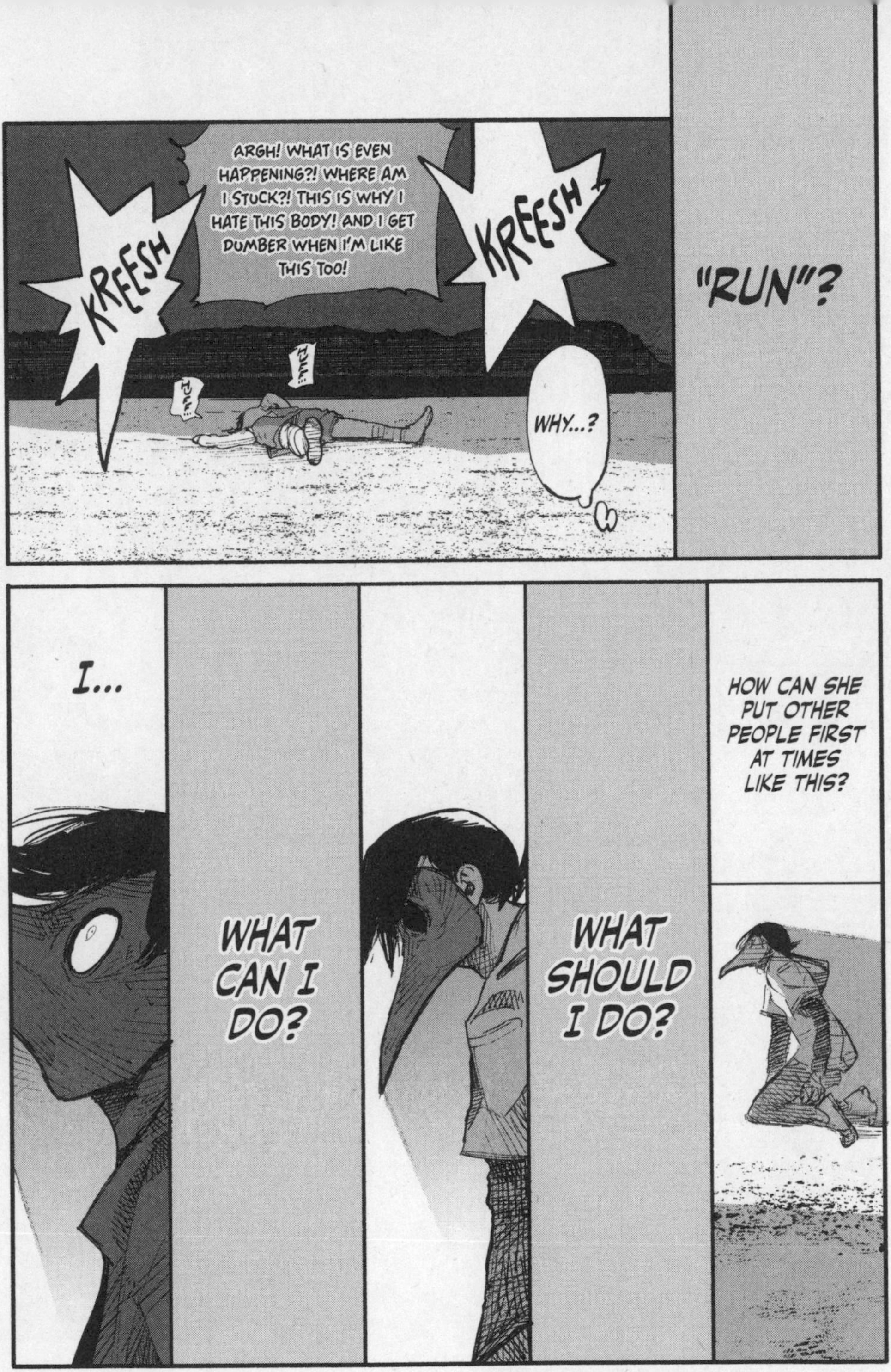
"RUN"?
KREESH
ARGH! WHAT IS EVEN HAPPENING?! WHERE AM I STUCK?! THIS IS WHY I HATE THIS BODY! AND I GET DUMBER WHEN I'M LIKE THIS TOO!
KREESH
WHY...?
HOW CAN SHE PUT OTHER PEOPLE FIRST AT TIMES LIKE THIS?
WHAT SHOULD I DO?
WHAT CAN I DO?
I...

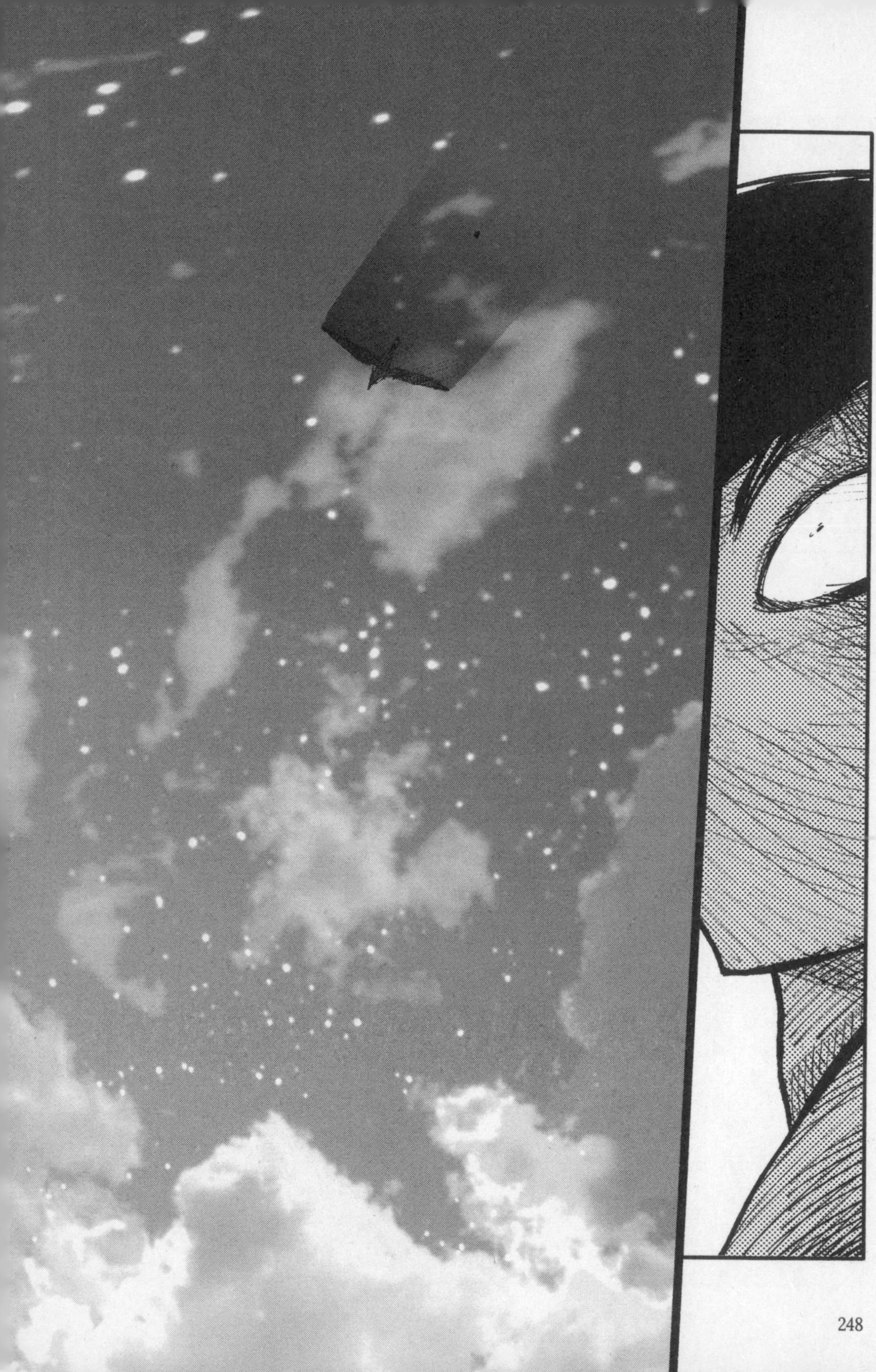

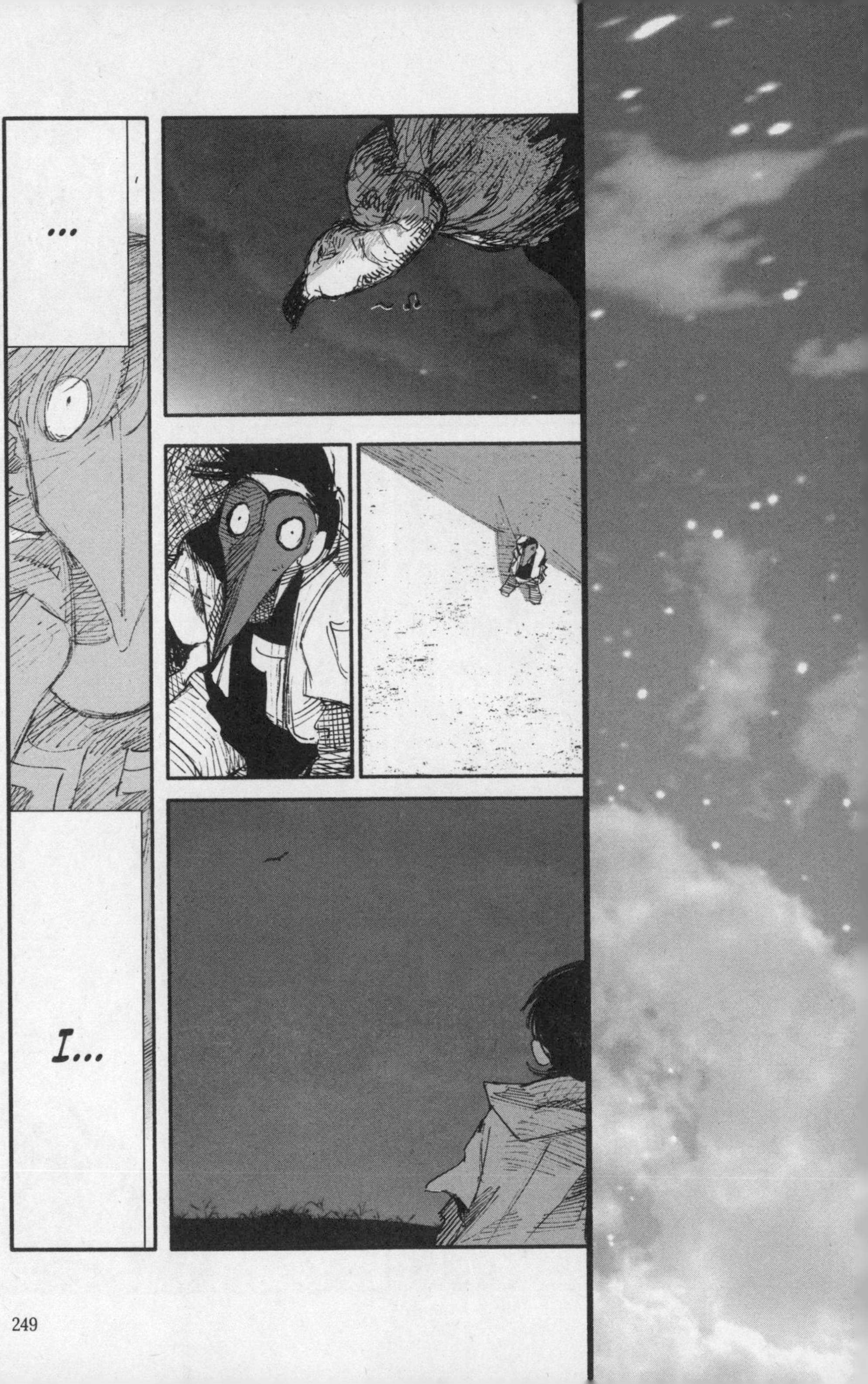
...
I...

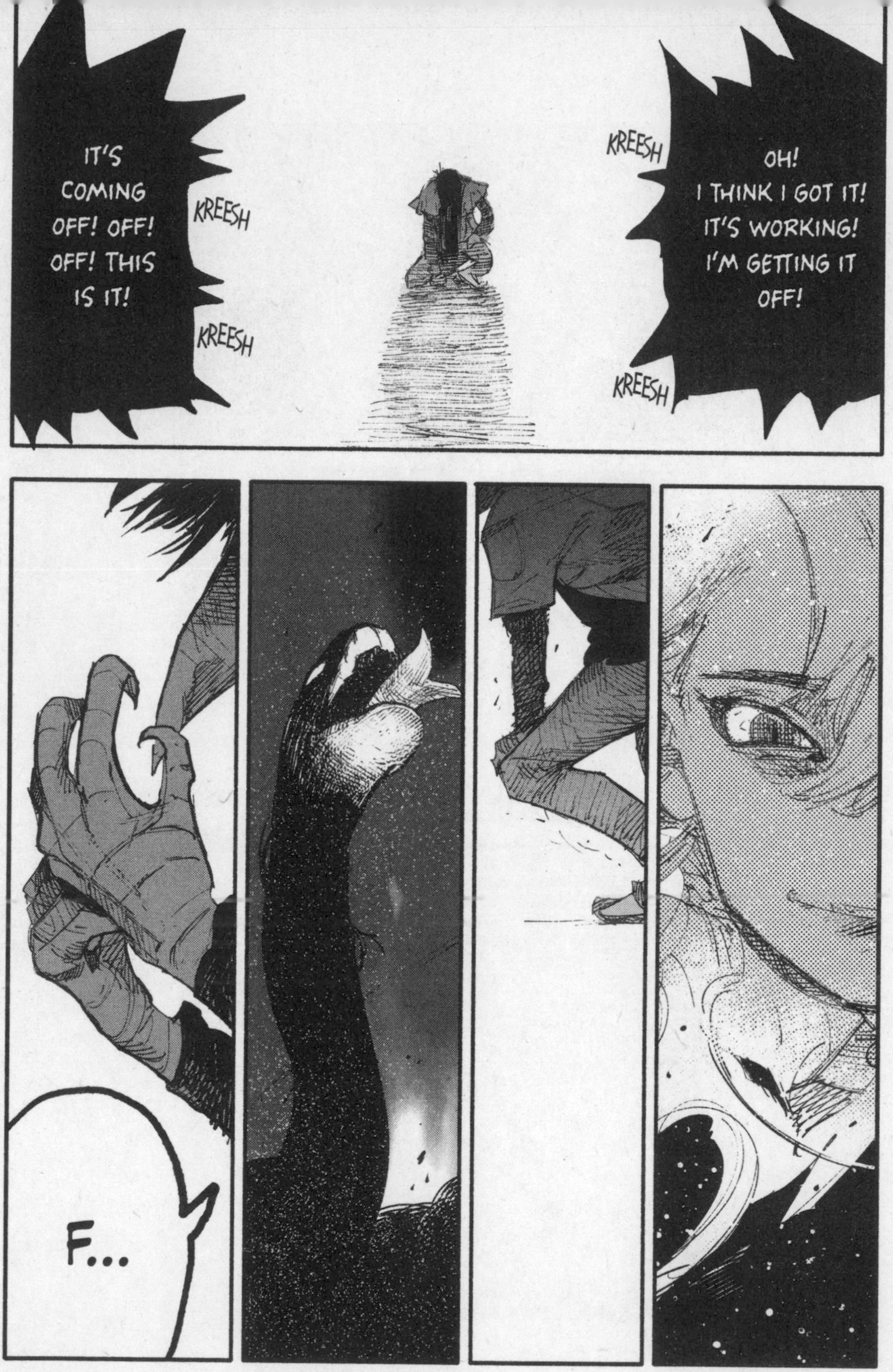
KREESH
OH! I THINK I GOT IT! IT'S WORKING! I'M GETTING IT OFF!
KREESH
KREESH
IT'S COMING OFF! OFF! OFF! THIS IS IT!
KREESH
F...

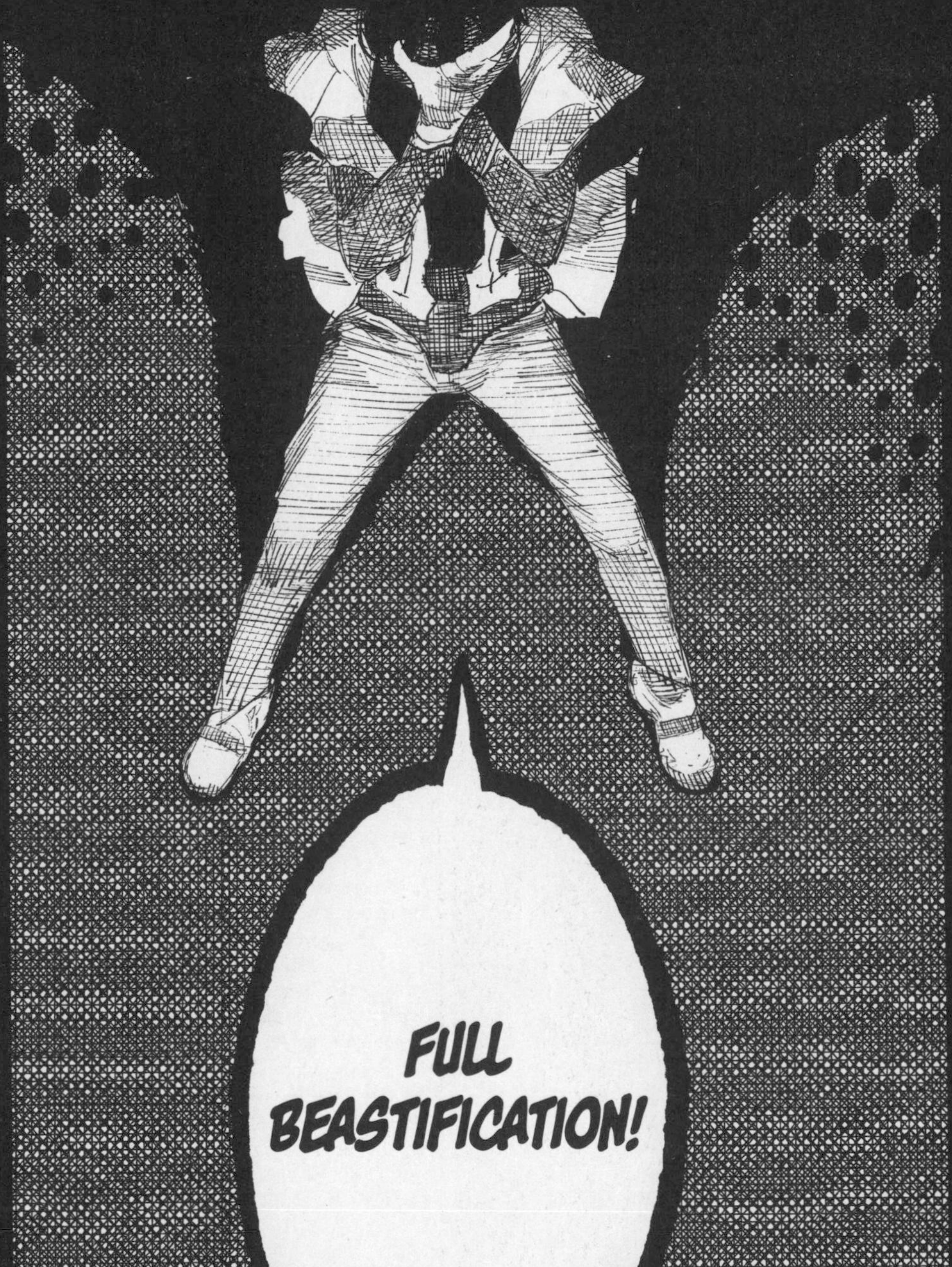
FULL BEASTIFICATION!

Choujin X volume 1 — The End

TOKIO KUROHARA

Age: 16 (in June 1998, the present day)
Birthday: January 13, 1982
175 cm, 57 kg

Hometown: Kita City, Yamato Prefecture
Affiliation: Tsuru Prefectural High, Year 2, Class A
Family: Tobisuke (father), Kinako (sister), Yuzuho (mother, killed in a traffic accident when Tokio was five).

Relationships:
♦ Azuma, the friend he looks up to
Friends since childhood when Azuma saved him from his usual bullies.

Azuma's strong sense of justice and well-rounded accomplishments in school and sports spark aspirations in Tokio for the very first time.

In striving to become more like his friend, Tokio adopts all of Azuma's interests as his own. However, he also gives up before he even knows whether he's capable of accomplishing anything.

That being said, Tsuru High is one of Yamato's leading schools, and the fact that Tokio was accepted might mean that he's more competent than he thinks.

He always hides in Azuma's shadow and tries to keep out of sight.

Tokio	
♦ Base Stats	
Constitution	13
Perception	8
Reaction	2
Strength	1
Endurance	0
Influence	1
Intelligence	6
Determination	3
Luck	5

Azuma

◆ Base Stats

Constitution	22
Perception	9
Reaction	13
Strength	5
Endurance	0
Influence	8
Intelligence	9
Determination	12
Luck	2

◆ Combat Skills

Karate
Judo
...

AZUMA HIGASHI

Age: 16 (in June 1998)
Birthday: December 25, 1981
158 cm, 55 kg

Hometown: Hojo, Kita City, Yamato Prefecture
Affiliation: Tsuru Prefectural High, Year 2, Class A
Family: Father (Toji, the deputy commissioner of the Yamato police department [three ranks from the top]), mother, younger sister

Worries: His height

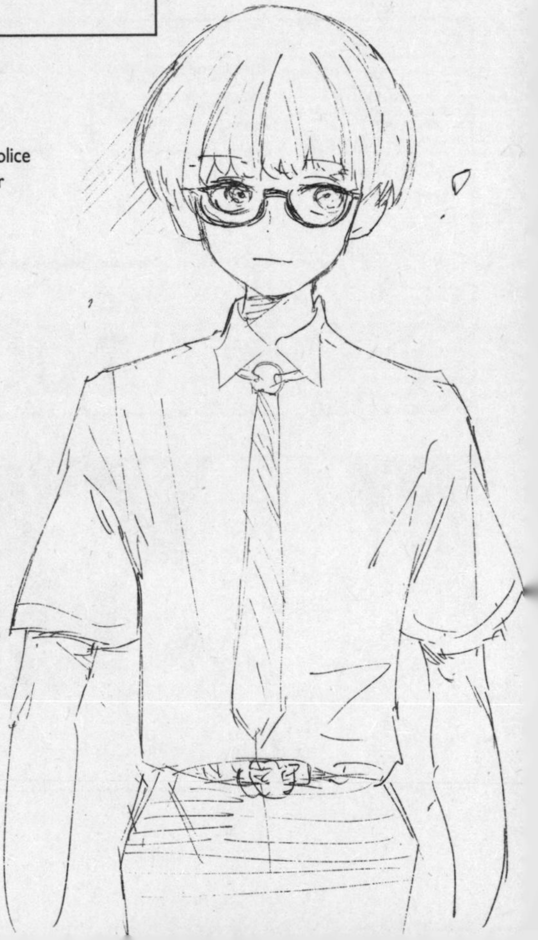

Relationships:

◆ Toji, his stern father

"Shirking justice is an act of cowardice."
Having been raised to adhere to this motto by his father, Azuma has a strong sense of justice himself.
An eager and diligent student, he has high standards for himself in academics and sports.

His life's work is helping others. Finding and subduing bad people is a part of his everyday life. He keeps a scrapbook of newspaper clippings about crimes.

◆ Tokio, his close childhood friend

Azuma tries to act strong and just in front of others, but Tokio is one of the few friends he can open his heart to.

They joke around together. Tokio goes with him when he's trying out new hobbies and they spend time being silly together when Azuma isn't saving people.

CHOUJIN CRIB SHEET VOL.1

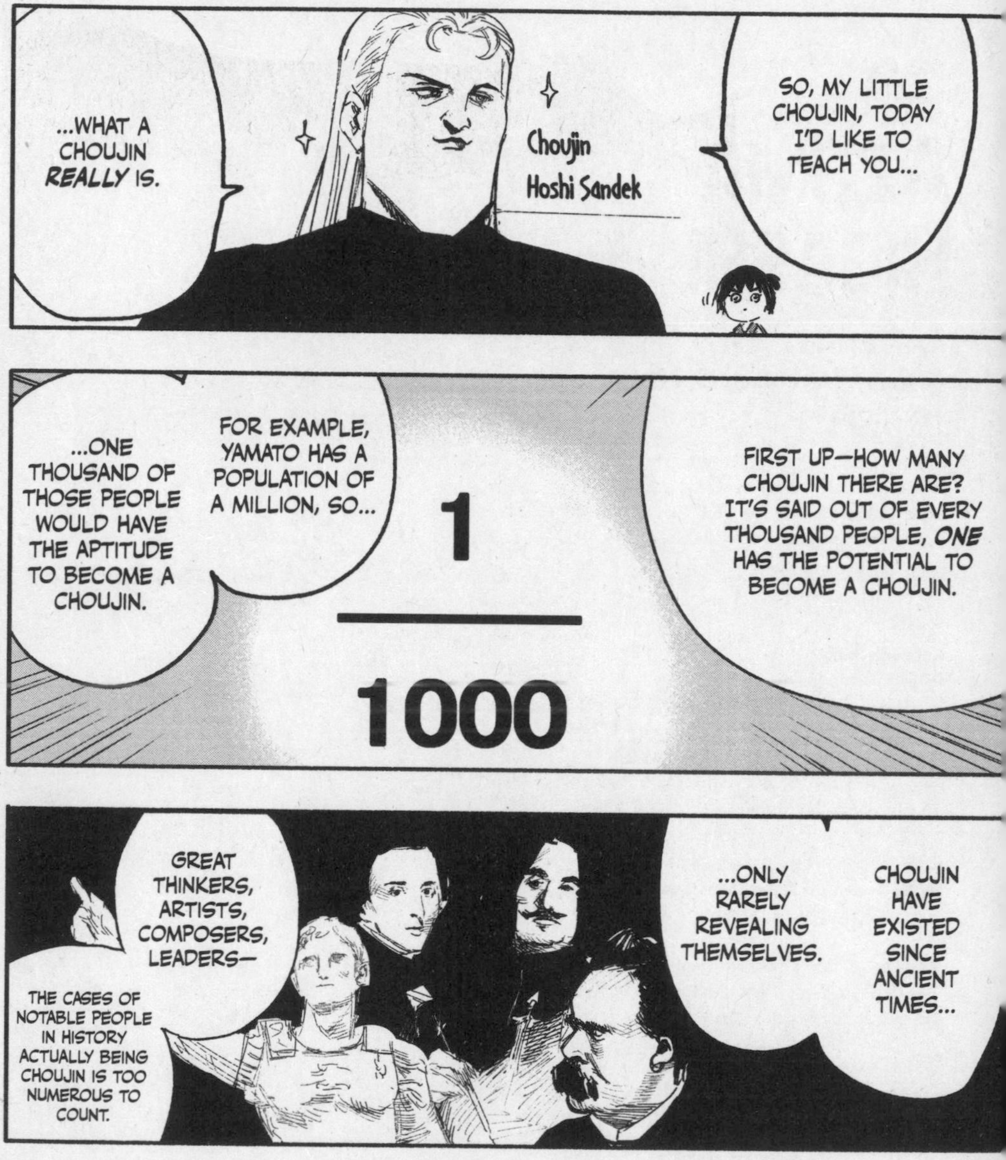

SO, MY LITTLE CHOUJIN, TODAY I'D LIKE TO TEACH YOU...
Choujin Hoshi Sandek
...WHAT A CHOUJIN *REALLY* IS.
FIRST UP—HOW MANY CHOUJIN THERE ARE? IT'S SAID OUT OF EVERY THOUSAND PEOPLE, *ONE* HAS THE POTENTIAL TO BECOME A CHOUJIN.
1
1000
FOR EXAMPLE, YAMATO HAS A POPULATION OF A MILLION, SO...
...ONE THOUSAND OF THOSE PEOPLE WOULD HAVE THE APTITUDE TO BECOME A CHOUJIN.
CHOUJIN HAVE EXISTED SINCE ANCIENT TIMES...
...ONLY RARELY REVEALING THEMSELVES.
GREAT THINKERS, ARTISTS, COMPOSERS, LEADERS—
THE CASES OF NOTABLE PEOPLE IN HISTORY ACTUALLY BEING CHOUJIN IS TOO NUMEROUS TO COUNT.

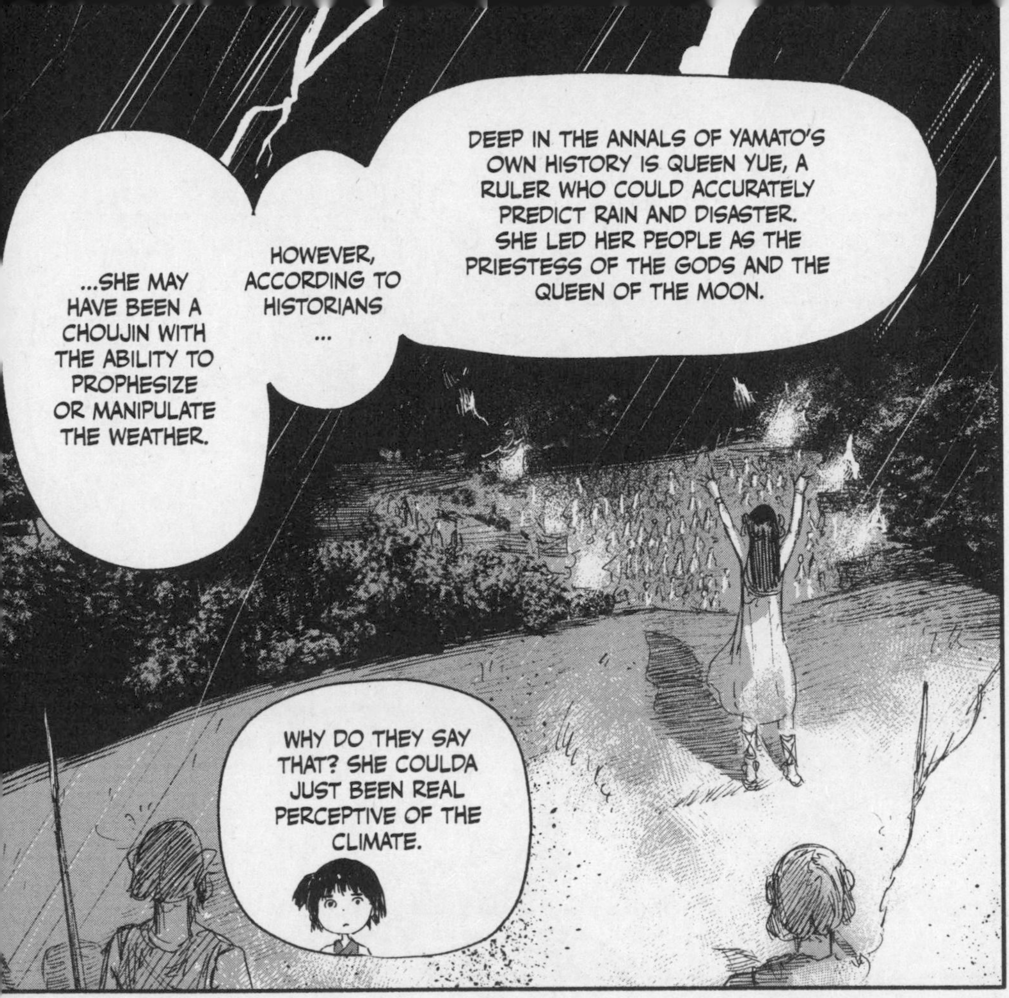
DEEP IN THE ANNALS OF YAMATO'S OWN HISTORY IS QUEEN YUE, A RULER WHO COULD ACCURATELY PREDICT RAIN AND DISASTER. SHE LED HER PEOPLE AS THE PRIESTESS OF THE GODS AND THE QUEEN OF THE MOON.
HOWEVER, ACCORDING TO HISTORIANS ...
...SHE MAY HAVE BEEN A CHOUJIN WITH THE ABILITY TO PROPHESIZE OR MANIPULATE THE WEATHER.
WHY DO THEY SAY THAT? SHE COULDA JUST BEEN REAL PERCEPTIVE OF THE CLIMATE.

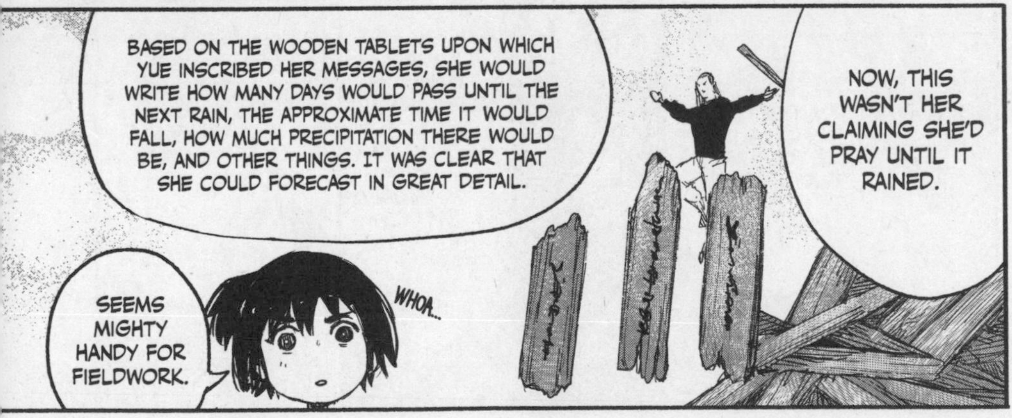
NOW, THIS WASN'T HER CLAIMING SHE'D PRAY UNTIL IT RAINED.
BASED ON THE WOODEN TABLETS UPON WHICH YUE INSCRIBED HER MESSAGES, SHE WOULD WRITE HOW MANY DAYS WOULD PASS UNTIL THE NEXT RAIN, THE APPROXIMATE TIME IT WOULD FALL, HOW MUCH PRECIPITATION THERE WOULD BE, AND OTHER THINGS. IT WAS CLEAR THAT SHE COULD FORECAST IN GREAT DETAIL.
WHOA...
SEEMS MIGHTY HANDY FOR FIELDWORK.

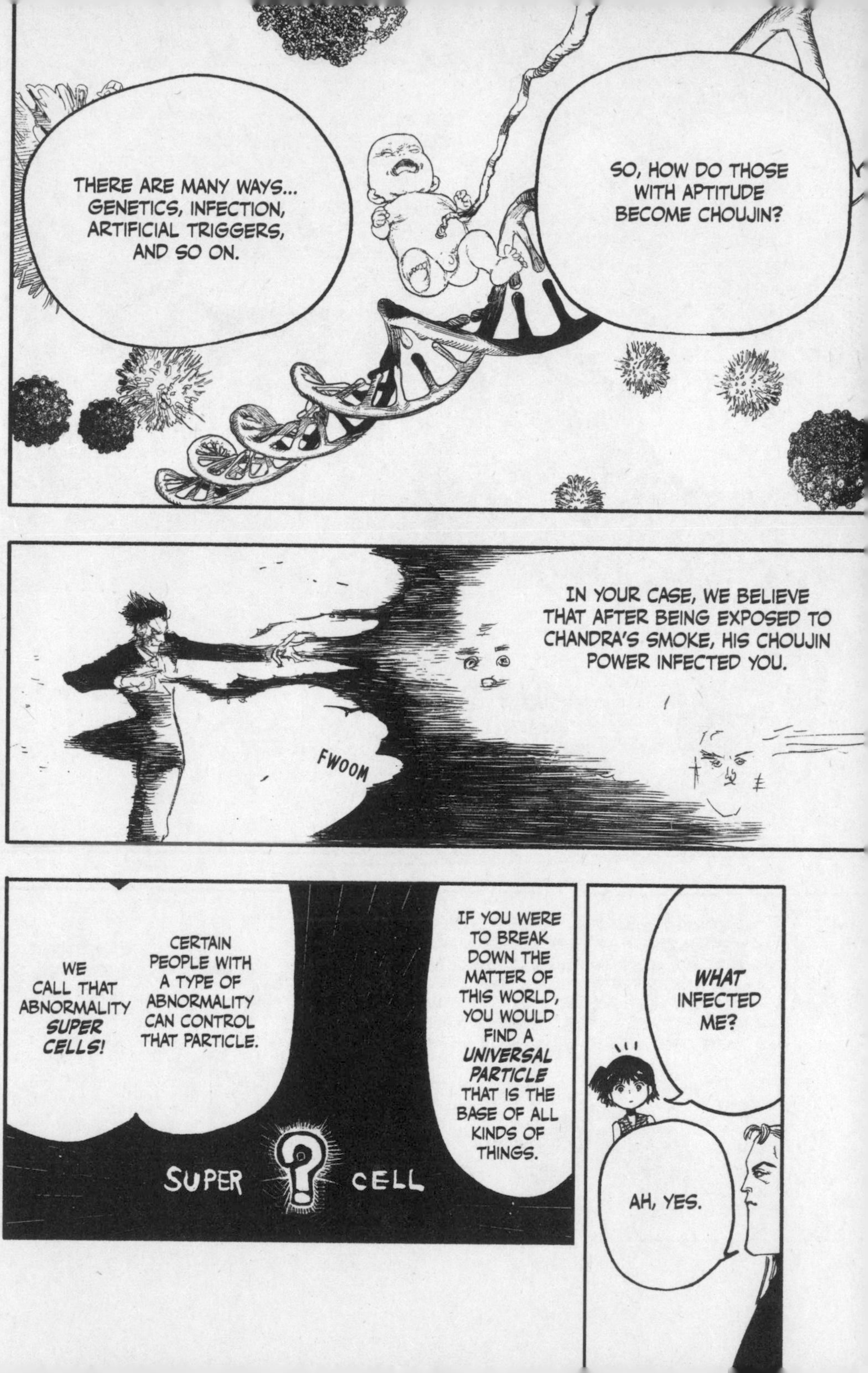
SO, HOW DO THOSE WITH APTITUDE BECOME CHOUJIN?
THERE ARE MANY WAYS... GENETICS, INFECTION, ARTIFICIAL TRIGGERS, AND SO ON.
IN YOUR CASE, WE BELIEVE THAT AFTER BEING EXPOSED TO CHANDRA'S SMOKE, HIS CHOUJIN POWER INFECTED YOU.
FWOOM
WHAT INFECTED ME?
AH, YES.
IF YOU WERE TO BREAK DOWN THE MATTER OF THIS WORLD, YOU WOULD FIND A *UNIVERSAL PARTICLE* THAT IS THE BASE OF ALL KINDS OF THINGS.
CERTAIN PEOPLE WITH A TYPE OF ABNORMALITY CAN CONTROL THAT PARTICLE.
WE CALL THAT ABNORMALITY *SUPER CELLS!*
SUPER ? CELL

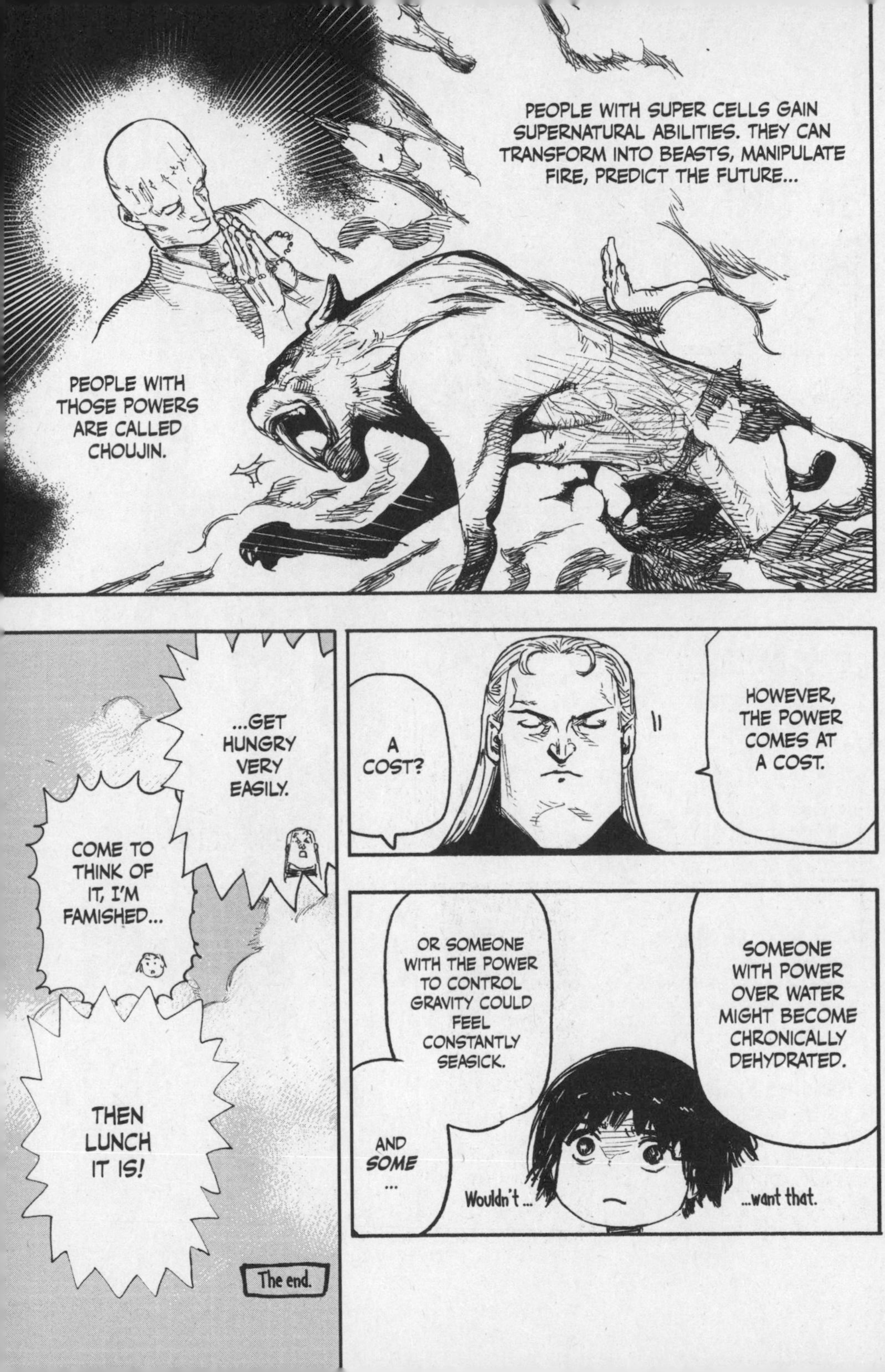
PEOPLE WITH SUPER CELLS GAIN SUPERNATURAL ABILITIES. THEY CAN TRANSFORM INTO BEASTS, MANIPULATE FIRE, PREDICT THE FUTURE...
PEOPLE WITH THOSE POWERS ARE CALLED CHOUJIN.
HOWEVER, THE POWER COMES AT A COST.
A COST?
SOMEONE WITH POWER OVER WATER MIGHT BECOME CHRONICALLY DEHYDRATED.
OR SOMEONE WITH THE POWER TO CONTROL GRAVITY COULD FEEL CONSTANTLY SEASICK.
AND *SOME* ...
Wouldn't ...
...want that.
...GET HUNGRY VERY EASILY.
COME TO THINK OF IT, I'M FAMISHED...
THEN LUNCH IT IS!
The end.

CHANDRA HUME

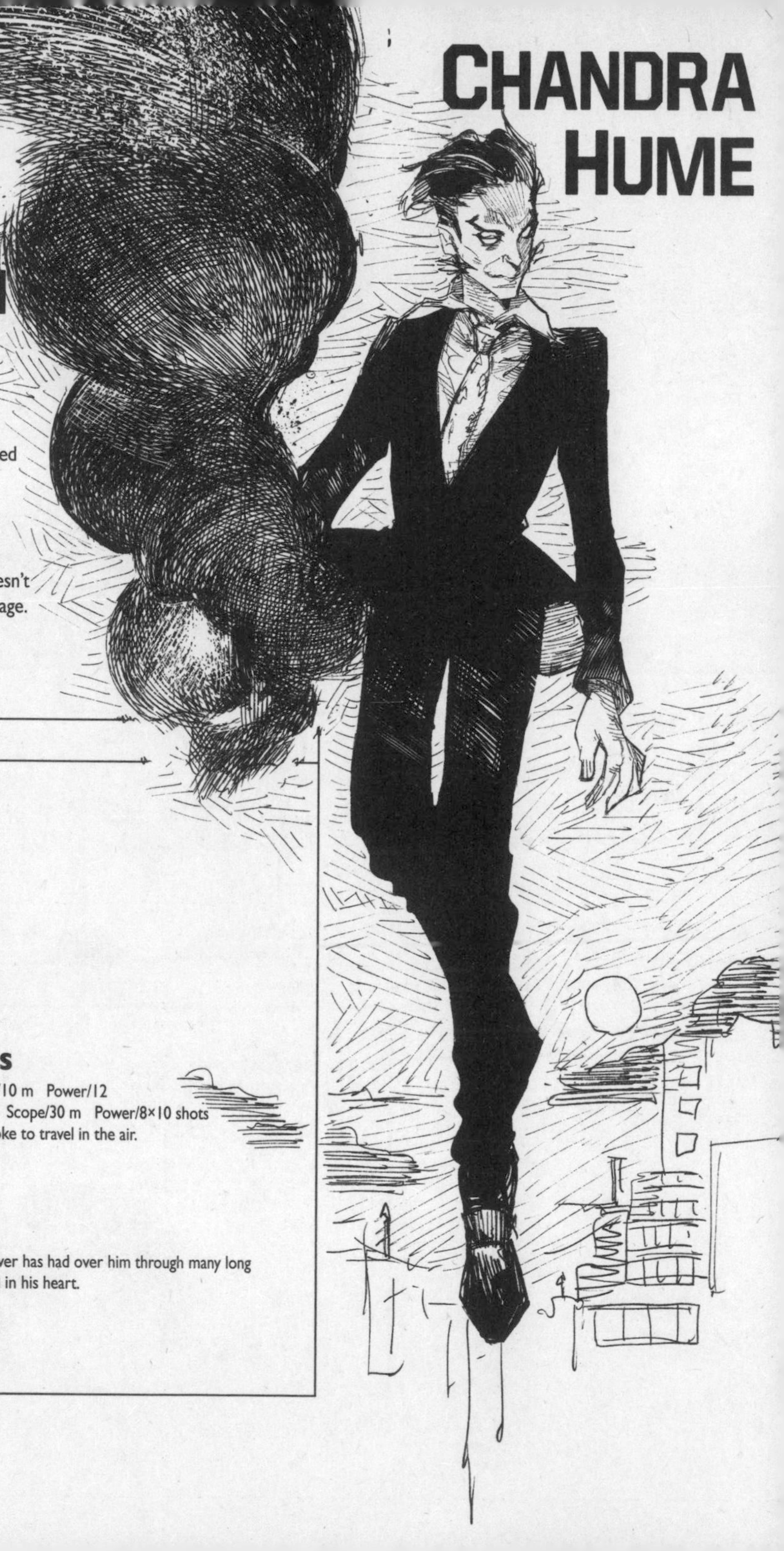

SMOKE CHOUJIN

Age: 42
178 cm, 53 kg

A cruel choujin who attacked the plane Ely was on.

He has a strong sense of aesthetic and when he encounters anything he doesn't care for, he goes on a rampage.

◆ Base Stats

Constitution	97
Perception	18
Reaction	15
Strength	35
Endurance	3
Influence	18
Intelligence	22
Determination	20
Luck	1
Choujin Proficiency	765

◆ Combat Skills

Fumes Range/Mid Scope/10 m Power/12
Smoke Reams Range/Far Scope/30 m Power/8×10 shots
Smoke Gliding Ejects smoke to travel in the air.
Raise ???
...etc.

◆ Passive Skill

Rage The influence his power has had over him through many long years has caused rage to roil in his heart.

NARI

BESTIAL CHOUJIN

Age: 19

164 cm, 49 kg, G Cup

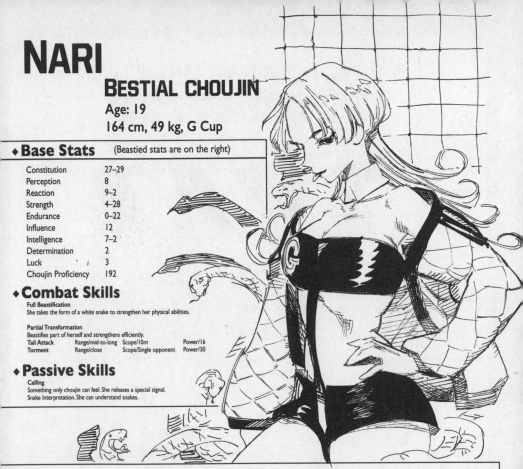

◆ Base Stats (Beastied stats are on the right)

Constitution	27–29	
Perception	8	
Reaction	9–2	
Strength	4–28	
Endurance	0–22	
Influence	12	
Intelligence	7–2	
Determination	2	
Luck	3	
Choujin Proficiency	192	

◆ Combat Skills

Full Beastification
She takes the form of a white snake to strengthen her physical abilities.

Partial Transformation
Beastifies part of herself and strengthens efficiently.

Tail Attack	Range/mid-to-long	Scope/10m	Power/16
Torment	Range/close	Scope/Single opponent	Power/30

◆ Passive Skills

Calling
Something only choujin can feel. She releases a special signal.
Snake Interpretation. She can understand snakes.

■ How to Read the Attribute Values

◆ Base Stats

Constitution Vitality, stamina, endurance, the overall ability to maintain function. This would be HP in a game.

Perception The speed and extent to which they notice to abnormalities. Insight and powers of inference. Takes into account how sharp their senses are.

Reaction Reflex speed. The ability to immediately react when an event occurs.

Strength Physical strength of limbs used when taking down a foe. This stat includes the effect choujin abilities have on them.

Endurance Physical fortitude, defenses. Regular bodies are normally 0-2 but could be higher with an ability that provides enhancement.

The average person's Constitution is 20 and the other stats are 5.

Influence Charisma, charm, sexiness, etc. The ability to manipulate a situation. Those with higher influence are more likely to become the center of attention.

Intelligence Mental acuity, analytical skills and inquisitiveness that takes into account their general abundance of knowledge. The higher this is, the faster their abilities will grow. Also advantageous in battle.

Determination The ability to withstand influence. Fortitude against wavering. A higher value indicates more tenacity.

Luck In this case, indicates not their environment or the situation into which they were born, but their luck in the moment. Also includes trivial situations, such as how often they win free ice cream. (However, their luck may influence everything in their life.)

Choujin Proficiency Their life experience as a choujin. How much time and hands-on experience they have had. Indispensable for growing their abilities and skills.

◆ Combat Skills Powers and techniques that can be used in battle.

◆ Passive Skills Routinely (and unconsciously) manifesting powers.

A NATIONLESS WORLD

Global chaos brought forth by Guelta

1918   Guelta Commonwealth forms a battalion of over 300 choujin to unify the neighboring states (the Great Gueltan Ideology).

1919   Queem Macman, commanding officer of Guelta's choujin battalion, incites rebellion and seizes control of the Gueltan Commonwealth.

1920   Great Guelta is formed when the neighboring nations are assimilated. Queem becomes its first choujin president and around that time dubs himself the "War Choujin." (Queem keeps his real nature concealed and purges those who know his actual powers, so it is unclear what his true abilities were.)

1924   With plans to further expand his territory, Queem declares war upon the neighboring nations. This leads to the outbreak of a world war, to which Greater Asia lends its support.

1927   Each nation deploys their own choujin, leading to mayhem.
Queem is assassinated by the choujin Antitise, the general of the volunteer allied forces. Great Guelta collapses. The war does not cease, however, and the choujin soldiers continue their path of destruction.
The concept of nations collapses worldwide.

1946   Self-governed prefectures are established.

1998   Present Day.

President of Guelta, Queem, appearing for an address (center).
In his final years, he stood at a towering 2.8 meters.
In the right photo, during (what is believed to be) his commissioned officer days, his skin was hardening but he still appeared human.

Chapter Sountracks

#1
"Sincere Parade"/
Bitei Matsuki

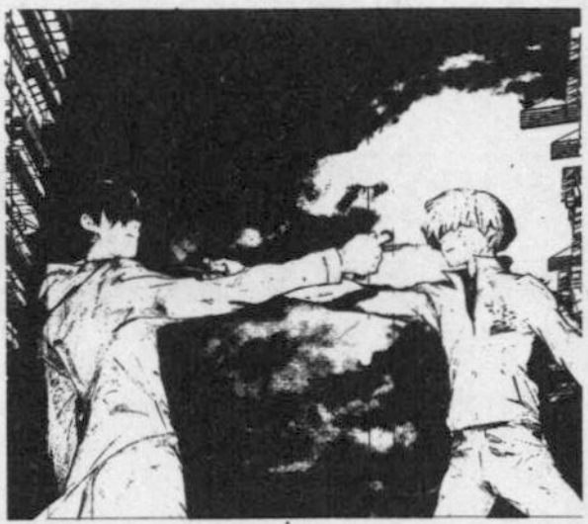

#2
"Thus We Fight"/
Noein (Hikaru Nanase)

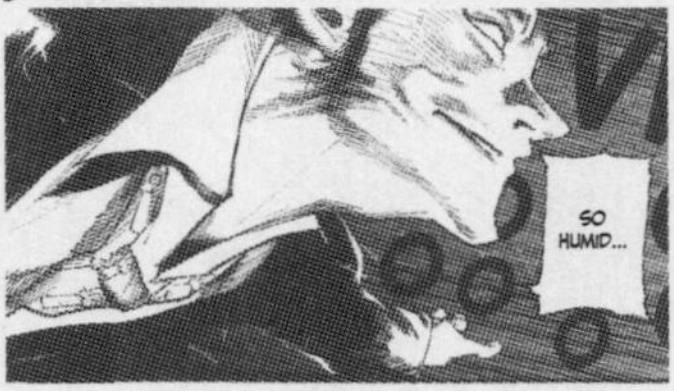
SO HUMID...

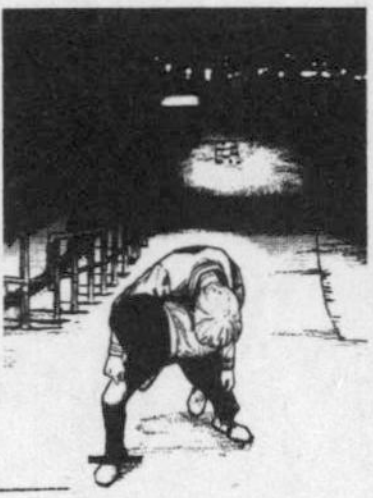

#3
"Time's Profile"/Junichi Matsumoto
"Lofi Type Beat Self-Harm"/rentaka

#4
"in the park"/
Kurubukko-chan

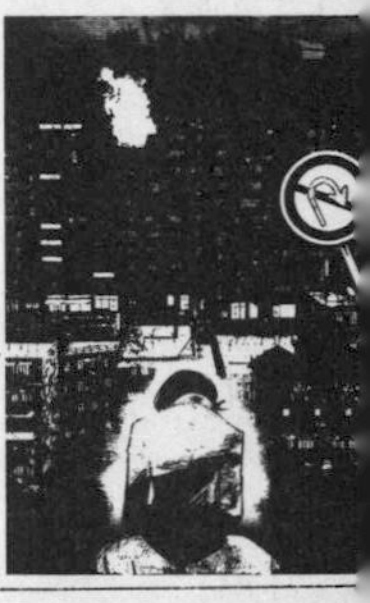

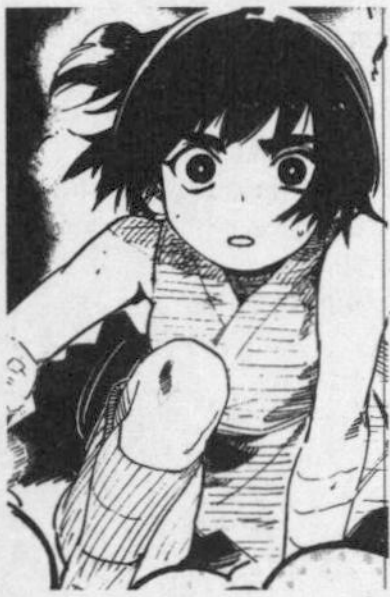

#5
"Honesty"/
Hallman

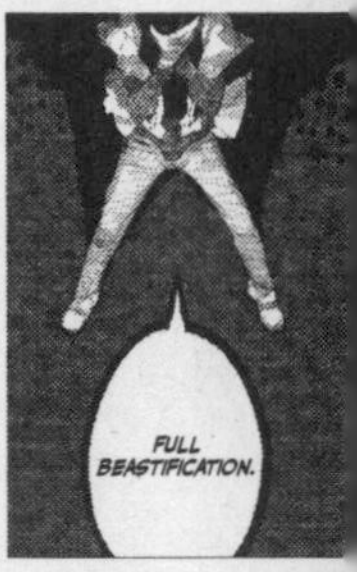
FULL BEASTIFICATION.

#6
"WHOO WHOO WHOO"/
Mrs. GREEN APPLE

THANK YOU FOR PICKING UP THE FIRST VOLUME OF *CHOUJIN X*. THIS STORY BEGAN SERIALIZING ON THE WEBSITE *TONARI NO YOUNG JUMP* ON MAY 10, 2021.

IT'S BEEN THREE YEARS SINCE THE COMPLETEION OF MY LAST WORK. DURING THAT TIME I MADE A GAME AND COMPOSED SOME SONGS. IT WAS A CURIOUS EXPERIENCE.

AND I THINK IT ALSO WAS A TIME FOR ME TO THINK ABOUT MY RELATION-SHIP WITH MANGA.

AFTER SO LONG, I DIDN'T KNOW MY RIGHT FROM MY LEFT WHEN IT CAME TO MANGA, BUT I SOMEHOW MANAGED TO PRODUCE SOMETHING.

THIS WAS POSSIBLE THANKS TO THE PEOPLE EARNESTLY READING MANGA AROUND ME AND SUPPORTING ME. I'D LIKE TO TAKE THE OPPORTUNITY TO EXPRESS MY GRATITUDE HERE. THANK YOU SO VERY MUCH. WELL THEN, LET'S MEET IN THE SECOND VOLUME.

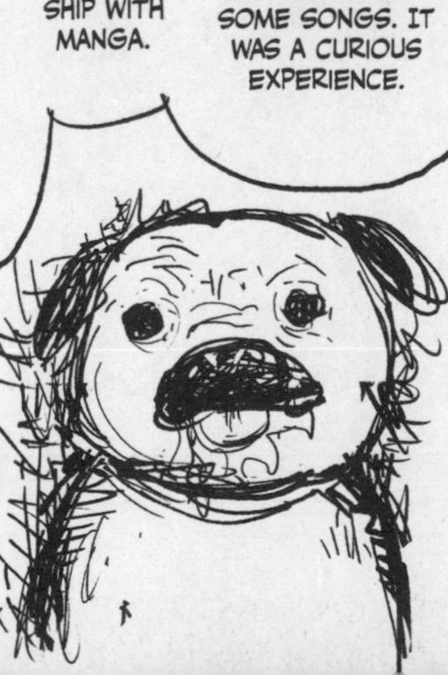

PEACE!!

2021.12.7
Sui Ishida

Thank you for the people who let me consult with them and who supported me!!

Editor
Ninohira
Matsuo

THIS IS THE END OF THE BOOK!

Choujin X reads from right to left, starting in the upper-right corner. Japanese is read from right to left, meaning that action, sound effects and word-balloon order are completely reversed from English order.

CHOUJIN X

VOLUME 1

VIZ SIGNATURE EDITION
Story and Art by Sui Ishida

Translation × Jan Mitsuko Cash
SJ Touch-Up Art & Lettering × Snir Aharon
GN Touch-Up Art & Lettering × Evan Waldinger
Design × Jimmy Presler
Editor × Pancha Diaz

CHOUJIN X © 2021 by Sui Ishida
All rights reserved.
First published in Japan in 2021 by SHUEISHA Inc., Tokyo.
English translation rights arranged by SHUEISHA Inc.

Printed in Canada

Published by VIZ Media, LLC
P.O. Box 77010
San Francisco, CA 94107

10 9 8 7 6 5 4 3 2
First printing, February 2023
Second printing, February 2023

 MEDIA 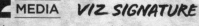 *VIZ SIGNATURE*

viz.com   vizsignature.com